W9-BBB-048

Economic Report
of the President

Together with

The Annual Report

of the

Council of Economic Advisers

January 2021

Bernan does not claim copyright in U.S. government information.

978-1-63671-008-2

Contents

---

*For a detailed table of contents of the Council's *Report*, see page 23.

Economic Report of the President

Economic Report of the President

To the Congress of the United States:

Four years ago, on the steps of the United States Capitol, I pledged to the citizens of this country to return our Nation to greatness, and to thereby enable, secure, and enhance the prosperity of all Americans. While this would require us to confront challenges and hardships, I knew that the American spirit, set free from overbearing taxation and regulation, would drive the country forward to unimaginable economic success. I was right. Over the course of this Administration, the American people demonstrated an indomitable will to prevail and drove our economy to record heights.

Since my first day in office, I have been steadfast in my commitment to put America First. The economic pillars of this movement—sweeping tax reform, extensive deregulatory actions, and fair and reciprocal trade agreements—promoted a robust middle class and led to the longest expansion and strongest recovery in history.

Before the coronavirus came to our country from China, our economy created more than 7 million jobs, nearly 12,000 factories returned to our shores, and wealth for Americans hit all-time highs. Inequality decreased as wage growth for blue-collar workers outpaced that of their managers, and earnings for those in the bottom 10 percent grew faster than earnings for the top 10 percent, reversing the trends of past Administrations. Since the start of my Administration, median household income grew by more than $6,000, lifting up people no matter their race, ethnicity, educational background, or age group. In 2019 alone, median household income rose $4,400—more in one year than in the entire 16 years through 2016. Even as more than 2 million people returned from the sidelines to enter the labor force, the unemployment rate plummeted to 3.5 percent in February 2020—the lowest level in more than half a century.

This past year, our Nation has faced trials the likes of which many have never experienced. Through these challenges, however, we have witnessed once again the resilience of the American people. In just 2 months this year, more than 23 million people saw their livelihoods threatened through no fault of their own, as the unemployment rate peaked at 14.7 percent. Since this spring, we have seen more than 12 million jobs return and gross domestic product increase by a record-shattering 33 percent in the third quarter alone, thanks to the largest and fastest economic policy response in history.

When the virus hit, my Administration launched the largest industrial mobilization since World War II. We have created the world's most innovative testing system, pioneered groundbreaking therapies and treatments, and, most importantly, we have developed and manufactured gold standard vaccines in record time. The pandemic may have begun in China, but we are ending it in America.

Thanks to the pro-growth policies of my Administration, our Nation's economy has exceeded expectations at every turn, and despite the economic shock due to the China Virus, our great American comeback is well underway.

The Renaissance of American Greatness: Rebuilding Our Country

For decades, political leaders and privileged elites worked to silence American workers and families even as opportunity—and with it hope—slipped from the shores of our great Nation. Almost 5 million manufacturing jobs and 60,000 factories fled our country following the establishment of Permanent Normal Trade Relations with China in 2000. Massive tax burdens and overregulation encouraged businesses to invest elsewhere. For decades, multinational corporations flooded our Nation with imported goods, stripping millions of American families of their livelihoods and their dignity. Decades of these damaging policies led to the prevalence of "Made in China," as China's leaders (and those from other countries) took advantage of establishment politicians who did not have the best interests of American workers at heart.

Before I took office, politicians and their adherence to a globalist doctrine converted our borders and national sovereignty into mere negotiable concepts to be traded away or simply ignored when in conflict with establishment interests. Anti-American ideology flooded into schools, universities, and media, while American wealth, intellectual property, and innovation rushed out of our country. Cities corroded by years of neglect and mismanagement became commonplace, each complete with an allotment of lawless streets that were devoid of prospect, educational choice, and liberty. International financial crises became matters not of "if" but of "when," yet the attention of those charged with governing turned elsewhere and the American people were forgotten.

Since taking office, rather than apologize for America, I have stood up for America. From day one of my Presidency, I have put America First, and I have fought for the American worker harder than anyone ever has. My Administration has adhered to the two simple rules of "Buy American" and "Hire American," we have built the most secure border in history, and I took the toughest-ever action to stand up to China.

I have worked every day to restore promise to our Nation through an economic agenda that lifts up all Americans. In just 3 years, my Administration's policies brought more than 6.6 million people out of poverty; created prosperity through record low unemployment rates for Black Americans, Hispanic Americans, Asian Americans, and those without a college degree; reduced homelessness among the general population and our veterans; and saved thousands of lives by stemming the tide of opioid-related deaths. We committed to breaking a cycle that for too long held children's education hostage on the basis of affluence and class background—denying children knowledge and unrealized potential. And my Administration returned economic freedom to the American people as we have cut nearly eight regulations for every new, significant rule—weakening the power of the regulatory state and stifling stealth taxation. The power of fracking has forged the path for American energy independence and delivered personal prosperity alongside national security, contributing to a 10 percent decline in the global price of oil. We also created the U.S. Space Force—the sixth branch of the military—and have given new meaning to "Peace through Strength" by expanding our capabilities and restoring American leadership in space.

We unleashed record prosperity at home, while also negotiating fair and reciprocal trade agreements. The passage of the Tax Cuts and Jobs Act increased wages for blue-collar workers, and the implementation of the United States–Mexico–Canada Agreement elevated American competitiveness with respect to our regional trading partners. We took the toughest, boldest, and strongest actions against China in American history, and the United States is now collecting billions of dollars in tariff revenue on imports of Chinese goods.

I took unprecedented action to reduce drug prices and ensure that Americans never pay more for life-saving medicines than consumers in other countries. And my Administration took action to end surprise medical billing. We also eliminated the harmful individual mandate from the so-called Affordable Care Act, as between 1.2 and 4.6 million Americans gained employment sponsored health coverage from 2018 to 2019. These actions, along with countless other taken by my Administration, have not only boosted economic growth and wage gains for all Americans, but they have also protected the American people from foreign competitors trying to take advantage of them.

A Great American Comeback Underway

The virus from China required us to close up the greatest economy in the history of the world. Understanding the risks our Nation faced, I took bold action to ban travel from China and then later Europe, saving countless American lives.

In a matter of days and weeks, the global economy ceased to exist as we knew it. Nations around the world locked down as uncertainty generated tremendous fear. In order to prepare our frontline responders in hospitals and health facilities across the United States, we prioritized the safety of the American people over the strength of our economy. In March of this year, we implemented an initial plan to slow the spread of the virus, in coordination with governors across the Nation. During that time, my Administration facilitated the delivery of thousands of ventilators and millions of gloves, masks, and protective gear to States and territories, working to get Americans life-saving medical equipment.

We promised that no patient suffering from the virus would have to pay for their treatment out of pocket, and we provided billions of dollars to hospitals and healthcare providers so that uninsured patients would have access to critical care. By the end of March, the Food and Drug Administration issued Emergency Use Authorizations to fast-track more than 20 diagnostic tests and life-saving treatments. Thanks to our efforts, the case fatality rate today is more than 85 percent lower than its April peak. Meanwhile, Operation Warp Speed has harnessed the innovation of the private sector to develop and manufacture millions of doses of life-saving vaccines, decreasing the average development time from 3 years to less than 9 months. This record-shattering work has cleared the path for an end to this cruel pandemic, saving millions of lives around the world and trillions of dollars in health and other economic costs.

Through no fault of their own, Americans from all walks of life have been forced to confront the Invisible Enemy. To help the Nation through this difficult time, I championed and signed four pieces of legislation. These laws kept Americans connected to their jobs and reduced the economic harm to families and workers. In March, the Coronavirus Aid, Relief, and Economic Security (CARES) Act—the largest piece of economic relief legislation in history—authorized direct payments to citizens, expanded unemployment insurance, and deferred loans for those who needed it most. When Congress later abdicated its duty to expand and extend this relief, for short-sided political gain, I signed four executive actions to continue providing for the families, students, and workers of our country. Additionally, my Administration worked hand-in-hand with the private sector, invoking the Defense Production Act and related authorities more than 100 times to surge production and distribution of ventilators, protective equipment, and other materials, including therapeutics and vaccines.

The Paycheck Protection Program, a core piece of the CARES Act, saved or supported more than 51 million American jobs by providing more than 5.2 million critical loans to small businesses. These loans were crucial lifelines to business owners and their employees that averted widespread bankruptcies. This effort alone meant that more than 80 percent of March and April layoffs were temporary, as over 80 percent of these businesses that received them are still open today. In addition, Economic Impact Payments sent to more than 159 million Americans surged liquidity to every corner of our Nation, and provided nearly three months of income to households in the bottom 10 percent of the income distribution. And our Farmers to Families Food Box Program delivered more than 90 million boxes to families, children, and businesses, protecting millions of Americans from food insecurity.

For the last 4 years, I have fought for you, the American people, in all that I do. The *Economic Report of the President* that follows describes the policies that have made our country so successful and lays out steps we can take to continue the great American comeback in response to the China Virus. This year's *Report* is a testament to the resolve of the American people, who never falter in the face of adversity, and whose courage and relentless drive forge our destiny.

The White House
January 2021

The Annual Report

of the

Council of Economic Advisers

Letter of Transmittal

Council of Economic Advisers

Washington, January 15, 2021

Mr. President:

The Council of Economic Advisers herewith submits its 2021 *Annual Report* in accordance with the Employment Act of 1946, as amended by the Full Employment and Balanced Growth Act of 1978.

Sincerely yours,

Rachael Seidenschnur Slobodien
Chief of Staff

Introduction

In 2020, the U.S. economy experienced its worst macroeconomic shock since the Great Depression. As a direct result of the arrival of COVID-19—and consequent measures to contain and mitigate viral transmission, real output was on pace to contract by as much as 12.3 percent in 2020, which would have constituted the worst economic contraction since 1932. Professional forecasters projected that the unemployment rate would reach as high as 25.0 percent in May 2020, its worst level since the Great Depression and more than twice its peak in the aftermath of the 2008–9 global financial crisis. The Congressional Budget Office (CBO) forecasted a contraction of almost 6 percent during the four quarters of 2020, and that the unemployment rate would remain over 11 percent through the end of the year.

In the face of this exogenous economic shock of historically unprecedented scale and speed that abruptly terminated the U.S. economy's record expansion, the Trump Administration responded with equally unprecedented scale and speed. As a result of this response, real gross domestic product (GDP) in the third quarter of 2020 was down 3.5 percent from its prepandemic level—less than half the drop in the early projections—and high-frequency forecasts

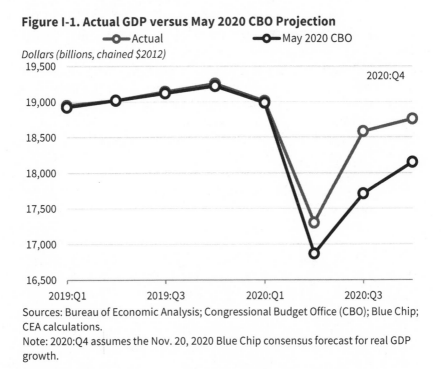

Figure I-1. Actual GDP versus May 2020 CBO Projection

Sources: Bureau of Economic Analysis; Congressional Budget Office (CBO); Blue Chip; CEA calculations.
Note: 2020:Q4 assumes the Nov. 20, 2020 Blue Chip consensus forecast for real GDP growth.

Figure I-2. Actual Payroll Employment versus May 2020 CBO Projection

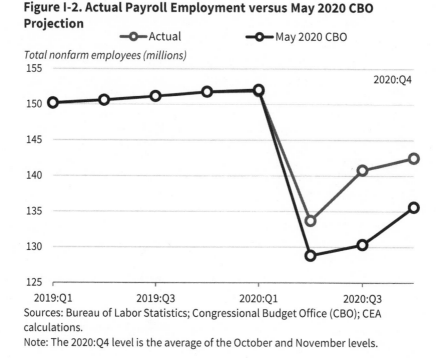

Total nonfarm employees (millions)

Sources: Bureau of Labor Statistics; Congressional Budget Office (CBO); CEA calculations.
Note: The 2020:Q4 level is the average of the October and November levels.

for the fourth quarter imply a calendar-year decline of 2.3 percent—less than one-third the projected decline (figure I-1). In seven months, the U.S. labor market recovered 12.3 million jobs, or 56 percent of job losses in March and April (figure I-2). The unemployment rate declined from a peak of 14.7 percent in April to 6.7 percent in November, almost 5 percentage points below the year-end unemployment rate projected by the CBO in May. After peaking at 22.8 percent in April, U-6, the broadest measure of labor market underutilization, had declined to 12.0 percent, a level lower than that of July 2014, more than five years into the previous recovery. Aided by unparalleled fiscal support for households, by July 2020 retail and new and existing home sales had regained their prepandemic levels.

The COVID-19 pandemic brought to an end the longest economic expansion in recorded U.S. history—which, for the first time since the 2008–9 financial crisis, was exceeding expectations and delivering real economic gains across the income and wealth distributions (figure I-3). In the three years before the pandemic, the U.S. economy added 7 million jobs—5 million more than projected by the nonpartisan CBO in August 2016. In the first 2 months of 2020 alone, the U.S. economy added more jobs (465,000) than the CBO projected would be created in the entire 12 months of 2020 (figure I-4).

Through 2019, real median household income rose $6,000—more than five times total gains under the preceding eight years—while wage, income, and wealth inequality declined, and the wage gap between African Americans

Figure I-3. Actual GDP versus August 2016 CBO Projection

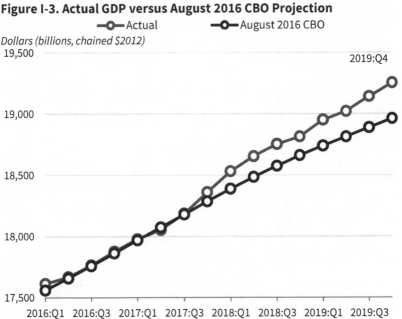

Sources: Bureau of Economic Analysis; Congressional Budget Office (CBO); CEA calculations.

Figure I-4. Actual Payroll Employment versus August 2016 CBO Projection

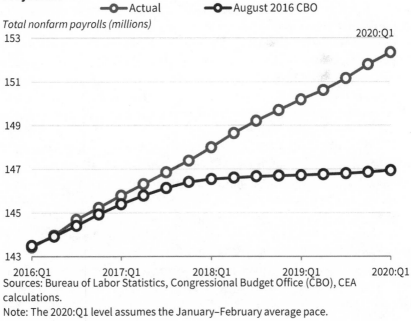

Sources: Bureau of Labor Statistics, Congressional Budget Office (CBO), CEA calculations.

Note: The 2020:Q1 level assumes the January–February average pace.

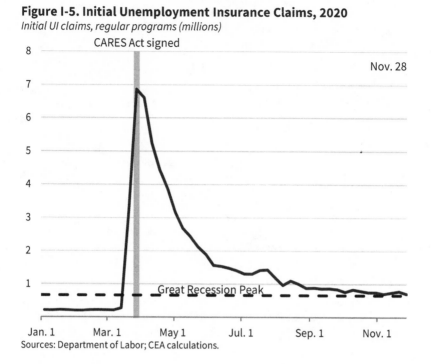

Figure I-5. Initial Unemployment Insurance Claims, 2020

Initial UI claims, regular programs (millions)

Sources: Department of Labor; CEA calculations.

and White Americans narrowed. After landmark tax reform in 2017, real wealth for the bottom 50 percent of households had risen three times faster than that of the top 1 percent, while real wages for the bottom 10 percent grew almost twice as fast as for the top 10 percent—marking stark reversals from the preceding expansion, when wage, income, and wealth inequality all rose. Although wealth rose across the income distribution, the bottom 50 percent's share of real net worth increased—while that of the top 1 percent decreased, labor's share of income rose, and capital's share decreased. In February 2020, just before the pandemic hit in force, the unemployment rate declined to 3.5 percent—its lowest level in more than 50 years, and a full 1.5 percentage points below the CBO's final 2016 forecast.

COVID-19 constituted an exogenous shock that abruptly terminated this record expansion, though it was met with a similarly swift policy response. Within a week of the first reported COVID fatality, Congress passed, and President Trump signed into law, the Coronavirus Preparedness and Response Supplemental Appropriations Act. Within four weeks, the President signed into law two more pieces of economic legislation, including the Coronavirus Aid, Relief, and Economic Security (CARES) Act, which provided $2.2 trillion in direct financial support to American firms, households, medical facilities, and State and local governments. These historic policy responses to the adverse shock of COVID-19, as well as the historic strength of the pre-COVID U.S. economy,

Figure I-6. Index of Household Income by Percentile, 2020

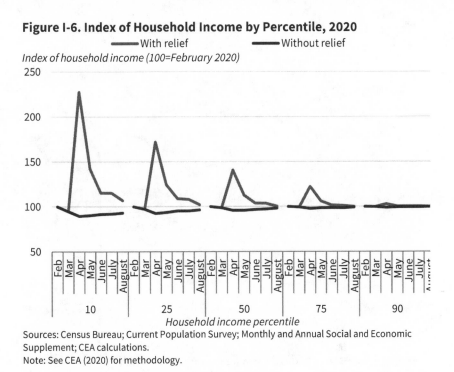

Index of household income (100=February 2020)

Sources: Census Bureau; Current Population Survey; Monthly and Annual Social and Economic Supplement; CEA calculations.

Note: See CEA (2020) for methodology.

mitigated what was on pace to be a macroeconomic contraction on par with the Great Depression. In particular, measures designed to preserve employer-employee relationships, most significantly the Paycheck Protection Program (PPP) and employee retention tax credit, played a key role in allowing firms to retain workers on leave. By limiting eligibility to small and medium-sized enterprises, the PPP targeted aid to those employers that were most at risk of needing to terminate employees (figure I-5).

Meanwhile, income replacement and cost mitigation helped to cushion the shock to household incomes and thereby facilitated stabilization and recovery of consumer spending, which alone constitutes 70 percent of the U.S. economy. Federal assistance programs, including expanded and enhanced Unemployment Insurance and Economic Impact Payments to households earning below set income thresholds, largely offset declines in household compensation due to economic shutdowns. Income replacement rates were highest at the lower end of the income distribution, indicating that relief was targeted toward households that were more vulnerable to an adverse income shock (figure I-6). Upon expiration of these provisions and in the absence of Congressional action, the Trump Administration extended further relief through four executive actions, providing supplemental payments through lost wages assistance to unemployed Americans, temporary payroll tax relief, and extended relief and protection for student borrowers and renters at risk of eviction.

Figure I-7. Labor Market Recovery Comparisons by Recessions

Level of employment (index, prerecession peak = 100)

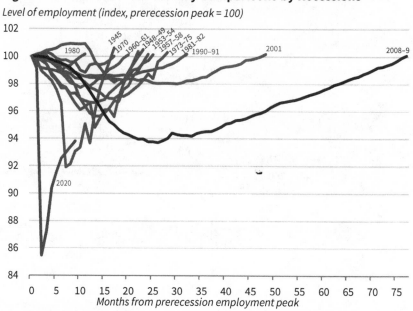

Sources: Bureau of Labor Statistics; National Bureau of Economic Research; CEA calculations.

Though the pace of the recovery vastly exceeded expectations and con-stituted the most rapid economic recovery on record (figure I-7), in the face of the continuing global COVID-19 pandemic, U.S. employment and produc-tion remained below prepandemic levels at the end of 2020. Recognizing the remaining challenges to full economic recovery, most importantly the ongoing COVID-19 pandemic, the Administration supports and consistently supported additional fiscal relief, including an additional round of the PPP to support small business payroll retention, an expanded employee retention tax credit, a continuation of enhanced Unemployment Insurance benefits, a second round of Economic Impact Payments, targeted aid to schools and State and local governments, additional nutritional support, and temporary relief to specific adversely affected industries. At the time of this writing, the U.S. Congress had not agreed to these measures.

In chapter 1 of this *Report*, we discuss the historic economic gains in the United States on the eve of the pandemic, before quantifying the magnitude of the economic shock that hit the U.S. economy in 2020 and situating this shock in historical context. In chapters 2, 3, and 4, we then document and estimate the economic effect of the Administration's response to the shock, focusing first on households and labor markets, then on business and financial markets, and finally on healthcare. We then turn, in the next five chapters, to the role of pre-COVID-19 Administration policies—specifically in the areas of Opportunity

Zones, deregulation, school choice, space innovation and exploration, and international trade—in establishing the foundations for longer-run potential economic growth. Finally, we review the U.S. economy in 2020 and discuss the economic outlook, including potential risks, before concluding with a discussion of potential future policies to promote further economic recovery and subsequent growth.

In chapter 1, we document that the beginning of 2020 ushered in a strong U.S. economy that was delivering job, income, and wealth gains to Americans of all backgrounds, with historically low unemployment and poverty along with record gains in median income for workers across the socioeconomic spectrum. Moreover, the robust state of the economy led forecasters to expect healthy growth through 2020 and beyond. However, the arrival of COVID-19, with origins in the People's Republic of China, brought with it an unprecedented economic and public health crisis. This chapter describes the health of the pre-COVID Trump economy and the nature of the economic shock from COVID-19, and gives an overview of the swift and bold fiscal response undertaken by the Trump Administration to provide relief and lay the foundation for the most rapid economic rebound to date in modern U.S. history.

We analyze these issues in greater depth in chapter 2. We find that the Trump Administration's pro-growth policies contributed to substantial gains for U.S. households between 2016 and 2019. Median net worth increased by 18 percent, median income increased by 9.7 percent, and poverty reached a record low. As the COVID-19 pandemic brought the historic expansion to a potentially catastrophic halt, the Trump Administration helped protect the livelihoods of Americans through legislation and executive actions. Even as the unemployment rate climbed from a 50-year low of 3.5 percent in February 2020 to a record high of 14.7 percent in April, household incomes increased across the distribution, especially for lower-income households, thanks to Economic Impact Payments and expanded and enhanced Unemployment Insurance. Protections against evictions and student loan defaults helped keep people in their homes and out of default. The ultimate success of these efforts will depend on how quickly the economy recovers. Between April and November, the unemployment rate fell by 8.0 percentage points, the fastest six-month decline on record, paving the way to attaining the same strong economy that prevailed during the first three years of the Trump Administration.

Chapter 3 analyzes the effects of the economic policy response on businesses and employer-employee ties. The CARES Act, which was signed into law by President Trump only two weeks after he issued a National Emergency Declaration, provided record economic relief to families and businesses to mitigate the shock from the COVID-19 crisis. In total, the fiscal response to COVID-19 stands out as the most rapid and robust crisis-related economic policy mobilization in the post–World War II era. Two central objectives have constituted the Trump Administration's approach to combating the economic fallout from COVID-19: the alleviation of financial distress to reduce hardship, and the preservation of underlying economic health to facilitate a faster recovery. Ensuring the vitality and resilience of small businesses plays an essential role in achieving these objectives. This chapter describes the fiscal relief provisions aimed at helping small businesses and their workers—principally the PPP—and their success in fueling what has been thus far the fastest employment and GDP rebound in U.S. history.

In chapter 4, we examine how the COVID-19 pandemic constituted a rapidly evolving health and economic crisis in the healthcare sector and for working families across the Nation. The Trump Administration's response to address this multifaceted crisis involved a complementary two-pronged policy approach. First, by enacting several pieces of bipartisan legislation, the Administration secured significant funding to alleviate the financial burden experienced by hospitals, offered tax credits to private employers with fewer than 500 employees to enable them to provide emergency paid family and sick leave for their workers, and fully covered the cost of COVID-19 testing and treatment for many low-income and uninsured individuals. Second, through a series of deregulatory actions, the Administration expanded the use of telemedicine for both COVID-19 screenings and many other health concerns, supported the relaxation of occupational licensing requirements for nurse practitioners, issued Emergency Use Authorizations for COVID-19 diagnostic tests, and accelerated the development, authorization, and deployment of therapeutics and vaccines for COVID-19. This included the Administration's Operation Warp Speed, which the CEA estimates could result in as much as $2.4 trillion in economic benefit through the accelerated availability of an effective vaccine. This chapter explores the various effects of these healthcare policy innovations and achievements, some of which are likely to pay dividends after the COVID-19 pandemic is resolved.

Beginning with chapter 5, we discuss the role of pre-COVID Administration policies in establishing the foundations for longer-run potential economic growth. The Tax Cuts and Jobs Act of 2017 not only broadly lowered taxes for businesses and individuals but also made targeted cuts to spur investment in economically distressed communities designated as Opportunity Zones (OZs). This chapter compares the advantages of OZs with those of other Federal antipoverty programs and documents the characteristics of the nearly 8,800 low-income communities designated as OZs. The CEA finds that $75 billion has been invested in funds for OZs, and that this investment is already benefiting OZ residents and potentially having only a small effect on the current Federal budget.

In chapter 6, we revisit the issue of economic regulation. During the Trump Administration, Federal agencies have demonstrated a sustained commitment to regulatory reform. As a result, the Administration's regulatory efforts have helped reduce red tape for small businesses and middle-income households. One of the most important deregulatory actions the Administration finalized in 2020 is the Safer Affordable Fuel Efficient (SAFE) Vehicles Rule, which we estimate will lead to an increase in real incomes, and raise GDP by $53 billion annually, or about 0.3 percent. The CEA also finds that the benefits of deregulations, such as the SAFE Vehicles Rule, tend to favor the lower income quintiles, suggesting that lower-income households may have benefited the most, relative to household income, from the Administration's deregulatory actions.

In chapter 7, we examine the topic of school choice. During the past 30 years, school choice programs have undergone dramatic expansion in the United States. These programs—organized at the Federal, State, and local levels—share a common goal of expanding access to education options that exist alongside and ultimately improve public school options for primary and secondary education. The programs have altered primary and secondary education in fundamental ways by increasing competition in the school system and by enhancing educational opportunities for all students, especially those from disadvantaged groups. We document the development and expansion of school choice programs and discuss the role of Federal policy, including recent actions by the Trump Administration to further this expansion. We explain how educational competition empowers families and incentivizes schools to deliver more value, and we document the growing empirical evidence that carefully crafted school choice programs do improve educational outcomes for all students.

Chapter 8 analyzes important developments in a frontier of economic potential, namely, innovation and opportunity in the space economy. We review advancements in spaceflight and space policy made during the past year, including the first commercial human spaceflight in history and implications for the private sector's role in the space economy. We also discuss the role of the Administration's policies—specifically the Executive Order on "Encouraging International Support for the Recovery and Use of Space Resources" and the Artemis Accords—in strengthening investor confidence in the space economy and thereby enabling expansion of the private space sector. After an extensive review of the economic theory of property rights and the empirical property rights literature, we find substantial evidence that improving investor expectations in a novel economic sector such as space increases investment in that sector. In addition, we estimate that private space investment could as much as double in the next eight years, due to the Administration's executive actions and other enhancements of property rights in space.

In chapter 9, we examine how the Administration has promoted U.S. interests in international trade by forging new bilateral trade agreements with China, Japan, and South Korea, and reshaped regional trade by modernizing the trade agreement with our most important trading partners, Canada and Mexico. The United States–Mexico–Canada Agreement achieves new safeguards for U.S. interests across a range of areas including digital services, intellectual property, and labor protections. These agreements go well beyond formal tariff barriers that have been the focus of past trade agreements by addressing structural and technical barriers to free and fair trade. We also review how the COVID-19 pandemic reduced international trade overall and has brought into focus underappreciated risks of global supply chains.

In chapter 10, we build on chapters 1, 2, and 3 by summarizing the main macroeconomic developments of 2020, and discuss the economic outlook for the years ahead, with particular attention to upside and downside risks. We find that though the U.S. economy in 2020 was hit with the biggest adverse macroeconomic shock since the Great Depression—with effects on output, labor, capital, housing, and energy markets all of historic magnitudes—the subsequent recovery to date has also been of historic speed, breadth, and magnitude. We highlight that though official and private forecasters currently project continued strong recovery in 2021—aided by an unprecedented economic policy response in 2020, a strong pre-COVID economy, and the availability of vaccines through Operation Warp Speed—substantial risks remain, including both pandemic and policy risks.

In the near term, the single greatest downside economic risk is rising COVID-19 cases before the widespread availability of vaccines, and the policy and behavioral responses to viral resurgences. Already, in December 2020, several State and local governments have reimposed shelter-in-place orders in response to rising cases in November and December. For this reason, the Administration continues to articulate support for additional fiscal measures to provide a bridge to the widespread availability of vaccine candidates developed under Operation Warp Speed. Over the longer term, failure to maintain or implement the types of pro-growth policies discussed in this *Report* and in the 2018, 2019, and 2020 editions of the *Economic Report of the President* would constitute additional potential downside risks. But the continuation and expansion of the Administration's pro-growth policies in support of full labor market recovery offer the upside potential for a rapid return to the levels of employment, production, and real income growth that prevailed on the eve of the pandemic.

We conclude this *Report*, in chapter 11, by reviewing a collection of policy areas highlighted by the COVID-19 pandemic, and we analyze reforms that might meet the ongoing economic challenges faced by the United States. In particular, we review potential policies to strengthen connections to the labor force, support a balance between work and family, advance international coordination to address 21st-century challenges, create a more effective healthcare system, build a dynamic economy through infrastructure improvement, and generate a more skilled and resilient workforce. We find that solving these challenges can ensure that the United States not only recovers to its prepandemic levels of prosperity but also builds a fairer, more dynamic, and more resilient economy that benefits all Americans.

Contents

Appendixes

Figures

Tables

Boxes

Confronting the Largest Postwar Economic Shock: The Federal Response to Mitigate the COVID-19 Pandemic

Chapter 1

Creating the Fastest Economic Recovery

The beginning of 2020 ushered in a strong U.S. economy that was delivering job, income, and wealth gains to Americans of all backgrounds. By February 2020, the unemployment rate had fallen to 3.5 percent—the lowest in 50 years—and unemployment rates for minority groups and historically disadvantaged Americans were at or near their lowest points in recorded history. Wages were rising faster for workers than for managers, income and wealth inequality were on the decline, and median incomes for minority households were experiencing especially rapid gains. The fruits of this strong labor market expansion from 2017 to 2019 also included lifting 6.6 million people out of poverty, which is the largest three-year drop to start any presidency since the War on Poverty began in 1964. These accomplishments highlight the success of the Trump Administration's pro-growth, pro-worker policies.

The robust state of the U.S. economy in the three years through 2019 led almost all forecasters to expect continued healthy growth through 2020 and beyond. However, in late 2019 and the early months of 2020, the novel coronavirus that causes COVID-19, with origins in the People's Republic of China, began spreading around the globe and eventually within the United States, causing a pandemic and bringing with it an unprecedented economic and public health crisis. Both the demand and supply sides of the economy suffered sudden and massive shocks due to the pandemic. During the springtime lockdowns aimed at "flattening the curve," the labor market lost 22.2 million jobs, and the unemployment rate jumped 11.2 percentage points, to 14.7 percent—the largest monthly changes in the series' histories.

The healthy foundation of the Trump Administration's prepandemic economy, coupled with strong and decisive action during the crisis, helped the Nation weather the catastrophic COVID-19 shock and rebound faster than either official or private forecasters had projected. After a sharp contraction in the second quarter of 2020, the U.S. economy posted a 33.1 percent annualized gain in gross domestic product (GDP) in the third quarter—the largest jump on record, and nearly double the previous record from 70 years ago. As a result, the U.S. economy has recovered two-thirds of the GDP damage from COVID-19 in just one quarter.

This chapter first documents the strength and resilience of the U.S. economy leading up to the COVID-19 pandemic, both in absolute and relative senses. The chapter demonstrates that the U.S. economy under the Trump Administration suffered from fewer macroeconomic vulnerabilities than the pre–Great Recession economy and that the economic experience during the pandemic would have been even worse if it had not been for the economic improvement from 2017 to the beginning of 2020.

In addition, this chapter details how, relative to the Great Recession, the Federal Government acted with greater speed and provided more robust relief in response to the COVID-19 crisis. In particular, the $2.2 trillion Coronavirus Aid, Relief, and Economic Security (CARES) Act—passed by Congress within two weeks of the President's National Emergency Declaration—delivered the most extensive fiscal relief in U.S. history. Moreover, it was targeted primarily to vulnerable families, workers, and small businesses, in stark contrast to the larger focus on banks and big businesses in the fiscal response to the Great Recession.

Two overarching objectives have characterized the Federal Government's approach to combating the economic consequences of COVID-19: the alleviation of financial distress to reduce hardship, and the preservation of underlying economic health to facilitate a faster recovery. For example, enhanced unemployment insurance benefits and eviction moratoriums supported household balance sheets, and the Paycheck Protection Program strengthened the connective tissue of the labor market by helping maintain matches between employers and furloughed employees, setting the stage for the fastest employment rebound in U.S. history.

Chapters 2, 3, and 4 of this *Report* analyze the specific responses that this Administration has implemented to address the dual public health and economic crises resulting from the COVID-19 pandemic.

The U.S. economy entered 2020 with historically low unemployment and poverty, declining inequality, and some of the strongest household income and wealth gains on record. In short, the American economy was delivering greater opportunity to people across the socioeconomic spectrum. At the time, leading forecasters were predicting this prosperity to continue in 2020 and beyond with healthy GDP growth. However, COVID-19 interrupted this boom after it spread beyond the borders of China and instigated the most severe global public health and economic crisis in almost a century. This chapter describes the healthy state of the U.S. economy before COVID-19 reached American shores, the evolution of what has become the largest shock to the U.S. economy since the Great Depression, and the historic range of policies that were quickly passed into law to support the economy and lay the foundation for a robust recovery.

Before delving into each of these issues individually, it is worth taking stock of the broader economic account of 2020 and just how far the U.S. economy has recovered since the peak crisis period of the spring shutdowns. As shown in figure 1-1, leading forecasters had been forecasting healthy 2 percent GDP growth for 2020 at the beginning of the year. Then, as the pandemic worsened, they sharply revised their forecasts down, predicting the worst contraction in annual GDP in the post–World War II period. However, in the face of a much stronger recovery to date than almost anyone had predicted, forecasters have responded by substantially revising their predictions for the year upward, especially in light of the 33.1 percent annualized GDP rebound in the third quarter that eclipsed the prior record from 70 years ago.

Figure 1-2 puts into stark relief the differences in economic behavior during the COVID-19 pandemic versus during the Great Recession. Each curve plots real GDP indexed to its level five quarters before the trough of each downturn. As shown by the time-0 point on the horizontal axis, the onset of COVID-19 led to a drop in indexed GDP more than twice as large as that of the Great Recession. However, the figure also reveals the much more dramatic rebound in economic fortunes during the pandemic thus far, driven by the Federal government's swift and bold economic interventions to deliver relief

Figure 1-1. Evolution of 2020's Gross Domestic Product Forecast, 2020

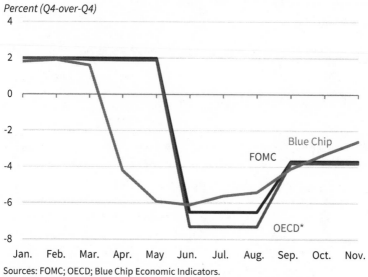

Percent (Q4-over-Q4)

Sources: FOMC; OECD; Blue Chip Economic Indicators.
Note: FOMC = Federal Open Market Committee; OECD = Organization for Economic Cooperation and Development. *The OECD's GDP forecast is the year-over-year percent change.

Figure 1-2. Real Gross Domestic Product Fell and Rose More Sharply Now Than during the Great Recession

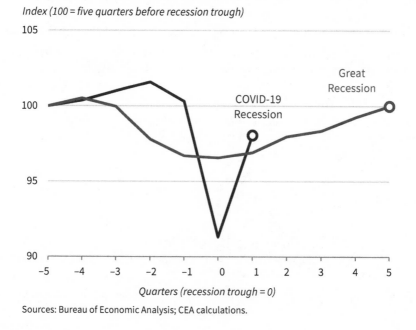

Index (100 = five quarters before recession trough)

Sources: Bureau of Economic Analysis; CEA calculations.

particularly to households and small businesses. Provided that the economy continues to receive appropriate and responsive fiscal support, the recovery is poised to remain on a healthy trajectory. In contrast, in the aftermath of the Great Recession, the economy suffered from a weaker and more protracted recovery—especially when viewed through the lens of the labor market, as this chapter discusses later.

The Historic Strength of the U.S. Economy before COVID-19

Before the COVID-19 pandemic, the U.S. economy under President Trump was surpassing milestone after milestone, delivering broad-based economic gains to Americans of all backgrounds. After years of historically slow recovery following the Great Recession, the unemployment rate fell below 4 percent for the first time since December 2000, reaching 3.5 percent at the end of 2019. The more comprehensive "U-6" unemployment rate—which includes people not looking for work but wanting a job and people working part-time who would prefer to have a full-time job—reached an all-time low of 6.7 percent in December 2019.

Moreover, the advances in labor market opportunity extended to all corners of American society. The unemployment rate for African Americans fell to 5.4 percent in late 2019, down from 7.5 percent when President Trump took office and the lowest level on record. For reference, the lowest rate achieved under any previous administration was 7.0 percent in April 2000. Hispanic Americans also enjoyed the lowest unemployment rate on record, with the rate dropping to 3.9 percent in late 2019. Those with a less formal education were also beneficiaries of a labor market of unparalleled strength, with the unemployment rate for people with less than a high school diploma reaching 4.8 percent in late 2019, and Americans with only a high school degree facing a 3.6 percent rate.

These strong pre-COVID labor market conditions were no mere coincidence; nor were they a passive continuation of economic momentum carried over from the preceding years of the expansion. Although the unemployment rate had managed to fall below 5 percent after six years of the slowest labor market recovery in recorded history, the Congressional Budget Office and the Federal Open Market Committee issued forecasts before the 2016 election showing that the unemployment rate would flatten and stay well above 4 percent, as shown in figure 1-3. However, the combination of the landmark Tax Cuts and Jobs Act in 2017 and the implementation of President Trump's pro-growth deregulatory agenda laid the groundwork for the economy to surpass

Figure 1-3. The Unemployment Rate versus Preelection Forecasts, 2011–19

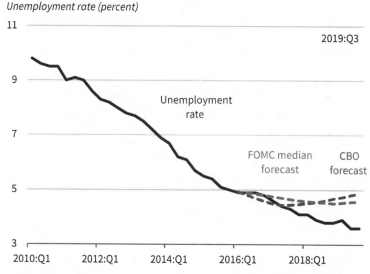

Unemployment rate (percent)

Sources: Congressional Budget Office; Bureau of Labor Statistics; Federal Reserve.
Note: CBO = Congressional Budget Office; FOMC = Federal Open Market Committee.
The CBO forecast is from August 2016; the FOMC forecast is from September 2016.

these expectations by boosting economic competitiveness and dynamism (CEA 2019, 2020a).[1]

Besides increasing the abundance of job opportunities, a low unemployment rate also confers greater bargaining power on workers when they are negotiating pay with employers. Both when looking to recruit new workers and retain existing talent, employers must offer a compelling pay package when unemployment is low or else risk losing valuable workers to their competitors. In fact, 2019 data from the Job Openings and Labor Turnover Survey (JOLTS) shows the highest quit rate since 2001—a sign of a challenging environment for employers to retain workers who were availing themselves of the tight competition for their services. Table 1-1 compares the magnitude of earnings growth for different types of workers under the pre-COVID Trump economy with the expansion period from the previous administration. Table 1-1 shows that earnings growth was higher across the board in the period since 2017 to before COVID-19, and on top of that, workers' earnings were outpacing those of managers, and the bottom 10 percent of wage earners were experiencing more rapid earnings growth than the top 10 percent.

---

[1] Chapter 1 in both the 2019 and 2020 editions of the *Economic Report of the President* provides a comprehensive analysis of the pro-growth benefits of the Tax Cuts and Jobs Act. Chapter 3 of the 2020 *Report* discusses the benefits of the Trump Administration's focus on deregulation for household income.

Table 1-1. Growth in Earnings, 2009–20

Group	Pre-COVID Economy (Jan. 2017–Feb. 2020)	Previous Expansion Period (Jul. 2009–Dec. 2016)
Workers	3.3	2.3
Managers	2.7	2.5
	(2017:Q1–2019:Q4)	(2009:Q3–2016:Q4)
No bachelor's	3.0	1.3
Bachelor's or more	2.9	1.5
Bottom 10% wage earners	4.9	1.9
Top 10% wage earners	3.3	2.4

Sources: Bureau of Labor Statistics; CEA calculations.

Note: Data represent a compound annual growth rate for 2009:Q3–2016:Q4 or July 2009–December 2016 and 2017:Q1–2019:Q4 or January 2017–January 2020. For workers and managers, earnings are defined as average weekly earnings. For all other categories, earnings are defined as median usual weekly earnings.

The CEA finds that higher earnings growth among low-wage workers is a result of rising labor demand in the Trump economy. Although some assert the importance of State-level minimum wage increases based on cross-state comparisons of wage growth since 2016 (Van Dam and Siegel 2020; Nunn and Shambaugh 2020; Tung 2020; Tedeschi 2020), there are serious limitations and flaws in these analyses that undermine their conclusions. In particular, the limitation of these studies is that they do not show that the timing of wage increases aligns with the timing of minimum wage hikes in States that have instituted such hikes. Thus, the studies do not distinguish wage growth that occurred before a minimum wage hike from wage growth that occurred after a hike. Because of their failure to consider this timing issue, these studies do not provide strong evidence that minimum wage hikes are responsible for wage growth. Additionally, wage growth could have been higher in the States that increased their minimum wages even without the increases.

In contrast, the CEA's analysis uses detailed microdata from the Current Population Survey to identify workers with direct exposure to minimum wage hikes based on their position in the wage distribution. The CEA then calculates the effect of the minimum wage by estimating what wage growth for the directly-affected group would have been had no minimum wage hike occurred. Based on these calculations and a sensitivity analysis, the CEA attributes as an upper bound only 0.2 percentage points of wage growth among workers in the bottom third of the wage distribution to minimum wage hikes. To put this number in perspective, such workers experienced total annual wage growth of 3.8 percent between 2017 and 2019.

In support of the view that strong labor market conditions—not minimum wages—drove the observed wage gains, research by the Federal Reserve Bank of Atlanta compares wage growth in States that increased their minimum

Figure 1-4. Real Median Household Income by Householder Race, 1967–2019

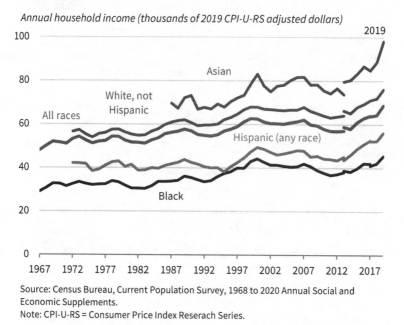

Annual household income (thousands of 2019 CPI-U-RS adjusted dollars)

Source: Census Bureau, Current Population Survey, 1968 to 2020 Annual Social and Economic Supplements.
Note: CPI-U-RS = Consumer Price Index Reserach Series.

wages with those that did not. Robertson (2019) examines the ratio of the 12.5th percentile wage (i.e., the median wage of the lowest quartile) relative to the median wage for all workers. Between 2014 and 2019, this ratio was increasing, indicating faster wage growth at the bottom of the distribution. Notably, the ratio was increasing at about the same rate among States that increased their minimum wages and among States that did not. Robertson (2019) concludes, "The increased tightness of labor markets, or some other factor than hikes in State minimum wages, is playing a role in pushing up the pay for those in lower-wage jobs."

Looking back further than just the previous administration, the $4,400 jump in real median income in 2019 marked the largest one-year increase on record, capping a nearly 10 percent increase since 2016 after adjusting for the U.S. Census's redesign in 2017. Moreover, figure 1-4 reveals that the boost to household incomes occurred for all races, with minorities experiencing outsized gains. Specifically, in 2019 real median income for Black households rose by 7.9 percent, Hispanic Americans saw a 7.1 percent boost, and Asian Americans enjoyed an even larger 10.6 percent increase, while White households experienced a smaller but still substantial 5.7 percent jump. Each of these figures represents record increases and record absolute levels.

The broad-based income and employment gains before COVID-19 also fueled rising household net worth, lower income and wealth concentration,

Figure 1-5. Share of Total Net Worth by Percentile, 2007–19

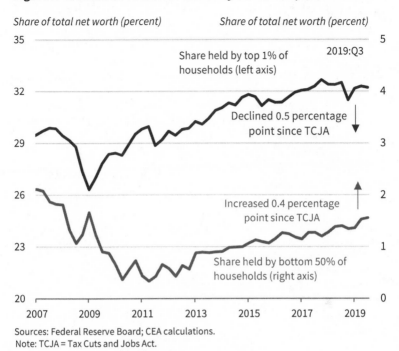

Share of total net worth (percent)　　　Share of total net worth (percent)

Share held by top 1% of households (left axis)

2019:Q3

Declined 0.5 percentage point since TCJA

Increased 0.4 percentage point since TCJA

Share held by bottom 50% of households (right axis)

Sources: Federal Reserve Board; CEA calculations.
Note: TCJA = Tax Cuts and Jobs Act.

and a record fall in the official poverty rate. Through the fourth quarter of 2019, the net worth of the bottom 50 percent increased by 38.9 percent during President Trump's first term, while it increased by 20.1 percent for the top 1 percent. Since the Tax Cuts and Jobs Act passed, the wealth share of the top 1 percent fell by 0.5 percentage point, while that of the bottom 50 percent rose by 0.4 percentage point, as shown in figure 1-5. This broad increase in net worth partly reflects the stark turnaround in the homeownership rate, which reached 65.1 percent in 2019 after recovering from a 2016 trough of 62.9 percent. Income concentration also fell, with the Gini coefficient—a widely used measure of concentration that ranges between 0 and 1—declining from 0.489 in 2017 to 0.484 in 2019. Data from the 2019 Survey of Consumer Finances reveal broad wealth increases driven by the lower earners, with median net worth in the lower two income quintiles up by over 30 percent since 2016. Hispanics and African Americans enjoyed respective gains of 64 percent and 32 percent.

At the bottom of the income distribution, the robust labor market expansion between 2016 and 2019 lifted 6.6 million people out of poverty, which is the largest three-year reduction to start any presidency since the War on Poverty began in 1964. As a proportion of the population, the poverty rate fell to an all-time low of 10.5 percent in 2019—with especially large poverty declines for African Americans, Hispanics, and Asians—as figure 1-6 makes

Figure 1-6. Poverty Rates by Race and Hispanic Origin, 1959–2019

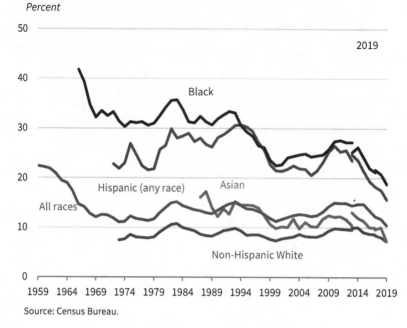

Percent

Source: Census Bureau.

Figure 1-7. U.S. Real Gross Domestic Product, 2014–19

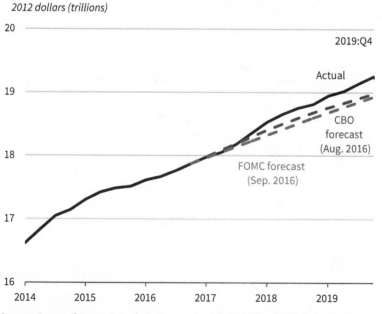

2012 dollars (trillions)

Sources: Bureau of Economic Analysis; Congressional Budget Office (CBO); Federal Open Market Committee (FOMC).

evident. Moreover, 2.8 million children were lifted out of poverty between 2016 and 2019, driving the child poverty rate down to a 50-year low of 14.4 percent.

In the years immediately preceding the pandemic, the United States experienced robust GDP growth that exceeded what the Congressional Budget Office and the Federal Open Market Committee had previously forecast for those years, as seen in figure 1-7. Real GDP grew 2.5 and 2.3 percent in 2018 and 2019, respectively, faster than any other Group of Seven country. Entering 2020, many forecasters slated U.S. output to grow at a healthy pace of about 2 percent in 2020, though it is entirely plausible that the U.S. economy could have continued exceeding projections if the global economy had not been hit with the COVID-19 pandemic—the largest exogenous shock since the Great Depression.

The Early Economic Effects of COVID-19

On January 7, 2020, Chinese researchers announced the discovery of the severe acute respiratory syndrome coronavirus 2 (SARS-CoV-2)—which causes the disease COVID-19—in the travel hub city of Wuhan, China.[2] On January 21, the first case of a person contracting the new coronavirus after traveling from Wuhan was reported in the United States.[3] By late February, the Centers for Disease Control and Prevention had confirmed the first possible instance of community transmission in the United States, and the Standard & Poor's 500 began a sharp sell-off that continued through March 23, losing 33.9 percent of its value compared with its peak just before the outbreak.[4]

The Trump Administration responded by promptly putting in place non-pharmaceutical intervention policies to contain the virus.[5] Travel restrictions on China were imposed on January 31, and the restrictions were subsequently expanded to 26 countries in Europe and several other countries by mid-March (White House 2020a, 2020b). On March 13, President Trump declared COVID-19 a national emergency (White House 2020c). The adoption of a host of social-distancing measures—which included school closures, bans on group gatherings, and closures of restaurants—became prevalent across States shortly thereafter. By March 23, Statewide school closures and restrictions on bars and restaurants had affected over 90 percent of the U.S. population (figure

---

[2] Chinese researchers isolated and confirmed a novel coronavirus after identifying a cluster of acute respiratory illnesses in Wuhan on December 31, 2019 (Patel, Jernigan, and 2019-nCov CDC Response Team 2020).

[3] The CDC announced the first case in the United States when a traveler sought treatment after returning from Wuhan to Washington State a few days earlier (CDC 2020a).

[4] The first case of COVID-19 with no prior travel to infected regions was confirmed by the CDC (2020b).

[5] The CDC defines nonpharmaceutical interventions as actions, apart from vaccination and taking medicine, that people and communities can take to slow the spread of illnesses like the COVID-19 pandemic (CDC 2020c).

Figure 1-8. Percentage of the U.S. Population under Statewide Restrictions, 2020

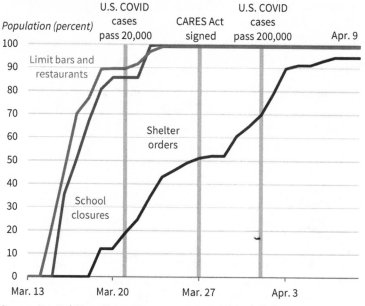

Sources: *New York Times*; State policy announcements; CEA calculations.

1-8). By March 30, 30 States had issued stay-at-home orders, with an additional 13 States having issued these orders for State sections. By early April, over 90 percent of the U.S. population lived in a State that had issued a stay-at-home order.[6]

Studies of the economic effects of past pandemics indicate that there are three main channels through which pandemics affect economic activity:[7] (1) increased mortality, (2) illness and absenteeism, and (3) avoidance behavior to reduce infection. These shocks reduce the size of the labor force, aggregate productivity, and aggregate demand. Consistent with these observations, the economy has experienced sudden, large, and simultaneous shocks to supply and demand as a result of the COVID-19 outbreak in the United States.

On the supply side, many businesses were shuttered by social-distancing measures that States and local authorities put in place or businesses

---

[6] After the Administration's efforts to inform the American public, States began introducing restrictive mandates and regulations dictating protective behavior. The CEA finds that 67 to 100 percent of the observed total increases in a variety of protective behaviors appears to have been driven by the American people's voluntary decisions and the Administration's efforts to encourage these voluntary decisions, and only 33 percent to be accounted for by restrictive State mandates.

[7] See Jonas (2013); Kilbourne (2006); Burns, van der Mensbrugghe, and Timmer (2006); Verikios et al. (2011); McKibbin and Sidorenko (2006); CEA (2019); and McKibbin (2009).

Figure 1-9. Retail Spending during the Early Stages of the Pandemic, Seven-Day Average, 2020

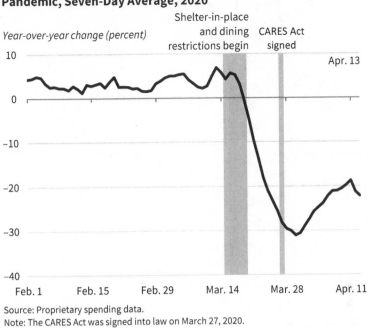

Source: Proprietary spending data.
Note: The CARES Act was signed into law on March 27, 2020.

voluntarily adopted to stop the spread of the virus and "flatten the curve."[8] Those that remained open faced supply disruptions that prevented them from operating normally. On the demand side, many consumers faced stay-at-home orders or voluntarily limited their economic activity to reduce the risk of contracting the disease.[9] Consumers also changed the composition of their demand; for example, they replaced restaurant meals with home-cooked meals and increased their demand for cleaning supplies.

High-frequency indicators that serve as proxies for demand across various economic activities show that the downturn began in early March, in some cases before Statewide social-distancing measures were implemented, and reached its trough at the end of April. Daily retail spending data started plunging in mid-March and bottomed out at a 30 percent year-over-year decline at the end of March (figure 1-9). By the time shelter-in-place orders and dining

---

[8] E.g., on March 11 (before President Trump's announcement of COVID-19 as a national emergency), the NBA had already suspended basketball games indefinitely. The following day, Major League Baseball delayed the start of its season, the National Hockey League suspended games, and March Madness was canceled.

[9] Baqaee and Farhi (2020) model the distinct shocks to supply and demand and study how the combination of supply and demand shocks explains the data. They argue that without the negative shock to aggregate demand, the United States could have experienced stagflation, or a combination of rising unemployment and rising prices. Instead, the negative shock to aggregate demand has limited inflation.

Figure 1-10. Traffic Congestion during the Early Stages of the Pandemic, Median across All States, Seven-Day Average, 2020

Year-over-year change (percent)

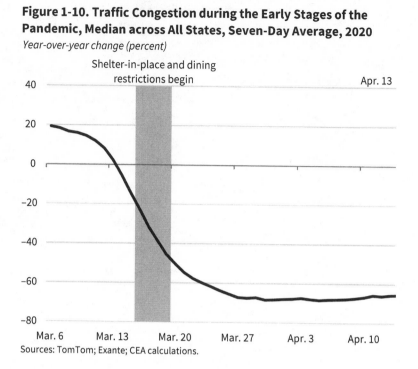

Sources: TomTom; Exante; CEA calculations.

restrictions began, daily traffic congestion (figure 1-10) and seated diners (figure 1-11) across all States had already dropped over 20 percent year-over-year. Similarly, weekly hotel occupancy had dropped 56 percent year-over-year in the week these shelter-in-place measures began (figure 1-12).

Supply indicators—the number of small businesses that were open, the number of hourly employees who were working, and number of hours worked—also saw the steepest year-over-year contraction in March and April. Figure 1-13 illustrates how these indicators compared with a January pre-COVID-19 baseline, as reported by Homebase.[10] After shelter-in-place orders became widespread in mid-March, the proportion of employees working fell from about 15 percent below normal conditions to about 55 to 60 percent.

As the indicators discussed above show, the restrictions on mobility and the shift toward social distancing played a major role in limiting economic activity. Academic research conducted since the COVID-19 pandemic began attempts to quantify the extent to which government restrictions versus voluntary mitigation behaviors can account for the decline in mobility during the

---

[10] Homebase is a company that provides software to help small business owners manage employee timesheets. Since the start of the pandemic, Homebase has maintained a database of U.S. small business employment using data from more than 60,000 businesses that use its software. The data cover more than 1 million employees that were active in the United States in January 2020. Most Homebase customers are businesses that are individually owned or operator-managed restaurants, food and beverages businesses, retail outlets, and service establishments.

Figure 1-11. Seated Diners in U.S. Restaurants, per OpenTable, during the Early Stages of the Pandemic, Seven-Day Average, 2020

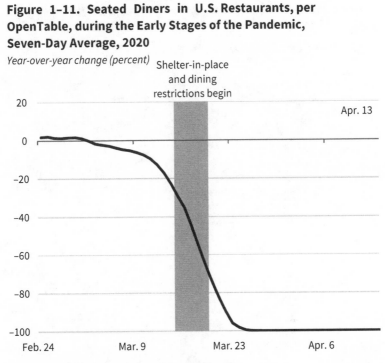

Sources: OpenTable; *New York Times*; CEA calculations.

spring. For example, Goolsbee and Syverson (2020) examine cellular phone records data on customer visits to individual businesses across contiguous boundaries with different policies. They conclude that consumer traffic started to decline before State and local restrictions were put in place, that the degree of private mitigation behavior was tied to the local severity of the virus (i.e., number of deaths in the county), and that, overall, legal restrictions explained only a small fraction of the total decline in activity. However, they do find that the shutdown orders caused a reallocation of consumer activity from "nonessential" to "essential" businesses and from restaurants and bars to groceries. Another study by Cronin and Evans (2020) contains similar findings, concluding that private, self-regulating behavior explained more than three-quarters of the decline in foot traffic but that regulations had large effects on foot traffic to restaurants, hotels, and nonessential retail.

The pandemic also caused significant disruptions to the labor market and to macroeconomic activity. Due to their short reporting lag, initial claims for Unemployment Insurance (UI) provide timely information on how the COVID-19 pandemic and containment measures have affected the labor market. In March, job losses occurred at a level not seen since the Great Depression, with initial UI claims spiking from 282,000 the week ending March 14 to 6.9 million two weeks later.

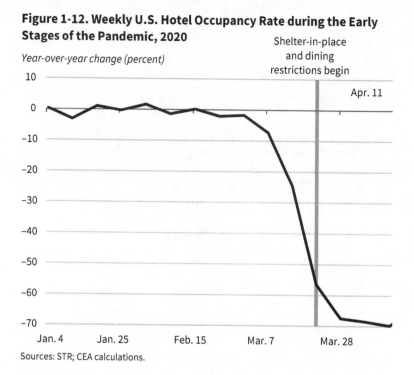

Figure 1-12. Weekly U.S. Hotel Occupancy Rate during the Early Stages of the Pandemic, 2020

Year-over-year change (percent)

Shelter-in-place and dining restrictions begin

Apr. 11

Sources: STR; CEA calculations.

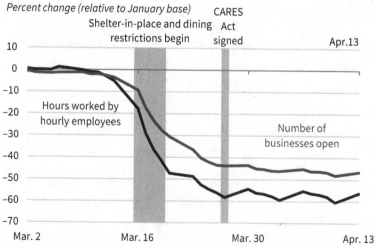

Figure 1-13. Percent Change in Small Businesses That Are Open and Hourly Employees Who Are Working in the Early Stages of the Pandemic, 2020

Percent change (relative to January base)

Shelter-in-place and dining restrictions begin

CARES Act signed

Apr.13

Hours worked by hourly employees

Number of businesses open

Source: Homebase.

Note: All rates compare a given date versus the median for that day of the week during the period January 4–31, 2020. The number of hourly employees working traces hours worked by hourly employees.

Data on total economic output also reflect the enormous negative shock that the COVID-19 pandemic and containment measures had on the economy. First-quarter real GDP declined at an annualized rate of 5.0 percent—itself significant—but this drop would later be dwarfed by the annualized 31.4 percent collapse in second-quarter GDP. In early June, the Organization for Economic Cooperation and Development (OECD) estimated that the COVID-19 pandemic and containment measures would decrease U.S. Q4-over-Q4 GDP by 7.4 percent in 2020 in the absence of a second wave in the fall (single-hit scenario), or 12.3 percent if such a wave were to occur (double-hit scenario). This forecast was more pessimistic than those provided by the Congressional Budget Office and the Blue Chip survey of the private sector in July, which were still large, at 5.9 and 5.6 percent decreases, respectively.

The U.S. Economy's Resilience in Weathering the COVID-19 Shock

Beyond the immediate prosperity that Americans were enjoying before COVID-19, the vibrant state of the U.S. economy rendered it more resilient and better prepared to weather the COVID-19 shock than if it had occurred in earlier years. To quantify this resilience, the CEA simulates the likely path of the unemployment rate if the COVID-19 shock had occurred under the weaker economic conditions of 2016 instead of the stronger actual 2020 pre-COVID conditions. To construct this simulation, the CEA uses Current Population Survey data to measure the monthly probability that workers transit between employment, unemployment, and not being in the labor force. The CEA's analysis assumes that any year-over-year deterioration in transition probabilities from 2019 to 2020 is attributable to COVID-19, which makes it possible to isolate the magnitude of the COVID-19 shock to labor flows. Then, the CEA applies this measured COVID-19 shock to monthly 2016 labor market transition probabilities to arrive at likely counterfactual labor market flows and ultimately unemployment dynamics if COVID-19 had occurred under 2016 economic conditions.

The solid blue line in figure 1-14 shows the actual observed path of unemployment, and the solid green line shows the simulated path of the unemployment response to COVID-19 under full 2016 conditions—specifically, starting from the 4.9 percent February 2016 unemployment rate (compared with 3.5 percent in February 2020) and with the worse baseline (without COVID-19) labor dynamism from 2016. As the figure shows, if COVID-19 had arrived with the U.S. economy in its 2016 state, the unemployment rate would likely have peaked at a higher rate and been nearly 2 percentage points above the actual level in October. If, instead, the U.S. economy had entered the COVID-19 crisis with the 2016 level of unemployment but the healthier Trump labor market flows—as shown in the red dashed curve in the figure—the dynamics of unemployment would not have looked substantially different than what has actually

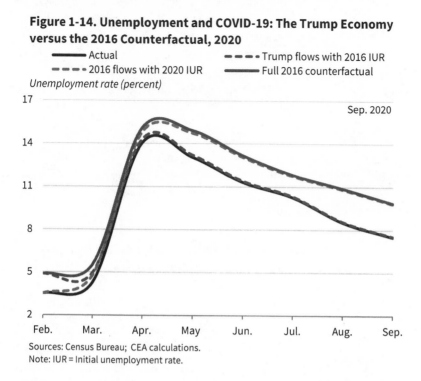

Figure 1-14. Unemployment and COVID-19: The Trump Economy versus the 2016 Counterfactual, 2020

Actual ━━━ Trump flows with 2016 IUR
2016 flows with 2020 IUR ━━━ Full 2016 counterfactual

Unemployment rate (percent)

Sep. 2020

Feb. Mar. Apr. May Jun. Jul. Aug. Sep.

Sources: Census Bureau; CEA calculations.
Note: IUR = Initial unemployment rate.

occurred. In other words, the difference in initial unemployment rates is not the crux of the superior resilience of the Trump economy. To the contrary, the gold dashed curve shows that, holding fixed the initial February unemployment rate at 3.6 percent, the unemployment rate would have followed a much worse trajectory if the economy had suffered from the worse underlying dynamism of the 2016 economy.

Comparing the COVID–19 Recession and the Great Recession

The pre-COVID U.S. economy possessed fewer macroeconomic vulnerabilities than it had in the lead-up to the Great Recession, when overextended household borrowers and a highly leveraged financial sector precipitated the Great Recession. Unlike the previous recession, the COVID-19 crisis was not the consequence of underlying economic imbalances, and the greater resilience of the pre-COVID U.S. economy coupled with the superior fiscal response augurs well for the continuing prospects of a much more robust recovery. This section sheds light on the comparative health of the U.S. economy before the current crisis relative to the years before the 2007–9 financial crisis and Great Recession.

The State of the Economy before the Crises

This subsection looks at various sectors of the U.S. economy before the crises. We consider households, nonfinancial businesses, and banks.

Households. The financial situation of the household sector was stronger in early 2020 than at the start of the Great Recession. From 2000 to 2008, household liabilities as a share of personal disposable income rose from 96 percent to 136 percent before falling back to below 100 percent before COVID-19, according to the Federal Reserve's Flow of Funds data. However, examining only aggregates can obscure the true level of risk, which is captured more accurately by the tails of the distribution. Even along this dimension, however, the U.S. economy was in a stronger position before the COVID-19 crisis than it was back in 2006 before the start of the financial crisis. The share of mortgages with debt-to-income ratios above 50 percent fell from 11.0 percent in 2006 to only 6.9 percent in 2018. Though the loan-to-value ratio for new mortgages was similar to what it was in 2006, credit had shifted toward borrowers with high credit scores. Whereas 14.1 percent of borrowers taking out a mortgage had below a 620 credit score in 2006, that share was only 3.3 percent in 2018. Borrowers were also taking out safer loans by 2018. The share of mortgages with less than full amortization fell from 29.2 percent in 2006 to 0.6 percent in 2018, and mortgages for which borrowers were only required to provide minimal documentation at origination saw their share drop from 34.5 percent in 2006 to 1.8 percent in 2018 (Davis et al. 2019). Looking beyond mortgages, the share of credit card volume going to subprime borrowers was under 2.5 percent in 2019, compared with 3.4 percent before the financial crisis, according to the Consumer Financial Protection Bureau. The bureau also shows that, for automobile loans, the share going to subprime borrowers was under 15 percent in 2019 before COVID-19, versus nearly 20 percent in 2006.

Before COVID-19, researchers ran stress tests on households to examine how negative shocks to the economy would translate into defaults on household debt. One study simulates a fall in house prices similar to what occurred in the Great Recession and generates a much smaller peak in foreclosures; the average shocked stressed default rate—which represents, for a particular loan, its expected default rate if it were hit shortly after origination with a replay of the financial crisis—was 9.7 percent in 2018 compared with 34.8 percent in 2006 (Davis et al. 2019). Another study simulates a large house price decline and unemployment spike meant to mimic the financial crisis. When faced with the same shocks from 2007 to 2009, the simulated 2020 economic response generates fewer defaults because of healthier household balance sheets (Bhutta et al. 2019). Although the COVID-19 economic shock differs from that of the last crisis, the combined effect of stronger household balance sheets and a bolder fiscal response has greatly reduced the amount of actual financial distress that one would expect from such a large disruption.

Figure 1–15. Ratio of Household Sector and Nonfinancial Business Debt to Gross Domestic Product, 2006:Q4–2020:Q2

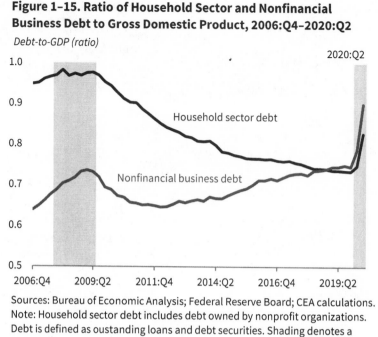

Debt-to-GDP (ratio)

Household sector debt

Nonfinancial business debt

2020:Q2

Sources: Bureau of Economic Analysis; Federal Reserve Board; CEA calculations.
Note: Household sector debt includes debt owned by nonprofit organizations.
Debt is defined as oustanding loans and debt securities. Shading denotes a recession.

Nonfinancial businesses. Although households were in good shape before the COVID-19 pandemic, the nonfinancial business sector had become more leveraged. By early 2020, the aggregate debt-to-GDP ratio for nonfinancial businesses had reached levels not seen since the financial crisis (figure 1-15).[11]

One reason nonfinancial business debt has risen, however, is that interest rates are at historic lows. This reduces the burden of servicing debt. A basic measure of the debt burden is the ratio of company earnings to their interest payments, or the interest coverage ratio. In the years leading up to the pandemic, the interest coverage ratio for the median firm remained high (Federal Reserve 2020). The sales-weighted shares of nonfinancial public corporations that use more than 30 percent, 40 percent, or 50 percent of their earnings to make interest payments were all declining; and in early 2020, at the onset of COVID-19, these shares were all lower than at the start of the Great Recession (Crouzet and Gourio 2020).

Despite historically low costs of borrowing, the Federal Reserve and the International Monetary Fund have expressed concern about the quality of corporate debt. In early 2020, about 50 percent of investment-grade debt was rated BBB, an amount that was near a historical high. BBB is the lowest rating category for investment-grade debt, and thus carries more risk of default than higher-grade debt. Another concern is that in recent years, loans to large

---

[11] These ratios spiked in the second quarter of 2020 as GDP contracted sharply.

corporations have increasingly focused on highly leveraged firms. In February 2020 at the onset of the pandemic recession, the rate was higher than at the start of the Great Recession (Federal Reserve 2020; IMF 2019, 2020). Overall, the second quarter of 2020 had the highest quarterly volume of defaults in leveraged loans since the first quarter of 2009 (LCD News 2020).

Banks. The banking sector was well capitalized at the start of the COVID-19 pandemic. According to data compiled by the Federal Deposit Insurance Corporation, as of the fourth quarter of 2019, the commercial banking and savings and loan sector stood at a record, or near-record, in various measures of industry solvency and liquidity. This status was largely attributable to the continuous growth in the economy since the end of the Great Recession and the passage and continuing implementation of the Dodd-Frank Act of 2010, which dramatically raised regulatory oversight and capital standards for the industry.

The number of banks on the Federal Deposit Insurance Corporation's "Problem Bank List" leading up to COVID-19 was exceptionally low. The number of problem banks fell from 76 in 2007:Q4 to 51 by 2019:Q4, the lowest number of problem banks since 2006:Q4. Total assets of problem banks increased from $22 billion in 2007 to $46 billion in 2019. The commercial banking sector also entered the crisis with stable indicators of asset quality.

The Origins and Progression

This subsection reviews the different origins of the COVID-19-induced recession and the Great Recession, and the important differences in how these shocks played out over time. The financial crisis and resulting Great Recession of 2007–9 started with an overheated housing market. In 2006, housing market weakness began to emerge, first in the form of longer selling delays—indicating a deterioration in housing liquidity—followed by deceleration and reversal in house price growth. The weakness in housing then spilled over into the rest of the economy because of the damage it wreaked on household and bank balance sheets alike.

By March 2007, there were reports that the housing slump had hit some hedge funds hard. In their book *First Responders*, Bernanke, Geithner, and Paulson (2020, 12) state that "if we had to pick the date that the crisis began, it would be August 9, 2007, when the French bank BNP Paribas froze withdrawals from three funds that held securities backed by U.S. subprime mortgages." By the late summer of 2007, the investment bank Bear Stearns was liquidating two hedge funds that were heavily invested in subprime mortgages. Over the next year, the contagion spread to every corner of financial markets and turned into a full-blown crisis. Facing deteriorating balance sheets and frozen markets, lenders cut the supply of credit to the economy, which caused households and businesses to curtail spending. As the economy hemorrhaged jobs, higher unemployment accelerated the collapse in the housing market, which further fueled the cascading spiral of economic misery.

The unemployment rate increased from 4.7 percent in November 2007 to a peak of 10.0 percent in October 2009. Moreover, unemployment remained above 9 percent for two years after the technical end of the recession (i.e., when GDP stopped contracting), and the average duration of unemployment for jobless workers stayed near historic highs. Households saw their housing wealth evaporate as prices fell by nearly 30 percent on average—with larger declines on the coasts and in several Sun Belt States—at the same time that their retirement portfolios suffered a 50 percent drop in the Dow Jones from peak to trough on March 9, 2009. In addition, 3.8 million homes were foreclosed between 2007 and 2010 (Dharmasankar and Mazumder 2016). Even with all the major interventions that were considered unprecedented at the time, it took years for the U.S. economy to fully recover as scars from the crisis persisted.

Both the origins of the COVID-19 recession and the progression of the recovery have been quite different from those of the Great Recession. First, as discussed above, the pre-COVID U.S. economy was in a much healthier state, lacking the household balance sheet vulnerabilities that exacerbated the wave of defaults and financial distress during the 2007–9 financial crisis. House prices have also remained remarkably stable—likely buoyed by the surge in personal income fueled by the CARES Act—and these prices are boosting family finances and have helped prevent a repeated wave of foreclosures like the one that ripped through the economy during the Great Recession. Most important, the speed of the recovery to date has been dramatically faster, with the unemployment rate spending only 4 months above 9 percent during the COVID-19 pandemic, compared with the over two years it hovered above 9 percent during the sclerotic recovery from the last recession. In the 7 months of data since the trough of employment during COVID-19, the U.S. economy has already recovered 56 percent of the lost jobs. By comparison, it took 30 months to gain back more than half the jobs lost in the aftermath of the Great Recession. Moreover, the broader "U-6" unemployment rate spent five years above 13 percent during the slow recovery from the Great Recession, whereas during COVID-19, the rate fell below that level after just 5 months.

Fiscal and Monetary Responses

Despite the health and resilience of the U.S. economy at the beginning of 2020, the initial negative shock was unprecedented. Moreover, even though the immediate economic losses were concentrated in the second quarter of 2020, when shutdowns were widely in place throughout the United States, the Federal Government took action to combat the short-term liquidity crisis and minimize the extent to which it could turn into a widespread solvency crisis for families and businesses with long-lasting negative effects on bankruptcies, unemployment, and production. This subsection compares the speed and scale of the Federal response to COVID-19 with the actions taken to combat the Great Recession. Later chapters analyze the economic effect of the specific COVID-19 economic interventions.

The Federal Government's policies to address the financial crisis of 2007–9 evolved over a number of years, and they ranged from the fiscal stimulus of increased government expenditures for infrastructure, health, education, energy independence, tax rebates targeting low- and middle-income families and tax incentives for business investment; to assistance on refinancing or modifying mortgages to monetary open market operations and liquidity-enhancing programs to bailouts and subsidies of various entities; and, finally, to substantial regulatory changes. On the monetary policy side, the Federal Reserve employed open market operations and later a program of large-scale asset purchases (commonly referred to as quantitative easing) after the Federal Funds rate hit the zero lower bound. The Federal Reserve also took a variety of approaches to help provide liquidity to various markets and market participants, primarily through the creation of several funding, credit, liquidity, and loan facilities.

Besides these and other Federal Reserve interventions, Congress passed significant stimulus bills over the course of the crisis. In February 2008, in an effort to ameliorate the growing crisis, the Economic Stimulus Act of 2008 was passed, offering tax recovery rebates to individuals and their dependents, and targeting low- and middle-income taxpayers. The act also created incentives for business investment by permitting the accelerated depreciation or immediate expensing for certain assets. In October 2008, the Emergency Economic Stabilization Act of 2008 was passed, allocating $700 billion to address the financial crisis by purchasing or insuring troubled assets and attempting to avert the failure of financial institutions identified as systemically important. This established the Troubled Asset Relief Program, known as TARP. In 2009, the American Recovery and Reinvestment Act was passed, which included tax cuts and government expenditures totaling over $800 billion, for national infrastructure, energy independence, education, health care, and tax relief. The Federal Government also stepped in to bail out the automobile industry. In 2010, the Dodd-Frank Wall Street Reform and Consumer Protection Act was enacted, entailing substantial changes to the regulatory architecture of U.S. financial markets.

In addition, the Federal Government took several actions to directly aid the housing market. It instituted the First-Time Homebuyer Tax Credit between 2008 and 2010, with the goal of stimulating home buying and house prices. The government also created the Home Affordable Modification Program (HAMP) and Home Affordable Refinance Program (HARP) to prevent distressed or underwater borrowers from going into foreclosure. The main distinction between the two was that HAMP modified a borrower's existing mortgage contract—often by extending the term or lowering the rate to reduce payments—whereas HARP loosened underwriting requirements to allow underwater

Figure 1-16. Timelines for the Fiscal and Monetary Responses to COVID-19 and the Financial Crisis

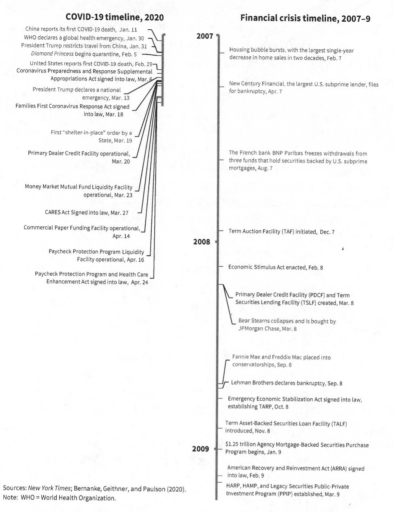

COVID-19 timeline, 2020

China reports its first COVID-19 death, Jan. 11
WHO declares a global health emergency, Jan. 30
President Trump restricts travel from China, Jan. 31
Diamond Princess begins quarantine, Feb. 5
United States reports first COVID-19 death, Feb. 29
Coronavirus Preparedness and Response Supplemental Appropriations Act signed into law, Mar. 6
President Trump declares a national emergency, Mar. 13
Families First Coronavirus Response Act signed into law, Mar. 18

First "shelter-in-place" order by a State, Mar. 19

Primary Dealer Credit Facility operational, Mar. 20

Money Market Mutual Fund Liquidity Facility operational, Mar. 23

CARES Act Signed into law, Mar. 27

Commercial Paper Funding Facility operational, Apr. 14

Paycheck Protection Program Liquidity Facility operational, Apr. 16

Paycheck Protection Program and Health Care Enhancement Act signed into law, Apr. 24

Financial crisis timeline, 2007–9

2007

Housing bubble bursts, with the largest single-year decrease in home sales in two decades, Feb. 7

New Century Financial, the largest U.S. subprime lender, files for bankruptcy, Apr. 7

The French bank BNP Paribas freezes withdrawals from three funds that hold securities backed by U.S. subprime mortgages, Aug. 7

Term Auction Facility (TAF) initiated, Dec. 7

2008

Economic Stimulus Act enacted, Feb. 8

Primary Dealer Credit Facility (PDCF) and Term Securities Lending Facility (TSLF) created, Mar. 8

Bear Stearns collapses and is bought by JPMorgan Chase, Mar. 8

Fannie Mae and Freddie Mac placed into conservatorships, Sep. 8

Lehman Brothers declares bankruptcy, Sep. 8

Emergency Economic Stabilization Act signed into law, establishing TARP, Oct. 8

Term Asset-Backed Securities Loan Facility (TALF) introduced, Nov. 8

$1.25 trillion Agency Mortgage-Backed Securities Purchase Program begins, Jan. 9

2009

American Recovery and Reinvestment Act (ARRA) signed into law, Feb. 9

HARP, HAMP, and Legacy Securities Public-Private Investment Program (PPIP) established, Mar. 9

Sources: *New York Times*; Bernanke, Geithner, and Paulson (2020).
Note: WHO = World Health Organization.

borrowers with negative home equity to take advantage of lower interest rates through refinancing.

Relative to the Great Recession, the Federal Government has responded with even greater speed and coordination to COVID-19, and with an even more expansive range of policies (figure 1-16). The Federal Reserve rapidly cut the Federal Funds rate target range to 0 percent at the effective lower bound (0.00–0.25 percent), and it began to reactivate liquidity facilities that it had set up during the 2007–9 financial crisis. In a matter of just a couple of months, the Federal Reserve's balance sheet jumped by over $3 trillion compared with the five years it took to expand by that amount during the Great Recession. The

Table 1-2. The Federal Response during the Great Recession and COVID-19

Relief Category	Stimulus Checks	Unemployment Insurance	Household Debt Relief	Mid-and-Large Business Relief	Small Business Relief	Healthcare	Education	Tax Cuts, Credits and Deferrals	State and Local Government Aid	Total Legislative Fiscal Relief
Great Recession (Nominal)	$1,200 to joint filers and $300 per dependent ($260 billion)	$25 weekly supplement; up to 99 week extension	Home Affordable Modification Program; Home Affordable Refinance Program	TARP ($700 billion allocated, $420 billion dispersed); Federal Reserve facilities; Bank, insurance and credit market insurance; Auto industry support	SBA loan adjustments	Healthcare subsidization ($128 billion)	K-12 school payroll and facility spending ($109 billion)	Temporary employee-side, 2-percentage-point payroll tax cut Income tax rebate	Funds for programs (some highlighted throughout this table) administered by States and local governments, paid out by the Federal government ($282 billion)	$1.4 trillion ($152 billion ESA 2008, $787 billion ARRA, $475 billion TARP)
COVID-19 Pandemic (Nominal)	$2,400 to joint filers and $500 per dependent (~$300 billion)	$600 weekly supplement; 13-week extension; expanded to include self-employed and others who do not qualify for regular UI ($268 billion)	Foreclosure moratorium; Eviction moratorium	Federal Reserve facilities ($454 billion); Airline loan guarantee and payroll grant; National security critical business loan guarantee ($32 billion)	Paycheck Protection Program ($649 billion); Employee Retention Tax Credit; SBA loan expansion/modification	HHS public health and research appropriation; Provider Relief Fund ($175 billion)	Education Stabilization Fund ($31 billion); Student debt deferral	Temporary employer-side full payroll tax deferral; Temporary expansion of Net Operating Loss carrybacks; Deferred payments of Social Security taxes through December 2020	Coronavirus Relief Fund ($150 billion)	$2.7 trillion ($192 billion FFCRA, $2.2 trillion CARES, $321 billion PPHCEA)

Sources: Great Recession: Economic Stimulus Act of 2008 (ESA 2008); American Recovery and Reinvestment Act, 2009; Troubled Asset Relief Program (TARP, 2008); COVID-19: Families First Coronavirus Response Act; CARES Act; Paycheck Protection and Health Care Enhancement Act.

Federal Reserve has also created Main Street Lending Facilities to direct relief to a larger swath of small and mid-sized firms.

The fiscal response to COVID-19 has also been swifter and larger (figure 1-16). During the Great Recession, a fiscal stimulus was rolled out in phases over the course of a year: the Economic Stimulus Act (ESA) in February 2008, the Emergency Economic Stabilization Act in October 2008, and the American Reinvestment and Recovery Act (ARRA) in February 2009. By contrast, during COVID-19 the Federal government passed the Families First COVID-19 Response Act and the CARES Act both within March 2020 (along with the smaller Coronavirus Preparedness and Response Supplemental Appropriations Act). Moreover, the CARES Act delivered $2.2 trillion in fiscal relief, compared with a bit over $800 billion by the ARRA (or about $970 billion after adjusting for inflation). In terms of composition, both fiscal packages delivered direct aid to households in the form of rebates and unemployment insurance. The ARRA also contained a payroll tax cut and direct aid to States to address revenue shortfalls. Unlike in the Great Recession, however, the CARES Act during COVID-19 established the Paycheck Protection Program (PPP), which has disbursed $525 billion in loans to small businesses to help them maintain payrolls and avoid insolvency.

Table 1-2 provides a summary comparison of the fiscal response to COVID-19 to that of the Great Recession. As is evident, not only has the magnitude of legislative fiscal relief during COVID-19 been nearly twice as large overall, but the increased aid has also gone primarily to households and small businesses, with more generous unemployment insurance and Economic Impact Payments to the former and the novel PPP to the latter. The next subsection provides a more detailed account of how the policy response to COVID-19 has been unprecedented in the support provided to low-income workers.

Federal Support for Low-Income Households

A primary focus of the CARES Act and other relief bills has been the provision of cash and economic support to economically vulnerable households. This subsection compares these unprecedented measures with those adopted during the Great Recession.

Economic Impact Payments and other tax provisions. In both the COVID-19 recession and the Great Recession, the Federal Government used tax provisions to provide economic support to households. The Economic Stimulus Act of 2008 (ESA), passed during the Bush Administration, included an individual income tax "recovery rebate." The rebates were sent to taxpayers in the form of stimulus checks. The typical tax filer received a credit of up to $600 for single filers or up to $1,200 for joint filers. Eligible individuals received an additional $300 per dependent child. Individuals without a net tax liability were still eligible for the rebate, but only if they had earnings of at least $3,000 annually. The rebate was phased out at a rate of 5 percent for incomes over $75,000, and

$150,000 for those filing jointly (the same as the CARES Act). ARRA, passed in 2009 under the Obama Administration, authorized a Making Work Pay personal tax credit for 2009 and 2010, which provided a refundable tax credit of up to $400 for single working individuals and up to $800 per couple. The credit was phased out for incomes over $75,000 (or $150,000 for joint filers) at a rate of 2 cents per $1 of higher income. ARRA also included one-time stimulus payments of $250 for seniors, persons with disabilities, and veterans.

During the COVID-19 recession, the Federal Government has also used tax provisions to provide economic relief to households. The support was larger in monetary value than in the ESA or ARRA, and it was not limited to households with Federal income tax liability, so it thereby extended relief to the lowest-income households. In the CARES Act, the U.S. government provided swift Economic Impact Payments to individuals generally based on 2018 and 2019 tax return information. Those not receiving the advance payments in 2020 can file for them as a tax credit on 2020 taxes. Although the phase-out rate and income thresholds are the same as under ESA and ARRA, the CARES Act payments were significantly larger, offering up to $1,200 to individuals and $2,400 to joint filers (El-Sibaie et al. 2020). The CARES Act payments were also larger for eligible individuals with children. ESA offered an extra $300 tax credit per dependent child, while ARRA expanded eligibility for the child tax credit. The CARES Act, by comparison, provided a $500 tax rebate per dependent child using the same eligibility criteria for dependent children as the child tax credit. Unlike the ESA tax credit, the CARES tax rebate does not require a minimum tax liability to receive the full rebate (Marr et al. 2020), meaning that those at the very lowest end of the income distribution received income support.

Some types of tax relief enacted under ARRA were not paralleled in the CARES Act. ARRA enhanced the Earned Income Tax Credit by expanding its coverage and raising the credit claimed by workers with three or more children. Although these changes were initially enacted on a temporary basis, Congress later made them permanent. ARRA also subsidized the purchase of cars and first-time homeowners through an automobile sales tax credit ($1.7 billion total) and a homeownership tax credit ($6.6 billion).

Workforce programs. In its response to both recessions, the Federal Government provided support for the Nation's workforce. Overall, the CARES Act provided significantly more support. The support was also targeted to reflect the different nature of the crisis. In the Great Recession, out of the $787 billion ARRA stimulus package, about $12 billion helped finance various public workforce programs to accommodate expanded participation (table 1-3). State unemployment insurance agencies received $500 million in administrative support funding and $7 billion in modernization funds to address increased demand (BLS 2014). By comparison, the Families First COVID-19 Response Act authorized $1 billion in additional funding to support UI administration

Table 1-3. Funding of Major Workforce Program Initiatives under the America Reinvestment and Recovery Act, 2009

Act Funding Category	Funding Amount (billions of dollars)
UI Administration	0.5
UI Modernization	7.0
Wagner–Peyser Act grants to States	0.15
Wagner–Peyser Act reemployment services	0.25
WIA Adult	0.5
WIA Dislocated Worker	1.25
WIA Dislocated Worker National Reserve	0.2
High Growth and Emerging Industry grants	0.75
WIA Youth	1.2
Job Corps	0.25
YouthBuild	0.05
Senior Community Service Employment Program	0.12

Sources: Bureau of Labor Statistics; Bradley and Lordeman (2009).
Note: WIA = Workforce Investment Act.

to assist States with processing increased caseloads and expanded programs (Emsellem and Evermore 2020; Goger, Loh, and George 2020).

Congress also funded additional enhancements and extensions to the Unemployment Insurance program. In response to the rise in the number of workers unemployed for more than 26 weeks, Congress enacted a temporary extension UI. The Emergency Unemployment Compensation Act of 2008 and its extensions included additional tiers of benefit weeks to supplement regular State UI and expanded Extended Benefits programs. In combination, between November 2009 and September 2012, these programs extended the maximum number of weeks UI recipients could receive benefits for up to 99 weeks.

In 2009, ARRA added to these benefits, providing both for expanded UI duration and an additional benefit of $25 per eligible worker in weekly UI benefits through temporary Emergency Unemployment Compensation. This benefit enhancement cost the Federal Government $20.1 billion during the period 2009–11. The permanent Extended Benefits program became completely federally funded through January 1, 2010, and State eligibility rules were relaxed to make more unemployed workers eligible. These Extended Benefits cost the Federal Government $24 billion during 2009–11. ARRA also temporarily suspended the taxation of the first $2,400 of UI benefits.

In response to the COVID-19 recession, Congress both temporarily extended the duration of UI benefits and increased their level considerably relative to the Great Recession. Under the CARES Act, UI benefits were extended for up to an additional 13 weeks and States were allowed to eliminate the mandatory 1-week waiting period before benefits can be released to recipients. The CARES Act also offered a considerable increase in additional UI income—24 times greater than the additional benefit of $25 that was offered during the Great Recession. Workers claiming UI received a $600 weekly supplement through July 15, 2020. Furthermore, unlike the Recovery Act, the CARES Act added a new program to expand eligibility for UI benefits to include the self-employed, gig workers, workers with limited work history, and other types of workers who would not otherwise qualify for regular UI benefits. After the $600 weekly supplement expired in July and in the absence of Congressional action, the Trump Administration extended relief to unemployed workers by issuing a Presidential Memorandum creating the Lost Wages Assistance Program, which authorized the use of Disaster Relief Funds to make supplemental payments of up to $400 ($300 Federal contribution, $100 optional State contribution) per week for lost wages. Forty-nine states along with Washington, DC and some US territories ultimately signed up for the program, which provided six weeks' worth of benefits to every State and territory that applied by September 10.

During the Great Recession, under ARRA, individuals eligible for UI were referred to the Employment Service for job referral and reemployment services. ARRA allocated an additional $250 million in Reemployment Services Grants to local employment offices to better serve UI recipients. The Bureau of Labor Statistics notes that, despite increased funding, the local offices still faced major constraints, which resulted in increased enrollment in low-cost services (e.g., orientations, assessments), but smaller increases in expensive and labor-intensive services (e.g. counseling, education, training). Other employment services, such as the Workforce Innovation Dislocated Worker program and the Workforce Innovation Adult program, also received increased funding (table 1-3).

The CARES Act does not have a parallel to ARRA's increase in funding for Reemployment Services Grants and Workforce Innovation and Opportunity Act formula programs. As outlined in a previous CEA report (2019), many government training programs lack rigorous evidence-based results that demonstrate their effectiveness in training or retraining workers and helping them find employment. The CARES Act does, however, provide $345 million in Dislocated Worker Grants to prevent, prepare for, and respond to COVID-19. In addition, the act offers incentives to States to adopt or make better-use of short-time compensation programs, which would allow employers to avoid laying off their employees by reducing their hours. Under these programs, workers would still be eligible for UI benefits to make up for their reduced working hours.

The CARES Act goes far beyond ARRA to support the workforce through its funding of the PPP. The program was designed to support small business employers and their employees during the pandemic. The CARES Act authorized $349 billion in PPP loans to support payroll and other expenses for America's small businesses, self-employed individuals, Tribal business concerns, and nonprofit/veterans' organizations. As part of the PPP and Health Care Enhancement Act, an additional $310 billion was authorized, bringing the total amount authorized for the PPP to $659 billion. While the funds will be used to guarantee and forgive loans, a condition for making the loans fully forgivable is that no less than 60 percent (originally 75 percent) of the funds be spent on payroll expenses within a 24-week (originally 8-week) period.

Healthcare. The Federal response to support healthcare during the COVID-19 recession has been much different from its response in the Great Recession because of the need to directly address the effects of the COVID-19 health crisis. There was no parallel to this in the Great Recession, which was driven by a financial crisis rather than a health-related crisis.

During the Great Recession, the Federal response for healthcare focused on temporarily increasing healthcare benefits for people who lost their jobs. Before the Great Recession, the Consolidated Omnibus Budget Reconciliation Act (COBRA) required many employers to provide continued healthcare coverage to workers (and their dependents) who lost their jobs, but it did not require employers to continue subsidizing the premium payments. ARRA provided a 65 percent subsidy for employers to help cover the premium payments of most COBRA-eligible workers who lost their jobs between September 2008 and May 2010. This subsidy covered workers and their dependents for up to 9 months (later extended to 15 months). The CARES Act did not change the terms of COBRA, but the Department of Labor temporarily extended deadlines for workers who lost their jobs to sign up for coverage and pay premiums.

To respond directly to the COVID-19 health-crisis, the CARES Act established the Provider Relief Fund to support healthcare providers in the midst of the pandemic. The CARES Act, through the Department of Health and Human Services, allotted $100 billion to hospitals and other healthcare providers. The Paycheck Protection Program and Health Care Enhancement Act provided an additional $75 billion for the Provider Relief Fund to healthcare providers to reimburse heightened costs and lost revenues that are attributable to COVID-19. The Department of Health and Human Services is currently allocating this $175 billion in aid. The aid includes specific programs to provide safety net relief to hospitals that serve the most vulnerable segment of the population as well as rural hospitals and those in small metropolitan areas.

Although this aid is substantial, the portion going to hospitals is unlikely to fully offset the losses that hospitals have experienced during the pandemic. The American Hospital Association estimates that the pandemic imposed over $200 billion in losses on the American healthcare system in the four-month period between March 1 and June 30. Over 80 percent of this estimated cost is due to revenue losses from canceled surgeries and other services. This includes both elective and nonelective procedures, outpatient treatments, and emergency department services. The remaining 20 or so percent of estimated losses are based on the direct costs of COVID-19 to hospitals: losses from COVID-19 hospitalizations, additional purchases of personal protective equipment, and additional support that hospitals provide to their front-line workers.

The CARES Act also provided $25 billion to help increase COVID-19 testing. This includes up to $1 billion to reimburse the cost of testing uninsured individuals, in addition to the $1 billion previously appropriated for this purpose by the Families First Coronavirus Relief Act (FFCRA). The FFCRA also, as amended by the CARES Act, requires Medicare Part B, State Medicaid and Children's Health Insurance Programs, and group health plans and health insurance issuers to cover COVID-19 diagnostic testing without cost sharing for patients. Uninsured individuals may also obtain COVID-19 diagnostic testing free of charge under State Medicaid programs, if a State offers this option. The Centers for Medicare & Medicaid Services has made an accessible and easy-to-use toolkit for States to amend their Medicaid programs in order to offer this service.

Education. During the Great Recession, the Federal Government directed a considerable portion of stimulus spending to education, allocating $100 billion in additional spending under ARRA. A central goal of the funding was to avert layoffs in school districts and universities. About half the funding was allocated to State governors for use in primary, secondary, and higher education through the State Fiscal Stabilization Fund. An additional $10 billion was targeted to low-income students and about $12 billion was designated to support students with disabilities. About $17 billion was used to increase the funding available for Pell Grants for higher education that support students from low-income households. ARRA also established the American Opportunity Tax Credit, which modified an existing education credit (the HOPE credit) by relaxing income-based eligibility limits to cover more students, qualifying more expenses for the credit, and allowing the credit to be claimed not only for study at two-year institutions but also for study at four-year higher education institutions.

Under the CARES Act, the Federal Government provided $31 billion in emergency relief to educational institutions. This includes about $13 billion for K-12 schools allocated mainly in proportion to a State's enrollments of low-income students. Another $14 billion is allocated to higher education, with most of the allocation based on an institution's share of Pell Grant recipients, but with about $1 billion allocated to Historically Black Colleges and Universities and other institutions serving students of color, which are discussed further in chapter 11 of this *Report*. Another $3 billion in relief is for governors to distribute to schools or higher educational institutions that have been particularly affected by COVID-19.

A major difference between the Great Recession and the current crisis is the large number of school closures across the country in response to the pandemic. Between the first and third weeks of March, close to 100 percent of kindergarten, primary, and secondary schools were shut down. These closures have had a substantial negative effect both on the U.S. economy and on children themselves. Prorated estimates based on analyses by Angrist and Krueger (1992) and Bhuller, Mogstad, and Salvanes (2017) suggest that children are likely to experience a persistent 2.3–3.7 percent decline in future earnings as a result of lower human capital accumulation from the shortened school year. Meanwhile, parents who have had to miss work entirely because of childcare duties induced by school closures may also experience a reduction in lifetime earnings. The CEA estimates that 18 percent of the workforce may experience a persistent 1 percent drop in lifetime earnings because of lost job experience due to school closures. The effects are likely to be particularly severe for early-career single mothers, who will experience not just lower earnings but also less secure job prospects. Accordingly, the safe reopening of schools will help to boost the economy and support economically vulnerable students and their families.

Supplemental Nutrition Assistance Program. The Federal Response in both recessions included support for the Supplemental Nutrition Assistance Program (SNAP), the Federal program that provides nutritional assistance to help America's neediest families purchase food. During the Great Recession, ARRA allocated $40 billion in additional SNAP benefits for all participants and raised the minimum benefits. As a result of these changes, in 2009, the average monthly SNAP benefit increased by $21. In addition to increasing the monthly benefit, ARRA suspended work requirements for nondisabled, childless adults between April 2009 and September 2010.

The Families First COVID-19 Response Act provided authority for work requirement waivers and SNAP benefit increases up to the maximum allotment for households not already receiving the maximum. The CARES Act provided over $15 billion in additional contingency funding for the increased costs associated with the FFCRA provisions, as well as anticipated increased participation in SNAP. As provided by the FFCRA and the CARES Act, the Department of Agriculture also provided waivers of certain requirements so that nutrition programs could reach families and children during the social-distancing restrictions. The FFCRA also suspended work requirements for nondisabled, childless adults through the month after the end of the COVID-19 public health emergency.

Housing assistance programs. During the Great Recession, the Federal response under ARRA provided $13.6 billion for programs administered by the Department of Housing and Urban Development (HUD), including $1.5 billion for the Homelessness Prevention and Rapid Re-Housing Program. As discussed in chapter 2 of this *Report*, the CARES Act provided housing relief to homeowners and renters in the form of forbearance for federally backed mortgages and a 120-day eviction moratorium that was subsequently extended by the Trump Administration via Executive Order 13945, Fighting the Spread of COVID-19 by Providing Assistance to Renters and Homeowners. The CARES

Act also allocated $12.4 billion for programs administered by HUD for fiscal year 2020. The funding includes $4 billion for the homeless who are among the most vulnerable and hardest hit by the pandemic. These funds will support the Emergency Solutions Grants program, which assists homeless populations or populations at risk of becoming homeless. About $3 billion of these funds are being used to operate emergency shelters (covering food, rent, security, etc.), make even more emergency shelters available, provide essential services to homeless populations (including childcare, employment assistance, and mental health services), and prevent individuals from becoming homeless through rapid rehousing.

Conclusion

The COVID-19 pandemic has had a profound effect on what had been a robust U.S. economy at the start of 2020. The Blue Chip panel of professional forecasters immediately began to sharply revise down its 2020 GDP projections in March as the pandemic was taking hold, as did the Federal Reserve and the OECD when updating their forecasts. Instead of predicting GDP growth of about 2 percent for 2020, all three issued dire warnings of a GDP contraction of about 6 percent to as much as 12 percent—which would have marked the steepest contraction since the 1930s. However, the swift and dramatic fiscal interventions implemented in late March and early April by the Federal Government paid dividends throughout the summer, and the U.S. economy consistently outperformed expectations.

As a result, as of the fall of 2020, all three leading forecasters were taking a much more sanguine view of GDP growth for the year, predicting that GDP will end up falling by less than 4 percent. Whether this robust recovery maintains a healthy pace depends partly on the progression of virus mitigation efforts and the continuation of appropriate and responsive levels of fiscal support. The chapters that follow provide an in-depth discussion of the major components of the fiscal response and their ensuing effects on different aspects of the U.S. economy.

Chapter 2

Prioritizing America's Households

The economic and health crises stemming from the COVID-19 pandemic required a coordinated response from all levels of government to protect the livelihoods of Americans. The Trump Administration took decisive action and worked with Congress to pass and sign three major bills in March 2020—the largest of which was the Coronavirus Aid, Relief, and Economic Security (CARES) Act—to address the economic fallout from the pandemic. As CARES Act provisions began to expire or dissipate in August, and in the absence of further Congressional action, President Trump followed up with a series of executive actions that extended further relief to American households.

A key goal of these policies was to provide financial support to American households weathering the sharp pandemic-fueled economic contraction. These policies were highly successful against this unprecedented event. Even as the unemployment rate climbed from a 50-year low of 3.5 percent in February 2020 to 14.7 percent two months later in April 2020, household incomes increased, thanks to Economic Impact Payments and to expanded and enhanced Unemployment Insurance. Lower-income households generally experienced the largest percentage income increases, and their monthly income in every month through at least August 2020 exceeded pre-COVID levels.

In addition to providing direct financial relief, the CARES Act and follow-up executive branch actions from the Trump Administration protected Americans against the risk of eviction and student loan defaults. Evictions fell below pre-COVID levels in cities across the United States, averting bouts of homelessness or shared housing that could pose additional health risks in the midst of the pandemic.

The long-run success of actions taken to support households will depend on the pace and depth of the economic recovery. Between April and November, the unemployment rate fell by 8.0 percentage points, from 14.7 percent to 6.7 percent, the largest seven-month decline on record. Almost 60 percent of all jobs lost between February and April had been recovered by November, as employment increased by 12 million over this period.

Continued economic recovery, supported by President Trump's executive actions designed to extend assistance beyond the expiration of CARES Act provisions, can pave the way back to the same strong economy that prevailed during the first three years of the Trump Administration, which was spurred in part by the Tax Cuts and Jobs Act and other pro-growth policies. Between 2016 and 2019, median net worth increased by 18 percent, with an increase of 32 percent for Black-headed households and 64 percent for Hispanic-headed households. Median income increased by 9.7 percent between 2016 and 2019, and the one-year 6.8 percent increase in 2019 was the largest one-year increase ever recorded. Poverty hit a record low in 2019 for all racial and ethnic groups, and fell by the largest amount (1.3 percentage points) in over 50 years. With continued pro-growth policies, including deregulation and the continued benefits of the Tax Cuts and Jobs Act, the pre-COVID economy can be attained again, and households will continue to benefit from the gains experienced during the first three years of the Trump Administration.

The partial shutdown of the U.S. economy in response to COVID-19 was unprecedented. Over 90 percent of Americans were affected by statewide school closures and restrictions on bars and restaurants by late March and were subject to State-level stay-at-home orders by early April. As a result of these events, between February 2020 and April 2020 the unemployment rate increased from the lowest level in over 50 years (3.5 percent) to the highest level since the Great Depression (14.7 percent). Aggregate, pretransfer disposable income in the United States fell by 9 percent between February and April, the largest two-month reduction ever recorded. Because job losses were concentrated among lower-wage workers, the reduction in pretransfer income hit lower-income households the hardest, threatening their ability to pay for rent, food, and other basic necessities.

Due to the rapid and unprecedented actions taken by President Trump and Congress, these harmful effects on American households were strongly mitigated. On March 20, 2020, President Trump delayed Tax Day, providing liquidity to Americans with tax liabilities. And following two other important pieces of legislation, on March 27, 2020, President Trump signed the Coronavirus Aid, Relief, and Economic Security (CARES) Act into law, providing $2.2 trillion in relief for households and businesses. A family with two children and an income below $150,000 received an Economic Impact Payment of $3,400, almost twice as much as the maximum $1,800 stimulus checks provided during the Great Recession. And unlike the Great Recession stimulus payments, full Economic Impact Payments were available to the lowest-income households with no tax liability. The CARES Act also provided unprecedented relief to those workers who lost their jobs. A supplemental $600 weekly Unemployment Insurance (UI) payment ensured that most workers who lost their jobs did not experience a reduction in income, and eligibility was expanded to workers not typically eligible for UI benefits. The CARES Act further placed a moratorium on foreclosures and evictions in homes with federally backed mortgages. Earlier legislation extended paid leave benefits for families that could not work due to illness or to care for children affected by school closures.

President Trump provided additional relief to households when CARES Act provisions expired, and Congress was unable to reach a consensus on extensions. He issued several important executive actions on August 8, 2020, providing $300 a week in supplemental Federal assistance to unemployed workers; deferring the employee portion of payroll taxes through the end of 2020; issuing an order to assist renters unable to pay their rent, and ultimately imposing a moratorium on evictions from all rental housing through the end of 2020; and extending the deferral of student loan payments with no interest through the end of 2020. These executive branch actions ensured that many households would continue to receive relief in the absence of further legislative packages.

Due to the CARES Act and subsequent executive action by the Trump Administration, poverty and income inequality fell, and most workers who lost their jobs experienced no income loss while receiving supplemental unemployment benefits. In the months immediately after passage of the CARES Act, households across the income distribution saw an increase in income relative to pre-COVID levels. The gains were largest for the lowest-income households. For example, for households at the 25th percentile, monthly incomes spiked by 127 percent in April, largely due to Economic Impact Payments; and these households were still above pre-COVID levels from May through August, largely due to expanded UI benefits. In fact, Economic Impact Payments alone were large enough to keep a family of four out of poverty for 1.5 months even if they lost all other income. Expanded UI benefits ensured that the vast majority of unemployed workers received at least as much from UI as they did from working. Though these UI payments would typically create strong work disincentives, the partial economic shutdown between April and July mitigated such concerns (Altonji et al. 2020; Bartik et al. 2020; Marinescu, Skandalis, and Zhao 2020). The somewhat reduced emergency lost wages assistance issued under President Trump's executive action in August alleviated some of the work disincentives of the $600 payments as the recovery from March and April proceeded, while continuing to provide additional support to unemployed workers.

These actions helped pave the way for a strong economic recovery. Between April and November, the unemployment rate fell by 8.0 percentage points, from 14.7 percent to 6.7 percent, the largest seven-month decline on record. Continued economic recovery, combined with President Trump's executive actions extending assistance to many households beyond the expiration of key CARES Act provisions, can pave the way to attaining the historically strong pre-COVID labor market and overall economy.

A strong economy is the most effective tool for lifting up households in the long term. From when President Trump was elected in 2016 until 2019, median net worth increased by 18 percent, with the biggest gains for minority groups. Median net worth increased by 32 percent for Black-headed households and by 64 percent for Hispanic-headed households (Federal Reserve Board of Governors (2020a, 2020c). Median income increased by 9.7 percent between 2016 and 2019, and increased by 6.8 percent in 2019 alone, the largest one-year increase ever recorded. In 2019, poverty fell by the largest amount (1.3 percentage points) in over 50 years and hit a record low. Black poverty fell below 20 percent for the first time ever. Continued pro-growth policies, including deregulation and the continued benefits of the Tax Cuts and Jobs Act (TCJA), can help ensure that the pre-COVID economy can be attained again, allowing households to continue seeing the gains experienced during the first three years of the Trump Administration.[1]

The Strength of the Pre-COVID
Economy and the COVID-19 Shock

The Trump Administration's policies have focused on spurring economic growth and job creation. Deregulation has reduced the costs for businesses to invest and hire workers. Tax reform has encouraged new capital investment and has reduced taxes on households that impose high effective tax rates on work, particularly at the lower end of the income distribution. Other policies—such as expanded childcare assistance for low-income workers, Opportunity Zones, and record investments to lessen the opioid epidemic—have helped

---

[1] The CEA previously released research on some of the topics discussed in this chapter. The text of this chapter builds on the CEA report "Evaluating the Effects of the Economic Response to COVID-19" (CEA 2020).

spur job growth for those remaining on the sidelines of the labor market. Until COVID-19 struck, the result of these policies was higher economic growth and a strong labor market, especially for the most disadvantaged Americans.

Between January 2017, when President Trump took office, and February 2020, the U.S. unemployment rate fell from 4.7 to 3.5 percent, the lowest level in 50 years. Traditionally, disadvantaged Americans experienced the largest labor market gains. Between January 2017 and February 2020, the unemployment rate for Black Americans fell by 1.7 percentage points and for Hispanic Americans by 1.4 percentage points, which was even larger than the overall decline of 1.2 percentage points.

The rise in labor demand not only brought more workers into the workforce but also increased wages. Real average hourly earnings rose 3.2 percent between January 2017 and February 2020. Wage growth was fastest for the lowest-wage workers, who through the first three years of the Trump Administration saw a nominal wage increase of 11.7 percent—4.2 percentage points higher than the growth of median wages for all workers during the same period.

Increased employment and wages translated into large income gains for households. Between 2016 and 2019, U.S. median pretax household income increased by 9.7 percent. Due to the TCJA, after-tax income grew even faster. For example, a family of four with an income of $82,500 now pays $2,300 less in taxes than before the TCJA, according to the Tax Policy Center's Tax Cuts and Jobs Act Calculator.

Households across the income distribution experienced income gains during the first three years of the Trump Administration. Pro-growth policies reduced poverty by 2.2 percentage points (6.6 million people) between 2016 and 2019. And the poverty rate reached an all-time record low of 10.5 percent in 2019. All racial and ethnic groups reached record low poverty rates, with the Black poverty rate falling below 20 percent for the first time ever.

Family wealth also increased during the Trump Administration. Between 2016 and 2019, overall median net worth increased by 18 percent, with increases of 32 percent for Black-headed families and 64 percent for Hispanic-headed families. Net worth increased the most for lower-middle-wealth families (those between the 25th and 50th percentiles of net worth), who saw a 22 percent increase in mean net worth. Homeownership increased by 1.2 percentage points between 2016 and 2019, the first three-year increase documented by the Survey of Consumer Finances since 2004 (Federal Reserve Board of Governors 2020b, 2020d).

The strong economic growth that lifted up all households between 2016 and 2019 was disrupted by the COVID-19 pandemic. Between February 2020 and April 2020, the unemployment rate spiked, from 3.5 percent to 14.7 percent—and this 11.2-percentage-point increase alone was larger than the peak unemployment rate reached during the Great Recession. Job vacancies fell more than 40 percent by late April (Forsythe et al. 2020). The Congressional Budget Office forecasted in May 2020 that the unemployment rate would be 15.8 percent in 2020:Q3 and 11.5 percent in 2020:Q4, which would mean an unemployment rate that continued to exceed the Great Recession's peak for the remainder of 2020. In reality, the unemployment rate fell lower than these predictions; in November, it was only 6.7 percent, well below what the office (CBO 2020) had predicted.

Policy Responses Providing Household Relief

In response to the sudden and severe shock caused by COVID-19, Congress quickly passed and President Trump signed into law three pieces of legislation in March 2020: the Coronavirus Preparedness and Response Supplemental Appropriations Act, on March 6, 2020; the Families First Coronavirus Response Act, on March 18, 2020; and the CARES Act, on March 27, 2020 (which was supplemented in April by the Paycheck Protection and Health Care Enhancement Act). After certain provisions of these acts expired, and in the absence of forthcoming legislation, President Trump issued a series of important executive actions on August 8, 2020: an Executive Order on Fighting the Spread of COVID-19 by Providing Assistance to Renters and Homeowners (White House 2020a); a Memorandum on Deferring Payroll Tax Obligations in Light of the Ongoing COVID-19 Disaster (White House 2020d); a Memorandum on Authorizing the Other Needs Assistance Program for Major Disaster Declarations Related to Coronavirus Disease 2019 (White House 2020b); and a Memorandum on Continued Student Loan Payment Relief During the COVID-19 Pandemic (White House 2020c). This section summarizes the provisions of these laws and executive actions that have provided direct relief to American households.

March 2020 Legislative Acts

The Coronavirus Preparedness and Response Supplemental Appropriations Act, which was signed into law by President Trump on March 6, 2020, provided $8.3 billion to fund the initial health response to COVID-19. The funding focused on vaccines, therapeutics, testing, and general responses to the health emergency, in addition to funding international relief efforts.

The Families First Coronavirus Response Act (FFCRA), which was signed into law by President Trump on March 18, 2020, provided assistance for households and State governments at an estimated cost of $192 billion. The FFCRA required certain employers with fewer than 500 employees to provide their employees with paid sick and family leave for COVID-related work absences, which would be fully reimbursed by the Federal government through refundable tax credits. To help fund the provision of leave benefits up front, firms were allowed to access tax withholdings that would otherwise be required to be deposited with the Internal Revenue Service (IRS), or to receive the tax credit as an advanced payment from the IRS for the amount not covered by previously withheld taxes. Workers were entitled to 2 weeks of paid sick leave covering up to 100 percent of wages, and to an additional 10 weeks of paid family and medical leave covering up to 67 percent of wages, with certain caps on wages. The FFCRA also increased Federal funding for Unemployment Insurance Extended Benefits and Medicaid, suspended work requirements in the Supplemental Nutrition Assistance Program, and provided no-fee COVID-19 testing and emergency care for all Americans covered by Medicare, Medicaid, and the Children's Health Insurance Program.

The largest legislative package was the CARES Act, which was signed into law by President Trump on March 27, 2020. The CARES Act provided $2.2 trillion in relief to households and businesses affected by COVID-19. For context, the major legislative response to the Great Recession, the American Recovery and Reinvestment Act of 2009, provided $836 billion over 10 years (in 2009 dollars).

Economic Impact Payments, at a cost of $292.4 billion (JCT 2020), were a key provision of the CARES Act intended to provide immediate relief to households. Each eligible adult could receive up to $1,200 and $500 for each qualifying child, and these payments were phased out at higher incomes. A family making less than $150,000 a year with two parents and two children would receive $3,400, even if they had no tax liability. By contrast, stimulus payments during the Great Recession offered a family of four a maximum of $1,800 and offered no payment at all to those with no tax liability and less than $3,000 in qualifying income. Economic Impact Payments were distributed quickly, with the IRS reporting that it had sent out nearly $267 billion in payments to 159 million Americans by June 3.

The CARES Act provided an additional $347 billion in targeted relief to Americans who lost their jobs. Federal Pandemic Unemployment Compensation (FPUC) offered every beneficiary of unemployment insurance an additional $600 a week in unemployment benefits from March 29, 2020 through July 31, 2020. For example, a worker typically earning $400 a week may receive $200 in regular UI benefits upon becoming unemployed. Under FPUC, the worker would receive an additional $600, for a total of $800 per week. Pandemic Emergency Unemployment Compensation provided an additional 13 weeks of UI benefits for workers who exhaust their regular State benefits, for a total of 39 weeks of coverage in most States (in addition to potential coverage by Extended Benefits). Pandemic Unemployment Assistance granted UI benefits to workers not eligible for regular State unemployment insurance benefits, such as self-employed workers, gig workers, business owners, independent contractors not participating in the UI elective coverage program, and workers with insufficient work history to normally receive unemployment benefits. This assistance for unemployed workers was complemented by the Paycheck Protection Program (PPP), which helped ensure that businesses could keep their workers on payroll and avoid the need to draw unemployment assistance.

The CARES Act also provided loan repayment assistance. Homeowners with federally backed mortgages who experienced financial hardship due to COVID-19 were allowed to suspend payments for up to 180 days, with the possibility of an extension of up to 180 more days. During this period, no interest or fees would accrue. The CARES Act also prohibited foreclosures on homes with federally backed single-family mortgages for at least 60 days starting on March 18, 2020, and prohibited evictions of tenants in certain federally supported rental properties for 120 days starting March 27, 2020. To allow families to borrow money if needed, holders of individual retirement accounts (IRAs) that were adversely affected by COVID-19 could take a distribution from their IRA and treat this distribution as a tax-free rollover, provided they recontribute the amount within three years. The CARES Act also ensured that consumers' credit did not suffer due to the virus; if consumers had an agreement with their lender to delay payments or make a partial repayment, they would not receive a negative credit report.

The CARES Act also included provisions to protect student loan borrowers. Employers were provided with the ability to make up to $5,250 in student loan payments through December 31, 2020 for each employee without incurring taxes. In addition, through September 30, 2020, student loan payments and interest accruals for Department of Education-held Federal student loans were suspended, and involuntary collections related to student loans through wage garnishments, tax refund reductions, and negative credit reporting were also suspended for loans held by the Department of Education.

Finally, the CARES Act also allowed for $150 billion in State and local government aid. Because many State and local governments, particularly those without savings or whose revenues rely heavily on sales taxes, have struggled to retain employees during the pandemic, this measure is estimated to have saved over 400,000 public sector jobs (Green and Loualiche 2020).

President Trump's Executive Actions

Key CARES Act provisions expired in July, and, although the economy was in the midst of a strong recovery, a substantial share of Americans had yet to return to work. The last week of July was the final week for which the CARES Act provided enhanced UI benefits to unemployed workers. The moratorium on evictions and foreclosures in homes with federally backed mortgages expired on July 24. In the absence of Congressional action, the Trump Administration took a series of executive actions on August 8, 2020.

President Trump's Memorandum on Authorizing the Other Needs Assistance Program for Major Disaster Declarations Related to Coronavirus Disease 2019 directed up to $44 billion to be provided in Federal lost wages assistance. In order to be eligible for Federal lost wages assistance, claimants were required to self-certify that they were unemployed or partially unemployed due to COVID-19 and that they had already received at least $100 a week in benefits. As a result, in addition to their regular UI benefits, claimants were eligible for up to another $400 a week, $300 of which was provided by the Federal Government. These benefits were set to terminate when Federal funds were exhausted, but no later than December 6, 2020.

Executive Order 13945 aimed to minimize evictions and foreclosures and thereby prevent homelessness or shared housing situations during the pandemic. The Centers for Disease Control and Prevention (CDC) reported that some racial and ethnic groups were disproportionately more likely to be evicted, and that homeless shelters and shared housing are particularly susceptible to COVID outbreaks. The order authorized the CDC Director to temporarily halt evictions for failure to pay rent, the Secretary of the Treasury and the Secretary of Housing and Urban Development (HUD) to identify available Federal funds for temporary financial assistance to homeowners suffering financial hardship resulting from COVID, and the Secretary of HUD to aid homeowners and renters in avoiding foreclosure, for example, by providing housing authorities or landlords with financial assistance.

In addition, the Director of the Federal Housing Finance Agency (FHFA) was directed to review resources that might be used to prevent evictions and foreclosures due to COVID-19. In response to Executive Order 13945, FHFA extended the moratorium on foreclosures in homes with federally backed mortgages through the end of 2020, and CDC declared that eligible renters in any type of property facing potential homelessness or shared housing situations could not be evicted.

President Trump's Memorandum on Deferring Payroll Tax Obligations in Light of the Ongoing COVID-19 Disaster authorized the Secretary of the Treasury to defer certain payroll tax obligations for Americans in need, relaxing temporary liquidity constraints for workers. At the employer's discretion, this deferral was available to employees with pretax biweekly wages below $4,000. In addition, President Trump instructed the Secretary of the Treasury to explore additional avenues to eliminate the obligation to eventually pay these deferred taxes.

Finally, President Trump's Memorandum on Continued Student Loan Payment Relief During the COVID-19 Pandemic extended the deferment of payments and waived interest on student loans held by the Department of Education through December 31, 2020.

The Impact of Policies in Providing Relief to Households

Due to their magnitude and coverage, the legislative acts and executive actions taken to counter the negative consequences of COVID-19 had large effects on U.S. households. As shown in figure 2-1, in 2020 real disposable income *excluding* government transfers experienced the largest two-month decline on record

Figure 2-1. Monthly Disposable Personal Income, 2020

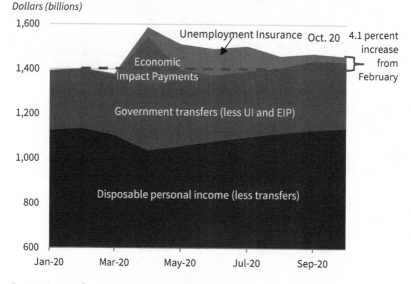

Sources: Bureau of Economic Analysis; CEA calculations.
Note: UI = Unemployment Insurance benefits; EIPs = Economic Impact Payments.

between February and April (8.7 percent) and remained suppressed through August. However, real disposable income *including* government transfers experienced the largest two-month increase on record between February and April (13.1 percent) and remained elevated through the time of publication.

The historic rise in posttransfer disposable income was a result of CARES Act provisions that provided relief to households. In combination, total Economic Impact Payments and Unemployment Insurance benefits paid between April and August were over twice as large as the loss in pretransfer disposable income incurred over the same period. Economic Impact Payments alone replaced 79 percent of the total reduction in pretransfer disposable income, and UI benefits on their own replaced 126 percent of the total reduction in pretransfer disposable income. This is largely a result of the $600 Federal UI weekly supplement. Ganong, Noel, and Vavra (2020) estimate that 76 percent of workers who were eligible for regular UI benefits in April through July received more in unemployment assistance than they would have received from their typical earnings. Though such assistance would normally create severe employment disincentives, these concerns were mitigated by the health benefits of staying home during the pandemic.

As a result of the Federal Government's unprecedented response to the pandemic-induced economic crisis, lower-income households experienced the largest income gains during the COVID crisis. Figure 2-2 simulates the trajectory of household income at different points of the income distribution—with and

Figure 2-2. Index of Household Income by Percentile, 2020

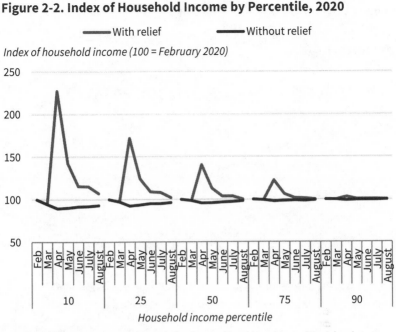

Index of household income (100 = February 2020)

Sources: Census Bureau, Current Population Survey, Monthly and Annual Social and Economic Supplement; CEA calculations.
Note: For the methodology used here, see CEA (2020).

without Economic Impact Payments and expanded UI. Without these provisions, a household at the 10th percentile of the income distribution would have experienced a 10 percent reduction in income in April 2020 compared with its February 2020 level, and its income would have remained 7 percent lower by August. However, because of expanded UI and the Economic Impact Payments, its monthly income was 127 percent higher in April, 42 percent higher in May, 15 percent higher in June and July, and 7 percent higher in August compared with February 2020. The spike in income in April is largely a result of the Economic Impact Payments, while the continued elevated income in May through August is largely a result of expanded UI.

Because figure 2-2 includes all households, it does not show how important the CARES Act and later executive actions were for preserving the income of households experiencing job losses. Figure 2-3 provides a more specific example of a household with two adults and two children, with one worker who loses their job starting in April 2020 and where all income is assumed to come from earnings. The worker in the "low-wage" household is assumed to earn $500 a week, and the worker in the "high-wage" household is assumed to earn $1,500 a week.

Without expanded UI and the Economic Impact Payment, the illustrative low-wage household would have experienced a 50 percent reduction in income

Figure 2-3. Index of Household Income for Example Households, 2020

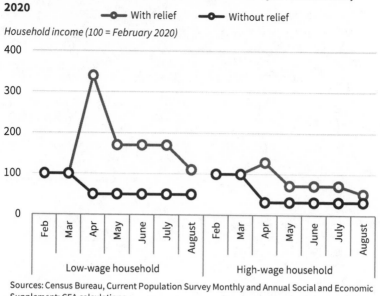

Household income (100 = February 2020)

Sources: Census Bureau, Current Population Survey Monthly and Annual Social and Economic Supplement; CEA calculations.

Note: A low-wage household earns $500 a week, and a high-wage one earns $1,500. For the methodology used here, see CEA (2020).

in April through August, while the illustrative high-wage household would have experienced a 68 percent reduction in these two months. As a result of Federal action, the low-wage household instead experiences a 240 percent increase in income in April, a 70 percent increase in May through July, and a 10 percent increase in August relative to its income in February. The high-wage household instead experiences a 28 percent increase in April, a 28 percent decrease in May through July, and a 48 percent decrease in August. Thus, not only did Federal action provide greater income protection for both households relative to the counterfactual scenario with no CARES Act, but also provided greater income protection for lower-wage households than higher-wage households.

The especially large increases in incomes for lower-income households can also be seen in reductions in poverty in the months immediately following the CARES Act. Han, Meyer, and Sullivan (2020) use near real-time data from the monthly Current Population Survey to estimate poverty rates each month based on the previous 12 months of income. In updated analysis, they find that the poverty rate in every month between March and September was near or below the pre-COVID poverty rate of 11.0 percent in February 2020 (see figure 2-4). Han, Meyer, and Sullivan estimate that CARES Act provisions reduced the poverty rate by 4.0 percentage points in the 12 months ending June 2020. Parolin, Curran, and Wimer (2020) project that CARES Act provisions could significantly reduce the poverty rate for calendar year 2020.

Figure 2-4. Percent Below Federal Poverty Line, 2019–20

Population below 100 percent of the Federal poverty line (percent)

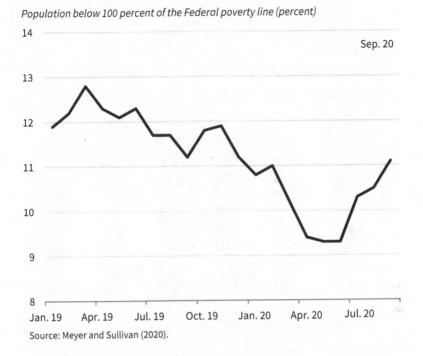

Source: Meyer and Sullivan (2020).

As of June 16, data from the Census Bureau Household Pulse Survey indicate that the vast majority (85.3 percent) of households had received an Economic Impact Payment (figure 2-5). The quick timing of Economic Impact Payments helped ensure that households could meet their basic needs. Indeed, as of June 16, only 12.8 percent of households reported mostly using their Economic Impact Payment to add to their savings accounts, and 13.5 percent mostly used it to pay off debt such as car loans, student loans, and credit cards. By contrast, about 59.1 percent of households used their Economic Impact Payment to pay for expenses such as food, clothing, and shelter. Baker and others (2020) show that over 20 percent of Economic Impact Payments were spent within 10 days of receipt, and spending increased the most for food, rent, bills, and nondurables. Chetty and others (2020) find that Economic Impact Payments had a large effect on spending by low-income households, allowing them to return their spending levels to pre-COVID levels by late April.

In addition to helping ensure that households did not experience income losses, the CARES Act attempted to help households maintain housing stability by halting all foreclosures and evictions for properties with federally backed mortgages. Estimates by the Federal Reserve Bank of Atlanta suggest that this covered between 28 and 46 percent of all rental units. This partial eviction moratorium, in combination with local eviction moratoriums in many cities,

Figure 2-5. Households' Receipt and Use of Economic Impact Payment, 2020

- Did not and does not expect to receive a stimulus payment
- Mostly to add to savings
- Mostly to pay off debt (car loans, student loans, credit cards)
- Mostly to pay for expenses (food, clothing, shelter, etc.)

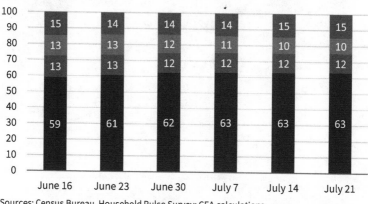

Households (percent)

	June 16	June 23	June 30	July 7	July 14	July 21
Did not	15	14	14	14	15	15
Savings	13	13	12	11	10	10
Debt	13	13	12	12	12	12
Expenses	59	61	62	63	63	63

Sources: Census Bureau, Household Pulse Survey; CEA calculations.

helped reduce evictions to below pre-COVID levels. According to data from the Eviction Lab, evictions in all the cities that it tracks were on average 66 percent lower in April through August 2020 than in February (figure 2-6).

The Trump Administration's temporary nationwide moratorium on evictions for eligible renters beginning on September 4 appears to have helped reduce evictions as well. Figure 2-7 shows evictions in the nine cities tracked by the Eviction Lab that did not have a local eviction moratorium at the time of the CDC order. Relative to the total number of evictions in these nine cities during the week beginning August 30 (before the CDC order), evictions were 41 percent, 11 percent, and 30 percent lower during the next three weeks.

One risk with an eviction moratorium is that nonpayment of rent could have increased, leaving landlords unable to pay mortgages and other costs. However, unprecedented income support via Economic Impact Payments and expanded UI benefits may have mitigated this problem. In fact, data from the National Multifamily Housing Council (2020) show that the rate of missed rental payments in multifamily housing properties had increased by only 1 to 2 percentage points in May through September of 2020, compared with the same month one year earlier.

Figure 2-6. Evictions in Selected Cities by Month, 2020

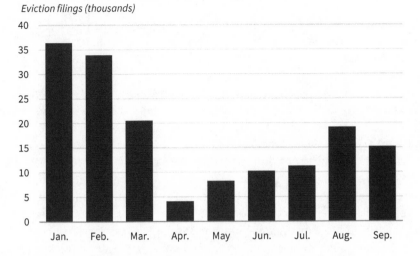

Eviction filings (thousands)

Sources: Hepburn, Louis, and Desmond (2020); CEA calculations.
Note: Eviction counts are for Austin, Boston, Bridgeport, Charleston, Cincinnati, Cleveland, Columbus, Fort Worth, Gainesville, Hartford, Houston, Jacksonville, Kansas City, Memphis, Milwaukee, Phoenix, Pittsburgh, Richmond, Saint Louis, Tampa, and Wilmington.

Figure 2-7. Eviction Filings in Selected Cities, 2020

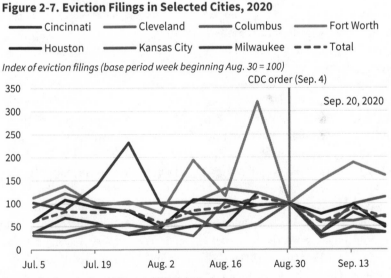

Index of eviction filings (base period week beginning Aug. 30 = 100)

Sources: Hepburn, Louis, and Desmond (2020); CEA calculations.
Note: Data are weekly; dates correspond to the first day of the reference week. The base period, the week of August 30–September 6, is equal to 100 for all series. On September 4, a CDC order temporarily halting evictions across the country went into effect.

Spurring a Return to the Pre-COVID Economy

Provisions in the CARES Act and other legislation, along with President Trump's executive actions, provided immediate relief to U.S. households. However, the most important way to ensure long-term gains in living standards is a rapid economic recovery.

A central CARES Act component intended to promote a rapid recovery was the Paycheck Protection Program, which helped keep workers employed by authorizing $349 billion to support payroll and other expenses for small businesses, self-employed individuals, Tribal business concerns, and nonprofit or veterans' organizations during the COVID-19 crisis. As part of the PPP and Health Care Enhancement Act, an additional $310 billion was appropriated to the program. Although the funds were issued as loans, they could be fully forgiven if no less than 60 percent (originally, 75 percent) of the funds were used for payroll. Other expenses eligible for loan forgiveness included mortgage interest, rent, and utilities. To further encourage employers to maintain ties with workers, employers whose operations were disrupted by COVID-19 but did not receive a PPP loan were offered an employee retention tax credit worth up to $5,000 per retained employee.

As discussed further in chapter 3 of this *Report*, these policies helped hasten the economic recovery. For example, Autor and others (2020) use administrative payroll data to compare employment changes at firms that were somewhat below and somewhat above the 500-employee cutoff for PPP loan eligibility. They find that the PPP saved between 1.4 million and 3.2 million jobs through the first week of June, based on an assumption that firms somewhat below the eligibility cutoff would have seen employment changes similar to those experienced by firms somewhat above the eligibility cutoff. If, however, smaller firms would have experienced larger employment losses than larger firms in the absence of the PPP, then the true impact of the PPP would be significantly larger than that estimated by the authors. Other studies find a range of early effects of PPP on employment (Bartik et al. 2020; Chetty et al. 2020; Granja et al. 2020). It is important to note that because PPP stemmed business closures, the total employment effect is likely to be considerably larger over time as those salvaged businesses rehire furloughed workers. In total, Standard & Poor's U.S. Chief Economist Beth Ann Bovino estimates that PPP could have saved upward of 13.6 million jobs, and JPMorgan Chase's Jamie Dimon estimates that PPP saved 35 million jobs (Fox et al. 2020; Ruhle, Miranda, and Capetta 2020).

After the unemployment rate rose from 3.5 percent in February 2020 to 14.7 percent in April 2020, forecasters expected that it would continue increasing and remain above 10 percent for the remainder of 2020. However, contrary to expectations, the unemployment rate fell to 6.7 percent just seven months later. By comparison, after the unemployment reached its peak in October

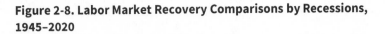

Figure 2-8. Labor Market Recovery Comparisons by Recessions, 1945–2020

Indexed employment level (pre-recession peak = 100)

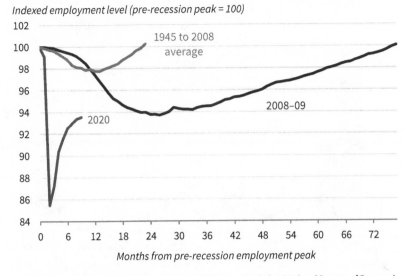

Months from pre-recession employment peak

Sources: Bureau of Labor Statistics, Current Employment Statistics; National Bureau of Economic Research; CEA calculations.

2009 during the Great Recession, in over a decade it had still not fallen by as much as it did between April and November 2020. Figure 2-8 shows that the recovery from the COVID shock has been much faster than that from the Great Recession and all other postwar recessions in regaining lost employment.

Workers in every major private sector industry have experienced employment gains. Between April and November, the leisure and hospitality industry regained 59 percent (4.9 million) of jobs lost; trade, transportation and utilities regained 71 percent (2.4 million); and education and health services regained 55 percent (1.5 million) (figure 2-9). Black workers have regained 53 percent, Hispanic workers have regained 66 percent, Asian American workers have regained 66 percent, and White workers have regained 66 percent of jobs lost.

The policy response to the most sudden and severe economic downturn since the Great Depression was unprecedented. It provided extensive relief to households that would otherwise have suffered substantial losses of income, and it set the economic recovery on a strong footing. Of course, continued progress is needed to return to the strong pre-COVID economy. In addition, there is near-term risk that policy and behavioral responses to a resurgence of COVID-19 could disrupt the considerable labor market recovery observed to date. For this reason, in late 2020 the Administration continued to articulate support for additional fiscal measures to provide a bridge to the widespread availability of vaccine candidates developed under Operation Warp Speed (Goodspeed and Navarro 2020).

Figure 2-9. Private Payroll Job Losses by Sector since February 2020

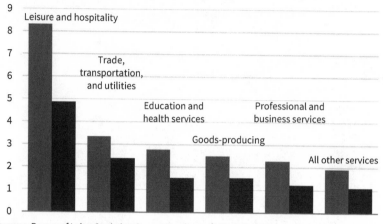

■ Loss from February to April ■ Gain from April to November

Employment change (millions)

Sources: Bureau of Labor Statistics, Current Employment Statistics; CEA calculations.
Note: "All other services" is the sum of the financial activities, information, and "other services" categories.

Conclusion

The COVID-19 pandemic and subsequent lockdowns caused a historic shock to the U.S. economy. The unemployment rate increased from a 50-year low of 3.5 percent in February 2020 to 14.7 percent just two months later. Experts forecasted that the unemployment rate would remain above 10 percent for the remainder of 2020. Without policy action, the loss in employment and earnings threatened the ability of millions of American households to pay for food, housing, and other basic necessities.

Fortunately, the policy response from the Federal Government was immediate, unprecedented in scale, and targeted to the most vulnerable households and firms. The Trump Administration worked with Congress to pass and sign three major bills in March 2020, providing over $2 trillion in relief to fund direct payments to U.S. households, assistance to employers to keep workers on payroll, expanded and enhanced unemployment assistance, measures to prevent housing foreclosures and evictions, and a number of other measures intended to provide relief to Americans and bolster the economy's recovery. In August 2020, President Trump followed up with a series of executive actions that extended further relief to American households, including providing lost wages assistance and a moratorium on residential evictions.

These actions led to historic *increases* in household incomes, especially at the lower end of the income distribution, along with decreases in poverty and evictions. In the long run, however, the success of actions taken to support households will depend on how quickly the economy recovers. Between April and November, the unemployment rate fell by 8.0 percentage points, from 14.7 to 6.7 percent, the largest seven-month decline on record. Although more progress is needed, the economy has recovered much more quickly than forecasters initially expected. Fortunately, the strong pre-COVID economy—in which unemployment fell to a 50-year low, labor force participation grew stronger, the poverty rate reached a record low, and median income experienced the largest one-year increase in 50 years—together with unprecedented Federal action during the COVID-19 crisis, has paved the way for a strong economic recovery.

Chapter 3

Assisting Entrepreneurs and Workers through Aid to Businesses

The Coronavirus Aid, Relief, and Economic Security (CARES) Act, which was signed into law by President Trump in March 2020, has authorized unprecedented levels of financial support, providing much-needed relief to families and workers during the COVID-19 pandemic. The Federal Government has also implemented, through the CARES Act and additional means, several critical measures to support small businesses as they have weathered this unique and exogenous economic shock. With businesses facing a significant loss in revenue and demand as a result of stay-at-home orders and social distancing by households, the Trump Administration has taken decisive actions to keep small businesses afloat, thus far averting a swath of bankruptcies and a collapse of the financial system similar to the Great Recession.

In one of the CARES Act's most significant provisions to help American small businesses, the Paycheck Protection Program (PPP) authorized hundreds of billions of dollars in forgivable loans to boost the retention of employees and preserve the relationships between employers and their workers. This program was successful in targeting the small businesses that needed loans the most; 5.21 million small businesses and nonprofit organizations received a loan, and the vast majority of loans went to small businesses and organizations with very few employees. Estimates find that the PPP has saved or supported tens of millions of jobs.

In addition to the PPP, the CARES Act funded several measures to provide liquidity to businesses in the midst of this economic shock. As a result, the economy in 2020 did not see a wave of bankruptcies like during the Great

Recession. Indeed, though bankruptcies did spike during the pandemic, they increased at a much lower rate than during the Great Recession, despite the fact that the pandemic caused an economic shock significantly larger than that of 2008. The robust labor market before the pandemic helped enable businesses and households to better weather this crisis, further contributing to the lower rates of small business bankruptcies during the pandemic.

The Department of the Treasury and the Federal Reserve also played critical roles in easing financial strain and ensuring access to liquidity for businesses. To accomplish this, the CARES Act authorized emergency actions to stabilize the financial system and to provide direct support for credit. In doing so, the act has helped avert a potential collapse of the financial system similar to what occurred during the Great Recession, thereby greatly improving the outlook for a swift economic recovery.

In analyzing numerous financial and economic indicators related to the pandemic, this chapter demonstrates that the CARES Act and the Trump Administration's actions have preserved American businesses and saved millions of jobs. These actions have been historic in their speed and magnitude, and the data show that small businesses have benefited the most from these unprecedented actions. As a result, the economy has recovered more rapidly than many people anticipated and is poised to continue its return to the level of prosperity it experienced before the COVID-19 pandemic provided that fiscal policy continues to provide appropriate support.

This chapter focuses on the effects that the extraordinary actions taken by the Federal Government in response to the COVID-19 pandemic have had on businesses, with a particular focus on small businesses. Just as forecasters have significantly revised their expectations for 2020 gross domestic product (GDP) upward, so too did businesses experience an uptick in their outlook. Between April and October, the small business optimism index compiled by the National Federation of Independent Business rose from 90.9 to 104.0—one of the steepest annual increases in the index's history. The federation attributes some of the improvement to the loan forgiveness feature of the

Paycheck Protection Program (PPP), which is discussed here, along with other business-oriented provisions of the CARES Act.

Summary of Policies to Assist American Businesses and Their Workers

Much of the analysis in this chapter focuses on the PPP and the Federal Reserve's lending facilities—given that these are the largest business provisions and have received the most attention by academic researchers—but here we also include a summary of several of the main provisions in the CARES Act directed at small, mid-sized, and large businesses. In total, $1.6 trillion was allocated (excluding Federal Reserve lending facilities), and about $930 billion has been disbursed as of October 2020.

The Paycheck Protection Program

The CARES Act authorized $349 billion in forgivable PPP loans to support payroll and other expenses for America's small businesses, self-employed individuals, Tribal businesses, and nonprofit/veterans' organizations. As part of the Paycheck Protection Program and Health Care Enhancement Act, which was signed into law by President Trump in April 2020, an additional $310 billion was authorized, bringing the total amount for the PPP to $659 billion. Though the funds are used to guarantee and forgive loans, a condition for full loan forgiveness is that recipient businesses must spend no less than 60 percent of the loaned funds on payroll expenses within a 24-week span called the covered period.[1] Other expenses eligible for loan forgiveness include interest on mortgages, rent, and utilities.

Employee Retention Tax Credits

The CARES Act provided refundable tax credits against payroll taxes for employers that either were required to shut down because of COVID-19-related government mandates or suffered at least a 50 percent decline in year-over-year revenue during a quarter. The credit amount is 50 percent of qualified wages, up to a maximum of $5,000. Like the PPP, these credits act as a wage subsidy to boost retention, and the Joint Committee on Taxation estimated a $55 billion cost of the provision in March, although it is unclear how high the uptake will end up being, in light of eligibility restrictions. In addition, qualified wages of firms with more than 100 workers include only wages paid to inactive employees (e.g., those furloughed).

---

[1] Before the Paycheck Protection Flexibility Act of 2020, which was signed into law by President Trump in June 2020, the forgiveness criteria required a 75 percent payroll requirement and an eight-week covered period.

Economic Injury Disaster Loans and Advances

The Economic Injury Disaster Loans and Advances (EIDL) program of the U.S. Small Business Administration (SBA), which predates the COVID-19 crisis, provides relief to small businesses and nonprofit organizations experiencing a temporary loss of revenue. Relative to PPP loans, EIDL loans tend to be longer in duration, have a higher interest rate, and are not forgivable outside the advance itself—that is, the loan must be repaid in full. The Coronavirus Preparedness and Response Supplemental Appropriations Act, which preceded the CARES Act, made COVID-19 losses an eligible disaster under the SBA disaster program, allowing affected businesses to apply for the program's loans. The CARES Act, along with the Paycheck Protection Program and Healthcare Enhancement Act, then expanded eligibility and eased application requirements. The acts also added $20 billion in funds to allow more entities to receive the $10,000 EIDL advances. As of November 23, $194 billion in EIDL loans had been approved for just over 3.6 million loans.

The Federal Reserve's Lending Facilities

The U.S. Department of the Treasury made available $454 billion via the CARES Act to backstop some of the emergency lending facilities set up by the Federal Reserve under Section 13(3) of the Federal Reserve Act. The purpose of this Treasury backing was to ensure that the Federal Reserve would not be put in a position to need to absorb losses. For the facilities created by this collaboration, Federal Reserve Banks lend to private firms, to nonprofit organizations, or to State and local governments.

The facilities can broadly be divided into two groups: those that are aimed at supplying credit to the macroeconomy (which rely on CARES Act capital funding)—the Primary and Secondary Market Corporate Credit Facilities, the Term Asset-Backed Securities Loan Facility, the Municipal Liquidity Facility, and the Main Street Lending Program—and those that are aimed at funding markets (which are backed by funding from the Treasury's Exchange Stabilization Fund (ESF) or are secured by collateral)—the Money Market Mutual Fund Liquidity Facility and the Commercial Paper Funding Facility. The Federal Reserve also created the Primary Dealer Credit Facility and the Paycheck Protection Program Liquidity Facility, neither of which received economic support or investments from the Treasury. This chapter goes into greater depth on these facilities in a later section.

Other Programs

Small Business Administration debt relief. The CARES Act appropriated $17 billion to go toward debt relief for new and existing SBA borrowers. Specifically, the SBA is required under this provision to pay the principal, interest, and fees owed on specified loans for six months. This debt relief is distinct from the conditional forgiveness offered for newly created PPP loans.

Deferral of employer payroll taxes. The CARES Act allowed employers to defer payment of their portion of payroll taxes incurred from March 27, 2020, through December 31, 2020. Businesses will repay their deferred liabilities in two installments, in December 2021 and 2022. This deferral is a de facto loan to businesses, giving them short-term liquidity without directly altering their long-term financial situation, except to the extent that the injection of liquidity is necessary for some of them to survive the crisis.

Modifications for net operating losses. The CARES Act permitted taxpayers to offset 100 percent of taxable income in taxable years beginning after 2017 and before 2021 with net operating losses (NOLs). Before the CARES Act, taxpayers' NOLs from taxable years beginning after 2017 were limited to offsetting 80 percent of taxable income in such years. The CARES Act also temporarily allowed taxpayers to carry back recently computed NOLs to offset income (and potentially claim refunds of all or part of their tax liabilities) for the previous five taxable years, if the losses were incurred in taxable years beginning after 2017 and before 2021.[2] The Joint Committee on Taxation estimated that this provision would reduce revenues by $154 billion in 2020 and by $161 billion during the 2020–30 window.

Direct sector-specific aid. The CARES Act authorized $46 billion in loans, loan guarantees, and other investments for certain affected industries. Specifically, the CARES Act authorized $25 billion for passenger air carriers, $4 billion for cargo air carriers, and $17 billion for businesses deemed critical to maintaining national security. In exchange for receiving these funds, passenger air carriers agreed to certain conditions, including a requirement not to reduce employment by more than 10 percent through September 2020.

Measuring Small Business's Utilization of Selected CARES Act Business Provisions

Table 3-1 illustrates the percentage of small businesses that have accessed different programs since March 13, 2020, as reported in the Census Small Business Pulse Survey. Small businesses may also have accessed Economic Impact Payments and Unemployment Insurance or Pandemic Unemployment Assistance.

As of August 8, at the time of the PPP's closing, the SBA had approved over 5.2 million small business loans worth more than $525 billion, supporting an estimated 51 million jobs and representing 80 percent of the small business payroll in all 50 States. The average loan size was about $101,000. The loans were overwhelmingly distributed to small businesses with few employees. More than 87 percent of the total approved loans, totaling over one-quarter of the total approved loan amount, were for $150,000 or less (table 3-2). Over 94

---

[2] In addition to the NOL rule changes, the CARES Act included a separate rule change that deferred limits on owners' losses from pass-through businesses, which could have an impact on individuals' computation of their NOLs.

Table 3-1. Liquidity Programs for Small Businesses during COVID-19

Program	Percentage of Small Businesses Receiving Assistance
Paycheck Protection Program (PPP)	73.2
Economic Injury Disaster Loans (EIDL)	23.8
Small Business Administration (SBA) debt relief	10.2
Other Federal programs	2.4
This business has not received financial assistance from any Federal program	22.0

Sources: Census Bureau; CEA calculations.
Note: The sum of these do not equal 100 because businesses could select multiple answers. Survey results are for the period November 23–29, 2020. The U.S. Census defines a small business as "a single location business with employment between 1 and 499 and receipts of at least $1,000." The sample consists of about 885,000 businesses.

Table 3-2. PPP Loan Size by Amount, First and Second Round Combined (data as of Aug. 8, 2020)

Loan Size (thousands of dollars)	Approved Loans (count)	Approved Loan Total Amount (billion dollars)	Percentage of Count	Percentage of Amount
50 and under	3,574,110	62.7	68.6	12.0
50–100	683,785	48.7	13.1	9.3
100–150	294,557	36.1	5.7	6.9
150–350	377,797	84.8	7.2	16.1
350–1,000	199,679	113.6	3.8	21.6
1,000–2,000	53,218	73.9	1.0	14.1
2,000–5,000	24,248	72.2	0.5	13.7
More than 5,000	4,734	33.1	0.1	6.3
Total	5,212,128	525.0		

Source: U.S. Small Business Administration.
Note: PPP = Paycheck Protection Program.

percent of the total approved loans, totaling more than 44 percent of the total approved loan amount, were for $350,000 or less. Because the maximum loan for which a business can apply is a function of its total payroll costs, the vast majority of PPP loans were approved for small businesses and organizations with very few employees.

The first round of the PPP, which ended April 16 when funds ran out, approved fewer loans but consisted of a larger share of the total loan amounts (figure 3-1). Round 2 had a change in the composition of which firms received the loans, with a shift toward smaller businesses. Conditional on participation,

Figure 3-1. Share of Total PPP Loan Counts and PPP Loan Amounts by Round

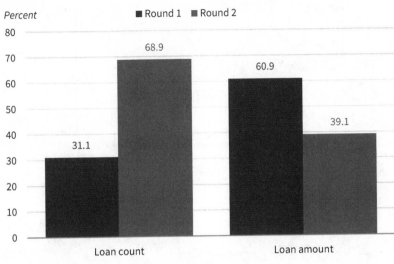

Sources: U.S. Small Business Administration (SBA); CEA calculations.
Note: The loan counts and amounts for round 1 are derived using the SBA's August 8 update, which shares data specific to round 2.

the average loan size fell from $197,462 in round 1 to $57,095 in round 2. Overall, 73.2 percent of small businesses received PPP loans, as indicated in table 3-1. Moreover, at the time the program closed, over $130 billion in authorized PPP funds remained unspent, which provides suggestive evidence that most small businesses that were eligible and applied for a PPP loan received one. The presence of leftover funds does not indicate that PPP demand is satiated, however. Rather, the leftover funds are more likely in part a consequence of the restriction against businesses receiving more than one PPP loan—for example, against businesses receiving a second loan to carry themselves through the fall after receiving an initial loan to get through the spring and early summer. Further legislation would need to provide such authorization.

Recent research by Autor and others (2020) provides evidence that, through just the first week of June 2020, the PPP saved between 1.4 and 3.2 million jobs. The rehiring of furloughed workers in the months since, in order to qualify for PPP loan forgiveness, is likely to result in a much higher total number of jobs saved attributable to the PPP. In total, Standard & Poor's (S&P) U.S. Chief Economist Beth Ann Bovino estimates that PPP could have saved upward of 13.6 million jobs, while JPMorgan Chase CEO Jamie Dimon suggests an even larger figure of 35 million jobs (Fox et al. 2020; Ruhle, Miranda, and Cappetta 2020). As of August 8, healthcare and social assistance; professional, scientific, and technical services; construction; and manufacturing accounted

Table 3-3. PPP Loans by Industry

NAICS Subsector Description	Approved Loans	Approved Dollars (billions)	Percentage of Loans	Percentage of Amount
Health care and social assistance	532,775	67.8	10.2	12.9
Professional, scientific, and technical services	681,111	66.8	13.1	12.7
Construction	496,551	65.1	9.5	12.4
Manufacturing	238,494	54.1	4.6	10.3
Accommodation and food services	383,561	42.5	7.4	8.1
Retail trade	472,418	40.6	9.1	7.7
Other services (except public administration)	583,385	31.7	11.2	6.0
Wholesale trade	174,707	27.7	3.4	5.3
Administrative and support and waste management and remediation services	258,907	26.6	5.0	5.1
Transportation and warehousing	229,565	17.5	4.4	3.3
Real estate and rental and leasing	262,921	15.7	5.0	3.0
Finance and insurance	181,493	12.2	3.5	2.3
Educational services	88,022	12.1	1.7	2.3
Unclassified establishments	219,502	9.7	4.2	1.8
Information	73,824	9.3	1.4	1.8
Arts, entertainment, and recreation	130,760	8.2	2.5	1.6
Agriculture, forestry, fishing, and hunting	149,535	8.1	2.9	1.6
Mining	22,503	4.5	0.4	0.9
Public administration	14,291	1.8	0.3	0.3
Management of companies and enterprises	9,472	1.6	0.2	0.3
Utilities	8,331	1.5	0.2	0.3
Total	5,212,128	525.0		

Sources: U.S. Small Business Administration; CEA calculations.
Note: NAICS = North American Industry Classification System; PPP = Paycheck Protection Program.

for 48 percent of the total amount of approved dollars in both rounds of PPP (table 3-3).

Figure 3-2 shows PPP coverage for each State as a percentage of total payroll expenses incurred over a 2.5-month period by businesses with fewer than 500 employees (the duration used to determine PPP loan size and the firm size cutoff for eligibility).[3] Those States with most if not all their small

[3] An early analysis of the PPP program found that some funds initially flowed to geographic regions that were less adversely impacted by the pandemic (Granja et al. 2020).

Figure 3-2. Percentage of Small Businesses Receiving a PPP Loan, through August 8, 2020

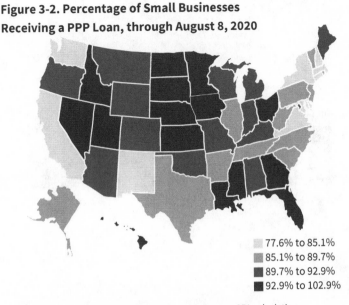

77.6% to 85.1%
85.1% to 89.7%
89.7% to 92.9%
92.9% to 102.9%

Sources: U.S. Small Business Administration; U.S. Census; CEA calculations.
Note: The amount of payroll comes from Census's 2017 SUBS survey adjusted to 2019 dollars and then reduced to 2.5 months' worth. Small businesses are defined as employment of 1 to 499 people. Sole proprietorships also received PPP loans, so some states received more than 100 percent of this payroll.

businesses payroll covered by PPP are predominantly in the Southeast and Midwest. As data on retail consumer spending reveal, PPP loans went especially to States that saw more drastic declines in consumer spending. The Census Small Business Pulse Survey reports that 73.2 percent of small businesses nationwide have received a PPP loan since the spring.

Comparing Expected and Actual Small Business Bankruptcies during the COVID–19 Pandemic

There are signs that the disruptive effects of the COVID-19 pandemic have led to greater business churn, with the Census Bureau reporting that business applications in 2020 are twice as high as they have been at any point in the past decade. However, measuring business exits is far more challenging, both because of an absence of live-tracking data, and because of the unique nature of the economic shock from COVID-19.[4] In particular, it is difficult to distinguish between businesses that have exited permanently from those which have closed temporarily. Bankruptcies can serve as a proxy for the subset of business exits caused by the inability of owners to meet debt obligations. This

---

[4] Crane et al. (2020) discuss some of these measurement challenges as well as a range of alternative measures and indicators of business exit.

Figure 3-3. Total Chapter 11 Bankruptcy Filings by U.S. Small Businesses, 2020

Percent change in 2020 from average of 2017 to 2019

Sources: U.S. Department of Justice; CEA calculations.
Note: Due to weekly reporting, the July period is June 28–August 2 and the August period is August 3–30.

section compares observed bankruptcies with what an empirical analysis of historical economic relationships predicts are the volume of bankruptcies we would expect to observe in the United States, given the magnitude of the COVID-19 economic shock.

Data from the Department of Justice make it possible to monitor weekly changes in small business bankruptcies (specifically, those filed under Chapter 11) and also to compare the monthly totals for 2020 with the same month in prior years to see if small business bankruptcies have spiked as a result of the crisis.[5] Figure 3-3 shows a spike in February and March, before COVID-19 had begun to wreak havoc, likely due to a new Subchapter 5 provision that came into effect in February.[6] The data then show a sharp decline in April, when most of the country was under lockdowns, which may have prevented business own-ers from physically filing for bankruptcy due to social-distancing measures, or courts being unable to accept filings for the same reason (Tett 2020). Businesses may also have been waiting to see how economic uncertainty would unfold before filing for bankruptcy (Keshner 2020). In addition, the strong economy before the pandemic likely put businesses in a better position to survive for

---

[5] When referred to as "small business," the data reflect businesses that classify themselves as small when they are filing for a Chapter 11 bankruptcy.

[6] Subchapter 5 of Chapter 11 makes it easier for smaller businesses to reorganize under Chapter 11 bankruptcy. Under the CARES Act, the threshold debt level for businesses that could apply for Subchapter 5 bankruptcy was raised further, allowing more small businesses to be eligible for this chapter.

**Figure 3-4. Percent Change in Small Business Chapter 11
Bankruptcies, FY 2020, from FYs 2017–19 Average**

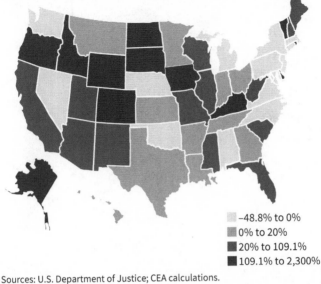

- ▨ −48.8% to 0%
- ▧ 0% to 20%
- ▦ 20% to 109.1%
- ■ 109.1% to 2,300%

Sources: U.S. Department of Justice; CEA calculations.
Note: Alabama and North Carolina have no data available as they are not under the jurisdiction of
the United States Trustee Program. The legend shows each quartile. FY = fiscal year.

some time, even in the face of COVID-related disruptions. Regardless of the
reasons for the April decline, bankruptcy filings started to rise in the late spring
and early summer, before showing a larger rise in July, August, September, and
October of, respectively, 69.3, 49.1, 82.3, and 63 percent. However, this level
was still 34 percent below that during the peak of the 2009 financial crisis.

Figure 3-4 shows which States saw an uptick in small business Chapter
11 bankruptcies in fiscal year (FY) 2020 through September 30, compared with
their 2017–19 averages. There are 36 States with higher FY 2020 small business
Chapter 11 bankruptcies than their averages between 2017 and 2019. These
States account for 72.9 percent of total small business Chapter 11 bankruptcies
in FY 2020.

Figure 3-5 uses the Department of Justice's data on small business
bankruptcy filings to compare bankruptcy dynamics with those during the
Great Recession and its aftermath. There was a large increase in small business
Chapter 11 bankruptcies during 2009 and 2010, and small business Chapter 11
bankruptcies fell as the recovery continued. The data for 2020 show a much
smaller initial uptick in bankruptcies, which is striking, given that second-
quarter gross domestic product fell by an annualized 31.4 percent during the
spring, compared with only 8.4 percent during the worst quarter of the Great
Recession (2008:Q4).

Figure 3-5. Small Business Chapter 11 Bankruptcies, FYs 2008–20

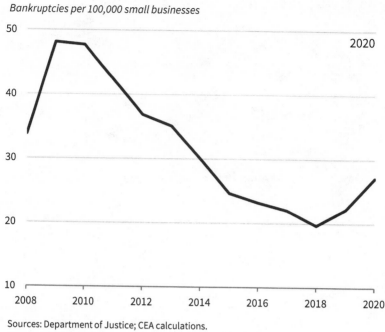

Bankruptcies per 100,000 small businesses

2020

Sources: Department of Justice; CEA calculations.
Note: FY = fiscal year.

Assessing how these observed bankruptcy filings compare with what one would expect given the disruption from COVID-19 requires a deeper analysis. The foremost explanation of why the increase in bankruptcies was not sharper is that the swift passage and implementation of record fiscal relief through the CARES Act helped businesses absorb the shock to cash flows that in the past would have forced them to declare bankruptcy; as we discuss below, in the absence of such a vigorous policy response, multitudes of companies would have been forced to permanently close.

One way to forecast small business Chapter 11 bankruptcies is through a vector autoregression estimate of unemployment insurance claims with three-month lags from January 2006 to December 2019. An advantage of this approach is that it can determine the lag between the negative economic shock and its effect on bankruptcies. In figure 3-6, the gap between actual and predicted bankruptcies represents "averted bankruptcies." Small business bankruptcies from April to September as a whole were predicted to increase by 181.8 percent, while actual filings rose by a much smaller 28.4 percent. This analysis suggests that the historic economic policy response in the spring and summer mitigated the macroeconomic shock and concomitant financial distress. However, this success does not preclude the possibility of a large future

Figure 3-6. Actual versus Predicted Small Business Chapter 11 Bankruptcy Filings, 2007–20

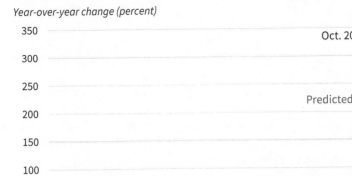

Year-over-year change (percent)

Sources: U.S. Department of Justice; U.S. Department of Labor; CEA calculations.
Note: Predicted filings are based on the vector autoregression results of a three-month lag using initial Unemployment Insurance claims.

bankruptcy spike, especially if the U.S. Congress fails to pass additional relief and recovery legislation in the coming months.

The CARES Act's Role in Facilitating Small Business Survival

The gap between predicted and actual bankruptcies through September (see figure 3-6) could arise from a number of factors. First, earlier in the pandemic, social-distancing mechanisms may have affected bankruptcy filing rates, both for the court systems and debtors. If business owners are unable to connect with lawyers or face difficulties submitting electronic filings, this could lead to filing delays that could show up as higher filings later in the data. At the same time, the courts' ability to take on cases was likely affected by State restrictions. A second important factor is the PPP's role in enabling businesses to stay afloat. By giving businesses loans that can be forgiven, the PPP allows them to meet expenses while facing a shock to cash flows. With this liquidity, many businesses that would otherwise have filed for bankruptcy are able to sustain themselves. The eligibility criterion disallowing firms in the process of filing for bankruptcy from accessing PPP loans also acts as a strong bankruptcy disincentive with considerable quantitative significance in light of the fact that nearly three-quarters of small businesses report having accessed PPP loans.

Finally, other elements of the CARES Act might have helped businesses avoid bankruptcy. For instance, Pandemic Unemployment Assistance extends unemployment insurance to the self-employed, sole proprietors, and others who may not qualify for traditional unemployment benefits, providing liquidity to help small businesses meet their monthly expenses. Their employees would be able to claim expanded unemployment insurance as well if they are placed on temporary furlough. The loan forbearance provision additionally enables businesses to defer certain expenses, such as rental and mortgage expenses. In other words, the PPP and other elements of the CARES Act have likely played a significant role in helping businesses avoid bankruptcy.

Recent academic estimates also highlight the promise and success of the PPP in keeping small businesses afloat. For example, Elenev, Landvoigt, and Van Nieuwerburgh (2020) simulate the effect of a PPP-type program in a general equilibrium macroeconomic model and show that it, along with a Main Street Lending–type program, successfully stems corporate bankruptcies. Using an instrumental variables approach, Bartik and others (2020) find that PPP loans led to a 14- to 30-percentage-point increase in a business' expected survival. Clearly, to the extent that the PPP helped mitigate business closures, it saved many of these businesses' jobs.

Although important, bankruptcies are only one measure of small business health during the crisis. The remainder of this section discusses data from Homebase that gives insight into a range of relevant small business metrics. Homebase is a company that provides software to help small business owners manage employee timesheets. Since the pandemic started, Homebase has maintained a database of U.S. small business employment using data from more than 60,000 businesses that use its software. The data cover more than 1 million employees who were active in the United States in January 2020. Most Homebase customers are restaurant, food and beverage, retail, and service businesses that are individually owned or managed by their operators.

The Homebase data show the dramatic effect of the COVID-19 pandemic on small businesses. Figure 3-7 illustrates the daily change in the number of hourly employees working at small businesses using Homebase compared with a January baseline. After shelter-in-place orders became widespread in mid-March, the number of employees working fell to a level about 55 to 60 percent lower than normal conditions. However, the passage of the CARES Act marked a significant inflection point that reversed this decline. The data reveal that small businesses have regained significant ground since then, though the number of hourly employees working at small businesses has plateaued, at about 20 percent below normal conditions, suggesting that a full small business recovery is still very much a work in progress.

Figure 3-7. Change in the Number of Small Business Hourly Employees Working, 2020

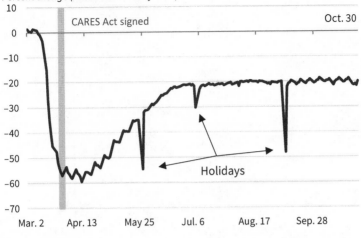

Percent change (relative to January base)

Source: Homebase.
Note: All the rates compare that day versus the median for the day of the week for the period January 4–31, 2020.

Company-specific data on PPP loan receipts and employment provide an insight into the role the program played in keeping workers attached to their employers, before which the extent was unclear.[7] Recent research by Autor and others (2020) using administrative payroll data finds that the PPP saved between 1.4 and 3.2 million jobs through just the first week of June. However, because the PPP has also stemmed business closures, the total employment effect is likely to be considerably larger over time as these businesses rehire furloughed workers. As stated above, the U.S. Chief Economist for S&P Global Ratings Services, Beth Ann Bovino, estimates that the PPP could have saved upward of 13.6 million jobs.

Opportunity Insights, a nonprofit research organization based at Harvard University, has also developed a data set to track the impact of COVID-19 on small businesses since January 2020. It pulls data from different sources of "credit card processors, payroll firms, and financial services firms" to construct a time series to track the effect of COVID-19 (Chetty et al. 2020). Figure 3-8 shows that by mid-April, the number of open small businesses had fallen over 40 percent compared with January. This trend began to increase in mid-April as initial PPP loans were disbursed and as States began to gradually lift restrictions on mobility and economic activity. As with the hourly employees

---

[7] Analysis by Chetty et al. (2020) shows a limited impact of PPP on employment levels at small businesses. However, their analysis is also constrained by the lack of firm-level data on PPP loan receipts and employment.

Figure 3-8. Change in the Number of Small Businesses Open, Seven-Day Average, 2020

Percent change (relative to January base)

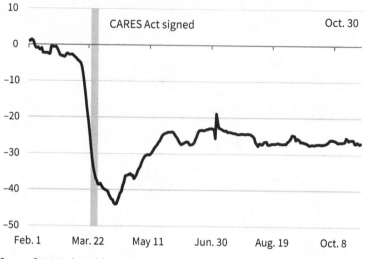

Source: Opportunity Insights.
Note: All the rates compare that day versus the median for the day of the week for the period January 4–31, 2020.

Figure 3-9. Change in Small Business Revenue, Seven-Day Average, 2020

Percent change (relative to January base)

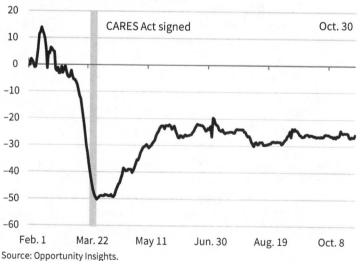

Source: Opportunity Insights.
Note: All the rates compare that day versus the median for the day of the week for the period January 4–31, 2020.

data discussed above, the number of open small businesses remains about 25 percent down from its pre-COVID levels. However, it is not currently possible to tell how many of these businesses have closed permanently versus how many remain temporarily inactive as a result either of residual or reimposed restrictions from State and local governments, or from continued lower-than-usual levels of demand.

Opportunity Insights also tracks how much total small business revenue has fallen (figure 3-9). At its trough in late March, small business revenue had fallen by nearly 50 percent. Between the end of April and early June, revenues recovered substantially, to about 25 percent below pre-COVID levels, but there has been no further progress since then for these data.

The Coronavirus Food Assistance Program's Impact on Farm Incomes

The CARES Act contained provisions that authorized support to farmers who were harmed by the consequences of the COVID-19 pandemic. These provisions took the form of the U.S. Department of Agriculture's Coronavirus Food Assistance Program (CFAP). The COVID-19 pandemic and the associated economic response disrupted food and agricultural markets, resulting in a

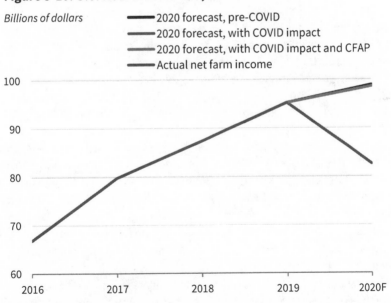

Figure 3-10. U.S. Net Farm Income, 2016–20

Sources: U.S. Department of Agriculture; Food and Agricultural Policy Research Institute; CEA calculations.
Note: "2020F" denotes a forecast; CFAP = Coronavirus Food Assistance Program.

dramatic drop in farm income for a wide array of agricultural products. CFAP made available $16 billion in financial assistance for producers of affected commodities, including $9.5 billion to compensate for losses due to commodity price reductions between mid-January and mid-April 2020 and another $6.5 billion for ongoing market disruptions. In early February 2020, before the extent of the pandemic's impact on agricultural markets was fully apparent, U.S. net farm income for 2020 was forecast to be $99 billion, which would have been a 4 percent increase over 2019 and the highest net farm income since 2013. By June, as the magnitude of the pandemic became evident, analysts had revised the forecast for 2020 net farm income down by more than $24 billion (25 percent), when CFAP payments are excluded. Including the $16 billion in emergency farm payments raises forecasts for net farm income to $99 billion (figure 3-10).

The Pandemic's Impact on the Financial Sector and Lending Facilities' Role

As the threat of the COVID-19 pandemic increased, the financial system came under stress in February and March 2020. Stock prices plummeted and market volatility rose. A recent analysis by Baker and others (2020) shows that COVID-19 has had an unprecedented effect on the stock market, especially in comparison with other infectious disease outbreaks, including that of Spanish Influenza in 1918–20 (figure 3-11). Businesses, which already held a historically high level of debt at the beginning of 2020, were suddenly at higher risk of default, leading to a decline in the availability of credit, and households' ability to repay their debts in the face of job and income loss became uncertain. With potential defaults looming, the risk of the real economic shock impairing assets of lenders and thereby infecting credit markets more broadly was substantial. Under these conditions, monetary or fiscal problems abroad—especially in Europe, China, and emerging market economies—could have spilled over to the United States, compounding the stress on the financial system.

The CARES Act, together with emergency powers under section 13(3) of the Federal Reserve Act, authorized the Federal Reserve and the Treasury Department to take actions to stabilize the system and prevent a financial crisis like that of the Great Recession. In accord with the Federal Reserve's *Financial Stability Report*, the Federal Reserve undertook aggressive monetary policy interventions and also took actions to stabilize short-term funding markets and provide direct support for credit. In addition, Chairman Jerome Powell testified that the Federal Reserve "took measures to allow and encourage banks to use their substantial capital and liquidity levels built up over the past decade to support the economy during this difficult time." Here we summarize some of the findings from the *Financial Stability Report* (Federal Reserve 2020).

Figure 3-11. Dow Jones Industrial Average Change during Various Pandemics

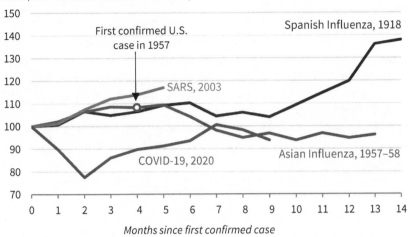

Index (100 = month of first confirmed case)

Sources: Dow Jones; CEA calculations.
Note: The *t* = 0 months were those with the first confirmed global cases, and were April 1918, February 1957, February 2003, and January 2020. All the pandemics except the Asian Influenza saw their first U.S. case within the same month as as their first global case.

Monetary policy interventions. The Federal Reserve lowered its policy rate close to zero to make borrowing less expensive. The Federal Open Market Committee began buying longer-term Treasury securities as well as agency mortgage-backed securities and commercial mortgage-backed securities after investors moved toward cash and short-term government securities because of volatility and uncertainty, which had the effect of smoothing and improving market conditions.

Stabilizing short-term funding markets and providing direct credit support. In a dash for liquidity, investors stopped purchasing commercial paper and pulled out of money market mutual funds that hold such paper along with other short-term debt instruments, leading to a cash shortage for businesses that rely on commercial paper to help fund their operations. In response, and pursuant to Section 13(3) of the Federal Reserve Act and with Treasury's approval, the Federal Reserve established a number of emergency lending facilities to support the flow of credit to businesses, nonprofit organizations, States, and municipalities.

Several facilities commenced before the CARES Act. The Primary Dealer Credit Facility allows primary dealers to support smooth market functioning and facilitate the availability of credit to businesses and households. The Commercial Paper Funding Facility (CPFF) provides liquidity to short-term funding markets. The Money Market Mutual Fund Liquidity Facility (MMLF) makes loans available to eligible financial institutions secured by high-quality assets purchased by the financial institution from money market mutual funds.

A number of additional facilities commenced after enactment of the CARES Act. The Primary Market Corporate Credit Facility (PMCCF) and the Secondary Market Corporate Credit Facility (SMCCF, together with the PMCCF, the CCF) provide liquidity for investment grade corporate bonds (or the bonds of certain companies that were investment grade as of March 22, 2020) as well as for exchange traded funds (ETFs) whose objective is to provide broad exposure to the market for U.S. corporate bonds. The Term Asset-Backed Securities Loan Facility (TALF) supports the provision of credit to consumers and businesses by enabling the issuance of asset-backed securities backed by private student loans, automobile loans and leases, consumer and corporate credit card receivables, certain loans guaranteed by the Small Business Administration, and other assets. The Municipal Lending Facility (MLF) supports lending to State, city and county governments, certain multistate entities, and other issuers of municipal securities. The Paycheck Protection Program Liquidity Facility offers a source of liquidity to financial institution lenders that lend to small businesses through the Small Business Administration's Paycheck Protection Program. The Main Street Lending Program (MSLP) supports lending to small and medium-sized businesses and nonprofit organizations that were in sound financial condition before the onset of the COVID-19 pandemic. MSLP operates five subfacilities: the Main Street New Loan Facility, the Main Street Priority Loan Facility, the Main Street Expanded Loan Facility, the Nonprofit Organization New Loan Facility, and the Nonprofit Organization Expanded Loan Facility. In support of these facilities, the Treasury Department has made equity investments in the CPFF, CCF, TALF, MLF, and MSLP, and has provided a backstop commitment to the MMLF.

These facilities resulted in a drop in the issuance of overnight commercial paper and redemptions from money market funds, easing market strains. Commercial and industrial loans from the Nation's commercial banks grew by $726 billion during the nine weeks from March 4 through May 6, far in excess of the growth during any similar interval since records were first collected in 1973. Li, Strahan, and Zhang (2020) argue that banks were able to accommodate this demand because of Federal Reserve bank liquidity programs, strong preshock bank capital, and coincident inflows from depositors.

In addition, a variety of indicators of financial distress that spiked early in the COVID-19 pandemic period have receded as of October 2020. Although many other shocks have hit the economy, including news about the pandemic itself, one can argue that public policy has mitigated the contagion of the pandemic into financial markets.

The VIX (the Chicago Board Options Exchange's Volatility Index), an index of expected stock market volatility derived from options prices, spiked from 27 in late February to a peak of 83 on March 16 (figure 3-12). It has generally fallen

Figure 3-12. Market Volatility Index (VIX), 2007–20

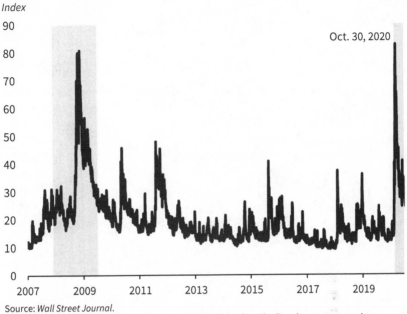

Source: *Wall Street Journal.*
Note: VIX = Chicago Board Options Exchange's Volatility Index. Shading denotes a recession.

since then, but remains somewhat elevated (as of October 30, the VIX was 38). Similarly, corporate bond spreads, such as the spread between BBB bonds relative to Treasury notes, show a similar pattern, peaking on about March 23 and then receding (figure 3-13).

The trends in these indicators, and others, suggest that lending facilities likely played an important role in easing financial market strain and ensuring access to liquidity for businesses in 2020. Recent academic work also confirms these findings. For example, Cox, Greenwald, and Ludvigson (2020) analyze stock market behavior in the early weeks of COVID-19 and attribute the large market swings to fluctuations in the pricing of risk, driven either by shifts in risk aversion or sentiment. They also find evidence that the Federal Reserve's "unconventional" monetary policy announcements outlining steps to support the economy played a role in the market turnabout, leading to gains of 8 percent in the S&P 500 and 12 percent in the Russell 2000 index. Importantly, they conclude that much of the benefit came from the signaling value of the Federal Reserve's statements, even as only a fraction of the credit that it has stood ready to provide has been extended. Haddad, Moreira, and Muir (2020) trace the recovery in the corporate bond market to the unprecedented actions the Fed took to purchase bonds, finding that the announcement on March 23 to buy investment-grade debt boosted prices and lowered bond spreads. The announcement on April 9 had a large effect both on investment-grade and

Figure 3-13. BBB Corporate Bond and 10-Year Treasury Note Spread, 2006–20

Percentage points

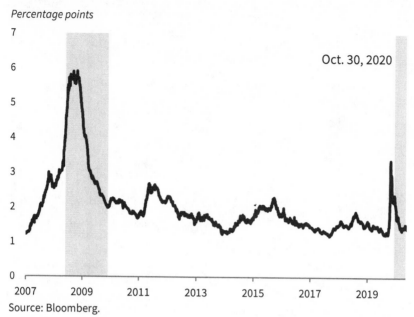

Oct. 30, 2020

Source: Bloomberg.

high-yield bonds, even for the riskier end. Gilchrist and others (2020) come to similar conclusions, finding that the announcements regarding the Secondary Market Corporate Credit Facility led to a reduction in credit spreads on bonds eligible for purchase by 70 basis points.

Finally, the large-scale income and small business revenue replacement, debt relief, and cost mitigation provisions in the CARES Act had a salutary impact on financial market stability. Such extensive relief helped ameliorate financial distress that could have created widespread default activity that would have threatened the proper functioning of secondary debt markets. Such liquidity provision helped buffer households and small businesses against the immediate shock to cash flows from COVID-19 and also helped preserve the health of their underlying balance sheets, thereby improving their long-term ability to service their financial obligations.

Conclusion

The health of U.S. businesses has seen a dramatic turnaround from the depths of the COVID-19 crisis during the spring 2020 lockdowns. The number of employees working at small businesses, the number of open businesses, and small business revenue have all recovered more than half the losses experienced in April. The Federal Government's decisive and bold action to inject more than $2 trillion into targeted income replacement and other key programs helped bolster the ability of businesses to remain financially viable, to retain or rehire their employees, and ultimately to restart activities. At this stage, there is still considerable ground to regain to return to the historic level of prosperity that existed just before the pandemic, but all indicators thus far point to a much more rapid recovery with fewer scars than in the aftermath of the Great Recession, despite an adverse shock several orders of magnitude greater than that experienced in 2008–9.

Additional fiscal support to mitigate business closures, stem layoffs, and accelerate the pace of hiring would further reduce the risk of economic scars. For example, allowing hard-hit and at-risk small businesses to receive second-round PPP loans would help them to survive and emerge healthy from the pandemic. In fact, an October 29 survey by the National Federation of Independent Business found that 75 percent of small businesses would apply or consider applying for a second-round PPP loan if allowed to do so. Also, expanding the eligibility of the Employee Retention Tax Credit (ERTC), but targeting it to reward only net retention and hiring, could significantly accelerate hiring. With regard to eligibility, if the main objective of the ERTC is to maximize hiring, then restricting access to businesses suffering significant revenue losses leaves out many employers that are willing and able to hire workers out of unemployment but may need the extra push from the ERTC incentive in light of ongoing economic uncertainty.

This problem is especially salient given that businesses in the direst straits may or may not be those with the highest propensity to hire, depending on the outlook for them individually and for their industry. As for the design of the incentive itself, subsidizing the retention of a business's entire workforce means paying the business to retain inframarginal workers that it likely would have kept anyway, unless it was on the verge of shutting down. Redesigning the ERTC to only subsidize net expansion above a company's head count or wage bill in some statutorily specified benchmark would specifically reward firms for returning to or exceeding the size of their pre-COVID workforce, thus accelerating the reabsorption of unemployed workers into gainful employment. This design especially benefits hard-hit firms that have the deepest employment hole from which to recover while also mobilizing other businesses to step up their recruiting. Recent research by Hamilton (2020) also finds promising labor market benefits from ERTC expansion. Both these policy actions would support the continuation of the fastest recovery on record as the economy regains its full potential.

Chapter 4

Advancing the Quality and Efficiency of America's Healthcare System

In the face of the global COVID-19 pandemic, the Trump Administration has taken decisive action to address the strain the health and economic crisis placed on the healthcare sector and on working families. This response has been twofold: financial support for hospitals and workers, and deregulation within the healthcare sector to accelerate the availability of testing and the development of vaccines and advanced therapeutics.

In March 2020, President Trump signed the bipartisan CARES Act, which appropriated $100 billion for healthcare providers, and which has alleviated the financial burden hospitals are experiencing during the COVID-19 pandemic. This was supplemented by an additional $75 billion for the Provider Relief Fund as part of the Paycheck Protection Program and Health Care Enhancement Act, and also funding for testing provided by the Families First Coronavirus Relief Act, resulting in $175 billion in direct aid to the healthcare sector. As a result, the CEA finds that the healthcare system has been one of the most resilient industries during the COVID-19 pandemic. The Administration also established emergency paid family and sick leave through tax credits available to private employers with fewer than 500 employees for leave payments through December 31, 2020. This has served to protect public health by encouraging workers to stay home rather than working while ill, and has allowed employees to care for sick family members without trading off work hours. In addition, the Administration provided funds to offer COVID-19 testing and treatment at no cost to uninsured patients, removing cost barriers for low-income and high-risk individuals—and, in turn, helped the United States identify positive COVID-19 cases and mitigate the effects of the COVID-19 pandemic.

When the United States needed to ramp up its testing capabilities for the virus at the onset of the COVID-19 pandemic, the Trump Administration, through the Food and Drug Administration (FDA), took action to issue Emergency Use Authorizations for COVID-19 diagnostic tests. As a result, the FDA permitted the use of over 20 diagnostic COVID-19 tests by the end of March 2020, helping public health officials track the spread of the coronavirus throughout the United States.

Similarly, the Centers for Medicare & Medicaid Services relaxed many of the regulations surrounding the use of telemedicine to allow patients seeking COVID-19 screening or advice on non-life-threatening conditions to do so from the safety of their homes. This reduced nonessential in-person healthcare visits, decreasing the strain on overburdened healthcare facilities and diminishing the potential transmission of COVID-19 throughout hospitals and healthcare facilities.

In one of the largest efforts during the pandemic, the Trump Administration mobilized the public and private sectors through Operation Warp Speed (OWS) in order to accelerate the development, production, and distribution of a safe and effective COVID-19 vaccine. OWS accomplishes this by identifying promising vaccines earlier in development, standardizing testing protocols, preparing manufacturing capacity, and funding infrastructure for vaccine distribution. Not only will the accelerated vaccine timeline provide an enormous benefit to public health, but the CEA estimates that OWS could provide an economic benefit of $155 billion if it pushes the arrival of the vaccine one month earlier, or $2.4 trillion if scientists were to deliver the vaccine by January 1, 2021. As of mid-November 2020, four vaccine candidates had entered Phase III clinical trials. The highly promising results of interim analyses of these candidates raise the possibility that researchers may develop a vaccine before the end of 2020 for widespread use among a set of targeted populations.

The deregulatory actions of the Trump Administration can continue to improve healthcare outcomes for the American people far beyond the scope of the COVID-19 pandemic. For example, the CEA estimates that more widespread adoption of telemedicine would allow rural Americans to save $130 per visit in travel-related opportunity costs while increasing their access to high-quality healthcare nationwide. In addition, the CEA estimates that a permanent reduction in FDA approval times by one, two, or three years for new drugs would provide trillions of dollars in social surplus. Moreover, the CEA calculates that expanding occupational licensing deregulation for nurse practitioners nationwide could result in $62 billion in cost savings annually. Also, this chapter explores the effects of several healthcare policy achievements beyond the response to the COVID-19 pandemic that will promote additional choice and competition in the market. Permanently deregulating aspects of the healthcare sector will provide better healthcare options and higher monetary savings for Americans as the Nation emerges from the COVID-19 pandemic.

The United States endured a major adverse health and economic shock in 2020 due to the arrival of the SARS-CoV-2 virus in the United States. The impact of this pandemic is likely to persist past 2020 as widespread mitigation takes hold. COVID-19—the disease stemming from the novel coronavirus—led to a global pandemic that, as of November 2020, has resulted in over 50 million confirmed cases worldwide and a global death toll of at least 1.25 million people. In the United States, there have been over 10 million confirmed cases and over 230,000 deaths. This disease has taken a toll on the American people that has been manifested not just as a tremendous mortality and morbidity burden, but also as a significant economic burden that affects the Nation at every level. In the first and second quarters of 2020, the U.S. economy contracted by 10.2 percent, and total employment declined by 14.5 percent between February and April 2020 after a record 20.8 million decrease in employment in April. At its peak, the unemployment rate was 14.7 percent in April. Initial claims for regular State unemployment insurance peaked in the week ending March 28, at 6.9 million, whereas insured unemployment in regular State programs peaked in the week ending May 9, at 24.9 million. This unprecedented level of economic disruption resulted in the highest levels of unemployment since the Great Depression, and had a direct impact on the economic well-being of millions of Americans.

COVID-19's dual effects on public health and the economy necessitated a response on two fronts. The first one, as discussed in the previous chapters of this *Report*, has consisted of efforts to address the economic effects of the crisis. The second front, which this chapter discusses, is the Trump Administration's efforts to address the underlying health crisis itself.

The resolution of any healthcare crisis relies largely on the efforts of three groups of people. First, it relies on the efforts of scientists to develop new treatments and tests for the disease. Second, it relies on the efforts of healthcare providers and healthcare systems to treat affected patients. And third, it relies on the efforts of the public to take appropriate actions during the crisis. These efforts require coordinated governance at the local, State, and Federal levels.

At the Federal level, the Trump Administration moved to eliminate regulatory barriers that could hinder the development of new treatments or the ability of healthcare providers to care for their patients. The CEA finds that these deregulatory efforts have had tremendous economic value. For example, the Centers for Medicare & Medicaid Services (CMS) relaxed many of the regulations surrounding the use of telemedicine and the share of telemedicine Medicare primary care visits increased dramatically, from 0.1 percent in February to 43.5 percent in April.

In addition, understanding that healthcare during a pandemic requires an economically strong healthcare system, the Administration moved to ensure the financial security of the healthcare system. Under the CARES Act and the Paycheck Protection Program and Health Care Enhancement Act (PPP/ HCE Act), Congress made up to $175 billion available for healthcare providers to support their financial health and livelihood. As a result of this and other Administration actions, the CEA finds that the healthcare system has been one of the most resilient industries during the first three quarters of 2020 based on employment, and indeed appears to be one of the industries that recovered most quickly from the initial shock caused by COVID-19. A key threat to the healthcare system early during the pandemic was sudden surges in demand for healthcare services that overwhelmed locally available resources. To combat this risk and slow the spread of the virus more broadly, local and State governments began implementing lockdown orders and other restrictions to combat the spread at the cost of economic activity. As the pandemic spread throughout the country, lockdown measures expanded commensurately, with over 99 percent of the population residing in States that had closed schools and limited bar and restaurant activity by March 24, and with over 90 percent residing in States that had issued shelter-in-place orders by April 4 (figure 4-1).

Finally, the Trump Administration's efforts focused on protecting Americans from the costs of care related to COVID-19 and on providing incentives for Americans to engage in appropriate behaviors during the crisis. For example, the Administration established emergency paid family and sick leave for COVID-19 patients to encourage these patients to stay at home instead of

Figure 4-1. Percentage of U.S. Population under Statewide Restrictions, 2020

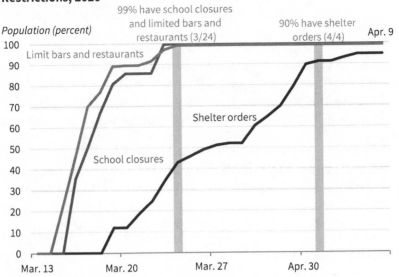

Sources: *New York Times*; State policy announcements; CEA calculations.

working while ill. This also allowed family members to take leave so they could look after those affected by COVID-19. Similarly, though much has been written on the Administration's effort to increase testing capacity, from an economic perspective, other important—and overlooked—parts of its approach were its efforts to decrease the barriers for Americans to receive testing. In the absence of treatment, testing may be of limited value to the individual, because a positive test will have little impact on disease management. However, testing does provide social value from a public health perspective, because it enables public health approaches that can limit the spread of the disease such as quarantining and contact tracing for infected individuals. Because individuals do not face the full social incentives for testing, making COVID-19 testing free at point-of-care by requiring that it be covered by insurers and reimbursing providers for the cost of testing for the uninsured are an important way to align the individual and social incentives for testing. The Kaiser Family Foundation found that, in July 2020, data from 78 hospitals revealed that COVID-19 diagnostic test prices ranged from $20 to $850 per diagnostic test, with a median cost of $127. The Administration's subsidies probably increased the likelihood of COVID-19 testing, especially for lower-income Americans.

The President's response to the unique dual health and economic crises caused by COVID-19 include an agenda for healthcare reform and deregulation. Although regulation is intended to benefit the public, whether it actually does so in practice is an empirical question, one that has been partly answered by the Administration's efforts to suspend and relax many regulations to address COVID-19. The benefits of deregulation to bolster the pandemic response are clear. For example, effective treatments and vaccines for COVID-19 have been and will be introduced at an extremely fast pace, and healthcare providers face fewer restrictions in providing care. If the absence of many regulations has improved social welfare, a natural question is why these regulations need to be reimposed when the pandemic subsides. Indeed, the CEA finds substantial benefits from extending many of the existing deregulatory efforts. For example, the CEA finds that expanding occupational licensing deregulation nationwide could result in $62 billion in cost savings annually.

This chapter begins with an overview of the Administration's efforts to promote research and development for COVID treatments and vaccines, followed by a discussion of the Administration's efforts to support the healthcare system. Next, we discuss the Administration's effort to protect the broader American public by subsidizing appropriate behaviors and the cost of COVID care. Finally, we conclude with an analysis of how healthcare can be improved by extending COVID-19 related reforms.

Expediting Research and Development for Novel Therapies and Tests for COVID-19

One important aspect of research and development for COVID-19 treatments and vaccines is the issuance of Emergency Use Authorizations to facilitate availability of pharmaceutical products in the event of an emergency. In addition, to accelerate the availability of effective COVID-19 therapeutics and vaccines, the Administration launched Operation Warp Speed, a public-private partnership to support the development, production, and distribution of treatments, diagnostics, and vaccines.

Emergency Use Authorizations

Ultimately, the solution to any healthcare crisis is to find a treatment for the underlying disease, and the Trump Administration moved aggressively to field treatments as quickly and in as widespread a manner as possible. A key roadblock in the development of treatments is the heavily regulated drug and vaccine development processes. On average, it takes 10 years to bring a new drug or vaccine to market, with just the preclinical phase of vaccine development taking six months to three years (André 2002; CEA 2019; DiMasi, Grabowski, and Hansen 2016; Grady et al. 2020; Mullard 2020; Plotkin et al. 2017; Pronker et al. 2013). These timelines are not tenable in the face of a global pandemic.

Early returns from these efforts appear promising. For example, Remdesivir, an antiviral, received an Emergency Use Authorization (EUA) from the Food and Drug Administration (FDA) on May 1—within 3.5 months of the first reported case of COVID-19 in the United States. By October 22, Remdesivir had been approved by the FDA for treatment of COVID-19. Similarly, the Trump Administration quickly solved early COVID-19 testing capacity problems. Pre-pandemic FDA rules required that the FDA provide premarket clearance, approval, or EUA review for COVID-19 diagnostic tests before their use in clinical labs, which led to significant delays in adequate testing capacity at the onset of the COVID-19 pandemic. Indeed, in February, only CDC's COVID-19 diagnostic test had been authorized by the FDA for emergency use in labs across the nation. While it can take years for the FDA to ultimately approve new diagnostic tests, by the end of March 2020, the FDA had issued EUAs permitting the emergency use of over 20 diagnostic tests for COVID-19 (FDA 2020; Ivanov 2013). This rapid access to numerous COVID-19 tests was made possible by FDA granting unprecedented flexibility to manufacturers and labs, including allowing labs to begin developing and using their own tests before FDA review of their validation data. And finally, as of September 2020, four vaccine candidates had entered Phase III clinical trials, raising the possibility that a vaccine may be developed before the end of 2020 (Milken Institute 2020).

Emergency Use Authorization is an authority granted to the FDA by the Federal Food Drug and Cosmetic Act, and it allows the FDA to permit the production and distribution of an unapproved product or temporarily allow an unapproved use of an approved product during a state of emergency. This does not constitute approval of the new product or use and can be revoked by the FDA once the emergency has ended or evidence arises that suggests that the EUA is not in accordance with public health. EUAs have been employed in previous pandemics, including for the development of influenza testing and treatment as well as the test for the Novel Coronavirus 2012, more commonly known as Middle East Respiratory Syndrome (MERS).

Operation Warp Speed

The Trump Administration also worked to expedite the development and large-scale production of new vaccine treatments. Operation Warp Speed (OWS) is a public-private partnership that encompasses most of these Administration efforts to expedite the availability of vaccines. OWS accelerated vaccine deployment by identifying promising vaccines earlier in development, standardizing safety and efficacy protocols, preparing manufacturing capacity, and funding infrastructure for vaccine distribution.

Under a traditional timeline, a COVID-19 vaccine would likely not be ready until September 2021. But under OWS, initial doses of the vaccine could become available as early as the end of December 2020 or beginning of January 2021. If OWS accelerates initial vaccine deployment by these 8 months, the CEA estimates that OWS would save $2.4 trillion in economic and health costs. Even if OWS only accelerates a vaccine by one month, OWS still provides an expected benefit of $155 billion.

Traditionally, vaccine candidates are developed individually by different firms and are not compared with each other until after they are approved and commercialized. However, under OWS, animal studies of candidate vaccines were compared with each other (before additional testing in humans) to ensure that resources were directed toward the most promising candidates. As of August 31, the Federal government financially supported and approved additional testing for seven vaccine candidates. Notably, OWS does not change the number or types of trials required for vaccines, nor their safety and efficacy tests, but it does change when they can occur.

Moreover, manufacturing and distribution infrastructure are typically not established until a vaccine has demonstrated safety and efficacy in clinical trials, leading to additional delays in vaccine deployment. But under OWS, the Federal government invested in manufacturing capacity for the promising vaccine candidates while they were still being tested, rather than waiting until they were approved. Manufacturing capacity that is developed will be used for whatever vaccine is eventually successful, if possible given the nature of the successful product, regardless of which firms have developed the capacity. OWS also preemptively expands the supplies of materials that are necessary to scale up production of any vaccine, such as glass vials. On October 16, the President announced that the department of Health and Human Services (HHS) and the Department of Defense will form a partnership with CVS and Walgreens to deliver the vaccine once it is available to vulnerable Americans in long-term-care facilities, free of charge.

The CEA estimates that OWS has the potential to bring tremendous economic benefits, given COVID-19's unprecedented costs. Figure 4-2 provides an estimate of the daily cost to the United States of not having a vaccine, separated into the costs due to COVID-19 deaths (health costs) and the costs due to lower economic activity (economic costs). As is common for many infectious diseases, the economic costs of preventing a disease are often of comparable magnitudes to the direct mortality and health costs induced by the disease. Daily costs were highest in early April due to the peak of COVID-19 deaths at that time. However, one prominent model, that of the Institute for Health Metrics and Evaluation (IHME), projects a second wave in 2021, which suggests the possibility of additional high future costs. Though IHME is just one among several COVID-19 forecasting models currently used by public health authorities, it is the only one that has released 2021 projections.

Figure 4-2 demonstrates why even small delays in vaccine deployment can be costly. Consider a vaccine that has initial doses deployed on January 1, 2021, which is shown by the gray vertical line. In this case, the value of the vaccine is equal to the sum of the daily health costs for all days January 2, 2021, or later, plus the sum of the daily gross domestic product costs through April 1, 2021, or later—assuming that it will take 90 days for the economy to return to normal. However, the vaccine cannot reverse damage that has already

Figure 4-2. Daily Health and Economic Costs of COVID-19 to the United States If No Vaccine Is Found

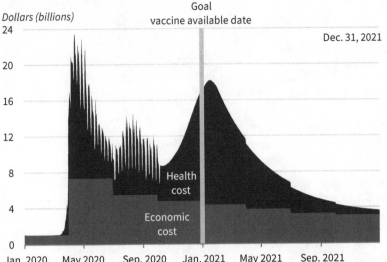

Sources: Institute for Health Metrics and Evaluation; Centers for Disease Control and Prevention; Congressional Budget Office; CEA calculations.

occurred, so the costs to the left of the gray line cannot be recovered, even with the introduction of a vaccine in January 2021.

Figure 4-3 demonstrates the value of faster vaccine development. We assume that without OWS, a vaccine would be available in September 2021, based on internal HHS projections. However, this should be viewed as a lower-bound estimate of the benefits of OWS, given that vaccines traditionally take 10 years to develop. The vertical axis gives the dollar value of an earlier vaccine, depending on the date at which it becomes initially available (horizontal axis). If OWS could accelerate vaccine deployment by 8 months (from September 1, 2021, to January 1, 2021), then the CEA estimates that the benefits would be $2.4 trillion above traditional deployment (the intersection of the red line and the left vertical gray line in figure 4-3).

The full value of the vaccine on January 1, 2021, would be $3.8 trillion. Some estimates suggest that traditional vaccine development processes would not result in a COVID-19 vaccine until September 2021, at which point it would provide benefits of $1.4 trillion. The benefit of the eight-month accelera-tion from OWS ($2.4 trillion) is the difference between the $3.8 trillion value in January and the $1.4 trillion value in September.

The CEA's methodology to create figures 4-2 and 4-3 has two aspects. First, for the value of lives lost (the health cost), the CEA used a widely cited model developed by the IHME. The model's most recent update reports the actual number of COVID-19 deaths in the United States for each day between

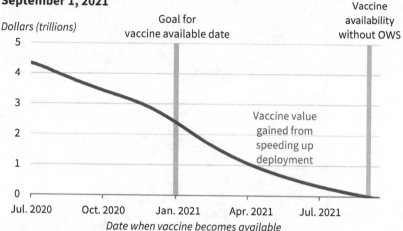

Figure 4-3. Value of Speeding Up a COVID-19 Vaccine Starting September 1, 2021

Sources: Institute for Health Metrics and Evaluation; Centers for Disease Control and Prevention; Congressional Budget Office; CEA calculations.
Note: OWS = Operation Warp Speed.

February 4 and October 19, 2020, and then projects the daily number of deaths for each day through February 1, 2021. The CEA lacks information on what will happen after February 1, and thus assumes, for this exercise (absent a vaccine), a 1 percent daily decline in deaths after February 1, 2021, recognizing that costs would be greater or less if the future path of pandemic mortality were more or less severe. The CEA then converted the number of deaths for each day to an economic cost by using the age-adjusted value of a statistical life, which is the standard way of evaluating economic costs of mortality (CEA 2019). The CEA assumes that as soon as the vaccine becomes available, it will immediately eliminate the health costs of COVID-19. However, because the vaccine will take time to deploy, only critical populations will get access to it first, and many will not take the vaccine at all, the CEA notes that this is a very optimistic scenario.

Second, to estimate the value of forgone gross domestic product (the economic cost), the CEA used the Congressional Budget Office's forecasts (CBO 2020) through 2022 to calculate the output losses between the current and pre-COVID baseline (January 2020) projections. These projections only take into account current law, meaning that the projections do not take any additional fiscal relief packages into account. Once a vaccine is available, for the sake of simplicity, the CEA optimistically assumes that the economy will return to pre-COVID conditions after 90 days, although it is likely that COVID-19 may have inflicted some permanent scarring on the economy.

Although the CEA makes these optimistic assumptions for simplicity, they do not significantly bias the estimate of the value of OWS. This is because they apply equally to both the case that a vaccine is developed by January

2021 and the counterfactual comparison without OWS that it is not developed until September. The CEA's analysis likely underestimates the true value of a COVID-19 vaccine because it does not include harder-to-measure factors such as loss of human capital and non-COVID negative health effects or the value of a vaccine to countries other than the United States.

Supporting the Healthcare System

Along with the Administration's efforts directly related to the COVID-19 pandemic, it is undertaking deregulatory initiatives to support the healthcare system more broadly. In addition, providing financial support to healthcare providers is critical to avoid exacerbating health risks for Americans.

Deregulation

Beyond working toward a vaccine, the Trump Administration has expanded short-term supply of healthcare services to meet the needs of the pandemic by enacting a variety of deregulatory actions across Federal agencies. Some of the larger changes, such as granting nurse practitioners more autonomy by loosening scope-of-practice regulations and removing restrictions on the provision of telemedicine, are dealt with more thoroughly later in this chapter because they represent significant opportunities for long-term improvements in the regulatory space. In addition to these major actions, regulators at various agencies within HHS took a number of less quantifiable but significant actions that increased the capacity of healthcare providers to meet the needs of their communities.

One of the primary public health concerns at the onset of the pandemic was the dearth of testing capabilities. To quickly expand diagnostic capacity, the FDA utilized EUA procedures and allowed for the production of tests earlier in their life cycle. To supplement these actions on the production side, the Trump Administration increased consumers' ability to access COVID-19 diagnostic testing by relaxing scope-of-practice regulations with regard to which healthcare providers were able to administer testing and by reducing or eliminating the out-of-pocket cost of testing through the CARES Act. The National Institutes of Health expanded on diagnostic efforts by investing in improvements in rapid testing technology.

As some localities began to be hit hard by COVID-19 outbreaks, one of the key public health risks was the limited supply of healthcare providers. To address this concern, CMS relaxed a plethora of occupational licensing restrictions to increase the number of providers. The supply of doctors and nurses was increased by allowing those with licenses that had expired or were still under review to practice. CMS also used deregulatory action to increase the supply of other healthcare workers by waiving certain licensing requirements for positions like nurse aides and paid feeding assistants. Such actions were particularly beneficial for hard-hit long-term-care facilities, whose patients are disproportionately at risk from COVID-19. CMS also encouraged out-of-State practitioners to assist in harder-hit areas by removing Federal restrictions on their ability to provide care to Medicare beneficiaries outside their State of licensure.

The Administration also helped to mitigate dangerous shortages of personal protective equipment (PPE). During the early months of the pandemic, a key risk to healthcare workers was the limited supply of PPE and stringent Federal regulations on how it must be used. To provide a temporary increase in the supply of PPE and protect healthcare providers working in settings that put them at high risk of contracting COVID-19, the FDA's EUA and the Families First Coronavirus Relief Act (FFCRA) allowed for highly protective facemasks initially designed for use in industrial settings to also be used in medical settings. Furthermore, CMS removed regulations that limited the ability of healthcare providers to store and reuse masks, which gave hospitals increased autonomy in determining what PPE policies they wanted to implement and substantially decreased demand for new masks in facilities that chose to capitalize on the deregulation.

In addition to using deregulation to increase the number of healthcare providers and the supply of PPE, the Trump Administration loosened regulations of hospital classifications and facilities. To reduce the spread of COVID-19 within hospitals, HHS allowed hospitals to screen potential patients offsite to prevent the spread of COVID-19. As hotspots arose in large cities, CMS allowed for the expansion of patient care areas to respond to sudden increases in demand for medical services. CMS also waived eligibility requirements for several classifications of rural hospitals to allow them to expand their capacity and serve their communities during the pandemic. Many of CMS's deregulatory actions for facilities benefited long-term-care facilities, including waiving resident group requirements for in-person meetings, statutory limitations on transfers and discharges, and requirements to honor resident roommate requests. All these actions were undertaken to decrease the risk of COVID-19 spreading among both the patient and provider populations.

Finally, CMS temporarily waived a number of paperwork and bureaucratic requirements during the pandemic to allow healthcare providers to make informed decisions about how to prioritize their time and best meet their patients' needs. These included regulations of the time frame for reporting requirements, the necessity of verbal orders, discharge planning, emergency preparedness plans, patient privacy, utilization reviews, and food plans.

Financial Support for Healthcare Providers

The COVID-19 pandemic represented a threat to the financial solvency of healthcare providers across the country, restricting their ability to ensure high-quality care for patients in their communities. In response, the Administration worked with Congress to pass the CARES Act, which established the Provider Relief Fund to help healthcare providers in the midst of the pandemic. The CARES Act, through HHS, made up to $100 billion available to eligible hospitals and other healthcare providers, which constituted about 4.5 percent of spending from the bill. The PPP/HCE Act provided an additional $75 billion for the Provider Relief Fund to reimburse healthcare providers for expenses related to healthcare and lost revenues that are attributable to COVID-19. In addition, the PPP/HCE Act provided $25 billion to help increase COVID-19 testing. This includes up to $1 billion to reimburse the cost of testing uninsured individuals, in addition to the $1 billion previously appropriated for this purpose by the FFCRA.

The FFCRA also, as amended by the CARES Act, requires Medicare Part B, State Medicaid, Children's Health Insurance Programs (CHIP), and group health plans and health insurance issuers to cover COVID-19 diagnostic testing without cost sharing for patients. Uninsured individuals may also obtain COVID-19 diagnostic testing free of charge under the State Medicaid programs, if the State offers this option. CMS has developed an accessible, easy-to-use toolkit for States to amend their Medicaid programs so they can offer this service. The CARES Act also appropriated $150 billion for the Coronavirus Relief Fund, which is administered by the Department of the Treasury, to reimburse expenses incurred by State, local, and Tribal governments as part of their response to the COVID-19 pandemic.

With funding allocated by the CARES Act and the PPP/HCE Act, HHS can allocate up to $175 billion of aid to eligible hospitals and other healthcare providers to offset these costs. Over $100 billion had been paid to hospitals and other providers by early October. This includes relief to hospitals that serve the most vulnerable segment of the population as well as rural hospitals and those in small metropolitan areas.

Canceling elective surgeries played a major role in declining revenue for many providers. Following the advice of both State-level policymakers and the surgeon general, in mid-March, elective surgeries were canceled or postponed as part of the effort to curb the spread of COVID-19 and prevent the potential straining of healthcare infrastructure and resources during the pandemic. Figure 4-4 shows the decline and subsequent recovery of five types of visits of Medicare patients relative to the comparable week in 2019, with total knee arthroplasties reaching as low as 3.2 percent of their baseline volume in mid-April. As restrictions were lifted throughout the summer, elective surgery volumes rebounded, with most at or near their baseline figures by early July. This likely represents a temporary surge in volume for those who rescheduled surgeries immediately after the end of restrictions but an overall lower demand for elective surgeries in the Medicare population.

However, due in part to the financial support that was provided to providers, healthcare has proven to be one of the most resilient labor markets

Figure 4-4. National Medicare Utilization, Jan. 10–Oct. 30, 2020

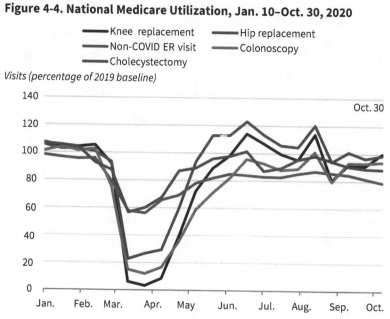

Sources: Department of Health and Human Services; CEA calculations.
Note: ER = emergency room.

during the pandemic. Figure 4-5 shows employment by sector for each month of 2020 as a percentage of the 2019 baseline using data from the Bureau of Labor Statistics (BLS). Healthcare employment fell to 92.2 percent of its 2019 level in April, the second-smallest decline of any sector. In contrast, average employment in all sectors in April was 86.6 percent and employment in leisure and hospitality was particularly volatile, falling to 51.8 percent. Healthcare has so far remained the second-most-resilient sector, after financial services, for the duration of the recovery and has steadily regained employment, rising to 97.2 percent of its 2019 level in October.

One major concern from the rapid job losses in March and April due to COVID-19 was the loss of health insurance for those obtaining benefits through employment. As of May 2, the Kaiser Family Foundation estimated that 47.5 million people who were covered by employer-sponsored insurance (ESI) were part of a family in which someone had lost a job (CBO 2020; Garfield et al. 2020). Of this group, about 26.8 million could potentially lose their health insurance, with the remaining 20.8 million retaining ESI though another worker in their family or another source of coverage. Given this consideration, all but 5.7 million would then be eligible for publicly subsidized coverage via Medicaid or marketplace subsidies, significantly reducing the share of job losses that result in a lack of health insurance.

Figure 4-5. Monthly Employment by Sector, 2020

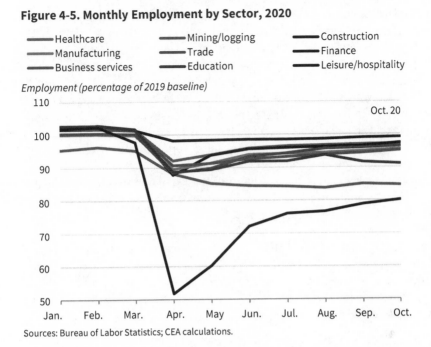

Sources: Bureau of Labor Statistics; CEA calculations.

However, these projections have not been borne out in the data thus far. Data from Americans in the Household Pulse Survey from the Census Bureau showed minimal changes in ESI coverage between the end of April and the end of September, as Americans reported being both insured and uninsured at slightly lower rates, with a substantial increase in those who did not report or reported "don't know." In fact, between the end of April and the end of August, Pulse results showed that uninsurance rates had actually declined by 0.6 percentage point. The disparity between the observed changes in ESI coverage and initial projections may in part be due to the PPP/HCE Act allowing forgivable loans to employers to cover payroll costs, including employer contributions to health insurance coverage. Ultimately, although microsimulation modeling can be used to approximate the decline in health insurance coverage due to COVID-19, survey data to quantify the effect remains inconclusive at this time.

Subsidizing Beneficial Behaviors and the Cost of COVID-19 Care

Testing is essential to identifying positive COVID-19 cases, quarantining and treating sick patients, and implementing contact tracing protocols. Test costs may be a barrier to some members of the public, which could thwart efforts to contain a pandemic. Passage of the FFCRA on March 18, 2020, reduced this potential cost barrier for American families. Nearly all public and private insurance plans are required by this legislation to cover FDA-approved COVID-19 tests and any costs associated with diagnostic testing with no cost sharing, as long as the test is deemed medically appropriate by an attending health care provider and the federally declared public health emergency is in effect. The CARES Act, which was enacted on March 27, 2020, further mandated that private plans reimburse out-of-network COVID-19 tests up to a publicly reported cash price. The FFCRA Relief Fund includes up to $2 billion ($1 billion appropriated through the FFCRA, and up to $1 billion appropriated through the PPP/HCE Act) to reimburse healthcare providers who conduct COVID-19 testing for uninsured individuals, which could raise the likelihood that these individuals seek testing when they feel ill and therefore contribute to the nation's public health objective of mitigating the COVID-19 pandemic. As of September 22, 2020, the CDC has awarded over $12 billion to States, Tribes, localities, and territories. This total includes $10.25 billion for critical support to enhance COVID-19 testing and related activities at the State and local levels. All these Federal protections have reduced the cost barriers of COVID-19 testing—which, in turn, has helped the United States identify positive COVID-19 cases and deliver care to individuals who have contracted COVID-19.

Emergency Paid Sick and Medical Leave

To slow the spread and contain the COVID-19 pandemic, the Administration has encouraged members of the public to stay home when they are sick or caring for a family member who is sick. At the same time, the Administration has firmly acted to prevent American workers from trading off work hours for their own or a family member's health and the broader public's health protection. As provided by the FFCRA, on April 1, 2020, the U.S. Department of Labor announced that private employers with fewer than 500 employees are eligible for tax credits for costs associated with providing paid leave for COVID-19 until December 31, 2020. These dollar-for-dollar reimbursements through tax credits enable employers to keep their workers on the payroll when their employees become sick or are caring for someone with COVID-19 and are unable to work, which promotes public health and maintains the flow of financial support to both employers and employees. For employers that could not cover the cost of paid leave with funds they would otherwise pay to the Internal Revenue Service in payroll taxes, the FFCRA enabled employers to seek an expedited advance from the Internal Revenue Service through streamlined reimbursement claims.

Subsidizing the Cost of COVID-19 Care

In addition to financing the detection of COVID-19 in order to implement containment and mitigation procedures, the Administration has also provided Federal support to reduce the cost of COVID-19 treatment. The Administration has responded in several ways to ensure that individuals seek the care that they need.

Many private Medicare health plans, known as Medicare Advantage plans, have expanded coverage to meet the unique needs of Medicare beneficiaries during a pandemic, including telehealth and medical transportation benefits. These types of support are especially important for lower-income individuals in the elderly population who would otherwise face cost or mobility constraints that would make obtaining medical care for COVID-19 difficult.

In addition, through the use of "1135 waivers," the Administration has created greater flexibility for Medicaid, Medicare, and CHIP requirements that can sometimes pose challenges for healthcare providers to provide medical care and for States to manage their Medicaid and CHIP programs during a national emergency such as the COVID-19 pandemic. The reduced administrative burden facilitated by these waivers has helped providers deliver medical care in these high-risk medical populations. When granted, the ultimate goal of these is to improve the ability of States and the healthcare sector to meet the needs of Medicare, Medicaid, and CHIP beneficiaries and expand access to medical services for these beneficiaries during the COVID-19 pandemic.

Finally, the Administration has taken actions to address the significant out-of-pocket medical cost burden faced by uninsured individuals when they become ill. Life during a pandemic is especially daunting for the uninsured because they do not have an insurance buffer in the event that they are exposed to COVID-19 and end up suffering from it. As noted above, a total of up to $2 billion in Federal funds appropriated by the FFCRA and the PPP/HCE Act reduce testing cost barriers among the uninsured population. However, the Administration has also acted to address treatment cost barriers for these Americans. HHS is providing claims reimbursement to healthcare providers that treat uninsured patients with COVID-19. As of November 9, $1.76 billion had been distributed to providers to reimburse the cost of testing and treating uninsured COVID-19 patients. Of this amount, representing almost 25,000 claims, $677 million was for testing and $1.1 billion was for treatment. The CARES Act established and appropriated a total of $100 billion to the Provider Relief Fund, and the PPP/HCE Act appropriated an additional $75 billion in relief funds. A portion of the Provider Relief Fund was used to reimburse providers that are treating uninsured individuals with COVID-19. In April 2020, the Administration began requiring providers to certify that, as a condition for supplemental COVID-19 funding, they would not seek to collect out-of-pocket expenses from a patient in an amount greater than what the patient would have otherwise been required to pay for in-network care.

COVID-19 and Future Healthcare Reform

Several other key initiatives are related to COVID-19 and the future of healthcare reform. These include reform of the FDA drug approval process, the expansion of telemedicine, and the deregulation of scope-of-practice requirements for nurse practitioners.

FDA Reform

The pandemic has also shown the value of speed in the development of new medical breakthroughs and the key role that deregulation can play in such efforts. At the onset of COVID-19, one of the reasons that testing was limited was extensive Federal regulations, including the long FDA approval process. To combat this, the Trump Administration took action through the FDA to issue EUAs for COVID-19 diagnostic tests. Such decisive actions played a key role in quickly ramping up testing capacity after initial delays, and they demonstrate the value of expedited the approval of medical breakthroughs. Currently, the United States has some of the most stringent regulations of new drugs in the world, with some approvals taking roughly 12 years from FDA application to market entry. As with COVID-19 testing and treatment, other new drugs have the potential to save lives and substantially improve well-being, which creates high opportunity costs for a long approval process. The CEA estimates that the net present value of the social surplus gained by decreasing FDA drug approval times by one, two, or three years would be $1.9 trillion, $3.9 trillion, and $5.9 trillion, respectively. Experience with the Prescription Drug User Fee Act (PDUFA) in the 1990s suggests that changes in policy can reduce approval times on this scale.

To estimate the value of shorter approval times, the CEA first estimates the annual social surplus generated by a drug for each year it is under patent protection. Because the FDA's approval time does not directly affect the patent expiration date of the average drug, the utility gained after postpatent expiration is assumed to be unchanged. Furthermore, the CEA's estimates of the value produced by such a policy change likely understates the true value because the number of new drugs introduced is treated as exogenous. In reality, shorter approval times increase the profitability of new entrants and would lead to further advances in medical technology, providing additional value for both consumers and pharmaceutical companies. (All dollar amounts are 2019 dollars.)

Figure 4-6 shows an average drug's life cycle, broken down into costs, producer surplus, and consumer surplus. The model updates the average drug revenue profile described by Philipson and others (2008)—using data from the FDA, BLS, and the Saint Louis Federal Reserve on the change in the number and prices of new drug approvals. Using this updated drug revenue profile, the CEA applies further calculations (described below) to estimate the producer and consumer surplus generated by the average drug. Of course, in reality most drugs will have very different revenue profiles, but the constructed average drug in the model uses data on average total revenue over the course

Figure 4-6. Average Drug Life Cycle during the Patent Period

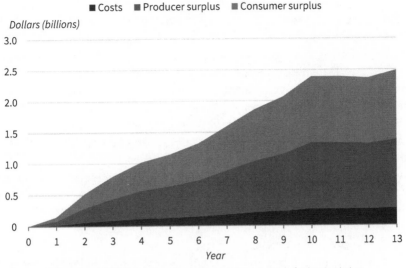

■ Costs ■ Producer surplus ■ Consumer surplus

Dollars (billions)

Year

Sources: Philipson et al. (2008); Food and Drug Administration; Bureau of Labor Statistics; Saint Louis Federal Reserve Bank; CEA calculations.

of the patent period and average share of revenue in each year to construct a representative example.

Although overall revenue profiles can be easily estimated using publicly available data on consumer expenditures, it is more difficult to calculate precise measures of producer and consumer surpluses, in large part due to the wide variation of producers and products in the pharmaceutical industry. The CEA estimates that the producer surplus in each year of the patent period is 80 percent of revenues, based on the finding that marginal costs are roughly 20 percent of revenue (Berndt, Cockburn, and Griliches 1996; Caves, Whinston, and Hurwitz 1991; Grabowski and Vernon 1992; Philipson et al. 2012). Of course, pharmaceutical companies also face high fixed costs early on in the life cycle of a drug in the form of research-and-development costs for both successful and unsuccessful products, approval application fees, and marketing expenditures (Kennedy 2018). A reduction in approval time may result in lower costs associated with the approval process if the preapproval time frame has nonnegligible marginal costs over time. However, to ensure that the result represents a true lower bound, the CEA does not include any reduction of fixed costs in the total benefit estimate.

To arrive at an estimate of total social surplus, the CEA conservatively assumes that consumer surplus is equal to producer surplus. It is well documented that consumers enjoy greater benefits from the development of new drugs than the profits made by their producers (CBO 2006; Lichtenberg 2014; Philipson and Jena 2006; Philipson et al. 2012; Roebuck et al. 2011). In fact, the literature suggests that consumers capture the vast majority of the social surplus generated by new drugs, meaning that the CEA may substantially underestimate the total value to consumers of reducing drug approval times. Under these assumptions, the CEA finds that once an average drug has reached maturity in the market, it will generate about $2.1 billion in social surplus annually.

Figure 4-7 demonstrates how decreasing drug approval time by one, two, or three years would affect this annual social surplus. The figure also accounts for the time value of money by using an annual discount rate of 3 percent. That is, $1 in year one is worth 97 cents in year zero. Using a discount factor accounts for the fact that both the consumers and producers of a product would rather have it sooner rather than later. By allowing earlier entry into the market, drugs reach maturity in the market and provide maximum social surplus earlier than in the status quo. The maximum social surplus is reached earlier and attains a higher value due to the discounting of future periods, which represents the increased value for both consumers and producers.

Some critics of FDA reform suggest that decreased approval times would result in more unsafe products being brought to market and therefore an increase in approval withdrawals. However, approval times decreased by over one year under PDUFA, and Phillipson and others (2008) found no evidence of an increase in withdrawals after the reduction in approval times, but did not account for potential adverse effects on safety that do not result in withdrawal. Qureshi and others (2011) found that safety-related withdrawals accounted for less than a quarter of all withdrawals between 1980 and 2009. The CEA's analysis using an expanded data set of safety-related withdrawals also did not find an increase in withdrawals after the decreased approval times of PDUFA. Given the absence of data on the distribution of withdrawals by drug revenue, the CEA applies the overall drug withdrawal rate of 15.9 percent as a reduction to the potential increase in social surplus. This likely overstates the extent to which withdrawals would decrease potential benefit due to the skewed distribution of revenue by different drugs. Although the FDA's approval is withdrawn for a small share of drugs for safety reasons, almost 80 percent are voluntarily withdrawn by their producers for commercial reasons. In reality, the more successful drugs that generate larger surpluses for both producers and consumers are less likely to be withdrawn, resulting in a conservative estimate of the overall benefit.

Using the estimate of the net present value of a drug's life cycle shown in figure 4-7, the CEA calculates the marginal cumulative net present value of social surplus generated by reducing FDA approval times, as shown in figure 4-8. The model uses the five-year average from 2015 to 2019 of 44 new drugs per year by the FDA. As noted above, by increasing the returns on investment in research, reducing FDA approval times would likely increase the number of new applicants, and hence approvals. Therefore, the static model that holds new drugs constant at 44 a year results in a conservative estimate of the value

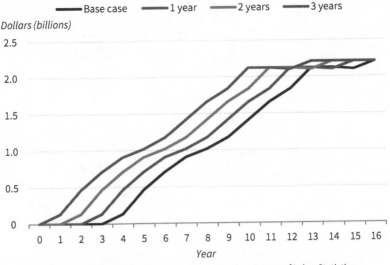

Figure 4-7. Average Annual Social Surplus by Approval Time Decrease

Sources: Philipson et al. (2008); Food and Drug Administration; Bureau of Labor Statistics; Saint Louis Federal Reserve Bank; CEA calculations.

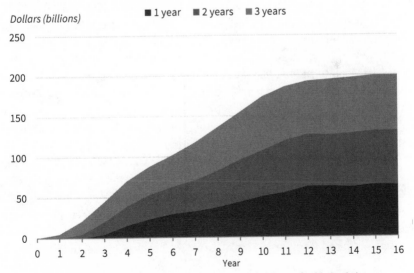

Figure 4-8. Cumulative Aggregate Net Present Value of Increased Social Welfare by Approval Time Decrease

Sources: Phillipson et al. (2008); Food and Drug Administration; Bureau of Labor Statistics; Saint Louis Federal Reserve; CEA calculations.

Table 4-1. Estimated Social Surplus by FDA Approval Time Reduction, 2025–40 (billions of real 2019 dollars)

Year	Approval Time Reduction		
	1 Year	2 Years	3 Years
Net present value	1,905.8	3,870.5	5,896.0
2025	0.0	0.0	4.9
2026	0.0	4.9	22.1
2027	4.9	22.1	48.3
2028	17.2	43.4	76.9
2029	26.2	59.7	97.3
2030	33.5	71.2	114.5
2031	37.6	81.0	133.3
2032	43.4	95.7	157.0
2033	52.3	113.7	181.6
2034	61.3	129.2	207.8
2035	67.9	146.4	224.9
2036	78.5	157.0	234.8
2037	78.5	156.2	238.0
2038	77.7	159.5	241.3
2039	81.8	163.6	245.4
2040	81.8	163.6	245.4

Sources: Philipson, et al. (2008); Food and Drug Administration; Bureau of Labor Statistics; Saint Louis Federal Reserve Bank; CEA calculations.

of deregulation, especially considering the fact that new approvals have been trending upward since 2005. The results, given in figure 4-8, represent the increase in social surplus for one year of drug approvals depending on whether the approval time for the drugs is reduced by one, two, or three years.

To calculate aggregate gain in social surplus, it is necessary to sum the gains in social surplus associated with quicker drug approvals over time. Because policies to reduce approval time may be difficult to implement immediately, the CEA assumes that the reductions in approval time would begin applying to drugs that would otherwise be approved in 2028. Under these assumptions, table 4-1 displays the nondiscounted gain in social surplus from a one-, two-, or three-year reduction in approval times for each year from 2025 to 2040, as well as the net present value in 2020 of such a policy change. The CEA estimates that the net present value of the increase in social surplus from a permanent reduction in approval times by one, two, or three years for new drugs would be $1.9 trillion, $3.9 trillion, or $5.9 trillion, respectively.

Telemedicine Deregulation

One of the most substantial deregulatory opportunities for long-term healthcare improvement that has been highlighted during the pandemic is telemedicine.

Early during the pandemic, HHS took four key deregulatory actions to increase the availability of telemedicine opportunities. First, the Office for Civil Rights (OCR) announced that it would relax enforcement of HIPAA regulations to allow health professionals to communicate with patients and provide telehealth services via remote communication technologies that may not fully comply with HIPAA privacy rules. Though the laws remain unchanged, OCR used its enforcement discretion to allow any covered health professionals to use a wide array of commercially available communication technology (e.g., Zoom or Skype) as part of a good faith effort to provide telehealth services during the pandemic, regardless of whether the services are directly related to the diagnosis or treatment of COVID-19.

Second, President Trump's emergency declaration allows HHS to relax Federal licensing restrictions so many health professionals can provide care virtually to patients in other States. This has created a large pool of potential health professionals available to any given patient who is seeking telehealth services, increasing access to medical services in the States with the greatest need. Finally, CMS took two significant deregulatory actions to promote telehealth by temporarily expanding the scope of Medicare telehealth to allow Medicare beneficiaries across the country—not just in rural areas—to receive telehealth services from any location, including their homes, as well as adding over 135 allowable services, more than doubling the number of services that beneficiaries could receive via telehealth (Verma 2020). The CMS temporarily waived statutory and regulatory provisions that restrict reimbursement for telemedicine services to those furnished in certain healthcare facilities, allowing healthcare professionals to be paid for providing telehealth services regardless of location. CMS also allowed for a broader range of services to be provided via video or audio call, including emergency department visits, therapy services, and initial nursing facility and discharge visits. These measures are designed to promote the use of telemedicine and ensure that patients have access to healthcare while remaining safely at home.

During the beginning stages of the pandemic, quick deregulatory action mitigated disruptions in care for patients in hotspot areas and those in the greatest need. Mann and others (2020) found that telemedicine visits increased almost sevenfold during the period of maximal COVID-19 active cases in New York City. Many of these online visits were directly related to COVID-19, which advanced three key public health goals. First, telemedicine allows for comparatively inexpensive and efficient screening for patients before they arrive in the emergency room. This lowers costs and prevents unnecessary healthcare visits, which decrease the strain on already-overburdened healthcare providers and the potential transmission of COVID-19 to other patients and healthcare workers. Second, expanding access to telemedicine provides useful data to public health officials who are trying to track the spread of the disease and predict future hotspots, an approach that has been shown in the past to provide a useful picture of the spread of influenza (Chauhan et al. 2020). Third, provision of telehealth services that is not directly related to COVID-19 is particularly necessary for patients who are actively quarantining and require healthcare, because in-person visits with such patients increase the risk of exposure for healthcare workers and their patients.

Telemedicine visits have also been useful in maintaining access to essential care services when physical access to medical services has been limited. For seniors who are at a heightened risk of serious illness from COVID-19, telemedicine has offered an appealing substitute due to the deregulatory actions of CMS. Telehealth visits constituted 43.5 percent of Medicare primary care visits in April, compared with just 0.1 percent of such visits before the pandemic in February. Urban areas that have had higher levels of COVID-19 hospitalizations have utilized telehealth services at a higher rate, suggesting that this uptake has been at least partly driven by concerns over COVID-19. With uncertainty and unemployment rising during the pandemic, telehealth services have also provided a safe and efficient method to meet rising demand for mental health services among patients of all ages. During the February-to-April period, increases in Medicare telehealth utilization for primary care visits were dramatic in every State; for example, visits went from 0.20 percent to 43.9 percent in Texas and from 0.03 percent to 69.7 percent in Massachusetts.

According to survey data from McKinsey & Company, 11 percent of U.S. consumers used telehealth services in 2019 (Bestsennyy et al. 2020). As of April 2020, 46 percent of U.S. consumers reported that they had already used telehealth to replace canceled in-person healthcare visits in 2020. Though telehealth has helped expand access to care at a time when COVID-19 has restricted patients' ability to see their doctors, there has been strong interest in making telehealth services a permanent option; 76 percent of U.S. consumers report being interested in using telehealth in the future. The enthusiasm for telehealth on the demand side is matched by favorable reviews of telehealth on the supply side; 57 percent of providers view telehealth more favorably than they did before COVID-19, and 64 percent are more comfortable using it. The positive reaction to exercising telehealth options is likely to increase over time as awareness and experience with virtual healthcare services grow and existing challenges (e.g., lower mobile and computer capabilities in lower-income communities and security concerns) are resolved.

The immediate and pressing nature of the COVID-19 pandemic has demanded that the healthcare system embrace telemedicine on a greatly accelerated timeline. Though the availability of telehealth services has been increasing consistently over time, the additional infrastructure built and deregulatory actions taken provide an opportunity to more strongly embrace telehealth as a key part of the future of healthcare. In 2019, the American Hospital Association identified Medicare reimbursement differentials and regulatory barriers as two key barriers to wider adoption of telemedicine in the United States. Many of these regulatory burdens have been temporarily removed, and healthcare systems have already implemented telemedicine programs in response to the pandemic, so they can use them beyond COVID-19 without incurring additional setup costs if HHS's deregulatory actions become permanent. Although the benefits to individuals in quarantine and those at a high risk of contracting COVID-19 will decrease once the threat of the pandemic has passed, other benefits will remain. Studies of telemedicine programs have found that they increase patient satisfaction, decrease the loss of work time (which decreases the opportunity costs for patients to seek care they need), and decrease the unnecessary use of the emergency department due to prescreening arrivals, which lowers costs and improves the quality of care for patients who need it most.

In addition, though the greatest beneficiaries of increased availability of telemedicine during the pandemic have been patients in urban areas, the long-term benefits of normalizing telemedicine will be highest among rural Americans who do not reside near major medical centers. The Department of Veterans Affairs found that 45 percent of its telemedicine utilization came from rural veterans. Telemedicine would allow greater access to specialists with knowledge in a particular area of medicine, even when doctors are not at the same hospital or region of the country. Furthermore, rural populations are particularly subject to high opportunity costs for medical care, including lost wages, transportation costs, and childcare expenses. On the basis of a study of this phenomenon by Bynum and others (2003), the CEA estimates that rural Americans would on average save $130 per visit in opportunity costs such as fuel, wages, and other family expenses if their visits could be replaced by telemedicine. Rural patients who would otherwise make the national average 2.8 physician's office visits a year would therefore save up to $362 annually. Though rural patients may empirically make fewer physician visits per year (Spoont et al. 2011), the increased access provided by telemedicine may reduce the geographic disparity between rural and urban Americans.

Given both consumers' and providers' interest in continued access to telemedicine, it is a potentially significant source of future economic value. McKinsey & Company estimates that before the COVID-19, the total annual revenue of U.S. telehealth players was about $3 billion, with the largest vendors being focused on virtual urgent care (Bestsennyy et al. 2020). They estimate that going beyond this segment of virtual healthcare may allow up to $250 billion, or $1 in $5 current healthcare dollars, to be virtualized.

Scope-of-Practice Deregulation

During the COVID pandemic, relaxing stringent scope-of-practice (SOP) requirements allowed hospitals and other health providers to increase the amount of care that they could provide for their communities. Before the outbreak of COVID-19, 22 States and 2 territories allowed full practice for nurse practitioners (NPs), meaning that NPs in those States and territories are authorized by their boards of nursing to evaluate and diagnose patients, order and interpret diagnostic tests, and manage treatments (including prescribing medication) without a physician. Increased demand from virus patients combined with decreased supply due to practitioners being out sick threatened to overwhelm hospital systems across the country. In contrast, States with more restrictive SOP guidelines place restrictions on NPs in one or more of these areas, generally in the form of prohibitions or physician supervision requirements. In response, State governments and Federal agencies relaxed SOP guidelines that prevented nurse practitioners from performing certain routine tasks without the supervision of a licensed physician. By April 24, 2020, another 22 States had temporarily relaxed their SOP requirements. In addition, CMS temporarily relaxed its SOP guidelines in March 2020. Medicare and Medicaid reimbursement payments are critical for the survival of many hospitals, and State regulations are always binding. Because of this, hospitals tend to operate under the more rigid regulations when their State and CMS regulations are in conflict. This has enabled providers in areas that have been hit hardest by COVID-19 to respond with increased labor flexibility in meeting the needs of their communities.

Existing SOP restrictions on NPs display a strong geographic correlation (figure 4-9). This is likely due to the greater benefits associated with broadening SOP in rural areas relative to urban communities, given that full practice was primarily allowed in New England, the northern Great Plains, the Mountain West, and the Pacific Northwest. Rural areas rely more heavily on NPs and grant them greater autonomy than urban areas because they tend to have fewer physicians to oversee the NPs (Rosenblatt and Hart 2000). This shortage of physicians can prevent the opening of community health centers (CHCs). The opening of new CHCs in rural areas was associated with relaxed SOP requirements. Furthermore, CHCs in States with relaxed SOP guidelines have more NPs relative to physicians than CHCs in States with rigid SOP guidelines (Shi and Samuels 1997). More CHCs mean better access to care in rural areas. And because relaxing SOP allows more CHCs to open and more CHCs mean better access to care, deregulating SOP would improve the ability for rural populations to access healthcare.

In addition to expanding access, relaxing SOP regulations drives down healthcare costs. Such restrictions increase the cost of healthcare, because NPs are unable to perform certain tasks without the supervision of a physician and physicians' time is expensive. Rigid regulations requiring physicians to perform some tasks increased the cost of well-child medical exams by 3-16 percent (Kleiner et al. 2016) Another analysis found that costs were lower in States with reduced and full SOP than in States with restrictive SOP (Spetz et al. 2013).

To estimate the economic benefit of relaxing SOP guidelines for NPs nationwide, the CEA uses interstate cost comparisons from Poghosyan and

Figure 4-9. State Scope-of-Practice Deregulation

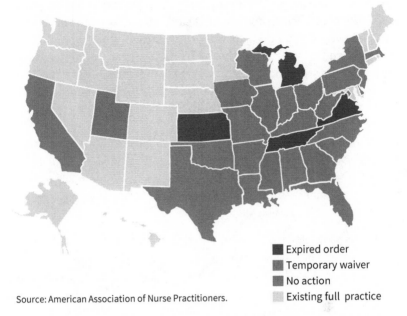

Source: American Association of Nurse Practitioners.

■ Expired order
■ Temporary waiver
■ No action
▨ Existing full practice

others (2019), who estimate the difference in outpatient and prescription drug costs for Medicaid patients between States that allow for full, reduced, and restricted practice for NPs. Using these figures, along with data from BLS and the Kaiser Family Foundation, the CEA estimates that allowing full practice nationwide would reduce outpatient costs by $33.96 billion a year and prescription drug costs by $27.73 billion a year across patients enrolled in employer health plans, nongroup plans, or Medicaid. This would lead to a reduction in national prescription drug spending of 5.3 percent and, combined, represent a reduction in national healthcare expenditures of 1.7 percent. Due to the limited supply of NPs, this number represents the potential long-run benefit once the labor market for NPs has expanded to match the increased demand. However, the supply of NPs has been flexible, more than doubling the past 15 years as States have removed SOP restrictions.

The CEA's estimate likely understates the total benefit in two ways. First, Medicaid spending per capita is lower than the privately insured population, so the savings for the general population in dollar terms may be larger than for Medicaid enrollees. Second, the CEA's analysis only accounts for individuals who are members of employer health plans, nongroup plans, or Medicaid. It is likely that relaxing SOP for NPs would also reduce costs for other groups, including those insured by military plans or Medicare, as well as the uninsured population.

The impact of relaxing SOP on health outcomes could go one of three ways. If relaxing SOP restrictions causes NPs to provide lower-quality care in the absence of physician supervision, then relaxing SOP would have a negative effect on health outcomes. If, instead, NPs performed just as well as doctors, then there would be no effect on health outcomes. In addition, if NPs could now perform more critical health actions, which previously could not have been performed due to a shortage of physicians to provide supervision, then one would expect health outcomes to improve when SOP restrictions are relaxed.

Empirical evidence suggests that allowing nurse practitioners full practice nationwide would not compromise the quality of patient care. State-level SOP restrictions had no effect on infant mortality or malpractice insurance premiums (Kleiner et al. 2016). Taking a broader approach, another study found that

> the considerable variation in the results for the measures included in each of the domains of primary care quality indicators we assessed—chronic disease management, cancer screening, ambulatory care–sensitive hospital admissions, and adverse outcomes—did not reveal a consistent pattern or relationship with state-level SOP. (Perloff et al. 2017)

In rural areas, the results of one analysis suggested a positive relationship between health outcomes and relaxed SOP guidelines (Ortiz et al. 2018). A wealth of literature analyzing the difference in patient outcomes between NPs and physicians has consistently found that, for most patients, NPs provide equivalent or better care at a lower cost (Lenz et al. 2004; Martin-Misener et al. 2015; Mundinger et al. 2000; Oliver et al. 2014; Stanik-Hutt et al. 2013). The States and Federal agencies that have temporarily relaxed their SOP guidelines during the COVID-19 pandemic could seize this opportunity to improve the access and affordability of healthcare for their citizens.

Additional Changes to Promote Choice and Competition

Beyond the response to the COVID-19 health crisis, the Trump Administration has championed several healthcare reforms to promote additional choice and competition in the market. These policies will provide tangible reform to Americans and play a critical part in the swift comeback for the U.S. economy.

First, CMS introduced site-neutral payment in 2019 for clinic services delivered by hospitals. Site-neutral payments were part of the 2019 Hospital Outpatient Prospective Payment System final rule and address unnecessary increases in utilization of clinic visits in off-campus, hospital-based departments. Medicare and beneficiaries often pay more for the same type of clinic visit in the hospital outpatient setting than in the physician office setting. The rule was challenged by a coalition of hospitals led by the American Hospital

Association in Federal court. In September 2019, the U.S. District Court for the District of Columbia ruled that CMS had overstepped its statutory authority in making the changes. However, a July 2020 decision issued by the U.S. Court of Appeals for the District of Columbia Circuit overturned the lower court's ruling, clearing the path for implementation. Site-neutral payments are estimated to generate healthcare savings that have a direct and positive impact on beneficiaries, the Medicare program, employers, and American taxpayers. An evaluation by CMS that has been extrapolated by the CEA shows that site-neutral payments for evaluation and management services are projected to save the Medicare program an estimated $330 million and lower patient copayments by $88 million in 2021.

Second, prescription drugs saw their largest annual price decrease in nearly half a century in 2019. For three consecutive years, the FDA has approved a record number of generic drugs. The CEA estimates that these approvals saved patients $26 billion in 2017 and 2018. The 2020 Creating and Restoring Equal Access to Equivalent Samples Act will also create opportunities for greater savings from generic drugs by increasing access to samples for testing. The CEA estimates that the projected savings to American taxpayers will be $3.5 billion from 2020 to 2030.

Also, in July 2019, the Trump Administration issued an Executive Order aimed at improving the care of patients with chronic kidney disease. In 2020, the Department of Health and Human Services published multiple rules that attempted to streamline the renal care system by removing regulatory barriers, increasing oversight of Organ Procurement Organizations, and encouraging living kidney donors. HHS estimates that its changes to the system of these organizations alone could generate up to 4,500 additional kidney transplants by 2026. The CEA estimates that these initiatives could have substantial health and economic benefits. Because each kidney transplant reduces lifetime medical spending by an estimated $136,000 and creates health benefits, such as increased longevity, that are worth an estimated $1.8 million, the net present value of these kidney transplants would be roughly $8.8 billion a year. Moreover, efforts to promote peritoneal dialysis could result in savings of $130 million to $450 million annually. When combined with the value of health gains and savings from kidney transplants, the CEA finds that the Administration's initiatives could provide societal benefits with a net present value of nearly $9.3 billion.

Conclusion

Although COVID-19 has imposed significant health and economic costs throughout 2020, the Trump Administration has been able to take decisive actions to mitigate its effects. Expediting the development of testing and treatment capabilities has played a key role in curbing the human cost of the virus, while the removal of burdensome regulation and provision of financial support have helped the healthcare sector adjust to the adverse shock. The Nation's experience with COVID-19 provides opportunities for extending the suspension of harmful regulations, which will further encourage economic recovery and provide long-term health and financial benefits. In particular, the CEA finds that reforming the FDA drug approval process to reduce approval times, encouraging the widespread continuation of telemedicine, and removing harmful scope-of-practice regulations would generate significant savings and improve the health of Americans in the future.

Part II

The Renaissance of American Greatness

Chapter 5

Assessing the Early Impact of Opportunity Zones

The Tax Cuts and Jobs Act of 2017 not only cut taxes for businesses and individuals broadly but also made targeted cuts to spur investment in economically distressed communities designated as Opportunity Zones (OZs). In this chapter, the Council of Economic Advisers (CEA) compares the advantages of OZs with those of other Federal antipoverty programs and documents the characteristics of the nearly 8,800 low-income communities designated as OZs. It also quantifies the effect of OZs investment and finds that a large increase is already benefiting OZ residents while potentially having only a small effect on the Federal budget.

OZs chart a new course in Federal policy aimed at uplifting distressed communities. Antipoverty transfer programs subsidize the consumption of goods such as housing and healthcare but can lead to reduced economic activity by raising taxes and discouraging eligible, working-age participants from seeking jobs. Also, under other existing place-based development programs, the Federal government selects who receives grants or tax credits and narrowly prescribes their use. By comparison, OZs cut taxes to increase economic activity by spurring private sector investment, job creation, and self-sufficiency. They also give greater scope for market forces to guide entrepreneurs and investors because they have no cap on participation and require no government approval.

The CEA finds that OZs, which are census tracts nominated by State governors and certified by the U.S. Department of the Treasury to be eligible for the investment tax cuts, are among the poorest communities in the United States. These communities have an average poverty rate more than double that of all other communities and are home to a higher share of African Americans, Hispanics, and high school dropouts. Even among all the communities eligible to be an OZ under Federal law, every State selected communities that, on average, had a median household income less than that of communities that were not selected.

The CEA also finds that the OZ tax cuts have spurred a large investment response. This chapter estimates that Qualified Opportunity Funds raised $75 billion in private capital by the end of 2019, most of which would not have entered OZs without the incentive. This new capital represents 21 percent of total annual investment in OZs and helps explain why the CEA also finds that private equity investment in OZ businesses grew 29 percent relative to the comparison group of businesses in eligible communities that were not selected as OZs.

The growth in investment has already made OZs more attractive to their residents, as reflected in what buyers are willing to pay for homes located in OZs. The CEA estimates that Opportunity Zone designation alone has caused a 1.1 percent increase in housing values. Greater amenities and economic opportunity behind the housing value increase will be broadly enjoyed, and for the nearly half of OZ residents who own their homes, the increase provides an estimated $11 billion in new wealth.

With regard to effects on the Federal budget, the CEA finds that each $1 raised by Qualified Opportunity Funds through 2019 has a direct forgone Federal revenue effect of 15 cents. By comparison, each $1 in investment spurred by the New Markets Tax Credit, an existing Federal program with similar goals, results in 18 cents of forgone revenue. Including indirect effects, the CEA estimates that the OZ incentive could be revenue neutral, with economic growth in low-income communities reducing transfer payments and offsetting forgone revenues from taxes on capital gains. Thus, the CEA projects that the capital already raised by Qualified Opportunity Funds could lift 1 million people out of poverty and into self-sufficiency, decreasing poverty in OZs by 11 percent.

The COVID-19 pandemic slowed investment everywhere in the second quarter of 2020, including in Opportunity Zones, but the initial evidence suggests that the OZ model has power to mobilize investors; engage State, local, and tribal stakeholders; and improve the outlook for low-income communities—all with limited prescription from the Federal Government. This chapter's findings highlight the potential for the Opportunity Zone model to help spur the post-COVID-19 recovery in thousands of distressed communities across the United States.

One of the main provisions of the Tax Cuts and Jobs Act, which was signed in December 2017, reduced U.S. corporate income tax rates to bring them in line with international levels. Lowering the corporate tax rate decreases the cost of capital, thereby stimulating investment and growth in gross domestic product and wages (CEA 2017). The Opportunity Zones (OZs) provision of the act mirrored this effort to lower capital taxes but with a focus on distressed communities. By reducing taxes on the capital gains invested in such communities, the provision lowers the cost of capital for businesses, which is expected to lead to new investment, jobs, and economic opportunity that has been lacking for decades. This CEA chapter compares the advantages of OZs relative to other Federal antipoverty programs, and it documents the characteristics of the nearly 8,800 low-income communities designated as OZs. The CEA also quantifies the effect of OZs on investment, finding a large increase that is already benefiting residents while potentially having only a small effect on the Federal budget.

To stimulate investment in OZs, the provision provides three potential tax benefits to investors that invest capital gains in Qualified Opportunity Funds, which are vehicles for investing in qualified OZ properties. The first benefit of investing in these funds is that the investor can defer paying taxes on capital gains rolled into OZs until potentially as late as 2026. Second, when these taxes are paid, the investor may omit 10 percent (15 percent) of the original gain if the investment is held there for at least five (seven) years.[1] Finally, and most important, any capital gains that accrue to investments in a Qualified Opportunity Fund are tax free if the investment is held for at least 10 years.

Funds can make equity investments in partnerships or corporations that operate in OZs as determined by various tests, such as where they generate

---

[1] Because an investor must pay capital gains taxes on the original gain by 2026, the original option to pay taxes on only 85 percent of the original has expired and would not apply to investments made in 2020. This is because the investments could not be held for the original seven years before having to pay the tax.

income or where their assets lie. A Qualified Opportunity Fund can also directly purchase tangible property for use in the fund's trade or business, but the property must have its original use begin with the fund or the fund must substantially improve the property. For example, a Qualified Opportunity Fund could purchase and install new solar panels in an OZ, or it could buy an apartment building and substantially improve it.

Although the Federal tax incentive described here is at the core of OZs, all levels of government have worked to complement this incentive. At the Federal level, on December 12, 2018, President Trump signed Executive Order 13853, which established the White House Opportunity and Revitalization Council.[2] The order gave the council the mission of leading efforts across executive departments and agencies "to engage with State, local, and tribal governments to find ways to better use public funds to revitalize urban and economically distressed communities." In its one-year report to the President, the council made 223 recommendations to this end and, as of August 2020 has taken more than 270 related actions.

Complementary efforts have also occurred at the State and local levels. For example, the Alabama Incentives Modernization Act provides additional State tax breaks for Qualified Opportunity Funds, and the State of New Jersey has created an OZ website and data tool with resources for local governments, investors, and businesses. The city of Erie, Pennsylvania, along with local businesses and nonprofit leaders, has created the Flagship Opportunity Zone Development Company to encourage investment in the city's OZs. And the city of Cleveland has taken a similar approach by creating the Opportunity CLE initiative to promote local OZ investments.

The CEA finds that OZs, which are census tracts selected by governors to be eligible for the investment tax cuts, are among the poorest communities in the United States. These communities have an average poverty rate that is more than double that of other communities and are home to a higher share of African Americans, Hispanics, and high school dropouts. Even among all the communities that were eligible to be an OZ under Federal law, every State selected communities that, on average, had a lower median household income than did eligible communities that were not selected.

The CEA also finds that the OZ tax cuts have spurred a large investment response. The chapter estimates that Qualified Opportunity Funds raised $75 billion in private capital by the end of 2019, most of which would not have entered OZs without this incentive. This new capital represents 21 percent of total annual investment in OZs and helps explain why the CEA also finds that private equity investment in OZ businesses grew 29 percent relative to eligible communities that were not selected as OZs and thus act as a control group.

---

[2] The council's various efforts are highlighted on the interagency website OpportunityZones.gov.

This growth in investment has already made OZs more attractive to their residents as reflected in the prices buyers are willing to pay for homes located in OZs. The CEA estimates that OZ designation alone has caused a 1.1 percent increase in housing values. The greater amenities and economic opportunity behind this housing value increase will be broadly enjoyed, and for the nearly half of OZ residents who own their homes, the increase provides an estimated $11 billion in new wealth.

With regard to effects on the Federal budget, the CEA finds that each $1 raised by Qualified Opportunity Funds through 2019 has had a direct forgone Federal revenue effect of 15 cents. By comparison, each $1 in investment spurred by the New Markets Tax Credit, an existing Federal program with similar goals, results in 18 cents in forgone revenue. Including indirect effects, the CEA estimates that the Opportunity Zone incentive could be revenue neutral, with economic growth in low-income communities reducing transfer payments and offsetting forgone revenues from taxes on capital gains. Also, the CEA projects that the capital already raised by Qualified Opportunity Funds could lift 1 million people out of poverty into self-sufficiency, decreasing poverty in OZs by 11 percent. These findings are complemented by recent research by Arefeva and others (2020) showing that in metropolitan areas, the OZ designation boosted employment growth relative to comparable tracts by between 3.0 and 4.5 percentage points, creating new jobs across a wide range of industries and education levels.

Comparing Opportunity Zones with Other Antipoverty or Place-Based Programs

Unlike antipoverty transfer programs—which raise taxes and reduce the incentive for program recipients to participate in productive economic activity—OZs lower taxes to stimulate economic activity in distressed areas. Relative to other place-based policies, the OZ incentives are more open-ended and less top-down in their design, which makes OZs more effective at attracting investment to communities most in need.

Antipoverty Transfer Policies

Antipoverty transfer programs provide cash grants or subsidies for the consumption of goods. Notable examples are housing vouchers, food stamps, cash assistance for needy families, and Medicaid. Although these programs support many Americans in need, they can also weaken the incentive for working-age adults to find employment. Because of eligibility requirements linked to income, taking a job or working more hours can cause a participant to become ineligible if his or her income exceeds a program's threshold. Considerable evidence confirms that such programs typically discourage employment (e.g., Hoynes and Schanzenbach 2012; Jacob and Ludwig 2012; Bloom and Michalopoulos 2001).

Antipoverty transfer programs also raise taxes to fund these transfers. Even if the transfers and associated eligibility requirements did not discourage work, they would still come at a cost. Each $1 raised through taxes costs society more than $1 because of the positive marginal cost of public funds. This cost captures the effect of a tax in driving a wedge between the market value of what an extra hour of labor produces and the worker's value of that hour (i.e., his or her opportunity cost). Given this tax wedge, each $1 in funds raised by taxes costs society an estimated 50 cents in forgone value (Dahlby 2008; CEA 2019).

The rules governing OZs do not create a disincentive to work because eligibility is based on community-wide measures of poverty and income rather than those of any particular individual. Nor does the OZ incentive have the same marginal cost of public funds associated with transfers funded by tax revenues. The incentive cuts taxes on capital supplied to low-income communities, which reduces the tax wedge associated with the supply and demand for capital. The forgone Federal revenue might be made up through higher taxes elsewhere, or it could be offset by declines in government transfers because of rising incomes in poor neighborhoods, which is considered in a later section.

OZs, nonetheless, are not a substitute for cash grants or subsidies. Not everyone can work, and most people living in poverty do not live in OZs. To the extent that transfer programs have appropriate work requirements for those who are able to work, OZs complement such programs by fostering job creation.

OZs also complement the Earned Income Tax Credit (EITC), which is an antipoverty tax incentive. The EITC targets low-income workers, especially those with children, and is phased out as a family's income rises. Because the EITC is only provided to low-income families with earnings, it encourages people to enter the workforce. Empirical research confirms that the EITC increases workforce participation for single mothers, who benefit the most from the credit (Nichols and Rothstein 2015). In this sense, the EITC increases the supply of labor, while OZs stimulate demand for it.

Federal Place–Based Policies: The New Markets Tax Credit Program

The Federal program most comparable to Opportunity Zones is the New Markets Tax Credit (NMTC), though OZs offer improvements over the NMTC program. Both use tax incentives to encourage private investment in low-income communities, but the total tax benefit available through the NMTC program is capped, limiting how much investment it can spur.[3] In most years since 2007, Congress has authorized the NMTC program to award tax credits to support about $3.5 billion in place-based investments. On average, these credits account for about half of total project costs, so the program supports roughly $7 billion in investment annually. As of 2016, nearly 3,400 census tracts have received NMTC program credits since the program's inception in the early 2000s (Tax Policy Center 2020).

In addition to being smaller in scale than the OZ initiative, the NMTC program has a top-down approach to distributing tax benefits. The U.S. Department of the Treasury administers the NMTC program through its Community Development Financial Institutions Fund (CDFI), which ultimately selects what applicants can receive tax credits. Community development entities must first apply to the CDFI to be qualified for the program. Those that are qualified then identify investment opportunities and submit applications to compete for a limited pool of credits. In 2018, development entities requested $14.8 billion in NMTC funds, but only $3.5 billion were available, and only about a third of all applicants received funding (Lowry and Marples 2019).

Even for approved applicants, the NMTC program places greater restrictions on investors. Funds must remain invested and compliant with program requirements for seven years or else forgo all their tax benefits (with interest and penalties). With OZs, funds can liquidate one investment and roll the proceeds into a new one without penalty, though standard taxes apply to any capital gains. OZs are also flexible in other ways; investors can contribute funds up to any size, and they can pool their funds with any number of other investors (Vardell 2019; Bernstein and Hassett 2015).

Many of the participants in the NMTC program are large financial intermediaries equipped to navigate the CDFI's application process and manage compliance risk (Vardell 2019; Hula and Jordan 2018). To manage the risk, most NMTC transactions use a complex leverage model that combines debt and equity. According to Hula and Jordan (2018, 23), the model requires "a team of accountants and attorneys" with relevant expertise to structure the investment. By contrast, any investor with eligible capital gains can invest in a Qualified Opportunity Fund. These funds, in turn, need only self-certify their investments on their tax returns and follow the broad guidelines provided by the Department of the Treasury's regulations.[4]

Although the NMTC program is more prescriptive than OZs, it is more flexible than the economic development grants given by the CDFI Fund. Harger, Ross, and Stephens (2019) find that the tax credits—but not the grants—increased the number of new businesses in low-income communities. They attribute the difference in part to the greater flexibility of the tax credit relative

---

[3] NMTCs are a limited allotment of tax credits that reduce investors' Federal tax obligations. Tax credits differ from tax deductions, which decrease the amount of income subject to being taxed.

[4] The final regulations are available at www.irs.gov/pub/irs-drop/td-9889.pdf.

to the grants. At the same time, the authors found that even the NMTC program may not have had much effect on local employment.

Other Federal Place–Based Development Programs

Along with Opportunity Zones, in recent decades three other Federal programs have also relied on tax policy to spur economic development in specific places: empowerment zones (EZs), enterprise communities (ECs), and renewal communities (RCs). EZs and ECs date to 1993, while RCs were authorized in 2000. These programs extended a mix of tax benefits and grants to businesses in designated census tracts. These programs had a smaller geographic reach, with many States having little or no participation in them. A key tax benefit among these programs was an employment tax credit of up to $3,000 on the wages paid to people who lived and worked in the designated tract. Other tax benefits included increased limits for expensed deductions, tax-exempt bond financing, and exemptions from certain capital gains taxes (CRS 2011). The EC and RC programs have both ended, and only the tax benefits associated with the EZ program continue. Early research on the effects of the programs showed little evidence of success, but more recent studies have documented beneficial effects on unemployment, wages, and poverty (CRS 2011; Ham et al. 2011; Busso, Gregory, and Kline 2013).

The Federal Government also supports place-based economic development through grant programs, with the largest being the Community Development Block Grant program. The U.S. Department of Housing and Urban Development (HUD) administers the program and provides about $3 billion a year in block grants. The program's structure makes rigorous evaluation difficult, and few systematic evaluations have been done, especially in recent years (Theodos, Stacy, and Ho 2017). HUD allocates funds using a formula based on population, poverty, housing conditions, and other factors. State and local government grantees have considerable discretion, within broad guidelines, on how to use the funding, such as that at least 70 percent of the funds must be used to benefit low- and moderate-income persons. The flexibility of the program is similar to OZs, but its design is very different in that it relies solely on public funding and does not seek to incentivize private investment.

The Economic Development Administration (EDA) of the U.S. Department of Commerce also administers grants for economic development. EDA's 2019 appropriation was roughly $300 million, but the Coronavirus Aid, Relief, and Economic Security Act (CARES Act) appropriated an additional $1.5 billion to administer grants to States and communities adversely affected by the COVID-19 pandemic. As with the HUD grants, few rigorous evaluations have been done of EDA's grants (Markusen and Glasmeier 2008).

Characteristics of Opportunity Zones

The census tracts designated as OZs have some of the most entrenched poverty in the United States. These communities had an average median income just over half of the U.S. average in 2000 and they fell further behind over the subsequent 16 years.

The Opportunity Zone Selection Process

As prescribed by law, governors nominated which census tracts should be designated as Opportunity Zones by the U.S. Department of the Treasury. To be eligible for designation, a census tract must:

- Have a poverty rate of at least 20 percent; or
- Have a median income below 80 percent of that in the State or metropolitan area, or for rural census tracts, 80 percent of that in the entire State; or
- Be contiguous with a census tract meeting one of the above conditions and have a median income less than 125 percent of the qualifying contiguous census tract.

Governors could designate up to 25 percent of their qualifying census tracts, or up to 25 tracts for those States with fewer than 100 eligible tracts. Eligible, contiguous tracts were restricted to make up no more than 5 percent of designated OZs in any State.

Aside from these restrictions, States could determine how, and which, census tracts would be designated as OZs, thereby drawing on State and local

Figure 5-1. The Geography of Opportunity Zones

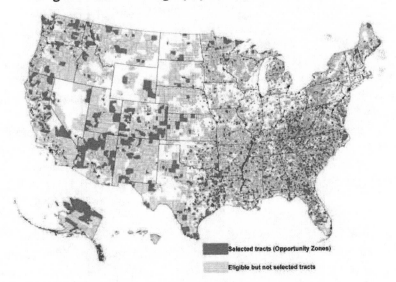

Selected tracts (Opportunity Zones)

Eligible but not selected tracts

Sources: U.S. Department of the Treasury; U.S. Census Bureau.

expertise. With this Federal design, States took diverse approaches in nominating their OZs. Arizona, for example, tasked the Arizona Commerce Authority with meeting with city, county, and tribal governments to select tracts. Kansas took a different approach, with its Department of Commerce requesting "Letters of Interest" from communities seeking OZ designation, allowing communities to explain their need and their ability to attract investment.

All governors submitted tracts for consideration to the U.S. Department of the Treasury by the end of April 2018. The Treasury ultimately designated a total of 8,766 tracts as OZs, with nearly all designations occurring between April and June 2018. Almost all OZs (8,537 tracts) met one of the criteria for low-income communities; the remaining 229, or 2.6 percent of all designated census tracts, were eligible for selection based on contiguity with a low-income tract. Figure 5-1 highlights the OZ tracts (in green) and the eligible tracts that were not selected (in gray).

The Economic State of Opportunity Zones

This subsection reports on the CEA's overall findings that census tracts selected as Opportunity Zones are among the poorest communities in the United States. The CEA finds that they have an average poverty rate more than double that of all other census tracts and are home to a higher share of African Americans, Hispanics, and high school dropouts (figure 5-2).

The economic woes of OZs are not new. In 2000, census tracts that later became OZs had an average median household income that was 57 percent of the average in other tracts, $39,305 compared with $68,726 as given in the 2000 Decennial Census. In real terms, median household income in the average OZ fell by 11 percent from 2000 to 2012–16, compared with a 6 percent drop in the average non-OZ census tract (figure 5-3).

The poverty and income criteria for eligibility explain some of the lower income in selected census tracts; but even among eligible tracts, States consistently nominated low-income tracts. In each of the 50 States and in the District of Columbia, median household income in OZs was lower than in eligible-but-not-selected tracts and considerably lower than in ineligible tracts (figure 5-4).

Figures 5-2 through 5-4 indicate that, as a whole, OZs encompass economically distressed areas. Although average values can mask diversity within the OZ group, only 3.2 percent of OZs experienced rapid socioeconomic change according to a metric developed by the Urban Institute (2018). This metric considers changes in income, demographics, educational attainment, and housing affordability.

The patterns shown in figure 5-5 suggest that States selected tracts that were both economically distressed and demonstrated a potential to attract fruitful investments. They selected tracts with varying levels of poverty, not focusing solely on those with the least poverty (among eligible tracts) nor on those with the highest poverty rates. The strategy has an economic rationale:

Figure 5-2. Demographics of Opportunity Zones (OZs), 2012–16

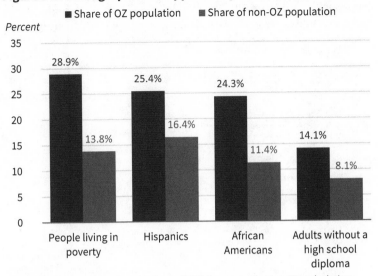

■ Share of OZ population ■ Share of non-OZ population

Percent

Sources: 2016 American Community Survey (ACS) five-year estimates; CEA calculations.
Note: This analysis excludes census tracts in Puerto Rico, American Samoa, the U.S. Virgin Islands, Guam, and the Northern Mariana Islands. In addition, the 2016 ACS is based on a five-year estimate from 2012 to 2016.

Figure 5-3. Average Median Household Income by Census Tract Designation, 2000–2016

Household income index (2000 = 100)

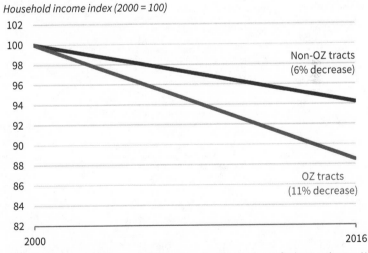

Sources: 2000 Decennial Census; 2016 American Community Survey five-year estimates; U.S. Department of the Treasury; CEA calculations.
Note: This analysis excludes census tracts in Puerto Rico, American Samoa, the U.S. Virgin Islands, Guam, and the Northern Mariana Islands. The 2016 ACS is based on a five-year estimate from 2012 to 2016.

Assessing the Early Impact of Opportunity Zones | 155

Figure 5-4. Average Median Household Income by Tract Designation and State, 2012–16

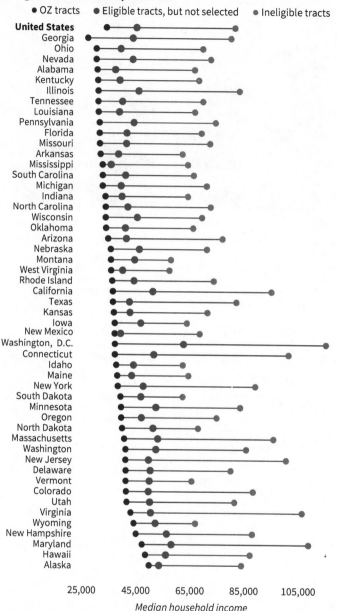

● OZ tracts   ● Eligible tracts, but not selected   ● Ineligible tracts

United States
Georgia
Ohio
Nevada
Alabama
Kentucky
Illinois
Tennessee
Louisiana
Pennsylvania
Florida
Missouri
Arkansas
Mississippi
South Carolina
Michigan
Indiana
North Carolina
Wisconsin
Oklahoma
Arizona
Nebraska
Montana
West Virginia
Rhode Island
California
Texas
Kansas
Iowa
New Mexico
Washington, D.C.
Connecticut
Idaho
Maine
New York
South Dakota
Minnesota
Oregon
North Dakota
Massachusetts
Washington
New Jersey
Delaware
Vermont
Colorado
Utah
Virginia
Wyoming
New Hampshire
Maryland
Hawaii
Alaska

25,000   45,000   65,000   85,000   105,000

Median household income

Sources: 2012–16 American Community Survey (ACS), five-year estimates; U.S. Department of the Treasury ; CEA calculations.

Note: This analysis excludes census tracts in Puerto Rico, American Samoa, the U.S. Virgin Islands, Guam, and the Northern Mariana Islands. The 2016 ACS is based on a five-year estimate from 2012 to 2016. Eligible but not selected tracts include those eligible based on low-income status or on contiguity with low-income tracts.

Figure 5-5. Population by Poverty Rates and Census Tract Designation

■ Opportunity Zones ■ Eligible tracts, but not selected ■ Ineligible tracts

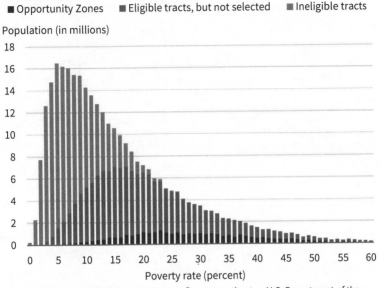

Sources: 2016 American Community Survey, five-year estimates; U.S. Department of the Treasury; CEA calculations.

States would benefit little from OZs if they selected tracts where a designation was unlikely to spur investment.

Opportunity Zones' Effect on Total Investment

The CEA estimates that by the end of 2019, Qualified Opportunity Funds had raised $75 billion in private capital. Although some of this capital may have occurred without the incentive, the CEA estimates that $52 billion—or 70 percent—of the $75 billion is new investment.

Capital Raised by Qualified Opportunity Funds

The $75 billion estimate for private capital raised is based on two different samples that track these funds over time. To extrapolate from sample values to population values, we rely on the total number of these funds in existence, as estimated by the Department of the Treasury based on tax filings (1,500 funds in 2018).[5] Both samples and estimation approaches give a roughly similar estimate for the capital raised by these funds, with the average being $75 billion.

---

[5] The count of Qualified Opportunity Funds in the population (1,500) is based on a Treasury Department's estimate based on preliminary counts of filings of Form 8996. The Treasury may adjust this count as more information becomes available.

The first sample covers Qualified Opportunity Funds voluntarily reporting data to Novogradac, a national professional services organization that has tracked funds since May 2019. As of January 17, 2020, the sample had 513 of these funds, a small subset of all funds, which had collectively raised $7.6 billion in capital.[6] Qualified Opportunity Funds voluntarily reporting data might not be representative of the general population of funds. However, comparisons with a non-voluntary sample, as discussed below, suggests that it is reasonably representative.

The second sample is based on data from the Securities and Exchange Commission (SEC). The SEC considers investment interests in Qualified Opportunity Funds as securities, which means that funds must register with the SEC unless they file for an exemption. Qualified Opportunity Funds seeking an exemption can file Form D within 15 days of the first sale of securities in an offering. In filing Form D, these funds provide information such as the amount sold in the offering, but they are not asked to identify themselves as funds. To create a sample of these funds from the Form D data, we select all funds with "Opportunity Zone" or similar words (e.g., "OZ Fund" or "QOZF") in their name. This yields 197 Qualified Opportunity Funds that had filed Form D by the close of 2019, 153 of which had raised capital, totaling about $2.9 billion. If Qualified Opportunity Fund names are uncorrelated with other fund characteristics, our sample should be reasonably representative of the broader population of funds seeking an exemption from SEC registration.[7]

The Novogradac and SEC samples show similar growth in the number of Qualified Opportunity Funds and capital raised. From May 2019, when Novogradac began tracking these funds, until Novogradac's January 17, 2020, report, the number of funds increased by 277 percent. The SEC data show a 271 percent increase in the number of these funds from 2018 to 2019, based on information on when each fund was incorporated. Additionally, the capital reported by Novogradac Qualified Opportunity Funds increased by 858 percent over the reporting period, while the capital raised by the SEC sample of funds increased by 1,523 percent from 2018 to 2019. See figure 5-6.

The two samples of Qualified Opportunity Funds inform two different approaches for estimating the total capital raised by funds. The first approach, based on the self-reported Novogradac data, is to multiply the Novogradac total equity amount ($7.6 billion) by an expansion factor, defined as the number of Qualified Opportunity Funds in the population divided by the number of funds in the Novogradac database. This factor reflects how much of the fund

---

[6] Although our analysis is for the close of 2019, more recent data from Novogradac show a 31 percent increase in capital raised from January to April 2020 and a roughly 20 percent increase for April to August 2020, which represents a 79 percent growth over the first eight months of 2020.
[7] Funds seeking to make public offerings of securities are generally not exempt from SEC registration and would not file a Form D. We expect such funds to be larger, on average, than those focused on private offerings.

Figure 5-6. Growth in Qualified Opportunity Funds, Novogradac and SEC Data

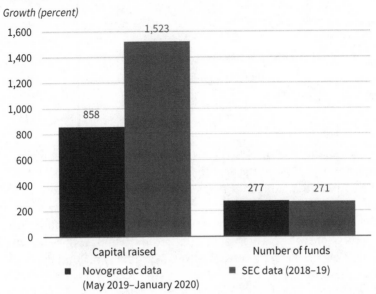

Growth (percent)

Sources: Novogradac; Securities and Exchange Commission (SEC); CEA calculations.

population is captured by Novogradac's database. The estimate of capital raised is then:

$$Capital\ Raised\ (Novo.) = Capital\ Raised_{Novo.}\ x\ \left(\frac{Population\ count\ of\ funds}{Novo.\ count\ of\ funds}\right)$$

$$= 7.6\ billion\ x\ \left(\frac{1,500\ funds}{136\ funds}\right)$$

$$= \$84\ billion$$

The number of Qualified Opportunity Funds (1,500) in the population comes from the Department of the Treasury and corresponds to the end of 2018, and the number of funds in the Novogradac database (136) is from May 2019, the earliest reporting of the Novogradac data. This estimation approach assumes that Qualified Opportunity Funds reporting to Novogradac are similar in size to funds not reporting to Novogradac. It also assumes that our expansion factor accurately reflects Novogradac's coverage of the Qualified Opportunity Fund population in January 2020.

The second estimation approach, which draws on the SEC sample, multiplies an estimate of the number of Qualified Opportunity Funds in existence at the close of 2019 by an estimate of the average amount of capital raised per fund, among those having raised capital. More specifically, it is:

$$Capital\ Raised\ (SEC)$$
$$= "Population\ count\ of\ Funds"_{2018}\ x\ "Growth\ in\ Fund\ count"_{2018-19}$$
$$x\ "Share\ of\ Funds\ with\ Capital"_{2019}\ x\ "Capital\ per\ Fund"_{2019}$$
$$= 1,500\ x\ 3.71\ x\ 0.60\ x\ 0.019$$
$$= \$63\ billion$$

The population count of Qualified Opportunity Funds is again from the Department of the Treasury, the growth in the fund count is based on the 2018 to 2019 growth in the number of funds incorporated (as reported in the SEC data); the share of funds with capital is as of January 2020 and comes from the Novogradac database; and capital per fund comes from the SEC data (0.019 billion per fund). For the share of Qualified Opportunity Funds with capital (0.60), we use the Novogradac data instead of the SEC data, which primarily cover funds that have already raised capital since that is what triggers their filing of the SEC form that generates the data. As such, funds that have raised at least some capital are likely to be overrepresented in the SEC data. In summary, the key assumptions of the second approach are that the SEC data provide a reliable estimate of the growth in the number of Qualified Opportunity Funds in the population and, among those with capital, their average capital raised. In line with the Novogradac data, the approach also assumes that 60 percent of all funds raised some capital by the close of 2019.

The standard error of the average amount of capital raised per Qualified Opportunity Fund permits providing a confidence interval around the SEC-based estimate of the total capital raised.[8] The resulting 90 percent confidence interval is $33 billion at the lower end and $93 billion at the higher end. It therefore includes the Novogradac-based estimate and the average of the two estimates, which is about $75 billion and is our preferred estimate. This is 21 percent of baseline annual investment in OZs, which is reported in the next subsection.

Estimated Investment Growth Caused by the Opportunity Zone Incentive

Not all the capital raised by Qualified Opportunity Funds is necessarily new to Opportunity Zones—some of it may have occurred without the incentive, and it is now occurring through a fund. In this subsection, the CEA draws from the

---

[8] The resulting confidence interval reflects uncertainty over the population value of capital per fund. It does not capture uncertainty over other parameters used in the calculation of total capital raised by funds in the population.

academic literature to estimate how much new investment is likely given the lower tax rates caused by the OZ incentive. We estimate that the incentives have brought $52 billion in new investment in OZs through 2019, representing 70 percent of the $75 billion raised by Qualified Opportunity Funds.

To estimate new investment, we calculate the reduction in the cost of capital caused by the cuts to capital gains tax rates. We then link the cost of capital to investment elasticities from the academic literature. This modeling of the OZ incentive illustrates how the incentive is similar to the corporate tax rate cuts resulting from the Tax Cuts and Jobs Act. These cuts were also projected to increase investment through a decline in the user cost of capital (CEA 2017).

The investment estimates come from first calculating the pretax rate of return needed to attract investors to supply funds in OZs. To achieve the same post-tax return inside OZs as outside them, investors would be willing to accept a lower pretax return because of lower effective tax rates in OZs. The second step of the estimation then calculates the increased investment from OZ businesses that occurs as they have access to new funding at a lower capital cost. Figure 5-7 illustrates the concepts behind the calculation, showing how the reduction in taxes makes investors willing to accept a lower pretax rate of return and still invest in OZs.

The numerical estimates rely on three parameters: baseline investment in OZ census tracts that predates the incentives, the post-tax rate of return that is required to attract funds, and the effective tax rate that prevails in OZs with the incentive. For the first parameter, we estimate baseline investment of $243 billion by apportioning national investment to counties based on gross domestic product, and then from counties to census tracts based on income and population. Second, using data that show a pretax 9.8 percent rate of return earned by investors outside OZs—which then face a capital gains tax rate of 21.3 percent—the required post-tax rate of return is 7.7 percent. We find that, to receive the same post-tax 7.7 percent rate of return in OZs—which feature only a 6.9 percent effective tax rate, as described below in the "Budgetary Effects of Opportunity Zones" subsection—investors only require a pretax rate of return equal to 8.3 percent (= 7.7/(1 − 0.069)) in 2019. Finally, we assume a −9.55 semielasticity of investment to the cost of capital, from Ohrn (2019). Over a one-and-a-half-year period, the increase to investment is then calculated as:

1.5 years x ($243 billion) x (8.3% − 9.8%) x (−9.55) = $52.2 billion.

The one-and-a-half-year period is used to reflect the time between the designation of Opportunity Zones (mid-2018) and the end of 2019.

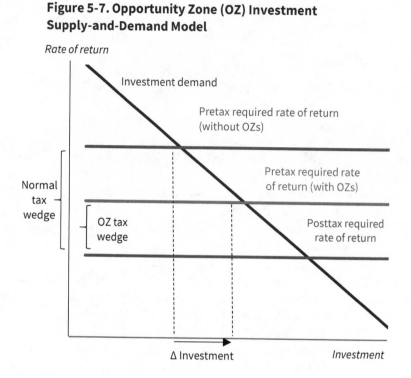

Figure 5-7. Opportunity Zone (OZ) Investment Supply-and-Demand Model

Rate of return

Investment demand

Pretax required rate of return (without OZs)

Pretax required rate of return (with OZs)

Normal tax wedge

OZ tax wedge

Posttax required rate of return

Δ Investment

Investment

The Industry Focus of Qualified Opportunity Funds

Recent data from the Securities and Exchange Commission allow us to describe the sectoral focus of a sample of Qualified Opportunity Funds, the same one described above. The SEC form completed by Qualified Opportunity Funds requires them to select one industry group. The selections, shown in figure 5-8, reveal the diverse focus of funds. Slightly less than half of them focus on real estate, with the majority targeting commercial real estate.[9] Another 45 percent describe their industry as a "Pooled Investment Fund," which suggests that they have investments across various industries. Finally, about 10 percent are in the "other" category, which includes funds that reported a focus on health care, technology, construction, and investing, and as well as those selecting the "other" option on the form.

The industry focus indicated by the SEC data are consistent with the types of projects seeking to attract Qualified Opportunity Fund investment, as evidenced by data from the Opportunity Exchange, which is a private organization that helps entities showcase OZ businesses and properties to stakeholders locally and nationally. As of February 2020, The Opportunity Exchange hosted $45 billion in proposed projects across 24 States. About 30 percent of the projects on the Opportunity Exchange are businesses seeking equity investments,

---

[9] Form D does not provide definitions for the industry categories that filers can select.

Figure 5-8. Percentage of Qualified Opportunity Funds, by Industry

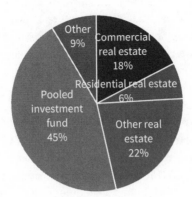

Sources: Securities and Exchange Commission; CEA calculations.
Note: "Other real estate" includes real estate inestment trusts and finance. "Other" includes healthcare, technology, construction, and investing.

26 percent are real estate projects with a development plan, and the rest are properties for sale without a development plan.

Opportunity Zones' Effects on Business Investment and Housing Values

The CEA finds that receiving an OZ designation led to a 29 percent relative increase in equity investment. Such communities have also benefited from larger house price appreciation, which creates $11 billion in additional housing wealth for homeowners and improved local amenities for renters.

Equity Investments in Opportunity Zone Businesses

Qualified Opportunity Funds can invest in Opportunity Zones by directly purchasing property or by making equity investments in operating businesses. In this subsection, we present data regarding private equity investment in businesses located in OZs compared with those located elsewhere. Investment data from the Securities and Exchange Commission show that OZ designation led to a 29 percent increase in equity investments in businesses whose principal place of business is in an OZ, compared with businesses in eligible-but-not-selected census tracts.

Many businesses pursuing equity investments must file the same SEC Form D that Qualified Opportunity Funds file. We use address information from this form, which gives the location of the principal place of business, to determine whether the business is located in an OZ census tract, an eligible-but-not-selected tract, or an ineligible tract. To capture nonfinancial operating businesses, we exclude entities that identified themselves as banks or investment funds.[10] To better measure systematic investment trends, as opposed to variation in the behavior of a few large firms, we focus on filings that raised less than $50 million in any quarter, which captures more than 96 percent of filings.[11] We then compile the total investment raised by businesses in each census tract type by quarter.

In figure 5-9, we present the four-quarter moving average of the total equity investment in each group of tracts, with values indexed to their value in the first quarter of 2018. The three groups had similar investment trends until the first half of 2018, when investment in OZ businesses spiked.[12] All States nominated census tracts in March and April 2018, and the Department of the Treasury finalized its formal designation of OZs by the second quarter of 2018. Over the seven quarters 2018:Q2–2019:Q4, equity investment in OZs was 41 percent higher than it was in the prior seven quarters. By comparison, investment was only 13 percent higher in eligible-but-not-selected tracts. This suggests that OZ designation led to a 29 percent increase in equity investment relative to comparable tracts (41.4–12.6 percent).[13]

Opportunity Zone Designation and Housing Values

Evidence from real estate markets suggests that the Opportunity Zones incentive is making many OZs more attractive for both residents and investors. This increase in housing value has led to an estimated $11 billion in additional wealth for the nearly half (47 percent) of OZ residents who own their housing.

Real Capital Analytics tracks commercial real estate properties and portfolios valued at $2.5 million or more. Its data show that year-over-year growth

---

[10] Specifically, we exclude all firms that identified their industry or their fund as "pooled investment fund," "commercial banking," "investment banking," "other banking and financial services," or "investing."

[11] Bauguess, Gullapalli, and Ivanov (2018) report that more than 96 percent of filings have an offering size of $50 million or less. An even larger percentage would actually raise less than $50 million.

[12] Not every businesses in an OZ is necessarily a Qualified Opportunity Zone Business as defined by statute and regulation.

[13] The location of a business in a particular OZ does not mean that the business's activities must be concentrated in that particular OZ. A business can achieve the status of a Qualified Opportunity Zone Business if 50 percent of its gross income is derived from its business activities in any OZ. Thus, a business could have multiple income-earning centers spread across various OZs. Alternatively, the business can qualify if at least 50 of the services purchased and used by the business (measured by hours or dollars) occur in OZs or if at least 50 percent of its tangible property and management functions are in OZs.

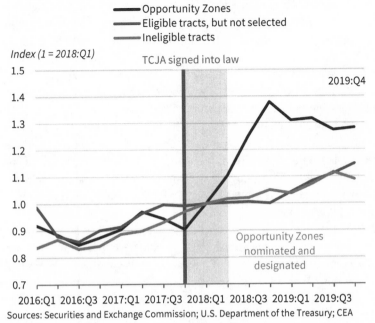

Figure 5-9. Private Equity Investment by Tract Group, 2016–19

Opportunity Zones
Eligible tracts, but not selected
Ineligible tracts

Index (1 = 2018:Q1)

TCJA signed into law

2019:Q4

1.5

1.4

1.3

1.2

1.1

1.0

0.9

0.8

0.7

Opportunity Zones
nominated and
designated

2016:Q1 2016:Q3 2017:Q1 2017:Q3 2018:Q1 2018:Q3 2019:Q1 2019:Q3

Sources: Securities and Exchange Commission; U.S. Department of the Treasury; CEA calculations.

Note: TCJA = Tax Cuts and Jobs Act.

in development site acquisitions surged in OZs by more than 50 percent late in 2018 after the Department of the Treasury had designated the OZs, greatly exceeding growth in the rest of the United States. Similarly, Sage, Langen, and Van de Minne (2019) use the same data and find that OZ designation led to a 14 percent increase in the price of redevelopment properties and a 20 percent increase in the price of vacant development sites as of early 2019.

Sage, Langen, and Van de Minne (2019) find a price increase only for particular property types and conclude that the OZ incentive is having limited economic spillovers in communities. Their data, however, only include commercial properties valued at $2.5 million or more. An analysis by Zillow, which was based on transactions of varying property types and values, suggests that the OZ incentive is having broader effects. After designation, the year-over-year change in the average sales price for properties in OZs rose to more than 25 percent while falling to below 10 percent in eligible-but-not-selected census tracts.

The Zillow analysis is limited in that it is based on changes in sales prices over time, without controlling for any changes in the composition of properties being sold. It is not based on price per square foot or, more ideally, on price changes for homes that are similar in many other dimensions. Chen, Glaeser, and Wessel (2019) provide a more rigorous assessment of effects on housing prices, though only through 2018. For a measure of housing prices, they use the Federal Housing Finance Agency (FHFA) repeat sales index for single-family homes. Their analysis centers on comparing OZs with eligible but not selected low-income tracts (thus excluding tracts whose eligibility was based solely on contiguity with low-income tracts). Across the two groups, they compare the growth in housing values in 2018 relative to that of prior years (2014–17). Their estimated effects are much smaller than those suggested by the Zillow analysis: their base model gives an estimate of 0.25 percent higher appreciation, with the estimates across models ranging from 0.09 to 0.74.

We replicate and extend the analysis done by Chen, Glaeser, and Wessel. First, we replicate the results from their base model and find a similar result (table 5-1, first and second columns). Then we reestimate the model with updated FHFA data released in May 2020. The update improves data from prior years and adds 2019 data.[14]

With the updated and expanded data, we estimate that OZ designation led to a higher annual appreciation of 0.53 percent. Over two years, this implies a roughly 1.1 percent (= $1.0053^2 - 1$) increase in values. This is a notable finding because it is based on OZ designation, not on whether a tract has actually received investment. Moreover, much of the investment raised by Qualified Opportunity Funds was probably not invested by the end of 2019. By comparison, Freedman (2012) looked at census tracts that had actually received investment through the New Markets Tax Credit and failed to find a statistically significant effect of investment on housing values over about five years, with the point estimate implying an annual effect of at most 0.5 percent.

The extra 1.1 percent appreciation implies $11 billion in additional wealth for the nearly half (47 percent) of OZ residents who own their housing. Homeowners can access newly found equity without selling their homes through cash-out refinancing, which has been common in the last two years. This does not mean that rising values only benefit homeowners. The causes of higher values—more local amenities and anticipated economic opportunities—will benefit many renters as well. The renovation of a blighted building, for example, benefits all who live nearby. Brummet and Reed (2019) draw a similar conclusion from a thorough analysis of Census microdata, finding that less exposure to poverty and rising values tend to benefit original residents and led to better outcomes for their children. Using a different data source from Medicaid records, Dragan, Ellen, and Glied (2019) draw a similar conclusion

---

[14] The data are available at www.fhfa.gov/DataTools/Downloads/Pages/House-Price-Index-Datasets.aspx; see "Census Tracts (Development Index; Not Seasonally Adjusted)." We also normalize the housing price index to make 2013 the base year (= 100). The renormalization ensures that that changes in the index are approximate percentage changes, with a 1-point change in the index corresponding to a 1 percent increase in values. If index values are about 300, which is typical in the original index, a 1-point increase represents a 0.3 percent increase in values. The renormalized values are also much less skewed than the original index values.

Table 5-1. The Effect of Opportunity Zone Designation on Home Value Appreciation

Characteristic	Chen et al. (2019)	CEA Estimates	
		Chen et al. Data	Updated Data
Opportunity Zone effect on housing values (percent)	0.25	0.25	0.53
Standard error	0.22	0.22	0.19
Number of Opportunity Zones	2,674	2,674	2,700
Number of eligible zones that were not selected	10,198	10,198	10,288

Sources: Chen, Glaeser, and Wessel (2019); Census Bureau, American Community Survey, 2012–16; Federal Housing Finance Agency; U.S. Department of the Treasury; CEA calculations.
Note: The estimated effect is based on comparing Opportunity Zones with low-income tracts that were eligible but not selected .

about the effects of rising housing values and neighborhood improvement on residents and their children.

Within Opportunity Zones, the distribution of the benefits from improved amenities is unclear. In some instances, the benefits may go primarily to low-income households. For example, Gamper-Rabindran and Timmins (2013) find that cheaper homes benefit the most from the cleanup of hazardous waste sites because such homes tend to be closer to such sites. In the same vein, the renovation of an abandoned warehouse would mostly benefit the residents in the immediate vicinity, who may also be among the poorest in the neighborhood.

Residents who rent their housing will generally benefit from improved amenities as long as the full value of the amenities enjoyed by residents is not passed on in the form of higher rents. Improved neighborhood conditions do not always result in rent increases for all renters (Brummet and Reed 2019), and sometimes improved amenities increase housing values more than they increase rents (e.g., Granger 2012).

Opportunity Zones' Effects on Poverty and the Budget

The CEA's estimate of new investment suggests that Opportunity Zones may lift about 1 million people out of poverty, an 11 percent decrease in the baseline population in poverty in OZs. This decline in poverty, and with it a reduction in transfer payments, may be sufficient to make the OZ incentive nearly revenue neutral.

Projected Effects of Opportunity Zones on Poverty

Census-tract-level data on poverty for 2019 will not be available for several years. The CEA therefore projects the effects on poverty using a prior study linking investment to poverty. Freedman (2012) uses tract-level data to estimate the effects of investment subsidized by the New Markets Tax Credit on tract-level outcomes. His empirical approach exploits the program's eligibility cutoffs to address the potential that subsidized investment went to tracts that would have performed better even without the subsidy. His most conservative estimate indicates that each $1 million in subsidized investment (in 2018 dollars) lifts 20 people out of poverty in the tract receiving it. Applying this finding to our estimate of new investment in Opportunity Zones ($52,000 million) suggests that 1 million people will be lifted out of poverty (= 52,000 x 20).

This effect is arguably applicable to OZ investment. The NMTC program has similar eligibility requirements for census tracts and rules to ensure that the subsidized investment happens in qualified tracts. The main difference is that community development entities must apply to and be selected by the Treasury Department, which only selects a portion of applicants. The Treasury scores applications using several criteria, including the expected effect of the project on jobs and economic growth in the community. It is possible that applicant reporting and Treasury selections result in the investments having larger effects on poverty. Conversely, the long-term net effects of a particular project on low-income populations is arguably hard to discern with consistency. In any case, our poverty projections are arguably conservative; we use the smallest estimated effect from Freedman (2012), which is about half the main estimate reported, and apply it to new investment as opposed to all subsidized investment, which is the basis of Freedman's estimate.

Budgetary Effects of Opportunity Zones

The CEA estimates that the Federal Government forgoes $0.15 for every $1 in capital gains invested in a Qualified Opportunity Fund before 2020, or about $11.2 billion for the $75 billion raised through the end of 2019. The forgone revenues stem from the deferment on the capital gains tax on the original gain, the reduction in taxes on the original gains when paid, and the lack of taxes on the gains earned while invested in the Qualified Opportunity Fund. In our calculation, we assume that taxpayers maximize their tax savings by waiting until 2026 to pay taxes on the original gains, the latest date allowed by law, and that they keep their money in the Qualified Opportunity Fund for at least 10 years.

Our calculations assume that capital gains would normally be taxed at a 21.3 percent rate, as opposed to an effective rate of 6.9 percent in 2019. This lower effective rate arises from the tax deferral and step-up in basis on funds that are invested in OZs to begin with, as well as the exclusion of capital gains taxes on the returns that accrue to those investments after they are held for at least 10 years. For funds invested in 2019, the present values of taxes paid on investments in an OZ are less than one-third what they would be if invested outside an OZ. These calculations are then repeated for each year to incorporate the dynamic nature of the OZ tax incentives, as discussed in a Congressional Research Service report (Lowry and Marples 2019).

When estimating overall revenue effects, any static calculation that uses only the difference in rates while assuming a fixed tax base gives an inflated measure of tax revenue losses. Therefore, in our approach, we incorporate the response of investment—and hence the tax base—to the incentive. Specifically, we estimate how much of the observed $75 billion would have occurred any-way—whether in an OZ or elsewhere in the country—versus how much is new investment. Investment that would have occurred anyway and been taxed at a 21.3 percent rate but that is now taxed at a lower rate because of the incentive unambiguously lowers revenues. However, new investment creates offsetting revenue gains, even when taxed at the lower OZ rate.

We employ a similar elasticity-based approach as in the investment sec-tion of this chapter. The approach suggests that of the $75 billion in Qualified Opportunity Fund capital, $22.8 billion would have occurred anyway in OZs, even without the incentive. Of the $52.2 billion balance, another $24.9 bil-lion is new to OZs but was shifted from elsewhere in the country, based on calculations using the elasticity-of-investment movement done by Koby and Wolf (2019). Thus, the incentive results in revenue losses from this $47.7 billion ($22.8 billion + $24.9 billion) but creates revenue gains from the entirely new $27.3 billion ($75 billion – $47.7 billion) in investment. On net, we estimate the present value of tax revenue losses on capital invested through 2019 to be $11.2 billion, which is 15 percent of the $75 billion in Qualified Opportunity Fund capital.

By comparison, the CEA estimates that for each $1 in investment associ-ated with the New Markets Tax Credit, the Federal government forgoes $0.18, more than the amount for OZs. Based on estimates from the Joint Committee on Taxation, the lost tax revenue for each $1 in tax credit authority is $0.26.[15]

---

[15] In December 2019, the Joint Committee on Taxation estimated the dynamic revenue effects from a $5 billion allocation for the NMTC (see the relevant line at www.jct.gov/publications.html?func=startdown&id=5237).

However, credit authority typically represents only 69 percent of total private investment associated with projects (Abravanel et al. 2013).[16] This implies about $0.18 in forgone revenue for each $1 in associated investment (= 0.26 x 0.69).

The previous calculations only consider the effect of the Opportunity Zone incentive on capital gains tax revenues. However, the incentive will have an offsetting effect on the Federal budget by stimulating the economies of low-income areas that receive a large share of transfer payments from the Federal Government. Using county-level data on transfer payments and poverty rates, the CEA estimates that an additional person living in poverty in a county is associated with about $8,240 additional Federal transfer payments to the county, including transfers related to income maintenance, unemployment insurance, and medical assistance (mainly Medicaid).[17] At this rate, economic growth that lifts 1 million people out of poverty for a little more than one year would save the Federal Government enough to offset the revenues forgone from the capital gains tax cuts (savings of $11.2 billion = a 1 million person reduction in poverty x 1.36 years x $8,240 per person).[18]

Conclusion

Much remains to study regarding the effects of Opportunity Zones on real estate markets, entrepreneurship, poverty, and income. In coming years, researchers will have ample data to assess the effects of OZs on diverse community outcomes. As of the 2019 tax year, the Internal Revenue Service's revised Form 8996 will collect detailed information on Qualified Opportunity Fund activity. This information will enable researchers to learn how much Qualified Opportunity Fund investment is occurring in particular census tracts and economic sectors. These data will permit the same rigorous empirical studies that have been done for the New Markets Tax Credit (Freedman 2012; Harger and Ross 2016), and they will add to the rigorous work already being done by Arefeva and others (2020) using other data sets to evaluate the impact of OZs.

---

[16] This is based on footnote 7 in a paper by Abravanel et al. (2013), which reports that qualified equity investments represent 53 percent of total project costs, while public funds represent 23 percent of project cost. This implies that qualified equity investment represents 69 percent of private project cost (= 0.53 / (1−0.23).

[17] This estimate is based on Bureau of Economic Analysis county-level data on Federal Government transfers and county-level population and poverty data from the Census Bureau. The average transfer per person in poverty, defined as total transfers in the county divided by the county population in poverty, over a seven-year period was about $11,500. However, regressing county-level transfers per capita on the poverty rate suggests that, at the margin, an extra person living in poverty is associated with $8,240 in greater transfers to residents of the county.

[18] Of course, this calculation should be viewed as illustrative because we lack an estimate of the causal impact of poverty reduction (via investment incentives) on total Federal spending.

The available evidence shows that Qualified Opportunity Funds are well positioned to invest in communities in 2020: they have raised considerable capital, and the final regulations from the Department of the Treasury, which were published in December 2019, have given further clarity on how the incentive and associated investments will function. However, numerous State-mandated restrictions and preventive behavior to slow the spread of the COVID-19 pandemic have prevented business as usual and have slowed investment everywhere, including in OZs.

A sizable amount of capital will enter Qualified Opportunity Funds in 2020. As noted above, the capital raised by these funds in the Novogradac sample grew by about 79 percent in the first eight months of 2020. Late in the first quarter, the pandemic prompted a massive selloff that likely generated capital gains for many investors exiting what had been a long bull market. And the rapid rebound in stock values has created the potential for more gains.

Pre-COVID-19 evidence suggests that the OZ model can help spur economic recovery in thousands of distressed communities across the United States. It has the power to mobilize investors, engage State and local stakeholders, and improve the outlook for low-income communities—all with limited prescription from the Federal Government. In other words, the OZ provision of the Tax Cuts and Jobs Act of 2017 is working as intended.

In nominating communities as Opportunity Zones, States selected places in need that had the potential to attract investment. The provision's incentives have helped mobilize the investment of $75 billion in private capital in Qualified Opportunity Funds, and some of this capital has already spurred growth in direct equity investments in businesses and real estate. Finally, OZ designation and the associated investment (both anticipated and realized) have made people more optimistic about these communities as places to live and to work in, with designation causing a 1.1 percent increase in housing values as of the close of 2019.

Such initial benefits underscore the potential of the Opportunity Zone model, which rests on private initiative; on engaged State, local, and tribal governments; and on limited Federal prescription—all to further prosperity and self-sufficiency in those areas that most lack it. This dynamic process will be important for helping the relatively poorer part of the population that has been most affected by the economic slowdown from the COVID-19 pandemic.

Chapter 6

Empowering Economic Freedom by Reducing Regulatory Burdens

Throughout the Trump Administration, Federal agencies have demonstrated a sustained commitment to regulatory reform. As a result, the Administration's regulatory efforts have reduced red tape for small businesses and the middle class. Although the Administration set the goal of eliminating two existing regulations for every one new regulation, it has far exceeded it. Between fiscal years 2017 and 2019, the executive branch agencies have issued roughly seven deregulations for every one significant regulatory action. The Administration's actions have served to lower costs for businesses and households while increasing competition and productivity in the American economy, leading to real gains, particularly at the middle and lower ends of the income distribution.

One of the most important deregulatory actions that the Trump Administration finalized in 2020 is the Safer Affordable Fuel Efficient (SAFE) Vehicles Rule. This joint rule from the Environmental Protection Agency and the U.S. Department of Transportation establishes tough, but reasonable, light vehicle carbon dioxide (CO_2) and fuel economy requirements for the 2021–26 model years. This regulatory approach continues to improve fuel economy year over year, while balancing efficiency, economic, and safety goals in a manner that gives the automobile industry greater flexibility to produce products that meet consumer demand and also creates meaningful savings for both manufacturers and customers. The Council of Economic Advisers (CEA) estimates that the SAFE Vehicles Rule will lead to $26 billion a year in savings for producers and consumers, and will deliver roughly 300,000 more new vehicles annually than the previous standards at a similar total cost. Taking market distortions into account, the CEA finds that the broader benefit of the SAFE Vehicles Rule is $39 billion a year, leading to an increase in real incomes and gross domestic product of $53 billion a year, or about 0.3 percent.

The CEA finds that the benefits of deregulation tend to skew toward the lower-income quintiles, suggesting that lower-income households may have benefited most, relative to household income, from the Administration's deregulatory actions. This finding is driven by the fact that deregulation often reduces the prices of economic necessities—such as groceries, electricity, prescription drugs, health insurance, and telecommunications—thereby making deregulatory actions progressive because lower-income quintiles spend a disproportionately larger fraction of their income, relative to higher-income quintiles, on necessities. Specifically, the gains from the deregulatory actions discussed in this chapter amount to 3.7 percent of the average income of the poorest fifth of households, compared with only 0.8 percent of the richest fifth, suggesting that they benefited the poorest households four times as much as the richest ones.

When the CEA examined the effect of a subset of the Trump Administration's deregulatory agenda for the 2020 *Economic Report of the President*, it estimated that, after 5 to 10 years, these deregulations would lead to an increase in real incomes of $3,100 per household a year. These previous findings, combined with our distributional analysis, suggest that the prioritization of sensible regulatory reform has particularly benefited the lowest-income households and allowed the U.S. economy to reach record-setting levels before the COVID-19 pandemic. A persistent focus on regulatory reform will play a critical role in the U.S. economy's return to the levels of economic prosperity it achieved before the COVID-19 pandemic.

n this chapter, we briefly review the Administration's regulatory reform progress and find that the Administration has slowed the pace of significant regulations issued compared with previous Administrations.[1] While executive agencies added an average of 275 significant regulations a year between presidential years (PYs) 2001 and 2016, President Trump added an average of only 74 per year, excluding deregulatory actions.[2] We also find that in fiscal year (FY) 2020, the Trump Administration is likely to achieve additional cost savings for a fourth consecutive year. We also discuss Executive Order 13891 (EO 13891), which directs executive branch agencies to publish their guidance documents on easily searchable public websites, marking an important step toward increasing the transparency and accessibility of the documentation that regulates all sectors of the U.S. economy.

In the next section, the CEA estimates the benefits associated with the SAFE Vehicles Rule, one of the Trump Administration's most significant deregulatory actions. This rule right-sizes CO_2 emissions standards for automobile manufacturers and establishes a slower rate of stringency increase through 2026. The CEA finds that compared with the 2012 rule, the SAFE Vehicles Rule will lead to $26 billion in savings a year for car manufacturers and consumers, and will deliver roughly 300,000 more new vehicles annually than the previous rule at a similar total cost. In addition, accounting for the effects of the rule on factor markets, the CEA estimates that the SAFE Vehicles Rule will increase the real incomes of Americans by $53 billion a year, or $416 per household a year, over the 2021–29 period.

Finally, the CEA examines how the gains from regulatory reform are distributed across income quintiles. Federal agencies must analyze whether a proposed deregulatory action reduces regulatory costs and whether the cost savings are larger than the benefits forgone from removing the regulation. Earlier, the CEA (2019) analyzed deregulatory actions that yield cost savings that are larger than the benefits forgone. In this chapter, the CEA finds that the cost savings from those regulations were distributed progressively. Specifically, we find that though regulatory reform benefits all households, those in the lowest income quintile likely benefit the most as a proportion of their income. The cost savings from the deregulatory actions we study amount to 3.7 percent of the average income of the lowest income quintile of households compared with only 0.8 percent for the highest income quintile of households. Our findings reaffirm that the Administration's regulatory reform efforts are helping consumers in low-income households, in part, because low-income

---

[1] The Office of Information and Regulatory Affairs deems a regulation significant when it may have an impact on the economy of at least $100 million, adversely affect the economy in a material way, raise novel legal or policy issues, or otherwise meet the criteria set forth in Section 3(f) of Executive Order 12866 from 1993. Among regulations deemed significant, those that are expected to have an impact on the economy of at least $100 million or adversely affect the economy in a material way are deemed economically significant.

[2] Presidential years begin on February 1 and end January 31 of the following year.

households spend a relatively large share of their budgets on necessities like groceries and medical care that are produced by heavily regulated sectors of the economy.

Regulation in Review

The Trump Administration's regulatory reform agenda has reduced unnecessary regulatory burdens while continuing to protect workers, public health, safety, and the environment. This section discusses three major executive orders that implement this agenda. As directed by Executive Order (EO) 13771 and EO 13777, executive branch agencies have sharply cut the rate at which they introduce new regulations and have adhered to regulatory budgets. Under EO 13891, executive branch agencies have improved public access to their regulatory guidance documents.

EO 13771, which was signed on January 30, 2017, requires executive branch agencies to remove two regulations for each new regulatory action.[3] EO 13777, which was signed on February 24, 2017, further requires agencies to evaluate their regulations on a periodic basis and to make recommendations to repeal, replace, or modify them to alleviate unnecessary regulatory burdens. The Administration surpassed its obligations under these EOs in FY 2019, with executive agencies issuing 150 deregulatory actions while issuing only 35 new significant regulatory actions. Between FYs 2017 and 2019, the Trump Administration achieved roughly a 7:1 ratio of deregulatory to significant regulatory actions. Focusing on significant regulations, the Administration has achieved a ratio of 2.5 significant deregulatory actions to 1 significant regulatory action between FYs 2017 and 2019.

Figure 6-1 shows the total numbers of significant rules, which include economically significant rules and other significant rules that meet part of the definition for economic significance or are important for other reasons described in EO 12866 (see note 1). During the Trump Administration, the average number of economically significant regulations, excluding deregulatory actions, was only 26 per PY. The Trump Administration's average number of economically significant regulations remains below the average of 52 economically significant regulatory actions per year between PYs 2001 and 2016. Including both economically significant and other significant rules, executive branch agencies added an average of 275 significant regulatory actions per year between PYs 2001 and 2016. Between PYs 2017 and 2019, the average number of significant regulations each year was only 74—excluding deregulatory

---

[3] The Office of Management and Budget defines an EO 13771 regulatory action as (1) a significant regulatory action as defined in Section 3(f) of EO 12866 that has been finalized and that imposes total costs greater than zero; or (2) a significant guidance document (e.g., significant interpretive guidance) reviewed by the Office of Information and Regulatory Affairs under the procedures of EO 12866 that have been finalized and that impose total costs greater than zero.

Figure 6-1. Significant Final Rules Excluding Deregulatory Actions, by Presidential Years 2001–19

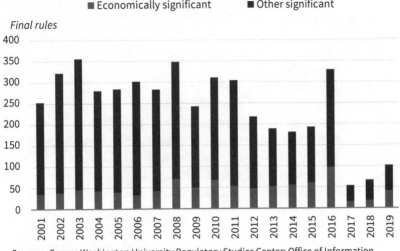

Sources: George Washington University Regulatory Studies Center; Office of Information and Regulatory Affairs; CEA calculations.

Note: Presidential years begin in February and end in January of the following year. Rule counts for 2017, 2018, and 2019 exclude rules that were considered significant deregulatory actions; before 2017, the CEA estimates that there was about one such action a year.

actions. This illustrates that the Trump Administration has slowed the pace of significant regulations more than any administration since 2001.

In addition to the two-for-one requirement, EO 13771 required executive branch agencies to adhere to annual regulatory budgets with cost savings targets set by the Office of Management and Budget. In FY 2019, the Trump Administration reached its cost savings targets for the third year in a row, with executive branch agencies eliminating $13.5 billion of regulatory costs. Between FYs 2017 and 2019, these agencies eliminated nearly $51 billion in regulatory costs. In FY 2020, the Administration is likely to achieve additional regulatory cost savings for a fourth year. This four-year stretch of regulatory reform significantly reduced the regulatory burdens that these agencies impose.

In 2019, President Trump issued EO 13891 to address the accumulation of regulatory guidance documents that Federal agencies use to clarify their regulations. EO 13891 requires executive branch agencies to make guidance documents more accessible to the public by building a "single, searchable, indexed website that contains, or links to, all of the agencies' respective guidance documents." To comply, agencies were given until June 27, 2020, after which they needed to submit any existing guidance documents that they had failed to publicly post as if they were new guidance. Crews (2020) estimates that agencies posted more than 54,010 documents as of July 7, 2020. Though many Federal agencies have asked for waivers on compliance deadlines, EO 13891 is a significant step toward bringing transparency and oversight to Federal guidance documents.

The Administration's regulatory agenda has differed from that of previous administrations due to its emphasis on limiting the burden of Federal government regulation. After four years of regulatory reform, there has been an observable change in the cost of and rate of regulation. The establishment of a regulatory budget and the commitment to removing two regulations for every one new significant regulatory action have led to significant cost savings for American firms and consumers. Supported by the improved public access to agency guidance, these changes are enhancing the Nation's economic efficiency and competitiveness. The CEA discussed the impact of many deregulatory actions on real income growth in an earlier report (CEA 2019). The next section examines one of the largest deregulatory actions finalized in 2020: the SAFE Vehicles Rule.

The Safer Affordable Fuel Efficient (SAFE) Vehicles Rule

The largest deregulatory action finalized under the Trump Administration has been the SAFE Vehicles Rule. This rule, which amended CO_2 emission standards for light vehicles and appropriately increased stringency, now gives automakers greater freedom to build and sell vehicles as demanded by consumers. It accomplishes this goal by reducing the CO_2 emission requirements for light vehicles produced by a manufacturer. Given the inherent relationship between CO_2 emissions and fuel economy, this has also had the effect of reducing the required minimum fuel economy standards (in miles per gallon, mpg). Though the SAFE Vehicles Rule promotes fuel efficiency, the fuel economy standards grow in stringency through 2026 at a lower rate than was prescribed by prior policy to appropriately balance policy considerations. This section estimates the potential cost savings associated with the SAFE Vehicles Rule as well as its distributional effects.

The corporate average fuel economy (CAFE) and greenhouse gas (GHG) regulations are written jointly by the U.S. Department of Transportation (DOT) and the Environmental Protection Agency (EPA) to ensure harmonization between the two standards, given the direct relationship between fuel used and GHG emissions.[4] More stringent GHG standards increase quality-adjusted automobile prices. In a supply-and-demand diagram, such as figure 6-2, the gold line represents the marginal cost of producing another vehicle and the red line represents consumers' willingness to pay for vehicles. The GHG standard

---

[4] Given the harmonization of the standards, we refer to these standards as GHG standards for brevity.

Figure 6-2. Vehicle Market Equilibrium with GHG Standards

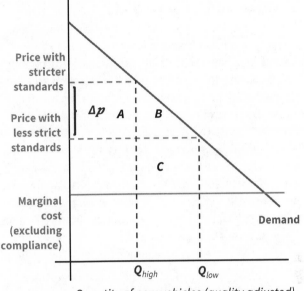

Price of new vehicles (quality adjusted)

Price with stricter standards

Δp A   B

Price with less strict standards

C

Marginal cost (excluding compliance)

Demand

Q_{high} Q_{low}

Quantity of new vehicles (quality adjusted)

Note: GHG = greenhouse gas.

drives a wedge between the marginal cost of producing a vehicle (excluding regulatory compliance costs) and the marginal willingness of consumers to purchase one, raising the price of the vehicle above the marginal cost of production. The 2012 rule would have increased the wedge by about $2,200 per vehicle by model year 2026 relative to the SAFE Vehicles rule, as represented by Δp in figure 6-2.

The EPA and DOT rules generally allow firms to comply by purchasing credits from other firms that have overcomplied, thus leading to the lowest overall cost of compliance for the industry. The approach to this analysis assumes that the price at which automakers buy and sell compliance credits reveals the private cost of meeting the standards, because it should incorporate both the cost of building marginally more efficient vehicles and the willingness of consumers to buy them. To estimate prices of compliance credits, the CEA draws from public records on nearly $700 million in credit transactions that occurred over seven years (2012–18), which provide a simple and transparent basis for our cost estimates.

Inferring costs and benefits based on actual firm behavior—in this case the price at which automakers buy and sell GHG compliance credits—eliminates a great deal of guesswork. Credit prices incorporate a wealth of information that is otherwise hard to observe, such as the extra cost of building a more efficient vehicle and the willingness of consumers to pay for such vehicles. This approach, also known as the revealed preference approach, differs from much of the existing literature on the costs of CAFE and GHG standards, which examines volumes of automotive engineering data and assesses consumer's driving habits, fuel-purchasing routines (including attempts to value consumers' time spent pumping fuel), and decisions about when to scrap a vehicle.[5]

In the revealed preference approach, we replace engineering assumptions with economic assumptions such as cost-minimization and pass-through of costs, in which case credit prices convey the information needed to estimate the private costs and benefits of complying with the standards.[6] To the extent that manufacturers minimize the cost of producing a given model and can freely trade credits, the observed credit price is equal to the marginal cost of reducing the manufacturer's fleet-wide emissions.[7] To the extent that the cost of GHG credits is reflected in the prices consumers pay for vehicles (i.e., pass-through), the cost also reflects consumers' willingness to have vehicles with more weight or other attributes that produce additional emissions as measured by the GHG program. This includes many dimensions of consumer preferences, including the value that consumers place on fuel savings over the life of a vehicle.

The costs and valuations permit quantifying the private net costs of changing the standards because the market complies with a stricter standard through some combination of changing vehicle attributes and adjusting prices to shift sales to lower-emission vehicles. These private net costs are pivotal for understanding the effects of the SAFE Vehicles Rule. Prior analyses of the standards show that private costs and benefits dwarf environmental costs and benefits (Bento et al. 2018).

The value of compliance credits equals the private net costs of changing the standards, which arise through some combination of changing vehicle attributes and skewing sales to lower-emission vehicles. These private net costs are pivotal for understanding the effects of the SAFE Vehicles Rule: prior analyses of the standards show that private costs and benefits dwarf environmental costs and benefits (Bento et al. 2018).

GHG Credit Transaction Data

The price at which automakers buy or sell GHG compliance credits is not publicly available. However, because credit revenue is significant for Tesla, it reports the revenues in its financial reports to the Securities and Exchange

---

[5] See, e.g., regulatory impact analyses (EPA/DOT 2012, 2020).

[6] EPA/DOT (2016, 2020) assume a one-for-one pass-through of compliance costs to consumer prices, as we do.

[7] Note that trading was quite limited in the initial years of the program, that these data are not widely available for every trade, and that some companies announced intentions to not trade, even when it represented a lower-cost way to comply.

Commission. The reports indicate that Tesla earned $695 million in revenues (in 2018 dollars) from the sale of GHG credits over the years 2012–18.[8] For the same period, EPA data show that Tesla was the second largest seller of GHG credits, after Honda, since GHG credit trading began in 2012. Tesla's sales have accounted for nearly a quarter of all sales in the U.S. credit market (EPA 2019). These revenue and sales numbers suggest that roughly $3 billion in credit transactions have occurred across the industry since the GHG credit trading program began.

Using Tesla's credit sales and revenues, we calculate the average credit price over the 2012–16 period.[9] We associate this price with the standards of the 2012–21 period because GHG credits earned during model years 2010–16 are used through model year 2021. Because credits are banked and traded across automakers and fleets, all model years 2012 through 2021 are effectively a single fleet for GHG compliance purposes.[10] Focusing on the 2012–16 price also has the advantage of the period being before President Trump's election, which would have changed expectations about the value of the credits later in the 2012–21 period.

When calculating the credit price, we adjust Tesla's 2012–16 credit revenues to incorporate their timing, using a 7 percent interest rate to standardize all revenues as if they were earned in 2016, which is when the industry's fleet shifted from performing above the standard and accumulating credits to performing below the standard and drawing down credits. Dividing total revenues by the quantity of credits sold over the period gives an average price of $86 per ton of CO_2 emissions, or $116 per mpg per vehicle (in 2018 dollars).[11] [12]

The $116 credit price is a lower-bound estimate of the actual average price at which Tesla sold its credits. Automakers are not required to report the timing of transactions, which complicates efforts to identify credit sales in individual years. However, automakers cannot sell credits that they do not have. Over the 2012–16 period, at most Tesla could have sold all the credits

---

[8] For several years, Tesla's annual filing with the Securities and Exchange Commission did not report revenues separately for zero emissions vehicle credits and GHG credits, but this breakout is available from the company's quarterly filings with the commission and was reported by *Forbes* (2017). This allows us to ensure that we are not including zero emissions vehicle revenues in our GHG revenues.

[9] We note that Leard and McConnell (2017) were the first to match Tesla credit revenue with trade volumes to infer credit prices.

[10] Because the GHG standard increased in each of the years 2012–21, we expect manufacturers to accumulate GHG credits in the early years and spend them in the later years. EPA records show this to be the case, with most manufacturers having a credit shortfall in model year 2017; see EPA (2019, figure 5.17).

[11] In 2014 Kia and Hyundai forfeited credits in a settlement with the EPA, which were valued at $51 per ton (in 2018 dollars and with interest until 2016). Because the price is not based on a market transaction, we do not include it in our estimation of the 2012–16 price.

[12] When calculating the credit price, we take into account the small number of GHG credits that Tesla sold in the Canadian GHG market and whose revenues would presumably be included in the credit revenues reported to the Securities and Exchange Commission.

that it earned through model year 2015, which is the quantity that we used to estimate the 2012–16 price. If Tesla sold any less, the estimated price would be higher because the same revenue would be divided by a smaller number of credits.

Estimating the Curve for the Marginal Cost of Compliance

Our credit price data and a prior study provide two relevant points that allows us to project what the market equilibrium price of compliance credits would be for any given standard.[13] The Tesla credit data described above provide one observation on compliance costs: credits cost $116 per mpg per vehicle when the standard was about 35 mpg, the average over the 2012–21 period.[14] The second data point is for model year 2006, for which Anderson and Sallee (2011) estimate the average marginal cost of tightening CAFE standards by 1 mpg to be $18 per vehicle. The CAFE standard during that year was 24.8 mpg.[15]

With two observations on compliance costs at different standards, we can project the relationship between the standard measured in mpg and the marginal effect of the standard on the marginal (production and opportunity) cost of manufacturing a vehicle (figure 6-3).[16] The horizontal axis measures the standard, while the vertical axis measures additions to the marginal cost of each vehicle. The area under the curve measures the additional cost of the standard per vehicle. The SAFE Vehicles Rule will raise standards for 2021–26 at a rate of 1.5 percent a year. Using fleet data from the 2012 rule rather than the SAFE Vehicles final rule, the standards reach 45.6 in 2026, while the 2012 rule prescribed a standard of 54.5 for model year 2025, which we assume will also apply to model year 2026.

If going from 24.8 to 35.8 mpg increased the marginal cost of tightening the standard from $18 to $116, then the marginal cost of further increasing the standard must be greater than $116. From the linear credit-supply assumption, the CEA projects that the credit price would be $203 per mpg for model year 2026 under the standards established in the SAFE Vehicles Rule (a standard of 45.6 mpg), as compared with about $283 per mpg for model year 2026 under

---

[13] The CEA's theoretical analysis of models with constant elasticity of substitution between types of vehicles has shown a linear credit-supply schedule (with respect to mpg) to be a good approximation of the actual schedule, except when the standard is especially tight, in which case linear supply underestimates compliance costs. This suggests that our estimate of the marginal cost of complying with the 2012 rule is likely conservative.

[14] Some manufacturers let credits expire in 2014, which may suggest that the standard may not have been binding at that time. However, 2009 credits could not be traded among automakers. In addition, the credits that expired were 2009 credits that could only be banked for five years, unlike credits earned in model years 2010–16, which could be banked and used through model year 2021.

[15] Although this estimate of the marginal cost of compliance is for CAFE standards, it remains our best estimate of the cost of compliance of a GHG standard of 24.8 mpg, given that there was not a GHG standard at the time.

[16] Figure 6-3 is labeled with fuel economy standards rather than emissions standards because mpg are more familiar to readers than tons of GHG.

Figure 6-3. GHG Credit Market Equilibrium for Various Standards

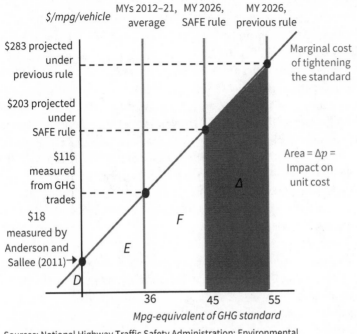

Sources: National Highway Traffic Safety Administration; Environmental Protection Agency; Leard and McConnell (2017); CEA calculations.
Note: GHG = greenhouse gas; MY = model year.

the tighter standard originally put in place by the 2012 rule (a standard of about 54.5 mpg). For each year of the 2021–29 period, we use the average of the two marginal costs, which can then be multiplied by the mpg difference in the standards to give the savings per vehicle from the SAFE Rule. The resulting value is equivalent to the green area in figure 6-3.

The CEA estimates that areas A, B, and C of figure 6-2 represent $26 billion a year in costs to new automobile consumers and producers. Relative to the SAFE Vehicles Rule, the 2012 rule results in roughly 300,000 fewer new vehicles delivered to consumers every year at a similar total cost, including fuel costs and the opportunity costs of vehicle features.

The rectangular area A of figure 6-2 accounts for the largest portion and is the product of the number of vehicles sold and the effect of changing the standards on costs per vehicle. The marginal cost of compliance curve shown in figure 6-3 allows us to calculate the cost of the 2012 rule per vehicle (for model year 2025) compared with the cost of the SAFE Vehicles Rule. Doing so indicates that phasing in the higher standard would eventually increase average quality-adjusted prices by about $2,200.[17] For the years 2021–29, the average annualized quality-adjusted price increase would be about $1,600. This amount corresponds to in figure 6-2.[18]

Applying the $1,600 average annual savings to the more than 16 million new vehicles sold annually in the United States gives an annualized average increase in consumer benefits of $25 billion each year for model years 2021–29, equivalent to area A in figure 6-2.[19]

Areas B and C of figure 6-2 are also part of the cost of increasing the standards. Estimating them requires an estimate of the impact of increasing the standards on vehicle sales. To identify the new quantity of vehicles sold annually, the CEA uses a price elasticity of demand for new vehicles of −0.4 (Berry, Levinsohn, and Pakes 2004), model-year-specific increments to vehicle costs (derived as above) relative to the average 2018 vehicle sales price, and model-year-specific projections of vehicle sales.[20] The sales impact is roughly 300,000 vehicles a year, which makes area B about $0.3 billion a year. Area C requires an estimate of the effect of the SAFE Vehicle Rule standards, relative to no standards, costs per vehicle. This baseline private cost per vehicle is shown in figure 6-3 as areas D, E, and F. Applying it to the change in vehicle sales gives an estimate of figure 6-2's area C of roughly $0.4 billion a year.

Because the emissions and fuel-efficiency requirements are imposed on the supply chain rather than on the final consumer, it follows from the pass-through assumption that costs of the regulation are reflected in consumer prices. The $26 billion in annual private costs in the market for vehicles is therefore measured as a productivity loss, in the sense that the economy produces less private value when assessed at market prices, using the same factors of production—capital and labor.

The productivity loss is experienced by market participants that supply less capital in the long run and less labor in the short run.[21] This means even less real income and, to the extent that factor markets are distorted by taxes, additional private costs. Using a marginal cost of public funds of 0.5, the decline in labor and capital supplied adds $13 billion in private costs (0.5 x $26

---

[17] To the extent that compliance with tighter standards is achieved entirely by adding or changing model designs in ways that reduce emissions and increase fuel economy without other perceptible effects on consumers' valuation of the vehicles, the average price increase is the same as the average quality-adjusted price increase.

[18] If we assume a flat $116 per mpg per vehicle in compliance costs, the SAFE rule saves consumers $1,032 per car, which is similar to the EPA/DOT (2020) regulatory impact analysis estimate.

[19] We use a 7 percent real discount rate for the purposes of annualizing 0-year cost profiles. All amounts are in 2018 dollars.

[20] The average vehicle price is from the *Kelley Blue Book*. Model year 2020–29 sales forecasts are from EPA/DOT (2020, table VI-189).

[21] We adopt the "balanced growth" assumption that productivity has income and substitution effects on labor supply that offset in the long run. As people earn more, they demand more leisure (the income effect); but rising wages has the opposite effect, of increasing the value of work relative to leisure, which encourages more work and less leisure (the substitution effect).

Figure 6-4. Consumer Savings from the SAFE Vehicles Rule as a Percentage of Income, by Income Quintile

Reduction in new car expenditures as a percentage of income

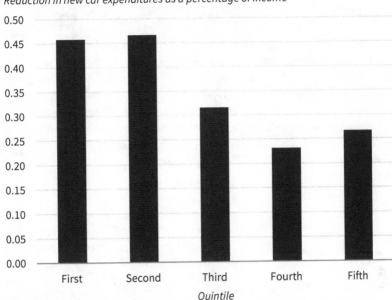

Sources: Bureau of Labor Statistics; CEA calculations.

billion). If the full market value of the factors supplied is considered, assuming a marginal tax rate of 0.48 (CEA 2019), the total gross domestic product loss in factor markets is about $27 billion ($13 billion / 0.48).

In total, the higher standards reduce real income and gross domestic product by $53 billion a year ($26 billion in the regulated market and $27 billion in factor markets), which is about 0.3 percent.[22] This makes the SAFE Vehicles Rule one of the single most effective deregulatory actions that the Trump Administration has finalized thus far (CEA 2019). The estimated $26 billion in consumer savings from the SAFE Vehicles Rule can be distributed among different household income groups. We allocate the savings across income quintiles based on each quintile's share of aggregate spending on new vehicles, as reported in the Consumer Expenditure Survey. Figure 6-4 depicts the savings as a percentage of the posttax income of each group. The savings from the SAFE Vehicles Rule disproportionately benefit lower-income consumers, with the savings in the lowest income quintile exceeding those of the highest quintile

---

[22] As with many of the other regulations that the CEA has analyzed previously (CEA 2019), the SAFE Vehicles Rule has an effect on real income whose dollar amount significantly exceeds the dollars of net (private and social) benefits. This is primarily because net benefits account for opportunity costs—for example, the value of leisure if not working—while real income does not.

by 66 percent. This is because a larger share of the posttax income of lower-income consumers goes toward the purchase of new vehicles.

The Potentially Regressive Nature of Regulation

Our analysis of the SAFE Vehicles Rule illustrates that the burden of regulatory costs can fall disproportionately on low-income households. And though a standard question in public finance is who bears the burden of the taxes needed to fund government expenditures, much less is known about who bears the burden of the costs of regulations. We find that deregulation can help consumers in low-income households by easing restrictions that disproportionately increase the prices of the goods and services they purchase. Because high-income households spend proportionally less on economic necessities than low-income households, the deregulation of such goods and services has progressive benefits.[23]

In 2019, the CEA studied 20 deregulatory actions of the Trump Administration and estimated that, after 5 to 10 years, they will together raise real incomes by 1.3 percent. In this section, we revisit 10 of these regulations to assess their distributional effect. We find that many of them will lower the prices of necessities—such as groceries, electricity, prescription drugs, health insurance, telecommunications, and other consumer goods and services—and will likely benefit lower-income households more than higher-income households. Specifically, we find that the cost savings from this subset of deregulatory actions—together with the SAFE Vehicles Rule—amount to 3.7 percent of the average income of the lowest income quintile of households compared with only 0.8 percent for the highest-income quintile of households (figure 6-10). This suggests that these deregulations benefited, relative to their income, the lowest-income quintile households four times as much as those in the highest-income quintile.

Progressive and Regressive Tax Structures

To evaluate how a tax burden is shared, public finance economists examine whether the burden increases with an individuals' capacity to pay (Duclos 2008). When the burden of a tax relative to income is higher for high-income individuals, the tax is described as progressive. In the United States, for example, Congress designed the Federal income tax to impose progressively higher marginal rates on earners with higher incomes. In tax year 2017, the lowest half of filers accounted for 11 percent of the adjusted gross income share while the highest quintile accounted for 63 percent. However, due to the progressive structure of the Federal income tax, the lowest half of filers represented less than 3 percent of total Federal income taxes, while filers with an adjusted gross

---

[23] The concept of economic necessities defined this way is broader than the way the word "necessity" is commonly used outside economics.

Figure 6-5. Illustrative Impact of a 15 Percent Grocery Tax, by Income Quintile

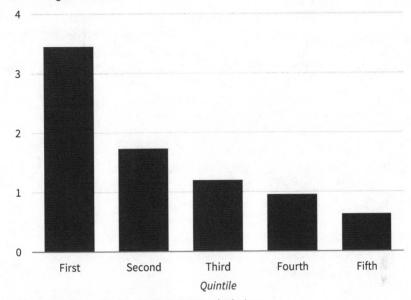

Percentage of income

Sources: Bureau of Labor Statistics; CEA calculations.

income in the highest quintile accounted for over 82 percent. Conversely, when the burden of a tax relative to income is lower for high-income individuals, the tax is considered regressive.

Sales taxes and other consumption-based taxes, such as the value-added tax, tend to be regressive. According to the technical economic definition, a good or service is a necessity when the income-elasticity of demand is less than 1—for example, when a 10 percent increase in income leads to an increase in consumption of less than 10 percent. Because low-income households spend a higher proportion of their incomes on necessities like groceries and medical care, sales taxes on these goods are regressive. Figure 6-5 illustrates the regressivity of a 15 percent sales tax on groceries. Households in the lowest fifth of the income distribution would pay 3.5 percent of their income in grocery sales taxes, while households in the top fifth would pay 0.6 percent. The grocery tax would have an impact on consumers in the lowest income quintile, which, relative to their income, is over five times larger than the impact on the highest-income quintile. To reduce the regressivity of sales taxes, most States exempt groceries and some other necessities from the sales tax (Figueroa and Waxman 2017). Other States offer credits or rebates to low-income households to help offset some of the regressivity of their sales taxes.

The Harm Regressive Regulation Systems Pose

Many regulations may be regressive because they increase the costs of producing goods and services that are necessities (e.g., groceries and medical care). When complying with regulations increases the costs of production, firms increase the prices charged to consumers. Because low-income households spend proportionately more of their income on necessities, these regulation-induced price hikes on necessities are similar to regressive sales taxes. However, the magnitude of the effect of a regulation on consumer prices depends on how firms respond to production cost increases, which in turn depends on market conditions. After a regulation, the market reaches a new equilibrium, where consumers pay a higher price for the good (figure 6-6).

In the case shown in figure 6-6, firms are able to pass their regulatory costs fully through to consumers through higher consumer prices. In other cases with different market structures (not shown), a full pass-through of regulatory costs does not always occur. For example, in response to a $1 increase in the cost of production, a firm might only raise prices by 50 cents due to competitive constraints. Figure 6-6 can also be reinterpreted to show another possible effect of regulation, where the regulation acts as a barrier to entry that limits new competition, resulting in a higher equilibrium price with above-normal profits or "economic rents" for established firms. In general, regulations will have effects on consumers and firms, conventionally measured by changes in consumer and producer surpluses. Tracing through the producer surplus effects to the distribution of the incomes of factors of production can be complex. (See box 6-1.)

Low-income households spend more of their income on goods and services in general because they have lower savings rates, making regulations that increase the price of these goods and services more regressive (Dynan, Skinner, and Zeldes 2004). Households in the lower-income quintiles spend larger fractions of their incomes for almost all the categories of goods and services tracked by the Consumer Expenditure Surveys (CEX). Thus, deregulation is often progressive because it removes regressive regulatory cost burdens that inflate the prices of necessities. Figure 6-7 shows spending patterns for some important categories of goods and services. Even when regulations do not intentionally target necessities, they can have the unintended consequence of imposing a regressive cost burden. Chambers, Collins, and Krause (2019) find that regulatory compliance costs increase the prices of necessities including energy, food, healthcare and health insurance, housing, and transportation. Unlike sales taxes, however, policymakers typically do not exempt the production of necessities from regulations.

Other regulations can be regressive because they intentionally target consumer choices that vary with income. Product standards are a common example because they mandate that products must have certain features or

Figure 6-6. The Impact of Regulation in a Competitive Market

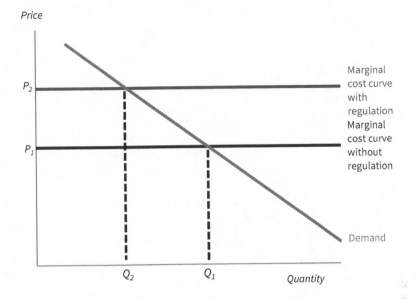

Figure 6-7. Percentage of Income Spent on Outlay Category, by Income Quintile

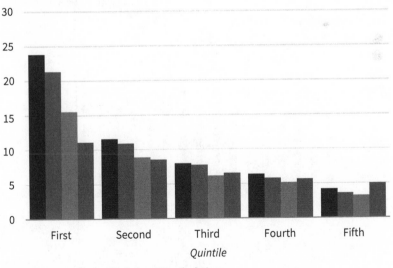

Sources: Bureau of Labor Statistics; CEA calculations.
Note: Utilities includes utilities, fuel, and public services.

Empowering Economic Freedom by Reducing Regulatory Burdens | 189

Box 6-1. Effects of Regulation on Small Businesses

Regulations can have regressive effects on small business because of economies of scale. For example, if a regulation requires that firms establish retirement accounts, larger firms' average costs will be lower because they can spread the fixed costs over a larger pool of employees. Given that the cost of retirement accounts are already lower for larger firms than for small firms, large firms, all else being equal, will be more likely to already have retirement accounts established before the regulation, thereby causing the regulation to have more of an impact on small than large firms.

Policymakers often attempt to offset regulatory burdens for small businesses by exempting businesses with a certain level of revenue or number of employees. However, the threshold exemptions distort the market and can cause businesses to cluster near the threshold limit. In France, where many regulations apply after a firm reaches 50 employees, Garicano, LeLarge, and Reene (2016) find that firms cluster below the employee threshold to enjoy regulatory exemptions. Though clustering reduces firm's regulatory burden, it also reduces total welfare and the productivity of the economy. In the United States, the Affordable Care Act used a similar approach by reducing the requirements imposed on businesses with fewer than 50 full-time employees.

Congress has passed several pieces of legislation that attempt to reduce the regulatory burden placed on small entities. The Regulatory Flexibility

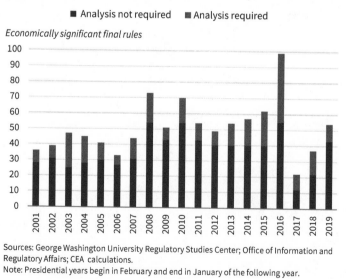

Figure 6-i. Economically Significant Final Rules with Regulatory Flexibility Analysis for Small Businesses, by Presidential Years 2001–19

Sources: George Washington University Regulatory Studies Center; Office of Information and Regulatory Affairs; CEA calculations.
Note: Presidential years begin in February and end in January of the following year.

Act of 1980 requires that agencies perform regulatory flexibility analyses for regulations that may have an effect on small entities, with specific attention to competitiveness and fairness; see figure 6-i. In 1996, Congress passed the Small Business Regulatory Enforcement Fairness Act, creating panels that enable small entities and regulatory agencies to interact with regulators during the regulatory process. In 2019, the Trump Administration issued EO 13891 and EO 13892, which required Federal agencies to make their guidance easily accessible and make sure that all enforcement actions are transparent and fair. These EOs are especially important for small businesses that may otherwise lack the capability to understand regulations relevant to their business.

attributes, whose desirability can depend on one's income. To the extent that the mandated features are normal goods (i.e., demand for the feature increases as income increases), high-income consumers would purchase more of the mandated feature even without the product standard. If their demand for the regulated feature is strong enough, the products purchased by high-income consumers will likely already meet the product standard. Although product standards are less binding or even nonbinding on high-income consumers, these standards impose costs on low-income households, which are required to pay higher prices for features they do not highly value.

Energy efficiency standards are another example of regulations that can be regressive due to the consumer choices they target. For instance, consumers who use their air conditioners on most days of the summer might find that energy savings pay back the higher price of a more efficient appliance within a few years. Low-income consumers who can only afford to use their air conditioners infrequently face a longer payback period and might be better off purchasing a lower-price and less-efficient appliance. Therefore, energy-efficient appliances and vehicles are more valuable to consumers who use their appliances and vehicles regularly. The CAFE standards, discussed above, have a similar effect. Levinson (2019) finds that high-income households purchase more fuel-efficient cars. Levison estimates that the CAFE standards disproportionately burden low-income households, which are less likely to prioritize fuel efficiency, absent CAFE. In other words, the CAFE standards may have less impact on high-income households because they already prefer to purchase more fuel-efficient cars.

Some health insurance regulations include product standards that can also be regressive. Health insurance regulations related to the Affordable Care Act (ACA) are notable examples. The ACA's individual mandate requires non-exempt consumers to have one of several enumerated forms of health insurance coverage. Through tax year 2018, the Internal Revenue Service enforced the individual mandate with a monetary penalty; the Tax Cuts and Jobs Act

Figure 6-8. Individual Mandate Penalties as a Percentage of Income, by Income Quintile

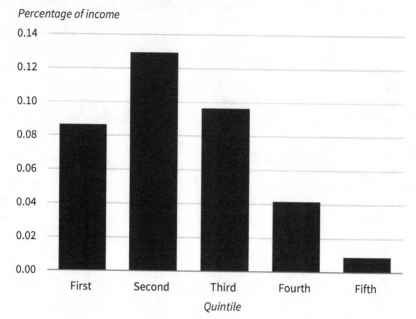

Percentage of income

Sources: Bureau of Labor Statistics; Internal Revenue Service; CEA calculations.

of 2017 set the mandate penalty to zero, becoming effective in the 2019 tax year. Because most high-income households already had coverage through ACA-compliant insurance plans, the mandate penalty fell disproportionately on lower- and middle-income households (figure 6-8). Households in the lowest income quintile bore a proportionately smaller burden than households in the second-lowest quintile because households in the lowest income quintile were more likely to be covered by Medicaid or receive subsidies to purchase ACA-compliant insurance. After the second lowest income quintile, the burden of the individual mandate penalty was steeply regressive. Other regulations—including the 2016 short-term, limited duration insurance rule—banned a number of insurance options that were popular among low-income households that made choices based on what was best for them.

Academic research provides several explanations for why the regulatory process leads to product standards and other forms of regulations that intentionally target certain consumer choices. Instead of always serving the general public interest, the regulatory apparatus may be prone to capture by special interests (Stigler 1971). Regulatory capture could cause policymakers to enact legislation and regulators to issue regulations that privilege certain groups, to the detriment of other groups, such as the public or their competitors. Mulligan and Philipson (2000) argue that wealthier portions of society may advocate for regulations that impose their preferences on the general population and offset some of those costs through a progressive tax system. Similarly, Thomas (2012) suggests that regulators may focus on prioritizing regulations that reduce risks for wealthier households at the cost of low-income households.

Lower-Income Households Often Gain the Most from Regulatory Reform

In an earlier report, the CEA estimated that the effect on real incomes associated with 20 deregulatory actions under the Trump Administration will total $235 billion a year (CEA 2019, 2020), which we also discussed in chapter 3 of the 2020 *Economic Report of the President*. We estimated that these 20 deregulatory actions will raise real incomes by reducing the prices of consumer goods, and by increasing competition, productivity, and wages. An important part of our earlier analysis was to account for the excess burden that regulatory actions impose on factor markets for labor and capital. In this section, we focus on the distributional implications of the reductions in the prices of consumer goods. The narrower scope of the analysis means that some of the deregulatory actions considered in the earlier CEA report are not part of this study (table 6-1). Though the CEA has not studied all the deregulatory actions taken since 2017, our analysis in this section builds upon our previous work, which used a sampling procedure to identify the largest deregulatory actions in terms of economic impact (CEA 2019, 2020).

We combine our estimates of the cost savings from deregulatory actions with data from the CEX. We attribute the reduction in industry costs to an expenditure category listed in the CEX shares of annual expenditures by income quintile. For example, we estimated that the Federal Communication Commission's (FCC) repeal of the Protecting and Promoting the Open Internet and issuance of Restoring Internet Freedom Order would provide $16.1 billion in cost savings to Internet users.[24] The expenditure category of the CEX for consumers most affected by Internet prices is the computer information services (Internet access) category. We used the expenditure shares by income quintile to calculate the reduction in Internet access expenditures as a fraction of total income (after tax) for each quintile. The results, shown in figure 6-9, show that relative to their incomes, the FCC's deregulation of internet access has an effect on consumers in the lowest income quintile that is five times larger than the effect on the highest income quintile.

---

[24] The CEA's distributional analysis focuses on regulatory cost savings that we predict are passed through to consumers who pay lower prices for the goods and services produced by the deregulated industries. Our earlier study finds substantial additional cost-savings in the markets for factors of production, i.e., in the labor and capital markets, as reported by the CEA (2019, table 6-1). Tracing through the factor market effects to their effects on the distribution of household incomes is a complex and challenging task that is beyond the scope of this *Report*. This narrower focus is only a portion of the total cost savings than we estimated in the earlier CEA report.

Figure 6-9. Consumer Savings on Internet Access from the Restoring Internet Freedom Rule, by Income Quintile

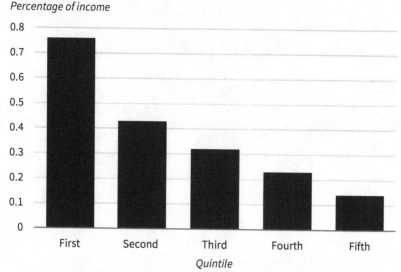

Percentage of income

Sources: Bureau of Labor Statistics; Bureau of Economic Analysis; CEA calculations.
Note: Values represent the CEA's estimates of consumer savings as a share of their income, which applied the Consumer Expenditure Survey's quintile and expenditure data to national income data.

We performed similar calculations for the set of deregulatory actions enacted since 2017 that reduced consumer prices (table 6-1). For some deregulatory actions, the distribution of the cost savings across income quintiles exactly follows the distribution of consumer expenditures in the relevant CEX category. Examples include deregulatory actions that we estimate will reduce the prices of electricity, prescription drugs, and Internet access. For other deregulatory actions, the distribution of cost savings across income quintiles reflects the fact that the original regulation targeted consumer choices that were more common among low-income households. Examples include health insurance deregulations and the deregulation of the short-term loan industry. We used additional information about consumer behavior in those markets to refine our estimates of the distribution of the cost savings across income quintiles.

When we total the results for the complete set of regulations we analyze, we find that the deregulatory actions are strongly progressive and reduce the disproportionate burden regulations impose on low-income households. We find that the gains from the deregulatory actions we study amount to 3.7 percent of the average income of the poorest fifth of households, compared with only 0.8 percent for the richest fifth (figure 6-10). The deregulatory actions have an effect on consumers in the lowest income quintile, which relative to

Table 6-1. Selected Deregulatory Actions' Annual Impact on Real Income

Name/Description	Impact on Real Income (in billion dollars a year)
Protecting the Privacy of Customers of Broadband and Other Telecommunications Services (Opt-In)	$22
Stream Protection Rule	$2
Definition of "Employer" Under Section 3(5) of ERISA- Association Health Plans (AHP Rule)	$17
Short-Term, Limited-Duration Insurance* (STLDI)	$13
Payday, Vehicle Title, and Certain High-Cost Installment Loans	$7
Scope of Sections 202(a) and (b) of Packers and Stockyards Act	$0
Waste Prevention, Production Subject to Royalties, and Resource Conservation; Rescission or Revision*	$0
Repeal of Protecting and Promoting the Open Internet and Issuance of Restoring Internet Freedom	$54
FDA and HHS Modernization Efforts	$32
The Tax Cuts and Jobs Act- Reduced the Individual Mandate Penalty to Zero	$28
Safer Affordable Fuel Efficient (SAFE) Vehicles Rule	$53
Total	$228

Source: CEA calculations.
Note: An asterisk (*) signifies the use of a shortened name for the regulation. All annual effects on real income are rounded to the nearest billion dollars. The impact on real incomes is estimated based on the full impact of the regulation, which may be realized in the future.

their income is over four times larger than the effect on the highest one. Above, we noted that we find that, with a hypothetical 15 percent tax on groceries, households in the lowest fifth of the income distribution would pay 3.5 percent of their income in grocery sales taxes, over five times larger than the effect on the highest-income quintile. The deregulatory actions we study removed cost burdens that were similar to a regressive tax on groceries.

Our analysis focuses on the distribution of the gains from regulatory reform that reduced the burdens costly regulations impose on consumers. Regulatory and deregulatory actions have both benefits and costs. The net effect of the actions on consumer welfare depends on the difference between benefits and costs, or the net benefits. The distribution of the net benefits of an action depends on the relative sizes of the benefits and costs and on the relative progressivity of how the benefits and costs are distributed (Bento, Freedman, and Lang 2015). Under Executive Order 12866 and Executive Order 13771, Federal agencies must analyze whether a proposed deregulatory action reduces regulatory costs and whether the cost savings are larger than the benefits forgone from removing the regulation. The CEA (2019, 2020) analyzed

Figure 6-10. Consumer Savings from Selected Deregulatory Actions and the SAFE Vehicles Rule, by Income Quintile

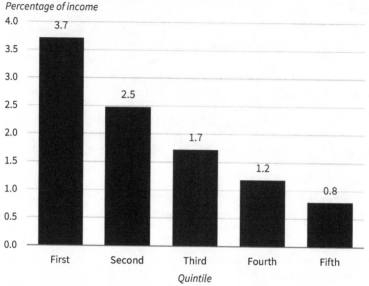

Percentage of income

Sources: Bureau of Labor Statistics; Bureau of Economic Analysis; CEA calculations.

deregulatory actions that yield cost savings that are larger than the benefits forgone, and we find that the cost savings are distributed progressively. Unless the forgone benefits of these rules were distributed more progressively than the costs, the distribution of the net benefits from these deregulations were progressive.

The Regressivity of Federal Regulation Offsets the Progressivity of Federal Taxes

Despite the deregulatory actions taken by the Trump Administration, a large amassed body of Federal regulations remains. The total cost of Federal regulations is difficult to estimate with precision. As of September 1, 2020, Federal agencies estimate that their regulations require that the U.S. public complete roughly 11.6 billion hours of paperwork at a cost of $150 billion each year. Between 2006 and 2018, the Federal Government issued an average of 3,600 regulations each year, not including guidance and other documents that some observers describe as "regulatory dark matter," which is another form of regulation that does not always include public participation (Crews 2017). Recent estimates of the total annual costs of Federal regulations range from

Figure 6-11. Consumer Savings from Deregulatory Actions Compared with the Federal Tax Rate, by Income Quintile

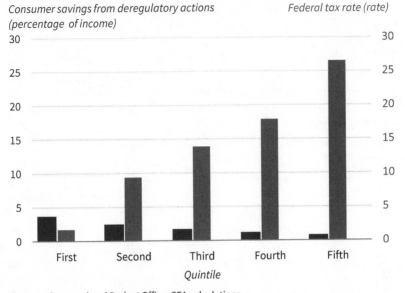

Consumer savings from deregulatory actions (percentage of income)

Federal tax rate (rate)

Quintile

Sources: Congressional Budget Office; CEA calculations.

Note: The CBO's estimates of each income quintile's average Federal tax rate includes individual income, payroll, corporate income, and excise taxes as of 2016.

almost half a trillion dollars into the trillions of dollars (CEA 2019).[25] Crain and Crain (2014) use a proxy measure of regulation to conclude that Federal regulations imposed a burden of roughly $2 trillion in 2012. Coffey, McLaughlin, and Peretto (2020) estimate the effect of regulations on 22 industries, between 1977 and 2012, and find that if regulations were held at 1980 levels, then the economy would have been $4 trillion larger in 2012.

The magnitude of regulatory burdens, in combination with their potential regressivity, implies that regulatory costs could largely offset the progressivity of Federal taxes. Regulatory cost estimates that range into the trillions of dollars are substantial compared with the $3.6 trillion in Federal tax revenues in fiscal year 2020. In fact, the distribution of the gains from the subset of deregulations we examined is almost the mirror image of the distribution of the burden of Federal taxation (figure 6-11). Thus, we find that continued regulatory reform has the potential to shift more of the total burden the Federal government imposes on businesses and consumers away from low-income households with less capacity to pay.

---

[25] No Federal agency attempts to estimate the cumulative cost of all Federal regulation; however, the Regulatory Right-to-Know act tasked the Office of Management and Budget to estimate the total cost and benefits of a subset of Federal rules that have been designated major rules. Federal regulatory agencies only monetize the costs and benefits of less than 1 percent of all the rules they issue.

Conclusion

This chapter has highlighted the Trump Administration's commitment to reducing the regulatory burden on households and businesses. The CEA finds that the benefits associated with one of fiscal year 2020's biggest deregulatory actions (the SAFE Vehicles Rule) will reduce prices for consumers by almost $2,200 per vehicle by 2026. Moreover, we find that the Administration's regulatory reform efforts may have benefited those in the lowest income quintile the most as a proportion of their income. Specifically, we conclude that the costs savings from the SAFE Vehicles Rule and other deregulatory actions we have studied amount to 3.7 percent of the average income of the lowest income quintile of households compared with 0.8 percent for the highest income quintile of households. Our findings provide evidence of the benefits of regulatory reform and reaffirm that deregulation can help consumers in low-income households—who spend a relatively large share of their budgets on necessities that are often in heavily regulated sectors of the economy—the most.

The regulatory reforms we have reviewed in this chapter were enacted before the COVID-19 pandemic and its effects on health and the U.S. economy. Although the longer-term consequences are hard to predict, evidence on the scope and nature of COVID-19's near-term effects are beginning to emerge. Unfortunately, the COVID-19 pandemic has hit low-income households particularly hard, in their health outcomes and in economic consequences including lost jobs and wages. The cost savings and distributional effects from the deregulations we discuss may have somewhat cushioned the blow to low-income households. Moreover, regulatory reform may help position the United States for a robust economic recovery and be a powerful tool to help lift up middle- and low-income Americans as the economy recovers from the COVID-19 pandemic.

Chapter 7

Expanding Educational Opportunity through Choice and Competition

During the last 30 years, school choice programs have undergone dramatic expansion in the United States. These programs—organized at the Federal, State, or local level—share a common goal of expanding access to education options that exist alongside and ultimately improve public school options for primary and secondary education. Under a district public school (DPS) system, students are assigned to schools based on where they live, and the only form of school choice requires physically moving to an area with better schools for those families that can afford to do so. School choice programs have altered this landscape in fundamental ways by increasing competition in the school system and enhancing educational opportunities for all students, especially those from disadvantaged groups.

One rapidly growing school choice option is charter schools. Charter schools are public schools that educate millions of students using public funding, but with operational autonomy from the local public school system. Additionally, scholarship programs—funded both publicly and privately—assist hundreds of thousands of students with tuition at private schools and can provide access to courses, work-based learning opportunities, concurrent and dual enrollment for college credit, home education, special education services and therapies, tutoring, and more. These and other choice programs are providing opportunities for families that lack them, thereby ensuring that all schools have an incentive to deliver a high-quality education.

This chapter documents the development and expansion of school choice programs since 1990, when the first major school choice program was introduced in this country. We provide an overview of school choice programs, describing the main types of programs with examples from around the country. We also discuss the role of Federal policy, including recent actions of the Trump Administration to further expand school choice.

We next explain the key benefit of expanding school choice policies: more educational competition that empowers families and pressures schools to deliver more value. School choice programs can extend competition to all areas, including those where families with lower incomes have little ability to move to more affluent areas in search of better schools. The programs enable families to hold accountable what in some cases is a failing local education monopoly. This can benefit the children who use school choice programs as well as the children who remain in a DPS, because all schools must compete for student enrollment by providing a higher-quality educational experience. We discuss the growing empirical evidence that carefully crafted school choice programs do improve educational outcomes for all students. In other words, competition can be the tide that lifts all boats.

School choice refers to policies, legislation, and organizations that foster alternatives to residentially assigned district public school (DPS) education. This chapter provides an overview of school choice programs in the United States and the role of Federal policy in helping to foster them. It also discusses the economic theory of competition that motivates these programs. And finally, it reviews the empirical research on the programs' impact.

The first major school choice programs were introduced in the early 1990s. The programs originated from concerns that students from low-income families had no alternatives to residentially assigned DPSs, especially in places where the local DPS had a poor performance record. In 1990, the State of Wisconsin enacted the Milwaukee Parental Choice Program, the first major voucher program in the Nation. This program, which continues to operate today, offers publicly funded vouchers to eligible students in Milwaukee who choose to attend private schools. In 1991, the State of Minnesota enacted the first charter school law, with the first public charter school opening in Saint Paul in 1992. Over time, demand for alternatives to residentially assigned DPSs has increased, and school choice programs have been introduced in many school districts throughout the country.

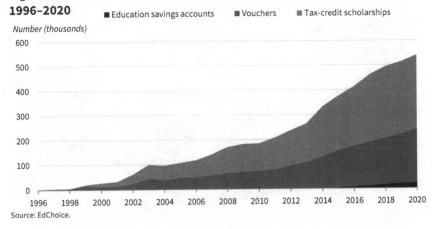

Figure 7-1. Number of ESAs, Vouchers, and Tax-Credit Scholarships, 1996–2020

■ Education savings accounts ■ Vouchers ■ Tax-credit scholarships

Number (thousands)

Source: EdChoice.

Today, private choice programs provide financial support that enables hundreds of thousands of students to attend private schools. As we discuss in more detail below, these programs include vouchers, tax-credit scholarships, and State-funded education savings accounts (ESAs) (figure 7-1), which together now number about 539,000 (EdChoice 2020a).

Public choice programs further allow millions of students to attend schools other than the DPS they would attend based on geographic residency. In addition to establishing public charter schools, States and local governments have introduced other public choice programs, such as magnet schools, which are public schools with specialized programs of study. Enrollment in public charter schools and magnet schools has grown over time (figure 7-2). In 2017–18, charter schools and magnet schools enrolled 3.1 million and 2.7 million students, respectively (NCES 2019a). Many public school systems have also introduced open enrollment programs that permit students to attend public schools other than a residentially assigned DPS.

Although Federal funding plays a relatively minor role in K-12 school funding, Federal policy does support State and local governments seeking to expand school choice. Below, we discuss the main Federal programs that support school choice, including the Magnet Schools Assistance Program and the Charter Schools Program. We also report on recent policies implemented under the Trump Administration to enhance this support, including the expansion of 529 ESAs to primary and secondary education under the 2017 Tax Cuts and Jobs Act (TCJA).

Although school choice programs have grown dramatically, the majority of students in K-12 school continue to attend a residentially assigned DPS. As shown in figure 7-3, the proportion of students attending a residentially assigned DPS fell by about 5 percentage points between 1999 and 2016. Over

Figure 7-2. Enrollment in Public Choice Programs over Time

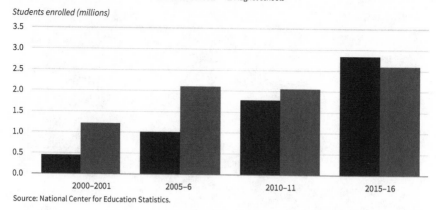

■ Charter schools　■ Magnet schools

Students enrolled (millions)

Source: National Center for Education Statistics.

the same period, the proportion of students attending a public school of their choosing rose by about 4 percentage points.

After providing an overview, we next discuss the economic theory of competition that motivates school choice. School choice programs are founded on the idea that when schools are exposed to increased competition, educational outcomes will improve. The intellectual foundation is often credited to the Nobel laureate Milton Friedman (1955), who argued that when public schools face competition, they have stronger incentives to provide a high-quality, cost-effective education. As described by Hoxby (2003), the beneficial effects of competition come into force through the power of choice. Because charter schools are not guaranteed any enrollment, they are spurred to provide a better education than competing DPSs in order to attract students. Private schools face similar incentives but, because they charge tuition, they are not financially accessible to some families. Private choice programs seek to expand access to private schools and make them more competitive with DPSs by subsidizing the cost. Far from acting as a one-way street, however, competition may also induce a response by DPSs. When faced with the threat of losing students to a competitive charter or private school, a DPS may work to improve its performance in order to retain students and the funding that comes with them.

As we explain in this chapter, the design of school choice programs can help ensure that competition leads to benefits for all students. In theory, choice programs could disproportionately entice away more advanced or more motivated students from the DPS system, leaving behind struggling students who lose the benefits of interacting with their high-performing peers. Similar to the default method of school choice—the ability to move to a more affluent area with better schools—this might create segmentation by family background that harms some students who remain in the DPS system. However, as we discuss, these theoretical concerns are not borne out by empirical research, in

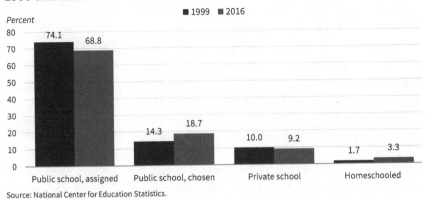

Figure 7-3. Percentage Distribution of Students Age 5–17 Years Attending Kindergarten through 12th Grade, by School Type, 1999 and 2016

Source: National Center for Education Statistics.

part because most school choice programs include design features that avoid such outcomes by targeting eligibility or providing more generous resources to relatively disadvantaged students.

In the last section of the chapter, we review the empirical evidence on the impact of school choice programs. For students participating in these programs, achievement results as measured by test scores are mixed, although several studies find large positive results for minority and low-income students. We explain that some positive outcomes of school choice emerge later in a child's development through higher educational attainment, and studies of these longer-term outcomes are generally more positive. Thus, policymakers should consider a broad range of outcomes when evaluating efforts to promote higher education quality through school choice. We also discuss studies of school choice relating to racial and ethnic integration, longer-term nonacademic outcomes, and fiscal effects. Finally, in terms of the impact on students who remain in their residentially assigned DPS, we discuss emerging empirical research suggesting that all students can benefit from the expansion of school choice programs in their local district, regardless of whether they participate themselves in the programs or decide to remain in their DPS. Thus, choice can be a tide that lifts all boats, not because of the inherent superiority of any one school type over another, but rather because competition pressures all schools to improve quality and deliver value.

Overview of School Choice Programs and Federal Policy

In this section, we describe the main types of private and public choice programs. Each type has unique advantages, which are highlighted in their respective subsections. We then provide examples of school choice in five regions of the country. Finally, we discuss Federal actions, including actions taken by the Trump Administration, to support school choice.

Private Choice Programs

There are three basic types of private choice programs: vouchers, tax-credit scholarships, and education savings accounts. Together, these programs enroll hundreds of thousands of students (figure 7-1) (EdChoice 2020a). Eight States also offer an individual tax deduction or tax credit for certain educational expenses, which are typically expended on one's own child.

Voucher programs provide a subsidy to parents to enroll their child in a private school. The voucher subsidy is typically set at a specific share of the public funding intended for that child's education. Though vouchers may not necessarily cover the full cost of tuition, they make private education more affordable for parents. During the 2018–19 school year, 28 voucher programs operated in 17 States, the District of Columbia, and Puerto Rico. Together, these programs served more than 188,000 students (EdChoice 2019). Many programs are targeted at low-income students or students with disabilities: seven States and the District of Columbia provide vouchers to low-income students, and eleven States provide vouchers for students with disabilities.

Tax-credit scholarships allow students to receive private funding from nonprofit organizations to attend private schools or may pay for other educational expenses, including tutoring, online learning, concurrent and dual enrollment for college credit, and homeschooling expenses. Individuals and businesses may donate to these nonprofit organizations and receive a State income tax credit in return. States limit the total amount of tax credits that will be offered for the year and/or the amount that each business or individual can claim. Tax-credit scholarships often target low-income students, students with disabilities, or students assigned to a low-performing DPS. During the 2018–19 school year, 23 programs operated in 18 States and served nearly 275,000 students (EdChoice 2019; Kaplan and Owings 2018). One of these programs, the Montana tax-credit scholarship program, became inoperable in late 2018 when the Montana Supreme Court ruled that the program violated the State's constitution. However, that decision was reversed by the Supreme Court of the United States in June 2020 (see box 7-1).

Education savings accounts (ESAs) are multiuse scholarships that allow participating parents to pay for current educational expenses, such as private school tuition, homeschool expenses, contracted services provided by a public school or school district, courses, concurrent and dual enrollment for college credit, special education services and therapies, and tutoring, as well as for future educational expenses such as college. During the 2018–19 school year, five programs operated in five States supporting more than 18,700 students. Most States restrict eligibility to students with disabilities. Arizona's program

> **Box 7-1. The Supreme Court's *Espinoza v. Montana Department of Revenue* Decision**
>
> In June 2020, the Supreme Court of the United States (SCOTUS) reversed the decision of the Montana Supreme Court in *Espinoza v. Montana Department of Revenue* (Supreme Court of the United States 2019). The central judgment, taken from Chief Justice Roberts's majority opinion, is that "a State need not subsidize private education. But once a State decides to do so, it cannot disqualify some private schools solely because they are religious."
>
> The decision automatically reinstated a Montana tax credit scholarship program that the State court had ended because it violated a "no-aid" provision, also referred to as a Blaine amendment, in the State's constitution. SCOTUS found this particular application of the no-aid provision discriminatory against religious schools and their prospective pupils' families, and thus the application violated the U.S. Constitution's free exercise clause.
>
> The original Blaine amendment was a proposed amendment to the U.S. Constitution that narrowly failed Senate approval in 1875. The Blaine amendment, founded in anti-Catholic immigrant sentiment with the purpose of keeping schools Protestant, would have expanded the reach of the Establishment Clause in the First Amendment to explicitly prohibit public spending on religious schools or organizations. Subsequently, a majority of States added Blaine language to their State constitutions; Montana became a State in 1889 and included a Blaine clause in its original constitution.
>
> Montana's scholarship program, passed in 2015, provided for tax credits worth a maximum of $150 for gifts made to organizations that provide private school scholarships. All Montana students are eligible for the program. However, due to the litigation and the $150 maximum gift, only 25 students in Montana received funds from the program in the 2016–17 school year.

also includes other groups of students, including low-income students, students assigned to a low-performing DPS, students who are adopted or in foster care, students who live on a tribal land, and children of active-duty military or who were killed in the line of duty. The funding amount varies by State, with some States setting a flat amount per pupil, such as $6,500 in Mississippi, and others giving a portion of the State's education funds per pupil to the parents. In some States, higher scholarship amounts are provided to low-income students or students with disabilities. For example, in Arizona, students from households with income up to 250 percent of the Federal poverty line receive 100 percent of State per-pupil funding, whereas other eligible students receive 90 percent (EdChoice 2020a).

Public Choice Programs

Public choice programs include charter schools, magnet schools, and open enrollment policies. *Charter schools* are tuition-free public schools that operate independently from district public schools and thus have more autonomy over their educational programs, hiring, operations, and budget in exchange for greater accountability. Although the programs differ by State, many charter schools receive per-pupil funding that follows students from their residentially assigned DPS to the charter school. In addition to providing funding for charter schools, State governments grant entities the role of charter authorizers. Charter authorizers come in a variety of types, including independent chartering boards, nonprofit organizations, institutions of higher education, and State and local education agencies. The charter authorizers can then approve charter operators to run schools.

Most charter school operators are independent entities (e.g., a group of teachers or parents, or a local nonprofit or community organization), but about 35 percent of charter schools are operated by nonprofit or for-profit management organizations as part of larger networks of schools. Examples of such networks include the Knowledge Is Power Program (KIPP) and Charter Schools USA. Charter school operators are accountable to the organization that grants their charter, and the schools are subject to periodic reviews (Kaplan and Owings 2018; David 2018).

Because public charter schools operate outside the restraints that bind a DPS system, they can be more innovative than DPSs. Grube and Anderson (2018) discuss innovations such as Montessori schools and dual-language immersion schools. Charter schools based on the "no-excuse" approach have proved popular in urban settings. These schools include features such as uniforms, strong discipline, extended classroom hours, and intensive tutoring (Angrist et al. 2016). The KIPP Foundation is known for these schools.

In terms of enrollment, charter schools typically have a mandate to accept all eligible applicants and to use a lottery to select students if they are oversubscribed. The charter school segment has grown rapidly. Between the 2000–1 and 2017–18 school years, the number of charter schools increased by about 260 percent, with student enrollment increasing about 600 percent. As of the fall of 2017, more than 6 percent of students enrolled in public elementary and secondary schools attended these institutions. Enrollment in charter schools is generally higher in urban areas where minority and low-income student populations are higher (NCES 2019a).

Magnet schools are public schools that offer specialized programs meant to bring together students with common interests or skillsets. These schools specialize in specific areas, such as mathematics, science, and the performing arts. Some magnet schools also include niche subjects, such as the culinary arts or aerospace engineering. Originally, magnet schools were created to foster desegregation by intentionally enrolling students from diverse populations (OII 2004). Many magnet schools continue to serve this mission.

Enrollment in magnet schools is handled through various application frameworks. Some magnet schools have attendance zones, where part of the student population is enrolled based on geographic location while the remaining slots are filled by applicants from throughout the rest of the district. Other magnet schools do not have attendance zones and instead grant all seats through an application process. Admission may also be handled through a lottery system; some magnets use random lottery systems, while others use weighted lottery systems that prioritize students with certain qualifications (OII 2004; Ayscue et al. 2015). As of the 2017–18 academic year, there were 3,421 magnet schools in operation, enrolling 2.7 million students (NCES 2019a).

Open enrollment school districts facilitate interdistrict or intradistrict public school choice, which allows students to select the school they wish to attend instead of taking a DPS assignment. Intradistrict policies allow choice among schools within a student's designated district, while interdistrict policies give students the option to attend schools within a State or larger defined region (EdChoice 2020b). Open enrollment programs help households by giving students access to higher-quality public schools while also providing competition between public schools. Still, not all States and school districts cover the costs of traveling to nonneighborhood schools, and this may pose a barrier to some families, limiting their ability to exercise choice. As of 2018, most States had enacted policies related to open enrollment. In 34 States, school districts choose whether to participate, while 28 States mandate open enrollment in some cases (ECS 2018).

Other types of competition with DPSs include homeschooling and virtual school. The Department of Education defines homeschooling to include students who attend less than 25 hours of public/private school weekly. As of 2016, 1.7 million students were homeschooled, representing 3.3 percent of all students, up from 1.7 percent in 1999 (figure 7-3; NCES 2019b). Virtual school may include a hybrid of in-person and online instruction or be a fully online curriculum run by either private or public schools. In 2017, about 280,000 students were enrolled in virtual school (NCES 2019a). However, during the coronavirus pandemic, many more students are experiencing some form of virtual learning (EdSurge 2020).

Examples of School Choice

Although school choice has grown in communities throughout the United States, it is instructive to compare how school choice developed in specific places. Here, we consider several examples where school choice has come to play a particularly prominent role in the education environment: Milwaukee, Florida, New Orleans, Massachusetts, and the District of Columbia.

Milwaukee. The Milwaukee Parental Choice Program was established in 1990 as a voucher program targeted at low-income students. Initially, the program was restricted to families with incomes below 175 percent of the Federal poverty line. Enrollment was also limited to 1 percent of students in the Milwaukee public school district (MPS), with a randomized selection process for most students. The program did not initially include religious private schools, which made up about 80 percent of private school student enrollment in the area (Witte 1998). After 1998, when the Wisconsin Supreme Court ruled that the inclusion of religious schools in the voucher program did not violate the Wisconsin Constitution, the voucher program grew more quickly. Today, the program has expanded to allow families with incomes up to 300 percent of the poverty level, has no enrollment cap, and uses a lottery system for selection when particular schools are oversubscribed. As of 2019, there were 120 schools participating and more than 28,900 students enrolled (EdChoice 2020c).

Milwaukee introduced charter schools in 1996. Today, Milwaukee has 44 charter schools with an enrollment of more than 18,000 students (Wisconsin Department of Public Instruction 2020). Some of the schools are authorized by the MPS, while others are independent of it and are authorized by the University of Wisconsin–Milwaukee and the City of Milwaukee. The independent charter schools have more autonomy than those run by the MPS and make up almost half of all charter schools in Milwaukee. Milwaukee's choice schools have spurred new educational approaches. In 1999, the MPS began to introduce changes, such as opening new Montessori schools in response to the competitive pressure (Grube and Anderson 2018).

Florida. In 2001, the Florida legislature established the Florida Tax Credit Scholarship program. The program offers State tax credits to corporations that donate to nonprofit scholarship-funding organizations. The scholarships can be used for tuition and fees at private schools or for transportation to a public school outside a student's residential school district. When the program was initially passed, only students with household incomes below 185 percent of the Federal poverty line were eligible, and the program expenditures were capped at $50 million annually. The program has since been expanded so that students with household incomes between 200 and 260 percent of the Federal poverty line are eligible for partial scholarships, while students from lower-income families are eligible for full scholarships. In the 2018–19 school year, nearly $645 million in scholarships was awarded to 104,091 students attending 1,825 participating private schools (Florida Department of Education 2019c).

Florida has also established other State-funded school choice programs. The McKay Scholarship Program was established in 2000 as the Nation's first school voucher program for students with special needs. The program provides scholarships for students to attend a private school or to transfer to a different public school. In 2018–19, the program awarded about $220 million in scholarships to 30,695 students. The Gardiner Scholarship Program, established in

2014, is an ESA program that provides funds for special needs students to purchase products and services to support their learning. In 2018–19, the program awarded about $125 million in scholarships to about 12,188 students. The Family Empowerment Scholarship program, which was established this past year, provides scholarships for up to 18,000 students from disadvantaged families to attend private schools, with priority for students from households with incomes less than 185 percent of the Federal poverty line. Florida also operates the Statewide virtual school known as the Florida Virtual School. This is the largest virtual school in the country, with 215,505 students enrolled during the 2018–19 school year. Finally, Florida has a large public charter school sector that enrolled 313,000 students in the 2018–19 school year (Florida Department of Education 2019a, 2019b).

New Orleans. Before Hurricane Katrina, the New Orleans public schools had one of the worst performance records in the country. In the 2004–5 school year, only 35 percent of students in the New Orleans schools achieved proficient scores on State exams, and high school graduation rates were about 54 percent (Teach New Orleans 2020). In 2003, the New Orleans Recovery School District (RSD) was created as a way to reform the public schools. In 2005, in response to the devastation left by Katrina, the RSD assumed control of 114 low-performing schools. With the help of $20.9 million in funding from the Department of Education, New Orleans began to open new charter schools. Over time, the RSD eliminated some of the low-performing schools and converted others to charters. By 2014, all the RSD schools were charter schools, and nearly all educators had been replaced. Furthermore, district public school attendance zones were eliminated, making New Orleans the only all-choice school system in the country. The reforms led to dramatic gains among New Orleans schoolchildren. By the 2013–14 school year, student proficiency on State exams had increased to 62 percent. High school graduation rates, college entry rates, and college graduation rates all rose substantially (Harris and Larsen 2018).

In 2008, Louisiana also launched a voucher program for students in New Orleans, known today as the Louisiana Scholarship Program. The program was targeted to children in failing schools with family incomes at or below 250 percent of the poverty line. Over the first four years, it grew slowly, reaching about 1,900 in annual vouchers in the 2011–12 school year. In 2012, the program was expanded to the rest of the State, and by 2014, more than 6,500 vouchers were awarded.

Massachusetts. In 1993, the Massachusetts legislature passed the Education Reform Act, increasing the State's role in education. The act allowed for the creation of charter schools, reserving the right to authorize them for the Massachusetts Department of Elementary and Secondary Education. In the 2019–20 school year, 81 charter schools operated in Massachusetts, educating just under 48,000 students. The schools have proved popular, and spots are typically allocated by lottery. In the 2019–20 school year, 73 charter schools had waiting lists, and there were nearly 28,000 students on one or more of the lists (Massachusetts Department of Elementary and Secondary Education 2016, 2019). In 2010, Massachusetts passed legislation allowing charter schools with a successful track record to expand. In Boston, the number of charter schools doubled as a result. Despite the large expansion, a recent study finds that the new schools generated achievement gains on par with the original charter schools (Cohodes, Setren, and Walters 2019).

For grades 1 through 8, Boston's public school system also facilitates school choice through an assignment system, known as the Home-Based School Assignment Policy (Boston School Finder 2020). The policy seeks to find a balance between allowing students to attend a neighborhood school and giving more students a chance to attend high-quality schools. Families choose from a list of schools and are allowed to express preferences. A lottery mechanism is used to assign students to schools, taking these preferences into account. Over time, the mechanism has been adjusted in response to concerns about student travel times and persistent racial inequities (Abdulkadiroğlu et al. 2006).

District of Columbia. The voucher program in the District of Columbia is the only private school choice program run by the Federal Government. Signed into law by President George W. Bush in 2004, the D.C. School Choice Incentive Act created the D.C. Opportunity Scholarship Program, which is intended to improve education in the District of Columbia, especially for disadvantaged students. Although Congress has continuously funded the program, the Obama Administration sought to phase it out and prevented new students from enrolling in the 2009–10 and 2010–11 school years. However, the Trump Administration has strongly supported the program and helped increase participation by more than 40 percent between the 2016–17 and 2017–18 school years to more than 1,600 students (CRS 2019). In the 2020–21 school year, vouchers are worth up to $9,161 for K-8 students and up to $13,742 for high school students. In addition to the voucher program, Washington has a large public charter school sector that dates back to 1996. In the 2019–20 school year, these schools enrolled more than 43,500 students in grades pre–K-12 and adult learning programs (DCPCSB 2020).

The Role of Federal Policy in School Choice

In this subsection, we discuss the role of Federal policy in school choice. We first provide an overview of the organization of K-12 education, its funding, and the Federal contribution. We then describe the main Federal policies that are related to school choice. Finally, we highlight recent actions of the Trump Administration to further support and expand school choice.

State and local governments have the primary responsibility for K-12 education in the United States. Along with public and private organizations,

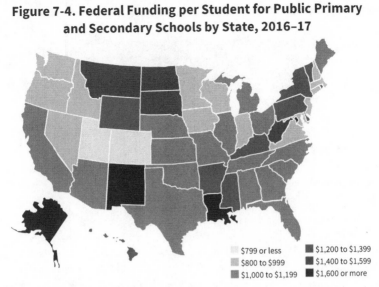

Figure 7-4. Federal Funding per Student for Public Primary and Secondary Schools by State, 2016–17

$799 or less	$1,200 to $1,399
$800 to $999	$1,400 to $1,599
$1,000 to $1,199	$1,600 or more

Source: National Center for Education Statistics.

they establish new schools, determine graduation standards, and develop curricula (U.S. Department of Education 2017). State and local governments also provide the primary financing for K-12 education. Of the $736 billion allocated for public elementary and secondary education for the 2016–17 school year, the majority was allocated from State and local governments—47 percent and 45 percent, respectively. Only $60 billion (8 percent) was from Federal sources (NCES 2020a).

More than half of Federal funding from the Department of Education supports students with low family incomes or disabilities. A large share of Federal funds, about 26 percent, is spent on Title I grants, which supplement State and local funding in school districts with a high share of low-income students. An additional 20 percent of Federal funding focuses on children with disabilities (NCES 2020b). Because States have different demographics, Federal funding per student varies by State. Figure 7-4 shows the Federal funding per student for public primary and secondary schools by State (NCES 2019c).

The Federal Government also provides resources to support school choice programs. The Department of Education oversees the key Federal programs that promote choice. These include the Magnet Schools Assistance Program and the Charter Schools Program, as well as the District of Columbia Opportunity Scholarship Program discussed above (U.S. Department of Education 2019a, 2019b, 2020a).

The Magnet Schools Assistance Program provides funding for magnet schools that are part of an approved plan to desegregate schools. These magnet schools are designed to bring students from different backgrounds

Figure 7-5. Number of Charter Schools Opened, 2006–7 to 2016–17

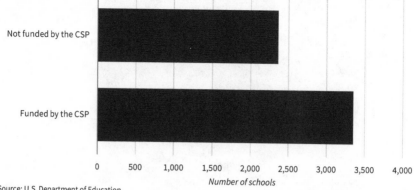

Source: U.S. Department of Education.
Note: CSP = Charter Schools Program.

together to reduce minority group isolation in schools with many minority students. As discussed, magnet schools are typically focused on specific academic areas—such as science, technology, engineering, and mathematics, known as STEM; the arts; language immersion—or implement alternative teaching philosophies, such as international baccalaureate programs or Montessori methods (U.S. Department of Education 2020a).

The Charter Schools Program (CSP) was established in 1994 to encourage the formation of new charter schools. Its initial budget of $4.5 million had grown to to $440 million as of 2019. In 2019, 85 percent of CSP funding went toward the creation of new charter schools, although the program also supports the expansion of existing charter schools. Between the 2006–7 and 2016–17 school years, the majority of new charter schools were started using funding from the CSP (figure 7-5). Charter schools funded by the CSP serve a higher percentage of Hispanic and Black students than residentially assigned district public schools (table 7-1) (U.S. Department of Education 2015, 2019b).

Some Federal programs interact with other Federal initiatives to enhance the total impact of Federal Government action. For example, earlier in 2020, the Department of Education provided an additional $65 million through the CSP, targeting charter schools in Opportunity Zones. These distressed areas have high poverty rates and low incomes. Currently, less than 30 percent of Opportunity Zones have at least one charter school. Additional funding for charter schools will complement tax incentives in Opportunity Zones to spur much-needed economic opportunity in these areas (U.S. Department of Education 2020b). A recent CEA report provides an initial assessment of the Opportunity Zone program (CEA 2020).

The Trump Administration has sought to further aid the expansion of State-based school choice. President Trump supports the proposed Education Freedom Scholarships and Opportunity Act, which would give Federal tax-credits

Table 7-1. Demographics of CSP-Funded Schools and District Public Schools, 2016–17

Demographics	CSP-Funded Schools (n = 3,129)		Residentially Assigned DPS (n = 88,320)	
	Students	Percent	Students	Percent
Hispanic	454,605	33.9	12,282,085	26.0
Black	409,010	30.5	6,901,043	14.6
White	371,462	27.7	23,268,443	49.2
Asian	50,637	3.8	2,440,986	5.2
Two or more races	43,410	3.2	1,719,774	3.6
American Indian / Alaska Native	7,759	0.6	482,088	1.0
Hawaiian Native / Pacific Islander	4,597	0.3	172,123	0.4
Total number of students	1,341,480	100	47,266,542	100

Source: U.S. Department of Education.
Note: CSP = Charter Schools Program.

to individuals and businesses that contribute to organizations that grant scholarships to students. States would designate qualified expenses, which can be for primary, secondary, career, and technical education. Expenses that might be recognized include advanced, remedial, and elective course fees; tuition at private schools; apprenticeships and industry certifications; concurrent and dual enrollment for college credit; private and home education; special education services and therapies; transportation to education providers outside of a family's zoned school; tutoring, especially for students in low-performing schools; and summer and after-school education programs (U.S. Department of Education 2019c). Individual taxpayers would be allowed to redeem a credit of up to 10 percent of their adjusted gross income, and corporations would be allowed to redeem a credit of up to 5 percent of their taxable income. States would have the responsibility to recognize scholarship-granting organizations and to decide the nature of the scholarships and eligibility criteria. For States with existing tax-credit scholarship programs, the program would incentivize additional private donations. State participation would be voluntary (Office of Senator Ted Cruz 2019). For a discussion of related legislation, see box 7-2.

The Trump Administration has also supported school choice as part of the 2017 Tax Cuts and Jobs Act (TCJA). The TCJA expanded the purview of the Qualified Tuition Program, known as a 529 program. Dating back to the 1990s, these programs have long allowed an individual to contribute money to an investment account from which a student's expenses for higher education (college or vocational school) can be paid without the earnings on the contributions being taxed. The TCJA allows 529 plans to be used to pay for primary and secondary education as well. Funds can be withdrawn tax-free to pay for up to $10,000 in tuition per beneficiary per year at any public, private, or parochial school (CRS 2018). The 529 program offers an alternative to Coverdell Education Savings Accounts. Coverdell ESAs similarly allow individuals to contribute money to an account that grows tax-free for use on qualified educational expenses for a student. However, there is a limit on how much can

> **Box 7-2. The School Choice Now Act**
>
> As part of ongoing COVID-relief legislative efforts, Senator Tim Scott and Senator Lamar Alexander introduced the School Choice Now Act on July 22, 2020. If passed, the bill would authorize the Department of Education to allocate 10 percent of its emergency CARES funding to States in the form of emergency education grants. The bill would also encourage donations to certain scholarship-granting organizations by establishing Federal tax credits.
>
> Bill proponents point out that more than 100, mostly Catholic, private schools—which enrolled more than 16,000 total students—have permanently closed because of the coronavirus. Adding all, or even a significant portion, of these 16,000 students to the public school population could strain already-delicate local government budgets at a critical time (McShane 2020).

be contributed per year (currently $2,000) and a phase-out by annual income of the contributor (CRS 2018).

School Choice and Competition

As we have seen, school choice programs have expanded significantly in the United States over the last three decades. In this section, we explain how school choice promotes competition among schools for students, which can ultimately lead to improved educational experiences for all children. We begin by explaining how mobility-based school choice has long existed in the DPS system for affluent families that can afford to move to higher-quality school districts. We next discuss how school choice programs introduce a different form of competition that can raise the educational quality received by all students, including those in less affluent neighborhoods, whether they participate in a choice program or remain in a DPS.

Competition between School Districts

Even before the school choice movement, parents exercised substantial discretion over where their children attend school, as families with the means to do so can move to higher-quality school districts. Tiebout (1956) describes how local governments compete with one another by adjusting levels of public good provision to meet the demand of potential residents. The model implies that families with the financial means to do so will live in certain kinds of communities based on their preferences for various public goods, including education. Localities will generally face pressure to increase quality, subject to a given level of cost, in order to increase their number of taxpaying residents. In the United States, school quality is an important factor for many parents in determining where to live. According to a 2018 survey, more than half (52 percent) of recent homebuyers with children considered the quality of schools when making their decision on the neighborhood in which to live (National Association of Realtors 2018). Studies of parental choices find that preferences for school quality are multidimensional, with parents placing different weights on factors such as academic performance, teaching quality, class size, safety, and discipline (Chakrabarti and Roy 2010).

Although this form of competition allows more affluent families to seek out a higher-quality education, the benefits may be financially out of reach for many less-affluent families. In fact, a Senate committee report finds that the median home price in neighborhoods with the highest-quality schools is about $486,000, which is four times larger than the median price of $122,000 in neighborhoods with the lowest-quality schools (JEC 2019). In addition, this form of competition can potentially have negative consequences for lower-income and minority students when it leads to increased segregation along racial and income lines (Urquiola 2005; Rothstein 2006).

Two important lessons emerge from the research on traditional mobility-based competition. First, because of the financial barriers that lower-income students' families face to moving, competition between districts for residents is likely insufficient on its own to substantially improve school quality for such students. Thus, additional school choice within a district may be needed to foster the procompetitive effects that hold schools accountable for delivering better outcomes. Second, to avoid negative consequences for students who remain in a residentially assigned DPS, school choice programs should be designed so that schools compete on their value added and not on their ability to siphon off students with more advantaged backgrounds from DPSs. Nonetheless, even when some selective sorting occurs, school choice programs may still outperform the traditional mobility-based system that relies on sorting across neighborhoods based in part on family affluence.

Designing School Choice Systems

We next explain why carefully designed school choice programs can improve the quality of education for all students within a district. In early research on school choice, Hoxby (2003) developed models to explain why exposing DPSs to competition can lead to better schools. The models characterize decisionmaking for different types of schools, but all of them rest on the basic assumption that for a given out-of-pocket cost, parents choose the school they value the most. This power of choice is the mechanism by which the beneficial effects of competition come in to play.

To illustrate, consider the case of a charter school that can receive a government payment for each student it attracts away from a DPS, although it is prevented from charging additional fees. Because the school cannot compete on price, it must compete on quality. By increasing its quality, the school can attract more students from DPSs and thus earn more revenue. Because quality is expensive to produce, the school faces a trade-off between attracting more students and keeping costs down. Where the school falls on this trade-off will depend on the structure of both demand (how much parents and students value quality) and supply (how expensive quality is to supply). At a minimum, however, a charter school must provide parents and students with at least as much value as the DPS.

This direct effect of school choice on program participants is distinguished from the indirect competitive effect that arises when a DPS responds to the competitive pressure from a charter or other choice school. As discussed by Hoxby (2003), if a DPS loses funding when students enroll in a different school, it should have an incentive to retain students. The strength of the effect will depend both on how much funding is lost and how many students are threatening to leave. If the competitive pressure is not robust, a DPS may not react to it. For example, choice programs that cap enrollment at low levels may not place much pressure on DPSs that are to a large extent guaranteed enrollment. This is quite different from the direct effect of school choice: any charter school, no matter how small, must compete with DPSs in order to enroll students.

When DPSs respond to competitive pressure from choice programs by increasing their value added, their students will benefit. However, it is not axiomatic that school choice will inevitably improve educational quality through competition in the same way that is often true in other markets. This is because of the important role that peer effects play in education provision. In most markets, the quality of a service that one person receives is not directly affected by the characteristics of the other people that consume that service. However, in education, students are both consumers and producers of education quality—not merely passive consumers—because of how peers have a direct impact on the education quality received by their classmates. As a result, school choice reforms that induce shifts in student sorting across schools could have large effects both on the students who leave and on those who remain in residentially assigned DPSs because of changes in peer composition. If a school choice program attracts highly motivated or affluent students, it might have negative effects on students who remain in DPSs surrounded by less-motivated, less-affluent peers.

However, as actually implemented, school choice programs often incorporate features designed to prevent such an outcome from occurring, and the empirical evidence finds little support for these theoretical concerns. For example, voucher programs often restrict participation to students from low-income families or provide resources that are more generous to relatively disadvantaged students, which directly limits the potential for income-related sorting. Designs that require oversubscribed schools to use lotteries to allocate slots also limit the potential for selective sorting. The result is that schools will compete based on value added rather than on their ability to select students. In the United States, many school choice programs incorporate these design features (Epple, Romano, and Urquiola 2017). Expanding school choice to more students while providing more generous assistance to disadvantaged families could further build upon these benefits (Epple and Romano 2008).

Evidence on the Impact of School Competition

Finally, we turn to the important question of whether the theoretical procompetitive benefits of school choice are borne out empirically. This evidence can help determine whether school choice program designs in different contexts have in fact promoted positive student outcomes, and it can help inform better school choice policies in the future. We first discuss the literature that examines the direct effects of school choice programs on the students who participate in them. We then discuss the literature that examines the indirect competitive effects of school choice programs on DPS students.

Direct Value-Added Effects

That charter schools must compete with DPSs is so basic that there is a sense in which we should not be surprised by evidence that they do. Simply put, if a charter school or voucher program does not offer parents and students additional value relative to the DPS, then it is unlikely to thrive (Hoxby 2003). Consistent with this, a recent survey finds that a larger share of children in private schools (77 percent) or in chosen public schools (60 percent) have parents who report being "very satisfied" with their schools compared with children in assigned public schools (54 percent) (NCES 2019b). That said, there is value for policymakers in understanding which types of school choice programs have worked best and for whom, as they test new approaches and encourage expansion of the most promising programs. Accordingly, a large body of literature has arisen to study the direct effects of school choice programs on their students. In our discussion, we divide the literature into studies of academic achievement as measured by test scores, studies of academic attainment such as graduation rates or college enrollment, studies of racial and ethnic integration, and studies of longer-term, nonacademic outcomes. We also discuss studies of the fiscal impact of choice programs.

Much of the literature on academic achievement focuses on student performance on national or Statewide tests. This may be surprising in light of the small role such tests play in the educational experiences of students. However, these test scores are more amenable to empirical study than measures that vary widely across schools, such as grades or pass rates for courses. Tests that are taken by most students are also more amenable for study than scores on national tests, such as the Scholastic Aptitude Test, that are taken by only a subset of high-performing students (Hoxby 2003). National accountability systems also emphasize performance on national and Statewide tests. However, test scores have been criticized as being a poor measure of the educational experience (Hitt, McShane, and Wolf 2018).

For private school choice programs, although results vary by individual study, Epple, Romano, and Urquiola (2017) conclude that most studies of voucher programs in the United States have not revealed large or statistically significant test score improvements for students in general. However, multiple studies uncover substantial test score improvements among Black students. For example, Mayer and others (2002) find that the School Choice Scholarship Foundation voucher program in New York City did not yield higher test scores on average for all students; but for Black students, test scores increased by about 6 percentage points. One notable exception to the positive findings for Black students is the Louisiana Scholarship Program (LSP). Abdulkadiroğlu, Pathak, and Walters (2018) find that the LSP led to a large decrease in math test scores among participants. They link this to the selection of low-quality, low-tuition schools into the program, pointing to the importance of program design for the success of private school choice.

For charter school programs, Epple, Romano, and Zimmer (2016) conclude that researchers have not reached a consensus on their effectiveness for academic achievement. Broad studies, including those by the Stanford Center for Research on Education Outcomes (CREDO 2009, 2013), do not reveal large or statistically significant test score improvements for charter school students on average (these studies compare test scores of students in charter schools with those of students that have similar observable attributes—"virtual twins"—in the fallback DPS). However, numerous studies of programs in urban areas find large, statistically significant gains. In particular, most studies of oversubscribed charter schools find positive effects on test scores. These studies are noted for the strength of their research design (they compare students who win the lottery with students that have similar observable attributes who lose the lottery; Epple, Romano, and Zimmer 2016). A recent study of a Massachusetts law allowing charter schools with a successful track record to expand finds that the new schools generate gains on par with the original schools (Cohodes, Setren, and Walters 2019). A study of Texas charter schools suggests that the effectiveness of charter schools is increasing over time, as successful charter schools expand and poorly performing schools exit (Baude et al. 2020). In both Massachusetts and Texas, many of the successful charter schools that have expanded use the "no excuses" approach, which features strong discipline, extended classroom instruction, and intensive tutoring. Of note, in a Boston study, Walters (2018) finds evidence that charter expansion programs are particularly effective when they target students who are unlikely to apply, including low achievers, as these students have the most to gain.

In comparison with test score studies, studies of educational attainment on the whole find more encouraging results. This is true for both voucher programs and charter programs (Epple, Romano, and Urquiola 2017; Epple,

Romano, and Zimmer 2016). For example, in a study of the Washington Opportunity Scholarship Program, Wolf and others (2010, 2013) estimate that vouchers raise high school graduation rates by 21 percentage points. As with test scores, vouchers appear to have an even more beneficial impact on the graduation rates of Black students. Shifting attention to college, Chingos and Peterson (2015) identify a 6-percentage-point boost to enrollment rates among Black students offered vouchers in New York City, although they find less evidence of an effect among a broader group of students. Sass and others (2016) find that students in Florida's charter schools stay in college longer than students in DPSs, reinforcing related findings by Booker Sass, and Zimmer (2011). Dobbie and Fryer (2015) find that students admitted to a high-performing charter school in the Harlem neighborhood of New York City are more likely to graduate from high school on time and enroll in college immediately after graduation, although they ultimately attain about the same amount of college education as DPS students.

The divergence between the results on test scores and the results on educational attainment leads some researchers to question whether test scores are a useful yardstick for evaluating school performance. Hitt, McShane, and Wolf (2018) review studies of a wide variety of school choice programs that measure test scores and educational attainment as part of the same study. They find little within-study correlation between results on test scores and educational attainment. Epple, Romano, and Zimmer (2016) also comment on this divergence, pointing to Wolf and others (2010) as an example of a study that finds no significant effects on test scores but strong positive effects on high school graduation rates.

Some studies address the impact of school choice on racial and ethnic integration. By separating the decision about where to attend school from the decision about where to live, school choice has the potential to reduce the role of income and race disparities in providing educational opportunity. Many school choice programs began in areas with high concentrations of minority and low-income students specifically to serve the needs of underserved communities with often poorly performing DPSs. As a result, charter schools educate a disproportionate number of such students relative to the national average. In the 2017–18 school year, Black and Hispanic students accounted for 26 percent and 33 percent of charter school enrollment, respectively, while accounting for only 15 and 27 percent, respectively, of enrollment across all public schools (NCES 2019d).

Regarding the impact of school choice on racial and ethnic stratification, Epple, Romano, and Zimmer (2016) discuss a large body of research and conclude that charter schools and public schools exhibit similar degrees of racial and ethnic segregation, with charter schools more likely to have a disproportionately nonwhite student population and DPSs more likely to have a disproportionately White student population. Moreover, Zimmer and others

(2009) conclude that charter schools have only modest effects on the racial mix of schools. Butler and others (2013) analyze the decision to attend charter schools and find a role for socioeconomic characteristics but not race as a driving factor. In terms of voucher programs, a recent study by Egalite, Mills, and Wolf (2017) assessing the Louisiana Scholarship Program finds that most students using the vouchers reduce racial stratification in the public schools that they leave and have only small effects on racial stratification in the schools to which they transfer. In addition, in school districts under Federal desegregation orders, voucher transfers cause a large drop in DPSs' racial stratification levels but have no impact on private schools.

Another body of literature focuses on the long-run benefit of school choice programs on outcomes such as civic engagement and criminal behavior. These studies are relatively rare because they require data from a period of many years. Two studies of the Milwaukee Parental Choice voucher program are worthy of note. DeAngelis and Wolf (2019) use data from the Milwaukee program to compare young adult voting behavior between program participants and similar students in DPS. They find no evidence of statistically different voting patterns, helping to allay potential concerns that private choice programs might provide less instruction in citizenship skills. DeAngelis and Wolf (2020) use the data from the Milwaukee program to analyze the prevalence of criminal activity. They find some evidence that voucher program participants are less likely to be involved in criminal activity relative to DPS students, including a large and statistically significant reduction in property damage convictions. Dobbie and Fryer (2015) find that for students admitted by lottery to a high-performing charter school in Harlem, New York City, female students are less likely to be pregnant as teenagers and male students are less likely to be incarcerated in comparison with similar students who are not admitted.

The discussion so far has focused on student outcomes in school choice programs. However, another relevant question is how much money is spent to achieve these outcomes. Several studies find that charter schools and voucher programs educate program participants at a lower cost per-pupil than DPSs. DeAngelis and others (2018) find that across 14 metropolitan areas, public charter schools received on average $5,828 less revenue per pupil than DPSs in the 2016 fiscal year. In a study of 16 voucher programs, Leuken (2018) finds that the voucher programs generated average savings of almost $3,100 per voucher recipient for State and local budgets in fiscal year 2015.

Indirect Procompetitive Effects

Finally, we turn to studies of the indirect procompetitive effects of school choice programs on DPSs. Such studies face several challenges. First, the penetration of choice programs in many areas of the United States is simply too small for robust procompetitive effects to have a reasonable chance of emerging. A DPS is little affected if it is only at risk of losing a handful of students to a choice program, in which case it does not face much market pressure to improve. Where school choice programs have reached sufficient penetration to enable study, researchers must try to distinguish competitive efforts by a DPS to improve its quality from effects related to changes in the DPS student composition and effects related to changes in DPS funding. However, the recent growth of school choice programs is enabling a growing number of well-designed empirical evaluations.

Figlio and Hart (2014) and Figlio, Hart, and Karbownik (2020) study the impact on DPS students of the Tax Credit Scholarship program in Florida. The latter study focuses on the scaling up of the program in recent years. They exploit the fact that some students are more exposed to this expansion due to the differing availability of nearby private schools before the policy is implemented. Public school students who are more heavily exposed to competition experience improved test scores as well as fewer suspensions and absences. Positive effects of increased competition from private schools are largest for students from low-income families whose parents have lower educational attainment. In addition, procompetitive effects on public schools increase over time as the program scales up. Similarly, Chakrabarti (2008) finds that the expansion of the private voucher program to religious schools in Milwaukee leads to larger increases in public school test scores. In a review of the literature, Epple, Romano, and Urquiola (2017) conclude that studies generally find that private school vouchers improve the performance of students in DPSs. They also find little evidence that school choice gives rise to adverse sorting. There are examples where the students who leave DPSs for a voucher program are of higher, lower, or equal ability relative to the peers they leave behind. Moreover, because voucher programs are often targeted to lower-income families, voucher students tend to come from families with lower or equal income to their peers in the DPSs that they leave behind. The empirical evidence on the positive returns from scaling up voucher programs and the absence of adverse sorting effects suggests that many more students could benefit from an expansion of voucher programs.

Positive competitive effects also arise for charter schools. Gilraine, Petronijevic, and Singleton (2019) find that when North Carolina lifted caps on new charter schools, students who lived closer to new charter schools experienced larger gains in test scores. Ridley and Terrier (2018) find that the Massachusetts reform that raised the cap on charter schools led to increased spending per pupil in DPSs and a shift in DPS spending from support services to instruction, and they similarly find small positive effects of charter schools on the test scores of DPS students. Dispelling concerns related to sorting and peer effects, Epple, Romano, and Zimmer (2016) synthesize the findings from several studies showing that students who transfer to charter schools have a similar or slightly lower ability relative to the DPS from which they are drawn. In a survey of further research on this topic vis-à-vis charter schools, Anderson

(2017) finds that charter schools often serve lower- or similarly performing students than DPSs.

Thus, the evidence from voucher and charter school studies alike suggest that there is little evidence to warrant fears about DPS students being left behind. Instead, such students tend to benefit from the improvement in their own schools that comes about from choice-induced educational competition.

As a final note, we return to the question of the fiscal effect of school choice programs on DPSs. As discussed, several studies find that public charter schools and voucher programs educate students with less per-pupil public funding than DPSs. This implies that when a student switches from the DPS to a choice program, the school district realizes savings that could be used to improve DPS education, although there may be an adjustment period before a district can realize those savings (Epple, Romano, and Zimmer 2016). To date, there has been relatively little research on this topic; but see Bifulco and Reback (2014) and Ladd and Singleton (2020) for case studies of New York and North Carolina. Buerger and Bifulco (2019) find that New York State school districts with larger charter school enrollments experience decreases in the cost of providing DPS education, both in the short run and the long run, though districts with only a small charter school presence can experience short-run increases in costs that are subsequently offset by efficiency gains. Some States provide temporary funding increases to DPSs to help them adjust to charter school expansion, including Massachusetts, as documented by Ridley and Terrier (2018).

Conclusion

School choice programs have grown dramatically over the past 30 years as evidence has accumulated about the benefits they provide. Parents are increasingly choosing alternatives to their assigned DPS as they seek out a higher-quality educational experience for their children. Federal policy has long supported school choice, both in the Trump Administration and in earlier administrations on both sides of the political aisle.

School choice can level the playing field and provide enhanced educational opportunity to all families, particularly when implemented to maximize competition and facilitate participation by disadvantaged students. The alternative to this modern form of school choice for everyone is the traditional system of school choice for the affluent and mobile, whereby those with financial means relocate to districts with better schools. In the traditional system, lower-income and minority students are disproportionately left behind in lower-performing schools, while other families may move away from neighborhoods that they enjoy solely to gain access to better schools. School choice programs that provide students with choices of public, charter, magnet, private, or home school can improve quality for all students, including those who remain in DPSs that are forced to adapt because of competitive pressure. Emerging empirical evidence has identified these positive effects at work in the United States.

As school choice continues to expand, lessons from existing programs can inform ways to maximize the benefits for children from all backgrounds. Research suggests that low-income and minority students tend to enjoy the greatest benefits, and the evidence on procompetitive effects suggests that substantial gains are possible from scaling up school choice. As a result, continuing to grow school choice programs is a promising way to reduce opportunity gaps and create a level playing field for all children. Research also suggests that a broader set of metrics should be used to assess school choice programs beyond standardized test scores in light of evidence that such choice programs can improve outcomes later in life. Parents themselves are also a source of wisdom in that they can incorporate other aspects of quality into their decisionmaking than the criteria that are officially measured. Ultimately, a focus on expanding opportunity for all students combined with a commitment to innovation that is grounded in evidence can help improve educational quality for all children.

Chapter 8

Exploring New Frontiers in Space Policy and Property Rights

The United States has been on the cutting edge of space exploration since the dawn of the space age and has become the world leader in commercial activity in space. In the 20th century, the United States became the first and only nation to send individuals to the Moon. After the end of the Apollo Program, the United States pioneered the Space Shuttle, the world's first reusable spacecraft. Now American engineers have become the first to demonstrate and operationalize the capabilities of commercial spacecraft for orbital cargo delivery, first-stage reusability, and human spaceflight.

In the 21st century, the United States has ushered in a new era of space exploration based on public-private partnerships and the success of private sector investment in space technologies. The Trump Administration recognizes the opportunities and benefits afforded by this new era and has advanced policies that encourage private sector innovation, collaboration with commercial companies, and a regulatory environment more conducive to investment in space. In doing so, this Administration is not only accelerating the development of the today's space industry; it is also laying the foundation for a viable space economy that can continue to develop and expand in the coming decades.

This past year has seen historic advances in spaceflight and space policy, even in the midst of the global COVID-19 pandemic. After the reestablishment of USSPACECOM as a combatant command for the space domain on August 19, 2019, President Trump established the U.S. Space Force (USSF), the sixth branch of the U.S. military, on December 20, 2019. The mission of USSF is to organize, train, and equip space forces to "protect U.S. and allied interests in space and to provide space capabilities to the joint force" (USSF n.d.). In addition, on May 30, 2020, and November 15, 2020, in major milestones for the partnership between the National Aeronautics and Space Administration (NASA) and the private sector, SpaceX launched a total of six astronauts from Cape Canaveral to the International Space Station (ISS). These missions, which represent the first commercial human spaceflights in history, are an important step for the private sector's role in the space economy.

In support of these achievements, the Trump Administration has advanced policies that strengthen investor confidence in the space economy to enable the private space sector to flourish. These new policies are creating an environment that spurs investment in innovation and encourages the responsible and sustainable use of space resources. In this spirit, the Administration has released the Artemis Accords, a practical set of principles that will create a safe, peaceful, prosperous, and open future in space. The initial tranche of signatories to these accords was announced on October 13, 2020, and included several other major spacefaring nations and international partners, with more to follow.

With regard to the economic theory of property rights and the large and diverse empirical literature on property rights, the Council of Economic Advisers finds substantial evidence that improving investors' expectations in a novel economic sector—like space—increases investment in that sector, leading to more innovation and greater benefits. The CEA estimates that private space investment could potentially double in the next eight years, due to President Trump's executive actions and other enhancements of property rights in space.

Much of the economic growth over the last five hundred years has occurred because economic actors have forgone present consumption to invest in the future. In support of this, a core tenet of the common law tradition is to ensure that future gains from investment accrue to the entities or individuals that make the investment and take on the subsequent risk. A fundamental role of government in this process is to set rules that create expectations about what the future holds for investors. Property rights form a legal and economic basis to support investment and provide a structure for the allocation and management of resources. Although new norms and systems will evolve with the growth of space exploration, the institution of property rights will be critical to encourage investment for the long-term development of the space economy.

This chapter highlights the Trump Administration's actions to enhance space property rights and maintain the United States' position on the frontier of innovation and economic development in space. A cornerstone of the Administration's policy is to encourage private investment in partnership with the Federal Government. The venture capital firm Space Capital estimated that companies invested $18 billion in space activities in 2019. The CEA projects that private investment in the space sector will reach $46 billion a year by 2028 as a result of the policies undertaken to clarify and improve the enforcement of property rights in space.

Property rights can be thought of as a "bundle of sticks," with each stick providing an aspect of the underlying rights that the owner can expect to receive (Barzel 1997). Sticks, in this case, could refer to the ability to transfer ownership of an asset, the right to earn income from the asset, or the right to restrict others from performing certain acts near the asset. As more sticks are added to the bundle, property rights are further specified, so that the owner can form more precise expectations of the value of a given investment. As activity has developed in space resources, new questions have arisen about property rights in space. The current system of international agreements does not require major changes, but it does need "carefully drafted additions and amendments" for clarification (Hertzfeld and von der Dunk 2005, 82). Recent actions by the Trump Administration seek to provide this clarification.

This chapter illustrates how recent U.S. space policy focuses on ensuring certainty and predictability for private investments in opportunities beyond Earth. The first section discusses current issues in space policy, and the second one addresses recent policy efforts and explains how they provide enhanced security and enforcement of property rights. The subsequent sections explain the economics of property rights theory and review the economic literature on how improving property rights affects investment. The chapter then projects future investment into space activities accounting for the effect of Federal Government policies on investment behavior. The chapter concludes by discussing the benefits of selecting the United States as the flag of choice—that is, the country whose frameworks a business finds most desirable—for space activity and how regulatory reform makes the market more competitive and innovative.

Current Issues in Space Policy
and the Space Economy

Today, most economic activity in space consists of satellites transmitting tele-communications and remote-sensing data to devices on Earth and the rockets launching these satellites into orbit. This orbital network of satellites has facilitated a variety of civil and economic activity on Earth, including weather forecasting, climate modeling, city planning, emergency response, precision agriculture, satellite television, satellite radio, global broadband Internet, and even app-based ridesharing services.

At this point in time, predicting some future industries in space is possible, but history suggests that anticipating all the emerging industries within the space economy is impossible. However, we can use recent developments in current technologies, such as in the satellite and rocket launch industries, to hypothesize what the future of the space economy could look like. For example, the process of mineral extraction on the Moon and other celestial bodies may become profitable as the costs of extraction fall and innovations in space manufacturing, habitation, and propulsion create a demand for resource availability in space. Space-based solar power is also a possibility, because orbiting solar panels can harness the sun's rays before they dissipate in Earth's atmosphere and can generate more electricity than terrestrially based solar panels. Finally, private companies are hoping to create a market for space tourism through partnerships with the Federal Government and innovations that lower costs, providing an experience quite literally like none other on Earth.

The beginnings of the space economy date to the mid–20th century, when the Soviet Union sent Sputnik 1 into orbit in 1957, spurring a flurry of investment into the space race from national governments. The National Aeronautics and Space Administration (NASA) began operations in 1958, sent the first American into space by 1961, and landed the first human on the Moon in 1969. These accomplishments occurred in parallel with a number of new United Nations treaties as countries around the globe contemplated the prospect of widespread activity in space. Because there were few profitable opportunities for the private sector at the time, the U.S. Government laid the groundwork for a space economy, and the industry developed based on projects funded by taxpayers (Weinzierl 2018).

Most space activity in the 1970s and 1980s involved the launch and operation of satellites for commercial telecommunications, reconnaissance, and surveillance purposes. In 1974, the first satellite of the forthcoming Global Positioning System (GPS) was launched into orbit (Pace et al. 1995). The Department of Defense initially utilized the GPS constellation purely for military purposes. However, in 1983, the United States announced that it would make GPS's standard positioning service available to the general public at no cost. This event initiated private, civilian uses of GPS that have since led to the

Figure 8-1. NASA Outlays and U.S. Private Investment, 2010–19

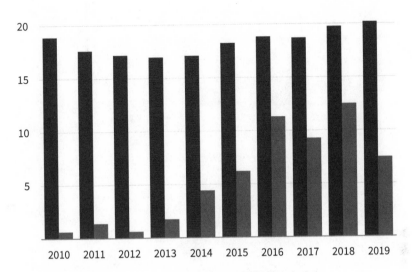

Dollars (billions) ■ NASA outlays   ■ U.S. private investment

Sources: Office of Management and Budget; Space Capital; CEA calculations.
Note: NASA = National Aeronautics and Space Administration.

creation of countless new firms, technologies, and applications. O'Connor and others (2019) estimate that GPS has generated about $1.4 trillion in economic benefits since being made available for civilian and commercial use.

Although governments initially funded all space activities, the private satellite industry grew throughout the second half of the 20th century as companies realized the market opportunity for satellite services, such as telecommunications, broadcasting, and data transmission. More recently, private industry has begun to offer other products and services that had been primarily owned and operated by the Federal Government, such as space launches, crew transportation, and remote sensing. For example, since the Space Shuttle was retired in 2011, private companies such as SpaceX and United Launch Alliance have provided launch services for civil, commercial, and national security space systems. Figure 8-1 shows that nongovernmental equity investment in U.S. space companies is rising in relation to the level of NASA outlays.

This shift from government launch vehicles toward commercial space launch services accelerated in 2005, when NASA began the $500 million Commercial Orbital Transportation Services (COTS) program. The COTS program operated on fixed-price payments rather than cost-plus procurement, which is intended to incentivize innovation and shift NASA's role from being

Table 8-1. Composition of Global Space Economy, 2019

Industry	Good or Service	Spending (billions of dollars)	Percentage of Space Economy
Satellite	Total	270.7	74.0
	Satellite ground equipment	130.3	35.6
	Television	92.0	25.1
	Fixed satellite services	17.7	4.8
	Satellite manufacturing	12.5	3.4
	Satellite radio	6.2	1.7
	Launch services	4.9	1.3
	Broadband	2.8	0.8
	Commercial remote sensing	2.3	0.6
	MSS	2.0	0.5
Nonsatellite	Total	95.3	26.0
	U.S. Government's space budget	57.9	16.0
	European space budget	12.0	3.3
	China's space budget	11.0	3.0
	Russia's space budget	4.1	1.1
	Rest of world's space budget	4.0	1.1
	Japan's space budget	3.1	0.8
	Commercial space flight	1.7	0.5
	India's space budget	1.5	0.4

Sources: Bryce Space and Technology; CEA calculations.

an owner and operator to being a customer for resupply services to the International Space Station. This method of procurement and the use of other contracting mechanisms have been gaining traction elsewhere in the space industry, in an effort to decrease costs and benefit from private innovation (box 8-1). Market competition has since provided stronger incentives for innovation than the existing government monopoly on launches. NASA estimates that the use of commercial services for ISS resupply services alone has saved taxpayers between $20 billion and $30 billion since 2011.

Annual estimates of the size of the space economy, incorporating both public and private activities, range from $360 billion to $415 billion. The current state of commercial activities still consists primarily of satellites and satellite services with industry revenues of nearly $270 billion as of 2019, making up 74 percent of the space economy (table 8-1). NASA's activities and procurements still drive a large amount of economic activities across the Nation, however,

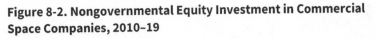

Figure 8-2. Nongovernmental Equity Investment in Commercial Space Companies, 2010–19

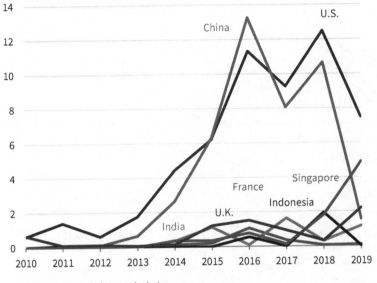

Dollars (billions)

Sources: Space Capital; CEA calculations.

with NASA's overall economic impact estimated at over $64 billion for financial year 2019 based on IMPLAN analysis. Recent technological developments will allow new industries to mature. For example, dramatic reductions in the cost of space launches are increasing the economic viability of private space activities such as tourism and mining. Technologies enabling the Moon, Mars, and asteroid surface operations will mark critical milestones for the next generation of space exploration. The reduced cost of access to space will broaden the set of countries that are able to take advantage of the opportunities in outer space and ensure benefit to people around the globe. Furthermore, in situ resource utilization of space resources derived from celestial bodies themselves for potable water, breathable air, and spacecraft propellant will allow longer-term survival away from Earth's surface. Once long-term survival in cislunar space is viable, further explorations deeper into space will be possible. And once technologies advance to make long-term survival viable, government policies clarifying property rights will provide the needed framework for a flourishing space economy.

Figure 8-2 shows nongovernmental equity investment in space companies from 2010 through 2019. Most private investment in space companies has occurred in the United States and China, with smaller levels of investment occurring in European and Asian economies. Investment in commercial space companies is only a small percentage of the total space economy, but it reflects

Box 8-1. Public-Private Partnerships for Human Spaceflight

The year 2020 has been historic for NASA, as the SpaceX Crew Dragon Demo-2 mission marked the first commercially developed crewed mission to the International Space Station as part of NASA's Commercial Crew Program. NASA has emphasized the implementation of public-private partnerships to advance space exploration through collaborations with the developing commercial space sector. After NASA's Space Shuttle program ended in 2011, the United States relied on the Russian-designed and operated Soyuz spacecraft to send American astronauts into space. However, the development of domestic commercial alternatives has allowed the U.S. government to regain its domestic human launch capability while supporting U.S. commercial companies.

The Commercial Crew Program, which supported the Crew Dragon mission by providing SpaceX with development funds, also used fixed-price contracts, with NASA working as a partner rather than supervisor. Cost reimbursement or cost-plus contracts had been more commonly used by NASA in the past, because technically complex and novel projects prevented it from receiving accurate advance estimates of risk and cost. However, these types of contracts provide weak incentives for innovation, given that any cost savings innovation undertaken by the firm leads to lower revenues and often incentivizes companies to increase the costs and lengths of their contracts. Fixed-price contracts, conversely, provide strong incentives for innovation and delivery of products or services on time and under budget. Per NASA's 2021 fiscal year budget request, fixed-price contracting is now considered the "first choice whenever possible" due to the incentives produced by placing increased responsibility on contractors.

Public-private partnerships have been shown to lower the costs of space products and services for taxpayers and to speed the growth of the space economy. The Commercial Crew Program's investment in the private sector has driven innovation, efficiency, and effective manufacturing and business techniques, and NASA has projected that it will save between $20 billion and $30 billion relative to the cost to develop its own crewed spacecraft. After the Space Shuttle program ended, the cost to fly an American astronaut on a Russian Soyuz rocket rose from $40 million in 2011 to about $90 million in 2020, given that the Russians held a monopoly on crewed launch vehicles. A SpaceX launch, by comparison, costs about $65 million per astronaut. SpaceX is able to reduce costs through new approaches to recover and reuse its spacecraft and launch vehicles.

In 2011, there were zero commercial launches in the United States, because the market was dominated by international competitors that were largely subsidized by their governments. Today, as a direct result of U.S. Government investments in the U.S. commercial space sector, most commercial space launches are conducted in the United States by companies such as SpaceX, which employs over 6,000 people throughout the country.

Looking to the future of public-private partnerships, NASA has been increasingly making the ISS available to commercial research and manufacturing activities, as supported by the ISS National Laboratory. In addition, NASA is allowing visits to the ISS by commercial astronauts aboard SpaceX's Dragon 2 and Boeing's Starliner. Companies are expected to purchase seats on private sector rockets for missions in low-Earth orbit and to the ISS in early 2022. These missions include opportunities for space tourism and commercial enterprise, and represent the next step in the space economy.

In addition, NASA will rely heavily on the private sector for the Artemis program in its mission to accomplish the next chapter in U.S. exploration of deep space: returning humans to the lunar surface by 2024. These include contracts for the Human Landing System to take astronauts to and from the Moon with stays lasting as long as two weeks.

the growing excitement about space companies and optimism for future returns on investment.

Although there has been large growth in economic activity in the space sector as a whole, a significant portion of space industry revenue is still made up of satellite services. As illustrated in table 8-1, over 75 percent of global spending in space is for the satellite industry, and the majority of the remainder is government spending. The only other category that is large enough to break out is the commercial human spaceflight industry.

Space Policy Developments

As investment and innovation grow in the space economy and we surpass new milestones in space exploration, the United States will continue to work to ensure the international and domestic framework for property rights in outer space resources develops in a manner that provides certainty and predictability for industry. Doing so will reinforce the progress the United States has made in the space sector that, based on CEA estimates, could double investment in space and accelerate new space technologies. Here, we first describe the main international treaties and domestic laws that have developed since the 1950s and provide a legal framework that supports the space economy. We then describe the efforts of the Trump Administration to advance and execute these agreements.

The United States is a party to four United Nations treaties on space. The United Nations Outer Space Treaty of 1967 laid the foundation for international space law, establishing outer space as a peaceful territory, designating astronauts as envoys of humankind, and declaring that each State bears responsibility for activities in space, "whether such activities are carried on by governmental agencies or by non-governmental entities." Whereas private entities are usually responsible for damages they impose, the Outer Space Treaty explicitly states that the country from which the object launches or the country that procures the launch bears responsibility for damages on Earth or in space.

The United States also approved the 1968 Rescue Agreement, which outlined the rescue provisions in the Outer Space Treaty requiring countries to assist personnel when landing within national borders or in places not under any jurisdiction, such as space. The Liability Convention, which entered into force in 1972, clarified the meaning of "launching State" to be the country "which launches or procures the launching of a space object" or "from whose territory or facility a space object is launched." The convention also defined what "damage" consists of and outlined a diplomatic process for resolving claims for compensation.

Finally, the United States agreed to be a party to the 1976 Registration Convention that instructs nations to register space objects launched into orbit or space. While the United States was a party to these four early United Nations treaties and resolutions establishing international space law, it did not ratify the United Nations Moon Agreement in 1979, which effectively banned private ownership of extraterrestrial property. Many other major spacefaring nations, including Russia and the People's Republic of China, are not parties to the Moon Agreement.

Domestically, the United States has gradually developed a framework of private property rights in space through legislative and executive action. U.S. space law was first codified in the 1958 National Aeronautics and Space Act, which created NASA, although military space activities were already under way within the Department of Defense. The Commercial Space Launch Act of 1984 created the process for licensing U.S. commercial space launches. The subsequent Commercial Space Launch Amendments of 1988 encouraged commercial space launches by providing Federal Government indemnification for damages exceeding $500 million to more than $2 billion.

Moving into the 21st century, three concrete policy achievements helped further codify property rights in space. First, the U.S. Commercial Space Launch Competitiveness Act of 2015 established the statutory framework for the Federal Government to permit domestic private entities to extract and use resources in space:

> A United States citizen engaged in commercial recovery of an asteroid resource or a space resource . . . shall be entitled to any asteroid resource or space resource obtained, including to possess, own, transport, use, and sell the asteroid resource or space resource obtained in accordance with applicable law, including the international obligations of the United States.

The U.S. Commercial Space Launch Competitiveness Act designates how the United States licenses and approves attempts to utilize space resources in line with authority granted to national governments in the Outer Space Treaty. Article VI of the Outer Space Treaty states that "activities of non-governmental entities in outer space . . . shall require authorization and continuing supervision by the appropriate State Party to the Treaty."

In 2020, the Trump Administration further clarified expectations and responsibilities for commercial activities in space by enumerating the U.S. position on property rights and laying out principles for international bilateral agreements. In April 2020, the Trump Administration announced Executive Order 13914, "Encouraging International Support for the Recovery and Use of Space Resources." This executive order announced the United States' intention to work with international partners to ensure that commercial exploration and the use of space resources is consistent with applicable laws. It also explicitly rejected the Moon Agreement, which the United States had not signed, because it was perceived to have prevented the application of private property rights to resources in space.

On October 13, 2020, the United States and seven partner spacefaring nations signed the Artemis Accords, a set of principles grounded in the Outer Space Treaty to ensure safety and avoid conflict. The principles of the Artemis Accords are peaceful exploration, transparency, interoperability, emergency assistance, registration of space objects, release of scientific data, preserving heritage, space resources, deconfliction of activities, and orbital debris. The Artemis Accords uphold that resource extraction and utilization must comply with the Outer Space Treaty, while also affirming that "extraction of space resources does not inherently constitute national appropriation under Article II of the Outer Space Treaty." The accords provide investors with more certainty when considering other countries' positions on resource extraction. Eight founding member nations signed the Artemis Accords: Australia, Canada, Italy, Japan, Luxembourg, the United Arab Emirates, the United Kingdom, and the United States. NASA anticipates that additional countries will join the Artemis Accords in the months and years ahead.

Taken together, these three policy developments built on past treaties and laws to further clarify outer space property rights. The increased security of property rights should lead to increased investment and economic activity, as individuals are able to form expectations and plan for future returns on that investment. As is discussed further below, the ability to make long-term plans has many direct and indirect positive effects.

The Economics of Property Rights

A large body of economic literature demonstrates the positive effects on investment from the initiation of policies that are similar to the space policy developments discussed above. The examples come from a wide range of geographies, natural resources, and time periods. This section provides an overview of the economic theory of property rights as well as several examples of the theory in practice, including how it applies to the space economy.

North (1991) considers the importance of institutions for shaping and constraining political, economic, and social interactions. Institutions guide economic change toward more growth, decline, or stagnation, depending on the incentive structure they enforce. Tangibly, government institutions determine and enforce property rights as rules governing the economy that shape the competitiveness and efficiency of markets. As rules for property rights are further specified, market participants interact with more certainty about the benefits and costs of potential activities.

The seminal work of Demsetz (1967) outlines the economics behind the evolution of property rights. Property rights bring clarity to people when they are weighing potential decisions. Accordingly, the benefits to setting and further clarifying property rights allow individuals to form more accurate expectations of how the rest of society will interact and respond to their actions. Property rights encourage an individual to undertake investments with the understanding of which benefits will accrue to that individual.

Establishing and enforcing property rights impose costs on society, as resources are devoted to monitoring and ensuring compliance. An individual's expectations are based on the understanding that the rest of society will comply with the rights specified, but if other parties are allowed to violate an individual's property right without recourse, then it will be difficult to set expectations.

As figure 8-3 shows, the optimal specification of property rights changes as the benefits and costs change. The figure depicts the optimal specification of property rights at two different points in time. In 1967, when the Outer Space Treaty was signed, there were only two entities engaged in outer space activity: the United States and Soviet Union. As access to space and other space technologies have increased, the benefits that companies can expect from engaging in economic activity in space have grown. These increase the benefits of property right specification, as ensuring investors have clear expectations about how benefits accrue across society will lead to higher gains from investment.

Advances in technology that improve monitoring and enforcement will lower the cost of further specifying property rights or adding more "sticks" to the bundle. This decrease in the cost of enforcement, along with the increase in the benefits from setting investment expectations, implies that the optimal level of property rights specification should increase (as shown in figure 8-3). The Artemis Accords, for example, are giving investors clearer guidance for how civil space activities will be conducted and the principles that will guide government decisionmaking. Although the Artemis Accords do not apply directly

Figure 8-3. Marginal Cost and Benefit of Property Rights Specification

Cost of enforcement

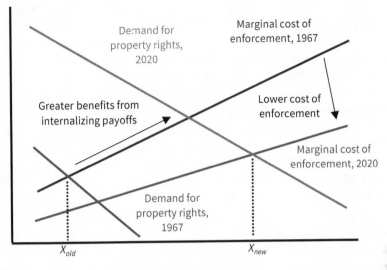

Level of property right specification

to the private sector, the United States is responsible, via Article VI of the 1967 Outer Space Treaty, for all individuals subject to its jurisdiction or control. In this regard, the principles of the Artemis Accords provide clarification to companies about the role of governments in space and eliminate uncertainty about public-private interactions.

Historical Examples of Property Rights Evolution

Historical examples of the development of property rights establish that without these extra sticks in the property rights bundle, we should expect to see higher costs and lower benefits from investments in the space economy, potentially hindering future developments in outer space.

The early history of oil drilling provides an example of how resources are likely to be wasted if property rights are not established in a timely manner. Until the early 20th century, oil was not considered property until it was extracted. This led to what Libecap and Smith (2002) call extractive anarchy. Companies drilled wells without concern for maximizing the amount of oil produced from a well, but instead sought to be the first to extract and claim ownership of the oil. Oil flows from a well because of the pressure inside the reservoir; if too many wells are drilled into one reservoir, then the pressure escapes too quickly to push the oil in the reservoir up the well. As a result, less oil is extracted. By 1914, the director of the Federal Bureau of Mines estimated that a quarter of the value of all petroleum production was being wasted due to the race to extract oil. Further, due to oil and natural gas being found together in a reservoir, the lower-valued natural gas was often vented into the atmosphere to ensure that the oil was extracted and thus ownership was secured. As time went on, the structure of property rights for oil and gas has changed to allow for increased value to be created from investments in resource extraction.

Without clear in situ property rights for subsurface resources, space could see a repeat of this behavior for its natural resources. Many elements that are common in space are frequently used in important technologies. Iron, aluminum, and titanium are elements critical to the production of electrical components. Silicon is a raw material for solar panels and computers. Extracted water can be broken down into hydrogen and oxygen to meet a variety of needs—oxygen is breathable, recombining hydrogen and oxygen generates electrical power, and liquid hydrogen and liquid oxygen can serve as propellants (Butow et al. 2020). Though it may sound futuristic, we can imagine a situation where mining expeditions recklessly extract resources from various celestial bodies, severely depleting the deposit of resources and diminishing the returns on future investment in mining. Therefore, defining property rights now to ensure the responsible use of resources in space could lead to future higher levels of demand and investment in exploration and a more sustainable space economy.

A similar story emerges for mineral rights in Nevada during the 19th century (Libecap 1978). As new deposits of minerals were found, especially those deposits further underground requiring increased investment for extraction, the specification and enforcement of property rights increased. One of the largest deposits in Nevada, the Comstock Lode, was discovered while Nevada was still a Federal territory. Property rights for discoveries on Federal lands were lacking at the time, so citizens created a series of local laws and eventually founded the State of Nevada to ensure these property rights. Libecap (1978) shows that as deposits increased in value, local property rights specification also increased. It may seem difficult to imagine how local property rights would be formed in space as in territorial Nevada, given the lack of settlements in space. However, this history implies that it is important to set these rules as economic actors spend extended time in space in order to maximize the future investment in the space economy.

Investment Responses to Property Right Enhancement

All the space policy developments discussed above have improved the ability of investors to set expectations for the manner in which benefits flow from investments in space. The historical examples given argue that further specifying property rights will bolster investment in the space economy. Increased investments in the space economy will lead to advances in space technology. In this subsection, we discuss the economics literature that addresses the effects of setting and strengthening property rights on both investment and economic growth. The research presented here aims to convey that the benefits for economic activity from improved setting of expectations that clarifies property rights is universal and not just due to specific circumstances of time and/or place.

Losses from short-term decisionmaking. A growing concern for future space exploration activities arises from a lack of property rights security leading to short-term decisionmaking, which may inhibit long-term human activity. Many empirical studies show that insecure property rights lead to investment decisions with lower values. Many of these studies have come from analyses of water rights in the western United States. In what is known as the Prior Appropriation Doctrine, water rights are handed out based on a "first in time, first in right" principle. Given that the amount of water available changes each year due to precipitation patterns, water rights holders that were, earlier in time, known as senior rights holders are more likely to receive their water allocation each year than those that were later in time, known as junior rights holders.

Leonard and Libecap (2019) argue that the Prior Appropriation Doctrine, with its clear rights for senior rights holders, allowed for investment in irrigation technologies. Given the climate of the western United States, large-scale investment in irrigation is required to maximize the productivity of large swaths of land. Leonard and Libecap estimate that 16 percent of western States' income in 1930 is attributable to investments made in irrigation that would not have occurred without secure property rights.

Another concern with insecure property rights is that owners of natural resources rush to extract them to ensure that they accrue the benefits of their investments. This rush to extract resources has a detrimental effect on the value obtained from those resources and other negative spillover effects on society. One example is the increase in the rate of deforestation that occurs when property rights for the land are insecure (Bohn and Deacon 2000). Ferreira (2004) finds that those countries with clearly defined property rights experience less deforestation than those with weaker protections. Kemal and Lange (2018) find that a reduced chance of oil well expropriation in Indonesia lowered the rate of extraction by up to 40 percent.

If short-term decisionmaking prevails in the initial incursions into space, the future of the space economy could be seriously harmed. Depleting the resources necessary to sustain life in space would mean having to transport these resources from Earth at a prohibitive cost and complexity. Therefore, protecting and responsibly using the resources available in space is more efficient in the long term. If done prudently, establishing property rights in space could diminish the risk of short-term decisionmaking and strengthen the ability of humans to receive benefits from space.

Enhanced investment and asset value. Frameworks such as the U.S. Commercial Space Launch Competitiveness Act and the Artemis Accords enhance property rights by providing clear expectations of the benefits one can receive from their investment and providing a list of principles that partner nations will follow as a way to encourage economic activity in space. One branch of the economics literature uses legal or legislative decisions that enhance or diminish property rights to determine how investment and asset values respond to a change in property rights specification. We discuss this literature here. Later in the chapter, we apply the conclusions of these studies to estimate the value of enhancing property rights in space.

Alston and Smith (2020) measure the effect of uncertain property rights resulting from the manner in which Northern Pacific Railroad's land grants were structured. The Federal Government provided generous land grants to railroad companies in hopes of ensuring the quick buildout of rail infrastructure. Northern Pacific was granted almost 16 percent of the land area in Montana, a State that requires coordination among its farmers and ranchers to irrigate any tract of land for productive use. Delays in the completion of the rail line in the 1870s led to uncertainty as to whether Northern Pacific owned (and could sell) land in its land grant or whether the land was the property of the Federal Government.

As a result of this uncertainty, completed irrigation projects averaged delays of four years, while investment in irrigation projects decreased by 28 percent. Insecure property rights affected the landowners whose rights were secure, because irrigation projects often require coordination among many parcels due to their high capital costs. The delay in undertaking irrigation investments led to these landowners being more junior water rights holders and, subsequently, holding less secure water rights. In total, Montana's economic activity was 6 percent lower in 1930 as a result of these insecure property rights.

Grainger and Costello (2014) compare the value of more secure property rights for fisheries in the United States, Canada, and New Zealand. New Zealand's regulations on quotas to operate in a given fishery explicitly state that these quotas are a property right, yet similar quota systems in the United States and Canada have regulations that explicitly state that the quotas are not property rights. The fact that the United States' and Canada's fishery quotas are not as secure as New Zealand's quotas leads to a lower perpetuity value of the quotas relative to their current annual value. Because U.S. and Canadian firms have the potential for their quotas to be taken away without recourse, their assets have lower values relative to New Zealand's firms. In an additional analysis, Grainger and Costello (2014) show that the increased security of property rights with the settling of an ownership dispute between native New Zealanders, known as the Maori, and New Zealanders of European descent improved the perpetuity value of fishing quotas by 50 percent. Ensuring that property rights will be honored is very important for market participants in understanding the value of their asset.

Galiani and Schargodsky (2010) use a court case in Argentina to estimate the effect of secure property rights for one's home on household decisions. Their results show that households that gained secure property rights increased their investments in the home structure. Investment in walls and roofs increased by 40 percent and 47 percent, respectively, as a result of households being granted title to the home. Though not directly related to space assets, the available evidence demonstrates that more secure property rights lead to other spillover benefits that are not directly related to the assets on which a property rights are granted. Galiani and Schargodsky (2010) find that when households had increased property rights security, they increased investment in their children's education. Children in households who obtained the secure property rights on their land achieved an extra 0.7 year of schooling on average. This is an important spillover effect given the large individual and societal benefits of extra years of education (see chapter 7 of this *Report*).

Telecommunications satellites orbiting Earth provide an example of positive spillovers from ensuring secure property rights in space. The International Telecommunication Union (ITU) is an organization that standardizes rules and regulations for a wide range of communications. Through the ITU, the United States was able to operate satellites that used specific frequencies to transmit information to Earth, thereby allowing companies to invest in utilizing those signals for commercial purposes. Communications satellites in geosynchronous orbit rely on the ITU to secure access to specific orbital slots as well as specific frequencies.

Protection against expropriation. A number of nongovernmental organizations produce indices that measure property rights protections or general institutional quality. The indices attempt to quantify the relative level of property rights characteristics, such as the rule of law or protection against expropriation risk, that are consistent across countries and time. A large body of economics literature uses these country-level indices of institutional quality to determine the extent to which improvements in property rights enforcement affect economic outcomes. Policies initiated under the Trump Administration would likely alter these indices in a measurable way if there were a property rights index for space.

Seminal work by Acemoglu, Johnson, and Robinson (2001) shows that improving the enforcement of property rights, in this case property rights that protect against expropriation risk, has large effects on gross domestic product (GDP). In their analysis, the authors show that a one-unit improvement in the protection against expropriation risk would lead to more than doubling GDP per capita 10 years later.

Similar results are found when researchers examine specific industries. For example, Cust and Harding (2020) show that firms drill for oil twice as often in countries with stronger property rights enforcement relative to their neighbors with weaker property rights. They also show that the effect of the enforcement of rights is most important for private international oil companies relative to national oil companies, highlighting the important role of stronger rights for harnessing private investment. Bohn and Deacon (2000) find a similar pattern for the effect on oil drilling as property rights security improves, with a 30 percent increase in security leading to a 60 percent increase in drilling per year.

Some changes in property rights enforcement come through improvements in technology. Hornbeck (2010) uses the invention and widespread use of barbed wire as a technology advancement that reduced the costs of enforcing property rights in agriculture. Importantly, Hornbeck compares areas that had access to timber for wooden fences with those that did not and finds a 23 percent relative improvement in crop productivity when barbed wire came into use, as barbed wire lowered the relative cost of fencing. Most of the gain came from farmers altering the type of crop that they planted once they were confident that livestock would not destroy the crop. This increased ability to effectively enforce property rights led to investments that increased the total area of farmland that had been improved by 19 percentage points, while also increasing land values. In many ways, this example of marking off territory is similar to the Artemis Accords' "Deconfliction of Activities" Principle. This principle prescribes setting "safety zones" to limit harmful interference and keep the probability of accidental loss to a minimum.

The Effects of Policies on Investment in Space Industries

The previous section detailed the expansive literature showing that more secure property rights increase both investment and economic activity. The examples discussed varied across time and space, leaving little doubt that the results are not driven by random chance; the studies as a whole reveal that the findings hold outside specific examples. Because the examples are numerous and varied, determining an average effect of more secure property rights on investment is difficult. Each study concerns a particular improvement in the security of property rights that is difficult to quantify. However, it is still a goal of this chapter to estimate the effect of the last year's space policy developments on future investment, given the available evidence.

Table 8-2 summarizes the effects of most of the studies discussed in the previous section. All these effects are large in magnitude. Another data point is the increase of investment in the space economy in the United States with the passage of the U.S. Commercial Space Launch Competitiveness Act in 2015 relative to investments in other countries. Using the Space Capital data discussed in the second section, and the historical examples given above, the CEA

Table 8-2. Summary of Effects of Property Rights Improvement

Study	Industry	Cause	Effect	Timing of Impact
Acemoglu, Johnson, and Robinson (2001)	All	Expropriation risk	GDP per capita increased 100%	10 years
Alston and Smith (2020)	Land	Tenure uncertainty	Investment delayed	5–10 years
Bohn and Deacon (2000)	Oil	Expropriation risk	Investment increased 100%	Immediate
Cust and Harding (2020)	Oil	Expropriation risk	Investment increased 200%	Immediate
Galiani and Schargodsky (2010)	Housing	Tenure uncertainty	Investment increased 40%	15 years
Grainger and Costello (2014)	Fisheries	Tenure uncertainty	Asset value increased 50%	Immediate
Hornbeck (2010)	Agriculture	Enforcement	Productivity increased 23%	5–10 years
Leonard and Libecap (2019)	Water	Tenure uncertainty	Income 16% higher	40 years

Note: This table summarizes the main findings of the papers discussed in the previous section of the main text. Each study has a different issue with property rights and the impact on the outcomes of interest.

estimates the increase in investment in the United States due to the improved property rights specification in 2015. Controlling for country and time period effects, the data show a statistically significant increase in investment of 92 percent—or roughly double—in the United States since passage of the U.S. Commercial Space Launch Competitiveness Act relative to countries that did not improve property specification. Together, these small improvements in the security of property rights have the potential to lead to large increases in investment. As an approximation, the CEA assumes that these improvements in property rights security will double the amount of investment in space. This number is in line with the evidence that has been discussed here.

To project the effect of the enhancements of property rights security that the Trump Administration's policies have achieved, the CEA starts with data from Space Capital on total private investment in space activities. Figure 8-4 illustrates the increasing rate of private investment in space activities.

The review of the literature discussed above shows that further property rights specification leads to increased investment and further economic

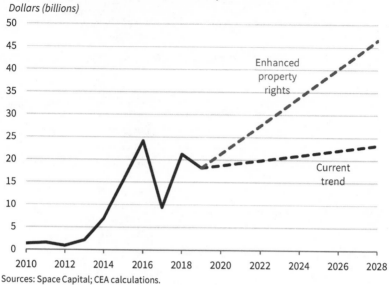

Figure 8-4. Nongovernmental Equity Investment in Commercial Space Companies in the United States, 2010–28

Dollars (billions)

Enhanced property rights

Current trend

Sources: Space Capital; CEA calculations.

Note: Data before 2020 reflect actual investment; subsequent years are forecasts.

activity. In figure 8-4, the diverging lines from 2020 to 2028 project the expected path of private investment as a result of policy developments in 2020.

The Space Capital data suggest that a linear projection of private investment in space would reach $23 billion in 2028, which is illustrated by the blue dashed line in figure 8-4. However, this does not take into account property rights enhancements that occurred in 2020 or will be occurring in the future. Therefore, the CEA projects that private investment in space will reach $46 billion by 2028. This projection is based on a doubling of investment over the eight-year period, which is in line with empirical estimates in the academic literature discussed above.

Establishing rights to distant resources with the goals of incentivizing economic development and investment has not always produced the desired results. The above-mentioned examples demonstrate how property rights specification and security can lead to increased investment. However, aligning incentives is a necessary but not sufficient condition in the short term. For example, the leading asteroid mining companies that were supporting the space resources language in the Commercial Space Launch Amendments Act of 2004 have both failed, despite the benefit of positive Federal legislation. In addition, the Deep Seabed Hard Mineral Resources Act, which was passed in 1980, established a legal system for extracting resources from the deep seabed with hopes of achieving economic viability before 2000. Forty years after the law's passage, the deep seabed mineral extraction industry still lacks the technology for economical extraction and does not bolster the argument that enhanced property rights typically unlock commercial value. Certain similarities do exist with the space industry, such as the need for technological innovation, the considerable distance to the resources, and some uncertainty about the types of resources for extraction.

Moreover, the space resource extraction industry currently lacks a customer base other than national governments, and even government demand will not become substantive until robust human and robotic operations on the lunar surface and elsewhere can be established. However, several key differences would support a space resource extraction industry. First, the commercial space industry benefits from public investment in civil space exploration, which might result in a decreased amount of investment necessary for the development of basic technologies. In addition, space exploration and research remain a national priority for many countries, which may drive further development of the industrial base. Moreover, space resource extraction potentially offers more valuable resources than deep sea mining (Barton and Recht 2018).

Looking Ahead

Increased investment, flowing from the enhancement of property rights, expands the possibilities of economic activity in space and transforms abstract issues into real considerations for national economies, companies, and individuals.

Flag of Choice

The origins of spacecraft and the settlement of international disputes beyond Earth's surface remain critical issues for space policy. The flag of choice in commercial space activity will depend on a nation's ability to provide the domestic infrastructure and international support needed to spur investment while mitigating risk. The development of a healthy space economy built on a strong industrial base, sensible regulatory environment, and the enforcement of property rights, along with national support in international disputes, will ensure that the United States becomes and remains the flag of choice for private space ventures.

Space vehicles, similar to naval vessels, are required to operate under the laws, or "flag," of a particular country. The process of flagging occurs when a company incorporates itself in a country or launches from that country. Once flagged, the vessel must abide by the flag state's laws, which include tax liabilities as well as labor and environmental regulations (Taghdiri 2013). The process of selecting a flag leads companies to seek flag countries with a legal, policy, and regulatory environment that is most favorable for their business activities.

The practice of finding a "flag of convenience" is one threat to maintaining a functional system of space travel, because companies could opt for flags of countries with little oversight, as is seen with waterborne vessels (Llinás 2016). Panama, for example, has become the flag of choice for ships, with more than double the number of ships of any other country due to an easy registration process and low-cost labor. In contrast to maritime law, which places the responsibility for redressing damages on private actors, the 1967 UN Outer Space Treaty established that countries assume the full responsibility and risk of spacecraft launching from their territory. This forces countries to weigh the costs and benefits of flagging spacecraft before allowing them to launch from their territories. Inevitably, accidents in space will occur, such as with the 2009 satellite collision between Iridium 33 and Cosmos 2251. The incident occurred when the Cosmos 2251, a derelict satellite from Russia, collided with Iridium 33, a commercial U.S. communications satellite, and both parties placed the blame on the other for not avoiding the collision. The United States and Russia were able to settle the potential dispute outside the Liability Convention, but this event highlighted the need for a predictable system for resolving disputes in space to provide the certainty needed for long-term investment in space ventures. Flying under the flag of the United States will provide companies with the backing of a sovereign state with substantial diplomatic capital that is willing to engage on their behalf, supporting a growing space economy in the United States (box 8-2).

Incentivizing the Private Sector

The Department of Defense continues to foster partnerships with the private sector through design competitions that award contracts to both large and small space technology companies, and through consulting programs that mentor small companies in competing for these contracts. These events and programs include the Space Enterprise Consortium; the Space Pitch Day, which awards grants to accelerate new technology; and the National Security Space Launch, which is helping to create new engines and launch vehicles. These partnerships help break down barriers to entry for smaller firms in this industry, which will drive competition and innovation, while decreasing the cost of operating within the space economy. To ensure that the United States maintains its leadership in space innovation and remains the flag of choice for space commerce, it must maintain a business-friendly regulatory environment that offers streamlined permitting, encourages innovation and risk-taking, and safeguards workers, the public, and property.

The Trump Administration has prioritized regulatory reform over the past four years, and it continues to focus on cutting red tape in the space sector. With regulatory authorities distributed among the Federal Aviation Administration, Federal Communications Commission, and National Oceanic Atmospheric Administration, the Trump Administration has made efforts to

Box 8-2. National Security and Space

Space-based capabilities are crucial for the United States' security. Space has become a primary component of U.S. military operations, including missile warning, geolocation and navigation, target identification, and activities to track adversaries. Remote-sensing satellites have greatly improved military and intelligence collection capabilities, thereby reducing other countries' ability to carry out covert military exercises and operations.

As advancements in the space sector occur, such as technological improvements and lower barriers to entry, foreign governments are developing capabilities that could threaten the United States' freedom to operate in space. In a 2020 report, the Defense Intelligence Agency points out how China and Russia, in particular, are trying to undermine the United States' advantage in space (DIA 2019). For example, Chinese and Russian military doctrines present a view that counterspace capabilities serve as a tool to reduce the effectiveness of U.S. and allied military forces. Both countries have developed extensive space surveillance networks that enable them to monitor, track, and target American and allied forces. Additionally, both China and Russia are working on their cyberspace and jamming capabilities.

The Trump Administration recognizes the importance of establishing and maintaining influence in space and providing space security for U.S. interests and the American people. In March 2018, the White House unveiled a new National Space Strategy that places an emphasis on "peace through strength in the space domain." Though adversaries are attempting to use space as a weapon, the United States' stance is to protect the space domain from conflict and secure the United States' vital interests in space—namely, the freedom of operation in space to advance security, economic prosperity, and scientific knowledge.

Although peace in the space domain is a top priority, the National Space Strategy affirms that the United States needs to be vigilant about any harmful interference within the space domain that negatively affects America's or its allies' vital interests and must "deter, counter, and defeat" any such threats.

Space systems are vital to the U.S. economy and national security, and they enable key functions such as global communications; positioning, navigation, and timing; scientific observation; exploration; weather monitoring; and multiple vital national defense applications. In September 2020, President Trump issued Space Policy Directive (SPD)–5, "Cybersecurity Principles for Space Systems," which provides guidance on the protection of space assets and supporting infrastructure from evolving cyber threats.

The National Space Strategy also emphasizes the importance of better leveraging and supporting the commercial sector to ensure that American companies are leaders in space technology. This is discussed more throughout this chapter.

To strengthen the United States' military position in the space domain, President Trump established the United States Space Force (USSF) as the sixth branch of the U.S. Armed Forces by signing the National Defense Authorization Act for fiscal year 2020. Vice President Pence has stated that the mission of the Space Force is to "develop and implement the unique strategy, doctrine, tactics, techniques and procedures our armed forces need to deter and defeat a new generation of threats in space" (Pence 2019). Its responsibilities include "developing military space professionals, acquiring military space systems, maturing the military doctrine for space power, and organizing space forces to present to our Combatant Commands" (USSF 2020).

modernize the authorization process for new space missions, as directed in Space Policy Directive-2. In addition, Federal Government procurement regulations are often complex and burdensome for the private sector. In fact, government-procured space systems were historically characterized by high costs, long program schedules, and frequent delays due to these regulations (Butow et al. 2020). This discouraged efficiency, innovation, and the entrance of new actors into the market. In the interest of increasing competition and innovation while reducing costs and bureaucracy, the Administration continues to remove undue regulatory barriers and increase the efficiency of existing processes. Doing so will foster a free and prosperous space economy, enable commercial space companies to operate more efficiently, and allow new firms to participate in the private space industry.

Furthermore, the Administration has recognized the important role the Federal Government plays in promoting an environment that encourages investment in the space economy. This starts with outlining clear and coordinated policy goals and stimulating public and private activity to achieve them. By increasingly shifting the role of the government in the space domain from that of owner and operator of technology to that of customer of private products and services, the United States increases demand for commercial activity and supports the growth of a viable space economy.

For example, NASA can use commercial service contracts within the Artemis Program, including those governing transportation, communications, and power systems to facilitate the return of manned missions to the lunar surface and to encourage their permanent operation there. The Department of Defense also serves a critical role in creating demand within the private sector because this Administration has prioritized the protection of national security in space. Applying the same concepts to space resources, the Federal Government can reduce risk to the private sector for new technologies such as space mining and manufacturing. By acting as an initial, substantial, and dependable customer for early entrants into space resource markets, the Federal Government can encourage private investment by offering to purchase products on forward contracts. With the assured revenue that comes from these contracts, private firms can use increased economies of scale to further reduce the costs of these new technologies, which opens the market to new customers.

Prioritizing regulatory reform and investment in the space sector builds a strong foundation for a thriving space economy. The Trump Administration has taken action to make this future a reality, and it will continue to foster the environment that spurs investment in the private space sector.

Conclusion

Secure property rights are a fundamental tenet of the U.S. economy. Property rights help individuals and firms set expectations for how the outcome of their investments will be distributed. However, there are costs for setting up and further specifying property rights. The literature on the economics of property rights discusses how to balance the benefits from improved expectation setting for individuals' investment decisions against the costs of enforcement. Although applications like space mining and space solar power satellites might be decades away from being profitable enterprises, it is worth laying the foundation for the emergence of future space industries now.

Economic activity in space will benefit from further property rights enhancement and specification, which is advantageous when net enforcement costs are exceeded by net benefits. To this end, the Trump Administration has initiated policies to enhance property rights and thus to encourage further investment in space. The Executive Order "Encouraging International Support for the Recovery and Use of Space Resources" and the Artemis Accords help to further property rights specification by rejecting an ineffective treaty that suggests communal property and by motivating other economies to follow the United States' lead in developing safe and sustainable best practices in space.

Recent policies to improve the ability of firms to gain certainty regarding their investments lay the foundation for further development of the space economy. The academic literature provides many examples across time, geographic range, and resource application of the large effects on investment and economic activity driven by enhanced property rights security. Based on these previous experiences with improvements in property rights security, the CEA estimates that recent Trump Administration policies will add an additional $23 billion to private investment in the space sector by 2028. Property rights enhancement, coupled with public-private partnerships, can solidify the long-term health of the commercial space economy.

Chapter 9

Pursuing Free, Fair, and Balanced Trade

As documented in the 2018 *Economic Report of the President*, the Trump Administration inherited a legacy of asymmetric trading arrangements that had imposed steep costs on U.S. manufacturing and segments of the labor market. Indeed, some recent academic literature finds that import displacement after the establishment of Permanent Normal Trade Relations with the People's Republic of China was the single biggest factor in the decline of the U.S. employment-to-population rate after 1999 (Abraham and Kearney 2020). Also, this shock was associated not only with a precipitous decline in previously relatively-stable U.S. manufacturing employment but also with increased mortality from drug overdoses in adversely affected communities (Autor, Dorn, and Hanson 2019; Case and Deaton 2017; Pierce and Schott 2020).

The Trump Administration has worked over the past four years to renegotiate unfair trading arrangements that have harmed, in particular, U.S. manufacturing and manufacturing employment. Much of this work came to fruition in 2020, with several historic trade agreements entering into force this year. This chapter details the benefits of the trade accomplishments of 2020 and shows that further work in renegotiating trade agreements to safeguard American workers will play a key part in returning the U.S. economy to the economic prosperity of the Great Expansion. In addition, we describe the changing global economic environment, punctuated by the COVID-19 pandemic, that has caused firms and governments to rethink existing configurations of global supply chains and, in some cases, bring production closer to home.

On January 15, 2020, President Trump joined Chinese Vice Premier Liu He in signing the U.S.-China Economic and Trade Agreement—the Phase One Agreement—a landmark deal that requires structural reforms and other changes to China's economic and trade systems in the areas of intellectual property, technology transfer, agriculture, financial services, and currency and foreign exchange. The centerpieces of the agreement include not only the numerous, specific commitments that China made in these areas but also China's agreement to expand trade by importing an additional $200 billion in U.S. goods and services on top of 2017 import levels. The United States maintains significant tariffs on $370 billion worth of Chinese imports because China has not ended all of its unfair trade practices, setting the stage for a Phase Two agreement in the future.

In addition to achieving this historic trade deal with China, the Trump Administration has followed through on its pledge to restore U.S. manufacturing, farming, and business by signing into law the United States–Mexico–Canada Agreement (USMCA) on January 29, 2020, overhauling the North American Free Trade Agreement. With the rules of the agreement entering into force on July 1, 2020, USMCA promises to better balance trade with our neighbors to the north and south. USMCA establishes requirements for digital trade, environmental standards, and standards for workers' rights between the three countries. Also, American agricultural exports will increase by $2.2 billion under USMCA thanks to better access to Canadian markets secured through the new agreement. Overall, pre-COVID estimates by the nonpartisan U.S. International Trade Commission found that under moderate assumptions, USMCA will increase U.S. gross domestic product by $68.2 billion (0.35 percent) and create 176,000 U.S. jobs.

Prepandemic analyses indicated that both the Phase One Agreement and USMCA would grow the U.S. economy. However, with the COVID-19 pandemic spreading from China around the globe, worldwide lockdowns temporarily disrupted the projected benefits from negotiating these trade deals and highlighted the substantial risk in centralizing supply chains in China. As China shut down factories in the city of Wuhan—a major manufacturing hub, and also the origin of the coronavirus—supply shocks rippled throughout the global economy and reached the United States long before the virus spread within the United States. This chapter examines COVID-19's effects on global supply chains and discusses evidence that companies are already reducing their reliance on Chinese manufacturing.

As the process of U.S. economic recovery continues, fair and reciprocal trade agreements will continue to be a critical component of returning to the economic prosperity of the Great Expansion. The Phase One Agreement, USMCA, an additional trade agreement with Japan, and a renegotiated trade agreement with South Korea, among others, underscore the Trump Administration's commitments to securing trade deals that drive growth in the economy and the labor market. These agreements are the culmination of the Administration's commitment to the American worker—addressing unfair trade practices that have adversely affected U.S. employment, while also incentivizing domestic hiring and capital formation.

International trade plays a critical role in driving economic growth, and thus in helping countries around the world achieve unprecedented prosperity in the 21st century. Institutions in which the United States plays a key leadership role, such as the World Trade Organization and its predecessor the General Agreement on Tariffs and Trade, established the institutional framework of the global trading system and facilitated growth in global trade. But the benefits of the global trading system have at times come at the cost of America's own national interest. The Trump Administration has actively pursued actions to make trade with the United States' international partners fairer and more sustainable. The Administration has imposed tariffs to protect national security and other U.S. economic interests. And by forging new trade agreements with China, our North American neighbors, and Japan, as well as a renegotiated agreement with South Korea and narrower agreements with several other countries, the Administration has ushered in a new international trade environment that promises to enhance U.S. economic growth and broad-based economic prosperity. The first three sections of this chapter examine these agreements.

Although growth in global trade has increasingly taken the form of trade in intermediate goods and the globalization of supply chains, events in recent years may slow that trend. The 2008 global recession, trade, and other geopolitical tensions (especially between the United States and China), and most recently the 2020 COVID-19 pandemic, have all underscored risks associated with trade that have prompted firms and governments around the world to reconsider the benefits and costs of their existing configurations of global supply chains. The Trump Administration's recent and ongoing activities focus on reaping the benefits of trade while advancing the interests of American industry and safeguarding national security. The last section of the chapter considers these issues related to global supply chains.

The Phase One Agreement with China

The U.S.-China Phase One Agreement is a first step in the resolution of U.S.-China trade disputes. These tensions came to the forefront in August 2017 with the announcement in the *Federal Register* of an investigation by the Office of the United States Trade Representative (USTR) into China's technology transfer and intellectual property (IP) protection policies under Section 301 of the Trade Act of 1974. This investigation led to a determination by the USTR that China engaged in certain unreasonable and discriminatory trade practices. The USTR took appropriate action by imposing tariffs on U.S. imports from China, triggering tariff increases by China and responsive tariff increases by the United States, from July 2018 to September 2019.

On December 13, 2019, the two countries agreed to the Phase One Agreement, which President Trump signed on January 15, 2020. This agreement has seven main chapters addressing structural reforms in the areas of IP, technology transfer, agricultural nontariff barriers, financial services, currency, and Chinese purchases of U.S. exports; and establishing a strong dispute resolution system. An eighth chapter provides details on amending the agreement, effective dates and termination, further negotiations, and "notice and comment" on implementing measures (USTR 2020b). The Chinese purchases of U.S. exports are an important component of this agreement, given that they were expected to provide immediate positive effects for U.S. producers. With the COVID-19 pandemic, Chinese purchases of U.S. exports this year started slowly but have increased significantly in recent months. The structural provisions are the important first steps in creating much-needed reform in the Chinese economy.

Background

In August 2017, the USTR opened an investigation into Chinese policies and practices regarding technology and IP under Section 301 of the Trade Act of 1974. The USTR issued a report in March 2018 that detailed a variety of unfair

Table 9-1. U.S. Tariff Actions against China, 2018–19

Tranche (month and year they took effect)	Value of Imports (billion dollars)	Tariff Rate (percent)	Retaliatory China Tariffs on U.S. Exports
1 (July 2018)	34	25	25% on $34 billion in goods
2 (August 2018)	16	25	25% on $16 billion in goods
3 (September 2018)	200	10; rose to 25 in June 2019	Range up to 25% on $53 billion in goods
4A (September 2019)	120	15	5–10% on $25 billion in goods

Source: Office of the U.S. Trade Representative.
Note: This table reflects the tariff rates when they went into effect, not necessarily the current state of play. Tranche 4B was set to take effect December 15, 2019, but due to the U.S.–China Phase 1 agreement, these tariffs were never imposed as noted in the text. Dollar values are in nominal terms.

Table 9-2. U.S. Bilateral Trade Deficit with China in Goods and Services

Type of Deficit	2018:Q2		2019:Q4		2020:Q3	
	Dollars (billions)	Share of GDP	Dollars (billions)	Share of GDP	Dollars (billions)	Share of GDP
Bilateral trade deficit in goods	−98.4	1.9	−77.4	1.4	−79.0	1.5
Bilateral trade deficit in goods and services	−88.7	1.7	−68.1	1.3	−74.6	1.4

Sources: Census Bureau; CEA calculations.
Note: The trade deficit is annualized to calculate the share of GDP. Dollar values are in nominal terms.

Chinese policies and practices: (1) forced technology transfer from U.S. inventors and companies to Chinese firms for market access in China; (2) nonmarket-based terms for technology licenses; (3) Chinese state-directed and facilitated acquisition of strategic U.S. assets; and (4) cyber-enabled intrusions into U.S. commercial networks to steal trade secrets for commercial gain (CEA 2019). Table 9-1 describes the four tranches of tariffs that the United States imposed to bring China to the negotiating table to reform these costly policies. China retaliated with its own tariff actions against the United States in each tranche. As part of the conclusion of the Phase One negotiations, the United States suspended a tariff rate increase from 25 percent to 30 percent on tranches 1 through 3 and reduced the tariff rate on tranche 4A from 15 percent to 7.5 percent. China also cut its 4A tranche tariff rates by half.

Since the Section 301 tariffs went into effect starting in July 2018, we have observed a decline in the bilateral trade deficit between the U.S. and China, from $88.7 billion ($354.8 at an annualized rate, or 1.7 percent of GDP) to $68.1 billion ($272.4 billion at an annualized rate, or 1.3 percent of GDP) at the end of 2019 (table 9-2). The bilateral trade deficit has increased slightly during the COVID-19 pandemic, particularly as international trade in goods has recovered faster than international trade in services, but remains below pre–Section 301 levels.

Major Provisions

On December 13, 2019, the United States and the People's Republic of China announced that they had reached the Phase One Trade Agreement. This agreement came just two days before the United States was set to impose tranche 4B, which would have imposed 15 percent tariff rates on an additional $160 billion worth of U.S. imports from China. As a part of the agreement, the United States suspended the tariffs set for December 15 and agreed to halve tranche 4A tariffs on $120 billion of Chinese goods to 7.5 percent (USTR 2019b). On January 15, 2020, President Trump signed the Phase One Agreement with the People's Republic of China, establishing a foundation for a fair and reciprocal trade relationship between the two countries. This agreement requires structural reforms and other changes to China's economic and trade policies in these seven areas, each of which corresponds to a chapter in the agreement:

1. Addressing concerns related to intellectual property,
2. Ending China's practice of forced foreign technology transfer,
3. Lowering structural barriers to agricultural trade,
4. Expanding market access for U.S. financial service companies in China,
5. Addressing unfair currency practices,
6. Expanding trade through Chinese purchase commitments, and
7. Introducing a dispute resolution mechanism to effectively implement and resolve issues arising under the agreement.

Chapters 1 and 2 of the Phase One Agreement address U.S. concerns relating to intellectual property theft and forced foreign technology transfer and should help create a fair market and protect U.S. companies operating in China. Chapters 4 and 5 require China to lower financial service barriers and end unfair currency practices. Chapter 6 sets forth purchase commitments, including purchase commitments for agricultural commodities, which China must meet to help create a more balanced and fairer trading relationship that benefits the United States. The removal of structural barriers to agricultural trade in Chapter 3 should help achieve these purchase commitments. Finally, Chapter 7, which addresses dispute resolution, creates a process for discussing implementation of, and resolving issues arising under, the Phase One Agreement.

Intellectual Property

Chapter 1 of the Phase One Agreement includes specific commitments to strengthen protection and enforcement of IP in China and reduce IP theft, including with respect to trade secrets, pharmaceutical-related IP, and enforcement against counterfeit and pirated goods. The Section 301 report found a $50 billion annual cost to the United States from IP theft (USTR 2018a). Several of the provisions in the Phase One Agreement are novel and require significant changes in China's practices. A large component of this addresses specific concerns regarding adequate and effective IP protection and enforcement in China. As part of China's implementation of the Phase One Agreement, China has published numerous draft measures for public comment and has issued final measures in areas including criminal prosecution standards for trade secret theft, civil enforcement of trade secrets, destruction of counterfeit and pirated goods, and online infringement on e-commerce platforms.

Reports from the Organization for Economic Cooperation and Development (OECD 2019) show China as the top source of counterfeit and pirated goods, endangering the public with goods that pose potential health and safety threats. The Phase One Agreement contains provisions on the expeditious takedown and destruction of counterfeit goods. The agreement also includes obligations for China to take effective action against e-commerce platforms that fail to take necessary measures against infringement and ensures that government agencies and state-owned enterprises use only licensed software.

Technology Transfer

In Chapter 2 of the Phase One Agreement, China agreed to end the practice of requiring or pressuring U.S. companies to transfer technology to Chinese entities, including in relation to joint ventures, acquisitions, or obtaining business licenses. These commitments extend to any informal, unwritten measures that China takes to force or pressure foreign companies to transfer their technology to Chinese entities, which is a key concern identified in the Section 301 investigation. China also committed to provide transparency, fairness, and due process in administrative proceedings and to ensure that any technology transfer and licensing take place on market terms. Moreover, China agreed not to support or direct outbound foreign direct investment activities aimed at acquiring foreign technology with respect to sectors and industries targeted by market-distorting industrial plans. Though Phase One negotiations were ongoing, China enacted its new Foreign Investment Law and amended its existing Administrative Licensing Law in order to address the use of "administrative means" to force technology transfer, and the disclosure of trade secrets and confidential business information submitted by administrative license applicants.

Agriculture

Chapter 3 of the Phase One Agreement lowers structural barriers to agriculture trade. As for nontariff agricultural barriers, China has removed many restrictive and burdensome import requirements, including lifting its effective ban on

Table 9-3. Agriculture Phase One Agreement Provisions

Product	Market Overview	Key Changes to Implement
Agricultural Biotechnology	Chinese demand for biotechnology, which is used for food and feed products, has drastically grown as Chinese wealth has grown. But existing regulations hinder U.S. exports.	Implement a transparent, predictable, efficient, science- and risk-based regulatory approval process for agricultural biotechnology products that contains strong administrative improvements. Limit approval wait times to an average of 24 months.
Animal feed	Chinese demand for feed has grown with its livestock supply, but U.S. feed exports have struggled due to restrictions in registering and licensing facilities and products.	Add 23 products to its list of allowable feed additive product imports. Streamline the registration-and-licensing process for U.S. feed exports.
Seafood	As Chinese seafood demand rises, regulations have held back U.S. seafood exports.	Legalize the importation of 26 new seafood products. Change seafood regulations so goods approved by the Food and Drug Administration and the National Oceanic and Atmospheric Administration can be imported by China.
Dairy and infant formula	Demand for imported dairy and infant formula products has a positive relationship with China's growing wealth, but strict regulations limit U.S. exports.	Streamline approval processes for U.S. facilities and products, and China's regulations will be simplified or eliminated.
Horticultural products	Although Chinese horticultural imports increased by 80% between 2013 and 2018, the U.S. market share of imports is only 10%.	Allow U.S. exports of potatoes, nectarines, blueberries, and avocados.
Meat, poultry, and live breeding cattle	After a 13-year ban, in 2017, China partially reopened its beef markets to U.S. exports, although regulatory restrictions remain. In 2015, China banned U.S. poultry, but this was partially removed in November 2019.	Expand market access for U.S. beef and poultry. Speed up and improve approval processes and health certifications. Hold necessary technical discussions for a protocol to allow U.S. live breeding cattle imports.
Pet food	Chinese poultry and bovine restrictions along with issues registering facilities have limited U.S. pet food exports in China, even as Chinese demand has grown.	Remove bans that restrict U.S. pet food exports. Streamline registration for U.S. facilities.
Rice	China is the world's largest importer of rice. Its tariff rate quota and phytosanitary protocol hurt U.S. exports.	Allow the importation of U.S. rice products within 20 days of their approval by the U.S. Department of Agriculture. Change how its tariff rate quota is applied so the quota is applied each year, and the process for allocation is not discriminatory and transparent for U.S. firms.

Source: U.S. Department of Agriculture (2020).

U.S. poultry products, which had been in place since 2015. Although not all the structural changes and commitments listed in table 9-3 have been completed, certain key changes have been made, resulting in improved market access for a number of U.S. agricultural products. The market overview for each product reveals that Chinese demand has continued to rise for these products, but before the Phase One Agreement, U.S. exports had been restricted. Changes made by China include the listing of additional U.S. food manufacturing and feed additive facilities eligible for export to China, recognition of the Food and Drug Administration's oversight of dairy food safety, and the removal of other sanitary and phytosanitary barriers. The lowering of barriers to agricultural trade, described in table 9-3, is necessary for the agricultural purchases China has promised.

Financial Services

Chapter 4 of the Phase One Agreement addresses long-standing barriers faced by a wide variety of U.S. financial services companies, including those in banking, insurance, securities, credit rating, and electronic payment services. These barriers include joint venture requirements, foreign equity limitations, and various discriminatory regulatory requirements. As one key example, China committed to allow U.S. securities, fund management, futures, and insurance companies to establish wholly foreign-owned companies in China, thereby providing the potential for U.S. companies to fully control and generate profits from their businesses. Removal of these barriers will allow U.S. financial services companies to compete on a more level playing field in China.

Currency

Chapter 5 of the Phase One Agreement includes policy and transparency commitments related to currency issues. The chapter addresses unfair currency practices by requiring strong commitments to refrain from competitive devaluations and targeting of exchange rates, while promoting transparency and providing mechanisms for accountability and enforcement. The enforcement mechanism enables either the U.S. Department of the Treasury or the People's Bank of China to refer exchange rate policy or transparency issues to the Bilateral Evaluation and Dispute Resolution Arrangement established in Chapter 7 of the agreement, which we discuss below.

China has a long history of pursuing a variety of economic and regulatory policies that provide their economy with a competitive advantage in international trade. This includes intervention in foreign exchange markets in concert with the maintenance of capital controls that together harm U.S. export competitiveness by facilitating the undervaluation of the renminbi. In August 2019, the U.S. Treasury ruled that China was manipulating its currency under the Omnibus Trade and Competitiveness Act of 1988.

After this determination, the U.S. Treasury and the People's Bank of China engaged in negotiations over currency issues to eliminate unfair Chinese practices that gain competitive advantages. More broadly, China made commitments in the Phase One Agreement to refrain from competitive devaluations and to not target its exchange rate for competitive purposes, and it agreed to publish relevant information related to exchange rates and external balances. In this context, in January 2020, the U.S. Treasury determined in its "Report to Congress on Macroeconomic and Foreign Exchange Policies of Major Trading Partners of the United States" that China would not be designated as a currency manipulator at that time.

Chinese Purchase Commitments

Chapter 6 of the Phase One Agreement specifies commitments for Chinese purchases of a selected group of U.S. goods and services. For the first year of the agreement, China has committed to purchase an additional $76.7 billion of U.S. goods and services over the 2017 baseline, followed by an additional $123.3 billion of purchases in the second year (table 9-4). Purchases are broken down into four sectors: manufactured goods (38.9 percent), energy (26.2 percent), services (19.0 percent), and agriculture (16.0 percent). From 2022 to 2025, the agreement states that the countries "project that the trajectory of increases in the amounts of manufactured goods, agricultural goods, energy products, and services purchased and imported into China from the United States will continue in calendar years 2022 through 2025."

As part of the trade deal, China will also reduce its structural trade barriers, which should result in an expansion of market-based access for U.S. goods and services aiding these purchase commitments, as described above for U.S. exports of agriculture. Because barriers to China's markets primarily take the form of nontariff barriers, specific purchase commitments help promote China's adherence to its structural reforms in the agreement. As a result of the Phase One Agreement, China has already begun taking actions to reduce its

Table 9-4. Additional U.S. Exports to China on Top of 2017 Baseline

Product Category	2020 (dollars, billions)	2021 (dollars, billions)	2020–21 Total (dollars, billions)	2020–21 Percentage of total
Manufactured goods	32.9	44.8	77.7	38.9
Energy	18.5	33.9	52.4	26.2
Services	12.8	25.1	37.9	19.0
Agriculture	12.5	19.5	32.0	16.0
Total	76.7	123.3	200.0	100.0

Source: "Trade Agreement between the United States of America and the People's Republic of China" (draft), Annex 6.1.
Note: the two-year percentage of of the total does not exactly add up to 100 due to rounding.

retaliatory tariffs, enabling greater market access and increased purchases. In two separate waves, China announced tariff reductions, or chose not to impose tariffs, on $75 billion worth of U.S. goods and available tariff exemptions on goods classified under 696 tariff codes (MOF 2020).

Due to the COVID-19 outbreak, international trade fell dramatically as economies around the world contracted. As a result, purchases from China early in the year were lower than anticipated. However, purchases have increased significantly in the past few months. The USTR (2020c) estimates that as of mid-October, China had purchased over $23 billion in U.S. agricultural products, about 71 percent of its target under the Phase One Agreement. Record or near-record U.S. exports to China are expected in 2020 for corn, pork, beef, pet food, alfalfa hay, pecans, peanuts, and prepared foods.

Dispute Resolution

Chapter 7 creates the Trade Framework Group, to be led by the United States Trade Representative with a designated Vice Premier of China. This group's purpose is to ensure implementation of the Phase One Agreement and resolve disputes in a fair and expeditious manner. The United States and China created the Bilateral Evaluation and Dispute Resolution Office to deal with day-to-day matters. Each party can file a complaint to the other for not acting in accordance with the agreement at the working level, and then escalate to the deputy and principal levels if no resolution is achieved. Each party may also raise matters of urgency directly at the principal level. Regular consultations are also set up to ensure compliance. Regular consultations are also set up to ensure compliance.

Unlike other trade agreements, the Phase One Agreement does not provide for independent third-party dispute resolution. If the two parties cannot resolve a dispute, then the complaining party is authorized under the agreement to take proportionate responsive action that it considers appropriate against the offending party. This can take the form of tariffs on goods imported from the other party or the suspension of a provision in the agreement benefiting that other party, among other actions. The responsive action may remain in effect until the resolution of the dispute. If the respondent party finds that the complaining party's action was taken in bad faith, its only recourse is withdrawal from the agreement upon 60 days' notice.

Chapter 7 of the Phase One Agreement provides for a series of meetings or telephone calls to ensure the success of the agreement, including monthly Designated Official calls, quarterly deputy calls, and twice-yearly principal-level calls. In addition, technical groups from the United States and China confer on a regular basis. During a principal-level call in August 2020, the parties noted sustained commitment to the success of the agreement as well as noticeable progress toward reaching the agreement's goals. They discussed China's steps to engender "greater protection for intellectual property rights, remove impediments to American companies in the areas of financial services and agriculture, and eliminate forced technology transfer" (USTR 2020d). This call also served as a discussion on the significant increases of Chinese purchases of U.S. products and any additional action needed to implement the Phase One Agreement. Both parties remain committed to the success of the agreement, with progress already made and a shared commitment to future necessary steps.

What Is Not in Phase One?

The Phase One Agreement with China is designed to lay the groundwork for a Phase Two negotiation. The Phase One Agreement does not address certain underlying structural issues, creating interest for a Phase Two Agreement in the future (White House 2020a). The two countries still have very different economic systems as China asserts the state as the principal actor in the economy, creating friction between the two countries. Despite some tariff concessions, the United States maintains most of the Section 301 tariffs still in effect because China has not addressed all the issues identified in the Section 301 investigation.

Some of the main issues remaining include China's massive government subsidies to and its preferential treatment of state-owned enterprises (SOEs). Many Chinese SOEs depend on government subsidies and loans from state-owned banks to compete with more efficient private firms. Important sectors in China's economy are state-directed, leading to policies and practices that provide significant artificial advantages to domestic companies while discriminating against or otherwise disadvantaging foreign competitors. China's "Made in China 2025" program is a plan announced in 2015 that aims to make China a global high-technology manufacturing power (McBride and Chatzky 2019). Many see this as a threat to U.S. leadership in high-technology industries, citing China's subsidies, the setting of market share targets for Chinese companies, and the use of policies designed to substitute Chinese products for other countries' products in the Chinese market and eventually abroad. China has released a list of 33 areas in which investment by foreign firms is extremely limited or not allowed. These areas include infrastructure, the media, agriculture, and some types of scientific research.

Another issue of concern is China's engagement in cyber-enabled theft and its intrusions into U.S. commercial computer networks for commercial purposes. According to the U.S. Department of Justice, China is involved in more than 90 percent of economic espionage cases and more than 67 percent of the trade secret theft cases the department has overseen since 2011 (DOJ 2018). National security concerns regarding technology and cyberspace are also significant issues, including concerns related to the Chinese companies Huawei and ZTE. The United States has banned the use of Huawei and ZTE 5G equipment by U.S. companies and citizens, and has been urging its allies to follow suit by not investing in Huawei's 5G technology services due to the potential for China to spy on customers (Vaswani 2020). Australia, New Zealand, and the United Kingdom are other major countries that have banned Huawei from their 5G networks.

The United States–Mexico–Canada Agreement

The United States–Mexico–Canada Agreement (USMCA), which took effect on July 1, 2020, is a new agreement that replaces the North American Free Trade Agreement (NAFTA). Free trade agreements establish areas between two or more countries "in which the duties and other restrictive regulations of commerce . . . are eliminated on substantially all the trade between the constituent territories in products originating in such territories" (WTO 2020). NAFTA established free trade in goods and services between the United States, Canada, and Mexico. The ability to maintain free trade in goods and services in the NAFTA area depends on rules pertaining to everything from customs administration to identification of the scope of covered services to dispute settlement. The original NAFTA rules were more than 25 years old.

USMCA updated these rules in order to reflect the lessons learned under NAFTA and other trade agreements, as well as economic and technological developments. Among these, USMCA ensures the free movement of data across borders, improves trade facilitation, strengthens intellectual property protection for U.S. firms, limits access to international arbitration in investment disputes (thus steering such disputes to the courts of the country hosting the investment), and modifies the requirements for an automobile to be eligible for duty-free treatment. In particular, the agreement requires that a higher percentage of an automobile's parts be sourced within the USMCA region for production if the vehicle is to qualify for duty-free treatment. Altogether, over the next five years, USMCA is projected to increase U.S. gross domestic product (GDP) by $68.2 billion (0.35 percent) and create 176,000 U.S. jobs, according to pre-COVID estimates by the independent, nonpartisan U.S. International Trade Commission (USITC).

Rules of Origin for Automobile Production

For certain products, USMCA revises the rules of origin, which establish the value that must be added, or processes that must occur, in the territory of one or more USMCA parties for a good to be considered a USMCA-originating good. If considered a USMCA-originating good, it will be entitled to preferential duty-free treatment upon importation into the territory of a USMCA party (USTR 2020a). In particular, USMCA increases the regional content requirements for automobiles traded under the agreement. NAFTA required 62.5 percent (by value) of an automobile's parts to be sourced in North America, and USMCA raises the requirement to 75 percent, depending on the vehicle type (USTIC

2019). In addition, under USMCA, North American auto manufacturers that trade under the agreement must purchase at least 70 percent of their steel and aluminum from the United States and its territories, Canada, or Mexico. Finally, annually 40 to 45 percent of the manufacturing costs of imported automobiles must be produced by workers who earn at least $16 per hour.

Although the USITC estimates that these provisions will create on net 28,000 jobs in the U.S. automobile industry, they will likely reduce growth in other sectors of the economy. And though these negative effects are more than offset by other USMCA provisions, these provisions will collectively raise the costs of producing automobiles in the United States, and thus increasing the consumer prices of cars and reducing real incomes (USITC 2019).

Digital Trade

USMCA contains the most comprehensive set of provisions for digital trade in a U.S. trade agreement. The agreement prohibits discriminatory restrictions on trade in digital products and services between USMCA partners and ensures the free movement of data across borders. Moreover, a U.S. company is not required to disclose proprietary source codes and algorithms to USMCA partners or to locate its computing facilities in their territory as a condition of doing business (USITC 2019). Altogether, these provisions are designed to reduce barriers to U.S. investment in Mexico and Canada, including in the financial services sector. The data transfer provisions are estimated to reduce U.S. trade costs by between 0.6 and 4.5 percentage points for a broad class of sectors, ranging from agriculture to manufacturing to business services (USITC 2019).

Many of the economic benefits of USMCA are generated through these digital trade provisions. Specifically, the USITC estimates that these provisions will reduce "trade policy uncertainty" (USITC 2019). Although the agreement prevents USMCA partners from establishing restrictions on trade in digital services, data flowed freely among the United States, Canada, and Mexico before the signing of the agreement. Nonetheless, research suggests that uncertainty about whether such regulations will eventually be imposed can reduce trade and investment between countries, and a reduction in this uncertainty can yield economic benefits (USITC 2019).

Intellectual Property Protection

USMCA introduces many provisions to enhance the protection and enforcement of the IP rights of U.S. firms. First, USMCA requires that countries grant patent extensions in response to unreasonable delays in their patent-granting offices (USITC 2019). USMCA also provides procedural safeguards for the recognition of new geographical indications, including strong standards for protection against issuances of geographical indications that would prevent U.S. producers from using common names, such as mozzarella, as well as establish a mechanism for consultation between the parties on future geographical indications pursuant to international agreements (CRS 2020a; USTR 2020a). In addition, the agreement calls for a minimum copyright term of life of the author plus 70 years, and for those works with a copyright term that is not based on the life of a person, a minimum of 75 years after first authorized publication (USTR 2020a).

The USMCA provides for the most comprehensive protection for trade secrets of any prior U.S. trade agreement. It requires countries to provide, including with respect to trade secret theft by SOEs, civil procedures and remedies, criminal procedures and penalties, prohibitions against impeding licensing of trade secrets, judicial procedures to prevent disclosure of trade secrets during the litigation process, and penalties for government officials for the unauthorized disclosure of trade secrets (USTR 2018c). USMCA confirms that the enforcement of IP also applies to the digital environment, ensuring that firms relying on digital trade receive adequate protection (USITC 2019).

Labor

USMCA enshrines core worker rights, which will have the most notable effect in Mexico. The Mexican labor market is hampered by a largely informal economy and a lack of protections for workers (ILO 2014). Many workers are part of undemocratic unions, also known as "ghost unions," that are not supported by the majority of the workers they allegedly represent. These unions form illegitimate collective bargaining agreements, alternately known as protection contracts, with an employer-dominated union, without workers seeing or ratifying the agreement. Such protective contracts are estimated to represent a significant percentage of collective bargaining agreements in Mexico. When workers try to form their own union, their employer tells them that they were already a part of one and subject to the parameters stipulated in the agreement they never had a chance to see (Mojtehedzadeh 2016). USMCA addresses each of these issues by supporting Mexico's creation of independent bodies to resolve labor disputes—guaranteeing democratic worker representation and collective bargaining rights—and providing enforcement tools to ensure that Mexico meets the USMCA's labor obligations (USTR 2020a).

Although these provisions will primarily affect Mexico by promoting higher wages and improving labor market conditions for workers, the U.S. economy could also benefit. To the extent that these provisions reduce this disparity between Mexican and U.S. wages, U.S. firms will be less likely to off-shore production to Mexico, increasing the bargaining power of U.S. workers. In addition, U.S. export markets may benefit from the increased purchasing power of the Mexican consumer (USITC 2019).

Reform of the Investor-State Dispute Mechanism

NAFTA contained provisions allowing an investor of one NAFTA party to submit to international arbitration claims that another NAFTA party (the host party)

Table 9-5. The Impact of Canada and Mexico Increasing De Minimis Thresholds

Model Results	Canada (dollars, millions)	Mexico (dollars, millions)
Current value of all e-commerce shipments	22,000	8,715
Current value of U.S. e-commerce shipments	7,260	2,527
Expected change in value of U.S. e-commerce shipments	332	91

Source: U.S. International Trade Commission.

had breached investment-related obligations in NAFTA and thereby harmed the investor or its investment in the territory of the host party. This arbitration mechanism, known as the Investor-State Dispute Settlement (ISDS), raised concerns about its effect on the ability of host state regulators to exercise their prerogative to regulate in the public interest. Under USMCA, the ISDS will no longer be available between the United States and Canada after June 30, 2023. Instead, investment-related claims by U.S. investors against Canada and by Canadian investors against the United States will need to be filed in local courts (USITC 2019).

For disputes between U.S. and Mexican investors, USMCA limits the scope of claims that can be submitted to ISDS, except where investors have certain government contracts in specific economic sectors. When such conditions are met, it is the view of the United States and Mexico that the risk of breach of investment-related obligations and consequent harm warrant maintaining the availability of ISDS. When these conditions are not met, aggrieved U.S. and Mexican investors must first attempt to resolve their disputes in domestic courts. Only if these efforts are unsuccessful after a period of 30 months may they have recourse to ISDS. The USITC estimates that these changes to ISDS for Mexico will reduce both domestic and foreign capital investment in Mexico by $2.9 billion (0.44 percent) while slightly increasing investment in the United States (USITC 2019).

Agricultural Provisions

Agricultural trade among member countries that was already duty-free under NAFTA will continue to be duty-free under USMCA. Moreover USMCA expands market access opportunities for U.S. dairy, poultry, and egg exports to Canada. Canada imposes tariff rate quotas (TRQs) on dairy products, which restrict the amount of dairy products it can import from other countries. Although Canada will be permitted to retain its TRQs, USMCA will boost exports of U.S. dairy products to Canada. Similarly, the agreement will preserve U.S. TRQs for sugar, while slightly increasing U.S. imports of sugar from Canada (USITC 2019). USMCA also provides a mechanism for biotechnology cooperation and fair treatment in quality grading for American wheat and nondiscrimination and transparency commitments regarding the sale and distribution of alcoholic beverages. In total, USMCA is expected to increase U.S. agricultural exports by $2.2 billion per year (1.1 percent) (USITC 2019).

Table 9-6. U.S. Employment Sector Effects of the United States–Mexico–Canada Agreement

Sector	Value (thousands)	Percent Increase over Five Years
Employment, overall	175.7	0.12
Agriculture	1.7	0.12
Manufacturing and mining	49.7	0.37
Services	124.3	0.09

Source: U.S. International Trade Commission.

Table 9-7. Effects of the United States–Mexico–Canada Agreement on U.S. Trade (percent changes relative to the baseline in 2017)

Aspect of Trade	Exports (percent)	Exports (dollars, billions)	Imports (percent)	Imports (dollars, billions)
U.S. trade with Canada	5.9	19.1	4.8	19.1
U.S. trade with Mexico	6.7	14.2	3.8	12.4

Source: U.S. International Trade Commission.

Trade Facilitation

Several USMCA provisions will improve "trade facilitation"—that is, the administrative procedures that enable traded goods to be processed quickly and efficiently at the border. USMCA changes the threshold below which goods are exempt from formal customs procedures (the de minimis threshold) for goods entering Canada and Mexico, while the United States will retain its current thresholds for imports from these countries (USITC 2019). This will help expedite the customs process for low- and moderate-value packages (i.e., with a value under $2,500), which will benefit U.S. e-commerce firms in particular by lowering processing costs. Other measures will boost trade facilitation for e-commerce firms, for example by permitting electronic authentication for transactions, e-signatures, and paperless trading. Altogether, these provisions will boost U.S. e-commerce exports by $424 million (USITC 2019).

Overall Economic Effects

USMCA will have a positive effect on many industries in the U.S. economy, creating jobs and increasing wages for U.S. workers in the agricultural, manufacturing, and services sectors. Over the next five years, USMCA will increase U.S. GDP by $68.2 billion (0.35 percent) and will create 176,000 jobs across a broad range of sectors, according to pre-COVID estimates by the USITC (table 9-6). It will also boost exports to and imports from USMCA partners by $64.8 billion (table 9-7).

Box 9-1. Bahrain's and the United Arab Emirates' Agreements with Israel

On September 15, 2020, the United States hosted representatives from Bahrain and the United Arab Emirates as they signed agreements to normalize relations with Israel. The President of the United Arab Emirates subsequently issued a decree stating that the United Arab Emirates' law requiring a boycott of Israel was repealed. Since the founding of Israel in 1948, the Arab League has maintained a boycott of the country. (The Arab League consists of 22 Middle Eastern and African countries and entities: Algeria, Bahrain, Comoros, Djibouti, Egypt, Iraq, Jordan, Kuwait, Lebanon, Libya, Mauritania, Morocco, Oman, the Palestinian Authority, Qatar, Saudi Arabia, Somalia, Sudan, Syria (suspended since 2011), Tunisia, the United Arab Emirates, and Yemen.)

Due to the boycott, both Israel and the boycotting countries miss opportunities for increased trade relations. Before 2020, only two Arab states had normalized relations with Israel: Egypt (1979) and Jordan (1994). (There was also a secondary boycott of companies that did business with Israel. It ended with the Oslo Accords in 1993.) The Palestinian Authority also maintains relations with Israel. A literature review of the Arab boycott found that it imposed trade costs on Israel of roughly $1 billion a year (Anthony et al. 2015).

If trade between Israel and Bahrain and the United Arab Emirates grows in line with other countries that have normalized relations with Israel, it would increase by an estimated $537 million annually. In order to estimate the trade effect of Bahrain and the United Arab Emirates normalizing relations with Israel, we use the examples of Egypt and Jordan. In 2019, Israel imported $195 million worth of goods from Egypt and Jordan, and exported $209 million of goods to them. This is roughly 0.12 percent of Egypt and Jordan's combined GDP. The CEA estimates that if Israeli imports and exports to Bahrain and the United Arab Emirates increased to this same percentage of Bahrain's and the United Arab Emirates' GDP, annual Israeli imports and exports with them would increase to $258 million and $278 million, respectively. The vast majority of this increase will occur with the United Arab Emirates, as its economy is much larger than Bahrain's.

Other Trade Agreements

Beyond USMCA and the Phase One agreement, the Trump Administration has sought to improve the United States' terms of trade with other countries. In 2018, the United States renegotiated parts of its trade deal with South Korea to ensure fair trade for the U.S. auto industry. In 2019, the United States reached a "Stage One" trade agreement with Japan to reduce or eliminate tariffs on many U.S. food and agricultural goods exports, and then in 2020 opened talks with the United Kingdom to pursue a free trade agreement. In addition, the United

States hosted representatives from Bahrain and the United Arab Emirates as they signed agreements to normalize relations with Israel (see box 9-1).

U.S.–Japan Trade Agreements

On October 7, 2019, the United States and Japan signed a "Stage One" outcome from bilateral negotiations consisting of two individual agreements: the U.S.-Japan Trade Agreement (USJTA), and the U.S.-Japan Digital Trade Agreement (USTR 2019c, 2019d). The USJTA provides for Japan cutting or eliminating agricultural tariffs and quota restrictions for scores of U.S. products, such as beef and nuts, in return for limited cuts and the elimination of import tariffs on U.S. industrial and agricultural goods (CRS 2019; Schott 2019). Each side respectively agreed to remove or reduce restrictions on about $7.2 billion in imports ($14.4 billion total), covering roughly 5 percent of all trade between the countries (CRS 2019).

The Digital Trade Agreement covers $40 billion in digital trade, and negotiators modeled many of the provisions in the deal after those in the USMCA (USTR 2020e). The agreement ensures barrier-free data flows, prohibits data localization laws that mandate having domestic computing facilities, and prohibits arbitrary disclosures of imported source codes and algorithms. Other provisions include prohibitions on customs duties on electronic transmissions (CRS 2019).

Several topics were not included in negotiations and were left for a larger, future deal (CRS 2019). A key Japanese trade objective revolves around automobiles, Japan's top export to the United States. Japan hopes to reduce current U.S. tariffs on its auto exports, as was originally negotiated in the Trans-Pacific Partnership, and to ensure that new tariffs are not imposed (Goodman et al. 2019). Although Japan imposes no tariffs on U.S. auto exports, the United States maintains that nontariff barriers, such as certain testing protocols for automobiles, limit U.S. exports with the result that Japan's automotive exports to the U.S. are 23 times higher than its imports from the United States (USTR 2019a; CRS 2019). Consistent with recent practice, the United States will also seek provisions on exchange rate issues (USTR 2018b).

The U.S.–South Korea Free Trade Agreement

On September 24, 2018, the United States and South Korea signed an agreement to revise the U.S.–South Korea Free Trade Agreement (KORUS). The agreement mainly focuses on automobile trade, considering that the largest share of the $9 billion trade deficit that the U.S. has with South Korea is concentrated in the automobile sector (Tankersley 2018; Overby et al. 2020). For example, a key provision centers on U.S. auto exports to South Korea that adhere to U.S. safety regulations. Under the renegotiated agreement, South Korea's allowance for U.S. exports of automobiles meeting U.S. safety standards doubled, from 25,000 to 50,000 per manufacturer per year, allowing U.S.

exporters to ramp up sales and marketing for future exports and thus avoid concerns about reaching the 25,000 limit. The United States will maintain its 25 percent tariff on Korean trucks through 2041 (USTR 2018e).

Beyond automobiles, KORUS and accompanying side letters also address several other issues. These include updating certain trade remedy provisions and improving customs procedures in South Korea related to verification of U.S. origin, something that is necessary for U.S. exporters to claim tariff benefits under the agreement without unnecessary delays (CRS 2018; USTR 2018d).

Limited Trade Agreements with Brazil and Ecuador

On October 19, 2020, the United States and Brazil reached an agreement that focuses on trade rules and transparency, contributing to the elimination of nontariff barriers between the two countries. The deal will facilitate the processing of goods at the countries' borders, enhance regulatory transparency, promote good regulatory practices, and strengthen rules addressing corruption. Other trade issues are expected to be addressed in a more comprehensive agreement, including those related to IP and agricultural issues (CRS 2020b).

On December 8, 2020, the United States and Ecuador signed an agreement that builds on the U.S.-Ecuador Trade and Investment Council Agreement that has been in effect since 1990. Like the agreement with Brazil, the new agreement with Ecuador will promote bilateral trade by updating trade facilitation between the two countries, enhancing regulatory transparency, and strengthening anticorruption efforts. The new agreement also seeks to foster trade and investment opportunities for small and medium-sized enterprises in the two countries.

U.S.-U.K. Negotiations

The United Kingdom formally exited the European Union on January 31, 2020, but has remained in a "status quo" transition period through December 31, 2020 (Henley, Rankin, and O'Carroll 2020). Consequently, the U.K. began negotiating its own trade agreements in 2020, which could enter into force from January 1, 2021. In May 2020, the U.S. and the U.K. launched negotiations on a comprehensive free trade agreement and conducted intensive negotiations throughout 2020. The United States' objectives for the agreement are to reduce or eliminate market access barriers to U.S. industrial, agricultural, services, and digital products to the U.K., including regulatory differences that impede bilateral trade, and to deepen the already-extensive economic relationship between the U.S. and the U.K. to support employment and economic growth (USTR 2020f). Though the U.S. and the U.K. share the goal of an ambitious agreement, the U.K. has political sensitivities in areas such as agricultural market access and regulations governing product standards and food safety (Packard 2020).

Separately, after the transition period between the United Kingdom and the European Union ends on January 1, 2021, the U.K. will no longer be covered by existing EU agreements with other countries, including the United States. Therefore, the U.S. and the U.K. completed new bilateral agreements and mechanisms to ensure that there is no disruption to trade in certain products—such as wine, distilled spirits, and marine and telecommunications equipment—all of which are covered by existing U.S.-EU agreements (USTR 2020f). Finally, the United States and the United Kingdom have other bilateral trade differences, including the U.K.'s implementation of digital services taxes targeting U.S. multinational firms, unresolved World Trade Organization disputes on large civil aircraft that have resulted in retaliatory tariffs on both U.S. and U.K. exports to each other, and U.S. tariffs on steel and aluminum imports and the resulting EU (and U.K.) retaliatory tariffs (CEA 2019; Elliott and Mason 2020; Isaac 2020).

The Rise of Global Supply Chains

In early 2020, the global economic outlook changed dramatically as the coronavirus responsible for the COVID-19 spread first through china and then through much of the rest of the world. The COVID-19 pandemic disrupted economic activity everywhere it spread, as people restricted their movement to avoid health risks, and governments closed schools and nonessential businesses in order to mitigate the public health threat. Moreover, in an increasingly globalized economy, localized outbreaks of the virus created effects that rippled beyond local borders to the rest of the world. The emergence of global supply chains over the past decades meant, for example, that covid-19 disrupted production in auto assembly plants in north america even before the pandemic spread to the United States, as plants in North America assembled parts produced in wuhan, china. The risks posed by disease, natural disasters, and trade wars have caused firms and governments to rethink global supply chains and, in some cases, bring production closer to home (Schlesinger 2020).

China and the Emergence of Global Supply Chains

The past three decades have seen a rapid expansion of international trade, and in particular, the use of global supply chains, as firms in the United States and around the world have relocated production off shore to take advantage of lower costs of labor and other inputs. Global supply chains have allowed for specialization and net gains from trade, resulting in increased productivity and lower costs for consumers (Grossman and Rossi-Hansberg 2008). Firms seeking lower manufacturing costs often found them in China, with its large supply of labor and resulting low labor costs (Cui, Meng, and Lu 2018).

Although U.S. consumers and importing firms, as well as competitive exporters, have benefited from globalized supply chains, some recent academic literature indicates that the establishment of Permanent Normal Trade Relations (PNTR) with China at the end of 2001 imposed steep costs on U.S. manufacturing employment and innovation (Pierce and Schott 2016; Autor, Dorn, and Hanson 2019). PNTR status meant that the United States extends permanently nondiscriminatory treatment to the products of China (GPO 2000). Import competition from countries with low labor costs including China has exacerbated a reduction in U.S. manufacturing employment, accounting for a quarter of the total decline in U.S. manufacturing employment between 1990 and 2007 and causing lower labor force participation, higher unemployment, and lower wages in affected communities (Autor, Dorn, and Hanson 2013). Abraham and Kearney (2020) find that import displacement after the establishment of PNTR with China was the single biggest factor in the decline of the overall U.S. employment-to-population rate after 1999, although automation also played a role.

Displaced American workers have struggled to transition to new opportunities, resulting in higher utilization of government safety net programs, including unemployment, disability, and healthcare benefits (Autor, Dorn, and Hanson 2013). The lack of valuable work reduced young males' marriage prospects, which was a factor in there being a greater share of single-headed households in communities affected by the China trade shock (Autor, Dorn, and Hanson 2019). Moreover, the worsening labor market conditions exacerbated socioeconomic distress, leading to substance abuse and increased mortality from drug overdoses, suicides, and liver diseases (Autor, Dorn, and Hanson 2019; Case and Deaton 2017; Pierce and Schott 2020).

U.S. Firms Begin to Hedge the Risks of Global Supply Chains

There are, however, some indications that the globalization of American supply chains has begun to partially reverse. First, the 2008 financial crisis was an unprecedented shock to the global economy, from which the expanding use of global supply chains has never quite recovered. The expansion of global supply chains, measured as a share of trade, slowed after the crisis and even reversed in 2015, the most recent year for which data are available, due to slowing economic growth and trade reforms (World Bank 2020). More recently, tensions between the United States and China and the global COVID-19 pandemic have brought into focus some of the risks of global supply chains, causing firms and governments to look for ways to reduce exposure to these risks (Lund et al. 2020).

The Trade Slowdown in Response to COVID-19

As the COVID-19 pandemic spread around the globe, it disrupted economic activity through private and public responses to quell its transmission. Real GDP for all the OECD countries fell 12.2 percent in the first half of 2020, while U.S. real GDP fell 10.2 percent (not at an annualized rate). Reductions in trade

Figure 9-1. U.S. Imports, 2020

Year-over-year change (percent)

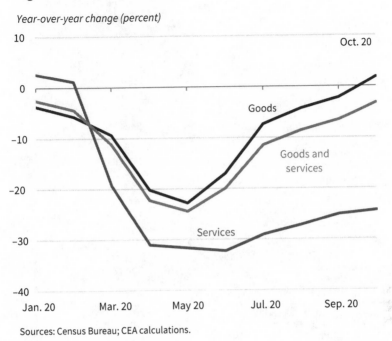

Sources: Census Bureau; CEA calculations.

Figure 9-2. U.S. Exports, 2020

Year-over-year change (percent)

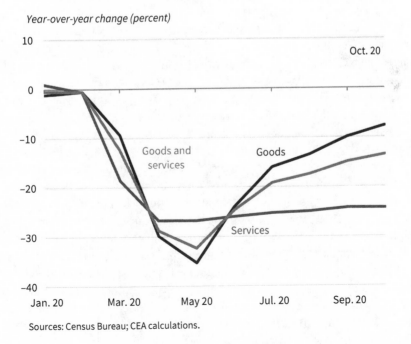

Sources: Census Bureau; CEA calculations.

Table 9-8. Imports and Exports of Services by Sector, through September 2020

Sector	Imports		Exports	
	2020 Level (dollars, billions)	2020 Change from 2019 (percent)	2020 Level (dollars, billions)	2020 Change from 2019 (percent)
Travel	33.8	−69.8	67.1	−58.4
Transportation	58.7	−34.6	47.7	−37.2
Maintenance and repair services	4.7	−27.1	12.7	−44.7
Construction	0.8	−26.6	2.0	−28.1
Telecommunications, computers, and information services	30.5	−16.0	45.1	−2.1
Financial services	32.8	−2.4	113.0	0.2
Charges for use of intellectual property	35.9	0.7	95.3	−2.1
Government goods and services	20.5	2.4	19.2	3.3
Other business services	95.6	1.0	155.1	−1.7
Personal, cultural, and recreational services	19.8	13.3	15.1	−22.1
Insurance services	49.7	17.8	12.4	−10.4
Total	383.0	−21.8	584.5	−19.7

Sources: Census Bureau; CEA calculations.

exacerbated declines in GDP. Global merchandise exports as reported by the World Trade Organization fell 14.0 percent in the first half of 2020 compared with the first half of 2019, and U.S. merchandise trade (exports plus imports) fell by 13.6 percent over the same period.

Total U.S. trade of goods and services (exports plus imports) through October was $645 billion (13.7 percent) below 2019 levels, with the second quarter falling $355 billion (25.1 percent). The drop in trade was largest in May, with imports down 24.4 percent year-over-year and exports down 32.3 percent (figures 9-1 and 9-2). Separating U.S. trade by goods and services reveals that the pandemic had a particularly large effect on trade in services. Moreover, though monthly trade in goods has shown signs of recovering, trade in services has remained over 20 percent below the previous year.

Trade in services, a major sector of the U.S. economy, was hit particularly hard by the international travel restrictions implemented by the United States and many other countries around the globe to prevent or slow the spread of COVID-19. The impact, however, has been concentrated in travel and transportation, with other service sectors seeing relatively lower declines in trade. On January 31, 2020, President Trump issued a travel ban for most non-U.S. citizens coming from China (White House 2020b). Then, on March 11, President Trump issued a travel ban for most non-U.S. citizens coming from the Schengen Area, which consists of 26 European countries with a common visa policy (White House 2020c). Also, effective March 14, the Centers for Disease

Figure 9-3. U.S. Imports of Goods Percent Change from Selected Countries, 2020

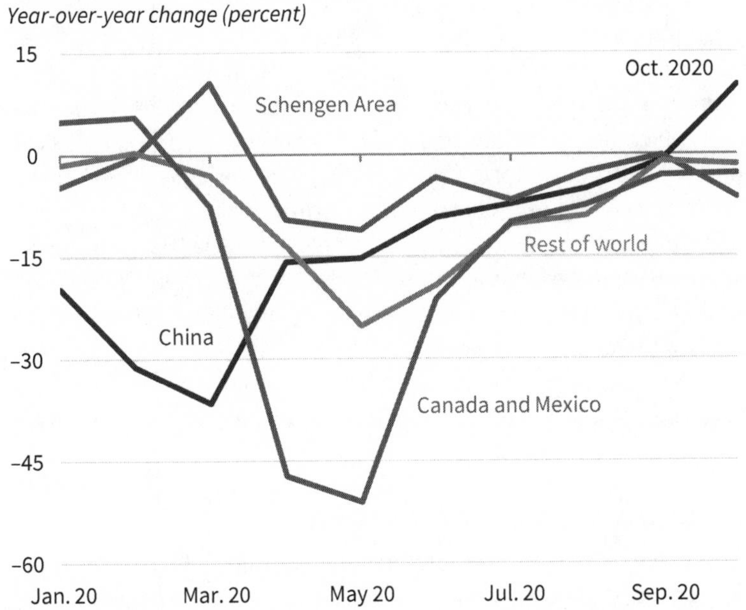

Year-over-year change (percent)

Sources: Census Bureau; CEA calculations.

Control and Prevention (CDC) issued a no sail order for all cruise ships (CDC 2020). International tourism and passenger travel services have taken the largest hit from COVID-19.

The effect of the travel restrictions and the private sector's response to COVID-19 is apparent when looking at the level of service trade broken down by the type of service. As discussed, the largest decreases are in travel and transportation services (table 9-8). Imports and exports of travel have fallen 69.8 percent and 58.4 percent, respectively, accounting for over two-thirds of the total drop in service trade. The European Union, much of which was covered by the Schengen ban, has seen the largest decline in service trade with the United States, with imports from the EU down 47.4 percent and exports to the EU down 37.8 percent in 2020 through September.

Through October 2020, imports of goods to the United States have decreased by 9.2 percent year-over-year. Most of the drop came in the second quarter, when nominal U.S. imports of goods fell by 20.0 percent. However, imports to the United States have fallen at different times for different countries (figure 9-3).

In the first quarter of 2020, imports from China plummeted reaching their lowest point in March at 36.5 percent below their March 2019 value. This quarter was also when COVID-19 was widely present in China, and China shut down its economy to address the health crisis. By comparison, in March, U.S. imports of goods from the rest of the world were only 1.3 percent below their March 2019 value, indicating that the economic effect of COVID-19 was mainly concentrated in China but had begun spreading to other countries.

In the second quarter of 2020, U.S. imports of goods saw their steepest declines in total. In April and May, imports were down 23.4 percent compared with the same period a year earlier. This drop was primarily driven by a 48.0 percent drop in imports from Canada and Mexico. Imports from the Schengen Area and the rest of the world also dropped, while imports from China rebounded, although they remained below 2019 levels. This pattern of imports may be explained by the fact that China was reopening its economy in the second quarter, while many other countries, including the United States, were shutting theirs down beginning in March. As governments around the world imposed shelter-in-place orders shuttering many businesses, imports fell. Imports of goods began to rebound in June and July as governments lifted these orders.

The Decline in Imports of Intermediate Goods

As discussed above, the emergence of global supply chains has driven a dramatic increase in international trade in recent years. Global supply chains drive trade in intermediate goods, which are goods used in the production of finished goods. The COVID-19 pandemic has had a particularly disruptive effect on supply chains through its effects on trade in intermediate goods.

Because global supply chains intricately connect distant locations, localized shutdowns due to COVID-19 disrupted economic activity around the world through "supply chain contagion" (Baldwin and Tomiura 2020). On January 23, 2020, China closed the city of Wuhan, a major manufacturing hub in Hubei Province, and locked down additional cities shortly thereafter, leading to supply chain disruptions in the United States as Chinese businesses ceased production of intermediate goods intended for the U.S. (Xie 2020). Luo and Tsang (2020) use a network model to estimate that about 40 percent of the impact of the Hubei lockdown on global output occurred through the effect on supply chains both inside and outside China.

The pandemic's effect on supply chains can be seen by analyzing data on international trade flows. These data are segmented into categories of goods—consumption, capital, and intermediate goods—using the broad economic categories defined by UN Comtrade (2016). Consumption goods are finished goods that are durable (long lasting) or nondurable (one-time use) goods that are readily available to a consumer to purchase directly or through a retailer or wholesaler. Capital goods are durable goods used in the production of other goods. Finally, as discussed, intermediate goods are goods used as inputs in the production of finished goods, and accordingly are important for supply chains.

Table 9-9. U.S. Imports: Change from 2019 Levels for Selected Countries and Regions, by Type of Good, through October 2020

Country or Region	Capital		Consumption		Intermediate	
	Dollars (billions)	Percent	Dollars (billions)	Percent	Dollars (billions)	Percent
Canada	−3.2	−16.7	−0.8	−3.1	−27.0	-18.3
China	−11.1	−7.9	−18.9	−16.8	−14.9	-14.2
Mexico	−10.6	−11.5	0.3	0.7	−17.2	-14.8
Schengen Area	6.3	10.0	−7.7	−8.8	4.7	3.2
Rest of world	9.5	8.0	−4.6	−2.6	−39.6	-11.8
World	−9.0	−2.1	−31.7	−7.1	−94.0	-11.1

Sources: Census Bureau; CEA calculations.

As discussed above, early in 2020, imports of goods to the United States declined, primarily as a result of China's lockdowns. In April and May, as the pandemic spread and governments around the world adopted shelter-in-place orders, imports of goods slowed down more dramatically. Imports began to recover in June and July as governments lifted their shelter-in-place orders. However, while imports of consumption goods rebounded sharply in June, imports of intermediate goods remained at about 15 percent below 2019 levels. By October, imports of consumption goods were 3 percent above 2019 levels; however, imports of intermediate goods continued to lag behind, at 3 percent below 2019 levels.

Through October 2020, U.S. imports of intermediate goods from the world decreased 11.1 percent year-over-year, primarily driven by the declines in imports from Canada, Mexico, and China (table 9-9). Imports of consumption goods are down only $31.7 billion from 2019 levels, while intermediate goods are down $94.0 billion.

Imports of consumption goods may have rebounded faster than imports of intermediate goods because as governments lifted shelter-in-place orders, consumers were able to increase their spending faster than firms were able to ramp up their production. As production continues to rebound, it is not yet clear whether U.S. imports of intermediate goods will return to pre-pandemic levels, or whether some supply chains will relocate to the United States.

Evidence That Firms Are Reducing Their Exposure to China

With the COVID-19 pandemic and trade policy uncertainty highlighting risks in global supply chains, U.S. businesses are considering moving production away from China to either other Asian countries, closer to the U.S. (near-shoring), or back to the U.S. (reshoring). Although a lag in the data commonly used to measure global supply chains prevents the CEA from directly observing recent changes in supply chains, surveys can provide a leading indicator of firms'

Figure 9-4. U.S. Imports of Goods from the World by Type of Good, 2020

Year-over-year change (percent)

Sources: Census Bureau; CEA calculations.

plans to locate facilities. In the past year, several surveys have attempted to evaluate the extent to which firms in the United States and elsewhere plan to change supply chains through the relocation of production or the diversification of input sourcing.

In January 2020, before the full extent of the COVID-19 pandemic was known, the Bank of America surveyed analysts covering 3,000 firms ($67 trillion in market capitalization) across North America, Europe, the Asia-Pacific region (excluding China), and China, finding "clear evidence" of movement in global supply chains. Across 12 sectors, 80 percent of firms with global supply chains ($22 trillion in market capitalization) are expected to shift "at least a portion of their supply chains" from current locations. The report concludes that "the trend is clear: global supply chains are on course to be uprooted and brought home, or transplanted to strategic allies." In a July update, the Bank of America found that three quarters of that 80 percent were expanding their reshoring plans (Bank of America 2020a, 2020b).

A March UBS survey of chief financial officers (CFOs) in the U.S., North Asia, and China suggests that 20 to 30 percent of capacity represented by these executives will relocate from China (UBS 2020). If actuated, this would move between $500 billion and $750 billion in current Chinese exports out of China. A June 2020 UBS survey shows that, among U.S. firms with manufacturing in China, 76 percent have moved or are planning to move some of their manufacturing capacity out of China. Leading candidate destinations for relocation are the United States, Canada, Japan, and Mexico.

Among North Asian (excluding Chinese) firms responding to the UBS survey, 85 percent of CFOs have moved or are planning to move capacity from China to home markets in Japan, Taiwan, and South Korea (UBS 2020). This represents over 30 percent of the Chinese production among the firms in the survey. The CFOs identified Vietnam, Thailand, and India as potential locations. Even Chinese firms have relocated or are planning to do so—60 percent of CFOs indicated that they would relocate a combined 30 percent of their Chinese production. Further, respondents reported plans to establish or expand supply chains closer to customers.

Among U.S. firms, 34 percent of CFOs reported that they had manufacturing in China, of whom 76 percent have moved or are planning to move capacity out of China. For those planning to move, they indicated that they would shift a combined 46 percent of their Chinese production. Plans to relocate are most common among healthcare firms (92 percent), consumer staples (89 percent), and technology (80 percent), followed by consumer discretionary (76 percent), industrials (69 percent), and materials (57 percent). The Bank of America (2020a) finds similar results for the Asia-Pacific region (excluding Chinese) firms. Half of the sectors have firms that have already moved or intend to move, largely to Southeast Asia and India. The survey finds that firms in 83 percent of U.S. sectors representing $3.8 trillion in market capitalization have already moved or are intending to do so.

Recent data on manufactured imports from low-cost Asian producers support the survey evidence that firms are moving supply chains out of China. The management consulting company Kearney reports the ratio of the value of manufactured goods imported to the U.S. from 14 low-cost Asian countries relative to the value of U.S. domestic gross output of manufactured goods (Kearney 2020). A decline in this manufacturing import ratio does not necessarily indicate that production is reshoring to the U.S., but it does indicate substitution away from supply chains running through these 14 countries.

In 2019, the manufacturing import ratio fell for the first time since 2011 (figure 9-5). The decline, from 13.1 percent in 2018 to 12.1 percent in 2019, was driven by a 7 percent contraction in imports from the low-cost Asian countries (the numerator), with U.S. domestic gross output of manufactured goods (the denominator) essentially unchanged. The decline in imports was led by a 17 percent contraction in trade with China. Whereas 65 percent of goods imported from the 14 Asian low-cost countries came from China in 2018:Q4, only 56 percent did so as of 2019:Q4. Though transshipment, where goods are altered slightly to change their originating status, is likely a partial factor, this cannot explain the entirety of the shift.

Another Kearney measure, the "near-to-far" ratio, measures the value of U.S. imports from Mexico divided by the value of imports from the same

Figure 9-5. U.S. Manufacturing Import Ratio, 2008–19

Ratio (percent)

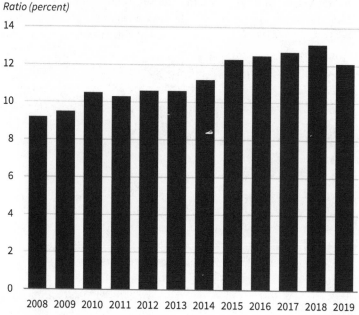

Sources: USITC; Bureau of Economic Analysis; Kearney (2020).

Figure 9-6. U.S. Near-to-far Ratio, 2009–19

Percent (imports from Mexico / imports from Asian low-cost countries)

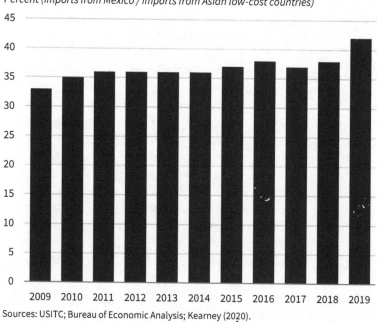

Sources: USITC; Bureau of Economic Analysis; Kearney (2020).

14 Asian low-cost countries. An increase in the ratio indicates greater near-sourcing from Mexico relative to Asia (figure 9-6). Much like the reshoring index, the near-to-far ratio jumped in 2019 as U.S. importers substituted away from Asia and toward imports from Mexico.

Drivers of Shifting Supply Chains

Although no single factor is responsible for global supply chain dynamics, the confluence of higher wages in China, technology and automation, trade policy tensions and tariffs, and the COVID-19 pandemic have all been factors in a change in how firms evaluate supply chains. In this section, we briefly discuss these factors and interactions between them.

Wages in China have risen relative to many other countries in recent years. In the 1970s, observers noted the seemingly "unlimited" labor supply in China as workers migrated from rural China to urban areas (Cui, Meng, and Lu 2018). Whereas 80 percent of the population lived in rural areas in the 1970s, the rural share of the population had shrunk to 43.9 percent by 2015. Owing partially to China's "one child" policy, China's population is aging, exacerbating a restriction in labor supply now and in the future. The resulting rising wages are eroding Chinese cost competitiveness (figure 9-7) and incentivizing firms to consider manufacturing in Southeast Asia or closer to home with

Figure 9-7. Average Monthly Nominal Wages in U.S. Dollars, 2000–2019

Wages (nominal U.S. dollars)

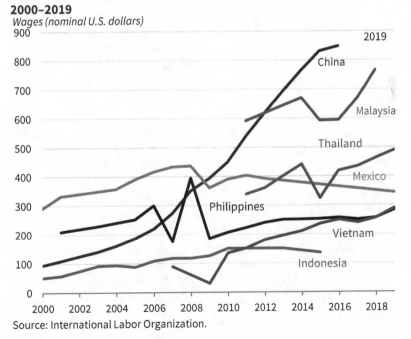

Source: International Labor Organization.

greater automation. Higher Chinese wages in comparison with other manufacturing centers persist, even when controlling for productivity.

Businesses are also increasingly aware of growing geopolitical tension between the U.S. and China. Even if the U.S. and China remove tariffs in the short term, businesses are adjusting for long-term tensions. COVID-19 has compounded these concerns, as firms recognize the need to increase resiliency. As firms consider moving out of China, they may look to automation to make up differences in labor productivity or to offset wage costs from relocating supply chains to countries with higher wages. The Bank of America estimates that by 2025, global robot installations will increase by 2.5 million, doubling 2019 levels (Bank of America 2020a).

U.S. tariffs on Chinese goods have been factors in the relocation of supply chains. In addition to tariffs, businesses are also aware of the broader geopolitical context of the U.S.-China relationship, and believe that regardless of near-term tariff policy, the two countries will face frictions. For this reason, Bank of America analysts cite both tariffs and national security as primary reasons for anticipated reconfigurations of global supply chains, with U.S.-China tariffs expected to persist regardless of the Phase One trade deal (Bank of America 2020b). Since the Bank of America published its survey, the COVID-19 pandemic appears to have further exacerbated U.S.-China tensions. As evidence of the role of national security concerns in driving supply chain relocation, Intel and TSMC (manufacturers of computer chips) have located plants in the United States, despite higher labor and capital costs (Wu 2020).

Conclusion

The Trump Administration has reasserted U.S. interests in international trade policy by forging new bilateral trade agreements with China and Japan, renegotiating the U.S. trade deal with South Korea, and reshaping regional trade by modernizing the United States' trade agreement with its most important trading partners, Canada and Mexico. The Phase One Agreement with China, when fully implemented, promises to achieve an unprecedented expansion of U.S. exports to China, and commits China to internal reforms that will make the country an improved trading partner for the United States. USMCA achieves new protections for U.S. interests across a range of areas, including digital services, intellectual property, and labor. These agreements go well beyond the lower tariffs that have been the focus of past trade agreements by addressing structural and technical barriers to free and fair trade. Along with progress on other trade agreements, these two major milestones will continue to drive U.S. economic growth and create American jobs.

The COVID-19 pandemic reduced overall international trade and has brought into sharp focus some risks of existing global supply chain configurations that previously may not have been fully priced in. These supply chains have the potential to tap into countries' comparative advantages to create mutual gains from trade. But global supply chains are susceptible to disruptions from pandemics, along with natural disasters and geopolitical tensions. As the private sector considers the relocation of supply chains, governments must weigh the benefits for some consumers and firms against the emerging understanding of the full costs to sectors facing import competition, as well as the costs associated with the risks of supply chain disruption.

Part III

An Effort to Rebuild Our Country

Chapter 10

The Year in Review and the Years Ahead

In 2020, the U.S. economy experienced the single largest adverse economic shock since the Great Depression due to COVID-19. The Business Cycle Dating Committee of the National Bureau of Economic Research determined that the economy peaked in February 2020, bringing to an end the economic expansion that began in June 2009—the longest such expansion in U.S. history. There were record declines in real gross domestic product (GDP) and payroll employment in the second quarter of 2020. Despite the sharpest rebound in real GDP and payroll employment since the Great Depression during third quarter, the U.S. economy has only partially recovered from its April 2020 nadir.

Declines in payroll employment were concentrated among low-wage workers. Overall, inflation in 2020 was similar to that in previous years, given that several months of substantial deflation early in the year were offset by higher-than-average inflation in later months. Housing markets and interest rates were affected by the pandemic, but not to the same extent as real GDP or employment.

As of the writing of this *Report*, fourth-quarter data for most indicators are not yet available. Blue Chip forecasts anticipate strong compensatory growth in 2021. However, GDP forecasts and the slowing pace of the recovery of labor force participation show that many of these issues will persist through at least 2021.

The first three chapters of this *Report* provide deep analysis of the major macroeconomic developments in the U.S. economy during 2020. It is the purpose of this chapter to provide a more succinct and summary review of the main macroeconomic indicators for the U.S. economy during 2020. The chapter then discusses the U.S. economy's future outlook, including potential economic gains in the event of full implementation of the President's complete economic policy agenda, as well as potential downside risks, particularly near-term risks from the ongoing COVID-19 pandemic.

The Year in Review

This section summarizes the main U.S. macroeconomic indicators during 2020, with a focus on total economic output, the labor market, inflation, the housing market, financial markets, and oil markets.

Components of Economic Output

Real GDP fell by 4.6 percent at an annualized rate during the first three quarters of 2020 (3.5 percent nonannualized). This decline was driven by an unprecedented contraction as a result of COVID-19 and measures taken to control the virus in the second quarter, which saw real GDP fall at an annualized rate of 31.4 percent (9.0 percent nonannualized)—the largest quarterly decline since the series began in 1947. The second quarter's record decline followed a 5.0 percent annualized contraction in the first quarter of 2020. In the third quarter, real GDP grew 33.1 percent at an annualized rate (7.4 percent nonannualized), the largest single quarter of economic growth on record and roughly twice the prior record of 16.7 percent at an annualized rate (3.9 percent nonannualized) set in the first quarter of 1950. With growth in the third quarter, the United States has recovered two-thirds of the economic output lost in the first half of the year due to the pandemic.

The decline in real GDP was widespread, touching nearly every facet of the economy and component of output (figure 10-1). Consumer spending, which accounts for roughly 70 percent of the U.S. economy, contributed most to the decline, accounting for 2.2 percentage points of the 3.5 percent (nonannualized) decline. Third quarter consumption recovered 71 percent of its decline during the first half of 2020. Investment contributed 0.5 percentage point to the 3.5 percent (nonannualized) decline in real GDP, as increased residential investment and inventories were more than offset by a drop-off in nonresidential investment during the first three quarters. In the third quarter, the level of investment recovered 82 percent of its decline from the first half of 2020. Net exports made up 0.5 percentage point (nonannualized) of the 3.5 percent decline in real GDP, and government spending made up 0.06 percentage point (nonannualized) of this decline. Government spending (which rose in the second quarter) and net exports both fell in the third quarter of 2020.

Figure 10-1. Components of Real GDP, 1990–2020

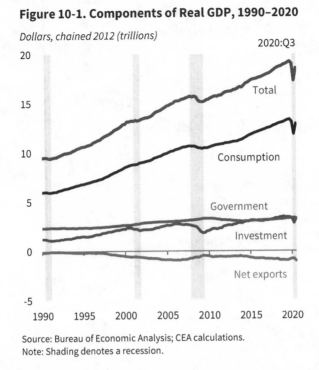

Source: Bureau of Economic Analysis; CEA calculations.
Note: Shading denotes a recession.

Consumer spending. Consumer spending fell markedly during 2020. Over the course of the first three quarters, personal consumption expenditures fell by 3.3 percent (nonannualized). Throughout the last 50 years, personal consumption expenditures have remained between 80 to 95 percent of disposable personal income, but fell to 74 percent of disposable personal income in the second quarter—its lowest level on record (figure 10-2). As a result, the personal saving rate—personal saving as a percentage of disposable personal income—surged from 7.3 percent in the fourth quarter of 2019 to 26.0 percent in the second quarter of 2020, before declining to 16.1 percent in the third quarter. On a monthly basis, the personal saving rate peaked in April 2020, setting a record high of 33.7 percent. Total net wealth (consisting of stock market wealth, housing wealth, and other wealth, less liabilities) also fell in the second quarter. Wealth data for the third quarter were not available as of the writing of this *Report*.

Consumer spending, which as noted above accounts for roughly 70 percent of GDP, provided the largest contribution to the GDP decline in the first two quarters of 2020 as well as to the GDP expansion in the third quarter. The patterns in consumption reveal the uneven way that COVID-19 and measures taken to control the virus affected economic activity. Declines in some components of services were particularly affected: travel industries, physician, and dental services. In addition, motor vehicle purchases also fell drastically. Real

Figure 10-2. Consumption and Wealth Relative Share of Disposable Personal Income (DPI), 1952–2020

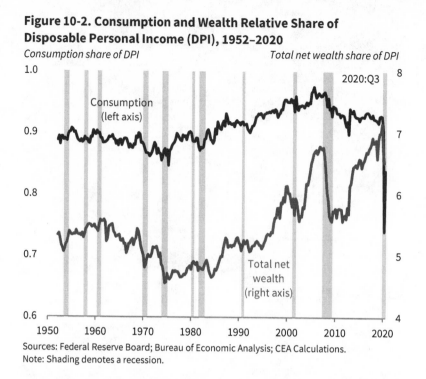

Sources: Federal Reserve Board; Bureau of Economic Analysis; CEA Calculations.
Note: Shading denotes a recession.

personal consumption expenditures accounted for 76.5 percent of the decline in real GDP during the second quarter, having declined by 9.0 percent (nonannualized). While consumer spending on goods contracted 2.8 percent (nonannualized) in the second quarter, spending on services plummeted 12.7 percent (nonannualized). A resurgence in personal consumption expenditures in the third quarter of 2020 reflected the partial reopening of businesses impacted by closures in the first and second quarters. Real personal consumption expenditures increased 7.4 percent (nonannualized) in the third quarter, accounting for 76.2 percent of real GDP growth in that quarter. Consumer spending in the services sector alone accounted for 47.5 percent of GDP growth in the third quarter.

Investment. During the first three quarters of 2020, private investment fell by 2.9 percent (nonannualized). The declines in the first and second quarters of 2.3 and 14.7 percent (nonannualized), respectively, were followed by a strong rebound (16.6 percent, nonannualized) in the third. The drop in total investment was mirrored across each of the three main types of investment: nonresidential, residential, and inventories (figure 10-3). Notably, the decline in investment was not as steep as during the Great Recession, and investment rebounded more quickly, though generally remained below prepandemic levels as of the third quarter.

Figure 10-3. Components of Investment, 1990–2020

Dollars (trillions)

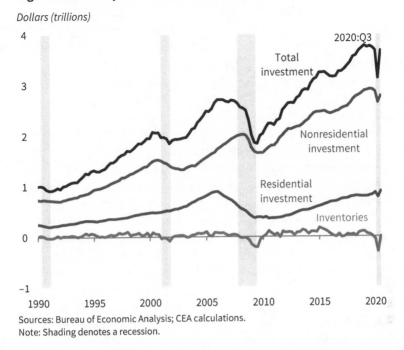

Sources: Bureau of Economic Analysis; CEA calculations.
Note: Shading denotes a recession.

Nonresidential investment contracted 1.7 and 7.6 percent (nonannualized) in the first and second quarters, respectively, and then rebounded 5.1 percent (nonannualized) in the third quarter so that the third quarter was 4.6 percent below the 2019:Q4 level. Within nonresidential investment, investment in structures declined in the first three quarters of 2020, and as of the third quarter was 14.3 percent below its 2019 year-end level. Declining investment in oil and gas exploration and production weighed heavily on investment in structures, with investment in mining exploration, shafts, and wells declining 49.7 percent (nonannualized) in the first three quarters of 2020.

Nonresidential investment in equipment contracted by 14.1 percent (nonannualized) in the first two quarters of 2020, though unlike investment in structures, it began to rebound in the third quarter, increasing 13.6 percent (nonannualized). As of the third quarter, nonresidential investment in equipment was 2.5 percent below its 2019:Q4 level with investment in information processing equipment surging to 13.4 percent above the 2019:Q4 level, though industrial and transportation equipment investment were 3.8 and 22.8 percent, respectively, below their 2019:Q4 level as of the third quarter of 2020. After edging up in the first quarter and declining in the second quarter, nonresidential investment in intellectual property products increased in the third quarter and was 1.0 percent below its 2019:Q4 level in the third quarter.

In the first quarter of 2020, residential investment increased 4.4 percent (nonannualized), the largest single-quarter increase since 2012:Q4. After contracting by 10.4 percent (nonannualized) in the second quarter, residential investment surged by 12.9 percent (nonannualized) in the third quarter to a level 5.6 percent above its 2019:Q4 level.

Inventory investment, or the change between goods produced (or imported) and goods sold (or exported), contributed negatively to real GDP growth in the first and second quarters of 2020. As firms invested to rebuild inventories, private inventory investment accounted for 6.6 percentage points, or 19.8 percent, of annualized real GDP growth in the third quarter.

Government purchases. Compared with other components of GDP, there was very little change in government purchases in 2020. During the first three quarters of 2020, government purchases fell by 0.2 percent (nonannualized). As a share of GDP, government purchases grew by 3 percent over this period, with all three categories of government purchases experiencing increases as a share of GDP (figure 10-4). Federal Government purchases increased substantially in the second quarter, supported by the Coronavirus Aid, Relief, and Economic Security (CARES) Act and other types of emergency coronavirus funding (see chapters 1 through 3 of this *Report*).

Although Federal spending rose during the first three quarters of 2020, State and local spending fell. Quarterly Federal Government nondefense consumption rose by $49 billion (in chained 2012 dollars) (13 percent, nonannualized) from the fourth quarter of 2019 to a peak in the second quarter of 2020. Similarly, during the first three quarters of 2020, quarterly Federal Government nondefense gross investment rose by $2.9 billion (in chained 2012 dollars) (2 percent, nonannualized). By comparison, during the first three quarters of 2020, quarterly state and local government consumption fell by $47 billion (in chained 2012 dollars) (3 percent, nonannualized), which outweighed the increase of $4 billion (in chained 2012 dollars) (1 percent, nonannualized) in quarterly State and local government gross investment.

Net exports. The first three quarters of 2020 saw a large drop in imports and an even larger drop in exports. Real net exports (exports minus imports) increased in the second quarter but fell in the third quarter. Overall, net exports fell for the first three quarters because the decline in exports was larger than the decline in imports. During the first three quarters of 2020, real exports of goods and services fell by $391 billion (in chained 2012 dollars) (15 percent, nonannualized), while imports fell by $242 billion (7 percent, nonannualized). As a result, net exports fell by $149 billion over this period.

Trade in goods recovered faster than trade in services. During the first three quarters of 2020, real exports of goods fell by $176 billion (in chained 2012 dollars) (25 percent, nonannualized) and real imports of goods fell by $46 billion (in chained 2012 dollars) (18 percent, nonannualized). During the same period, real exports of services fell by $191 billion (in chained 2012 dollars) (25

Figure 10-4. Government Purchases as a Share of GDP, 1948–2020

Percentage of GDP

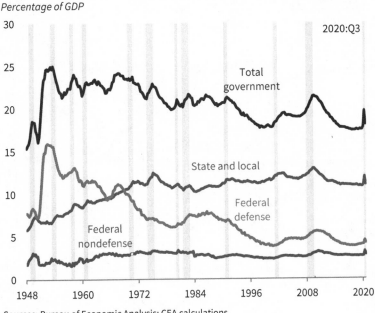

Sources: Bureau of Economic Analysis; CEA calculations.
Note: Shading denotes a recession.

percent, nonannualized) and real imports of services fell by $152 billion (in chained 2012 dollars) (32 percent, nonannualized). By the third quarter of 2020, real exports and imports of goods had both rebounded by about 20 percent from their pandemic lows. By comparison, during the same period, real exports of services had rebounded by less than 1 percent of pandemic lows, and real imports of services had rebounded by roughly six percent.

The Labor Market

The U.S. labor market experienced historically unprecedented declines in employment in March and April before posting a strong but partial recovery in the months immediately thereafter, accentuated by record employment gains in May and June. The labor force participation rate also fell dramatically before retracing part of its earlier decline.

Unemployment. The scale and speed of the increase and decrease in unemployment in 2020 were unprecedented. In February 2020, before the COVID-19 pandemic struck, the unemployment rate stood at 3.5 percent. It surged to 14.7 percent in April 2020 before falling sharply in the following months. As of November 2020, the unemployment rate (U-3) had fallen to 6.7 percent (figure 10-5). During the Great Recession, the unemployment rate peaked at 10.0 percent in October 2009, but it took more than four years to fall to 6.7 percent (December 2013). The data for unemployment insurance

Figure 10-5. Unemployment Rate, 1990–2020

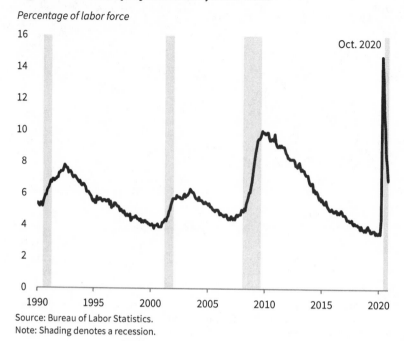

Percentage of labor force

Oct. 2020

Source: Bureau of Labor Statistics.
Note: Shading denotes a recession.

claims during 2020 are also historic: the week of March 21, 2020, saw a tenfold increase in unemployment claims, from 282,000 to 3,307,000, the largest increase on record.

The Bureau of Labor Statistics publishes several measures of the unemployment rate. U-3, the official unemployment rate, measures the share of people in the labor force actively looking for a job who are unable to find one. U-6 includes all these people, but also those who (1) want a job and are available for work and have looked for a job in the prior 12 months but not in the past 4 weeks, or (2) have given up looking for a job in the past 4 weeks because they are discouraged by job prospects, or (3) want a full-time job but are forced to work part time for economic reasons. As a result, U-6 is a much broader measure of unemployment and labor underutilization. In February 2020, before the pandemic struck, the U-6 rate stood at 7 percent. It rocketed to 22.8 percent in April 2020 before falling sharply in the immediately subsequent months. As of November 2020, U-6 had fallen to 12.0 percent, almost half its pandemic high but still higher than at any prepandemic point since August 2014—more than five years into the preceding expansion. Whereas the gap between U-3 and U-6 was small in February 2020, at 3.5 percentage points, it has widened over the course of the pandemic and stood at 5.2 percentage points in October.

Labor force participation. The labor force participation rate—the fraction of people who are either working or actively looking for work—fell in 2020,

Figure 10-6. Labor Force Participation Rate, 1990–2020

Percent

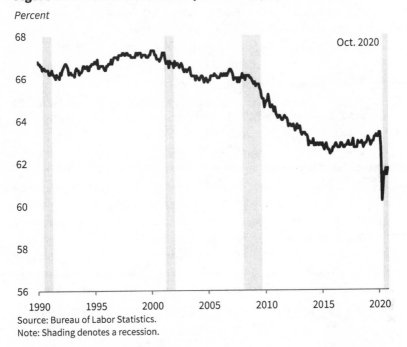

Oct. 2020

Source: Bureau of Labor Statistics.
Note: Shading denotes a recession.

Figure 10-7. Nominal Compensation and Earnings for Private Industry Workers, 2006–20

Percent change (12-month)

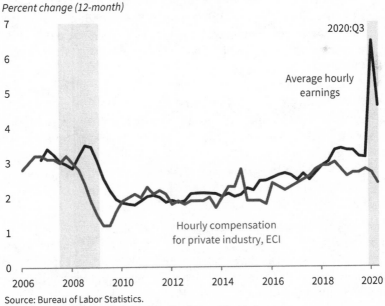

2020:Q3

Average hourly earnings

Hourly compensation for private industry, ECI

Source: Bureau of Labor Statistics.
Note: Shading denotes a recession. ECI = Employment Cost Index.

after rising in 2018 and 2019 and during the first two months of 2020, reversing a previous downward trend. From February to October 2020, the rate fell by 1.7 percentage points. It fell to 60.2 percent in April 2020, but had recovered 1.5 percentage points by October (figure 10-6). Notably, most of the recovery occurred in June. The rate did not recover much further between June and October 2020. This suggests the possibility that the 1.7-percentage-point drop in participation may be persistent. Consistent with this hypothesis, Coibion, Gorodnichenko, and Weber (2020) find that a wave of early retirements explains much of the drop in participation.

Wages. Average hourly real wages rose by 3 percent during the first three quarters of 2020, primarily because layoffs were concentrated among low-wage workers (Crust, Daly, and Hobijn 2020) (figure 10-7). While this pattern is not unique to the current recession, the change in average hourly real wages is more pronounced now than in previous recessions given the magnitude of the employment losses in March and April. That the rise in average hourly earnings is due to the composition of the workforce can be seen in the contrast with the measure of wages from the Employment Cost Index, which measures wages directly for a fixed sample of job categories. This fixed-weighted measure, increased only 2.7 percent during the 12 months through September.

Inflation

Overall, inflation in 2020 was below the average for 2019. The Federal Reserve has a target of 2 percent inflation for the Personal Consumption Expenditures Chain-Type Price Index (the PCE Price Index). But this index rose by only 1.4 percent during the 12 months through October, which was little changed from the year-earlier rate (figure 10-8). The total PCE Price Index includes volatile food and energy components, and if these are excluded (yielding the "core" PCE Price Index), inflation rose by only 1.5 percent during those 12 months, also little changed from the year earlier rate.

Looking at 2020 in detail, some months had negative inflation. In particular, month-over-month inflation was negative in March (–0.1 percent) and April (–0.4 percent). This deflation was driven primarily by changes in nondurable prices, which fell 1.1 percent in March and April. However, inflation rose at above-trend rates in June, July, and August, leading the overall 12-month change to rise back to the year-earlier rate of about 1.4 percent.

The Housing Market

Home construction and sales were substantially disrupted during the early part of the year as a result of COVID-19. This disruption did not translate into a decline in house prices, however, because tight housing supply—partly a consequence of the pandemic—and strong demand from low mortgage rates stabilized market conditions in the spring (Gascon and Haas 2020). Indeed, house prices have actually risen 6.8 percent through the first nine months of

Figure 10-8. Consumer Price Inflation (PCE Price Index), 2012–20

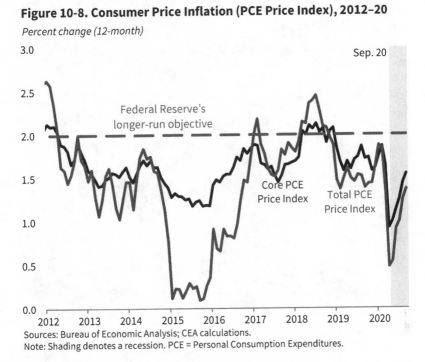

Sources: Bureau of Economic Analysis; CEA calculations.
Note: Shading denotes a recession. PCE = Personal Consumption Expenditures.

Figure 10-9. U.S. Housing Price Index, 1990–2020

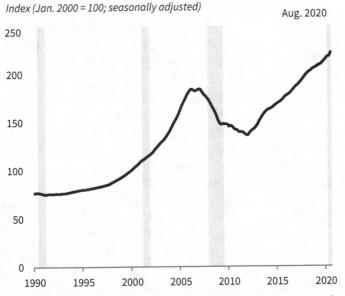

Source: Standard & Poor's—S&P CoreLogic Case-Shiller National Home Price Index.
Note: Shading denotes a recession.

Figure 10-10. U.S. New Housing Formation and Single-Family Home Sales, 1990–2020

Thousands of units (seasonally adjusted)

Sources: Census Bureau; National Association of Realtors; CEA calculations.

the year, according to the S&P Corelogic Case-Shiller Home Price Index (figure 10-9). The disruption caused a severe but short-lived drop in housing sales, housing starts, and permits, followed by a complete recovery (figure 10-10).

New housing starts peaked in January 2020 at 1.617 million units (seasonally adjusted, annualized) and fell by 683,000 units (seasonally adjusted, annualized) or 42 percent by April before recovering 87 percent of its loss to 1.530 million units (seasonally adjusted, annualized) by October. New housing permits reached a prepandemic peak in January 2020 at 1.536 million units (seasonally adjusted, annualized) and fell by 470,000 units (seasonally adjusted, annualized) or about 30 percent by April before recovering to 1.545 million units (seasonally adjusted, annualized) by October, slightly above the prepandemic peak. Total housing starts reached a prepandemic peak in January 2020 at 1.305 million units (seasonally adjusted, annualized) and fell by 125,000 units (seasonally adjusted, annualized) or about 10 percent by May before recovering to 1.343 million units (seasonally adjusted, annualized) by October, roughly 3 percent above the prepandemic peak.

Existing home sales reached a prepandemic peak in February 2020 at 5.760 million units (seasonally adjusted, annualized) and fell by 1.850 million units (seasonally adjusted, annualized) or about 32 percent by May before recovering to 6.850 million units (seasonally adjusted, annualized) by October, roughly 19 percent above the prepandemic peak. New home sales reached

Figure 10-11. U.S. Homeownership Rate, 1990–2020

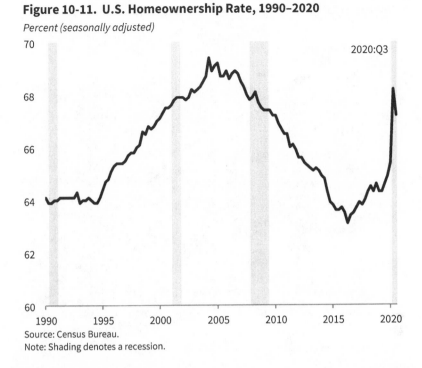

Percent (seasonally adjusted)

2020:Q3

Source: Census Bureau.
Note: Shading denotes a recession.

a prepandemic peak in January 2020 at 774,000 units (seasonally adjusted, annualized) and fell by 204,000 units (seasonally adjusted, annualized) or about 26 percent by April before recovering to and stabilizing at about 1 million units (seasonally adjusted, annualized) by August, roughly 30 percent above the prepandemic peak. Brokers' commissions and other ownership transfer costs for real residential investment contracted 22.7 percent in the second quarter of 2020, the largest single quarter contraction on record. However, in the third quarter commissions jumped up 45.3 percent, boosting commissions above prepandemic levels. The third quarter jump was the largest single-quarter expansion on record. Brokers' commissions for real nonresidential investment fell 6.8 percent in the first three quarters of 2020. This drop is in the same range as other three-quarter declines experienced during the past three years.

Evictions fell during the 2020 pandemic (see figure 2-6 in chapter 2 of this *Report*), due to the CARES Act and the President's Executive Order 13945 (August 8, 2020), which placed a moratorium on evictions until the end of 2020. The homeownership rate appears to have increased dramatically (figure 10-11), though there have been questions about data reliability because the U.S. Census Bureau temporarily suspended (though June) personal visits for the survey, which reduced response rates. The percentage of rental units making rent payments in 2020 remained relatively stable compared with the same

Figure 10-12. Percentage of Rent Payments Made, 2019–20

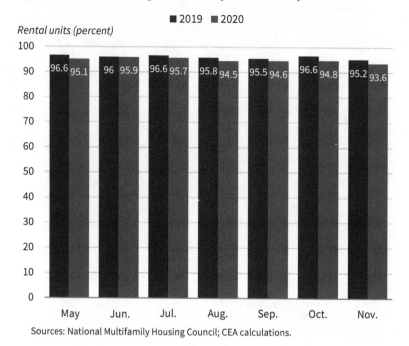

Sources: National Multifamily Housing Council; CEA calculations.

month in 2019, ranging from a drop of 0.1 to 1.8 percentage points (figure 10-12).

Financial Markets

In 2020, U.S. equity markets experienced substantial volatility but ultimately recovered from losses experienced during the pandemic. On February 19, the Standard & Poor's 500 index closed at 3,386, a prepandemic peak in 2020. However, by March 23, 2020, the S&P 500 index had fallen by 31 percent for the year. Yet, by August 18, it closed at a higher level than on February 19 and, following brief downswings in September and October, achieved several all-time highs starting in mid-November and continuing into at least early December. The Dow Jones Industrial Average index, which measures performance of shares of the 30 largest U.S. corporations, followed a similar trend, closing at a prepandemic peak of 29,551 on February 12, falling 37 percent by March 23, and achieving all-time highs starting in mid-November and continuing through at least early December. The NASDAQ index, which is heavily weighted with shares of technology firms, experienced shallower losses and a larger recovery, closing at a prepandemic peak of 9,817 on February 19, falling roughly 30 percent by March 20, and achieving an all-time high of 12,056 on September 2, roughly 23 percent above the prepandemic high.

Figure 10-13. Market Volatility Index (VIX), 2007–20

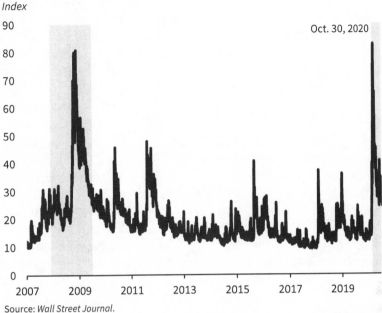

Index

Oct. 30, 2020

Source: *Wall Street Journal*.
Note: Shading denotes a recession; VIX = Chicago Board Options Exchange's Volatility Index.

Stock market volatility increased during the pandemic and remained elevated through at least October 30. The Chicago Board Options Exchange's Market Volatility Index measures the market's assessment of the volatility of the stock market (derived from options prices). This measure of volatility rose from 12.5 on January 2, to reach a peak of 82.7 on March 16, before dropping to 38.0 by October 30 (figure 10-13). As concerns over COVID-19 escalated in February and March, enormous selling pressures led to a precipitous deterioration in corporate bond market liquidity conditions. In the two weeks prior to the Federal Reserve's announcement of numerous credit and liquidity facilities on 23 March, bond transaction costs soared in both high-yield and investment grade bonds. Over those two weeks, the average cost for investment-grade bond transactions tripled, jumping from 30 basis points in February to a peak of almost 90 basis points in mid-March. Similarly, transaction costs among high-yield bonds jumped up from around 50 basis points in February to nearly 110 basis points in mid-March (Sharpe and Zhou 2020).

The spread between corporate bond yields and comparable Treasury yields took a similar path. High-yield corporate bond spreads rose from just below 4 percentage points in early February to just below 11 percentage points in Mid-march. Investment grade spreads quadrupled to 4 percent in mid-March from 1 percent in February. After the announcement and implementation of several credit facilities, corporate bond spreads substantially eased and transaction costs saw initial declines. As the Federal Reserve's lending facilities continued to offer relief, corporate bond yield spreads generally continued to fall throughout the rest of the year, reaching pre-pandemic levels in both investment-grade and high-yield bonds. Chapter 3 of this report discusses the specific Federal Reserve lending facilities implemented to address the corporate bond market crises.

Interest Rates

U.S. Treasury notes are the main form of debt issued by the Federal Government, and their interest rates are relevant to Federal interest expenses. Because corporate debt usually move roughly in parallel with government debt, these rates affect the cost of business borrowing as well.

The Federal Reserve's Open Market Committee (FOMC) lowered its target for the Federal funds rate by 150 basis points to 0.125 percent at unscheduled meetings on March 3 and March 15. Most short-term rates dropped by similar amounts. For example, the yield on 3-month Treasury bills fell by 145 basis points during March. The yield on 10-year Treasury notes (which averages the expected value of short-term rates during the next 10 years), fell by 48 basis points in March and another 20 basis points in April.

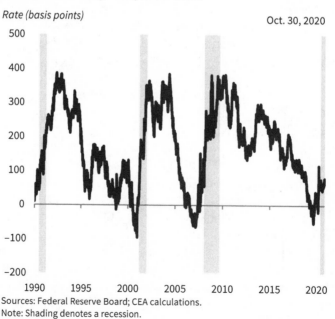

Figure 10-14. Ten-Year Minus Three-Month Treasury Constant Maturity Rate, 1990–2020

Rate (basis points)   Oct. 30, 2020

Sources: Federal Reserve Board; CEA calculations.
Note: Shading denotes a recession.

The spread between yields on long- and short-term Treasury notes is useful as a forecasting tool. The yield spread between 10-year and 3-month Treasury notes began 2020 at low positive levels. Negative yield spreads have often preceded recessions, so they are generally thought of as a leading indicator of recessions. In February the spread narrowed to zero (foreshadowing a recession), but has since rebounded to 80 basis points, a positive signal (figure 10-14).

Interest rates are also important because the Federal Reserve often adjusts interest rates as one of its main methods to support its dual mandate of price stability and maximum sustainable employment. However, short-term nominal interest rates in 2020 were near zero. The Federal Reserve may not be able to lower nominal interest rates below this "zero lower bound." If it cannot, then interest rates near zero could take away one of its primary tools for stimulating economic growth. See chapter 3 of this *Report* for a discussion of methods used by the Federal Reserve to combat the current recession at the zero lower bound.

Oil Markets

Worldwide oil consumption fell 8 percent during the first three quarters of 2020, following the typical pattern of energy demand falling during recessions (EIA 2020). As a result, Brent crude oil prices fell from $66 per barrel on January 1, 2020, to a low of $19 per barrel on April 21, before recovering to $38 as of October 30. The price of West Texas Intermediate, an important U.S. oil benchmark, actually went negative for the first time in history on April 20, driven by fears of insufficient storage capacity (BBC 2020). In response, world production of crude oil and liquid fuels fell by 10 percent between 2019 Q4 and 2020 Q3 (EIA 2020).

The Global Macroeconomic Situation

The global economy contracted in 2020 as a consequence of the COVID-19 pandemic. In its October 2020 *World Economic Outlook*, the International Monetary Fund forecast that global output would contract at a 4.4 percent rate (year-over-year) (IMF 2020a). Due in part to China's rapid return to growth and faster than expected growth among developed countries in the third quarter, the outlook improved slightly from June when the IMF expected global output to fall 4.9 percent (IMF 2020b). A separate forecast published by the Organization for Economic Cooperation and Development (OECD 2020) in December expects the global economy to contract 4.2 percent in 2020. With this economic contraction, the World Bank (2020) anticipates an additional 88 to 115 million people worldwide will fall into extreme poverty. These forecasts are highly uncertain and depend critically on any resurgence of the virus, intensity of social distancing policies, and the efficiency and efficacy of vaccination programs.

Unprecedented fiscal and monetary policy undertaken by governments and central banks helped to avoid or dampen the adverse financial transmission mechanisms of the Great Recession. Fiscal measures in advanced economies were equivalent to 9 percent of output, while liquidity supports alone were equivalent to 11 percent (IMF 2020a). Though smaller as a share of output, fiscal and monetary support among emerging and developing economies was sizeable as well, with fiscal measures equaling 3.5 percent of output and liquidity measures equaling 2 percent.

Despite the vast spread of COVID-19, there were notable differences in the timing and size of economic contractions. China, which experienced the first outbreak of the virus, experienced a 10.7 percent (nonannualized) contraction in the first quarter of 2020 before officially rebounding to its 2019 level in the second quarter of 2020. Other countries, including the United States, experienced their largest contractions in the second quarter as the virus spread from China. Differences in output in the second quarter among these countries can be explained, in part, by changes in the stringency of measures undertaken to contain the virus and subsequent changes in mobility (OECD 2020).

To consider the cumulative loss in real GDP across countries, the CEA calculated the percent of one year's real GDP lost during 2020 assuming a baseline with no growth during the first three quarters (table 10-1). This calculation represents the integral of real GDP losses during the first, second, and third quarters, as proposed by Fernández-Villaverde and Jones (2020). Using this approach, a country that experiences a 9 percent decline in output during the first quarter, and then experiences no growth in subsequent quarters, has suffered a loss three times greater than a country that experiences no decline in real GDP during the first two quarters but a 9 percent decline during the third quarter. This measure applies greater weight to contractions in growth at the beginning, as this results in a longer period of lower economic activity. By this measure, the United States has lost 3.7 percent of a year's real GDP through the first three quarters of 2020. China lost the lowest share of a year's GDP (1.7 percent), while Spain lost the largest share (9.1 percent), among countries for which data are available.

Advanced economies. Economic growth in advanced economies—such as Germany, France, Japan, the United Kingdom, and other European Union countries—are expected to contract by 5.8 percent in 2020, reflecting an upward revision of 2.3 percentage points from June to October. This change reflects less severe than expected contractions in the second quarter and growth that exceeded expectations in the third quarter. In 2021, economic growth among advanced economies is expected to reach 3.9 percent, leaving the group 2 percent below 2019 levels. However, there is substantial heterogeneity within the advanced economies. Asian countries that were better at containing the spread of COVID-19 are expected to see smaller declines in growth. Japan, for example, is forecast to contract 5.3 percent before rebounding with 7.2 percent

Table 10-1. Cumulative Losses of Real Gross Domestic Product, Selected Countries, through 2020:Q3

Country (or Group)	Decline (percentage of annual GDP)
China	−1.7
South Korea	−2.0
Norway	−2.3
Sweden	−2.6
Japan	−3.4
Israel	−3.6
United States	−3.7
Germany	−4.4
European Union (27 members)	−5.5
Mexico	−6.8
Italy	−6.9
France	−7.1
India	−8.4
United Kingdom	−8.5
Iceland	−8.5
Spain	−9.1

Source: CEA calculations.

Note: Countries are shown for which data are available.

growth in 2021. Euro area countries that were comparatively worse at containing the virus, like Spain, are expected to see growth contract by 9.8 percent in 2020 before growing at 5.9 percent in 2021, according to the IMF (2020a).

Emerging markets and developing economies. The IMF anticipates that emerging markets and developing economies will contract 3.3 percent in 2020 before growing at 6 percent in 2021. However, this forecast is buoyed by China, which experienced a strong rebound in the second quarter, according to official statistics. The IMF forecasts that China will grow at 1.9 percent in 2020. When China is excluded from emerging markets and developing countries, the forecast contraction in 2020 is 5.7 percent while the forecast growth in 2021 is 5.5 percent.

India experienced a high volume of COVID-19 cases and undertook severe measures to control the spread of the virus. Subsequent real GDP growth was worse than expected in the second quarter of 2020, leading the IMF to revise downward its forecast for 2020. India's economy is expected to contract 10.3 percent in 2020, before returning to positive growth in 2021 at an 8.8 percent pace (IMF 2020a).

The Future Economic Outlook

The United States is in the midst of a recovery from what has been a very severe recession triggered by the exogenous shock of the COVID-19 pandemic. Strong compensating growth is anticipated in 2021, buoyed by complementary fiscal

Table 10-2. Economic Forecasts, 2019–31

Year	Real GDP (chain-type) CBO	Blue Chip* Top	Blue Chip* Consensus	Blue Chip* Bottom	FOMC	Nominal GDP CBO	Nominal GDP BC*	GDP Price Index (chain-type) CBO	GDP Price Index BC*	Consumer Price Index CBO	Consumer Price Index BC*	Unemployment Rate (percent) CBO	Blue Chip Top	Blue Chip Consensus	Blue Chip Bottom	FOMC**	Interest Rate, 91-Day Treasury Bills (percent) CBO	BC	Interest Rate, 10-Year Treasury Notes (percent) CBO	BC
2019 (actual)	2.3	2.3	2.3	2.3	2.3	4.0	4.0	1.6	1.6	2.0	2.0	3.7	3.7	3.7	3.7	3.5	2.1	2.1	2.1	2.1
2020	-5.9	-2.0	-2.6	-3.3	-3.7	-5.7	-1.4	0.2	1.2	0.4	1.2	10.6	8.2	8.1	8.0	7.6	0.4	0.3	0.9	0.9
2021	4.8	6.0	3.6	1.5	4.0	6.2	5.5	1.3	1.8	1.6	2.0	8.4	6.7	6.1	5.5	5.5	0.2	0.1	0.9	1.1
2022	2.2	3.8	2.9	2.1	3.0	4.1	4.8	1.8	2.0	2.0	2.2	7.1	6.4	5.5	4.6	4.6	0.2	0.4	1.1	1.4
2023	2.1	2.9	2.3	1.9	2.5	4.1	4.4	1.9	2.1	2.2	2.2	6.5	5.5	4.8	4.1	4	0.2	0.6	1.4	1.7
2024	2.3	2.4	2.1	1.7	1.9	4.4	4.2	2.1	2.1	2.3	2.2	6.0	5.1	4.5	3.9	4.1	0.2	0.9	1.6	2.0
2025	2.4	2.3	2.0	1.6	1.9	4.5	4.1	2.1	2.1	2.2	2.2	5.6	4.9	4.3	3.8	4.1	0.2	1.1	1.9	2.2
2026	2.3	2.2	2.0	1.7	1.9	4.4	4.0	2.1	2.1	2.2	2.2	5.2	4.9	4.4	3.8	4.1	0.3	1.3	2.2	2.3
2027	2.3	2.2	1.9	1.7	1.9	4.4	4.1	2.0	2.1	2.2	2.2	4.8	4.7	4.3	3.9	4.1	0.6	1.7	2.6	2.5
2028	2.0	2.2	1.9	1.7	1.9	4.1	4.1	2.0	2.1	2.2	2.2	4.5	4.7	4.3	3.9	4.1	1.1	1.7	2.8	2.5
2029	1.8	2.2	1.9	1.7	1.9	3.9	4.1	2.0	2.1	2.2	2.2	4.4	4.7	4.3	3.9	4.1	1.6	1.7	3.0	2.5
2030	1.8	2.2	1.9	1.7	1.9	3.8	4.1	2.0	2.1	2.2	2.2	4.4	4.7	4.3	3.9	4.1	2.1	1.7	3.2	2.5
2031	2.2	2.2	1.9	1.7	1.9		4.1		2.1		2.2	4.7		4.3	3.9	4.1		1.7		2.5

Note: CBO = the Congressional Budget Office's July 2020 forecast; BC = Blue Chip Economic Indicators' December 2020 forecast, combined with its October 2020 forecast for long-term projections; FOMC = the Federal Open Market Committee's September 2020 forecast; Top = the average forecast of the 10 highest forecasters; Bottom = the average forecast for the 10 lowest forecasters. *The Blue Chip Forecasts for 2022 and beyond use October's 2020 year-over-year projections; **the FOMC's forecasted unemployment rate for the fourth quarter of that year.
Sources: Congressional Budget Office; Blue Chip Economic Indicators; Federal Reserve Board.

and monetary policy, as well as reductions in the disease burden as vaccine candidates become more widely available through Operation Warp Speed. This section reviews several economic forecasts, as detailed in table 10-2, and discusses upside and downside risks to the economic outlook.

Forecasts from the Blue Chip Consensus, the Congressional Budget Office, and the Federal Reserve Open Market Committee

Private and official forecasts anticipate GDP to bounce back strongly from the 2020 recession, with 4 percent or higher growth expected during the four quarters of 2021 by the July 2020 Congressional Budget Office's projection, the November Blue Chip consensus, and the September FOMC projection. The Blue Chip forecasters range from 1.7 percent, projected by the bottom 10 forecasters, to 5.3 percent, projected by the top 10, potentially indicating different assessments regarding the upside and downside risks discussed below, and the magnitude and composition of additional support from fiscal and monetary policy. After a strong short-term recovery, all forecasters predict that long-term growth rates will gradually fall back to averages of about 2 percent per year, although the Congressional Budget Office predicts a second growth rate peak in 2025, with a gradual decline to a long run average afterward.

The Federal Reserve expects increases in the Consumer Price Index to remain near target, though interest rates are projected to remain below their long-term levels until the second half of the decade. In August 2020, the FOMC announced that it would target an inflation rate that averages 2 percent, thereby allowing periods of higher than 2 percent inflation to compensate for periods when inflation fails to reach 2 percent. As a result, the FOMC may aim for inflation moderately above 2 percent if prior rates of inflation have persisted below 2 percent. This policy change means it will likely not preempt projected inflationary pressures with interest rate hikes, as was done between 2015 and 2019. This shift will give greater space for the labor market to strengthen before the FOMC considers raising interest rates relative to the FOMC's previous policy stance.

The unemployment rate is expected to continue to fall throughout the upcoming years, before settling at a long-run rate. There are substantial differences in estimates of what this long-run rate will be, with the top 10 Blue Chip estimates averaging 4.7 percent and the bottom 10 averaging 3.7 percent. These estimates are above the February 2020 observed unemployment rate of 3.5 percent, which was associated with a 12-month change in the Personal Consumption Expenditures Price Index of just 1.8 percent, below the Federal Reserve's target. As discussed below, the interaction between labor force participation and labor market slack will have large effects on the unemployment rate, wages, and inflationary pressures.

Economic Objectives and Policy

Economic prospects in the coming years depend critically on the Nation's economic policies. The Employment Act of 1946 called for the Federal Government to pursue the goal of maximum employment, production, and purchasing

Table 10-3. Policy-Inclusive Economic Projections, 2019-31

	Percent Change (Q4-to-Q4)				Level (calendar year)		
Year	Nominal GDP	Real GDP (chain-type)	GDP Price Index (chain-type)	Consumer Price Index	Unemployment Rate (percent)	Interest Rate, 91-Day Treasury Bills (percent)	Interest Rate, 10-Year Treasury Notes (percent)
2019 (actual)	4.0	2.3	1.6	2.0	3.7	2.1	2.1
2020	-1.0	-2.2	1.3	1.1	8.1	0.4	0.9
2021	7.4	5.3	2.0	2.3	5.2	0.1	0.8
2022	6.0	3.9	2.0	2.3	4.3	0.1	1.0
2023	5.4	3.3	2.0	2.3	4.1	0.1	1.2
2024	5.1	3.0	2.0	2.3	4.0	0.1	1.5
2025	5.0	2.9	2.0	2.3	4.0	0.1	1.7
2026	4.9	2.8	2.0	2.3	4.0	0.2	2.0
2027	4.9	2.8	2.0	2.3	4.0	0.5	2.2
2028	4.9	2.8	2.0	2.3	4.0	0.9	2.4
2029	4.9	2.8	2.0	2.3	4.0	1.3	2.6
2030	4.9	2.8	2.0	2.3	4.0	1.7	2.7
2031	4.9	2.8	2.0	2.3	4.0	2.1	2.8

Sources: Bureau of Economic Analysis; Bureau of Labor Statistics; Department of the Treasury; Office of Management and Budget; Council of Economic Advisers.

Note: Forecast was based on data available as of November 6, 2020. The interest rate on 91-day T-bills is measured on a secondary-market discount basis. GDP = gross domestic product.

power, and it established the Council of Economic Advisers to support the President in meeting this goal. Building on this, the Full Employment and Balanced Growth Act of 1978 called for the President to set forth annual numerical goals for several key economic indicators over a multiyear period, as well as a program of policies for achieving the prescribed objectives, regardless of the probability of that program being administratively or legislatively implemented.

The projections reported in table 10-3 reflect the Trump Administration's goal of achieving maximum employment, production, and purchasing power within the Federal budget window of ten years, consistent with the objectives of the 1946 and 1978 employment acts, and accordingly include the estimated impacts of the Administration's full economic policy agenda. Considering the economic challenges discussed in this *Report* and recent editions of the *Economic Report of the President*, these are very ambitious economic projections. Achieving these targets will require full implementation of the Administration's complete economic policy agenda, most of which requires Congressional legislation.

As discussed in the chapters of this *Report*—as well as in the 2018, 2019, and 2020 editions of the *Economic Report of the President*—the ambitious economic projections reflect the fact that the Administration's economic policy agenda has been similarly ambitious. In the very near-term, the agenda includes full implementation of further legislation to support economic recovery from the COVID-19 pandemic. Specifically, the projections reported in table 10-3 assume passage of additional legislation to provide for reauthorization and expansion of the Paycheck Protection Program to support small business employment, an expanded employee retention tax credit, a reemployment bonus, and a temporary extension of targeted fiscal support to State and local governments, schools, and low- and middle-income households and households with unemployed workers.

In the near term, the economic targets reported here also assume enactment of the President's $1.5 trillion infrastructure proposal, as analyzed in the 2018 *Economic Report of the President*. They also assume that all provisions of the 2017 Tax Cuts and Jobs Act that are currently scheduled to sunset or expire are instead made permanent. These include, but are not limited to, full expensing of new equipment investment, the near-doubling of the standard deduction, reductions of personal income tax rates across multiple brackets, doubling of and expanded eligibility for the Child Tax Credit, and a 20 percent small business tax deduction. In addition, the numeric targets assume enactment of a new middle-class tax cut, as discussed in chapter 11 of this *Report*, including elimination of the second-earner penalty, further raising the standard deduction, and reducing income tax liability in the lowest personal income tax rate brackets, offset at higher incomes by rate and threshold adjustments to ensure targeted tax cuts with no net tax increases. Such a design would target tax relief to lower- and middle-income taxpayers, who face some of the highest effective marginal personal income tax rates, thereby substantially raising labor force participation rates, particularly among women and low-income workers. This is reflected in the supply-side components reported in table 10-4.

The economic targets also assume enactment of skills-based immigration reform, a continuation of the Administration's comprehensive deregulatory agenda, improved bilateral trade agreements with major trading partners, and longer-run fiscal consolidation, as discussed in the 2020 *Economic Report of the President*. They further assume additional labor market policies to incentivize

Table 10-4. Supply-Side Components of Actual and Potential Real Output Growth, 1953–2031

Component	Growth Rate (percentage points)				
	1953:Q2 to 2019:Q4	1990:Q3 to 2001:Q1	2001:Q1 to 2007:Q4	2007:Q4 to 2019:Q4	2019:Q4 to 2031:Q4
1 Civilian noninstitutional population age 16+	1.3	1.2	1.1	1.0	0.7
2 Labor force participation rate	0.1	0.1	-0.3	-0.4	-0.2
3 Employed share of the labor force	0.0	0.1	0.1	0.1	-0.0
4 Ratio of nonfarm business employment to household employment	0.0	0.3	0.4	0.1	0.1
5 Average weekly hours (nonfarm business)	-0.2	-0.1	-0.2	-0.1	0.0
6 Output per hour (productivity, nonfarm business)	2.0	2.4	2.5	1.4	2.7
7 Ratio of real GDO to nonfarm business output	-0.3	-0.6	-0.2	-0.2	-0.5
8 Sum: actual real GDO[a]	3.0	3.5	2.4	1.7	2.7
Memo:					
9 Output per worker differential: GDO vs. nonfarm**	-0.3	-0.3	-0.6	-0.3	-0.4

Sources: Bureau of Labor Statistics; Bureau of Economic Analysis; Department of the Treasury; Office of Management and Budget; CEA calculations.

[a] Real GDO and real nonfarm business output are measured as the average of income- and product-side measures.

**The output-per-worker differential (row 9) is the difference between output-per-worker growth in the economy as a whole and output-per-worker growth in the nonfarm business sector, and is also equal to row 4 + row 7.

Note: All contributions are in percentage points at an annual rate. The forecast is based on data available on November 9, 2020. The total may not add up due to rounding; 1953:Q2, 1990:Q3, 2001:Q1, 2007:Q4, and 2019:Q4 are all quarterly business-cycle peaks. Gross domestic output (GDO) is the average of GDP and gross domestic income. Population, labor force, and household employment have been adjusted for discontinuities in the population series.

higher labor force participation, including expanding work requirements for nondisabled, working-age recipients in noncash welfare programs; increasing childcare assistance for low-income families; and enhancing assistance for reskilling programs through the National Council for the American Worker.

By any measure, this is a very ambitious economic policy agenda. However, it reflects the bold requirements of the 1946 and 1978 acts: to set forth a program for achieving, as rapidly as possible, the goals of full employment, full production, and rising real incomes. Achieving these projected outcomes is therefore contingent on full implementation of the complete range of economic policies articulated here and in the 2018, 2019, and 2020 editions of the *Economic Report of the President*. In the absence of full implementation, not only does the CEA anticipate that economic growth in the coming years will be lower than the numeric targets reported in table 10-3, but also perhaps substantially lower, in line with the economic projections summarized in table 10-2.

Near–Term Upside and Downside Risks

As discussed throughout this *Report*, the emergence of COVID-19 in late 2019 has burdened the economic outlook and continues to present near-term downside risks. The burden of the virus is heaviest for elderly people and for individuals suffering from-co-morbidities, but extends to all segments of the population. The outlook is complicated further by the long-term health effects of COVID-19, which are not fully understood.

The COVID-19 pandemic dominated economic developments during 2020 and will continue to do so in 2021. In the near term, the biggest downside risk to the economic outlook is that policy and behavioral responses to a resurgence of COVID-19 disrupt the considerable recovery in output and labor markets observed to date. For this reason, in late 2020 the Administration continued to articulate support for additional fiscal measures, discussed above, to provide a bridge to the widespread availability of vaccine candidates developed under Operation Warp Speed (Goodspeed and Navarro 2020).

Upside risk to economic activity includes the possibility that an effective vaccine or vaccines will be rapidly distributed and administered to a high percentage of the population, which, thanks in part to Operation Warp Speed, looks highly probable. Indeed, multiple candidates have had successful trials, evincing high effectiveness. Preliminary results have exceeded expectations, and an Emergency Use Authorization (EUA) from the Food and Drug Administration has been issued for the Pfizer/BioNTech vaccine, with an EUA for the Moderna vaccine expected by the end of the year. In addition, treatment for COVID-19 has improved throughout 2020 and will likely continue to improve, thanks in part to EUAs of advanced therapeutics that reduce the illness severity and fatality rate for those affected. However, there remains the possibility of viral mutation, especially if the virus recrosses transspecies borders, removing the resistance afforded by immune system responses built by infection or vaccination. For example, Denmark has been forced to cull its mink populations to avoid such a result, and other animal populations may follow.

Substantial challenges to distributing vaccines remain. Several of the promising candidates require cold temperatures during transportation and storage to maintain effectiveness, an issue that will create challenges in many developing countries and some areas of the developed world. The distinct threat posed by misinformation regarding the safety and effectiveness of vaccination will also need to be addressed. Creating a vaccine is only useful if a high enough percentage of individuals use it to protect themselves and others.

Dramatic pandemic-related shocks were felt in the labor market during early 2020. The U.S. employment level fell from a record-high of 158.8 million in February 2020 to 133.4 million in April, a decline of over 25 million in 2 months. For comparison, during the Great Recession employment fell by 8.6 million in 25 months. However, since April many temporary layoffs and furloughed workers have been recalled. American entrepreneurship has met the challenge, as new high-propensity business applications (i.e., applications with a high probability of turning into businesses with a payroll) were 29,000 by week 47 of 2020 (a 23 percent increase from 2019) according to the Business Formation Statistics from the Census Bureau. These positive developments increased employment by 16.3 million from April to November and reduced the official unemployment rate from 14.7 to 6.7 percent.

In the near term, there is a risk that these trends temporarily reverse. Rising cases have prompted the reimposition of lockdown restrictions and endogenous individual social distancing, leading to a curtailment of expenditures on in-person consumer services. Even if case levels fall, further recovery may still be characterized by a slower pace. Many temporary employment separations have now been restored, increasing the proportion of the unemployed who will not be returning to their previous employment. Permanent separations require new search and matching as well as more structural adjustments, which become more difficult the longer they are without employment. For example, some workers may need to retrain for new industries that develop in response to permanent changes in consumer preferences.

Hall and Kudlyak (2020) observe that the labor market's recoveries from recessions have consistently been measured as roughly a reduction of 0.55 percentage point a year in the unemployment rate. As the labor market regains the temporary layoffs and begins to reallocate permanent layoffs, the rate of recovery will likely converge toward this rate. However, looking at output, Bordo and Haubrich (2017) find that typically the amplitude of a recovery is strongly correlated with the amplitude of the preceding contraction, with the recovery following the Great Recession constituting a notable exception of the past 140 years. As the long-term unemployed experience skill deterioration and potentially permanent income losses (Hamermesh 1989; Ruhm 1991), rapid action to reemploy the most people possible is needed to minimize lasting harm to the labor market. One area where layoffs may continue is State and local governments, which have seen reduced revenue in 2020.

Another variable that has shown partial recovery is labor force participation. The 12-month moving average of participation had risen to 63.1 percent in February 2020 from a nadir of 62.6 percent in January 2016. In recent years, the U.S. labor force participation has faced demographic headwinds from the retirement of the baby boom population, with rising participation on the eve of the pandemic driven by a 1.9-percentage-point increase in prime-age labor force participation. Even in February, participation remained well below (4.2 percentage points) its early 2000 peak of 67.3 percent, though it was only 1 percentage point lower for prime-age workers.

During the pandemic, participation fell 3.2 percentage points, and subsequently rose 1.5 percentage points during the recovery. Further recovery could be imperiled if the pandemic continues to encourage individuals near the age of retirement to retire early or encourages individuals to delay school or labor force entry. However, there could be greater gains in participation if individuals choose to work later in life due to a desire to accumulate more savings for retirement, if higher female participation rises during prime-age relative to previous cohorts, and if workplaces offer greater availability of physically accommodating occupations, including remote work. An additional upside risk is that some pandemic-induced investment in teleworking facilitates greater labor force participation from individuals who otherwise might face binding childcare constraints. Similarly, the decentralization of work could cause individuals to move to more affordable and less restrictive areas, which might increase economic activity in areas with lower costs of living, such as rural areas, and thereby improve family finances.

A tight labor market benefits workers by leading to higher wages and shorter spells of unemployment. A slack labor market does the opposite, leading to substantial downside risks for the American worker from a slower recovery and to upside risks from a faster recovery. The lack of consensus in the U.S. Congress to implement the President's economic policy objectives for additional fiscal support in response to the pandemic, particularly in the form of an additional round of the Paycheck Protection Program to help maintain employer-employee matches and organizational capital, is therefore a substantial downside risk in the near term.

Relatedly, in the absence of Congressional support for the Administration's near-term legislative priorities, there is a risk of mounting business insolvencies, particularly among small- and medium-sized firms adversely affected by the reimposition of lockdown restrictions. As losses incurred as a result of the pandemic and associated lockdowns are realized, there is a nontrivial risk that defaults and insolvencies may impair collateral assets in commercial credit markets, and therefore trigger downgrades of securities collateralized by those assets, which would elevate the risk of broader credit disintermediation, of the type discussed by Bernanke (1983). Tax code changes introduced by the CARES Act were designed to mitigate this risk by modifying the treatment of business tax assets, specifically by introducing a five-year carryback for net operating losses (NOLs) in 2018, 2019, and 2020; suspending the NOL limit of 80 percent of taxable income; and allowing pass-through business owners to use NOLs to offset non-business income above the prior limit in 2018, 2019, and 2020. These modifications were designed to mitigate the adverse shock to business cash flow in 2020 by allowing firms to spread losses over time.

Internationally, however, there is the risk that insolvency issues generated by severe and protracted lockdown restrictions abroad introduce new strains on fiscally weak sovereign governments, most notably in emerging markets and Europe. Such strains would elevate the risk of a replay of the sovereign debt concerns that emerged in the aftermath of the Great Recession.

Long-Term Upside and Downside Risks

A crucial variable for the long-run outlook for growth is the productivity of the workforce. This area has substantial upside risk for growth to outperform what would otherwise be forecasted based on the experiences of the post–Great Recession economy.

Productivity measures how much economic output is generated from a given amount of inputs. As shown in table 10-4, output per hour averaged annual growth of 2 percent between 1953:Q2 and 2019:Q4. By contrast, productivity growth averaged only 1.32 percent between 2007:Q4 and 2019:Q4. After the passage of the 2017 Tax Cuts and Jobs Act (TCJA), productivity growth averaged 1.52 percent annually between 2017:Q4 and 2019:Q4. Improving this rate of increase is of paramount importance for meeting goals of raising real incomes across the income distribution, as was observed in 2018-19. Chapter 11 of this *Report* discusses several possible prescriptions for achieving this result, such as incentivizing higher education institutions to better prepare students for the workforce, immigration reform, and infrastructure investment, as well as making permanent some of the provisions of TCJA that are currently legislated to phase out.

As mentioned above, demographic shifts continue to constitute a challenge to the supply-side potential of the U.S. labor market. The 65-and-older population grew by over a third (34.2 percent, or 13,787,044) during the past decade. The first cohort of the baby boom generation turned 65 in 2011, and the last cohort will turn 65 in 2029. These demographic shifts have generated downward pressure on the aggregate participation rate over the past decade, and will continue to generate downward pressure over the next decade. Whether these individuals retire early or continue to actively participate in the labor market will have a major impact on the economic trajectory over the next decade. Policies such as those described in chapter 11 of this *Report* can have a positive effect on participation, alleviating the demographic drag. As discussed in the 2019 and 2020 editions of the *Economic Report of the President*, making permanent the marginal personal income tax rate reductions in the TCJA can also incentivize continued participation among retirement and near-retirement age workers, who theoretical and empirical research indicate are more responsive to changes in marginal personal income tax rates.

The COVID-19 pandemic has highlighted shortcomings in the healthcare system in the United States that lead to both upside and downside risks for long-term growth. As the pandemic has dramatically illustrated, individuals with poor health are much more likely to suffer serious illness in the event of contracting the disease, and consequently face a higher mortality rate. Life expectancy among particular segments of the population in the United States was falling even before the pandemic, a trend that is the result in large part of drug overdoses (particularly from opioids), suicides, and liver diseases, which recent research suggests may be related to displacement effects of increased exposure to import competition from China following the establishment of permanent normal trade relations in 2000 (Pierce and Schott 2020). Addressing the underlying reasons for these disturbing trends provides an upside risk that the loss of social cohesion, mental health deterioration, and poor diet and exercise can be successfully reversed. However, there is also a downside risk that the situation gets worse, with losses in productivity and participation resulting from more sickness and death.

There is also an upside potential that pandemic-induced investments in healthcare research and the rapid deployment of new therapies and vaccines, as well as deregulatory actions to increase choice and access in the medical system, can lead to better health in the future. Examples of deregulatory actions include expanded access to telehealth services, increased scope of practice, and further mRNA-based interventions. Observations by individuals may also result in greater precautionary personal measures in future influenza seasons, reducing the annual burden of endemic disease.

An additional long-run risk is that the pandemic and associated lockdowns generate long-term economic scarring and amplify issues of economic inequality. Whereas—in a stark reversal of trends under way during the 2009–16 expansion—wage, income, and wealth inequality, including among races, were declining in the three years immediately preceding the pandemic, the extreme regressivity of lockdown restrictions and consequent loss of employment and disruption to human capital acquisition may exacerbate economic inequality for years to come. Although the CARES Act attenuated income inequality in the near term, over the long run, school closures, disparate access to remote learning, and losses of on-the-job training and skills acquisition may introduce human capital deficits that compound over time and have a particularly adverse impact on the lower end of the skills and income distributions. Long-term scarring that depresses future supply-side potential could also complicate the task of monetary policy if inflation expectations become unanchored (Kozlowski, Veldkamp, and Venkateswaran 2020).

Finally, to ensure robust long-term growth, the United States must also address its rising debt burden. Structural and taxation incentives for debt-financing investments have created a large increase in nonfinancial corporate debt, growing from $6.1 trillion at the end of 2010 to $11 trillion in 2020. The

TCJA codified several improvements in capital allocation mechanisms, including limiting the tax deductibility of interest payments on debt, precipitating upside risk that this will lead to improved productivity growth. Lower interest rates due to the pandemic are unlikely to substantially increase during much of the budget window, which may continue to incentivize debt-financing of business activity. The debt burden on individuals is also a cause of concern, especially loans used to finance higher education. Since 2003, inflation-adjusted student debt balances have more than doubled in nearly every State, and in parts of the Southeast they have nearly quadrupled, with the student loan delinquency rate rising commensurately (Hedlund 2019). This debt burden has been found to constrain occupational choice, reduce marriage prospects and homeownership, and increase the risk of bankruptcy (Rothstein and Rouse 2011; Gicheva 2016; Mezza et al. 2020; Gicheva and Thompson 2015). As students who have put off entry into higher education decide whether to return, the question of whether higher education will act as an expensive signaling device or as a skill-formulating institution has substantial upside and downside risks.

Conclusion

The events of the past 12 months have created a historically unprecedented year for the U.S. economy. Record declines in GDP and employment in the second quarter were followed by record increases in both of these economic indicators in the third quarter. Inflation, housing markets, and financial and energy markets were also affected, although to a lesser extent than output and labor markets. Strong compensatory growth is anticipated in 2021. However, GDP forecasts and the slowing pace of the recovery of labor force participation show that many of these issues will persist through at least 2021.

Despite the historic pace of the economic recovery observed to date, there remain risks to both the near- and long-term outlooks. In the near term, particularly in the face of viral resurgence, the Administration recognizes the need for further fiscal support to maintain attachments between employees and employers until the widespread availability of vaccines through Operation Warp Speed allows the resumption of normal levels of economic activity. Over the longer term, building on the historic economic gains observed in 2017, 2018, and especially 2019, a program of economic policies that continues to incentivize domestic capital formation and increased labor force participation will be essential for ensuring a rapid return to the economic conditions prevailing on the eve of the pandemic. As discussed throughout this *Report*, this program includes but is not limited to extending the provisions of the TCJA, investing in infrastructure, lowering high effective marginal income tax rates on lower-income workers, further regulatory reform, and continuing to upgrade bilateral trading arrangements. Such a program was instrumental in generating a historically tight labor market and broad-based real income gains in 2017-19, following what had been the weakest economic recovery in postwar U.S. history between 2009 and 2016.

Chapter 11

Policies to Secure Enduring Prosperity

This *Report* analyzes the unprecedented health and economic shock of the COVID-19 pandemic, and the historic policy responses to mitigate its impact on the Nation. The United States is making progress toward emerging from this crisis; however, our country continues to contend with an adverse shock of historic magnitude. The purpose of this final chapter is to review a collection of policy areas highlighted by the COVID-19 pandemic and to analyze potential reforms to meet the ongoing challenges facing the U.S. economy. We introduce these areas in this prefatory section, and then the full chapter presents them in detail.

Strengthening connections to the labor force. The U.S. labor market's recovery since the initial effect of COVID-19 has been unprecedented, with the unemployment rate falling by 8 percentage points in seven months. However, workers with a weaker prior connection to the labor force have experienced a slower recovery. This chapter discusses two important ways in which the tax code discourages lasting connections to the workforce: high effective taxes both on nonprimary earners in families and on low-income earners navigating the various Federal assistance programs.

Supporting balance between work and family. The recent suppression of economic activity has posed particular challenges for families. Parents of children whose schools were closed faced challenges in obtaining childcare while working. Parents who needed time off due to illness or to care for a sick relative faced difficult decisions regarding work and family responsibilities. This chapter discusses how, even in normal times, a lack of accessible paid leave and childcare for parents can lead to wider detrimental effects on society, and how this challenge could be addressed.

Enhancing international coordination to address 21st-century challenges. Both the health and economic consequences of COVID-19 cross national boundaries, given that disease transmission and supply chain disruptions in one country can have large effects on other countries. This chapter discusses how strong reciprocal trade relationships between the United States and other countries can preserve U.S. consumer access to foreign products and U.S. producer access to global supply chains, while ensuring that American entrepreneurs face an even playing field that protects U.S. economic interests.

Creating a more effective healthcare system. COVID-19 caused a public health crisis that exposed strains on the U.S. healthcare system. This chapter reviews mechanisms that inefficiently drive up costs and reduce access to quality health care. These include restrictions on the supply of healthcare professionals, information problems inherent in balance billing, and a disconnect between Medicare prices and competitive prices for some medical services.

Building a dynamic economy through infrastructure improvement. Continued adjustment to the potential reallocation of economic activity and factors of production in response to the pandemic requires strong and versatile infrastructure. The Federal Government can target investment to increase the productivity of American industry. This chapter discusses the structural factors that inhibit improvements in infrastructure along with mechanisms to resolve them.

Generating a more skilled and resilient workforce. COVID-19 is imposing a large reallocation shock on the U.S. economy because temporarily suppressed output and changes in consumer preferences may weaken some firms and industries and strengthen others. Highly skilled workers will be needed not only to take advantage of these new opportunities but also to create them. This chapter discusses two ways to expand the skilled workforce: moving toward a more transparent and merit-based immigration system, and improving human capital formation for Americans attending institutions of higher education. This chapter also highlights the success of Historically Black Colleges and Universities.

The American economy faces challenges that not only were exacerbated by the COVID-19 pandemic but also extend into the postpandemic future, as outlined above and as explained in detail below. Meeting these challenges will ensure that the United States not only recovers to its prepandemic levels of prosperity but also builds a more dynamic and resilient economy that will benefit all Americans.

Strengthening Connections to the Labor Force

The COVID-19 pandemic and subsequent economic shock decreased prime-age labor force participation by 3.2 percentage points, erasing the unanticipated gains of the preceding three years and reaching its lowest value in April 2020 since the early 1980s, before partially recovering. Increasing the labor force participation rate will require action addressing the elements of the Federal tax code that disproportionately deter labor force entry and skill upgrading. This section identifies two areas in which Federal policy changes can remove barriers to participation in the workforce. Taken together, these tax reforms would constitute a momentous middle class tax cut.

From the early 1960s until the turn of the century, the United States experienced a sustained and pronounced rise in the employment-to-population ratio—which measures the percentage of the civilian, noninstitutional population that is working—from 55 percent to nearly 65 percent. This trend was driven by the participation of females, many of whom were in two-earner households. However, over the past 20 years, this trend has been eroded by two recessions—in 2001 and 2008-09—and subsequent slow recoveries, coupled with an aging of the population. Even among the prime-age labor force of 25- to 54-year-olds, the employment-to-population ratio fell from a peak of over 80 percent in 2000 to only 75 percent in the immediate aftermath of the Great Recession. Only by 2019 did the U.S. economy nearly return to its 2000s peak under the historically strong labor market conditions that existed before the arrival of the COVID-19 shock. Figure 11-1 summarizes these dynamics.

Abraham and Kearney (2020) discuss several factors behind the stagnation and decline in the employment-to-population ratio between 1999 and 2018. These include the effects of import competition from China, automation, disability insurance programs, childcare costs, and shifting social norms reducing the stigma of not working (especially among men) on labor supply.

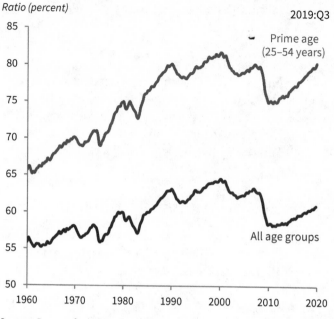

Figure 11-1. Employment-to-Population Ratio, 1960–2020

Ratio (percent)

2019:Q3

Prime age
(25–54 years)

All age groups

Sources: Bureau of Labor Statistics; FRED (2020).

In addition to these factors, the Federal Government's income tax code is an important impediment to the growth of the labor force due to both the way that second-earners are penalized by the system of joint taxation and the high combined effective marginal rates of Federal and State taxes faced by low-income earners. While the 2017 Tax Cuts and Jobs Act reduced hindrances to investment and brought more low-income earners out of Federal income tax liability altogether by nearly doubling the Standard Deduction, many filers in these two groups continue to face high effective marginal tax rates under the current code. This section discusses the negative effects of family taxation and the causes of the high effective marginal tax rates faced by many low-income earners (estimated to be as high as 70 percent by Altig et al. 2020, when taking into account Federal and State taxes along with phase-outs of credits and deductions). This section also provides a broad outline of possible tax reforms that could spur economic growth by stimulating labor market participation by second-earners and low-income earners, two groups with relatively high responsiveness to labor market incentives.

Dual-Earner Couples

Among married couples, the prevalence of dual-earners increased steadily during the postwar years (figure 11-2). This trend demonstrates the growing

Figure 11-2. Distribution of Joint Filers, 1962–2019

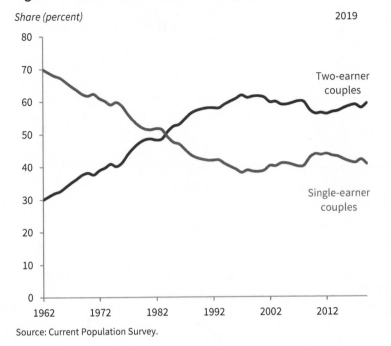

Share (percent)   2019

Source: Current Population Survey.

importance of two-earner couples, but also how their growth has stagnated since the 1990s. The female labor force participation rate in countries that do not differentiate between single-earner and dual-earners families, such as Sweden, also stagnated during this period, but remained at a higher level. Guner, Kaygusuz, and Ventura (2012a) find that the participation rate of married women in Sweden is nearly 15 percentage points higher than in the United States. Even though Sweden's overall tax burden on labor earnings is considerably higher, its system of separate taxation, which taxes individuals based on their own earnings instead of penalizing them for the earnings of their spouse, leads to noticeably lower marginal tax rates on second-earners—the individual in a dual-earner couple that has lower earnings. In some cases Sweden has a rate that is nearly 10 percent lower than in the United States, according to Bick and Fuchs-Schundeln (2017).

Before 1948, the United States levied income taxes at the individual level, although couples living in States with community property laws were taxed as if each spouse earned half of household income. As the tax system became much more progressive, concerns began to arise that wealthy husbands could engage in income-shifting to avoid heavy taxation in upper brackets. By transferring some of their assets to their wives (who generally had lower incomes), their transferred asset income being might be taxed in a lower tax bracket. The shift to joint taxation meant that couples added their income together when filing taxes. This switch greatly increased marginal tax rates on second-earners because the first dollar of the second-earner is effectively taxed at the marginal rate of the last dollar earned by the primary-earner. A 2008 study suggests that this switch depressed married female labor force participation by 2 percentage points in the postwar period among women most likely to be affected by the law, despite going into effect before the widespread acceptance of women in the workplace (LaLumia 2008). If the move from individual to joint taxation had occurred after the shift in norms, the effect would likely have been considerably larger.

The Marriage Penalty and the Second-Earner Penalty

The second-earner penalty is distinct from the marriage penalty that is more often discussed in that the former deals with marginal taxation and the distribution of work incentives within couples, whereas the latter is related to changes in the total tax burden a couple faces before and after they get married. For example, in 2016, before the 2017 TCJA, the increase in the tax rate from 25 to 28 percent occurred at $91,150 for single persons but at $151,900 for couples. Thus, if two individuals in a relationship each had $90,000 in taxable income, they would each fall into the 25 percent tax bracket before marriage but would be pushed well into the 28 percent bracket after marriage because of their combined $180,000 in taxable income. As a result, they would face a higher total tax bill as a married couple than they faced as individuals in a relationship before marriage (because each new tax bracket for married couples began at an income level at less than twice the income level for single persons). In other cases, a couple may have a marriage bonus if their tax burden under joint filing is lower than their combined tax burden when they filed two separate returns as unmarried individuals. The Office of Tax Analysis at the Treasury Department estimated that before the TCJA, roughly 40 percent of nonelderly married tax filers faced a marriage penalty while 51 percent enjoyed a marriage bonus. The TCJA greatly reduced this tax penalty for the vast majority of married couples by ensuring that the size of the standard deduction and the location of tax bracket thresholds for joint filers were double those for single filers.

In contrast, the second-earner penalty refers to the fact that, under a progressive tax code, joint filing imposes higher tax rates on second-earners than if they were filing taxes as a single person. Figures 11-3 and 11-4 plot the average combined income and payroll tax rate faced by single filers and second-earners without and with children based on current law. Single filers face an average tax rate—defined as total tax obligation divided by total income—that starts near 10 percent. If, however, that person gets married to someone earning $40,000, his or her average second-earner tax rate—defined as the added tax the joint household faces from the second-earner's decision to work divided by the amount of those second-earnings—starts at over 25 percent. If the single filer were to marry someone earning $120,000, he or she

Figure 11-3. Average Tax Rate on the Pretax Wages of Single Persons and Second-Earners (without Children), 2020

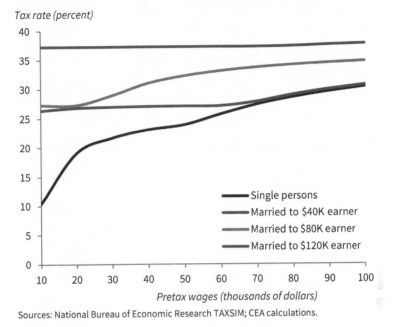

Tax rate (percent)

Pretax wages (thousands of dollars)

Sources: National Bureau of Economic Research TAXSIM; CEA calculations.

would be subjected to average second-earner tax rates starting at nearly 40 percent, with State income taxes further pushing up this rate. This does not take into account governmental aid programs, which impose a high effective tax rate on individuals who are in the phase-out range for governmental programs, as discussed below.

Figure 11-4 reveals that the second-earner penalty is even starker for people with children because of means-tested provisions in the tax code, such as the Earned Income Tax Credit (EITC), a refundable tax credit that subsidizes the wages of low-income households, especially those with children. The credit gradually rises with income in the phase-in region before eventually leveling off and then phasing out as household income continues to grow. The design of the EITC therefore incentivizes labor force participation. The net result for single filers with less than $35,000 is a negative total tax obligation, with average rates for some below –30 percent (i.e., a subsidy rate of over 30 percent, not including other governmental assistance programs). However, if the single filer gets married to a person earning $40,000, their joint income causes the EITC to shrink in addition to pushing the second-earner into a higher tax bracket—resulting in an average tax rate of about 35 percent, which represents an increase of nearly 70 percentage points for low-income second-earners.

Figure 11-4. Average Tax Rate on the Pretax Wages of Single Persons and Second-Earners (with Children), 2020

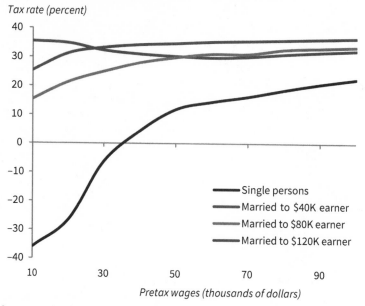

Tax rate (percent)

Pretax wages (thousands of dollars)

Sources: National Bureau of Economic Research TAXSIM; CEA calculations.

The joint nature of the income tax code introduces a bias toward single-earner families, encouraging them to specialize, with one spouse at work in the market and the other engaging in tax-free home production. This may not be an optimal allocation for the individual family or the overall labor force absent such a skewed taxation system. For example, both individuals may wish to work outside the home, but the tax penalty for doing so discourages them. The existence of a second-earner penalty is intrinsic to any progressive income tax code with joint filing, though the magnitude of the penalty can vary—the steeper the rate structure, the larger the second-earner penalty. For this reason, past tax reforms in the United States that lowered marginal rates also mitigated—but did not eliminate—the second-earner penalty.

For example, the 1981 and 1986 tax reforms, which brought the top marginal tax rate down from 70 percent to 31 percent and eliminated loopholes to broaden the taxable base, were responsible for at least one-fifth to one-quarter of the 13-percentage-point rise in labor force participation by married females during the 1980s, according to research by Kaygusuz (2010). This estimate is based only on the direct effects of the tax code change, but after taking into account the contribution of the tax cuts to higher wages, the effect may very well have been much larger. This same research attributes 62 to 64 percent of the rise in participation to rising female wages during the 1980s. Bronson and Mazzocco (2018) also conclude that the primary effect of the Reagan and

George W. Bush Administrations' tax cuts was to increase married female participation. Malkov (2020) finds that—along with the 1986, 2001, and 2003 tax reforms—the 2017 TCJA created welfare gains for married couples and reduced the second-earner penalty because of the overall lowering of the marginal tax rate schedule.

Tax Reforms to Mitigate the Second-Earner Penalty and Boost the Labor Supply

There are two ways to eliminate the second-earner penalty: reduce progressivity—which the Administration does not recommend—or move toward individual taxation. Guner, Kaygusuz, and Ventura (2012a) find large gains in economic output, welfare, and female labor supply (because women are more likely to be second earners) from moving to a proportional income tax. However, Bick and Fuchs-Schundeln (2017) point out that taxing two-earner labor income jointly acts as a greater impediment to female labor supply than does the progressivity of the tax code. They also find that moving completely to a system of individual instead of joint taxation—that is, replacing the current single, head of household, and joint filing statuses with one individual status that features a revamped system of deductions and tax brackets—would boost female labor supply by 7.8 percent. Guner, Kaygusuz, and Ventura (2012b) find a 10.4 percent increase in the supply of married women and 18.1 percent rise for married women with children in response to a shift from joint to individual taxation that eliminates the second-earner penalty. Similarly, Borella, De Nardi, and Yang (2019a, 2019b) estimate that shifting away from joint taxation completely would raise the labor force participation rate of married women by 20 percentage points for women under the age of 35 and by 10 percentage points for women between the ages of 45 and 60. These numbers are high, but research by Crossley and Jeon (2007) indicates that when Canada reformed its tax code in 1988 in a way that reduced the marginal tax rate for certain married women, that group's participation rate increased by nearly 10 percentage points.

Such a complete shift toward individual taxation would mark a dramatic reform for the United States. Moreover, Fruttero and others (2020) point out that eliminating the current joint tax rate schedule entirely could have a negative effect on single-earner households. This finding assumes that the tax rate schedule for the new, unified individual filing status that replaces it would have income brackets between those of the current single and joint brackets (if the new schedule instead adopted the current joint brackets, the static drop in income tax revenues would be larger).

As an alternative to universal individual taxation, the Federal Government could allow second-earners to directly protect their earned income through segmentation, whereby married couples filing jointly have the option of applying the joint rate schedule to the primary earners' income and the rate schedule for single persons to the earned income of the secondary (lower) earner. Other proposals include allowing a second-earner deduction or credit. Under segmentation, all deductions, credits, and dependents enter into the joint tax calculation based on the primary-earners' income (and any income not derived from wages, salary, or self-employment of the second-earner). The Federal Government could also use means-testing for the EITC to exclude the earnings of the second-earner, reducing the implicit tax in the phase-out region of the EITC for dual-earning couples, because each $1 in higher second-earner wages and salary income has no effect on the EITC amount received by the household.

Under this reform, the earnings of the secondary earner would be taxed as if earned by a single person having no children with only the standard deduction applicable. As a result, this tax reform option would allow families to protect the second-earner from tax penalties associated with the income of the primary earner. In other words, second-earners would owe the same amount of tax based on their paycheck income regardless of the earnings of their spouse or other sources of family income, thereby directly eliminating much of the second-earner penalty currently embedded in the tax code. Correcting this disincentive would create a situation wherein second-earners would be able to participate in the labor market on a basis similar to single persons.

High Marginal Rates for Low Earners

Perversely, some of the highest effective marginal tax rates on labor income fall upon low-income earners, individuals making at or slightly above the poverty line. Altig and others (2020) calculate that one in four low-wage workers face lifetime marginal tax rates above 70 percent, taking into account the combination of Federal, State, and local taxation and benefits programs. Over half of low-wage workers face lifetime marginal rates over 45 percent. Chien and Macartney (2019) find that among households just above the poverty line and that have children, the median marginal tax rate is 51 percent, as shown in figure 11-5. Some households face a marginal tax rate above 100 percent. As a result, a low-wage household that increases its earnings by $1 will lose more than $1 to combined explicit and implicit taxation. This mechanism locks households in a cycle of poverty and impedes their ability to climb into the middle class.

This situation is the result of a combination of the structure of benefit programs and Federal and State income taxes. U.S. Federal individual income taxes are progressive and the first 2 bracket rates (10 and 12 percent) are relatively low. States collect most of their revenue from sales and property taxes; however, 41 States also tax individuals' labor income, accounting for 24 percent of State and local government tax revenue. The lowest-bracket State-level income tax is as high as 5 percent in Illinois, Kentucky, Massachusetts, Oregon, and Utah; 5.3 percent in North Carolina; and 5.4 percent in Minnesota—thus

Figure 11-5. The Marginal Effective Rate on Low Earners

Median marginal tax rate (percent)

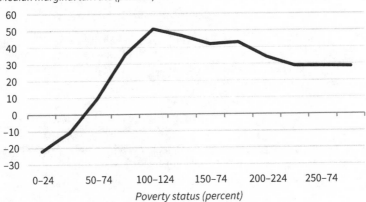

Poverty status (percent)

Sources: Chien and Macartney (2019); U.S. Department of Health and Human Services; CEA calculations.

Note: This figure shows the marginal tax rates on households below the poverty line after a $2,000 earnings increase. Because households with children are recipients of more government aid programs and, consequently, see a greater reduction in benefits, they pay a higher effective marginal tax than households without children. The most common combination of aid programs is SNAP, EITC, Child Tax Credits, and Medicaid / Children's Health Insurance Program. For a household of two, the dollar value of 100 percent poverty is $17,200 and of 200 percent poverty is $34,400.

increasing the tax burden on low-wage labor income. In addition, complex benefit programs often include phase-outs that can jointly create extreme losses in benefits as a result of gains in income. This reduction in benefits functions similarly to a tax on income. There are also programs in which earning above a certain threshold can result in a sudden large loss in benefits with no gradual phase-out.

Programs such as the EITC, Medicaid, Temporary Assistance to Needy Families (TANF), Supplemental Nutrition Assistance Program, Child Care Assistance, Section 8 Housing Vouchers, Energy Assistance, and Children's Health Insurance Program can provide valuable assistance but at the cost of a large administrative burden to the government and a complex web of procedures that families must navigate to receive aid. In combination, they also impose high costs on the acquisition of earnings-enhancing human capital, effectively punishing families for augmenting their human capital by rapidly withdrawing government assistance.

Altig and others (2020) illustrate the benefit cliff faced by a hypothetical mother with two children. She loses access to benefits as her income rises, with notable drop-offs in total benefits after $44,000 in annual earnings. In terms of net resources, she is nearly as well off financially earning $53,000 a year as when she is earning only $11,000 a year. This constitutes a severe impediment to the acquisition of new human capital through labor market advancement.

Box 11-1. Limiting Tax Expenditures to Facilitate Pro-Growth Reform: the SALT+MID Deduction

The 2017 TCJA combined lower taxation on investment, individual rate reductions, an increase in the Child Tax Credit, and a dramatic expansion in the standard deduction with the imposition of tighter caps on the State and local tax and mortgage interest deductions. Specifically, the TCJA increased the standard deduction from $6,500 to $12,000 for single filers and from $13,000 to $24,000 for joint filers while capping the State and local tax (SALT) deduction at $10,000 and reducing the maximum mortgage principal eligible for the mortgage interest deduction (MID) from $1 million to $750,000. These reforms weakened the MID and SALT deduction by both reducing the incentive to claim them relative to the larger standard deduction, and by reducing the maximum MID and SALT deductions that can be claimed.

One reason for limiting these tax expenditures is that they are skewed to high-income households, as shown in figure 11-i. In addition, they each create economic distortions. Specifically, the SALT deduction makes it easier for State and local governments to increase their revenue at the expense of taxpayers in other jurisdictions by diverting taxes that would otherwise be paid to the Federal Government into local receipts. This forces taxpayers in other locales to shoulder a greater share of the burden. Because local taxes are capitalized in local home prices, particularly in supply-inelastic markets, the partial defraying of tax increases causes the SALT deduction to artificially inflate housing prices in high-tax areas. The MID also fuels price increases

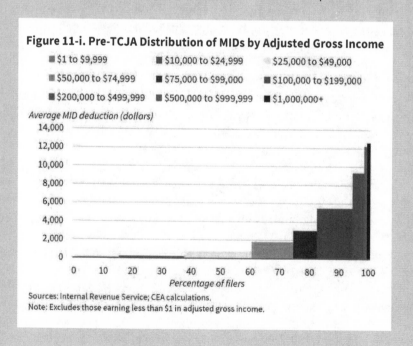

Figure 11-i. Pre-TCJA Distribution of MIDs by Adjusted Gross Income

■ $1 to $9,999   ■ $10,000 to $24,999 $25,000 to $49,000

■ $50,000 to $74,999   ■ $75,000 to $99,000   ■ $100,000 to $199,000

■ $200,000 to $499,999   ■ $500,000 to $999,999   ■ $1,000,000+

Sources: Internal Revenue Service; CEA calculations.
Note: Excludes those earning less than $1 in adjusted gross income.

while encouraging homeowners to finance their home purchases with debt instead of equity.

During the crafting and passage of the TCJA, some outside groups (e.g., National Association of Realtors n.d.) expressed concerns that the changes outlined above would diminish the tax benefits of homeownership by inducing people to switch from itemization to claiming the standard deduction. Indeed, the share of individual returns that claimed itemized deductions fell from 31 percent in 2017 to only 11.4 percent in 2018. Notably, the individuals who switched to claiming the standard deduction generally benefited, because they chose this option over claiming the still-existent MID. However, the housing market has proven incredibly strong and resilient in the years since passage of the TCJA. Homeownership has *increased* since 2017 after nearly a decade of consistent declines during and in the aftermath of the 2007–9 Great Recession.

As predicted, home price growth did weaken in some areas due to the TCJA reforms. Li and Yu (2020) find that the $10,000 SALT cap caused the growth rate of home values to decline by 0.8 percentage point per year in high-tax areas, with the effects felt most strongly within the medium range of properties on the market. Rappoport (2019) measures the response of house prices to all the deduction provisions mentioned above and estimates a 3 percent average reduction across 269 metropolitan areas. Martin (2018), in turn, finds an even larger average decline, of 5.7 percent, but with variation across zip codes and income classes. Each of these research papers comports with the assertion above that the SALT deduction and MID prop up home values, and thus their removal should create the opposite effect and make homeownership more affordable for Americans.

Although slowed home price growth reduces equity increases for incumbent homeowners in high-tax areas, first-time buyers gain easier admission into homeownership by facing more affordable housing choices and being able to make smaller down payments. In fact, 2017 marked the beginning of the turnaround in the U.S. homeownership rate, which had been on a stubborn downward path, from 68.2 percent in 2007 to 63.4 percent in 2016. By 2020:Q1, the homeownership rate had recovered to 67.4 percent. In fact, research by Hilber and Turner (2014) find that the MID has had no discernible effect on the overall level of U.S. homeownership. Sommer and Sullivan (2018) go even further, demonstrating that limiting the MID actually improves homeownership by making housing more affordable, which is particularly relevant to young prospective buyers who lack the accrued savings to make large down payments. Consistent with this finding, the data reveal that households under the age of 35 have experienced the largest homeownership gains.

Looking across states, the CEA finds that the period after the TCJA's enactment evinced relative homeownership gains—not declines—in states with high mortgage income plus State and local tax (MID + SALT) deduction intensity compared with States with lower MID + SALT deduction intensity.

Here, intensity is defined as the ratio of MID + SALT deductions to adjusted gross income in 2016. States with an above-median ratio (which equaled 7 percent in 2016) are considered to have high MID + SALT intensity, and those below the median are categorized as having low MID + SALT intensity.

Using State-level homeownership data from the Census Bureau covering the 2014:Q1 through 2020:Q2 period, the CEA employs regression analysis to measure changes in comparative homeownership dynamics between these two groups of States in the years after the TCJA compared with the years before. This analysis controls for permanent State differences as well as seasonality. The CEA finds that homeownership rates in States with high MID + SALT deduction intensity *increased* by an average of 0.9 percentage point per quarter in the period after the TCJA's enactment relative to States with lower MID + SALT deduction intensity, with the difference growing over time, as shown in figures 11-ii and 11-iii. States with high and lower MID + SALT deduction intensity had statistically indistinguishable homeownership rates in 2018 and the first half of 2019. Elevated homeownership in States with high MID + SALT deduction intensity began in 2019:Q3 (1 percentage point higher than in lower-tax States)—one and a half years after the TCJA's enactment—and was over 3.5 percentage points higher in 2020:Q2. The average 0.9-percentage-point increase in States with high MID + SALT deduction intensity translates into a 1.4 percent gain per quarter relative to the average homeownership rate of 66.2 percent across all States during the analysis period.

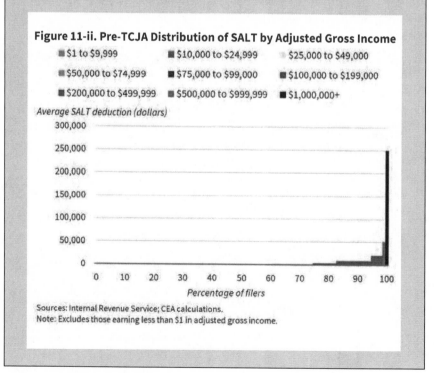

Figure 11-ii. Pre-TCJA Distribution of SALT by Adjusted Gross Income

- $1 to $9,999
- $10,000 to $24,999
- $25,000 to $49,000
- $50,000 to $74,999
- $75,000 to $99,000
- $100,000 to $199,000
- $200,000 to $499,999
- $500,000 to $999,999
- $1,000,000+

Average SALT deduction (dollars)

Percentage of filers

Sources: Internal Revenue Service; CEA calculations.
Note: Excludes those earning less than $1 in adjusted gross income.

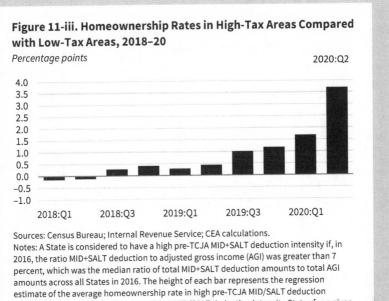

Figure 11-iii. Homeownership Rates in High-Tax Areas Compared with Low-Tax Areas, 2018–20

Percentage points   2020:Q2

Sources: Census Bureau; Internal Revenue Service; CEA calculations.
Notes: A State is considered to have a high pre-TCJA MID+SALT deduction intensity if, in 2016, the ratio MID+SALT deduction to adjusted gross income (AGI) was greater than 7 percent, which was the median ratio of total MID+SALT deduction amounts to total AGI amounts across all States in 2016. The height of each bar represents the regression estimate of the average homeownership rate in high pre-TCJA MID/SALT deduction intensity States relative to lower pre-TCJA MID/SALT deduction intensity States for a given quarter-year. An asterisk indicates that the regression estimate is statistically significant. Standard errors account for the possible correlation among observations within the same State over time. The regression includes controls for State dummy variables and month dummy variables.

Reducing the benefit cliffs faced by families receiving assistance can be accomplished by reforming these programs to ensure that there is a low or no penalty for improving wage income. Removing provisions that create nonconvexity and nonlinearity in benefit schedules and consolidating the patchwork of benefits into a more user-friendly system would be a substantial improvement. Allowing a grace period during which an individual maintains benefits after commencing a new job or receiving a raise can smooth the transition to a higher income level. When phase-outs do happen, starting them sooner and having them progress more slowly will reduce the disincentives they create.

Progress toward the goal of skill accrual and independence can be made by reducing the Federal labor tax rate on the lowest income tax brackets. Although it may appear at first glance that the burden of taxation is light on the lowest earners in the U.S. economy, the structure of benefit programs and the income tax system impose a high tax rate on low-earners' wage income. Removing impediments to increasing productivity and earning higher wages is of critical importance for the long-term recovery of the U.S. economy. In the spring of 2020, labor force participation dropped 3.2 percentage points, and has to date only partially recovered, by 1.3 percentage points. Increasing participation among marginalized groups can assist in reversing this trend.

The middle class tax cut discussed above would remove impediments to higher labor force participation and economic growth. However, it would likely reduce Federal tax revenues even when dynamic growth effects are taken into account. In the past, the U.S. has successfully increased fiscal capacity for pro-growth tax reform by coupling rate reductions and other broad-based relief provisions with the elimination or limitation of tax benefits. Such benefits act effectively as a form of spending, even if they are disguised as a broad reduction in tax liabilities. Proposals for reducing these tax expenditures have been subject to claims about pernicious results in the past. However, as detailed in box 11-1, this prediction did not come to pass after the 2017 limitation of the State and local tax (SALT) and mortgage interest deductions (MIDs).

Supporting a Balance between Work and Family

The COVID-19 crisis has had divergent effects on families with children. In April and May 2020, when most schools did not provide in-person learning opportunities, employed workers with children under 13 years of age were more likely than employed workers without children to work fewer hours (figure 11-6). The crisis has also illuminated an underlying issue with the lack of high-quality, affordable childcare and paid family leave. This absence not only hurts the labor market prospects of the parents or family members in question, but also affects the entire U.S. economy.

Family demographic changes and increased participation of women in the workforce have caused the lack of paid family and medical leave to generate costs, not only for workers and their families but also for society. From 1979 to 2019, the labor force participation rate increased for mothers with children younger than three years (+ 21.9 percentage points), younger than six (+ 19.8 percentage points), and younger than 18 (+ 15.3 percentage points). Families are facing increased pressure to balance caregiving needs at home with work demands. Paid family leave (PFL) policies attempt to ease this pressure by allowing families to take time off from work when a baby is born or adopted, or when someone in the family is ill and needs care. The lack of PFL is a serious issue that affects the most vulnerable workers, reducing their ability to engage in the workforce and meet family responsibilities.

This Administration helped to address these issues by offering tax credits to employers that voluntarily offer paid family and medical leave to employees earning below $75,000. Although this provision of the TCJA will sunset at the end of 2020, the COVID-19 pandemic and containment measures have expanded the need for such leave by altering the ways in which many Americans work and attend school. Individuals must look after their children more than before because schools and daycare centers are closed or have limited hours. In addition, the ability to take time off to recover from illness or help others recuperate is critical in containing the virus. The Families First

Figure 11-6. Change in Employed Workers with Actual Hours Lower Than Usual Hours, by Family Type, 2020

■ With child under 13　　■ Without child under 13

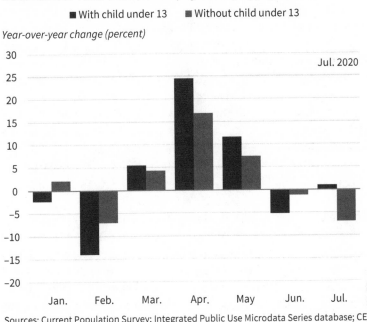

Year-over-year change (percent)

Jul. 2020

Sources: Current Population Survey; Integrated Public Use Microdata Series database; CEA calculations.

Coronavirus Response Act extended paid family and medical leave to employees of businesses with fewer than 500 employees, which allowed workers to take time off when they were ill or needed to care for family members. The act was a temporary action—set to expire at the end of 2020—funded by a refundable tax credit and advanced funds not already on deposit with the Internal Revenue Service. Paid leave remains an important policy issue as Americans continue to navigate the pandemic and look toward the future. However, access to such leave policies is often underprovided by private markets.

The market failure that any Federal paid leave program addresses centers on the positive externalities that paid leave programs generate. A paid leave program accrues some benefit to both the employer and employee, in the form of higher efficiency and productivity. This increase is often not large enough for low-wage workers to receive such benefits from their employers. However, there are additional benefits to provision that spill over and result in a positive externality for society. When workers are unable either to take leave or work while ill (which creates additional problems), they drop out of the workforce, lose income, contribute less in tax revenues and economic growth, become more dependent on the government's safety net, and may even live shorter lives.[1] Budig and England (2001) estimate that, of the 7 percent wage penalty mothers endure per child, about one-third can be explained by a loss of job experience due to time off or part-time work as a result of childrearing. Staff and Mortimer (2012) similarly conclude that loss in time spent either at work or in school is the greatest factor in explaining the motherhood pay gap. At the same time, these families suffer, and there may be adverse consequences for maternal and family health. Even though workers may realize the cost that such a lack of leave may impose on them, they may not account for external costs to the public healthcare system. Similarly, the costs for society of not giving workers access to paid leave are not internalized by businesses, which are focused on minimizing their own private costs of production. It may also be impossible for small businesses with liquidity and capacity constraints to offer paid leave, even if leave would generate a direct net benefit for their operations.

Aguirre and others (2012) find that if women's labor force participation rates increased to equal those of their male counterparts, U.S. gross domestic product (GDP) could increase by 5 percent. Houser and Vartanian (2012) estimate that women who take paid leave are 39 percent less likely to receive public assistance and 40 percent less likely to receive food stamps in the year after a child's birth, when compared with those who do not take any leave. Not only is paid leave associated with fewer dollars in public assistance spending, it reduces the chance that a family receiving public assistance will increase its use of public assistance after a child's birth.

Unequal Access to Paid Family and Medical Leave

The Family and Medical Leave Act of 1993 (FMLA) guarantees unpaid family and medical leave to 56 percent of American workers (U.S. Department of Labor 2020). The FMLA grants employees the right to take 12 weeks of unpaid leave to care for newborn children, seriously ill close family members, or themselves. Employers are not required by the Federal Government to provide paid leave for employees.

Figure 11-7 shows how access to PFL, regardless of whether provided through the FMLA, varies with wages, as of 2019. Generally, higher-income workers are more likely to have access to PFL; 30 percent of workers in the highest wage quartile have access to PFL, while only 9 percent of workers in the lowest quartile do.

Although the majority of workers were eligible for leave through the FMLA in 2018, access to leave through the FMLA is not uniformly distributed throughout the population. In 2018 those who worked for large employers were more likely to have access to FMLA leave because employers with fewer than 50

---

[1] Sullivan and von Wachter (2009) find a sharp increase in mortality rates for male workers as a result of work displacement, even 20 years after the displacement takes place. Displaced workers therefore have a lower life expectancy, by about 1 to 1.5 years.

Figure 11-7. Access to Paid Leave by Average Wage

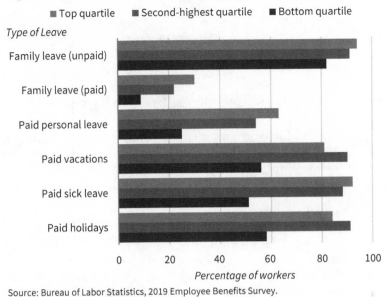

■ Top quartile ■ Second-highest quartile ■ Bottom quartile

Type of Leave

Source: Bureau of Labor Statistics, 2019 Employee Benefits Survey.
Note: Workers are grouped into quartiles by average wages. For example, 30 percent of workers whose averages wages fall in the top 25 percent of all workers have access to paid family leave.

employees are not required to offer it; 59 percent of private sector workers were eligible for FMLA, but they worked at only 10 percent of worksites. Low-wage workers were more likely to have an unmet need for FMLA leave. Nearly 1 in 10 (9 percent) workers who made less than $15 an hour reported that they needed to take leave but did not qualify for FMLA, compared with 6 percent of workers who made more than $15 an hour. Several States have supplemented unpaid leave through FMLA with paid leave programs of their own. As of January 2020, eight States have enacted PFL with divergent requirements and benefits.[2] This creates a patchwork system that generates a complex burden on employees and employers that could be alleviated with a nationwide paid leave policy. Worryingly, Sarin (2016) finds that employers may discriminate against female job candidates if paid leave is offered; prohibiting firms from firing employees for taking State-sanctioned paid family leave reduced the female share of new hires at large firms by 0.6 percentage point, or 1.1 percent. A paid leave program that is not directly paid for by the employer could reduce the incentive for such discrimination.

---

[2] These States are California, Connecticut, Massachusetts, New Jersey, New York, Oregon, Rhode Island, and Washington. A paid family leave law will be effective in the District of Columbia in July 2020, in Massachusetts in January 2021, in Connecticut in January 2022, and in Oregon in January 2023.

Effects of Paid Leave on Employment and Earnings

Because very few States in the United States have experience offering paid leave programs, the research on paid leave has either relied on household surveys like the Current Population Survey or State-level administrative data on actual take-up of leave. The empirical literature provides evidence that paid leave promotes employment, more hours worked, increased income, and breastfeeding. These factors often disproportionately benefit disadvantaged populations.

Many studies of paid family leave programs find that the programs do increase labor force participation, though some find no or negative effect. Jones and Wilcher (2019) study the effects of State-family leave policies in California and New Jersey and find that access to PFL increases maternal labor market participation by over 5 percent in the year of a birth, an effect that remained significant even five years later. However, Bailey and others (2019) study the short- and long-term effects of PFL in California and find that for first-time mothers who elected to take the paid leave, there was a negative effect on their employment of between 2.8 percent and 3.7 percent in the short term and between 5.4 and 6.9 percent in the long term. Rossin-Slater, Ruhm, and Waldfogel (2012) find that California's PFL initiative doubled the use of maternity leave, from three to six weeks on average. In addition, it increased working hours and wages for mothers of young children by between 10 and 17 percent. This effect was particularly pronounced in disadvantaged groups, a finding backed up by Bartel and others (2019), who find a disproportionately large difference between White and Hispanic access to paid leave and that under California's PFL, fathers of infants were 46 percent more likely to take leave, an effect particularly pronounced for fathers of first-born children. Finally, Bartel and others (2019) note that PFL increases breastfeeding by an average of 18 days, which might lead to long-term health benefits, particularly for disadvantaged families.

The effects of paid family leave on incomes and earnings are mixed. Even with PFL, families may suffer from lower earnings in the long run, although some lower-income women may benefit from a short-run wage boost. Bailey and others (2019) find that the earnings of first-time mothers with access to paid family leave were reduced by between $346 and $549 in the short term and between $541 and $791 in the long term relative to their mean level of pre-birth earnings. For first-time mothers who elected to take paid leave, the negative effect on their earnings was between $1,613 and $2,559 in the short term and $2,522 and $3,685 in the long term. Timpe (2019) similarly finds that expansion of disability insurance programs to cover pregnant women and mothers of infants caused women's wages to fall by 5 percent and led to decreases in family income for families in the middle of the income distribution. In contrast, Campbell and others (2017) study the effect of expanding temporary disability insurance to new mothers in Rhode Island and find no wage effects for women in households making less than $50,000 as a whole, but positive wage effects in the three years after giving birth for women for households making less than $20,000. For women in households making between $20,000 and $40,000, the wage effect was positive in the year after birth and indistinguishable from zero thereafter. Kleven and others (2020) find no long-term effect on female labor market outcomes, but that leave of longer duration can have a negative effect on the labor force penalty imposed by children.

Although the empirical evidence on paid leave shows varying effects, this could be a consequence of different empirical approaches, data used, and years covered. Analysis on this topic is often hindered by a lack of high-quality data on access to and take-up of paid leave, and the fact that few States currently offer a State paid leave plan. At the same time, while employers are starting to offer paid leave voluntarily, such programs are more common among larger employers in certain industries. Finally, while labor market outcomes are important for measuring the efficacy of paid-leave programs, gains in alternative metrics such as child health quality can be persuasive in determining whether net societal benefit is generated as a result of a program.

Implementation of Paid Leave

The 2017 TCJA incentivized private provision of paid leave by offering a tax credit to employers. Several members of Congress have proposed possible reforms to give more American workers additional access to paid leave. The Federal Employee Paid Leave Act (FEPLA), signed into law December 2019, expands the FMLA's 12-week paid leave benefit for the civil service to cover all FMLA leave, and to allow the Office of Personnel Management to grant an additional four weeks of leave. The FAMILY Act proposal would create a new payroll-tax financed wage insurance program that would pay cash to those caring for a new child or close family member. The New Parents and CRADLE Acts would instead allow those caring for newborn or newly adopted children to receive a portion of their Social Security benefits while on leave. Members

Table 11-1. Congressional FMLA Tax Proposals

Legislation Title	Overview
Advancing Support for Working Families Act	Up to $5,000 advance payment in the year of the child's birth or adoption
The Working Parents Flexibility Act of 2019	Creates tax-advantaged parental leave savings accounts
The Freedom for Families Act	Expands HSAs for family and medical leave use
The Support Working Families Act	Up to $6,000 tax credit for parental leave

Source: Congressional Research Service.
Note: FMLA = Family and Medical Leave Act of 1993 ; HSA = Health Savings Account.

Table 11-2. Annual Cost of Paid Parental and Medical Leave by Take-Up Scenario (billions of dollars)

Type of Leave	Scenario 1	Scenario 2	Scenario 3	Scenario 4
Medical	9.9	5.0	8.3	4.2
Parental	8.6	7.7	7.5	6.8
Total	18.5	12.7	15.8	11.0

Sources: American Enterprise Institute; Brookings Institution; CEA calculations.

Note: The four scenarios refer to assumptions about program use. Scenario 1's participation rates are similar to those observed under programs of the Family and Medical Leave Act. Scenario's 2 participation rates are more consistent with existing State-level paid leave programs. Scenario 3 assumes that half of the workers are on sick leave and 9 out of 10 workers on parental leave would participate. And scenario 4 assumes that 6 in 10 workers receiving paid leave would claim the benefits after four weeks of paid employer-provided leave.

of Congress have proposed four tax policy changes to support new parents, as seen in table 11-1.

The difference between the proposals hinges on the method of financing any new program of paid leave, as well as the scope of that program. In general, some proposals have favored using existing programs, such as Social Security or the Child Tax Credit, and allowing workers to access funds early. In contrast, other proposals have favored new types of financing, such as a new payroll tax on employers and employees, to finance paid leave. The proposal on paid leave sponsored by Senator Bill Cassidy, the Advancing Support for Working Families Act, would allow families to claim an advance payment, paid back over 10 years through lower child credits. This act would provide no additional money to families beyond the value of bringing a future payment forward in time (or qualified delayed or nonrepayment due to unfortunate circumstances faced by the family).

An additional policy to expand paid leave could be financed and distributed by State Unemployment Insurance (UI) programs, as proposed in the President's Budget, and would be scored at $21 billion for a UI-based proposal offering 6 weeks of leave. This estimate depends on the assumptions of take-up rates (table 11-2).[3] The cost ranges from $32 million in Wyoming to $2.3 billion in California, with a median cost of $241 million in Louisiana, using take-up assumptions based on the FMLA experience. The cost as a share of State wages ranges from 0.08 percent of annual 2018 wages in the District of Columbia to 0.32 percent in Idaho and Mississippi, with a median of 0.25 in Georgia, Maine, Missouri, Nebraska, Tennessee, and Vermont (figure 11-8).

---

[3] Estimates made using the American Enterprise Institute–Brookings Working Group on Paid Family Leave Calculator, available at https://www.aei.org/spotlight-panels/paid-family-and-medical-leave-cost-model/. The CEA further assumed a wage replacement rate of 70 percent, with maximum weekly benefits of $600, a one-week waiting period, and work requirements in line with those from FMLA.

Figure 11-8. Cost of Paid Family and Sick Leave as a Share of State Wages, 2019

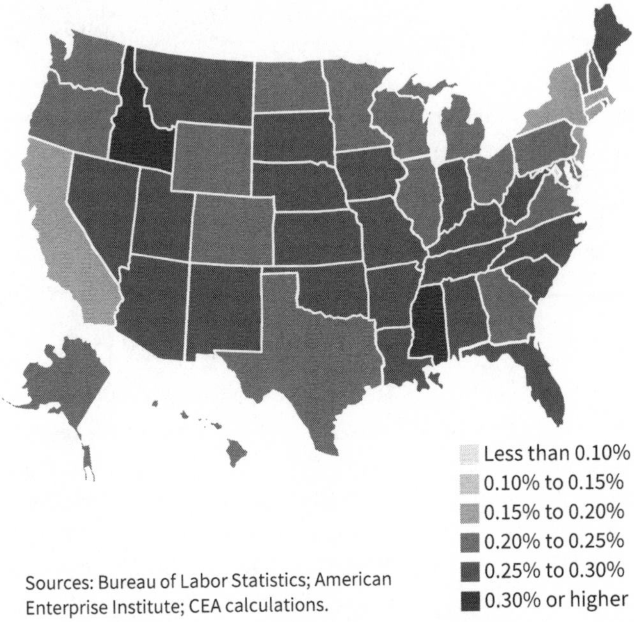

Less than 0.10%
0.10% to 0.15%
0.15% to 0.20%
0.20% to 0.25%
0.25% to 0.30%
0.30% or higher

Sources: Bureau of Labor Statistics; American Enterprise Institute; CEA calculations.

One potential issue with funding paid leave through State UI systems is that typically State programs vary significantly when it comes to eligibility, wage replacement rates, and the duration of benefits. This can lead to uncertainty and confusion for workers regarding their eligibility for paid leave. It can also be problematic for employers to understand if their employees have access to the State program or not, and can lead to different compliance requirements across states. Therefore, at a very minimum, to guarantee uniformity across states, it would be important to ensure that any leave taken for the explicit purposes of birth, adoption, fostering a child, or medical leave be subject to the same rules across State programs. Tenure eligibility could be similar to the FMLA program, so that workers need to work with an employer for about a year. Finally, as the current COVID-19 crisis has shown, State UI systems can come under significant pressure if additional programs are tacked onto them. Therefore, adopting this approach to paid leave provision would require additional planning and administration, and also an investment in State UI programs.

Paid leave could alternatively be offered through the EITC or the Child Tax Credit (CTC). Allowing parents to access the portion of the EITC and the CTC they normally receive as a tax refund at the time of birth instead of after filing taxes could help parents finance the costs of parental leave. Married parents making between $10,000 and $40,000 a year with two children could receive between $5,000 and $8,600 in advanced funds to fund parental leave. An additional $2,000 flat payment upon the birth of a child also could give parents of all income levels funds to cover their expenses and to take time off work, at an estimated annual cost of $7.6 billion.

This policy can be illustrated with a hypothetical two-parent, married family with two children under age 13. Both parents work, and it is assumed each parent makes the same amount of income and has only earned income. As noted above, the family can receive payments only from the refundable portion of each tax credit, since the nonrefundable portion can be used only to reduce actual tax liabilities and is not available as a cash transfer. Withholdings can be reduced to take into account these credits, thereby increasing take-home pay.

In 2019, for a family with annual income of $20,000, the EITC contributed $5,828 to their income, while the CTC contributed roughly half that. The combination of these credits could thus provide the family an advanced payment of $8,453, which could be used to meet childcare expenses associated with the birth of a child. In combination with the $2,000 bonus, the family receives over $10,000 toward meeting childcare expenses at the time of a birth or the adoption of a child. For a family earning $20,000, this is a significant means of financial support that enables them to provide care for the child for several weeks, even if they do not have paid leave from their employer.

According to the Centers for Disease Control and Prevention, nearly 3.8 million babies were born in the United States in 2018.[4] Offering a $2,000 baby bonus would cost an estimated $7.6 billion each year. Though this may not involve the need for new funding, advancing the CTC and EITC could increase improper payments and would increase administrative costs. In the past, the take-up rate of the advanced EITC was low, leading to an end to that program. However, that program was not specifically targeted at new parents.

The Lack of Childcare

Although paid leave is important for working parents who need time off immediately after the birth or adoption of a child, affordable childcare is often needed for parents to transition back into the workplace. In an earlier report, the CEA estimated that as of 2016, the high cost of childcare was preventing up to 3.8 million parents from joining the labor force (CEA 2019). Over 71 percent of these parents were married mothers, 21 percent were single mothers, 6 percent were married fathers, and 2 percent were single fathers. In addition to these 3.8 million parents, the CEA estimated that another 6.6 million non-disabled, working-age parents were working only part time and may require childcare to increase their working hours. Each of these 6.6 million parents had

---

[4] According to the U.S. Department of State, only 4,058 babies were adopted internationally in fiscal year 2018.

a child under age 13 and had no other potential nonworking caretaker in the household.

There are societal benefits to high-quality, affordable childcare that do not accrue solely to the parent and their employer. The positive externalities generated by higher labor force participation at the intensive and extensive margins, such as increased tax payments and reduced enrollment in assistance programs, provide a basis for government interventions that support childcare. Though substantial government assistance for childcare is currently offered through the tax code and transfer programs, the benefits are spread over multiple programs and may not necessarily reflect current childcare costs. The high cost of childcare is also a result of government regulation of childcare centers and providers. And though implementing a high standard of safety for caretakers is of paramount importance, excessive regulation and credentialing reduces the supply of childcare available, raising the costs above what some Americans can afford.

A large body of literature in economics has studied the effect of the high costs of childcare on labor force participation. One Federal program, discussed further below, is the Child Care and Development Fund (CCDF). A recent study by the U.S. Department of Health and Human Services finds that a 10 percent increase in the CCDF leads to a nearly 0.7 percent increase in maternal employment; this conclusion tracks with a meta-analysis (Morrissey 2017) finding that a 10 percent increase in the price of childcare reduces maternal employment by 0.5 to 2.5 percent. The effects were strongest for single mothers, mothers with young children under the age of four, and mothers with low incomes. A tripling of CCDF funds, for example, could bring an additional 300,000 mothers with young children into the labor force. Blau and Kahn (2013) show that the gap in labor force participation between women in the United States and other countries belonging to the Organization for Economic Cooperation and Development (OECD) could be explained by the lack of paid leave laws and childcare availability in the U.S.

An earlier report from the Pew Research Center (2014) showed that for families with working mothers, average weekly childcare expenses rose by 70 percent between 1985 and 2011, and that costs as a fraction of family income were much higher for lower-income families. In addition to its effect on labor force participation, the high cost of formal childcare is a possible reason why the U.S. has a higher reliance on informal care compared with other OECD countries.

Increasing Access to Childcare

As discussed in the last subsection, spending on childcare can be helpful for enabling work and improving labor force participation, especially for women. Today, families receive some support for meeting childcare expenses through the CCDF, as well as through various tax credit programs.

The CCDF is a consolidated block grant to States funded by both discretionary and mandatory Federal dollars that generally funds childcare by providing vouchers to families for use in childcare centers, family childcare homes, before- and after-school care, and in some informal settings. In total, the CCDF provided $8.7 billion in childcare assistance in 2016, with 75 percent of funds coming from the Federal government and 25 percent coming from the States. States additionally subsidize childcare directly through the TANF program. States provide additional funds to eligible families based on TANF rules, which vary by State but generally include only low-income families that meet program requirements. In 2018, $3.8 billion in TANF Federal block grant and State maintenance-of-effort funds were spent on childcare.

In addition to these subsidies, two tax benefits for households specifically subsidize childcare while enabling parental work or educational activities. The larger of these tax benefits is the Child and Dependent Care Tax Credit (CDCTC), which allows taxpayers to take a credit of up to $3,000 per child under age 13 for qualified childcare expenses for up to two children, for a total of $6,000.[5] This credit is worth a fixed proportion, which ranges from 20 to 35 percent of these qualified expenses and depends upon the taxpayer's adjusted gross income, with the higher percentages applying to lower incomes. The second tax benefit specifically tied to childcare is a provision whereby employers may allow employees to contribute up to $5,000 in pretax earnings to flexible spending arrangements, which can then be used to pay for childcare expenses.[6] However, expenses claimed for the exclusion may not be included among the childcare expenses claimed for the CDCTC. In combination, the CDCTC and flexible spending arrangements for childcare expenses benefited 6.9 million families in 2016, for an average benefit of $769 per family. The combined cost of the CDCTC and flexible spending arrangements was $5.3 billion in 2016.

Many of the policy ideas discussed above for funding paid leave could also be used to fund family childcare needs. For instance, tax credits like the EITC and the CTC added over $8,000 for two-parent, two-child families with annual incomes of $20,000 in 2019. If these credits were further expanded so that families could claim them in advance, this would allow families to pull forward money in a time of need. Of these, the EITC is the best targeted at lower-income households and is the most beneficial for covering their childcare costs because it is fully refundable. The CTC is only partly refundable and is not as targeted to lower-income households as the EITC. Its benefits extend well up the income ladder. Modifications of the CDCTC could increase its capacity to

---

[5] The CDCTC is nonrefundable and thus only kicks in once the taxpayer begins to pay income tax. Crucial to this credit, both spouses (if filing jointly) must earn income or be enrolled in school, and the childcare provider cannot be a spouse, parent, or other dependent. The CDCTC is also available for the care of disabled dependents.

[6] Flexible spending arrangements use the same qualifications for eligible expenses as the CDCTC. Employers may also fund the childcare flexible spending arrangement directly, up to the statutory limit.

cover childcare costs. Currently, the cap on the size of the credit has not kept pace with inflation, which means that while childcare costs have increased, the maximum benefit has not kept pace with these changes. In addition, the dependent care credit is nonrefundable, which means the lowest-income families cannot take advantage of it.

Federal policy could encourage an increase in the supply of high-quality childcare to reduce its cost to American families. Policy changes could allow more individuals to provide noninstitutional childcare to friends and neighbors, either by relaxing regulatory requirements or by ensuring that the burden of credentialing requirements for childcare providers is efficiently achieving the goals of safety and quality. Potential policies could include lowering the educational requirements for caretakers and increasing the ratio of students to teachers when it is consistent with safety and educational benefit to do so. As discussed in chapter 6 of this *Report*, the benefits of deregulation tend to favor households in the lower-income quintiles, and improving access to affordable childcare while maintaining a high standard of quality has the potential to greatly benefit lower-income parents.

Enhancing International Coordination to Meet 21st-Century Challenges

The COVID-19 pandemic caused a historically unprecedented simultaneous global supply and demand shock, reducing the output of each of the Group of Seven economies by about 10 to 20 percent. This section discusses issues with existing international bodies that were underscored during the response to the pandemic. Rather than a one-size-fits-all approach, this section analyzes the benefits of a narrow-deep relationship with the United States' trusted allies and friends, and a broad-shallow relationship with nations that do not share the same value systems as the United States. Incongruity in values takes on profound economic significance because the current global economy is driven by interwoven networks, a prominent example of which is the Internet itself. Although networks possess great economic potential, they also introduce vulnerabilities, and, as detailed below, tend to work best and most securely between trusted participants. These profound differences in fundamental values create distrust, and limit the extent to which it is beneficial to share systems. It is U.S. policy that multilateral institutions are useful, and they continue to be effective for implementing U.S. policy priorities. This section discusses the benefits of supplementing existing institutions with stronger bilateral ties with allies that share U.S. values.

The global economy is in the midst of the most profound technological revolution in history—the information revolution—which continues to transform communication, production, commerce, and conflict. Social and economic transformations continue to accelerate. The continued growth in connectivity and computing power is driving 5G, artificial intelligence, nano-technology, three-dimensional printing, and the Internet of Things—each a major revolution. Quantum computing, rapidly advancing biotechnology, and profound innovations in energy—all facilitated by, or a part of, the information revolution—loom on the near horizon. The international order is at a historical inflection point, fraught with both great opportunities and dangers. To ensure success, global and domestic strategies must be grounded in the economic realities of the 21st century. The choices made now will reverberate for a very long time.

The Economics of Networks, Coordination, and Standard Setting

Today's world is driven in large part by the economics of networks, which can be characterized as any economic or institutional relationship in which the greater the number of participants, the more valuable the network's function becomes to each participant. A classic example is a telephone system. If only a few people have access to a telephone system, its usefulness is obviously limited to calls between those few. If, in contrast, the vast bulk of the population of a region has access to the system, then its usefulness to any one user (and to all of them jointly) is vastly increased. Human languages themselves are networks—the more people who use a language, the more beneficial for all users it is to know that language. Any interconnected system of transportation, communication, or technologies constitutes a network, because the more linkages and connections there are, the more useful it is to all users. As noted above, the Internet is a network. Railroads are networks, as is the highway system; if a new, hardtop road more effectively connects a rural village to a superhighway, it also simultaneously more effectively connects the rest of the world to that rural village.

In their foundational work, Katz and Shapiro (1985, 1986) and Farrell and Saloner (1985, 1986) define network effects as positive consumption externalities, such that the benefit that a user derives from consuming a good is increasing in the number of other consumers that use the good. They distinguish between direct network effects, whereby a user's utility is directly dependent on the number of other users such as arise in a telephone system, and indirect or market-mediated network effects, such as arise in markets for operating systems where complementary goods such as software will be in better supply the more users adopt the system. They explain how the benefits of standardization and interoperability are rooted in such network effects. In this subsection, we use a broad definition of network effects to encompass any coordinated network of standards. When countries share the same standards, business is simpler to conduct between these separate jurisdictions, leading to benefits for all participants. The more members are sharing standards, the greater the gains for each participant, leading to a network effect working through the supply side. This definition of network effects includes any kind of widespread standard that generates benefits from interoperability.

For example, standardizing the manner in which computers can communicate with one another constitutes a network (the more users of the standard, the better for all concerned). If equipment, hardware, machinery, parts, or tools of any sort are standardized, then they constitute a network; for instance, the metric system is a network, and the more tools and machines that are built using the calibrations inherent in this system, the more valuable each of them is, because they are more interoperable. Networks mesh and overlap with one another, and they are used in various complementary combinations. One might use the English language (a communications network) to convey a message within an email message (part of a communications network) about purchasing a train ticket (employing a commercial and transportation network) and an intent to hire a ride-share car upon arrival (coordinated through a communications and commercial network).

Modern market economies are vast networks of networks that pull in entrepreneurs, labor, capital, materials, and legal infrastructure (among other factors) to meet the evolving demands of consumers and governments around the world in real time. What makes this broad network system tick are the many networks enmeshed within it. For example, what facilitates an exchange at arm's length—such as a credit card purchase of a pizza—is a set of trusted networks, including not only the confidence that the money will be moved among the pertinent accounts to render payment but also the legal remedies implied if the ingredients of the pizza are harmful due to negligence.

Similarly, international institutions and standards constitute networks of international trade, investment, communications, regulation, and procedures to resolve disputes. The Organization for Economic Cooperation and Development, which originated in 1948 as the Organization for European Economic Cooperation, was established in its original form to coordinate the administration of the U.S. Marshall Plan, and today serves as a network by which countries identify and discuss common problems (OECD 2011, n.d.). The Society for Worldwide Interbank Financial Transactions network allows financial institutions, including central banks, a secure means by which to communicate and transact (Cook and Soramäki 2014). More recently, the United States–Mexico–Canada Agreement (USMCA) is a network, setting standards for economic activity between the three joining countries (USITC 2019).

Whereas the purchaser of tainted pizza has recourse in U.S. courts, international networks can often fail to enforce standards. This is especially problematic when participants in international networks do not share the values of free societies and exploit these same networks to their advantage, disadvantaging the free societies. As a result, the effectiveness of networks at the international level is reduced. Economic activity will recede when international coordination and standard-setting create uncertainty. This Administration in particular has been focused on the failure of global networks to enforce intellectual property protection. It is of vital national interest that global networks—such as international trade, capital markets, and anti-money-laundering or antiterrorist financing—are aligned with the values of the United States. This necessitates working alongside like-minded allies and partners individually and within existing international frameworks to ensure that global standards do not disadvantage the United States.

The Current Paradigm for Coordination and Standard Setting

This Administration has both recognized the potential benefits of international coordination yet also highlighted the real limitations faced by international institutions in their coordination and standard-setting efforts. Recent successes include the update to the U.S.-Korea Trade Agreement (KORUS), the U.S.-Japan Trade Agreements, and USMCA. As discussed in chapter 9, trade agreements enhance U.S. firms' access to supply chains and foreign markets, allow U.S. consumers to enjoy a wider variety of goods and services, and generate gains for the U.S. economy.

At the same time, it has become increasingly difficult to work with some existing international institutions. Institutions made up of a broad membership with disparate goals, value sets, and trust structures are most vulnerable to suffer ossification and become ineffective. Although these institutions can and do provide broad value, they often fail to produce deep gains through enhanced cooperation between members, and are unable to allocate gains among competing interests. And though several international institutions are aptly characterized by these circumstances, the trade space provides an appropriate example. Rather than working through the WTO's Doha Round or multilaterally, balancing the interests of many parties, this Administration has focused on achieving gains through narrower agreements, as discussed above. In the case of the WTO, the Office of the U.S. Trade Representative (USTR) has noted in the most recent annual report on the WTO that the Appellate Body "has added to U.S. obligations and diminished U.S. rights" while "several of [the Appellate Body's] interpretations have directly harmed the ability of the United States to counteract economic distortions caused by nonmarket practices of countries like China" (USTR 2020a, 2020b). This is the predictable outcome of a network that includes countries with fundamentally different values and limited enforcement capabilities. More broadly, international organizations have faltered due to a confluence of factors, including the size of the organizations, the emerging multipolarity of international affairs, and the fact that existing organizations largely addressed "low-hanging fruit" early in their tenure. Large institutions contain members with wildly divergent situations and goals, increasing the frictions and transaction costs of achieving gains through coordination.

Table 11-3. Durations of GATT/WTO Rounds

Round	Initiated	Completed	Participants	Duration (months)
Geneva I	Apr. 1947	Oct. 1947	23	6
Annecy	Apr. 1949	Aug. 1949	13	4
Torquay	Sep. 1950	Apr. 1951	38	7
Geneva II	Jan. 1955	May 1956	26	16
Dillon	Sep. 1960	Jul. 1962	26	22
Kennedy	May 1964	Jun. 1967	62	37
Tokyo	Sep. 1973	Nov. 1979	102	74
Uruguay	Sep. 1986	Apr. 1994	123	91
Doha	Nov. 2001		153	> 229

Sources: Moser and Rose (2012); CEA calculations.
Note: GATT/WTO = General Agreement on Tariffs and Trade / World Trade Organization.

To illustrate this first point, consider the durations of the negotiation rounds of the General Agreement on Tariffs and Trade / World Trade Organization (GATT/WTO), shown in table 11-3. These rounds have increased steadily over time, alongside the number of participants—with the Doha round, initiated in November 2001, still outstanding (Moser and Rose 2012). Increased participation, an indicator of broader multipolarity in the WTO, is associated with longer negotiation durations. Measures of productivity, such as average tariff cut per year of negotiations, show a relative stability through the Uruguay round (Martin and Messerlin 2007) though there will need to be large cuts as part of the Doha round for this trend to continue.

This relationship makes clear the trade-off the United States faces in working through some broad international organizations. Though the potential for benefits rises with organization size, so do heterogeneity costs from increased diversity among these states (Posner and Sykes 2013; Bradford 2014). On the margin, a new member must be valued against the cost of reduced cohesion and ability to make decisions. It is important that international organizations reach optimal membership decisions, with failures of judgment resulting in a free-rider problem where countries are unwilling to contribute and unlikely to engage in voluntary arrangements (Buchanan 1965). This is not to say that the WTO or other international institutions would necessarily be better off as a result of a U.S. withdrawal. Aside from working to generate new gains for the U.S. through narrow cooperation, U.S. participation in broad international institutions also serves as an institutional safeguard against the possibility of those institutions taking actions that contradict American values and priorities, or becoming dominated by America's rivals. The United States' participation leverages heterogeneity costs to its advantage, making it difficult for countries with different values to co-opt existing institutions. The Trump Administration has recognized this, and thus has worked both within existing institutions and outside them to generate gains from deeper coordination.

Evaluating the costs and benefits of admitting new members to an organization or evaluating an agreement is complicated, because of changes in the global landscape and difficulty in enforcing international agreements. For example, the situation in 1947 was quite different than today. Many of the trade agreements of that period were made with a desire to support countries as a strategic counterbalance against totalitarian economies (Martin and Messerlin 2007). At that time, the United States was willing to accept nonreciprocal and unfavorable trade deals to benefit American allies (Baldwin 2006). However, this has proved harmful when international institutions have been unable to enforce compliance. The USTR has noted that "China's entry into the WTO [was] on terms that have proven to be ineffective in securing China's embrace of an open, market oriented trade regime" (USTR 2018, 2019, 2020a, 2020b). As detailed in the 2018 *Economic Report of the President*, the United States has very little negotiating power today within the existing WTO structure because the current U.S. trade barriers are so low. This makes the negotiating process exceptionally difficult for the United States.

Another difficulty is that enforcing agreements is made conditional on a country's accession to an international organization. Consider the case of China's accession to the WTO. As part of this agreement, the WTO engaged in consent tailoring, which involved requiring China to engage in economic reforms as part of the accession process. At the time, it was thought that through accession, China would also engage in economic reform. But this has not come to fruition. Neomercantilist nations, such as China, that engage in industrial policy create dangers in markets characterized by network economics. A government that is heavily subsidizing a champion company for a network niche, as China has been doing with Huawei and 5G, might exploit the dominance of the company to pursue geostrategic interests and might not be a trustworthy steward of a network upon which so many and so much will rely. These issues beg the question of how to proceed toward the goal of free, fair, and reciprocal trade within the broader network of trade agreements and international organizations.

Adam Smith stated in *The Theory of Moral Sentiments* (1759) that to make a market economy work, trust is an essential component. Successfully navigating the challenges inherent in this rivalrous global environment will necessitate economic partnerships with other like-minded and trusted nations in a deeper and more integrated manner than what has been done in the past. As Evensky (2011, 261) states: "When trust is shaken, individuals pull back and the market system contracts. Where trust grows, individual energy and creativity are unleashed and the system grows." This is the great geostrategic and economic challenge that confronts international economic structures today:

how to build, govern, and maintain extensive cross-jurisdictional networks while ensuring that they are secure, reliable, and based on well-founded trust.

Opportunities for Advancing Coordination

To remain nimble, future deep international partnerships must be based on economic and geostrategic interests as well as on shared values. Economic theory suggests a way forward. As opposed to seeking shallow agreements between countries with differing belief systems, the United States can generate gains through deep integration with countries with a similar economic situation and regulatory system (Buchanan 1965). One approach to this integration is to develop narrow collectives like the European Union and African Union that work in parallel to and in support of broad international organizations. These collectives rebalance the cost-benefit analysis by attempting to reduce heterogeneity costs and allowing for gains through deeper integration. This can be done by adopting global rules or creating rules from scratch to advance the goal of borderless markets (Davies and Green 2008).

Another approach is to create bilateral agreements between countries with similar economic values that can later be extended into multilateral agreements such as USMCA. Under this framework, political and monetary action would remain the prerogative of each country. Moreover, regulatory uniformity would not be enforced by an extranational government, but alignments could be achieved through mutual recognition and acceptance of equivalency in the outcome of each system. Nations may pursue two different methods of regulating industry, but can still reach regulatory convergence on key issues such as safe products, fair work environments, and well-stewarded natural resources. For example, in 2008 the United States and Australia entered a limited mutual recognition arrangement for regulatory exemptions that would permit U.S. and eligible Australian stock exchanges and broker-dealers to operate in both jurisdictions, without the need for these entities to be separately regulated in both countries (SEC 2008; Jackson 2015). This foundation of trust provides a model for international cooperation that could provide economic returns not captured by current multilateral efforts, while still constituting a laboratory for eventual broader, multinational efforts (Buchanan 1965).

These approaches have the potential to benefit all the countries involved, by allowing deep integration with aligned nations while maintaining an economic relationship with countries that are unable or unwilling to couple their economies under a framework of shared values and trust. As the importance of these collectives grow, they will offer greater benefits to membership, creating an incentive for countries to meet the criteria for joining (Bradford 2014).

The U.S. has the potential to generate particularly large gains through coordination with like-minded countries to help limit negative externalities from countries with different goals. The enforcement of intellectual property rights provides an example. The U.S. used Section 301 tariffs to enforce intellectual property rights against China. Intellectual property theft is quite costly: the OECD estimates in a 2019 study that international trade in counterfeit goods amounted to $509 billion in 2016. The IP Commission (2017) estimated in 2017 that the cost to the U.S. economy of counterfeit goods, pirated software, and theft of trade secrets is more than $225 billion a year. Assuming a discount rate of 3 percent, the cumulative cost of inaction is $7.5 trillion. The Office of the Director of National Intelligence estimated in November 2015 that economic espionage through hacking costs $400 billion a year. Although the U.S. has achieved enhanced protection of intellectual property through bilateral negotiations with China (discussed in chapter 9), additional gains could be achieved by working alongside like-minded countries that share the United States' perspective on intellectual property protection. By creating a collective to better enforce intellectual property rights against China, the U.S. can increase the gains and lower the costs.

Reorienting American policy from a broad-shallow framework to include narrow-deep coordination will allow for greater benefits and flexibility in making trade agreements. This will allow for the stagnation of the past decades to be overcome and create a higher-income and more closely linked world. As recovery from the COVID-19 pandemic continues, building international structures for a return to prosperity and prevention of future reoccurrences becomes of paramount importance.

Prospects for U.S.–U.K. Coordination

As an example of this new approach to economic partnerships, the U.S. could explore the potential for an explicit economic and geostrategic deep partnership with the United Kingdom. There are many possible nations with which the U.S. could partner in this way, and this is just one possibility. Although trade agreements like KORUS and USMCA provide excellent templates for future partnerships and highlight important areas of coordination for contemporary economies (see chapter 9 for a discussion of these agreements), future agreements could go beyond a trade deal. Blueprints for such cross-border arrangements have been outlined in depth by Tafara and Peterson (2007) in the context of financial market regulation.

The optimal economic result would be economic integration that increases gross trade flows and innovation. Trade in goods, services, labor, and ideas would be as free as possible, yet consistent with maintaining full sovereign independence. Facilitating this goal would involve intensive bilateral processes, such as a free flow of labor through streamlined processes facilitating citizens of the U.S. and U.K. to work and live in the other's jurisdictions or mutual recognition of financial institutions that would enhance the global reach of both markets. Another area of potential benefit is the security of devices, software, and networks. The U.S. and U.K. would benefit from coordination on determining what types of devices are not secure and pose a risk to the development of safe networks. Yet another area for enhanced coordination is institutions of higher learning, which provide the foundation for future innovation. A U.S.-U.K. consortium of universities might act as a catalyst for centers of innovation and further collaboration. The exchange and flow of faculty, students, and ideas would build tremendous technological momentum in itself. The U.S. and U.K. could vigorously and jointly prosecute the theft of intellectual property and coordinate remedies—like tariffs, sanctions, and prohibiting the operation of certain firms—to form a truly deep partnership.

The economic benefits of such a partnership could be substantial. As a narrow example, consider the 1958 agreement on automotive industry standards between the European Union, Japan, South Korea, and other countries (though not the United States), which increased automotive trade between partner countries by more than 20 percent through regulatory harmonization. In exploring the elimination of tariffs between the U.S. and the U.K., a 2000 report by the USITC found that U.S. imports from the U.K. would increase 7 to 12 percent, and U.K. imports from the U.S. by 11 to 16 percent, although the aggregate output effects were not substantial (USITC 2000). A broader review of the literature on mutual recognition agreements by the OECD found that, in almost all cases, such agreements boosted international trade flows between partner countries (Correia de Brito, Kauffmann, and Pelkmans 2016). The direct benefits of any agreement will be sensitive to the provisions therein. However, what is both more valuable, and more difficult to value, are the early and future network effects of such an agreement.

The U.S. is positioned to lead in the development of a new generation of flexible, bilateral economic partnerships that protect national sovereignty and interests while seeking to produce gains from cooperation. This stands in contrast to the expansion and sharing of networks with countries with which the U.S. has fundamental disagreements, and with which it does not share sufficient trust to warrant generating the vulnerabilities that are inherent in shared processes. Pursuing deep integration with allied nations will facilitate economic recovery from the COVID-19 pandemic and create a safer world where such a crisis can be addressed in a more coordinated fashion.

Creating a More Effective Healthcare System

The U.S. healthcare system faces several interwoven challenges. The current COVID-19 pandemic is focusing attention on the importance of a resilient and efficient healthcare system for maintaining a strong and vibrant economy. This section discusses several of these challenges and potential reforms that would increase the efficiency of the American healthcare system. Increasing transparency in healthcare markets and increasing the supply of healthcare will help individuals access treatment, both for any direct COVID-19 health effect and also for other diseases and injuries.

Rationalizing the Provision of Healthcare Professionals

Several elements of the current healthcare market structure impose large distortions on the mobility and training of healthcare professionals. These distortions limit the supply of medical practitioners, especially to underserved rural and low-income populations, artificially increasing medical costs. Alleviating these distortions could generate gains for many Americans.

Medical professionals currently face large hurdles to labor mobility due to restrictive licensing requirements. Because medical licensing is performed at the State level, providers cannot easily move between States as they face both monetary and temporal costs in the form of additional examinations, interviews, fees, and paperwork. This creates a strong distortionary effect on the labor market, which is particularly pronounced in metropolitan areas that cross State lines, where healthcare workers can face major bureaucratic and monetary barriers to taking a job only a few miles away. Such regulatory burdens on employment are associated with lower levels of job-switching, which may decrease upward economic mobility, result in higher rates of unemployment, and ultimately lead to higher prices for consumers.

Efforts are being made to limit the distortionary effects of these regulations within the health sector through interstate licensure compacts. These compacts aim to either provide portability or streamline the acquisition of licensure in other signatory states. However, the effectiveness of such plans is limited by incomplete adoption across states. Figure 11-9 demonstrates the patchwork nature of three of the largest licensing compacts for healthcare providers: the Nurse Licensure Compact (NLC), the Advanced Practice Nurse Compact (APRNC), and the Interstate Medical Licensure Compact (IMLC). The IMLC is further limited because it provides only a streamlined process for physicians to apply for licensure in other states, which decreases some of the bureaucratic obstacles but retains the negative effect of licensure fees on provider mobility. Further complicating the regulatory landscape, there are similar compacts for other healthcare professions, including social workers, mental health professionals, physical and occupational therapists, pharmacists, and dentists.

Efforts to combat the inefficiencies of individual state licensing have been ongoing for decades. When the Federal Government has taken targeted action to remove barriers, it has been successful. The Department of Veterans Affairs (VA) allows licensed physicians to practice in any state to increase the quality and decrease the cost of care, and the Health Resources and Services Administration award grants to State-licensing boards to encourage cooperation, which has resulted in the landscape of interstate compacts that can somewhat ameliorate the issue. More recently, the Centers for Medicare & Medicaid Services (CMS) has taken deregulatory actions spurred by the COVID-19 pandemic that allow licensed providers to care for Medicare patients across

Figure 11-9. The Free Movement of Health Care Labor, 2020

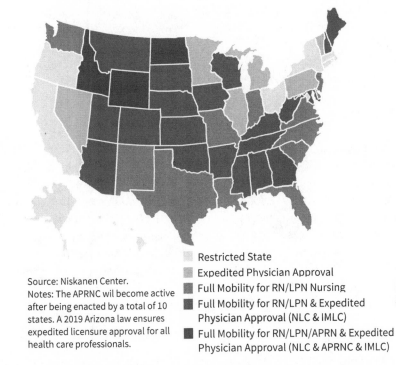

Source: Niskanen Center.
Notes: The APRNC wil become active after being enacted by a total of 10 states. A 2019 Arizona law ensures expedited licensure approval for all health care professionals.

Restricted State
Expedited Physician Approval
Full Mobility for RN/LPN Nursing
Full Mobility for RN/LPN & Expedited Physician Approval (NLC & IMLC)
Full Mobility for RN/LPN/APRN & Expedited Physician Approval (NLC & APRNC & IMLC)

State boundaries to facilitate increased care in hotspot areas and enable a nationwide expansion of telemedicine. The Federal Government may be able to increase the availability of care and decrease the cost of healthcare by playing a coordinating role. Creating incentives for States to either adopt stronger portability of licensure between States or encourage the usage of a Federal licensure system modeled on the approach of the VA are strong steps toward increasing access to care and curbing rising medical prices.

Other supply-side problems include the limited number of medical schools and accredited residency slots for medical school graduates. Of 53,030 medical school applicants, only 22,239 (42 percent) matriculated into a medical school in 2020. Though U.S. medical school enrollment has increased by 31 percent between 2002 and 2018, residency training positions have expanded at a rate of just 1 percent a year.

Reducing the barriers to entry for aspiring doctors and improving the educational process for individuals pursuing a medical profession would ensure that the United States has superior healthcare provision in the years to come. There would be positive feedback effects for patients from adding more doctors in historically underserved areas, because it would enable a lighter burden to be placed on each doctor, reducing burnout and encouraging more individuals to join the medical field as doctors, nurses, and other healthcare professionals. According to the Agency for Healthcare Research and Quality (2017), in recent years the rising prevalence of burnout among clinicians (over 50 percent in some studies) has led to concerns on negative effects to access care, patient safety, and care quality. Doctors suffering from burnout are more likely to leave their practice, which reduces patients' access to care. Burnout can also threaten patient safety and care quality when depersonalization leads to poor interactions with patients and when affected physicians suffer from impaired attention, memory, and executive function.

To address concerns that funding for graduate medical education (GME) is poorly allocated, this Administration has proposed, since fiscal year 2019, to consolidate all GME spending in the Medicare, Medicaid, and the Children's Hospital GME Payment Program into a new mandatory, capped Federal grant program. The distribution of funding to hospitals through this new grant program would depend on the proportion of residents training in priority specialties as well as other criteria identified by the Secretary of Health and Human Services. Such an improvement in the distribution of GME funds would serve to achieve a better distribution of healthcare specialties, address shortages in healthcare professionals nationally and especially in medically underserved communities, and incentivize better training of healthcare professionals.

Balance Billing

When a patient sees an out-of-network provider, they may be liable for the difference between what the provider charges and the amount their insurer would have paid an in-network provider. This difference, known as the "balance billed" amount, is owed in addition to any other out-of-pocket amounts such as deductibles and copayments. In some cases, patients actively choose to pay this additional amount in order to seek care from an out-of-network provider. When a consumer lacks key information or choice in what they are purchasing, such as when a patient unknowingly receives care from an out-of-network provider or when a patient does not have the ability to select an in-network provider, there is a market failure. This situation can arise even when a patient receives care at an in-network hospital, because different providers within a given hospital independently make decisions on which types of insurance to accept. Adopting network matching at the Federal level would require any provider that takes care of patients at a hospital to bill as in-network any patient who the hospital also considers to be in-network.

The Trump Administration has taken direct actions to address the issue of surprise billing. In June 2019, Executive Order 13877 directed agencies to ensure that patients have access to meaningful price and quality information before the delivery of care. Beginning in 2021, hospitals will be required to publish their real price for every service, and to publicly display—in a consumer-friendly, easy-to-understand format—the prices of at least 300 different common services that are able to be purchased in advance. In April 2020, the Administration began requiring providers to certify, as a condition for receiving supplemental COVID-19 funding, that they would not seek to collect out-of-pocket expenses from a patient for treatment related to COVID-19 in an amount greater than what the patient would have otherwise been required to pay an in-network provider. In May 2020, the Department of Health and Human Services released the Health Quality Roadmap to empower patients to make fully informed decisions about their healthcare by facilitating the availability of appropriate and meaningful price and quality information.

Several States have also taken action on balance billing, though many resort to price-setting or arbitration, which can alter the negotiating power of hospitals, insurers, and physicians. For example, California has attempted to limit patients' cost sharing for all nonemergency physician services at in-network hospitals from out-of-network physicians at the greater of the insurer's local average contracted rate or 125 percent of the Medicare rate for the given service. As a result, physicians have criticized the law for giving insurers the upper hand in negotiations and for decreasing patients' access to care. In addition, New York's arbitration system has been criticized for granting excessive bargaining power to providers in their rate negotiations with insurers, resulting in higher reimbursements and premiums. By contrast, an analysis by the Congressional Budget Office (CBO) found that network matching could actually lower costs by reducing the ability of healthcare providers to negotiate higher rates from insurers, avoiding New York and California's pitfalls by harnessing market forces to address the balance billing issue.

The CEA finds that protecting patients from balance billing could provide an economic benefit of $2.8 billion a year by creating greater predictability in healthcare expenses. A total of 11.1 percent of privately insured patients in a given year will seek emergency room care, and 6.2 percent will be admitted to the hospital. Data from a recent study indicates that, of these patients, about 42 percent can expect to receive a surprise balance bill with an average amount of $628 for emergency room care and $2,040 for inpatient admissions. The elimination of balance billing lowers uncertainty and increases transparency. Based on the statistics above, the actuarial value of this reduction in risk is $82.40 per patient a year, and patients value the elimination of uncertainty at 25 percent of this amount.[7] Thus, 25 percent of $82.40 per patient multiplied by the 137 million adults covered by private insurance yields an aggregate annual economic benefit of $2.8 billion from eliminating balance billing.

---

[7] This is calculated from the statistic that households willingly pay $1.25 in health insurance premiums for each $1 in average payouts.

Medicare Inpatient Rates

According to data on national health expenditures from CMS, Medicare hospital payment is currently one of the most regulated price mechanisms in the U.S. health economy, accounting for about $300 billion in government expenditures in 2019 alone. A recent proposal for a new Federal rule seeks to better calibrate the price mechanism to market prices. The existing pricing systems rely on estimates of growth rates of costs based on assumptions that often have little bearing on market prices outside Medicare Fee for Service. One proposed solution is to rely on data from Medicare Advantage pricing, which is partly based on private sector negotiations. However, there is a concern that Medicare Advantage pricing is closely linked to Medicare Fee for Service pricing. If the private sector negotiations are using prices set by the government as an anchor, then the price discovery is curtailed and the usefulness of the negotiated price is limited.

The CEA completed an analysis to compare private and government prices for the top 25 inpatient Diagnosis Related Groups (DRGs), based on the inpatient payment system used for Medicare fee for service (FFS) payment. A DRG is a patient classification system that standardizes prospective payment to hospitals and encourages cost containment initiatives. In general, a DRG payment covers all charges associated with an inpatient stay from the time of admission to discharge. Specifically, Medicare FFS average payments are compared with Medicare Advantage and Private Insurer data from 2015 using a publicly available data source (Parente 2018). Figure 11-10 displays the percent change in the relative price of Medicare FFS when compared with Medicare Advantage and Private Insurers. The relationship between Medicare FFS and private insurance payments and Medicare Advantage does not support using Medicare Advantage as a close substitute for competitive market pricing (i.e., prices set by private insurers). If they were close substitutes, the observations would cluster narrowly around the 45-degree line shown in the figure. This analysis supports furthering the development of the proposed Federal rule to integrate pricing that more closely matches competitive market prices.

Future policy analyses will be able to take advantage of the new all-payer insurer synthetic database created by the price transparency Executive Order 138777 of June 2019. This database could easily confirm and extend this initial analysis and provide strong evidence of the need to revisit the economic price control mechanism used to set Medicare FFS inpatient payment prices.

The health reforms discussed above would be complemented by a continuation of the health information technology reforms that took place this year (see box 11-2). Better storage and sharing of information about health care will increase transparency, reduce cost, and improve the experience of patients.

Figure 11-10. Percent Change in Medicare FFS DRG Payments Compared with Medicare Advantage and Private Insurers, Top 25 Diagnosis-Related Groups, 2015

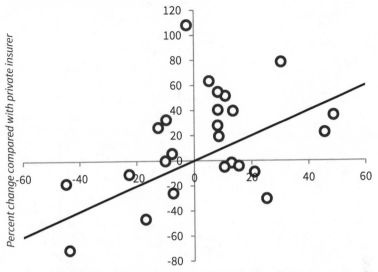

Percent change compared with private Medicare Advantage

Sources: SynUSA 2018; CEA calculations.

Building a Dynamic Economy through Infrastructure Improvement

The infrastructure of the United States is made up of physical elements like roads and ports, but also of less obvious components, like digital infrastructure. The COVID-19 pandemic highlighted the importance of high-quality infrastructure in responding to the crisis, as well as increasing the productivity of the American workforce. Locally planned and led infrastructure projects are desirable because of their ability to be responsive to the specific needs of local communities. However, when projects are too large for local financing, require coordination between multiple States, or are instrumental in achieving national goals, the Federal Government has a role to play. This section details the infrastructure investment channels in which the Federal Government's intervention would be beneficial.

The Federal Government's Role in Infrastructure Investment

Federal involvement in infrastructure investment can have a beneficial effect as a countervailing force in local politics. Local politicians often face strong incentives to prefer new projects over maintaining existing ones, and they may

Box 11-2. Continuing the Historic Modernization of Health Information Technology Begun during COVID-19

The decentralized nature of the U.S. healthcare system can create challenges for coordination in a national public health crisis. In March 2020, it became evident that more precise health data were needed to coordinate the COVID-19 response. Given the number of agencies needing these data, the Federal Government embarked on an ambitious plan to modernize the national health information technology (IT) infrastructure to facilitate the seamless, secure reporting of critical and sensitive health data from healthcare organizations and IT vendors. This effort led to the creation of the Federal data platform named HHS Protect that has allowed Federal agencies, along with State and local partners, to coordinate using shared data. This platform streamlines processes and connections to ensure data quality while eliminating time-intensive duplicative IT work.

HHS Protect contains, within a single portal, over 3.5 billion data elements across 200 different data sets. This information is available in real time to drive the Federal and State government responses to the COVID-19 pandemic. Having access to this real-time data allows the government to more accurately pinpoint patients in need, to identify regions and healthcare systems that are under strain, and to allocate treatments and resources more rapidly and efficiently. Having granular, hospital-level data in near real time has been critical for developing an understanding of the severity of the disease, the status of capacity and staffing constraints, and the supply and demand of personal protective equipment. The HHS Protect platform has also played a central role in the COVID-19 vaccine trials. Specifically, using data from claims and other sources, it allows analysts to algorithmically identify at-risk populations and locations on the verge of a COVID-19-surge to target data gathering so as to quickly and efficiently meet the necessary benchmarks for trial validity.

No such infrastructure existed before this massive data mobilization and IT modernization. In contrast to the prepandemic status quo, currently 99 percent of hospitals report data consistently and 94 percent report every single day. Similarly, automated connections now exist for case and laboratory reporting from State and local jurisdictions. In addition to the data and platform, the Federal Government has built out new and existing teams of experienced, well-trained analysts from HHS, the CDC, the U.S. Digital Service, and other agencies, as well as leveraging the expertise of trusted external partners to ensure that these data are available in an actionable, interpretable form to inform decisionmaking.

This groundbreaking effort will also prove useful for future pandemics and other health crises. For example, it can facilitate more in-depth exploration of the recent declines in American life expectancy and can target resources to combat opioid overdoses, suicides, and heart disease. One important innovation that has emerged is the creation of Health Information

Exchanges in multiple States that link real-time electronic health records data to track intensive care unit surge capacity for COVID-19 patients. This platform could combine data from public and private insurance transactions to greatly enhance the planning, execution, and response to future pandemics. As mentioned above, one policy proposal advocates the allocation of GME funding to areas with greater medical need. This platform could be adapted to identify those areas and ensure that they receive the healthcare professionals needed to provide a high quality of life for residents. The innovations developed during the fight against the COVID-19 pandemic will continue to serve Americans in the years to come.

also avoid imposing user fees that could be unpopular among frequent users (Kahn and Levinson 2011; Glaeser and Ponzetto 2017).

Over a short time horizon, maintenance is often a more effective use of funds than new capital investment. Keeping existing infrastructure in good repair is likely to have a larger economic effect than building new infrastructure, given that existing infrastructure is already woven into the fabric of high-output economic environments and generates a higher marginal return than new construction. Nadiri and Mamuneas (1996) find no evidence of overinvestment or underinvestment in highway capital by the end of the 1980s, indicating that maintaining the existing stock would ensure the correct amount of infrastructure intensity after that point, with new infrastructure only needing to be built at a rate commensurate with the growth of the population and economic needs. Every $1 spent to keep a road in good condition prevents $7 in costs when it has fallen into a poor condition (AASHTO and TRIP 2009). Given that estimated output multipliers for transfer payments to State and local governments for infrastructure range between 0.4 and 2.2, focusing funding on repair could have a positive effect on GDP (CBO 2015).

According to the CBO (2018), in 2017 the share of Federal spending on maintenance was just 27 percent of total Federal spending on transportation and water infrastructure, and the real dollar amount spent has remained flat since the 1980s, even as the stock of infrastructure has increased. State and local spending have not increased their growth rates to compensate. Currently, the Federal Government primarily funds road infrastructure through the Highway Trust Fund. But this fund is now facing insolvency, with a projected deficit of over $6 billion as soon as 2022. Zhao, Fonseca-Sarmiento, and Tan (2019) estimate that the current cost of deferred repairs might be as large as $873 billion, or 4.2 percent of GDP. Nongovernmental estimates find that $110 billion to $150 billion per year would be needed to cover the infrastructure investment gap through 2025 (McBride and Moss 2020; American Society of Civil Engineers 2016).

Simple and transparent metrics for discretionary grants would allow fulfillment of projects that have difficulty getting local funding because of their size or cross-jurisdictional nature. This would include projects across multiple States and that fulfill significant national goals. The process could expand upon the existing TIGER/BUILD model, which entails federally funded discretionary grants that attempt to achieve national objectives, but could improve on them by emphasizing numerical metrics for economic, safety, and environmental impact by using cost-benefit analysis that follows a consistent and clear evaluation process. The Federal Government can provide technical assistance to avoid biasing the process against smaller applicants and ensure adherence to best practices (U.S. Department of Transportation 2020).

As discussed in chapter 8 of this *Report*, public-private partnerships (PPPs) can enable provision of high value infrastructure at a low cost to the government. Well-designed PPPs are structured to ensure that the private partner has strong performance incentives at the same time that the public interest is protected (Istrate and Puentes 2011). For example, if the same entity builds and manages the project, this can align incentives to minimize operational costs in the design and implementation of the project. Best practices for PPPs include robust competition between private vendors to win the partnership and contractual terms that optimally divide the risk burden between the vendor and the government. If the private entity is allowed to earn a return to the investment through user fees, the partnership contract must carefully consider what, if any, role the public retains in terms of approving or setting the fees. If the infrastructure will be a natural monopoly—as a road on public land with few competing roads nearby—this issue is particularly important to address.

Finally, efforts can be made to avoid deterring private financing of infrastructure investment funded by user fees. The cost of capital of PPPs relative to public risk assumption and funding is high (Arezki et al. 2017). As detailed by Makovsek (2018), the government can take several actions to offset the risk and uncertainty private investors face when contemplating publically beneficial investment. Such hurdles include failure of environmental review, change in political situation, or other regulatory hurdles that introduce additional risk to the process of providing public infrastructure. In addition, the interest on State and local government debt instruments is exempted from taxation and government-owned entities providing infrastructure services are given preferential tax treatment. Offering guarantees against the unavoidable risk of infrastructure provision and equalizing taxation treatment could increase private investment.

Infrastructure and Productivity

Productivity, a measure of the ratio of outputs to inputs, is the result of a complex interaction between infrastructure, education, research, investment, and

Figure 11-11. U.S. Productivity, 1949–2019

Percent change at annual rate

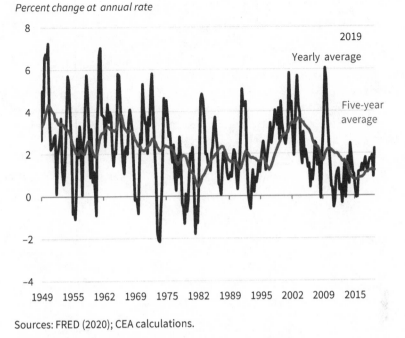

Sources: FRED (2020); CEA calculations.

implementation. Especially important for productivity growth and innovation are public infrastructure investments, because the choice of where and what to build has tremendous implications for the enterprises that rely on them. If productivity increases, an economy can create more with less. This leads to a higher-income economy with more leisure time and less environmental degradation for the same level of economic output.

For decades, there has been concern within the United States regarding a decline in labor productivity growth (Munnell 1990). As shown in figure 11-11, the late 1990s saw a rise in productivity growth as industry implemented new information technologies; but since the Great Recession, productivity growth has remained depressed. This decline in productivity growth does not appear to be due to mismeasurement (Byrne, Fernald, and Reinsdorf 2016; Syverson 2016). Research productivity has been found to be declining as a result of requiring more resources to advance the frontiers of scientific knowledge in existing fields (Bloom and others 2020). New fields such as artificial intelligence, quantum computing, and autonomous vehicles can reverse this trend when their benefits are diffused to the broader economy. However, there is a concern that dynamism is falling for cutting-edge fields. Astebro, Braguinsky, and Ding (2020) find that start-up formation by doctorate recipients in science and engineering has fallen, partly due to increased complexity and administrative costs.

Box 11-3. 5G Infrastructure

The United States has begun the transition to 5G technology for wireless communications. Far from a minor improvement on 4G, the next generation of wireless communications features vastly expanded data capacity and speed unleashing new opportunities for innovation and economic growth. As a simple example, movies will be downloaded over the Internet at speeds more than 10 times faster than is possible today. However, the technology may also enable transformative applications such as self-driving cars, remote surgery, and increasingly intelligent manufacturing. In a 2018 report, the Federal Communications Commission (FCC) describes the country as "at the brink of another technological revolution," in which 5G networks "will make possible once-unimaginable advances" (FCC 2018). The FCC further reports that the wireless industry is expected to invest more than $275 billion over 10 years to deploy infrastructure for 5G, that 3 million jobs will be created, and that the boost to GDP will be half a trillion dollars.

The integration of digital technologies with artificial intelligence and machine learning has been called the fourth industrial revolution (Schwab 2016). This integration will be enabled by 5G technology. Over time, 5G is expected to enable transformative applications through two novel facilities: massive, machine type communications (mMTC); and ultrareliable, low-latency communications (URLCC). The abbreviation mMTC refers to the capacity of the 5G infrastructure to support a very large number of devices in a network of sensors, known as the Internet of Things. For example, "smart cities" may deploy dense monitoring systems that reduce the cost of public services from city lighting to garbage collection by allowing for more efficient provision. URLLC refers to 5G performance standards that are designed to support "mission critical" communications. URLLC provides for data delivery at latencies as low as 1 millisecond with 99.9999 percent reliability. Use cases include automated energy distribution in a factory or energy grid, intelligent transportation systems, and bioelectronic medicine (Rysavy Research and 5G Americans 2020).

Although private providers—such as ATT, Verizon, and T-Mobile—are investing in and building out the 5G infrastructure, the Federal Government is playing a key role in organizing auctions for commercial licenses to the electromagnetic spectrum. This is a complex undertaking because 5G is designed to use different parts of the electromagnetic spectrum in combination. 5G providers will use high-band spectrum (frequencies above 24 gigahertz) to transmit vast amounts of data at high speeds with low latency. However, high-band spectrum does not travel far and cannot, for example, penetrate walls. Providers will use mid-band spectrum (frequencies between 1 and 6 gigahertz) to augment the high band spectrum for broader coverage at somewhat reduced speeds. Finally, providers will use low-band spectrum (frequencies below 1 gigahertz) to efficiently transmit data across very broad geographic areas at lower speeds.

The FCC has made significant progress in implementing its strategy named Facilitate America's Superiority in 5G Technology. In 2019 and 2020, the FCC ran three auctions (auctions 101, 102, and 103) that released almost 5 gigahertz of high-band spectrum to the market (FCC 2020a, 2020b, n.d.). These auctions generated about $10.3 billion in gross bids for just over 20,000 licenses. Winning bidders included ATT, Verizon, T-Mobile, and US Cellular, along with smaller wireless providers. On August 25, 2020, the FCC concluded its first auction (auction 105) of mid-band spectrum for 5G, releasing about 70 megahertz of spectrum in the range of 3.55 to 3.65 gigahertz. The auction generated $4.6 billion in gross bids for 20,625 licenses. Winning bidders included Verizon, the Dish Network, and several large cable companies. The FCC is currently organizing a spectrum auction to repurpose 280 megahertz of mid-band spectrum for use with 5G. The spectrum, which is in the range of 3.7 to 4.2 gigahertz, is currently used by fixed satellite service companies, primarily to deliver audio and video content to cable systems. As part of the auction process, the satellite companies will vacate the spectrum, allowing 5G providers to use it instead.

Despite the disruptions caused by the COVID-19 pandemic, the FCC has pursued an expedited schedule for the auction, finalizing bidding procedures in August, with bidding under way as of December 2020. The FCC is also working on targeted changes to facilitate 5G usage of low-band spectrum. Finally, the Department of Defense has contributed to the government's 5G efforts; in August, it announced that it will release 100 megahertz of mid-band spectrum in the range of 3.45 to 3.55 gigahertz, which was hitherto reserved for military use, to be auctioned in late 2021 with commercial use starting in 2022.

To the extent that the Federal Government can support the infrastructure necessary to ensure that these emerging fields can flourish, this will enhance productivity. However, government support for business structures that are no longer viable will decrease the rate of productivity by preventing "creative destruction," a process whereby innovative firms enter the market and stagnant firms exit (Acemoglu et al. 2018). Consequently, government operates optimally not when it invests in specific enterprises, favoring certain companies over others, but when it provides rules and transparency that allow companies to compete on an even playing field (see box 11-3 for a discussion of how the government allocates spectrum, allowing companies to fairly compete). Judicious government investments in infrastructure can fulfill this goal.

The Costs of Building Infrastructure

Foerster and others (2019) find that the annual rate of GDP growth has fallen more than 2 percentage points since 1950. As they argue, part of the reason for this is a decline in the trend in total factor productivity of the construction sector of 0.15 percentage point. Although this decline in productivity was reversed after 1999, the trend value of construction sector labor fell by 0.07 percentage point between 1999 and 2016. The cost of building highway infrastructure in the United States has risen 94 percent between 2003 and 2020, according to the National Highway Cost Construction Index. This increase began long before this period, having increased threefold from the 1960s to the 1980s (Brooks and Liscow 2019); these increases are partly driven by increased regulation (see box 11-4).

Labor regulations can also increase the overall cost of building infrastructure. For example, the 1931 Davis-Bacon Act requires the Federal Government to pay wages to construction workers that are no less than what they would earn working on similar projects in that area, known as "locally prevailing wages." This regulation can artificially increase labor costs, which can result in a nonoptimal allocation of capital. Although this was a Great Depression–era attempt to raise wages, Davis-Bacon also increases the burden of regulation, which discriminates against small firms. Reform could ensure that such regulations are achieving an appropriate balance between competing policy priorities.

In addition to the National Environmental Act in 1970, other environmentally focused legislation has increased the difficulty of developing on public lands, such as the 1973 Endangered Species Act and the 1972 Clean Water Act. Citizen organizations and environmental nonprofits have also increased since the 1970s, often opposing some development projects. Environmental impact reviews can delay projects or force developers to take expensive routes to fulfill the project, increasing overall costs (Brooks and Liscow 2019). While ensuring that new investment does not "steal" from the public by despoiling public goods is crucial, a rapid and transparent approval process could ensure that the capital is not tied up, but, if rejected, can be repurposed for alternate, more environmentally friendly projects.

Another factor in rising infrastructure costs is a lack of transparency and competitive processes. This limits public oversight and leads to wasteful and corrupt spending, which reduces the return on investment. For example, the Long Island Rail Road project has paid $3.5 billion for each mile of track, a rate seven times the world average. Schwartz and others (2020) estimate that 15 percent of advanced economy infrastructure investment is lost to waste.

The Critical Importance of User Fees

Certain goods have characteristics that are not amenable to pricing, and therefore must be financed by general revenues. Clean air, for example, cannot be priced for use because there is no practical way to exclude those who do not pay from breathing it. Moreover, there is no cost from additional consumption, as one's breathing it does not reduce another's ability to do so by a notable amount. Economists refer to such goods as "nonexcludable and nonrivalrous."

Box 11-4. Reforming the NEPA Process

The National Environmental Policy Act (NEPA), which was signed into law in 1970, requires Federal agencies to assess the environmental effects of their proposed actions and prepare an environmental impact statement (EIS) for actions that will significantly affect the quality of the human environment. For such actions, agencies must consider ways to minimize significant effects through reasonable alternatives or mitigation. The lead Federal agency must also solicit and consider public comments on potential environmental effects and alternatives. If it is completed, the entire EIS process takes about four and half years to complete on average, and averages over 600 pages in length.

The Council on Environmental Quality (CEQ) finalized reforms in 2020 to modernize its NEPA regulations and reduce delays in the environmental review and decisionmaking process. Changes include establishing a presumptive two-year time limit for the process, clarifying definitions and procedural requirements, codifying efficient agency practices to reduce unnecessary paperwork and delays, and updating the regulations to reflect current technologies. CEQ's updated NEPA regulations also include aspects of the Administration's One Federal Decision policy, established by Executive Order 13807, which addresses major infrastructure projects that require multiple agencies to approve permits. The One Federal Decision Executive Order, which is codified in the updated regulations, requires agencies issuing multiple permits for a project to develop a joint permitting schedule, develop one EIS, and then issue a joint record of decision for the project.

By reducing the time for completing NEPA reviews from 4 to 2 years, the CEA estimates that these policies will lead to $739 billion in benefits from infrastructure projects over the next 10 years. The benefits come from earlier completion and lower costs of financing projects, leading to improved infrastructure and amenities. The CEA bases the estimate on the $2.35 trillion in roads, airports, waterways, pipelines, and utility investments that are needed to modernize infrastructure in the next 10 years (American Society of Civil Engineers 2016). Though it is not clear that all these projects would require review under NEPA or preparation of an EIS, the CEA estimate is conservative in assuming that delays under the current NEPA permitting process are only 4 years rather than 4.5 years. Research by the CEA has shown that public infrastructure investments provide a marginal product to society at a rate of 12.9 percent a year.

Accordingly, the value of moving the benefits of $2.35 trillion in investments forward two years is $479 billion. An additional benefit of the reduced delay in the permitting process is that developers of this infrastructure do not need to hold loans for as many years, incurring interest on the principal loaned to undertake the project. The estimated reduction in financing costs is $260 billion for loans made on a principal of $2.35 trillion, or the difference in interest payments on a 4-year versus a 2-year loan. If the decision is made to not approve a proposed project, those resources can more quickly be reallocated to a more beneficial use.

The benefits from reform could be even larger than we have estimated because some permits are not just delayed by some years but instead are never issued at all, because the company requesting them moves into financial hardship while awaiting a response. Bear Lodge mine in Wyoming is one example. Rare Element Resources attempted to open a mine for rare earth minerals, which have been designated as a critical mineral, on U.S. Forest Service (USFS) land. The company submitted its plan of operations to the USFS in November 2012. In September 2013, the USFS accepted the initial plan and started the process of finding a contractor to undertake the EIS. In January 2016, Rare Element Resources suspended permitting efforts because the company had run out of money waiting for the project to be approved.

With so much attention being paid to reshoring critical industries (see chapter 9), simply capitalizing domestic natural resources responsibly would ensure access to many key commodities, improving the U.S. trade balance, mitigating U.S. reliance on vulnerable commodity supply chains, and ensuring that resources are extracted and used in a sustainable way. This would allow for more sustainable trading partnerships without imposing distortionary trade barriers that disrupt supply chains and impose costs on American consumers. It would also allow commodities to be produced in a more sustainable way than is often done in other countries.

However, when it is possible to exclude users and when additional consumption imposes costs on others, setting a price on a good can efficiently internalize the costs associated with its use. Roads, canals, and bridges are examples of goods that are both excludable and rivalrous, and therefore would benefit from pricing plans.

As detailed in the 2018 *Economic Report of the President*, it is optimal when the users of a public good are those who pay for it. This prevents overconsumption of public goods by ensuring that the costs of using them are borne by the users, and provides a source of funding for the maintenance and upkeep of these goods. Without a clear and sustainable funding stream, infrastructure can become a burden on future generations.

Although Federal gasoline taxes partly fund Federal infrastructure projects, and so partly align the users with the costs of use, most of these projects are financed through general revenues. Because drivers are not bearing the costs of driving on public roads and bridges, they do not have any incentive to economize their use of them, leading to congestion and high maintenance costs. User fees, such as tolls or fees based on vehicle miles traveled (with both scaled to the damage the use does to the infrastructure), reduce congestion and help provide a stable source of funding for infrastructure. Expanding their use, and other forms of congestion pricing, would yield further economic benefits.

The Federal Government has implemented several kinds of user fees over many decades to finance public infrastructure, although these have not adequately addressed the problems of depreciation and congestion. The Federal Government passed a gasoline tax in 1931, initially set at 3 cents a gallon, which then was roughly 10 percent of the price of gasoline. The Federal Highway Act and Highway Revenue Act of 1956 attached user fees explicitly to the Interstate Highway System. These included taxes on gasoline, diesel fuel, tires, and heavy vehicle use, though the vast majority of the Highway Trust Fund revenues depend on fuel taxes. However, these taxes are not pegged to inflation, and the Federal gasoline tax in particular has not been raised since October 1993, although the general price level (price index for GDP) has increased by a multiple of 1.65. The gasoline tax is now 18.4 cents a gallon, which was 17 percent of the cost of gasoline in 1993, and is currently roughly half that.

In addition, higher-mileage vehicles, including electric vehicles, render the gasoline tax an incomplete and flawed user fee. Higher-mileage vehicles depreciate physical assets, such as roads and bridges, as much as lower-mileage vehicles of equivalent mass, but pay less per mile when fuel taxes are utilized as a user fee. Though a gasoline tax may generate ancillary benefits by reducing pollution and greenhouse gas emissions, dependence on this tax to fund the maintenance of Federal roads and bridges is inadvisable.

Alternatively, Federal, State, and local governments could consider increasing their use of toll roads to finance public infrastructure and reduce congestion. These toll roads could vary their charges based on the vehicle type. One example of these is high-occupancy toll (HOT lanes). HOT lanes charge low occupancy vehicles a fee, while buses and emergency vehicles can use the lanes free of change. Currently, there are 10 HOT lanes operating across 8 States. Some academics and government officials have advocated converting high-occupancy vehicle (HOV) lanes, which restrict use to only qualifying vehicles, to HOT lanes to increase usage and reduce congestion in other lanes.

Research on the effectiveness of HOT lanes has been mixed, however. If the toll is set too low, a HOT lane may actually reduce the incentive to carpool and therefore generate more congestion, given that single occupants may be content to simply pay the toll to access the lane (Burris et al. 2014; Konishi and Mun 2010). In HOV lanes, these single-occupant vehicles would typically have been excluded. However, toll prices that are set optimally can reduce congestion and finance the maintenance of the public asset.

Governments could also consider varying toll prices based on the time of day. Variable tolls, as opposed to flat-rate tolls, charge drivers more during peak travel hours to reduce congestion. In Fort Myers, Florida, a 50 percent discount on the toll was offered on the Midpoint and Cape Coral bridges for a short period before and after the rush hours. Survey data revealed that, among those eligible for the discount, there was an increase in traffic of as much as 20 percent during the discount period before the morning rush hour, with corresponding drops in the rush hour itself.

A handful of cities and countries have embraced "cordon pricing," which charges drivers for entering certain areas. Instead of traditional tollbooths, vehicles are charged through transponders that are scanned by overhead antennas to detect entry. Currently, 70 to 80 percent of toll fees are collected this way in the United States. In Germany, highway authorities use Global Positioning System technology to administer truck tolls on its autobahns. An in-vehicle device records all the charges based on the location of the vehicle, and then the owner of the vehicle uploads the charge to a processing center. The costs of such systems are as much as $500 per vehicle in Germany, but their presence reduces the need for roadside equipment and labor for toll collection.

Cordon pricing has had considerable effects on congestion. Table 11-4 details the cities and countries that have embraced this form of congestion pricing, and summarizes the economic effects. In the year after implementation, traffic congestion fell in London by 30 percent. Bus service increased by 23 percent due to improved reliability and reduced travel times. Of the thousands of car trips that no longer traveled into the cordon zone, 50 percent shifted to public transit, 25 percent were diverted to other parts outside the cordon area, and the remainder shifted to carpooling, walking, biking, and traveling outside peak hours. These results have been sustained over time, despite nearly 20 percent population growth in London since 2000. The city has also achieved concomitant public health benefits, as carbon dioxide emissions declined 16 percent from 2002 to 2003. In Stockholm, traffic in the cordon area has fallen 20 percent and carbon dioxide emissions have fallen 14 percent.

Singapore's road pricing plan reduced congestion by 20 percent from 1975 to 1998, and generated revenues that were nearly nine times the costs of investment. When Singapore switched to its current electronic road pricing system in 1998, this reduced congestion even further, despite strong population growth since then. Congestion in the inner city has fallen by 24 percent, while average speeds have increased by more than 30 percent, and bus and train usage have increased by 15 percent. Revenues have been used to support public transit; street safety; and bus, rail, and bicycle infrastructure projects. However, Singapore also introduced stringent measures to restrict car ownership, requiring the purchase of a certificate that can cost as much as $37,000 that must be recertified every 10 years. Since 2018, Singapore has required new drivers to bid on existing certificates, as it will not allow any increase in car ownership.

Although most economists agree that congestion pricing would make the average person better off, many States and localities are reluctant to adopt such pricing mechanisms because of the system's perceived inequities. As of

Table 11-4. Congestion Pricing Initiatives Worldwide

City	Year Implemented	Policies	Impact
London	2003	8 square miles inside the city's Inner Ring Road Traffic cameras capture license plate numbers upon entry/exit; pay within next day Flat daily fee from 7 a.m.–6 p.m., Monday–Friday	Annual operating cost/net revenue: £130 million / £137 million 30 percent reduction in traffic congestion Bus ridership reached 50-year high in 2011
Stockholm	2006	Automatic tolling at main entry points to inner city Fees levied between 6:30 a.m. and 6:30 p.m. Monday–Friday, varying based on demand	Annual operating cost / net revenue: 100 million krona / 1.3 billion krona Traffic delays decreased 30–50 percent 80 percent resident opposition reversed after successful pilot; citizens voted to keep permanent
Gothenburg, Sweden	2013	Automatic tolling at main entry points to inner city Fees levied between 6:30 a.m. and 6:30 p.m. Monday–Friday, varying based on demand	Traffic declined 12 percent during charged hours Public transit use jumped 24 percent for commuters
Milan	2008	Flat daily charge applies to drivers entering the city between 7:30 a.m. and 7:30 p.m. Residents exempt for first 40 entries, then pay reduced charge Electric and hybrid cars exempt	More than 30 percent reduction in traffic 33 percent drop in black carbon emissions
Singapore	1975	Variable pricing scheme adjusts to congestion levels in real time from 7 a.m.–8 p.m., Monday–Saturday Vehicles equipped with dashboard devices storing fare Car ownership certificates (limited) can cost $50,000	Annual operating cost / net revenue: S$25 million / S$150 million Since 1998, traffic in inner city have dropped 24 percent Greenhouse gas emissions in cordon area reduced 10–15 percent
New York City	2021*	E-ZPass system—already used for bridge and tunnel tolls—charges vehicles entering Manhattan south of 60th Street Tax credits for residents earning less than $60,000 annually In addition to preexisting congestion fees for taxis and rideshares	

Note: New York City congestion pricing plans are still tentative.
Sources: Tri-State Transportation Campaign; European Commission; *New York Times*; Bloomberg CityLab.

Box 11-5. Digital Infrastructure

The COVID-19 crisis has revealed inadequacies in medical information systems, with some officials relying on fax machines to relay critically important health data (Kliff and Sanger-Katz 2020). Box 11-2 above details the digital infrastructure investment made in response to this need. As the American public suffered job losses of unprecedented scope, dated computer software was overwhelmed by skyrocketing State Unemployment Insurance claims.

Government agencies could be better served by modernizing data storage. For example, the Department of Veterans Affairs (VA) began creating an in-house records system amid the advent of personal computing in the 1970s. Though state-of-the-art in its prime, the VA's system continues to draw criticism from lawmakers concerned about maintenance costs and security issues related to commercially tested software alternatives. As currently implemented, despite several modernization attempts and billions of dollars in annual spending, the VA's information technology fails to adequately support its services and protect against security threats. However, a recent change in policy will allow veterans to have more access to private healthcare, which will require the VA to coordinate with other healthcare providers and reinforces the necessity of updating its outdated IT systems (Steinhauer 2019).

Without modernization, critical infrastructure like regional power grids and hospital medical records remain at risk for potentially catastrophic cyberattacks (GAO 2018). In 2017 alone, Federal executive branch civilian agencies reported more than 35,000 security incidents, ranging from email phishing to malicious software installations. The Government Accountability Office finds that legacy systems at the Department of Homeland Security pose 168 "high- or critical-risk" network vulnerabilities (GAO 2019). In many cases, foreign intelligence agencies spearhead such intrusions. As recently as October 2020, the Department of Justice indicted six Russian military officials for disrupting the 2017 French elections and the PyeongChang Winter Olympics, among other attacks (DOJ 2020).

Standardized data storage and streamlined information-sharing processes would foster more efficient interagency collaboration on government-wide initiatives like coronavirus relief. In addition, providing information for public use once it has been scrubbed of identifying characteristics would significantly benefit scientific research. Academics argue that providing direct access to administrative data can further strengthen the position of the United States on the forefront of academic progress (Card et al. 2011).

New digital infrastructure will also be needed in cutting edge sectors such as the autonomous vehicles industry. The Federal Government can ease the entry of new players in such sectors, thereby supporting competition, by supporting infrastructure investment. For the autonomous vehicles industry, this will involve ensuring that localities have the infrastructure in place to support autonomous vehicle technology for passenger cars, long-haul trucking, and short-range drones in a consistent and universal manner. Investing in unmanned traffic management systems and streamlining regulatory approval for engineers seeking airspace to test their inventions will be a major step toward a future of half-hour package deliveries and decongested roadways. Federal intervention can facilitate the development of robust national-scale systems instead of a State-by-State patchwork.

Altogether, advances in digital infrastructure could generate tremendous economic gains for the United States. The autonomous vehicle industry alone is expected to increase output by $1.2 trillion, or roughly $3,800 per person (Clements and Kockelman 2017). A Virginia Tech study found in a cross-sectional analysis of three large U.S. cities that drone delivery could produce $583 million in total time savings for consumers each year in those cities (Lyon-Hill et al. 2020).

2008, only 1 percent of roads in the United States used some type of congestion pricing beyond traditional tollroads. However, the Federal Government could incentivize State and local governments to adopt such policies by offering to match infrastructure investments if such pricing is adopted, or offer Federal support to help compensate low-income populations that might be adversely affected by congestion pricing.

An additional area in which government and private interests alike could benefit from increased Federal investment is in digital infrastructure. Relevant projects involving improved data gathering, enhanced security, and revolutionized computing efficiency. These public goods will increase the productivity of private industry and the well-being of the American citizenry (box 11-5).

Investing in Port Infrastructure

America's seaports serve as our economy's gateways to the vast maritime network that transports more than 90 percent of global trade tonnage. These 360 American ports facilitate more than 70 percent of America's international trade by weight and nearly 50 percent by value. They are absolutely vital for American prosperity and economic security. However, America's ports now lag far behind the competitiveness and productivity of the world's leading ports. As a result, increased transportation costs place American companies at a significant disadvantage, effectively locking the U.S. economy out of the world's lowest-cost trade routes. Over time, the poor state of the Nation's ports has taken a significant toll on America's position in global trade and manufacturing, and has adversely affected net exports. Because maritime commerce is the dominant global trade mode, competing nations have prioritized enhancements to their seaports to improve the flow of trade. Increasing the efficiency and productivity of ports decreases transportation costs and expands trade opportunities. Capital investment to modernize American ports is long overdue and would yield substantial returns for the Nation's trade and manufacturing competitiveness by supporting net exports, as high-quality port infrastructure benefits exports more than imports through supply chain interactions.

Container ships spend less time making port in Taiwan (0.46 day), China (0.62 day), Japan (0.35 day), Spain (0.66 day), and Norway (0.33 day) than in the United States, where it takes a full day on average. U.S. ports take longer than the world average in five out of six market segments (UNCTAD 2020). Deep channels, round-the-clock automated cargo handling, and constant competitive improvement enable nearly frictionless trade. Ports with these features serve, allowing tremendous economies of scale and complex supply chains to flourish. Low transportation costs are pivotal for the production of goods that require the movement of many players. For large parts and bulk goods—such as those required in aerospace, automotive, and industrial production—waterborne commerce often offers a transportation mode for intermediate inputs.

Conversely, higher transportation costs resulting from poor maritime infrastructure relegate host nation economies to favor less complex supply chains, the exporting of primary goods, and the importing of intermediate and finished goods. Over time, this can have the effect of deindustrializing a nation. Poor maritime logistics, (including the absence of entire classes of bulk transportation legs) leads to situations where hog farmers in North Carolina import feed grain from Brazil instead of America. The United States also leads the world in exporting scrap metal because the existing water transportation modes cannot move this cheap and abundant domestic strategic commodity to American minimills.

Half of all goods, by value, entered the U.S. in 2017 through maritime ports, and the Federal Maritime Commission estimates that these ports generated nearly $4.6 trillion in economic activity in 2014. Increased investment in infrastructure at U.S. seaports would speed the flow of goods, expand trade, and increase U.S. GDP. For example, the World Bank (2020) gives the United States a rating of 5.8 out of 7 on its port infrastructure and ranks the Netherlands number 1, with a 6.8 rating. Extrapolating from an analysis by Munim and Schramm (2018), the CEA finds that increasing the United States' port infrastructure by 1 point (to 6.8 out of 7) would increase U.S. real GDP by 0.3 percent ($56 billion).

In 2018, 5 of the 50 busiest seaports in the world were located in the United States (figure 11-12). By contrast, 16 were located in China, and 10 of these were busier than the United States' busiest port—Los Angeles. Whereas U.S. ports processed an average of 7 million 20-foot equivalent units of container traffic annually, Chinese ports averaged 38 million units.

Infrastructure investment plays a role in this discrepancy. The average service life of U.S. airports and seaports is 38 years, below the global average, and the required port investment forecast through 2040 is 90 percent higher than current port investment trends, according to a 2017 analysis by Oxford Economics, which concluded that the United States' gap between needed

Figure 11-12. Number of Seaports by Country among the Top 50 Busiest Seaports in the World, 2018

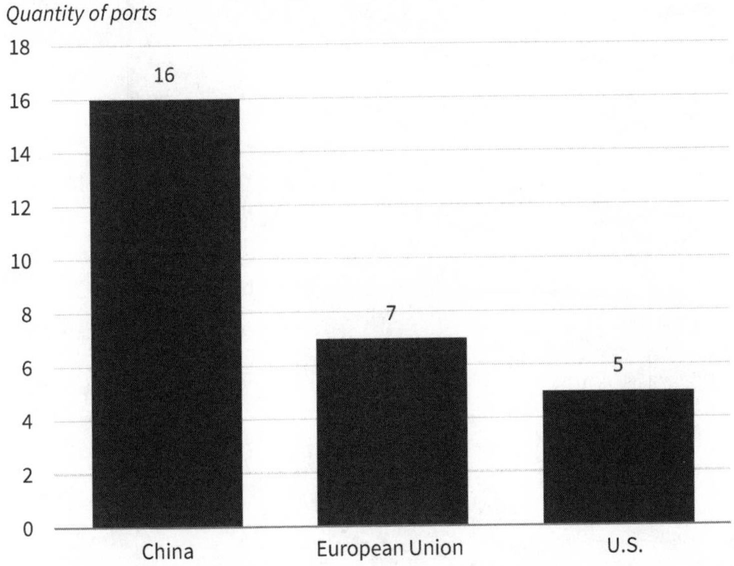

Quantity of ports

Source: World Shipping Council.
Note: The busiest seaports are as measured by tonnage.

and actual investment is one of the highest in the world. Over the last decade, increased trade volume has led to busier maritime ports and increased congestion. In 2014, the top three container ports alone accounted for nearly half of all containerized trade in the United States. The slower throughput caused by congestion has started to affect the performance of U.S. ports relative to other countries' ports and has begun to divert trade away from American ports through increasingly competitive Canadian and Mexican ports. Figure 11-13 shows the tonnage shipped out of the Port of Seattle against that shipped from the Port of Prince Rupert (one of the main ports on the West Coast of Canada). Although the Port of Seattle has seen increased traffic over the last four years, the growth in the Port of Prince Rupert's traffic is almost double that of Seattle. The Federal Maritime Commission estimates that if trade volumes at maritime ports continued to grow between 5 and 7 percent annually, the average growth rates for the East Coast and Gulf Coast ports since 2009, port capacity would need to double in the next decade to accommodate this growth.

The depth of shipping channels plays a significant role in the volumes and rates of the trade a port can facilitate. If a waterway is too shallow, large vessels benefiting from low unit transportation costs will be unable access the foreland infrastructure through the adjacent port. Many American ports are too shallow to facilitate trade with the large ships regularly used in the lowest cost trade routes internationally. Overall, due to inadequate dredging and

Figure 11-13. Cargo Volumes of the Port of Seattle Compared with the Port of Prince Rupert, 2015–18

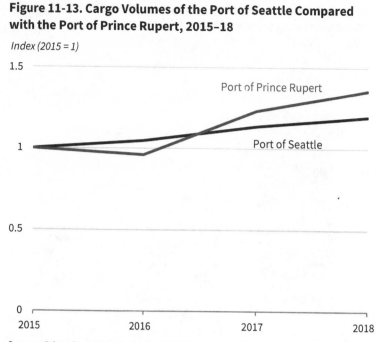

Index (2015 = 1)

Sources: Prince Rupert Port Authority; U.S. Department of Transportation; CEA calculations.

insufficient port depth, the U.S. likely forgoes $376 billion in trade annually, according to the U.S. Army Corps of Engineers (2017). This has become a major challenge for American energy producers in particular. Increased oil production in the United States has elevated the demand for oil transportation services via very large crude carriers (VLCCs) across Gulf Coast ports. However, all but one American oil export terminal have insufficient depth to handle VLCCs. As a result, Gulf Coast ports need to use smaller tankers to carry out costly and inefficient ship-to-ship oil transfers, thus loading VLCCs in open water, many miles offshore. Russian and Saudi producers are able to load VLCCs directly, reducing their oil's price per barrel and dramatically increasing their pace of exporting to market. This inefficient method of loading American oil exports generally adds several extra days and $1 million to shipping costs for each shipment of American oil exported from the Gulf Coast. This inefficiency translates into an additional $0.50 to $0.80 cost per barrel for American oil (Huchzermeyer 2018; Miller 2019). Updating and upgrading U.S. maritime laws to ensure adequate dredging capacity could therefore generate substantial economic gains.

Improving American trade competitiveness can be accelerated by leveraging the Nation's unique comparative advantages. The United States has rapidly emerged as the world's leading producer of natural gas and is becoming one of the world's top liquefied natural gas (LNG) exporters. Concurrently, the global deep-sea shipping industry has begun a seismic shift toward LNG as a marine propulsion fuel. Because fuel costs are typically the leading driver of operating expenses for vessel owners, the 15–30 percent reduction in costs realized by shifting from fuel oil to LNG has become a superior alternative. In addition to fuel conversions, dual-fuel- and LNG-powered vessels are becoming increasingly ubiquitous. This shift toward LNG as a marine fuel has not been matched with investment in the bunkering infrastructure that is necessary to fuel LNG-powered vessels except in the most modern competitive ports in Asia and Europe. Investing in U.S. port infrastructure to enable LNG refueling terminals would make American ports more attractive.

Other Federal regulations have exacerbated congestion at the ports. One of the largest amplifiers of this situation is the shortage of trailer truck beds, or chassis. Once the goods arrive at maritime ports, trucks are typically used to transport the goods to other destinations. Stricter Federal safety requirements introduced in 2009 were factors in creating a situation in which providing a chassis is too cost-prohibitive for ocean carriers. Known as the "roadability rule," this regulation placed the burden of the safety inspection of a chassis on drivers, increasing regulatory compliance costs. As a result, many of the carriers sold their chassis to third-party leasing companies, which now provide the majority of chassis at ports. Truckers must now make multiple trips to pick up and return chassis, leading to delays in the availability of chassis at any one time. This limits the amount of goods truckers can move in a timely manner. For example, in January 2019, chassis shortages led to large backlogs at the Los Angeles and Long Beach terminals.

Research demonstrates that improving port infrastructure increases trade. Countries that enhance their seaport efficiency can decrease shipping costs by up to 12 percent, leading to increased trade (Clark, Dollar, and Micco 2002). Cheaper shipping both increases firm sales and helps spread new technology (Lakshmanan 2011). These outcomes allow firms to scale up their activities and increase domestic output, which has positive spillover effects into the labor market and the rest of the economy.

There is also evidence that port infrastructure investment not only boosts total trade but also provides a larger boost to exports than imports. Improved port infrastructure increases exports by $4 for every $1 increase in imports (Wilson, Mann, and Otsuki 2004; Korinek and Sourdin 2011). Physical infrastructure has an even higher positive effect on exports as income grows (Portugal-Perez and Wilson 2012). Improved port efficiency has increased incomes in communities around ports by up to 70 percent (Brooks, Gendron-Carrier, and Rua 2018).

Generating a More Skilled and Resilient Workforce

As a result of the COVID-19 pandemic, an unprecedented fall in economic activity occurred in 2020. Although this was met by a rapid and massive policy response that focused on maintaining the social capital of employee-employer relationships, there is still work to be done. Improving the productivity of the U.S. workforce is more important than ever as the country recovers from the pandemic-induced recession. This section outlines two ways in which this can be done: increasing the skills of the immigrants who contribute to this country, and improving the institutions of higher-learning that equip millions of Americans for the labor market.

Points-Based Immigration

In contrast to other developed countries—such as Canada, Australia, and Japan—the United States immigration system limits the ability of high-skilled workers to immigrate to the United States if they do not have existing family relationships. Under current U.S. law, immigrants obtain lawful permanent resident (LPR) status (i.e., green cards) through immigration categories for familial relations, employment, the diversity lottery, and the refugee and asylum programs. Table 11-5 shows the distribution of those receiving LPR status in fiscal year 2018. The U.S. distribution of immigrant visas diverges significantly from countries with merit-based points systems where over half of permanent immigration visas were granted based on the employment or skills of the applicants (figure 11-14).

Points-based immigration systems select their employment-based immigrants by awarding points based on factors such as age, education, and earnings that are associated with positive outcomes. For example, Canada's merit-based immigrants earn more than other Canadian immigrants. Abbott and Beach (2011) find that the median 10-year average earnings of Canada's merit-based immigrants are 35 to 56 percent above the median 10-year average earnings of all immigrants in the most recent cohort they consider. The CEA's estimates, which are discussed below, and a review of the economic literature suggest that there is strong evidence that shifting the U.S. immigration system toward a merit-based system would lead to benefits for the U.S. economy—increasing growth, wages, and tax revenue.

Estimated Economic Benefits

In this subsection, the CEA estimates the economic and fiscal benefits if the United States prioritized the highest-skilled workers within the applicant pool and allocated 56 percent of green cards to high-skilled applicants, thereby putting the U.S. in line with the average percentage of employment-based visas offered by Japan, Australia, and Canada. In this modeling, it is assumed that

Table 11-5. Lawful Permanent Resident (LPR) Status Obtained by Broad Class of Admission, Fiscal Year 2018

Broad Class of Admission	Number of LPRs	Percentage of LPRs
Immediate relatives of U.S. citizens	478,961	44
Family-sponsored preferences	216,563	20
Employment-based preferences	138,171	13
Diversity	45,350	4
Refugees	155,734	14
Asylees	30,175	3
All other	31,657	3
Total	1,096,611	100

Sources: U.S. Department of Homeland Security; CEA calculations.

Figure 11-14. Share of Permanent Legal Immigration Based on Employment, 2017

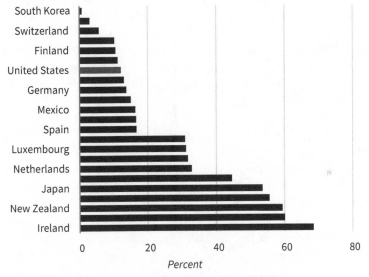

Sources: OECD International Migration Outlook 2019; CEA calculations.
Note: Data are for calendar year 2017. Employment base includes accompanying family members on work visas. Totals exclude permanent immigration from free movements.

immigrants receiving new high-skilled green cards would bring their spouse and dependent children and that these dependents would count against the total number of green cards. The total amount of immigration would remain consistent with the current flow.

The characteristics of recent immigrants to the United States are identified using data from the three most recent years of the American Community Survey from the Census Bureau from 2016 through 2018, as provided by the Integrated Public Use Microdata Series (known as IPUMS) database (Ruggles et al. 2019).

Figure 11-15 shows the educational characteristics of recent immigrants under the current system, among those admitted as new high-skilled workers, and among the anticipated composition resulting from a policy shift. Two assumptions are made. First, it is assumed that immigrants below the 85th percentile of wage earners continue to have the same characteristics despite their percentage of the overall immigration flow being smaller. Second, it is assumed that new immigrants on merit-based green cards match the characteristics of immigrants whose earnings are above 85th percentile in the American Community Survey.

Although 51 percent of recent immigrants have less than a bachelor's degree, increasing the share of green cards awarded to high-skilled immigrants suggests that the share with less than a bachelor's degree would fall to 33 percent (figure 11-15). By allocating a larger share of visas based on employment and skill, the employment rates of recent immigrants would also increase. Even including those arriving on non-skills-based visas, along with the spouses of new employment-based visas who may not be working, the employment rate of new immigrants rises by 8 percentage points from current rates (from 60 percent to 68 percent) and the average wage of employed recent immigrants increases from $49,000 to $94,000.

To estimate the effect of increased high-skilled immigration on national income and national income per capita over the next 10 years, the CEA approximated the contribution to national income of immigrant workers to the economy as their total compensation. For the subset of visas converted to high-skilled green cards, the existing employment and earnings rates are compared with those projected. Among new high-skilled recipients and their families, additional increases in employment rates in future years is not assumed.

Having determined the total wages of recent immigrants under the current system and in the new system, total compensation is estimated based on the Bureau of Labor Statistics' Employer Costs for Employee Compensation survey. The employer share of payroll taxes and fringe benefits (insurance, retirement benefits, and legally required benefits) represent over 20 percent of compensation. Thus, dividing wages by 0.8 leads to an estimate of total compensation. The change in total compensation from the introduction of additional high-skilled workers represents our estimate of national income growth in a single year. To project the contributions of immigrants in future years, it is assumed that the nominal compensation of new and recent immigrants grows by 3 percent a year, which is consistent with recent overall wage growth trends from the Bureau of Labor Statistics' Current Employment Statistics.

Figure 11-15. Estimated Educational Attainment of Recent Immigrants Age 25 Years and Older, 2016–18

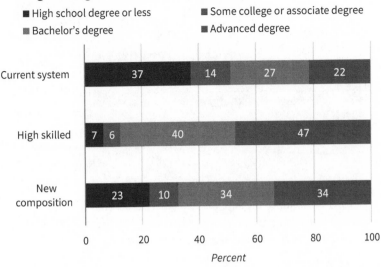

Sources: American Community Survey, 2016–18; Integrated Public Use Microdata Series database; CEA calculations.
Note: Estimates assume that the total visas issued remain at current levels. Estimates for recent immigrants are based on noncitizens who have been in the United States between one and three years.

Given that shifting toward high-skilled immigrants increases both innovation and the productivity of the existing U.S. workforce and capital, additional increases in national income are expected. While recognizing that there is substantial uncertainty about the magnitude of these productivity gains, the same 0.3 percent long-run increase in the productivity of domestic workers (about 0.03 percent increase a year) is included in the analysis of wage gains given above. This effect is slightly more than half the long-term productivity gains estimated by the CBO for the Border Security, Economic Opportunity, and Immigration Modernization Act.

Using this approach, the total increase in nominal national income in 2029 would be about $570 billion above the baseline (pre-COVID-19) forecast under the current immigration system. Relative to the baseline national income growth projections, this reflects an increase in national income growth of about 0.20 percentage point a year. In addition, using the baseline population forecast, and recognizing that the exercise does not change the total number of immigrants arriving legally in the United States, this increases nominal national income per capita by about $1,600 in 2029 (table 11-6). If, instead, these new immigrants have average characteristics that match those of the top 30 percent of recent immigrants, as opposed to the top 15 percent, national income per capita would still be nearly $1,200 above the baseline forecast. The

Table 11-6. National Income Increase from a Merit-Based Immigration System

	Increase in 10-Year Average National Income Growth (percentage points)	Increase in 2029 National Income per Capita (2029 dollars)	Increase in 2029 National Income (billions of 2029 dollars)
Projected change	0.15–0.20	1,200–1,600	430–570

Sources: American Community Survey, 2016–18; Integrated Public Use Microdata Series database; CEA calculations.

Notes: The CEA bases these estimates on pre-COVID-19 national income projections. The estimate of national income per capita is rounded to the nearest $100. Aggregate national income estimates are rounded to the nearest $10 billion.

average growth of national income per year would be 0.15 percentage point, and the total increase in nominal national income in 2029 would be $430 billion above the baseline national income growth projection.

Estimated Effects on the Wages of Domestic Workers

Through this shift to a merit-based immigration system, low- and middle-skilled existing U.S. workers would face less competition from substitutable foreign workers for employment. As of December 2019, there were 42 million people age 25 and older in the labor force with a high school degree or less, 37 million with some college or an associate degree, and 62 million with a bachelor's degree. The shift in the makeup of the immigrant population, along with the emigration of 2 to 3 percent of recently arrived immigrants each year (based on estimates from Schwabish 2009), means that after 10 years, there would be roughly 600,000 fewer permanent adult immigrants in the labor force with a high school degree or less. There would be 200,000 fewer immigrants with some college or an associate degree and 1.4 million more immigrants with at least a bachelor's degree. These changes represent a decline in the size of the labor force with less than a high school degree and with some college of about 1.5 percent and 0.4 percent, respectively, whereas the size of the work-force with at least a bachelor's degree would increase by about 2.3 percent.

Using de Brauw and Russell's (2014) updated elasticity from Borjas (2003) as the upper end of the likely wage elasticity from immigration—and using Longhi, Nijkamp, and Poot's (2010) estimate of the lower end of the likely range—wage effects before capital adjustments and any long-run productivity gains are estimated. The result is that the revised immigrant flows from this exercise would increase wages for those with some college by up to 0.1 percent and for those with a high-school degree or less by up to 0.3 percent. The reform would reduce the wages of existing U.S. workers with at least a bachelor's degree by between 0.1 and 0.5 percent after a decade, indicating that there would be some redistribution from highly educated workers to less educated workers as a result.

An alternative approach to estimate the change in relative wages between workers at different levels of education is to consider the effects on relative wages from a shift in relative supplies of labor. Based on the estimates by Katz and Murphy (1992) that log relative wages increase by about 0.1 percent for a 1.5 percent decline in relative supply, there would be a 0.15 percent decline in wages for workers with at least a bachelor's degree, a 0.1 percent increase in wages for workers with a high school degree or less, and a 0.03 percent increase in wages for workers with some college or an associate degree. These estimates are within the range of short-run relative wage changes using the wage elasticities from the immigration literature.

The CEA anticipates productivity gains once capital has adjusted, resulting in additional wage gains for individuals at all education levels. This is consistent with the estimates of the CBO (2013) finding that wage gains from changes in immigrant flows increase once capital adjusts to the number of workers. In its analysis of the Border Security, Economic Opportunity, and Immigration Modernization Act, which substantially increased both high-skilled and low-skilled immigration, the CBO (2013) projected that the proposal would increase productivity and result in a long-run increase in wages of 0.5 percentage point. These productivity gains would, consequently, mitigate and possibly reverse any shorter-run wage declines among high-skilled domestic workers, while further increasing the wage gains for low- and middle-skilled domestic workers. The CEA estimates that the productivity gains would be just over half of those estimated by the CBO for the larger changes in immigration flows in the 2013 Border Security, Economic Opportunity, and Immigration Modernization Act, and it is assumed that these productivity gains are distributed equally throughout the distribution, causing overall wages to increase by 0.3 percent.

The CEA expects the overall effect on wages for those with a bachelor's degree or above to be between a 0.2 percent decline and a 0.2 percent increase. Wages of those with a high school degree or less would increase by 0.3 to 0.6 percent, and wages of those with some college would increase by 0.3 to 0.4 percent. For a typical high school graduate working full time, this would result in an additional $130 to $230 per year of earnings. Furthermore, consistent with the observations by Moretti (2013) and Borjas (2017) that shifting toward high-skilled immigration would likely lead to a reduction in income inequality, this distribution of wage gains would reduce wage inequality among current U.S. workers.

These estimates are also broadly consistent with the long-run wage effects found by Chassamboulli and Peri (2018) from a shift in the composition of immigration flows toward high-skilled employment-based immigrants. In addition to these wage effects, they also find that the shift toward skilled

Table 11-7. 75-Year Net Present Value of Fiscal Benefits from Proposed Changes to the Permanent Legal Immigration System (billions of dollars)

	Federal Benefits	State and Local Benefits	Total
Projected change	840–1,320	260–300	1,010–1,620

Sources: National Academy of Sciences, Engineering, and Medicine (2017); American Community Survey, 2016–18; Integrated Public Use Microdata Series database; CEA calculations.

Note: Estimates assume that the total visas issued remain at current levels. Estimates are rounded to the nearest $10 billion.

immigration will decrease the unemployment rate for native workers at all skill levels. This suggests an even more positive effect on the outcomes for U.S. citizens than is seen through wages alone, and one that is especially important in light of high unemployment rates resulting from the economic consequences of COVID-19.

Estimated Effects on Government Revenue and Expenditures

The CEA estimates that tax revenues would rise and outlays for social welfare programs would fall as a result of these wage, productivity, and employment gains. Using average tax rates (JCT 2019), the proposed changes could increase tax revenues by $470 billion in the CEA's primary forecast, and by $340 billion in the conservative forecast. These estimates do not include potential gains for domestic worker productivity, and they are broadly consistent with those that would be derived by multiplying the total increase in national income over the 10-year budget window from the higher-skilled immigrants by the 16 percent revenue-to-GDP ratio in 2018. However, the actual revenue gains are larger once the progressivity of the U.S. tax system is accounted for, which means that the higher-income immigrants would pay a higher share of their income in taxes than the lower-income immigrants who arrive in the United States under the current system.

To estimate the long-run fiscal effects of this new composition, the CEA uses the average 75-year fiscal benefits of immigrants by education level, as estimated by the National Academy of Sciences (2017). This approach is similar to that taken by Borjas (2019) to illustrate the substantial increase in U.S. wealth that would result from increasing the education profile of the immigrant population. Although changes in the education levels of parents arriving in the United States will likely also increase the education levels of children arriving with them, only the long-run fiscal costs and benefits of adult immigrants age 25 to 64 and those 65+ are included. Based on these estimates, shifting the composition of permanent immigration toward more highly educated and younger individuals will, after 10 years, result in a net present value of between $840 billion and $1.3 trillion of fiscal benefits from immigration for the Federal Government (table 11-7). In addition, it will result in a further $260 billion to $300 billion in fiscal benefits for State and local governments.

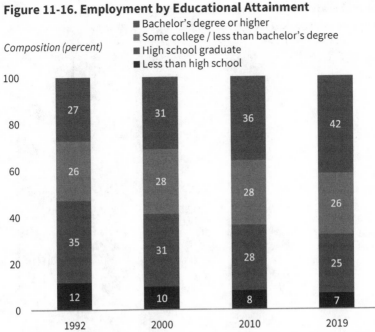

Figure 11-16. Employment by Educational Attainment

- Bachelor's degree or higher
- Some college / less than bachelor's degree
- High school graduate
- Less than high school

Composition (percent)

	1992	2000	2010	2019
Bachelor's degree or higher	27	31	36	42
Some college / less than bachelor's degree	26	28	28	26
High school graduate	35	31	28	25
Less than high school	12	10	8	7

Sources: Bureau of Labor Statistics; CEA calculations.

Improving Postsecondary Education and Skill Development

Postsecondary education and skill development are integral to the health of the U.S. economy. As shown in figure 11-16, an estimated 68 percent of all jobs require a postsecondary education, of which 42 percent require at least a bachelor's degree and an additional 26 percent require an associate degree or some form of higher education less than a bachelor's degree. In comparison, in 1992 only 53 percent of all jobs required a postsecondary education.

Wage premiums and job security often accompany education and skills attainment; however, the rising cost of college and increases in student loan balances erode the overall return that accompanies a college degree. Through the Higher Education Act of 1965, and subsequent reauthorizations since that time, the Federal Government has taken action to address the costs of higher education by subsidizing both students and educational institutions. Figure 11-17 shows the growth in the average level of student aid from Federal and other sources awarded to undergraduate students since 2010. As shown in figure 11-11 above, this took place during a time of stagnant productivity. Improved allocation of human capital investments could generate an increase in productivity and may be hindered due to distorted decisionmaking at higher education institutions.

Figure 11-17. Average Federal, State, Local, Institutional, or Other Sources of Grant Aid Awarded to Undergraduate Students, 2010–18

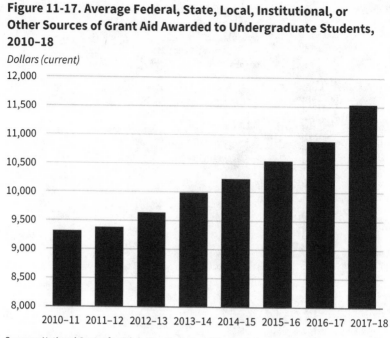

Sources: National Center for Education Statistics; CEA calculations.
Note: This includes four-year public and private nonprofit universities.

Federal regulatory reforms of higher education could better hold institutions accountable for the economic return that they provide to students, as well as assist students and families to make more informed decisions regarding their educational options. This section explains how this could be done by increasing incentives for schools to improve the economic return to students and by improving Federal support for educational programs that directly help more Americans secure well-paying jobs. This section also highlights the success of Historically Black Colleges and Universities (HBCUs) and illustrates the lessons of their experiences for the higher education system as a whole.

Increasing Incentives for Schools to Improve the Economic Gains of Students

Increased institutional accountability could improve the economic return to students. Investing in higher education generally provides substantial value for students and taxpayers. However, when an institution fails to deliver the type of high-quality education that enables students to repay their Federal student loans, this institution is not held responsible for losses. Instead, taxpayers are left to foot the bill. Institutions that lack a focus on generating positive value for their students exacerbate an increased rate of student loan default and stress throughout a student's career.

As currently configured, the credit risk associated with student loans is not efficiently distributed between all parties related to the transaction—that is, borrowers (students and parents), taxpayers, and the higher education institutions. The burden of repayment currently rests solely with the borrowers, who may face daunting loan payments if the expected education premium underdelivers, and with taxpayers, who foot the bill when the borrowers default or the loan is forgiven. Institutions of higher education bear none of the direct expenses of such failed outcomes and thus have limited incentive to assist students in optimizing educational skill development and career paths. The U.S. Department of Education (2020) provides useful institution-level data—such as annual costs, average earnings, and graduation rates—to help students avoid making poor investments in education. However, better accountability by the institutions themselves could further limit failed outcomes.

A reformed system could require postsecondary institutions that accept taxpayer funds to share in the financial responsibility associated with student loans. Such a risk-sharing arrangement could require postsecondary institutions to pay a small percentage of the value of the loans on which their former students have defaulted, or alternatively require institutions with worse repayment outcomes to pay fees. Such fees could be adjusted to account for variation in the composition of student intake so as to align institutions' interests with their students and incentivize them to improve repayment outcomes, but without disproportionately penalizing institutions serving higher-risk students.

There have been three major pieces of Federal legislation pertaining to risk-sharing on Federal student loans in recent years. A bipartisan bill, the Student Protection and Success Act, first introduced in 2015, would create a program where institutions are responsible for paying a percentage of the cohort nonrepayment balance, 2 percent in the 2019 version of the bill, for loans that had not paid down at least $1 of principal in three years. The legislation factors in the national unemployment rate and includes a list of exceptions for loans in deferment and mandatory forbearance. A Republican-sponsored bill, the PROSPER Act, introduced in 2017, would make changes to provisions for repayment of Federal student aid if a student withdraws from an institution of higher education, shifting 90 percent of the repayment responsibility to the institution (U.S. House of Representatives 2018). A Democratic-sponsored bill, the Protect Student Borrowers Act, first introduced in 2013, would require covered institutions to make risk-sharing payments on defaulted loans on a sliding scale based on the default rates of their students.

As shown in figure 11-18, education expenses have grown faster than inflation, with expenses for academic and institutional support (which includes expenses associated with noninstructional activities, such as admissions, student activities, libraries, administrative activities, and executive activities) growing faster than expenses for instruction and research. This trend may be driven by instances of mismanagement such as those uncovered in a 2017

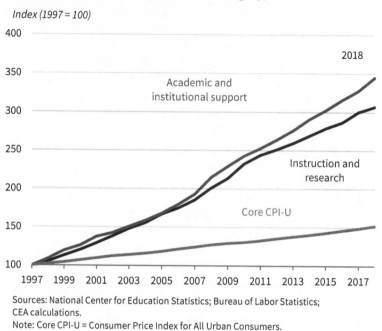

Figure 11-18. Growth in Four-Year Public and Private Universities' Expenses by Selected Category, 1997–2018

Index (1997 = 100)

2018

Academic and institutional support

Instruction and research

Core CPI-U

Sources: National Center for Education Statistics; Bureau of Labor Statistics; CEA calculations.
Note: Core CPI-U = Consumer Price Index for All Urban Consumers.

State audit of the University of California (2017). The audit found that the university's Office of the President had spent over $2 million on meeting and entertainment costs over five years and had awarded salaries and benefits to personnel far higher than salaries awarded for other comparable positions. As measured by the 2019–20 AAUP Faculty Compensation Survey, the salary for the average category I chief academic officer was $383,000, compared with $160,000 for a full-time professor.[8] The quantity of these hires has increased as well. Administrative hires increased 50 percent faster than classroom instructors between 2001 and 2011.

Improving Support for Educational Programs That Promote Skill Development

The Federal Government could also improve outcomes for students by better aligning education with the needs of today's workforce. The higher education system has been slow to adapt to the changing nature of work. In recent years, millions of jobs have remained unfilled, in part due to a lack of Americans with appropriate skills. Federal policy could better align higher education with the needs of today's workforce in multiple ways.

---

[8] This includes institutions that grant 30 or more doctoral-level degrees annually from at least three distinct programs. See AAUP (2020, n.d.).

Box 11-6. Historically Black Colleges and Universities

One example of higher education institutions delivering a high return for their students is that of Historically Black Colleges and Universities. HBCUs have played a crucial role in expanding educational opportunity for all students, especially for the African American students who make up 76 percent of their student populations. As of 2019, there were 101 accredited HBCUs across the United States. HBCUs enroll over 300,000 students, including around 80,000 non–African Americans (National Center for Education Statistics 2020). According to a 2017 economic impact report produced by the United Negro College Fund, HBCUs generated an employment contribution of 134,090 jobs, work-life earnings of $130 billion for HBCU students, and a total economic contribution to the U.S. economy of $14.8 billion.

HBCUs historically have served distinct student populations. HBCU students are largely low-income, first-generation-college students (nearly three in five students), and over a quarter of HBCUs are open admission. Open admission enrollment implies that all qualifying students (students with a high school degree or general education development certificate) are welcome to apply and enter the program without additional qualifications or performance benchmarks. This appeal to low- and moderate-income, first-generation students suggests that HBCUs have lower barriers to entry (e.g., costs of attendance, required test scores) than many comparable non-

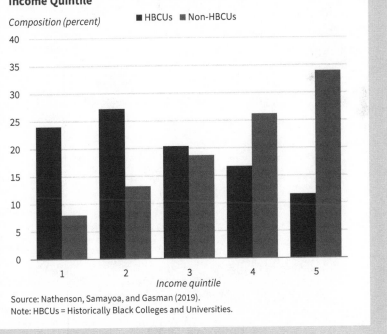

Figure 11-iv. Composition of Student Body Population by Income Quintile

Composition (percent) ■ HBCUs ■ Non-HBCUs

Income quintile

Source: Nathenson, Samayoa, and Gasman (2019).
Note: HBCUs = Historically Black Colleges and Universities.

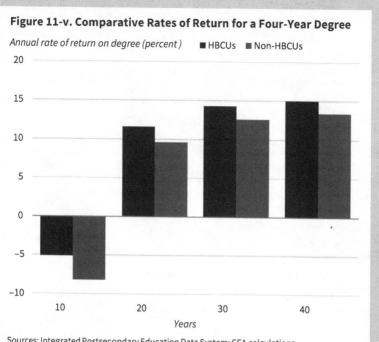

Figure 11-v. Comparative Rates of Return for a Four-Year Degree

Annual rate of return on degree (percent) ■ HBCUs ■ Non-HBCUs

Years

Sources: Integrated Postsecondary Education Data System; CEA calculations.
Note: Based on the most recent institution-level data as of June 1, 2020. HBCUs =
Historically Black Colleges and Universities.

HBCU institutions. HBCUs draw 24 percent of their student body's population from the lowest 20 percent of incomes. By this measure, HBCUs serve more economically disadvantaged populations than non-HBCU institutions, which are composed of only 8 percent of students in the bottom 20 percent.

Although HBCUs account for a mere 10 percent of the African American college student population, in 2014 they represented 17 percent of bachelor's degrees and 24 percent of STEM (science, technology, engineering, and mathematics) degrees earned by African Americans. From 2002 to 2011, the top eight institutions where African Americans earned PhDs in science and engineering were HBCUs.

Here, the CEA estimates the rates of return on an education from the HBCU system. The estimates use traditional approaches and are in keeping with the work of Mincer (1958), Schultz (1961), and Becker (1962) on differences in earnings across persons resulting from levels of human capital, accumulated primarily through education and training. Using institutional-level data obtained from the U.S. Department of Education's (2020) College Scorecard and the Federal Reserve's 2019 Survey of Consumer Finance, the CEA estimates the comparative rates of return over 40 years for graduates of four-year HBCUs and comparable non-HBCU institutions (figure 11-iv). Comparable institutions are located within the same commuting zone of at least one of these HBCUs and are of similar institutional selectivity, according to the Barron's Selectivity Index. The long-term rates of return for graduates receiving a college education at an HBCU are significantly positive and track those of graduates from a non-HBCU school. Short-term rates of return for students of HBCUs and non-HBCUs are significantly negative and vary largely to the extent that forgone income for non-HBCU graduates tends to be larger than it is for HBCU graduates. However, as time passes, both cohorts experience income growth and thus see an increase in their rates of return.

Although non-HBCU graduates initially benefit, on average, from higher incomes than do HBCU students, HBCU graduates tend on average to experience greater annual growth in income than non-HBCU graduates (figure 11-v). Thus, over the long run, alumni of HBCUs will tend to experience rates of return comparable to those for non-HBCU alumni. This shows that from a productivity standpoint, HBCUs can deliver comparable returns at a lower cost. HBCUs have a slightly lower level of earnings, which is attributable to the different student composition (e.g., the presence of first-generation students, and the selection of college majors). Figure 11-vi shows that graduates of HBCUs also track closely with graduates of non-HBCUs in cumulative earnings over time.

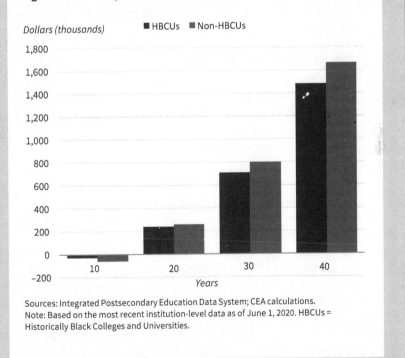

Figure 11-vi. Comparison of Real Cumulative Median Net Earnings

Dollars (thousands) ■ HBCUs ■ Non-HBCUs

Years

Sources: Integrated Postsecondary Education Data System; CEA calculations.
Note: Based on the most recent institution-level data as of June 1, 2020. HBCUs = Historically Black Colleges and Universities.

One approach would be for Congress to expand Pell Grant eligibility to include high-quality, short-term programs that provide students with a credential, certification, or license in a high-demand field and that demonstrate strong employment and earnings outcomes. Pell Grants are typically used to support students in traditional two- or four-year degree programs. Though some certificate programs are eligible for Pell Grants, programs must cover at least 15 weeks of instruction. Expanding support to shorter-term programs designed to teach skills specific to well-paying jobs could better meet the needs of students with near-term employment goals.

Federal program requirements could also encourage, rather than limit, partnerships between higher education providers and employers. Employers are most aware of the skills needed to succeed in the workplace. Congress could reform the Federal Work Study program to support workforce- and career-oriented opportunities for low-income undergraduate students. Work-based learning improves students' chances of developing important workplace skills, yet the Federal Work Study rules favor campus-based jobs.

Building on the successes of the National Council for the American Worker (NCAW) could promote multiple pathways to career success. Since January 2017, the NCAW has enrolled more than 750,000 apprentices; has modernized the Perkins Career and Technical Education Act to increase dual enrollment, work-based learning, and employer engagement; and has encouraged more than 400 companies to commit to providing 16 million employees with the training, reskilling, and career opportunities needed to increase productivity.

Improving the four-year degree to generate greater skill increases for students, as well as providing alternative paths for human capital accumulation, can avoid a one-size-fits-all approach that leaves individuals and groups behind. Apprenticeships, training programs, and four-year degrees are all paths to a more productive workforce and a higher quality of life for millions of Americans. Historically Black Colleges and Universities (HBCU) demonstrate how large gains from a high-quality education can be successfully provided to underserved groups (see box 11-6).

Conclusion

In this final chapter of the 2021 *Economic Report of the President*, the Council has identified various challenges for the American economy that not only were exacerbated by the pandemic, but also extend beyond the COVID-19 crisis into the postpandemic future. The policy ideas discussed here to potentially address these challenges can lead to a more resilient and prosperous economy for all Americans.

We have examined workers' connections to the labor force—relationships that COVID-19 strained and in millions of instances severed during the economic crisis—and how provisions of the tax code may discourage and disrupt these connections and their reconstitution. Reforming the provisions that disproportionately place the tax burden on second-earners and low-income earners could rebuild employees' relationships with their employers and therefore strengthen the current economic recovery.

In addition, we have discussed the importance of paid leave and childcare, not only in the context of the global health crisis, but also as a way to support a stronger workforce after the pandemic abates. These provisions have become especially relevant during the COVID-19 crisis as sick family members have required care at home and children have attended virtual school from home, creating barriers for working parents to return to their jobs. Although the Federal Government has passed temporary measures to mitigate the lack of access to paid leave and childcare during this crisis, this chapter demonstrates that permanent policies to provide such access would increase labor force participation and earnings beyond the current pandemic recession.

Furthermore, we have analyzed the effects of negotiating reciprocal trade agreements on consumers' and manufacturers' access to the international market and how deepening trade integration with like-minded U.S. allies can allow for future flexibility in negotiations and can assist the Nation in achieving its trade goals. In working to preserve America's economic interests on the world stage, the economy can achieve real gains from trade while protecting the economic security of American enterprise.

We have illustrated the strain COVID-19 has placed on the U.S. healthcare system in this *Report*. Historic financial relief from the Federal Government alleviated the worst of the crisis for hospitals and patients. Nevertheless, the COVID-19 pandemic has revealed persisting issues within the healthcare system that create distortions in the healthcare market. This chapter has examined how to increase the supply of healthcare and remove opaque pricing structures, which will provide patients and doctors alike with benefits.

We have also highlighted the Federal Government's role in participating in the creation and maintenance of a world-class infrastructure system. Fostering public-private partnerships to lower taxpayer costs, targeting funds to high-productivity areas such as ports, and reforming the country's ever-more-important digital infrastructure have all been explored in this chapter. Investing in infrastructure projects would not only increase the productivity of the American economy in and of itself, but would also have spillover benefits for all sectors of the economy.

Finally, we have showed that the American economy could support a more resilient workforce by shifting the U.S. immigration system toward a merit-based system for higher-skilled immigrants and by realigning the goals of higher education institutions to better equip students seeking nontraditional career paths. This would lead to increases in economic growth, wages, and tax revenue, and thus to prosperity for all Americans.

The policy reforms discussed in this chapter are designed to support the American economy and the American people long after the COVID-19 pandemic subsides. These policies would boost productivity for manufacturers, increase investment in workers, enhance labor force participation, and grow families' earnings. In accordance with its mandate to "recommend national economic policy to promote employment, production, and purchasing power under free competitive enterprise," the Council of Economic Advisers has used this chapter to analyze reforms that could provide substantial economic benefits for Americans in every walk of life. Solving the issues and challenges articulated in this chapter would aid in restoring the American economy to its prepandemic levels of prosperity and would offer a solid foundation upon which to build an even greater and more resilient economy for all Americans.

References

Chapter 1

Angrist, J., and A. Krueger. 1992, *Estimating the Payoff to Schooling Using the Vietnam-Era Draft Lottery*. NBER Working Paper 4067. Cambridge, MA: National Bureau of Economic Research.

Baqaee, D., and E. Farhi. 2020. *Nonlinear Production Networks with an Application to the COVID-19 Crisis*. CEPR Discussion Paper DP14742. London: Centre for Economic Policy Research.

BEA (Bureau of Economic Analysis). 2020. "Gross Domestic Product (Third Estimate), Corporate Profits (Revised), and GDP by Industry, Second Quarter 2020." https://www.bea.gov/news/2020/gross-domestic-product-third-estimate-corporate-profits-revised-and-gdp-industry-annual.

Bernanke, B., T. Geithner, and H. Paulson Jr., with J. Liang. 2020. *First Responders: Inside the U.S. Strategy for Fighting the 2007–2009 Global Financial Crisis*. New Haven, CT: Yale University Press.

Bhuller, M., M. Mogstad, and K. Salvanes. 2017. "Life-Cycle Earnings, Education Premiums, and Internal Rates of Return." *Journal of Labor Economics* 35, no 4: 993–1030.

Bhutta, N., J. Bricker, L. Dettling, J. Kelliher, and S. Laufer. 2019. *Stress Testing Household Debt*. Finance and Economics Discussion Series Working Paper 2019-008. Washington: Board of Governors of the Federal Reserve System.

BLS (Bureau of Labor Statistics). 2014. "Public Workforce Programs during the Great Recession." https://www.bls.gov/opub/mlr/2014/article/public-workforce-programs-during-the-greatrecession.htm.

Burns, A., D. van der Mensbrugghe, and H. Timmer. 2006. "Evaluating the Economic Consequences of Avian Influenza." World Bank. https://web.worldbank.org/archive/website01003/WEB/IMAGES/EVALUATI.PDF.

CDC (Centers for Disease Control and Prevention). 2020a. "First Travel-Related Case of 2019 Novel Coronavirus Detected in United States." https://www.cdc.gov/media/releases/2020/p0121-novel-coronavirus-travel-case.html.

———. 2020b. "CDC Confirms Possible Instance of Community Spread of COVID-19 in U.S." https://www.cdc.gov/media/releases/2020/s0226-Covid-19-spread.html.

———. 2020c. "Nonpharmaceutical Interventions (NPIs)." https://www.cdc.gov/nonpharmaceutical-interventions/index.html.

CEA (Council of Economic Advisers). 2019. *Economic Report of the President*. Washington: U.S. Government Publishing Office.

———. 2020a. *Economic Report of the President*. Washington: U.S. Government Publishing Office.

———. 2020b. "Evaluating the Effect of the Economic Response to COVID-19." https://www.whitehouse.gov/wp-content/uploads/2020/08/Evaluating-the-Effects-of-the-Economic-Response-to-COVID-19.pdf.

Cronin, C., and W. Evans. 2020. *Private Precaution and Public Restrictions: What Drives Social Distancing and Industry Foot Traffic in the COVID-19 Era?* NBER Working Paper 27531. Cambridge, MA: National Bureau of Economic Research.

Crouzet, N., and F. Gourio. 2020. "Financial Positions of U.S. Public Corporations: Part 1, Before the Pandemic." Federal Reserve Bank of Chicago.

Davis, M., W. Larson, S. Oliner, and B. Smith. 2019. *A Quarter Century of Mortgage Risk*. FHFA Working Paper 19-02. Washington: Federal Housing Finance Agency.

Dharmasankar, S., and B. Mazumder. 2016. "Have Borrowers Recovered from Foreclosures during the Great Recession?" *Chicago Fed Letter* 370: 1.

El-Sibaie, A., E. York, G. Watson, and T. LaJoie. 2020. "FAQ on Federal Coronavirus Relief Law (CARES Act)." Tax Foundation. https://taxfoundation.org/federal-coronavirus-relief-bill-caresact/#:~:text=Individuals%20with%20a%20Social%20Security,)%2C%20or%20%24112%2C500 %20(heads%20of.

Emsellem, M., and M. Evermore. 2020. "Understanding the Unemployment Provisions of the Families First Coronavirus Response Act." National Employment Law Project. https://www.nelp.org/publication/understanding-the-unemployment-provisions-of-thefamilies-first-coronavirus-response-act/.

Federal Reserve. 2020. "Financial Stability Report, May 2020." https://www.federalreserve.gov/publications/2020-may-financial-stability-report-purpose.htm.

Goger A., T. Loh, and C. George. 2020. "Unemployment Insurance Is Failing Workers during COVID-19. Here's How to Strengthen it." Brookings Institution. https://www.brookings.edu/research/unemployment-insurance-is-failing-workers-duringCOVID-19-heres-how-to-strengthen-it/.

Goolsbee, A., and C. Syverson. 2020. *Fear, Lockdown, and Diversion: Comparing Drivers of Pandemic Economic Decline 2020*. NBER Working Paper 27432. Cambridge, MA: National Bureau of Economic Research.

IMF (International Monetary Fund). 2019. *Global Financial Stability Report*. Washington: IMF. https://www.imf.org/en/Publications/GFSR/Issues/2019/03/27/Global-Financial-StabilityReport-April-2019.

———. 2020. *Global Financial Stability Report*. Washington: IMF. https://www.imf.org/en/Publications/GFSR/Issues/2020/04/14/Global-Financial-StabilityReport-April-2020-49020.

Jonas, O. 2013. "Pandemic Risk." Background paper, World Bank. https://www.worldbank.org/content/dam/Worldbank/document/HDN/Health/WDR14_bp_Pa ndemic_Risk_Jonas.pdf.

Kilbourne, E. 2006. "Influenza Pandemics of the 20th Century." *Emerging Infectious Diseases* 12, no. 1: 9–14.

Krueger, A. 1992. *Government Failures in Development*. NBER Working Paper 3340. Cambridge, MA: National Bureau of Economic Research.

LCD News. 2020. "U.S. Leveraged Loan Defaults Total $23B in Q2, the Most Since 2009." S&P Global, July 6.. https://www.spglobal.com/marketintelligence/en/news-insights/latest-newsheadlines/us-leveraged-loan-defaults-total-23b-in-q2-the-most-since-2009-59301227.

Marr, C., S. Jacoby, C. Huang, S. Hingtgen, A. Sherman, and J. Beltrán. 2020. "Future Stimulus Should Include Immigrants and Dependents Previously Left Out, Mandate Automatic Payments." Center on Budget and Policy Priorities. https://www.cbpp.org/research/economy/future-stimulus-should-include-immigrants-anddependents-previously-leftout.

McKibbin, W. 2009. "The Swine Flu Outbreak and Its Global Economic Impact." https://www.brookings.edu/on-the-record/the-swine-flu-outbreak-and-its-global-economicimpact/.

McKibbin, W., and A. Sidorenko. 2006. "Global Macroeconomic Consequences of Pandemic Influenza." Lowy Institute for International Policy. https://www.lowyinstitute.org/sites/default/files/pubfiles/McKibbin_Sidorenko%2C_Global_macroeconomic_1.pdf.

Nunn, R., and J. Shambaugh. 2020. "Whose Wages Are Rising and Why?" Brookings Institution. https://www.brookings.edu/policy2020/votervital/whose-wages-are-rising-and-why/.

Patel, A., D. Jernigan, and 2019-nCov CDC Response Team. 2020. "Initial Public Health Response and Interim Clinical Guidance for the 2019 Novel Coronavirus Outbreak—United States, December 31, 2019–February 4, 2020." *Morbidity and Mortality Weekly Report* 69, no. 5: 140–46.

Robertson, J. 2019. "Faster Wage Growth for the Lowest-Paid Workers." Federal Reserve Bank of Atlanta. https://www.frbatlanta.org/blogs/macroblog/2019/12/16/faster-wage-growth-for-the-lowest-paid-workers.

Tedeschi, E. 2020. "Pay Is Rising Fastest for Low Earners. One Reason? Minimum Wages." *New York Times*, January 1. https://www.nytimes.com/2020/01/03/upshot/minimum-wage-boost-bottom-earners.html.

Tung, I. 2020. "Minimum Wage Increases Reverse Post-Recession Wage Declines for Workers in Lowest-Paid Jobs." National Employment Law Project. https://www.nelp.org/publication/minimum-wage-increases-reverse-post-recession-wage-declines-workers-lowest-paid-jobs/.

Van Dam, A., and R. Siegel. 2020. "Minimum Wage Increases Fueling Faster Wage Growth for Those at the Bottom." *Washington Post*, January 2. https://www.washingtonpost.com/business/2020/01/02 /minimum-wage-increases-fueling-faster-wage-growth-those-bottom/.

Verikios, G., M. Sullivan, P. Stojanovski, J. Giesecke, and G. Woo. 2011. "The Global Economic Effects of Pandemic Influenza." https://static.rms.com/email/documents/liferisks/papers/the-globaleconomic-effects-of-pandemic-influenza.pdf.

White House. 2020a. "Proclamation on Suspension of Entry as Immigrants and Nonimmigrants of Persons who Pose a Risk of Transmitting 2019 Novel Coronavirus." https://www.whitehouse.gov/presidential-actions/proclamation-suspension-entry-immigrants-nonimmigrants-persons-pose-risk-transmitting-2019-novel-coronavirus/.

———. 2020b. "Proclamation: Suspension of Entry as Immigrants and Nonimmigrants of Certain Additional Persons Who Pose a Risk of Transmitting 2019 Novel Coronavirus." https://www.whitehouse.gov/presidential-actions/proclamation-suspension-entry-immigrants-nonimmigrants-certain-additional-persons-pose-risk-transmitting-2019-novel-coronavirus/.

———. 2020c. "Proclamation on Declaring a National Emergency Concerning the Novel Coronavirus Disease (COVID-19) Outbreak." https://www.whitehouse.gov/presidential-actions/proclamation-declaring-national-emergency-concerning-novel-coronavirus-disease-covid-19-outbreak/.

Chapter 2

Altonji, J., Z. Contractor, L. Finamor, R. Haygood, I. Lindenlaub, C. Meghir, C. O'Dea, D. Scott, L. Wang, and E. Washington. 2020. "Employment Effects of Unemployment Insurance Generosity during the Pandemic." Manuscript, Yale University, July 14.

Autor, D., D. Cho, L. Crane, M. Goldar, B. Lutz, J. Montes, W. Peterman, D. Ratner, D. Villar, and A. Yildirmaz. 2020. "An Evaluation of the Paycheck Protection Program Using Administrative Payroll Microdata." Working paper, Massachusetts Institute of Technology.

Baker, S., R. Farrokhnia, S. Meyer, M. Pagel, and C. Yannelis. 2020. *Income, Liquidity, and the Consumption Response to the 2020 Economic Stimulus Payments*. NBER Working Paper 27097. Cambridge, MA: National Bureau of Economic Research.

Bartik, A., M. Bertrand, F. Lin, J. Rothstein, and M. Unrath. 2020. *Measuring the Labor Market at the Onset of the COVID-19 Crisis*. NBER Working Paper 27613. Cambridge, MA: National Bureau of Economic Research.

CBO (Congressional Budget Office). 2020. "Interim Economic Projections for 2020 and 2021." https://www.cbo.gov/publication/56368#_idTextAnchor027.

CEA (Council of Economic Advisers). 2020. "Evaluating the Effects of the Economic Response to COVID-19." August. https://www.whitehouse.gov/wp-content/uploads/2020/08/Evaluating-the-Effects-of-the-Economic-Response-to-COVID-19.pdf.

Chetty R., J. Friedman, N. Hendren, M. Stepner, and Opportunity Insights Team. 2020. *How Did COVID-19 and Stabilization Policies Affect Spending and Employment? A New Real-Time Economic Tracker Based on Private Sector Data*. NBER Working Paper 27431. Cambridge, MA: National Bureau of Economic Research.

Federal Reserve Board of Governors. 2020a. "Net Worth by All Families." Survey of Consumer Finances, 1989–2019. https://www.federalreserve.gov/econres/scf/dataviz/scf/chart/#series:Net_Worth;demographic:all;population:all;units:median.

———. 2020b. "Net Worth by Percentile of Net Worth." Survey of Consumer Finances, 1989–2019. https://www.federalreserve.gov/econres/scf/dataviz/scf/chart/#series:Net_Worth;demographic:nwcat;population:1,2,3,4,5;units:mean.

———. 2020c. "Net Worth by Race or Ethnicity." Survey of Consumer Finances, 1989–2019. https://www.federalreserve.gov/econres/scf/dataviz/scf/chart/#series:Net_Worth;demographic:racecl4;population:all;units:median.

———. 2020d. "Primary Residence by All Families." Survey of Consumer Finances, 1989–2019. https://www.federalreserve.gov/econres/scf/dataviz/scf/chart/#series:Primary_Residence;demographic:all;population:1;units:have.

Forsythe, E., L. Kahn, F. Lange, and D. Wiczer. 2020. *Labor Demand in the Time of COVID-19: Evidence from Vacancy Postings and UI Claims*. NBER Working Paper 27061. Cambridge, MA: National Bureau of Economic Research.

Fox, Z., B. Yang, A. Sikander, and B. Scheid. 2020. "As Virus Crisis Persists, PPP recipients Lay Off Thousands." S&P Global Market Intelligence, July 30. https://www.spglobal.com/marketintelligence/en/news-insights/latest-news-headlines/as-virus-crisis-persists-ppp-recipients-lay-off-thousands-59602815.

Ganong, P., P. Noel, and J. Vavra. 2020. *U.S. Unemployment Insurance Replacement Rates During the Pandemic*. NBER Working Paper 27216. Cambridge, MA: National Bureau of Economic Research.

Goodspeed, T., and P. Navarro. 2020. "The White House Favors a Bridge to Recovery." *Wall Street Journal*, December 2. https://www.wsj.com/articles/the-white-house-favors-a-bridge-to-recovery-11606950989.

Granja, J., C. Makridis, C. Yannelis, and E. Zwick. 2020. *Did the Paycheck Protection Program Hit the Target?* NBER Working Paper 27095. Cambridge, MA: National Bureau of Economic Research.

Green, D. and E. Loualiche. 2020. *State and Local Government Employment in the COVID-19 Crisis*. HBS Working Paper 21-023. Cambridge, MA: Harvard Business School. https://papers.ssrn.com/sol3/papers.cfm?abstract_id=3651605.

Han, J., B. Meyer, and J. Sullivan. 2020. *Income and Poverty in the COVID-19 Pandemic.* NBER Working Paper 27729. Cambridge, MA: National Bureau of Economic Research. https://www.nber.org/papers/w27729.

Hepburn, P., R. Louis, and M. Desmond. 2020. "Eviction Tracking System: Version 1.0." Princeton University. www.evictionlab.org.

JCT (Joint Committee on Taxation). 2020. "Description of the Tax Provisions of Public Law 116-136, the Coronavirus Aid, Relief, and Economic Security ("CARES") Act." JCX-12R-20, April 23. https://www.jct.gov/publications/2020/jcx-12r-20/.

Marinescu, I., D. Skandalis, and D. Zhao. 2020. "Job Search, Job Posting and Unemployment Insurance During the COVID-19 Crisis." Working paper.

Meyer, B., and J. Sullivan. 2020. "Percent Below Federal Poverty Line or Multiple of the Federal Poverty Line, Basic Monthly CPS, January 2019 to Date." Near Real Time COVID-19 Income and Poverty Dashboard, Poverty Measurement. http://povertymeasurement.org/covid-19-poverty-dashboard/.

National Multifamily Housing Council. 2020. "NMHC Rent Payment Tracker Finds 79.4 Percent of Apartment Households Paid Rent as of October 6." https://www.nmhc.org/research-insight/nmhc-rent-payment-tracker/.

Parolin, Z., M. Curran, and C. Wimer. 2020. "The CARES Act and Poverty in the COVID-19 Crisis." *Poverty and Social Policy Brief* 4, no. 8.

Ruhle, S., L. Miranda, and M. Capetta. 2020. "PPP Likely Saved 35 Million Jobs, Says JPMorgan Chase CEO Jamie Dimon." NBC News, August 11. https://www.nbcnews.com/business/economy/ppp-likely-saved-35-million-jobs-says-jpmorgan-chase-ceo-n1236341.

White House. 2020a. "Executive Order on Fighting the Spread of COVID-19 by Providing Assistance to Renters and Homeowners." https://www.whitehouse.gov/presidential-actions/executive-order-fighting-spread-covid-19-providing-assistance-renters-homeowners/.

———. 2020b. "Memorandum on Authorizing the Other Needs Assistance Program for Major Disaster Declarations Related to Coronavirus Disease 2019." https://www.whitehouse.gov/presidential-actions/memorandum-authorizing-needs-assistance-program-major-disaster-declarations-related-coronavirus-disease-2019/.

———. 2020c. "Memorandum on Continued Student Loan Payment Relief During the COVID-19 Pandemic." https://www.whitehouse.gov/presidential-actions/memorandum-continued-student-loan-payment-relief-covid-19-pandemic/.

———. 2020d. "Memorandum on Deferring Payroll Tax Obligations in Light of the Ongoing COVID-19 Disaster." https://www.whitehouse.gov/presidential-actions/memorandum-deferring-payroll-tax-obligations-light-ongoing-covid-19-disaster/.

Chapter 3

Autor, D., D. Cho, L. Crane, M. Goldar, B. Lutz, J. Montes, W. Peterman, D. Ratner, D. Villar, and A. Yildirmaz. 2020. "An Evaluation of the Paycheck Protection Program Using Administrative Payroll Microdata." Working paper, Massachusetts Institute of Technology.

Baker, S., R. Farrokhnia, S. Meyer, M. Pagel, and C. Yannelis. 2020. *Income Liquidity, and the Consumption Response to the 2020 Economic Stimulus Payments.* NBER Working Paper 29097. Cambridge, MA: National Bureau of Economic Research.

Bartik, A., Z. Cullen, E. Glaeser, M. Luca, C. Stanton, and A. Sunderam. 2020. *The Targeting and Impact of Paycheck Protection Program Loans to Small Businesses.* NBER Working Paper 27623. Cambridge, MA: National Bureau of Economic Research.

Chetty, R., J. Friedman, N. Hendren, and M. Stepner. 2020. *How Did COVID-19 and Stabilization Policies Affect Spending and Employment? A New Real-Time Economic Tracker Based on Private Sector Data.* Working Paper 2020-05. Cambridge, MA: Opportunity Insights.

Cox, J., D. Greenwald, and S. Ludvigson. 2020. *What Explains the COVID-19 Stock Market?* NBER Working Paper 27784. Cambridge, MA: National Bureau of Economic Research.

Crane, L., R. Decker, A. Flaaen, A. Hamins-Puertolas, and C. Kurz. 2020. *Business Exit during the COVID-19 Pandemic: Non-Traditional Measures in Historical Context.* Finance and Economics Discussion Series Working Paper 2020-089. Washington: Board of Governors of the Federal Reserve System.

Elenev, V., T. Landvoigt, and S. Van Nieuwerburgh. 2020. *Can the Covid Bailouts Save the Economy?* NBER Working Paper 27207. Cambridge, MA: National Bureau of Economic Research.

Federal Reserve. 2020. "Financial Stability Report—May 2020." Washington: Board of Governors of the Federal Reserve System. https://www.federalreserve.gov/publications/files/financial-stability-report-20200515.pdf.

Fox, Z., B. Yung, A. Sikander, and B. Scheid. 2020. "As Virus Crisis Persists, PPP Recipients Lay Off Thousands." S&P Global Market Intelligence, July 30. https://www.spglobal.com/marketintelligence/en/news-insights/latest-news-headlines/as-virus-crisis-persists-ppp-recipients-lay-off-thousands-59602815.

Granja, J, C. Makridis, C. Yannelis, and E. Zwick. 2020. *Did the Paycheck Protection Program Hit the Target?* NBER Working Paper 27095. Cambridge, MA: National Bureau of Economic Research.

Gilchrist, S., B. Wei, V. Yue, and E. Zakrajsek. 2020. *The Fed Takes on Corporate Credit Risk: An Analysis of the Efficacy of the SMCCF.* NBER Working Paper 27809. Cambridge, MA: National Bureau of Economic Research.

Haddad, V., A. Moreira, and T. Muir. 2020. *When Selling Becomes Viral: Disruptions in Debt Markets in the COVID-19 Crisis and the Fed's Response*. NBER Working Paper 27168. Cambridge, MA: National Bureau of Economic Research.

Hamilton, S. 2020. "From Survival to Revival: How to Help Small Businesses through the COVID-19 Crisis." Hamilton Project. https://www.hamiltonproject.org/assets/files/PP_Hamilton_Final.pdf.

Keshner, A. 2020. "Coronavirus Has Rocked America's Economy—and It's Had a Surprising Effect on Bankruptcy Filings." MarketWatch, May 6. https://www.marketwatch.com/story/the-coronavirus-has-rocked-americas-economy-but-its-had-a-surprising-effect-on-bankruptcy-filings-2020-05-05.

Li, L., P. Strahan, and S. Zhang. 2020. *Banks as Lenders of First Resort: Evidence from the COVID-19 Crisis*. NBER Working Paper 27256. Cambridge, MA: National Bureau of Economic Research.

Ruhle, S., L. Miranda, and M. Cappetta. 2020. "PPP Likely Saved 35 Million Jobs, Says JPMorgan Chase CEO Jamie Dimon." NBC News, August 11. https://www.nbcnews.com/business/economy/ppp-likely-saved-35-million-jobs-says-jpmorgan-chase-ceo-n1236341.

Tett, G. 2020. "Swamped Bankruptcy Courts Threaten U.S. Recovery." *Financial Times*, May 14. https://www.ft.com/content/14b07c0e-95e3-11ea-af4b-499244625ac4.

Chapter 4

André, F. 2002. "How the Research-Based Industry Approaches Vaccine Development and Establishes Priorities." *Developmental Biology* 110: 25–29.

Berndt, E., I. Cockburn, and Z. Griliches. 1996. "Pharmaceutical Innovations and Market Dynamics: Tracking Effects on Price Indices for Antidepressant Drugs." *Brookings Papers on Economic Activity, Microeconomics*, no. 2: 133–99. https://www.brookings.edu/wp-content/uploads/1996/01/1996_bpeamicro_berndt.pdf.

Bestsennyy, O., G. Gilbert, A. Harris, and J. Rost. 2020. "Telehealth: A Quarter-Trillion-Dollar Post COVID-19 Reality?" McKinsey & Company. https://www.mckinsey.com/industries/healthcare-systems-and-services/our-insights/telehealth-a-quarter-trillion-dollar-post-covid-19-reality.

Bynum, A., C. Irwin, C. Cranford, and G. Denny. 2003. "The Impact of Telemedicine on Patients' Cost Savings: Some Preliminary Findings." *Telemedicine Journal and e-Health* 9 no. 4: 361–67. https://doi.org/10.1089/153056203772744680.

Caves, R., M. Whinston, and M. Hurwitz. 1991. "Patent Expiration, Entry, and Competition in the U.S. Pharmaceutical Industry." *Brookings Papers on Economic Activity, Microeconomics*, no. 1: 1–66. https://www.brookings.edu/wp-content/uploads/1991/01/1991_bpeamicro_caves.pdf.

CBO (Congressional Budget Office). 2006. "Research and Development in the Pharmaceutical Industry." https://www.cbo.gov/sites/default/files/109th-congress-2005-2006/reports/10-02-drugr-d.pdf.

———. 2020. "Federal Subsidies for Health Insurance Coverage for People Under 65: 2020 to 2030." https://www.cbo.gov/publication/56650.

CEA (Council of Economic Advisers). 2019. "Mitigating the Impact of a Pandemic Influenza through Vaccine Innovation." https://www.whitehouse.gov/wp-content/uploads/2019/09/Mitigating-the-Impact-of-Pandemic-Influenza-through-Vaccine-Innovation.pdf.

Chauhan, V., S. Galwankar, B. Arquilla, M. Garg, S. Di Somma, A. El-Menyar, V. Krishnan, J. Gerber, R. Holland, and S. Stawicki. 2020. "Novel Coronavirus (COVID-19): Leveraging Telemedicine to Optimize Care While Minimizing Exposures and Viral Transmission." *Journal of Emergencies, Trauma, and Shock* 13, no. 1: 20–24. https://doi.org/10.4103/JETS.JETS_32_20.

DiMasi, J., H. Grabowski, and R. Hansen. 2016. "Innovation in the Pharmaceutical industry: New Estimates of R&D Costs." *Journal of Health Economics* 47: 20–33. https://www.sciencedirect.com/science/article/abs/pii/S0167629616000291.

FDA (U.S. Food and Drug Administration). 2020. "In Vitro Diagnostic EUAs." https://www.fda.gov/medical-devices/coronavirus-disease-2019-covid-19-emergency-use-authorizations-medical-devices/vitro-diagnostics-euas.

Garfield, R., G. Claxton, A. Damico, and L. Levitt. 2020. "Eligibility for ACA Health Coverage Following Job Loss." Kaiser Family Foundation. https://www.kff.org/coronavirus-covid-19/issue-brief/eligibility-for-aca-health-coverage-following-job-loss/.

Grabowski, H., and J. Vernon. 1992. "Brand Loyalty, Entry, and Price Competition in Pharmaceuticals after the 1984 Drug Act." *Journal of Law and Economics* 32: 331–50. https://www.jstor.org/stable/725543.

Grady, C., S. Shah, F. Miller, M. Danis, M. Nicolini, J. Ochoa, Holly T., Dave W., and A. Rid. 2020. "So Much at Stake: Ethical Tradeoffs in Accelerating SARSCoV-2 Vaccine Development." *Vaccine* 8, no. 41: 6381–87. https://doi.org/10.1016/j.vaccine.2020.08.017.

Ivanov, A. 2013. "Barriers to the Introduction of New Medical Diagnostic Tests." *Laboratory Medicine* 44, no. 4: e132–e136. https://doi.org/10.1309/LMMHGYKY7LIUEEQ6.

Kennedy, J. 2018. "How to Ensure That America's Life-Sciences Sector Remains Globally Competitive." Information Technology and Innovation Foundation. https://itif.org/publications/2018/03/26/how-ensure-americas-life-sciences-sector-remains-globally-competitive.

Kleiner, M., A. Marier, K. Park, and C. Wing. 2016. "Relaxing Occupational Licensing Requirements: Analyzing Wages and Prices for a Medical Service." *Journal of Law and Economics* 59, no. 2. https://doi.org/10.1086/688093.

Lenz, E., M. Mundinger, R. Kane, S. Hopkins, and S. Lin. 2004. "Primary Care Outcomes in Patients Treated by Nurse Practitioners or Physicians: Two Year Follow Up." *Medical Care Research and Review* 61, no. 3: 332–51. https://journals.sagepub.com/doi/abs/10.1177/1077558704266821.

Lichtenberg, F. 2014. "The Impact of Pharmaceutical Innovation on Disability Days and the Use of Medical Services in the United States, 1997–2010." *Journal of Human Capital* 8, no. 4: 432–80. https://www.jstor.org/stable/10.1086/679110.

Mann, D., J. Chen, R. Chunara, P. Testa, and O. Nov. 2020. "COVID-19 Transforms Health Care through Telemedicine: Evidence from the Field." Journal of the American Medical Informatics Association 27, no. 7: 1132–35. https://doi.org/10.1093/jamia/ocaa072.

Martin-Misener, R., P. Harbman, F. Donald, K. Reid, K. Kilpatrick, N. Carter, D. Bryant-Lukosius, et al. 2015. "Cost-Effectiveness of Nurse Practitioners in Primary and Specialized Ambulatory Care: Systematic Review." BMJ Open. https://bmjopen.bmj.com/content/5/6/e007167.

Milken Institute. 2020. "COVID 19 Tracker." https://airtable.com/shrSAi6t5WFwqo3GM/tblEzPQS5fnc0FHYR/viweyymxOAtNvo7yH.

Mullard, A. 2020. "COVID-19 Vaccine Development Pipeline Gears Up." *The Lancet* 395, no. 10239: 1751–52. https://doi.org/10.1016/S0140-6736(20)31252-6.

Mundinger, M., R. Kane, E. Lenz, A. Totten, W. Tsai, P. Cleary, W. Friedewald, A. Siu, and M. Shelanski. 2000. "Primary Care Outcomes in Patients Treated by Nurse Practitioners or Physicians: A Randomized Trial." JAMA 283, no. 1: 59–68. https://doi.org/10.1001/jama.283.1.59.

Oliver, G., L. Pennington, S. Revelle, and M. Rantz. 2014. "Impact of Nurse Practitioners on Health Outcomes of Medicare and Medicaid Patients." *Nursing Outlook 62,* no. 6: 440-447. https://www.sciencedirect.com/science/article/abs/pii/S002965541400150X.

Ortiz, J., R. Hofler, A. Bushy, Y. Lin, A. Khanijahani, and A. Bitney. 2018. "Impact of Nurse Practitioner Practice Regulations on Rural Population Health Outcomes." *Healthcare* 6, no. 2: 65. https://doi.org/10.3390/healthcare6020065.

Perloff, J., S. Clarke, C. DesRoches, M. O'Reilly-Jacob, and P. Buerhaus. 2017. "Association of State-Level Restrictions in Nurse Practitioner Scope of Practice with the Quality of Primary Care Provided to Medicare Beneficiaries." *Medical Care Research and Review* 76, no. 5: 597–626. https://doi.org/10.1177/1077558717732402.

Philipson, T., E. Berndt, A. Gottschalk, and E. Sun. 2008. "Cost-Benefit Analysis of the FDA: The Case of the Prescription Drug User Fee Acts." *Journal of Public Economics* 92, nos. 5–6: 1306–25. https://doi.org/10.1016/j.jpubeco.2007.09.010.

Philipson, T., and A. Jena. 2006. "Who Benefits from New Medical Technologies? Estimates of Consumer and Producer Surpluses for HIV/AIDS Drugs." *Forum for Health Economics & Policy* 9, no. 2. https://doi.org/10.3386/w11810.

Philipson, T., E. Sun, D. Goldman, and A. Jena. 2012. "A Reexamination of the Costs of Medical R&D Regulation." *Forum for Health Economics & Policy* 15, no. 3: 132–159. https://doi.org/10.1515/fhep-2012-0020.

Plotkin, S., J. Robinson, G. Cunningham, R. Iqbal, and S. Larsen. 2017. "The Complexity and Cost of Vaccine Manufacturing: An Overview." *Vaccine* 35, no. 33: 4064–71. https://www.ncbi.nlm.nih.gov/pmc/articles/PMC5518734/.

Poghosyan, L., E. Timmons, C. Abraham, and G. Martsolf. 2019. "The Economic Impact of Nurse Practitioner Scope of Practice for Medicaid." *Journal of Nursing Regulation* 10, no. 1: 15–20. https://doi.org/10.1016/S2155-8256(19)30078-X.

Pronker, E., T. Weenen, H. Commandeur, E. Claassen, and A. Osterhaus. 2013. "Risk in Vaccine Research and Development Quantified." Plos One 8, no. 3: e57755. https://doi.org/10.1371/journal.pone.0057755.

Qureshi, Z., E. Seoane-Vazquez, R. Rodriguez-Monguio, K. Stevenson, and S. Szeinbach. 2011. "Market Withdrawal of New Molecular Entities Approved in the United States from 1980 to 2009." *Pharmacoepidemiology and Drug Safety* 20, no. 7: 772–77. https://doi.org/10.1002/pds.2155.

Roebuck, M., J. Liberman, M. Gemmill-Toyama, and T. Brennan. 2011. "Medication Adherence Leads to Lower Health Care Use and Costs Despite Increased Drug Spending." *Health Affairs* 30, no. 1. https://doi.org/10.1377.hlthaff.2009.1087.

Rosenblatt, R., and L. Hart. 2000. "Physicians and Rural America." *West Journal of Medicine* 173, no. 5: 348–51. https://doi.org/10.1136/ewjm.173.5.348.

Shi, L., and M. Samuels. 1997. "Practice Environment and the Employment of Nurse Practitioners, Physician Assistants, and Certified Nurse Midwives by Community Health Centers." *Journal of Allied Health* 26, no. 3: 105–11. PMID: 9358300. https://pubmed.ncbi.nlm.nih.gov/9358300/.

Spetz, J., S. Parente, R. Town, and D. Bazarko. 2013. "Scope-of-Practice Laws Far Nurse Practitioners Limit Cost Savings That Can Be Achieved in Retail Clinics." *Health Affairs* 32, no. 11. https://www.healthaffairs.org/doi/full/10.1377/hlthaff.2013.0544.

Spoont, M., N. Greer, J. Su, P. Fitzgerald, I. Rutks, and T. Wilt. 2011. *Rural vs. Urban Ambulatory Health Care: A Systematic Review*. Washington: U.S. Department of Veterans Affairs. https://www.ncbi.nlm.nih.gov/books/NBK56147/.

Stanik-Hutt, J., R. Newhouse, K. White, M. Johantgen, E. Bass, G. Zangaro, R. Wilson, et al. 2013. "The Quality and Effectiveness of Care Provided by Nurse Practitioners." *Journal of Nurse Practitioners* 9, no. 8: 492–500. https://doi.org/10.1016/j.nurpra.2013.07.004.

Verma, S. 2020. "Early Impact of CMS Expansion of Medicare Telehealth during COVID-19." Health Affairs Blog. https://www.healthaffairs.org/do/10.1377/hblog20200715.454789/full/.

Chapter 5

Abravanel, M., N. Pindus, B. Theodos, K. Bertumen, R. Brash, and Z. McDade. 2013. "New Markets Tax Credit NNMTC Program Evaluation Final Report." Urban Institute. https://www.urban.org/sites/default/files/publication/24211/412958-New-Markets-Tax-Credit-NMTC-Program-Evaluation.PDF.

Arefeva, A., M. Davis, A. Ghent, and M. Park. 2020. "Job Growth from Opportunity Zones." Working paper.

Bauguess, S., R. Gullapalli, and V. Ivanov. 2018. "Capital Raising in the U.S.: An Analysis of the Market for Unregistered Securities Offerings, 2009-2017." Securities Exchange Commission White Paper. https://www.sec.gov/files/DERA%20white%20paper_Regulation%20D_082018.pdf.

Bernstein, J., and K. Hassett. 2015. "Unlocking Private Capital to Facilitate Economic Growth in Distressed Areas." Economic Innovation Group. https://eig.org/wp-content/uploads/2015/04/Unlocking-Private-Capital-to-Facilitate-Growth.pdf.

Bloom, D., and C. Michalopoulos. 2001. "How Welfare and Work Policies Affect Employment and Income: A Synthesis of Research." MDRC. https://www.mdrc.org/publication/how-welfare-and-work-policies-affect-employment-and-income.

Brummet, Q., and D. Reed. 2019. *The Effects of Gentrification on the Well-Being and Opportunity of Original Resident Adults and Children*. Working Paper WP 19-30. Philadelphia: Federal Reserve Bank of Philadelphia. https://www.philadelphiafed.org/-/media/research-and-data/publications/working-papers/2019/wp19-30.pdf.

Busso, M., J. Gregory, and P. Kline. 2013. "Assessing the Incidence and Efficiency of a Prominent Place Based Policy." *American Economic Review* 103, no. 2: 897–947.

CEA (Council of Economic Advisers). 2017. "The Growth Effects of Corporate Tax Reform and Implications for Wages." https://www.whitehouse.gov/sites/whitehouse.gov/files/images/Corporate%20Tax%20Reform%20and%20Growth%20Final.pdf.

———. 2019. *Economic Report of the President*. https://www.whitehouse.gov/wp-content/uploads/2019/03/ERP-2019.pdf.

Chen, J., E. Glaeser, and D. Wessel. 2019. *The (Non-)Effect of Opportunity Zones on Housing Prices*. NBER Working Paper 26587. Cambridge, MA: National Bureau of Economic Research.

CRS (Congressional Research Service). 2011. "Empowerment Zones, Enterprise Communities, and Renewal Communities: Comparative Overview and Analysis." https://www.everycrsreport.com/files/20110214_R41639_b18ae5bf0fbe93505d7b6c2b13b744b76124b9ed.pdf.

Dahlby, B. 2008. *The Marginal Cost of Public Funds: Theory and Applications*. Cambridge, MA: MIT Press.

Dragan, K., Ellen, I. and S. Glied. 2019. *Does Gentrification Displace Poor Children? New Evidence from New York City Medicaid Data*. NBER Working Paper 25809. Cambridge, MA: National Bureau of Economic Research.

Freedman, M. 2012. "Teaching New Markets Old Tricks: The Effects of Subsidized Investment on Low-Income Neighborhoods." *Journal of Public Economics* 96, nos. 11–12: 1000–1014.

Gamper-Rabindran, S., and C. Timmins. 2013. "Does Cleanup of Hazardous Waste Sites Raise Housing Values? Evidence of Spatially Localized Benefits." *Journal of Environmental Economics and Management* 65, no. 3: 345–60.

GAO (Government Accountability Office). 2014. "New Market Tax Credit." GAO-14-500. https://www.gao.gov/assets/670/664717.pdf.

Grainger, C. 2012. "The Distributional Effects of Pollution Regulations: Do Renters Fully Pay for Cleaner Air?" *Journal of Public Economics* 96, nos. 9–10: 840–52.

Ham, J., C. Swenson, A. Imrohoroglu, and H. Song. 2011. "Government Programs Can Improve Local Labor Markets: Evidence from State Enterprise Zones, Federal Empowerment Zones and Federal Enterprise Community." *Journal of Public Economics* 95, no. 7: 779–97.

Harger, K., and A. Ross. 2016. "Do Capital Tax Incentives Attract New Businesses? Evidence Across Industries from the New Markets Tax Credit." *Journal of Regional Science* 56, no. 5: 733–53.

Harger, K., A. Ross, and H. Stephens. 2019. "What Matters the Most For Economic Development? Evidence from the Community Development Financial Institutions Fund." *Papers in Regional Science* 98, no. 2: 883–904.

Hoynes, H., and D. Schanzenbach. 2012. "Work Incentives and the Food Stamp Program." *Journal of Public Economics* 96, nos. 1–2: 151–62.

Hula, R., and M. Jordan. 2018. "Private Investment and Public Redevelopment: The Case of New Markets Tax Credits." *Poverty & Public Policy* 10 no. 1: 11–38.

Jacob, B., and J. Ludwig. 2012. "The Effects of Housing Assistance on Labor Supply: Evidence from a Voucher Lottery." *American Economic Review* 102, no. 1: 272–304.

Koby, Y., and K. Wolf. 2019. "Aggregation in Heterogeneous-Firm Models: Theory and Measurement." https://scholar.princeton.edu/sites/default/files/ckwolf/files/hetfirms_agg.pdf.

Lowry, S., and D. Marples. 2019. "Tax Incentives for Opportunity Zones: In Brief." *Congressional Research Service*, R45152.

Markusen, A., and A. Glasmeier, 2008. "Overhauling and Revitalizing Federal Economic Development Programs." *Economic Development Quarterly* 22, no. 2: 83–91.

Nichols, A., and Rothstein, J., 2015. "The Earned Income Tax Credit." In *Economics of Means-Tested Transfer Programs in the United States, Volume 1*. Chicago: University of Chicago Press.

Ohrn, E. 2019. "The Effect of Tax Incentives on U.S. Manufacturing: Evidence from State Accelerated Depreciation Policies." *Journal of Public Economics* 180, article 104804.

Sage, A., M. Langen, and A. Van de Minne. 2019. "Where Is the Opportunity in Opportunity Zones? Early Indicators of the Opportunity Zone Program's Impact on Commercial Property Prices." http://dx.doi.org/10.2139/ssrn.3385502.

Tax Policy Center. 2020. "What Is the New Market Tax Credit, and How Does It Work?" https://www.taxpolicycenter.org/briefing-book/what-new-markets-tax-credit-and-how-does-it-work.

Theodos, B., C. Stacy, and H. Ho. 2017. "Taking Stock of the Community Development Block Grant." Urban Institute. http://www.urban.org/sites/default/files/publication/89551/cdbg_brief.pdf.

Vardell, R. 2019. "The Land of Opportunity Zones: Deferring Taxable Capital Gains Through Investments in Low-Income Communities." *Missouri Law Review* 84, no 3: article 13.

Chapter 6

Anderson, S., and J. Sallee. 2011. "Using Loopholes to Reveal the Marginal Cost of Regulation: The Case of Fuel-Economy Standards." *American Economic Review* 101, no. 4: 1375–1409.

Berry, S., J. Levinsohn, and A. Pakes. 2004. "Differentiated Products Demand Systems from a Combination of Micro and Macro Data: The New Car Market." *Journal of Political Economy* 112, no. 1 (2004): 68–105.

Bento, A., M. Freedman, and C. Lang. 2015. "Who Benefits from Environmental Regulation? Evidence from the Clean Air Act Amendments." *Review of Economics and Statistics* 97, no. 3: 610–22.

Bento, A., et al. 2018. "Flawed Analyses of U.S. Auto Fuel Economy Standards." *Science Magazine* 362, no. 6419: 1119–21.

CEA (Council of Economic Advisers). 2019. "The Economic Effects of Federal Deregulation since January 2017: An Interim Report." https://www.whitehouse.gov/wp-content/uploads/2019/06/The-Economic-Effects-of-Federal-Deregulation-Interim-Report.pdf.

———. 2020. *Economic Report of the President*. Washington: U.S. Government Publishing Office.

Chambers, D., C. Collins, and A. Krause. 2019. "How Do Federal Regulations Affect Consumer Prices? An Analysis of the Regressive Effects of Regulation." *Public Choice* 180, no. 1: 57–90.

Coffey, B., P. McLaughlin, and P. Peretto. 2020. "The Cumulative Cost of Regulations." *Review of Economic Dynamics* 38: 1–21.

Crain, M., and N. Crain. 2014. "The Cost of Federal Regulation to the U.S. Economy, Manufacturing and Small Business." National Association of Manufacturers.

Crews, W. 2017. "Mapping Washington's Lawlessness; An Inventory of Regulatory Dark Matter." Competitive Enterprise Institute. https://cei.org/sites/default/files/Wayne%20Crews%20-%20Mapping%20Washington%27s%20Lawlessness%202017.pdf.

———. 2020. "The E.O. 13891 Guidance Document Portal: An Exercise in Utility." https://cei.org/blog/eo-13891-guidance-document-portal-exercise-utility.

Duclos, J. 2008 "Horizontal and Vertical Equity." In *The New Palgrave Dictionary of Economics.* https://link.springer.com/referenceworkentry/10.1057%2F978-1-349-95121-5_1961-1.

Dynan, K., J. Skinner, and S. Zeldes. 2004. "Do the Rich Save More?" *Journal of Political Economy* 112, no. 2: 397–444.

EPA (Environmental Protection Agency). 2016. "Proposed Determination on the Appropriateness of the Model Year 2022–2025 Light-Duty Vehicle Greenhouse Gas Emissions Standards under the Midterm Evaluation: Technical Support Document." https://nepis.epa.gov/Exe/ZyPDF.cgi?Dockey=P100Q3L4.pdf.

———. 2019. "The 2018 EPA Automotive Trends Report: Greenhouse Gas Emissions, Fuel Economy, and Technology since 1975." https://nepis.epa.gov/Exe/ZyPDF.cgi/P100W5C2.PDF?Dockey=P100W5C2.PDF.

EPA/DOT (U.S. Environmental Protection Agency / U.S. Department of Transportation). 2012. "Final Rulemaking for 2017–2025 Light-Duty Vehicle Greenhouse Gas Emission Standards and Corporate Average Fuel Economy Standards." https://nepis.epa.gov/Exe/ZyPDF.cgi/P100EZI1.PDF?Dockey=P100EZI1.PDF.

———. 2018. "The Safer Affordable Fuel-Efficient (SAFE) Vehicles Rule for Model Years 2021–2026 Passenger Cars and Light Trucks." Preliminary Regulatory Impact Analysis. https://www.nhtsa.gov/sites/nhtsa.dot.gov/files/documents/ld_cafe_my2021-26_pria_0.pdf.

———. 2020. "The Safer Affordable Fuel-Efficient (SAFE) Vehicles Rule for Model Years 2021–2026 Passenger Cars and Light Trucks." Final Regulatory Impact Analysis. https://www.nhtsa.gov/sites/nhtsa.dot.gov/files/documents/final_safe_fria_web_version_200701.pdf.

Figueroa, E., and S. Waxman. 2017. "Which States Tax the Sale of Food for Home Consumption in 2017?" Center on Budget and Policy Priorities. http://www.cbpp.org/research/state-budget-and-tax/which-states-tax-the-sale-of-food-for-home-consumption-in-2017.

Forbes. 2017. "Tesla's Lucrative ZEV Credits May Not Be Sustainable." https://www.forbes.com/sites/greatspeculations/2017/09/01/teslas-lucrative-zev-credits-may-not-be-sustainable/?sh=16b653416ed5.

Garicano, L., C. LeLarge, and J. Van Reenen. 2016. "Firm Size Distortions and the Productivity Distribution: Evidence from France." *American Economic Review* 106, no. 11: 3439–79.

Jacobsen, M. 2013. "Evaluating U.S. Fuel Economy Standards in a Model with Producer and Household Heterogeneity." *American Economic Journal: Economic Policy* 5, no. 2: 148–87.

Leard, B., and V. McConnell. 2017. "New Markets for Credit Trading under U.S. Automobile Greenhouse Gas and Fuel Economy Standards." *Review of Environmental Economics and Policy* 11, no. 2: 207–26.

Levinson, A. 2019. "Energy Efficiency Standards Are More Regressive Than Energy Taxes: Theory and Evidence." *Journal of the Association of Environmental and Resource Economists* 6, no. S1: S7–S36.

Mulligan, C., and T. Philipson. 2000. *Merit Motives and Government Intervention: Public Finance in Reverse.* NBER Working Paper 7698. Cambridge, MA: National Bureau of Economic Research.

Stigler, G. 1971. "The Theory of Economic Regulation." *Bell Journal of Economics and Management Science* 2, no. 1: 3–21.

Thomas, D. 2012. *Regressive Effects of Regulation.* Arlington, VA: Mercatus Center at George Mason University.

Chapter 7

Abdulkadiroğlu, A., P. Pathak, A. Roth, and T. Sönmez. 2006. *Changing the Boston School Choice Mechanism.* NBER Working Paper 11965. Cambridge, MA: National Bureau of Economic Research.

Abdulkadiroğlu, A., P. Pathak, and C. Walters. 2018. "Free to Choose: Can School Choice Reduce Student Achievement?" *American Economic Journal: Applied Economics* 10, no. 1: 175–206.

Anderson, K. 2017. "Evidence on Charter School Practices Related to Student Enrollment and Retention." *Journal of School Choice* 11, no. 4: 527–45.

Angrist, J., S. Cohodes, S. Dynarski, P. Pathak, and C. Walters. 2016. "Stand and Deliver: Effects of Boston's Charter High Schools on College Preparation, Entry, and Choice." *Journal of Labor Economics* 34, no. 2.

Ayscue, J., R. Levy, G. Siegel-Hawley, and B. Woodward. 2015. "Choices Worth Making: Creating, Sustaining, and Expanding Diverse Magnet Schools." Civil Rights Project / Proyecto Derechos Civiles.

Baude, P., M. Casey, E. Hanushek, G. Phelan, and S. Rivkin. 2020. "The Evolution of Charter School Quality." *Economica* 87, no. 345: 158–89.

Bifulco, R., and R. Reback. 2014. "Fiscal Impacts of Charter Schools: Lessons from New York." *Education Finance and Policy* 9, no. 1: 86–107.

Booker, K., T. Sass, and R. Zimmer. 2011. "The Effects of Charter High Schools on Educational Attainment." *Journal of Labor Economics* 29, no. 2: 377–415.

Boston School Finder. 2020. "What Is the Home-Based Assignment Policy (HBAP)?" https://www.bostonschoolfinder.org/home-based-assignment-policy-hbap.

Buerger, C., and R. Bifulco. 2019. "The Effect of Charter Schools on Districts' Student Composition, Costs, and Efficiency: The Case of New York State." *Economics of Education Review* 69: 61–72.

Butler, J., D. Carr, E. Toma, and R. Zimmer. 2013. "Choice in a World of New School Types." *Journal of Policy Analysis and Management* 32, no. 4: 785–806.

CEA (Council of Economic Advisers). 2020. "The Impact of Opportunity Zones: An Initial Assessment." https://www.whitehouse.gov/wp-content/uploads/2020/08/The-Impact-of-Opportunity-Zones-An-Initial-Assessment.pdf.

Chakrabarti, R. 2008. "Can Increasing Private School Participation and Monetary Loss in a Voucher Program Affect Public School Performance? Evidence from Milwaukee." *Journal of Public Economics* 92, nos. 5–6: 1371–93.

Chakrabarti, R., and J. Roy. 2010. "The Economics of Parental Choice." *Economics of Education* 3: 336–42.

Chingos, M., and P. Peterson. 2015. "Experimentally Estimated Impacts of School Vouchers on College Enrollment and Degree Attainment." *Journal of Public Economics* 122: 1–12.

Cohodes, S., E. Setren, and C. Walters. 2019. *Can Successful Schools Replicate? Scaling Up Boston's Charter School Sector*. NBER Working Paper 25796. Cambridge, MA: National Bureau of Economic Research.

CREDO (Center for Research on Education Outcomes). 2009. "Multiple Choice: Charter School Performance in 16 States." Stanford University.

———. 2013. "National Charter School Study." Stanford University. https://credo.stanford.edu/sites/g/files/sbiybj6481/f/ncss_2013_final_draft.pdf.

CRS (Congressional Research Service). 2018. "Higher Education Tax Benefits: Brief Overview and Budgetary Effects." https://files.eric.ed.gov/fulltext/ED593609.pdf.

———. 2019. "District of Columbia Opportunity Scholarship Program (DC OSP): Overview, Implementation, and Issues." https://fas.org/sgp/crs/misc/R45581.pdf.

David, R. 2018. "National Charter School Management Overview." National Alliance for Public Charter Schools. https://www.publiccharters.org/sites/default/files/documents/2019-06/napcs_management_report_web_06172019.pdf.

DeAngelis, C., and P. Wolf. 2019. "Will Democracy Endure Private School Choice? The Effect of the Milwaukee Parental Choice Program on Adult Voting Behavior." *Journal of Private Enterprise*.

———. 2020. "Private School Choice and Character: More Evidence from Milwaukee." *Journal of Private Enterprise*.

DeAngelis, C., P. Wolf, L. Maloney, and J. May. 2018. "Charter School Funding: (More) Inequity in the City." November. School Choice Demonstration Project.

Dobbie, W., and R. Fryer. 2015. "The Medium-Term Impacts of High-Achieving Charter Schools." *Journal of Political Economy* 123, no. 5: 985–1037.

DCPCSB (D.C. Public Charter School Board). 2020. "Student Enrollment." https://dcpcsb.org/student-enrollment.

ECS (Education Commission of the States). 2018. "Open Enrollment Quick Guide." https://www.ecs.org/wp-content/uploads/Open-Enrollment-Quick-Guide.pdf.

EdChoice. 2019. "Fast Facts on School Choice." https://www.edchoice.org/engage/fast-facts/.

———. 2020a. "The ABCs of School Choice." https://www.edchoice.org/wp-content/uploads/2020/01/2020-ABCs-of-School-Choice-WEB-OPTIMIZED-REVISED.pdf.

———. 2020b. "Types of School Choice." https://www.edchoice.org/school-choice/types-of-school-choice/.

———. 2020c. "Wisconsin—Milwaukee Parental Choice Program." https://www.edchoice.org/school-choice/programs/wisconsin-milwaukee-parental-choice-program/.

EdSurge. 2020. "What's the Plan? How K-12 School Districts Are Preparing to Resume and Reopen." https://www.edsurge.com/research/guides/what-s-the-plan-how-k-12-school-districts-are-preparing-to-resume-and-reopen.

Egalite, A., J. Mills, and P. Wolf. 2017. "The Impact of Targeted School Vouchers on Racial Stratification in Louisiana Schools." *Education and Urban Society* 49, no. 3: 271–96.

Epple, D., and R. Romano. 2008. "Educational Vouchers and Cream Skimming." *International Economic Review* 49, no. 4: 1395–1435.

Epple, D., R. Romano, and M. Urquiola. 2017. "School Vouchers: A Survey of the Economic Literature." *Journal of Economic Literature* 55, no. 2: 441–91.

Epple, D., R. Romano, and R. Zimmer. 2016. "Chapter 3: Charter Schools—A Survey of Research on Their Characteristics and Effectiveness." In *Handbook of the Economics of Education*, ed. G. Bulman and R.W. Fairlie. Amsterdam: Elsevier. Vol. 5, 139–208.

Figlio, D., and C. Hart. 2014. "Competitive Effects of Means-Tested School Vouchers." *American Economic Journal: Applied Economics* 6, no. 1: 133–56.

Figlio, D., C. Hart, and K. Karbownik. 2020. *Effects of Scaling Up Private School Choice Programs on Public School Students*. NBER Working Paper 26758. Cambridge, MA: National Bureau of Economic Research.

Florida Department of Education. 2019a. "School Choice." http://www.fldoe.org/schools/school-choice/.

———. 2019b. "Florida's Charter Schools." http://www.fldoe.org/core/fileparse.php/7696/urlt/Charter-Sept-2019.pdf.

———. 2019c. "Fact Sheet: Florida Tax Credit Scholarship Program." http://www.fldoe.org/core/fileparse.php/5606/urlt/FTC-Sept-2019-line.pdf.

Friedman, M. 1955. "The Role of Government in Education." In *Economics and the Public Interest*. New Brunswick, NJ: Rutgers University Press.

Gilraine, M., U. Petronijevic, and J. Singleton. 2019. *Horizontal Differentiation and the Policy Effect of Charter Schools*. EdWorkingPaper 19-80. https://edworkingpapers.com/sites/default/files/ai19-80.pdf.

Grube, L., and D. Anderson. 2018. "School Choice and Charter Schools in Review: What Have We Learned?" *Journal of Private Enterprise* 33, no. 4: 21–44.

Harris, D., and M. Larsen. 2018. "What Effect Did the New Orleans School Reforms Have on Student Achievement, High School Graduation, and College Outcomes?" Education Research Alliance for New Orleans. July 15. https://educationresearchalliancenola.org/files/publications/071518-Harris-Larsen-What-Effect-Did-the-New-Orleans-School-Reforms-Have-on-Student-Achievement-High-School-Graduation-and-College-Outcomes.pdf.

Hitt, C., M. McShane, and P. Wolf. 2018. "Do Impacts on Test Scores Even Matter? Lessons from Long-Run Outcomes in School Choice Research." American Enterprise Institute. https://www.aei.org/research-products/report/do-impacts-on-test-scores-even-matter-lessons-from-long-run-outcomes-in-school-choice-research/

Hoxby, C. 2003. "Chapter 8: School Choice and School Productivity: Could School Choice Be a Tide That Lifts All Boats?" In *The Economics of School Choice*, ed. C. Hoxby. Cambridge, MA: National Bureau of Economic Research.

JEC (Joint Economic Committee). 2019. *Zoned Out: How School and Residential Zoning Limit Educational Opportunity*. SCP Report 6-19.

Kaplan, L., and W. Owings. 2018. "Funding School Choice: Implications for American Education." *Journal of Education Finance* 44, no. 2: 199–217.

Ladd, H., and J. Singleton. 2020. "The Fiscal Externalities of Charter Schools: Evidence from North Carolina." *Education Finance and Policy* 15, no. 1: 191–208.

Leuken, M. 2018. *Fiscal Effects of School Vouchers: Examining the Savings and Costs of America's Private School Voucher Programs*. Indianapolis: EdChoice.

Massachusetts Department of Elementary and Secondary Education. 2016. "Enrollment Policy and Practice Frequently Asked Questions." http://www.doe.mass.edu/charter/guidance/2016-3-faq.html.

———. 2019. "Massachusetts Charter School Waitlist Initial Report for 2019–2020 (FY20)." March 15. http://www.doe.mass.edu/charter/enrollment/fy2020/waitlist.html#:~:text=73%20out%20of%2081%20charter,waitlists%2C%20representing%2027%2C743%20unique%20students.

Mayer, D., P. Peterson, D. Myers, C. Tuttle, and W. Howell. 2002. "School Choice in New York City after Three Years: An Evaluation of the School Choice Scholarships Program." Mathematica Policy Research.

McShane, M. 2020. "The School Choice Now Act and the Fate of Private Schools." *Forbes,* July 23. https://www.forbes.com/sites/mikemcshane/2020/07/23/the-school-choice-now-act-and-the-fate-of-private-schools/#2db492ef7278.

National Association of Realtors. 2018. "2018 Profile of Home Buyers and Sellers." https://nationalmortgageprofessional.com/sites/default/files/NAR_HBS_2018_10_29_18.pdf.

NCES (National Center for Education Statistics). 2019a. "Table 216.20. Number and Enrollment of Public Elementary and Secondary Schools by School Level, Type, and Charter, Magnet, and Virtual Status: Selected Years, 1990–91 through 2017–2018." https://nces.ed.gov/programs/digest/d19/tables/dt19_216.20.asp?current=yes.

———. 2019b. "School Choice in the United States: 2019." https://nces.ed.gov/programs/schoolchoice/ind_02.asp.

———. 2019c. "Table 235.20: Revenues for Public Elementary and Secondary Schools, by Source of Funds and State or Jurisdiction: 2016–2017." https://nces.ed.gov/programs/digest/d19/tables/dt19_235.20.asp?current=yes.

———. 2019d. "Table 216.30: Number and Percentage Distribution of Public Elementary and Secondary Students and Schools, by Traditional or Charter School Status and Selected Characteristics: Selected Years, 1999–2000 through 2017–18." https://nces.ed.gov/programs/digest/d19/tables/dt19_216.30.asp?current=yes

———. 2020a. "Public School Revenue Sources." https://nces.ed.gov/programs/coe/indicator_cma.asp.

———. 2020b." Revenues and Expenditures for Public Elementary and Secondary Education: FY 17." https://nces.ed.gov/pubs2020/2020303.pdf.

Office of Senator Ted Cruz. 2019. "Sen. Cruz Introduces Education Freedom Scholarships and Opportunity Act." February 28. https://www.cruz.senate.gov/?p=press_release&id=4343.

OII (Office of Innovation and Improvement). 2004. "Creating Successful Magnet School Programs." U.S. Department of Education. https://www2.ed.gov/admins/comm/choice/magnet/report.pdf.

Ridley, M., and C. Terrier. 2018. *Fiscal and Education Spillovers from Charter School Expansion*. NBER Working Paper 25070. Cambridge, MA: National Bureau of Economic Research.

Rothstein, J. 2006. "Good Principals or Good Peers? Parental Valuation of School Characteristics, Tiebout Equilibrium, and the Incentive Effects of Competition among Jurisdictions." *American Economic Review* 96, no. 4: 1333–49.

Sass, T., R. Zimmer, B. Gill, and T. Booker. 2016. "Charter High School's Effect on Long-Term Attainment and Earnings." *Journal of Policy Analysis and Management* 35, no. 3: 683–706.

Supreme Court of the United States. 2019. *Espinoza et al. v. Montana Department of Revenue*. https://www.supremecourt.gov/opinions/19pdf/18-1195_g314.pdf#page=23.

Teach New Orleans. 2020. "Nola by the Numbers." https://teachneworleans.net/nola-by-the-numbers/#:~:text=98%25%20of%20students%20attend%20charter,create%20its%20own%20unique%20culture.

Tiebout, C. 1956. "A Pure Theory of Local Expenditures." *Journal of Political Economy* 5: 416–24.

Urquiola, M. 2005. "Does School Choice Lead to Sorting? Evidence from Tiebout Variation." *American Economic Review* 95, no. 4: 1310–26.

U.S. Department of Education. 2015. "Welcome to ED's Charter Schools Program." https://www2.ed.gov/about/offices/list/oii/csp/index.html.

———. 2017. "The Federal Role in Education." https://www2.ed.gov/about/overview/fed/role.html.

———. 2019a. "School Choice Improvement Programs." https://oese.ed.gov/offices/office-of-discretionary-grants-support-services/school-choice-improvement-programs/.

———. 2019b. "The U.S. Department of Education's Charter Schools Program Overview." https://oese.ed.gov/files/2019/12/CSP-Data-Overview-WestEd-7.22.2019.pdf.

———. 2019c. "How Education Freedom Scholarships Can Expand Private and Home Education Options." https://sites.ed.gov/freedom/2019/09/26/how-education-freedom-scholarships-can-expand-private-and-home-education-options/

———. 2020a. "Magnet Schools Assistance Program." https://oese.ed.gov/offices/office-of-discretionary-grants-support-services/school-choice-improvement-programs-assistance-program-msap/.

———. 2020b. "Secretary DeVos Awards $65 Million to Create and Expand Public Charter Schools in Areas of Greatest Need." https://www.ed.gov/news/press-releases/secretary-devos-awards-65-million-create-and-expand-public-charter-schools-areas-greatest-need.

Walters, C. 2018. "The Demand for Effective Charter Schools." *Journal of Political Economy* 126, no. 6: 2179–2223.

Wisconsin Department of Public Instruction. 2020. "2019–2020 Charter School Enrollment." https://dpi.wi.gov/sms/charter-schools/current.

Witte, J. 1998. "The Milwaukee Voucher Experiment." *Educational Evaluation and Policy Analysis* 20, no. 4: 229–51.

Wolf, P., B. Gutmann, M. Puma, B. Kisida, L. Rizzo, N. Eissa., and M. Carr. 2010. "Evaluation of the DC Opportunity Scholarship Program." National Center for Education Evaluation and Regional Assistance. https://ies.ed.gov/ncee/pubs/20104018/pdf/20104018.pdf.

Wolf, P., B. Kisida, B. Gutmann, M. Puma, N. Eissa, and L. Rizzo. 2013. "School Vouchers and Student Outcomes: Experimental Evidence from Washington, DC." *Journal of Policy Analysis and Management* 32, no. 2: 246–70.

Zimmer, R., B. Gill, K. Booker, S. Lavertu, T. Sass, and J. Witte. 2009. "Charter Schools in Eight States: Effects on Achievement, Attainment, Integration, and Competition." RAND Corporation.

Chapter 8

Acemoglu, D., S. Johnson, and J. Robinson. 2001. "The Colonial Origins of Comparative Development: An Empirical Investigation." *American Economic Review* 91, no. 5: 1369–1401.

Alston, E., and S. Smith. 2020. "Development Derailed: Uncertain Property Rights and Asset-Specific Investment." Mountain West Economic History Conference.

Barton, S., and H. Recht. 2018. "The Massive Prize Luring Miners to the Stars." Bloomberg, March 8. https://www.bloomberg.com/graphics/2018-asteroid-mining/.

Barzel, Y. 1997. *Economic Analysis of Property Rights*. New York: Cambridge University Press.

Bohn, H., and R. Deacon. 2000. "Ownership Risk, Investment, and the Use of Natural Resources." *American Economic Review* 90, no. 3: 526–49.

Butow, S., T. Cooley, E. Felt, and J. Mozer. 2020. "State of the Space Industrial Base 2020: A Time for Action to Sustain US Economic & Military Leadership in Space." http://aerospace.csis.org/wp-content/uploads/2020/07/State-of-the-Space-Industrial-Base-2020-Report_July-2020_FINAL.pdf.

CEA (Council of Economic Advisers). 2020. "Expanding Educational Opportunity through Choice and Competition." https://www.whitehouse.gov/wp-content/uploads/2020/10/Expanding-Education-through-Choice.pdf.

Cust, J., and T. Harding. 2020. "Institutions and the Location of Oil Exploration." *Journal of the European Economic Association* 18, no. 3: 1321–50.

Demsetz, H. 1967. "Toward a Theory of Property Rights." *American Economic Review* 57, no. 2: 347–59.

DIA (Defense Intelligence Agency). 2019. "Challenges to Security in Space." https://www.dia.mil/Portals/27/Documents/News/Military%20Power%20Publications/Space_Threat_V14_020119_sm.pdf.

Ferreira, S. 2004. "Deforestation, Property Rights, and International Trade." *Land Economics* 80, no. 2: 174–93.

Galiani, S., and E. Schargrodsky. 2010. "Property Rights for the Poor: Effects of Land Titling." *Journal of Public Economics* 94, nos. 9–10: 700–729.

Grainger, C., and C. Costello. 2014. "Capitalizing Property Rights Insecurity in Natural Resource Assets." *Journal of Environmental Economics and Management* 67, no. 2: 224–40.

Hertzfeld, H., and F. von der Dunk. 2005. "Bringing Space Law into the Commercial World: Property Rights without Sovereignty." *Chicago Journal of International Law* 6, no. 1: 81–99.

Hornbeck, R. 2010. "Barbed Wire: Property Rights and Agricultural Development." *Quarterly Journal of Economics* 125, no. 2: 767–810.

Kemal, M., and I. Lange. 2018. "Changes in Institutional Design and Extraction Paths." *Environmental and Development Economics* 23, no. 4: 478–94.

Leonard, B., and G. Libecap. 2019. "Collective Action by Contract: Prior Appropriation and the Development of Irrigation in the Western United States." *Journal of Law and Economics* 62, no. 1: 67–115.

Libecap, G. 1978. "Economic Variables and the Development of Law: The Case of Western Mineral Rights." *Journal of Economic History* 38, no. 2: 338–62.

Libecap, G., and J. Smith. 2002. "The Economic Evolution of Petroleum Property Rights in the United States." *Journal of Legal Studies* 31, no. S2: S589–S608.

Llinás, C. 2016. "Pretending to Be Liberian and Panamanian; Flags of Convenience and the Weakening of the Nation-State on the High Seas." *Journal of Maritime Law & Commerce* 47, no. 1: 1–28.

North, D. 1991. "Institutions." *Journal of Economic Perspectives* 5, no. 1: 97–112.

O'Connor, A., M. Gallaher, K. Clark-Sutton, D. Lapidus, Z. Oliver, T. Scott, D. Wood, M. Gonzalez, E. Brown, and J. Fletcher. 2019. *Economic Benefits of the Global Positioning System (GPS)*. Research Triangle Park, NC: RTI International. https://www.space.commerce.gov/wp-content/uploads/2019-08-gps-presentation.pdf.

Pace, S., G. Frost, I. Lachow, D. Frelinger, D. Fossum, D. Wassem, and M. Pinto. 1995. *The Global Positioning System: Assessing National Priorities*. Santa Monica, CA: RAND Corporation.

Pence, M. 2019. "Mike Pence: It's Time for Congress to Establish the Space Force." *Washington Post*, March 1. https://www.washingtonpost.com/opinions/mike-pence-its-time-for-congress-to-establish-the-space-force/2019/03/01/50820a58-3c4e-11e9-a06c-3ec8ed509d15_story.html.

Taghdiri, A. 2013. "Flags of Convenience and the Commercial Space Flight Industry: The Inadequacy of Current International Law to Address the Opportune Registration of Space Vehicles in Flag States." *Journal of Science and Technology Law* 19, no. 2: 405–31.

USSF (U.S. Space Force). 2020. "About the United States Space Force." https://www.spaceforce.mil/About-Us/About-Space-Force.

Weinzierl, M. 2018. "Space, the Final Economic Frontier." *Journal of Economic Perspectives* 32, no. 2: 173–92.

Chapter 9

Abraham, K., and M. Kearney. 2020. "Explaining the Decline in the US Employment-to-Population Ratio: A Review of the Evidence." *Journal of Economic Literature* 58, no. 3: 585–643.

Anthony, C., et al. 2015. *The Costs of the Israeli-Palestinian Conflict*. Santa Monica, CA: RAND Corporation.

Autor, D., D. Dorn, and G. Hanson. 2013. "The China Syndrome: Local Labor Market Effects of Import Competition in the United States." *American Economic Review* 103, no. 6: 2121–68.

———. 2019. "When Work Disappears: Manufacturing Decline and the Falling Marriage Market Value of Young Men." *American Economic Review: Insights* 1, no. 2: 161–78.

Baldwin, R., and E. Tomiura. 2020. "Thinking Ahead About the Trade Impact of COVID-19." In *Economics in the Time of COVID-19*, ed. R. Baldwin and B. di Mauro. London: Centre for Economic Policy Research.

Bank of America. 2020a. "Tectonic Shifts in Global Supply Chains." February 4. Bank of America Global Research. https://www.bofaml.com/content/dam/boamlimages/documents/articles/ID20_0147/Tectonic_Shifts_in_Global_Supply_Chains.pdf.

———. 2020b. "The Cost of Remaking Supply Chains: Significant but not Prohibitive." July 23. Bank of America Global Research. https://www.bofaml.com/content/dam/boamlimages/documents/articles/ID20_0734/cost_of_remaking_supply_chains.pdf.

Case, A., and A. Deaton. 2017. "Mortality and Morbidity in the 21st Century." *Brookings Papers on Economic Activity*. casetextsp17bpea.pdf.

CDC (U.S. Centers for Disease Control and Prevention). 2020. "No Sail Order and Suspension of Further Embarkation." *Federal Register*. https://www.federalregister.gov/documents/2020/03/24/2020-06166/no-sail-order-and-suspension-of-further-embarkation.

CEA (Council of Economic Advisers). 2019. *Economic Report of the President*. Washington: U.S. Government Publishing Office.

CRS (Congressional Research Service). 2018. "U.S.-South Korea (KORUS) FTA." https://fas.org/sgp/crs/row/IF10733.pdf.

———. 2019. "'Stage One' U.S.-Japan Trade Agreements." https://fas.org/sgp/crs/row/R46140.pdf.

———. 2020a. "USMCA: Intellectual Property Rights (IPR)." https://crsreports.congress.gov/product/pdf/IF/IF11314#:~:text=Geographical%20Indications%20(GIs),-GIs%20are%20geographical&text=USMCA%20contains%20due%20process%20procedures,GI%20protection%20in%20international%20agreements.

———. 2020b. "U.S.-Brazil Trade Relations." https://crsreports.congress.gov/product/pdf/IF/IF10447.

Cui, Y., J. Meng, and C. Lu. 2018. "Recent Developments in China's Labor Market: Labor Shortage, Rising Wages, and Their Implications." *Review of Development Economics* 22, no. 3: 1217–38.

DOJ (U.S. Department of Justice). 2018. "Statement of John C. Demers Before the Committee on the Judiciary, United States Senate." https://www.justice.gov/sites/default/files/testimonies/witnesses/attachments/2018/12/18/12-05-2018_john_c._demers_testimony_re_china_non-traditional_espionage_against_the_united_states_the_threat_and_potential_policy_responses.pdf.

Elliott, L., and R. Mason. 2020. "U.K. to Impose Tax on Tech Giants but Risks U.S. Tariffs on Car Exports." *Guardian*, January 22. https://www.theguardian.com/business/2020/jan/22/uk-to-impose-tax-on-tech-giants-but-risks-us-tariffs-on-car-exports.

Goodman, M., D. Gerstel, N. Szechenyi, and M. Green. 2019. "The U.S.-Japan Trade Deal." Center for Strategic and International Studies. https://www.csis.org/analysis/us-japan-trade-deal.

GPO (U.S. Government Publishing Office). 2000. "Public Law 206–286—Oct. 20, 2000: Normal Trade Relations for the People's Republic of China." https://www.congress.gov/106/plaws/publ286/PLAW-106publ286.pdf.

Grossman, G., and E. Rossi-Hansberg. 2008. "Trading Tasks: A Simple Theory of Offshoring." *American Economic Review* 98, no. 5: 1978–97.

Henley, J., J. Rankin, and L. O'Carroll. 2020. "Brexit Explained: How It Happened and What Comes Next." *Guardian*, January 27. https://ustr.gov/countries-regions/europe-middle-east/europe/united-kingdom/us-uk-trade-agreement-negotiations.

ILO (International Labor Organization). 2014. "Informal Employment in Mexico: Current Situation, Policies, and Challenges." https://www.ilo.org/wcmsp5/groups/public/---americas/---ro-lima/documents/publication/wcms_245889.pdf.

Isaac, A. 2020. "U.K. Scrambles for Legal Route to Hit Back on U.S. Airbus Tariffs." *Politico*, December 1. https://www.politico.eu/article/uk-scrambles-for-legal-route-to-hit-back-on-us-airbus-tariffs/.

Kearney. 2020. "Trade War Spurs Sharp Reversal in 2019 Reshoring Index, Foreshadowing COVID-19 Test of Supply Chain Relience." https://www.kearney.com/operations-performance-transformation/us-reshoring-index/full-report.

Luo, S., and K. Tsang. 2020. "China and World Output Impact of the Hubei Lockdown During the Coronavirus Outbreak." *Contemporary Economic Policy*, forthcoming.

Lund, S., et al. 2020. "Risk, Resilience, and Rebalancing in Global Value Chains." McKinsey Global Institute, August 6. https://www.mckinsey.com/business-functions/operations/our-insights/risk-resilience-and-rebalancing-in-global-value-chains.

McBride, J., and A. Chatzky. 2019. "Is 'Made in China 2025' a Threat to Global Trade?" Council on Foreign Relations. https://www.cfr.org/backgrounder/made-china-2025-threat-global-trade.

MOF (Ministry of Finance of the People's Republic of China). 2020. "Announcement of the Customs Tariff Commission of the State Council on Adjusting Measures to Impose Tariffs on Certain Imported Commodities Originating in the United States." http://gss.mof.gov.cn/gzdt/zhengcefabu/202002/t20200206_3466540.htm.

Mojtehedzadeh, S. 2016. "Inside Mexico's 'Ghost' Unions." *Toronto Star*, May 22. https://www.thestar.com/news/gta/2016/05/22/inside-mexicos-ghost-unions.html.

OECD (Organization for Economic Cooperation and Development). 2019. "Trade in Fake Goods Is Now 3.3% of World Trade and Rising." https://www.oecd.org/newsroom/trade-in-fake-goods-is-now-33-of-world-trade-and-rising.htm.

Overby, T., S. Snyder, T. Stangarone, and E. Swicord. 2020. *Stabilizing the U.S.-Korea Trade Agenda Under Trump and Moon*. Washington: Council on Foreign Relations. https://efile.fara.gov/docs/3327-Informational-Materials-20200318-108.pdf.

Packard, C. 2020. "Trump and Johnson Can Quickly Strike a Trade Deal—If They Avoid the Pitfalls." *Foreign Policy*, March 11. https://foreignpolicy.com/2020/03/11/trump-johnson-us-britain-trade-agreement-fta/.

Pierce, J., and P. Schott. 2016. "The Surprisingly Swift Decline of U.S. Manufacturing Employment." *American Economic Review* 106, no. 7: 1632–62.

———. 2020. "Trade Liberalization and Mortality: Evidence from U.S. Counties." *American Economic Review: Insights* 2, no. 1: 47–64.

Schlesinger, J. 2020. "How the Coronavirus Will Reshape World Trade." *Wall Street Journal*, June 19. https://www.wsj.com/articles/how-the-coronavirus-will-reshape-world-trade-11592592995.

Schott, J. 2019. "Reinventing the Wheel: Phase One of the U.S.-Japan Trade Pact." Peterson Institute for International Economics. https://www.piie.com/blogs/trade-and-investment-policy-watch/reinventing-wheel-phase-one-us-japan-trade-pact.

Tankersley, J. 2018. "Trump Signs Revised Korean Trade Deal." *New York Times*, September 24. https://www.nytimes.com/2018/09/24/us/politics/south-korea-trump-trade-deal.html.

UBS. 2020. "Supply Chains Are Shifting: How Much and Where?" UBS Evidence Lab. https://www.ubs.com/global/en/investment-bank/in-focus/covid-19/2020/supply-chains-are-shifting.html.

UN Comtrade. 2016. "Classification by Broad Economic Categories Rev.5." https://unstats.un.org/unsd/trade/classifications/Manual%20of%20the%20Fifth%20Revision%20of%20the%20BEC%20(Unedited).pdf.

USITC (U.S. International Trade Commission). 2019. "U.S.-Mexico-Canada Trade Agreement: Likely Impact on the U.S. Economy and on Specific Industry Sectors." https://www.usitc.gov/publications/332/pub4889.pdf.

USTR (Office of the United States Trade Representative). 2018a. "Section 301 Investigation Fact Sheet." https://ustr.gov/about-us/policy-offices/press-office/fact-sheets/2018/june/section-301-investigation-fact-sheet.

———. 2018b. "United States–Japan Trade Agreement (USJTA) Negotiations: Summary of Specific Negotiating Objectives." https://ustr.gov/sites/default/files/2018.12.21_Summary_of_U.S.- Japan_Negotiating_Objectives.pdf.

———. 2018c. "United States–Mexico–Canada Trade Fact Sheet: Modernizing NAFTA into a 21st Century Trade Agreement." https://ustr.gov/about-us/policy-offices/press-office/fact-sheets/2018/october/united-states%E2%80%93mexico%E2%80%93canada-trade-fa-1.

———. 2018d. "New U.S. Trade Policy and National Security Outcomes with the Republic of Korea." https://ustr.gov/about-us/policy-offices/press-office/fact-sheets/2018/march/new-us-trade-policy-and-national.

———. 2018e. "Fact Sheet on U.S.-Korea Free Trade Agreement Outcomes." https://ustr.gov/about-us/policy-offices/press-office/fact-sheets/2018/september/fact-sheet-us-korea-free-trade.

———. 2019a. "2019 National Trade Estimate Report on Foreign Trade Barriers." https://ustr.gov/sites/default/files/2019_National_Trade_Estimate_Report.pdf.

———. 2019b. "United States and China Reach Phase One Trade Agreement." https://ustr.gov/about-us/policy-offices/press-office/press-releases/2019/december/united-states-and-china-reach.

———. 2019c. "U.S.-Japan Trade Agreement Text." https://ustr.gov/countries-regions/japan-korea-apec/japan/us-japan-trade-agreement-negotiations/us-japan-trade-agreement-text.

———. 2019d. "U.S.-Japan Digital Trade Agreement Text." https://ustr.gov/countries-regions/japan-korea-apec/japan/us-japan-trade-agreement-negotiations/us-japan-digital-trade-agreement-text.

———. 2020a. "United States–Mexico–Canada Agreement." https://ustr.gov/trade-agreements/free-trade-agreements/united-states-mexico-canada-agreement.

———. 2020b. "Economic and Trade Agreement between the United States of America and the People's Republic of China." https://ustr.gov/sites/default/files/files/agreements/phase%20one%20agreement/Economic_And_Trade_Agreement_Between_The_United_States_And_China_Text.pdf.

———. 2020c. "USTR and USDA Release Report on Agricultural Trade between the United States and China." https://ustr.gov/about-us/policy-offices/press-office/press-releases/2020/october/ustr-and-usda-release-report-agricultural-trade-between-united-states-and-china.

———. 2020d. "Statement on Call between the United States and China." https://ustr.gov/about-us/policy-offices/press-office/press-releases/2020/august/statement-call-between-united-states-and-china.

———. 2020e. "Fact Sheet on the 2020 National Trade Estimate: Removing Barriers to U.S. Exports Worldwide." https://ustr.gov/about-us/policy-offices/press-office/fact-sheets/2020/march/fact-sheet-2020-national-trade-estimate-removing-barriers-us-exports-worldwide.

———. 2020f. "U.S.-U.K. Trade Agreement Negotiations." https://ustr.gov/countries-regions/europe-middle-east/europe/united-kingdom/us-uk-trade-agreement-negotiations.

Vaswani, K. 2020. "U.S.-China Trade Deal: Five Things That Aren't in It." BBC News, January 16. https://www.bbc.com/news/business-51130434.

White House. 2020a. "Remarks by President Trump at Signing of the U.S.-China Phase One Trade Agreement." https://www.whitehouse.gov/briefings-statements/remarks-president-trump-signing-u-s-china-phase-one-trade-agreement-2/.

———. 2020b. "Proclamation on Suspension of Entry as Immigrants and Nonimmigrants of Persons Who Pose a Risk of Transmitting 2019 Novel Coronavirus." https://www.whitehouse.gov/presidential-actions/proclamation-suspension-entry-immigrants-nonimmigrants-persons-pose-risk-transmitting-2019-novel-coronavirus/.

———. 2020c. "Proclamation—Suspension of Entry as Immigrants and Nonimmigrants of Certain Additional Persons Who Pose a Risk of Transmitting 2019 Novel Coronavirus." https://www.whitehouse.gov/presidential-actions/proclamation-suspension-entry-immigrants-nonimmigrants-certain-additional-persons-pose-risk-transmitting-2019-novel-coronavirus/.

World Bank. 2020. *World Development Report 2020: Trading for Development in the Age of Global Value Chains*. Washington: World Bank. https://www.worldbank.org/en/publication/wdr2020.

WTO (World Trade Organization). 2020. "The General Agreement on Tariffs and Trade (GATT 1947)." https://www.wto.org/english/docs_e/legal_e/gatt47_01_e.htm.

Wu, D. 2020. "TSMC Scores Subsidies and Picks Site for $12 Billion U.S. Plant." *Bloomberg*, June 8. https://www.bloomberg.com/news/articles/2020-06-09/tsmc-confident-of-replacing-any-huawei-orders-lost-to-u-s-curbs

Xie, E. 2020. "Build-up to Coronavirus Lockdown: Inside China's Decision to Close Wuhan." *South China Morning Post*, April 2. https://www.scmp.com/news/china/society/article/3078189/build-coronavirus-lockdown-inside-chinas-decision-close-wuhan.

Chapter 10

BBC (British Broadcasting Corporation). 2020. "U.S. Oil Prices Turn Negative as Demand Dries Up." https://www.bbc.com/news/business-52350082.

Bernanke, B. 1983. "Nonmonetary Effects of the Financial Crisis in the Propagation of the Great Depression." *American Economic Review* 73, no. 3: 257–76.

Bordo, M., and J. Haubrich. 2017. "Deep Recessions, Fast Recoveries, and Financial Crises: Evidence from the American Record." *Economic Inquiry* 55: 527–41.

CEA (Council of Economic Advisers). 2018. *Economic Report of the President*. Washington: U.S. Government Publishing Office.

———. 2019. *Economic Report of the President*. Washington: U.S. Government Publishing Office.

———. 2020. *Economic Report of the President*. Washington: U.S. Government Publishing Office.

Chen, Y., A. Ebenstein, M. Greenstone, and H. Li. 2013. "Evidence on the Impact of Sustained Exposure to Air Pollution on Life Expectancy from China's Huai River Policy." *Proceedings of the National Academy of Sciences* 110, no. 32: 12936–41.

Coibion, O., Y. Gorodnichenko, and M. Weber. 2020. *Labor Markets during the COVID-19 Crisis: A Preliminary View*. NBER Working Paper 27017. Cambridge, MA: National Bureau of Economic Research.

Crust, E., M. Daly, and B. Hobijn. 2020. "The Illusion of Wage Growth." Federal Reserve Bank of San Francisco Economic Letter.

Deschenes, O., M. Greenstone, and J. Shapiro. 2017. "Defensive Investments and the Demand for Air Quality: Evidence from the NOx Budget Program." *American Economic Review* 107, no. 10: 2958–89.

EIA (Energy Information Administration). 2020. "Short-Term Energy Outlook." December 8. https://www.eia.gov/outlooks/steo/.

Fernández-Villaverde, J., and C. Jones. 2020. *Macroeconomic Outcomes and COVID-19: A Progress Report.* NBER Working Paper 28004. Cambridge, MA: National Bureau of Economic Research.

Gascon, C., and J. Haas. 2020. "The Impact of COVID-19 on the Residential Real Estate Market." Federal Reserve Bank of Saint Louis.

Gicheva, D. 2016. "Student Loans or Marriage? A Look at the Highly Educated." *Economics of Education Review* 53: 207–16.

Gicheva, D., and J. Thompson. 2015. "The Effects of Student Loans on Long-Term Household Financial Stability." In *Student Loans and the Dynamics of Debt,* edited by B. Hershbein and K. Hollenbeck. Kalamazoo: W. E. Upjohn Institute for Employment Research.

Goodspeed, T., and P. Navarro. "The White House Favors a Bridge to Recovery." *Wall Street Journal,* December 2. https://www.wsj.com/articles/the-white-house-favors-a-bridge-to-recovery-11606950989.

Hall, R., and M., Kudlyak. 2020. *Why Has the U.S. Economy Recovered So Consistently from Every Recession in the Past 70 Years?* NBER Working Paper 27234. Cambridge, MA: National Bureau of Economic Research.

Hamermesh, D. 1989. "What Do We Know About Worker Displacement in the U.S.?" *Industrial Relations: A Journal of Economy and Society* 28, no. 1: 51–59.

He, J., H. Liu, and A. Salvo. 2019. "Severe Air Pollution and Labor Productivity: Evidence from Industrial Towns in China." *American Economic Journal: Applied Economics* 11, no. 1: 173–201.

Hedlund, A. 2019. "Failure to Launch: Housing, Debt Overhang, and the Inflation Option." *American Economic Journal: Macroeconomics* 11, no. 2: 228–74.

IMF (International Monetary Fund). 2020a. *World Economic Outlook: A Long and Difficult Ascent.* Washington: IMF. https://www.imf.org/-/media/Files/Publications/WEO/2020/October/English/text.ashx.

———. 2020b. *World Economic Outlook Update: A Crisis Like No Other, An Uncertain Recovery.* Washington: IMF. https://www.imf.org/-/media/Files/Publications/WEO/2020/Update/June/English/WEOENG202006.ashx.

Kozlowski, J., L. Veldkamp, and V. Venkateswaran. 2020. *Scarring Body and Mind: The Long-Term Belief-Scarring Effects of COVID-19.* NBER Working Paper 27439. Cambridge, MA: National Bureau of Economic Research.

Mezza, A., D. Ringo, S. Sherlund, and K. Sommer. 2020. "Student Loans and Homeownership." *Journal of Labor Economics* 38, no. 1: 215–60.

OECD (Organization for Economic Cooperation and Development). 2020. *OECD Economic Outlook.* Vol. 2020, Issue 2. https://www.oecd-ilibrary.org/

deliver/39a88ab1-en.pdf?itemId=%2Fcontent%2Fpublication%2F39a
88ab1-en&mimeType=pdf.

O'Hara, M., and A. Zhou. 2020. "Anatomy of a Liquidity Crisis: Corporate Bonds in the COVID-19 Crisis." *Journal of Financial Economics*, forthcoming.

Pierce, J., and P. Schott. 2020. "Trade Liberalization and Mortality: Evidence from U.S. Counties." *American Economic Review: Insights* 2, no. 1: 47–64.

Rothstein, J., and C. Rouse. 2011. "Constrained after College: Student Loans and Early-Career Occupational Choices." *Journal of Public Economics* 95, nos. 1–2: 149–63.

Ruhm, C. 1991. "Are Workers Permanently Scarred By Job Displacements?" *American Economic Review* 81, no. 1: 319–24.

Sharpe, S., and X. Zhou, 2020. "The Corporate Bond Market Crises and the Government Response." *FEDS Notes* 2020-10-07-2. Board of Governors of the Federal Reserve System.

World Bank. 2020. "Reversals of Fortune: Poverty and Shared Prosperity 2020." https://openknowledge.worldbank.org/bitstream/handle/10986/34496/9781464816024.pdf.

Chapter 11

AASHTO (American Association of State Highway and Transportation Officials) and TRIP. 2009. "Rough Roads Ahead: Fix Them Now or Pay For It Later." Road Information Program. https://t2.unh.edu/sites/t2.unh.edu/files/documents/publications/RoughRoads_FullReport.pdf

AAUP (American Association of University Professors). 2020. "2019–20 Faculty Compensation Survey Results." https://www.aaup.org/2019-20-faculty-compensation-survey-results.

———. No date. "Explanation of Statistical Data." https://www.aaup.org/explanation-statistical-data-6.

Abbott, M., and C. Beach. 2011. "Do Admission Criteria and Economic Recessions Affect Immigrant Earnings?" Institute for Research on Public Policy Working Paper. https://irpp.org/research-studies/do-admission-criteria-and-economic-recessions-affect-immigrant-earnings/

Abraham, K., and M. Kearney. 2020. "Explaining the Decline in the U.S. Employment-to-Population Ratio: A Review of the Evidence." *Journal of Economic Literature* 58, no. 3: 585–643.

Acemoglu, D., U. Akcigit, H. Alp, N. Bloom, and W. Kerr. 2018. "Innovation, Realocation, and Growth." *American Economic Review* 108, no. 11: 3450–91.

Agency for Healthcare Research and Quality. 2017. "Physician Burnout." https://www.ahrq.gov/prevention/clinician/ahrq-works/burnout/index.htm.

Aguirre, D., L. Hoteit, C. Rupp, and K. Sabbagh. 2012. "Empowering the Third Billion. Women and the World of Work in 2012." Booz and Company. https://www.

hrtoday.ch/sites/hrtoday.ch/files/article_inline_images/BoozCo_
Empowering-the-Third-Billion_Full-Report.pdf.

Altig, D, A. Auerbach, L. Kotlikoff, E. Ilin, and V. Ye. 2020. *Marginal Net Taxation of Americans' Labor Supply*. NBER Working Paper 27164. Cambridge, MA: National Bureau of Economic Research.

American Society of Civil Engineers. 2016. *Failure to Act: Closing the Infrastructure Investment Gap for America's Economic Future*. Boston: Economic Development Research Group.

Arezki, R, P. Bolton, S. Peters, F. Samama, and J. Stiglitz. 2017. "From Global Savings Glut to Financing Infrastructure." *Economic Policy* 32, no. 90: 221–61.

Astebro, T., S. Braguinsky, and Y. Ding. 2020. *Declining Business Dynamism among Our Best Opportunities: The Role of the Burden of Knowledge*. NBER Working Paper 27787. Cambridge, MA: National Bureau of Economic Research. https://www.nber.org/system/files/working_papers/w27787/w27787.pdf.

Bailey, M., T. Byker, E. Patel, and S. Ramnath. 2019. *The Long-Term Effects of California's 2004 Paid Family Leave Act on Women's Careers: Evidence from U.S. Tax Data*. NBER Working Paper 26416. Cambridge, MA: National Bureau of Economic Research.

Baldwin, R. 2006. "Failure of the WTO Ministerial Conference at Cancun: Reasons and Remedies." *World Economy* 29, no. 6: 677–96.

Bartel, A., S. Kim, J. Nam, M. Rossin-Slater, C. Ruhm, and J. Waldfogel. 2019. "Racial and Ethnic Disparities in Access to and Use of Paid Family and Medical Leave: Evidence from Four Nationally Representative Datasets." *Monthly Labor Review*, January.

Becker, G. 1962. "Investment in Human Capital: A Theoretical Analysis." *Journal of Political Economy* 70, no. 5: 9–49.

Bick, A., and N. Fuchs-Schündeln. 2017. "Quantifying the Disincentive Effects of Joint Taxation on Married Women's Labor Supply." *American Economic Review* 107, no. 5: 100–104.

Blau, F., and L. Kahn. 2013. "Female Labor Supply: Why Is the United States Falling Behind?" *American Economic Review: Papers and Proceedings* 103, no. 3: 251–56.

Bloom, N., C. Jones, J. Van Reenen, and M. Webb. 2020. "Are Idea Getting Harder to Find?" *American Economic Review* 110, no. 4: 1104–44.

Borella, M., M. De Nardi, and F. Yang. 2019a. *Are Marriage-Related Taxes and Social Security Benefits Holding Back Female Labor Supply?* NBER Working Paper 26097. Cambridge, MA: National Bureau of Economic Research. https://www.nber.org/papers/w26097.

———. 2019b. "Marriage-Related Taxes and Social Security Benefits Are Holding Back Women's Labour Supply in the U.S." Vox EU and Centre for Economic Policy Research. https://voxeu.org/article/marriage-related-taxes-social-security-benefits-and-women-s-labour-supply-us.

Borjas, G. 2003. "The Labor Demand Curve Is Downward Sloping: Reexamining the Impact of Immigration on the Labor Market." *Quarterly Journal of Economics* 118, no. 4: 1335–74.

———. 2017. "Why Trump's New Immigration Bill Makes Sense; Hey, It Works in Canada." *Politico*, August 4. https://www.politico.com/magazine/story/2017/08/04/why-trumps-new-immigration-bill-makes-sense-215457

———. 2019. *Immigration and Economic Growth*. NBER Working Paper 25836. Cambridge, MA: National Bureau of Economic Research.

Bradford, A. 2014. "How International Institutions Evolve." *Chicago Journal of International Law* 15, no. 5: 47–83.

Bronson, M., and M. Mazzocco. 2018. "Taxation and Household Decisions: An Intertemporal Analysis." https://wpcarey.asu.edu/sites/default/files/taxation_sep_2018.pdf.

Brooks, L., N. Gendron-Carrier, and G. Rua. 2018. "The Local Impact of Containerization." Finance and Economics Discussion Series 2018-045. Board of Governors of the Federal Reserve System.

Brooks, L., and Z. Liscow. 2019. "Infrastructure Costs." http://leahbrooks.org/leahweb/papers/Brooks_Liscow_Infrastructure_Costs_2019-07-31.pdfhttp://leahbrooks.org/leahweb/papers/Brooks_Liscow_Infrastructure_Costs_2019-07-31.pdf

Buchanan, J. 1965. "An Economic Theory of Clubs." *Economica* 32, no. 125: 1–14.

Budig, M., and P. England. 2001. "The Wage Penalty for Motherhood." *American Sociological Review* 66, no. 2: 204–25. http://www.jstor.org/stable/2657415. http://www.jstor.org/stable/2657415.

Burris, M., N. Alemazkoor, R. Benz, and N. Wood. 2014. "The Impact of HOT Lanes on Carpools." *Research in Transportation Economics* 44: 43–51.

Byrne, D., J. Fernald, and M. Reinsdorf. 2016. "Does the United States have a Productivity Slowdown or a Measurement Problem?" Finance and Economics Discussion Series 2016-17. Board of Governors of the Federal Reserve System.

Campbell, Z., I. Chin, E. Chyn, and J. Hastings. 2017. *The Impact of Paid Sick Leave: Evidence from Temporary Disability Insurance in Rhode Island*. Cambridge, MA: National Bureau of Economic Research.

Card, D., R. Chetty, M. Feldstein, and E. Saez. 2011. "Expanding Access to Administrative Data for Research in the United States." In *American Economic Association, Ten Years and Beyond: Economists Answer NSF's Call for Long-Term Research Agendas*, ed. C. Shulze and D. Newlon. Maastricht: SSRN.

CBO (Congressional Budget Office). 2013. "The Economic Impact of S. 744, the Border Security, Economic Opportunity, and Immigration Modernization Act." https://www.cbo.gov/publication/44346.

———. 2015. "Estimated Impact of the American Recovery and Reinvestment Act on Employment and Economic Output in 2014." https://www.cbo.gov/sites/default/files/114th-congress-2015-2016/reports/49958-ARRA.pdf.

———. 2018. "Public Spending on Transportation and Water Infrastructure, 1956 to 2017." https://www.cbo.gov/system/files/2018-10/54539-Infrastructure.pdf.

CEA (Council of Economic Advisers). 2019. "The Role of Affordable Child Care in Promoting Work Outside the Home." https://www.whitehouse.gov/wp-content/uploads/2019/12/The-Role-of-Affordable-Child-Care-in-Promoting-Work-Outside-the-Home-1.pdf

Chassamboulli, A., and G. Peri. 2018. *The Economic Effect of Immigration Policies: Analyzing and Simulating the U.S. Case*. NBER Working Paper 25074. Cambridge, MA: National Bureau of Economic Research.

Chien, N., and S. Macartney. 2019. "What Happens When People Increase Their Earnings? Effective Marginal Tax Rates for Low-Income Households." Office of the Assistant Secretary for Planning and Evaluation, U.S. Department of Health and Human Services.

Clark, X., D. Dollar, and A. Micco. 2002. *Maritime Transport Costs and Port Efficiency*. Policy Research Working Paper 2781. Washington: World Bank.

Clements, L., and K. Kockelman. 2017. "Economic Effects of Automated Vehicles." *Transportation Research Record* 2606, no. 1: 106–14. https://doi.org/10.3141/2606-14.

Cook, S., and K. Soramäki. 2014. *The Global Network of Payment Flows*. Working Paper 2012-006. London: Swift Institute.

Correia de Brito, A., C. Kauffmann, and J. Pelkmans. 2016. *The Contribution of Mutual Recognition to International Regulatory Co-operation*. Regulatory Policy Working Paper 2. Paris: OECD Publishing.

Crossley, T., and S. Jeon. 2007. "Joint Taxation and the Labour Supply of Married Women: Evidence from the Canadian Tax Reform of 1988." *Fiscal Studies* 28, no. 3: 343–65.

Davies, H., and D. Green. 2008. *Global Financial Regulation: The Essential Guide*. Cambridge: Polity Press.

de Brauw, A., and J. Russell. 2014. "The Labor Demand Curve Is . . . Upward Sloping? The Wage Effects of Immigration and Women's Entry into the U.S. Labor Force, 1960–2010." Social Science Research Network.

DOJ (U.S. Department of Justice, Office of Public Affairs). 2020. "Six Russian GRU Officers Charged in Connection with Worldwide Deployment of Destructive Malware and Other Disruptive Actions in Cyberspace." https://www.justice.gov/opa/pr/six-russian-gru-officers-charged-connection-worldwide-deployment-destructive-malware-and.

Evensky, J. 2011. "Adam Smith's Essentials: On Trust, Faith, and Free Markets." *Journal of the History of Economic Thought* 33, no. 2: 249–68.

Farrell, J., and G. Saloner. 1985. "Standardization, Compatibility, and Innovation." *RAND Journal of Economics*, 70–83.

———. 1986. "Installed Base and Compatibility: Innovation, Product Preannouncements, and Predation." *American Economic Review* 76: 940–55.

https://www.jstor.org/stable/pdf/1816461.pdf?refreqid=excelsior%3A439e02c
544f7d7adedd3de6cd4d1e1d8.

FCC (Federal Communications Commission). 2018. "Accelerating Wireless Broadband
Deployment by Removing Barriers to Infrastructure Investment." Presented
before Federal Communications Commission, Washington, WT Docket 17-79.

———. 2020a. "FCC Concludes First 5G Mid-Band Spectrum Auction." *FCC News*. https://
docs.fcc.gov/public/attachments/DOC-366396A1.pdf.

———. 2020b. "FCC Fact Sheet: Auction 107—3.7 to 3.98 GHz; Public Notice, AU Docket
No. 20-25." https://docs.fcc.gov/public/attachments/DOC-365577A1.pdf.

———. No date. "The FCC's 5G FAST Plan." https://www.fcc.gov/5G.

Federal Reserve. 2019. "Survey of Consumer Finances." https://www.federalreserve.
gov/econres/scfindex.htm.

Foerster, A., A. Hornstein, P. Sarte, and M. Watson. 2019. *Aggregate Implications of
Changing Sectoral Trends*. NBER Working Paper 25867. Cambridge, MA:
National Bureau of Economic Research.

Fruttero, A., D. Gurara, L. Kolovich, V. Malta, M. Tavares, N. Tchelishvili, and S. Fabrizio.
2020. "Women in the Labor Force: The Role of Fiscal Policies." IMF Staff
Discussion Notes. https://www.imf.org/en/Publications/Staff-Discussion-
Notes/Issues/2020/02/11/
Women-in-the-Labor-Force-The-Role-of-Fiscal-Policies-46237.

GAO (U.S. Government Accountability Office). 2018. "High-Risk Series: Urgent Actions
Are Needed to Address Cybersecurity Challenges Facing the Nation." Report
to Congressional Requesters. GAO-18-622.

———. 2019. "Information Technologies: Agencies Need to Develop Modernization
Plans for Critical Legacy Systems." Report to Congressional Requesters.
GAO-19-471.

Glaeser, E., and G. Ponzetto. 2017. *The Political Economy of Transportation Investment*.
NBER Working Paper 23686. Cambridge, MA: National Bureau of Economic
Research.

Guner, N., R. Kaygusuz, and G. Ventura. 2012a. "Taxing Women: A Macroeconomic
Analysis." *Journal of Monetary Economics* 59, no. 1: 111–28.

———. 2012b. "Taxation and Household Labour Supply." *Review of Economic Studies* 79,
no. 3: 1113–49. https://doi.org/10.1093/restud/rdr049.

Hilber, C., and T. Turner. 2014 "The Mortgage Interest Deduction and Its Impact on
Homeownership Decisions." *Review of Economics and Statistics* 96, no. 4:
618–37. https://doi.org/doi:10.1162/REST_a_00427.

Houser, L., and T. Vartanian. 2012. "Pay Matters: The Positive Economic Impacts of Paid
Family Leave for Families, Businesses and the Public." Rutgers Center for
Women and Work. https://www.nationalpartnership.org/our-work/resources/
economic-justice/other/pay-matters.pdf.

Huchzermeyer, L. 2018. "The VLCC Race: US Midstream Companies Plan to Export More Oil Faster." S&P Global Platts. https://blogs.platts.com/2018/07/23/vlcc-midstream-us-crude-oil-export/.

IP Commission. 2017. "The Report of the Commission on the Theft of American Intellectual Property." National Bureau of Asian Research. https://www.nbr.org/wp-content/uploads/pdfs/publications/IP_Commission_Report_Update.pdf.

Istrate, E., and R. Puentes. 2011. "Moving Forward on Public Private Partnerships: U.S. and International Experience with PPP Units." Brookings-Rockefeller Project on State and Metropolitan Innovation.

Jackson, H. 2015. "Substituted Compliance: The Emergence, Challenges, and Evolution of a New Regulatory Paradigm." *Journal of Financial Regulation* 1, no. 2: 169–205.

JCT (Joint Committee on Taxation). 2019. "Distributional Effects of Public Law 115-97" Joint Committee on Taxation Report JCX-10-19.

Jones, K., and B. Wilcher. 2019. "Reducing Maternal Labor Market Detachment: A Role for Paid Family Leave." American University Department of Economics, Working Paper 2019-07.

Katz, L., and K. Murphy. 1992. "Changes in Relative Wages, 1963–1987: Supply and Demand Factors." *Quarterly Journal of Economics* 107, no. 1: 35–78.

Kahn, M., and D. Levinson. 2011. "Fix It First, Expand It Second, Reward It Third: A New Strategy for America's Highways." Brookings Institution, Hamilton Project, Report 2011-03.

Katz, M., and C. Shapiro. 1985. "Network Externalities, Competition, and Compatibility." *American Economic Review* 75, no. 3: 424–40.

———. 1986. "Technology Adoption in the Presence of Network Externalities." *Journal of Political Economy* 94, no. 4: 822–41.

Kaygusuz, R. 2010. "Taxes and Female Labor Supply." *Review of Economic Dynamics* 13, no. 4: 725–41.

Kleven, H., C. Landais, J. Posch, A. Steinhauer, and J. Zweimüller. 2020. *Do Family Policies Reduce Gender Inequality? Evidence from 60 Years of Policy Experimentation*. NBER Working Paper 28082. Cambridge, MA: National Bureau of Economic Research. https://www.nber.org/system/files/working_papers/w28082/w28082.pdf.

Kliff, S., and M. Sanger-Katz. 2020. "Bottleneck for U.S. Coronavirus Response: The Fax Machine." *New York Times*, July 13. https://www.nytimes.com/2020/07/13/upshot/coronavirus-response-fax-machines.html.

Konishi, H., and S. Mun. 2010. "Carpooling and Congestion Pricing: HOV and HOT Lanes." *Regional Science and Urban Economics* 40, no. 4: 173–86.

Korinek, J., and P. Sourdin. 2011. *To What Extent Are High-Quality Logistics Services Trade Facilitating?* Trade Policy Working Paper 108. Paris: Organization for Economic Cooperation and Development.

Lakshmanan, T. 2011. "The Broader Economic Consequences of Transport Infrastructure Investments." *Journal of Transport Geography* 19, no. 1: 1–12.

LaLumia, S. 2008. "The Effects of Joint Taxation of Married Couples on Labor Supply and Non-Wage Income." *Journal of Public Economics* 92, no. 7: 1698–1719.

Li, W., and W. Yu. 2020. *Real Estate Taxes and Home Value: Winners and Losers of TCJA.* Working Paper 20-12. Philadelphia: Federal Reserve Bank of Philadelphia. https://doi.org/10.21799/frbp.wp.2020.12.

Lyon-Hill, S., M. Tilashalski, K. Ellis, and E. Travis. 2020. "Measuring the Effects of Drone Delivery in the United States." Virginia Tech Office of Economic Development and Grado Engineering. https://www.newswise.com/pdf_docs/160018187481745_Virginia%20Tech%20%20Measuring%20the%20Effects%20of%20Drone%20Delivery%20in%20the%20United%20States_September%202020.pdf.

Makovšek, D. 2018. "Mobilizing Private Investment in Infrastructure: Investment De-Risking and Uncertainty." Organization for Economic Cooperation and Development. https://www.itf-oecd.org/sites/default/files/docs/mobilising-private-investment-infrastructure.pdf.

Malkov, E. 2020. *Welfare Effects of the Labor Income Tax Changes on Married Couples.* Working Paper 2020-03. Minneapolis: Federal Reserve Bank of Minneapolis.

Martin, H. 2018. *The Impact of the Tax Cuts and Jobs Act on Local Home Values.* Working Paper 18-06. Cleveland: Federal Reserve Bank of Cleveland. https://doi.org/10.26509/frbc-wp-201806.

Martin, W., and P. Messerlin. 2007. "Why Is It So Difficult? Trade Liberalization under the Doha Agenda." *Oxford Review of Economic Policy* 23, no. 3: 347–66.

McBride, J., and J. Moss. 2020. "The State of U.S. Infrastructure." Council on Foreign Relations. https://www.cfr.org/backgrounder/state-us-infrastructure.

Miller, G. 2019. "Bringing VLCCs to Port." *Petroleum Economist.* https://www.petroleum-economist.com/articles/midstream-downstream/transport/2019/bringing-vlccs-to-port

Mincer, J. 1958. "Investment in Human Capital and Personal Income Distribution." *Journal of Political Economy* 66, no. 4: 281–302.

Moretti, E. 2013. "Want to Reduce Income Inequality? Lower the Barriers to Talented Immigrants." *Forbes*, March 5. https://www.forbes.com/sites/realspin/2013/03/05/want-to-reduce-income-inequality-lower-the-barriers-to-talented-immigrants/#15d537487f14.

Morrissey, T. 2017. "Child Care and Parent Labor Force Participation: A Review of the Research Literature." *Review of Economics of the Household* 15, no. 1: 1–24.

Moser, C., and A. Rose. 2012. "Why Do Trade Negotiations Take So Long?" *Journal of Economic Integration* 27, no. 2: 280–90.

Munim, Z., and H. Schramm. 2018. "The Impacts of Port Infrastructure and Logistics Performance on Economic Growth: The Mediating Role of Seaborne Trade." *Journal of Shipping and Trade* 3, no. 1.

Munnell, A. 1990. "Why Has Productivity Growth Declined? Productivity and Public Investment." *New England Economic Review* (Federal Reserve Bank of Boston), January, 3–22.

Nadiri, M., and T. Mamuneas. 1996. "Contribution of Highway Capital to Industry and National Productivity Growth." U.S. Department of Transportation. https://www.fhwa.dot.gov/reports/growth.pdf.

NAS (National Academy of Sciences, Engineering, and Medicine). 2017. *The Economic and Fiscal Consequences of Immigration*. Washington: National Academy Press.

National Association of Realtors. No date. "The Tax Cuts and Jobs Act: What It Means for Homeowners and Real Estate Professionals." https://www.nar.realtor/tax-reform/the-tax-cuts-and-jobs-act-what-it-means-for-homeowners-and-real-estate-professionals.

National Center for Education Statistics. 2020. "Postsecondary Institution Expenses." Condition of Education. https://nces.ed.gov/programs/coe/indicator_cue.asp.

OECD (Organization for Economic Cooperation and Development). 2011. "Better Policies for Better Lives: The OECD at 50 and Beyond."

———. No date. "History." https://www.oecd.org/about/history/#d.en.194377.

Parente, S. 2018. "SynUSA Synthetic Health Insurance Analytic Files." SynUSA. http://synusa.com/SynUSA_Overview.pdf.

Pew Research Center. 2014. "Rising Cost of Child Care May Help Explain Recent Increase in Stay-at-Home Moms." https://www.pewresearch.org/fact-tank/2014/04/08/rising-cost-of-child-care-may-help-explain-increase-in-stay-at-home-moms/.

Portugal-Perez, A., and J. Wilson. 2012. "Export Performance and Trade Facilitation Reform: Hard and Soft Infrastructure." *World Development* 40, no. 8: 1295–1307.

Posner, E., and A. Sykes. 2013. *Economic Foundations of International Law*. Cambridge, MA: Harvard University Press.

Rappoport, D. 2019. "Tax Reform, Homeownership Costs, and House Prices." http://dx.doi.org/10.2139/ssrn.3308983.

Rossin-Slater, M., C. Ruhm, and J. Waldfogel. 2012. "The Effects of California's Paid Family Leave Program on Mothers' Leave-Taking and Subsequent Labor Market Outcomes." *Journal of Policy Analysis and Management* 32, no. 2: 224–45.

Ruggles, S., S. Flood, R. Goeken, J. Grover, E. Meyer, J. Pacas, and M. Sobek. 2019. IPUMS USA: Version 9.0. Data set. Minneapolis: IPUMS. https://doi.org/10.18128/D010.V9.0.

Rysavy Research and 5G Americas. 2020. "Global 5G: Rise of a Transformational Technology." https://www.5gamericas.org/wp-content/uploads/2020/09/Global-5G-Rise-of-a-transformational-technology.pdf.

Sarin, N. 2016. "The Impact of Paid Leave of Female Employment Outcomes." https://doi.org/10.2139/ssrn.2877015.

Schultz, T. 1961. "Investment in Human Capital." *American Economic Review* 51, no. 1: 1–17.

Schwab, K. 2016. *The Fourth Industrial Revolution*. New York: Crown.

Schwabish, J. 2009. "Identifying Rates of Emigration in the United States Using Administrative Earnings Records: Working Paper 2009-01." Congressional Budget Office. https://www.cbo.gov/sites/default/files/111th-congress-2009-2010/workingpaper/2009-01_1.pdf

Schwartz, G., M. Fouad, T. Hansen, and G. Verdier. 2020. "How Strong Infrastructure Governance Can End Waste in Public Investment." International Monetary Fund. https://blogs.imf.org/2020/09/03/how-strong-infrastructure-governance-can-end-waste-in-public-investment/.

SEC (U.S. Securities and Exchange Commission). 2008. "SEC, Australian Authorities Sign Mutual Recognition Agreement." https://www.sec.gov/news/press/2008/2008-182.htm.

Smith, A. 1759. *The Theory of Moral Sentiments*, ed. D. Raphael and A. Macfie. Republished: Oxford: Oxford University Press, 1976.

Sommer, K., and P. Sullivan. 2018. "Implications of U.S. Tax Policy for House Prices, Rents, and Homeownership." *American Economic Review* 108, no. 2: 241–74. https://doi.org/10.1257/aer.20141751.

Staff, J., and Mortimer, J. 2012. "Explaining the Motherhood Wage Penalty During the Early Occupational Career." *Demography* 49: 1–21. https://doi.org/10.1007/s13524-011-0068-6https://doi.org/10.1007/s13524-011-0068-6.

Steinhauer, J. 2019. "Veterans Will Have More Access to Private Health Care Under New V.A. Rules." *New York Times*, January 30. https://www.nytimes.com/2019/01/30/us/politics/veterans-health-care.html.

Sullivan, D., and T. Von Wachter. 2009. "Job Displacement and Mortality: An Analysis Using Administrative Data." *Quarterly Journal of Economics* 124, no. 3: 1265–1306.

Syverson, C. 2016. *Challenges to Mismeasurement Explanations for the U.S. Productivity Slowdown*. NBER Working Paper 21974. Cambridge, MA: National Bureau of Economic Research.

Tafara, E., and R. Peterson. 2007. "A Blueprint for Cross-Border Access to U.S. Investors: A New International Framework." *Harvard International Law Journal* 48, no. 1: 31–68.

Timpe, B. 2019. "The Long-Run Effects of America's First Paid Maternity Leave Policy." https://economics.ku.edu/sites/economics.ku.edu/files/files/Seminar/papers19_20/Timpe percent20draft percent202019.10.pdf.

UNCTAD (United Nations Conference on Trade and Development). 2020. "Review of Maritime Transport 2019." https://unctad.org/system/files/official-document/rmt2019_en.pdf.

University of California. 2017. "It Failed to Disclose Tens of Millions in Surplus Funds, and Its Budget Practices Are Misleading." Office of the President, Report 2016-130. https://www.auditor.ca.gov/pdfs/reports/2016-130.pdf.

U.S. Army Corps of Engineers. 2017. "Hopper Dredge Recapitalization Analysis Examination of the Corps and Industry Hopper Dredge Capacity: the Need, Composition, Location and Recapitalization of the Corps Hopper Dredge Fleet." https://bayplanningcoalition.org/wp-content/uploads/2018/07/HDRecapFinal.pdf.

U.S. Department of Education. 2020. "Technical Documentation: College Scorecard Institution-Level Data." College Scorecard, March. https://collegescorecard.ed.gov/assets/FullDataDocumentation.pdf.

U.S. Department of Labor. 2020. "Employee and Worksite Perspectives of the Family and Medical Leave Act." Abt Associates. https://www.dol.gov/sites/dolgov/files/OASP/evaluation/pdf/WHD_FMLA2018SurveyResults_FinalReport_Aug2020.pdf.

U.S. Department of Transportation. 2020. "About BUILD Grants." https://www.transportation.gov/BUILDgrants/about.

U.S. House of Representatives. 2018. "PROSPER Act." H.R. 4508, 115th Congress (2017–18). https://www.congress.gov/bill/115th-congress/house-bill/4508/text.

USITC (U.S. International Trade Commission). 2000. "The Impact on the U.S. Economy of Including the United Kingdom in a Free Trade Arrangement with the United States, Canada, and Mexico." Investigation 332-409.

———. 2019. "U.S.–Mexico–Canada Trade Agreement: Likely Impact on the U.S. Economy and on Specific Industry Sectors."

USTR (Office of the U.S. Trade Representative). 2018. "2018 Report to Congress on China's WTO Compliance." Executive Office of the President.

———. 2019. "2019 Report to Congress on China's WTO Compliance." Executive Office of the President.

———. 2020a. "Report on the Appellate Body of the World Trade Organization." Executive Office of the President.

———. 2020b. "2020 Report to Congress on China's WTO Compliance." Executive Office of the President.

Wilson, J., C. Mann, and T. Otsuki. 2004. *Assessing the Potential Benefit of Trade Facilitation: A Global Perspective*. Policy Research Working Paper 3224. Washington: World Bank.

World Bank. 2020. *Reversals of Fortune: Poverty and Shared Prosperity 2020*. Washington: World Bank. https://worldbank.org/en/publication/poverty-and-shared-prosperity.

Zhao, J., C. Fonseca-Sarmiento, and J. Tan. 2019. "America's Trillion-Dollar Repair Bill." Volcker Alliance. https://ceres-am.com/wp-content/uploads/2019/12/Ceres-Americas-Trillion-Dollar-Repair-Bill-Capital-Budgeting-and-the-Disclosure-of-State-Infrastructure-Needs-by-Volcker-Alliance-Nov-2019.pdf.

Appendix A

Report to the President on the Activities of the Council of Economic Advisers During 2020

Letter of Transmittal

Council of Economic Advisers
Washington, December 31, 2020

Mr. President:

The Council of Economic Advisers submits this report on its activities during calendar year 2020 in accordance with the requirements of Congress, as set forth by Section 10(d) of the Employment Act of 1946, as amended by the Full Employment and Balanced Growth Act of 1978.

Sincerely yours,

Rachael Seidenschnur Slobodien
Chief of Staff

Council Members and Their Dates of Service

Name	Position	Oath of office date	Separation date
Edwin G. Nourse	Chairman	August 9, 1946	November 1, 1949
Leon H. Keyserling	Vice Chairman	August 9, 1946	
	Acting Chairman	November 2, 1949	
	Chairman	May 10, 1950	January 20, 1953
John D. Clark	Member	August 9, 1946	
	Vice Chairman	May 10, 1950	February 11, 1953
Roy Blough	Member	June 29, 1950	August 20, 1952
Robert C. Turner	Member	September 8, 1952	January 20, 1953
Arthur F. Burns	Chairman	March 19, 1953	December 1, 1956
Neil H. Jacoby	Member	September 15, 1953	February 9, 1955
Walter W. Stewart	Member	December 2, 1953	April 29, 1955
Raymond J. Saulnier	Member	April 4, 1955	
	Chairman	December 3, 1956	January 20, 1961
Joseph S. Davis	Member	May 2, 1955	October 31, 1958
Paul W. McCracken	Member	December 3, 1956	January 31, 1959
Karl Brandt	Member	November 1, 1958	January 20, 1961
Henry C. Wallich	Member	May 7, 1959	January 20, 1961
Walter W. Heller	Chairman	January 29, 1961	November 15, 1964
James Tobin	Member	January 29, 1961	July 31, 1962
Kermit Gordon	Member	January 29, 1961	December 27, 1962
Gardner Ackley	Member	August 3, 1962	
	Chairman	November 16, 1964	February 15, 1968
John P. Lewis	Member	May 17, 1963	August 31, 1964
Otto Eckstein	Member	September 2, 1964	February 1, 1966
Arthur M. Okun	Member	November 16, 1964	
	Chairman	February 15, 1968	January 20, 1969
James S. Duesenberry	Member	February 2, 1966	June 30, 1968
Merton J. Peck	Member	February 15, 1968	January 20, 1969
Warren L. Smith	Member	July 1, 1968	January 20, 1969
Paul W. McCracken	Chairman	February 4, 1969	December 31, 1971
Hendrik S. Houthakker	Member	February 4, 1969	July 15, 1971
Herbert Stein	Member	February 4, 1969	
	Chairman	January 1, 1972	August 31, 1974
Ezra Solomon	Member	September 9, 1971	March 26, 1973
Marina v.N. Whitman	Member	March 13, 1972	August 15, 1973
Gary L. Seevers	Member	July 23, 1973	April 15, 1975
William J. Fellner	Member	October 31, 1973	February 25, 1975
Alan Greenspan	Chairman	September 4, 1974	January 20, 1977
Paul W. MacAvoy	Member	June 13, 1975	November 15, 1976
Burton G. Malkiel	Member	July 22, 1975	January 20, 1977
Charles L. Schultze	Chairman	January 22, 1977	January 20, 1981
William D. Nordhaus	Member	March 18, 1977	February 4, 1979
Lyle E. Gramley	Member	March 18, 1977	May 27, 1980
George C. Eads	Member	June 6, 1979	January 20, 1981
Stephen M. Goldfeld	Member	August 20, 1980	January 20, 1981
Murray L. Weidenbaum	Chairman	February 27, 1981	August 25, 1982
William A. Niskanen	Member	June 12, 1981	March 30, 1985
Jerry L. Jordan	Member	July 14, 1981	July 31, 1982
Martin Feldstein	Chairman	October 14, 1982	July 10, 1984
William Poole	Member	December 10, 1982	January 20, 1985
Beryl W. Sprinkel	Chairman	April 18, 1985	January 20, 1989

Council Members and Their Dates of Service

Name	Position	Oath of office date	Separation date
Thomas Gale Moore	Member	July 1, 1985	May 1, 1989
Michael L. Mussa	Member	August 18, 1986	September 19, 1988
Michael J. Boskin	Chairman	February 2, 1989	January 12, 1993
John B. Taylor	Member	June 9, 1989	August 2, 1991
Richard L. Schmalensee	Member	October 3, 1989	June 21, 1991
David F. Bradford	Member	November 13, 1991	January 20, 1993
Paul Wonnacott	Member	November 13, 1991	January 20, 1993
Laura D'Andrea Tyson	Chair	February 5, 1993	April 22, 1995
Alan S. Blinder	Member	July 27, 1993	June 26, 1994
Joseph E. Stiglitz	Member	July 27, 1993	
	Chairman	June 28, 1995	February 10, 1997
Martin N. Baily	Member	June 30, 1995	August 30, 1996
Alicia H. Munnell	Member	January 29, 1996	August 1, 1997
Janet L. Yellen	Chair	February 18, 1997	August 3, 1999
Jeffrey A. Frankel	Member	April 23, 1997	March 2, 1999
Rebecca M. Blank	Member	October 22, 1998	July 9, 1999
Martin N. Baily	Chairman	August 12, 1999	January 19, 2001
Robert Z. Lawrence	Member	August 12, 1999	January 12, 2001
Kathryn L. Shaw	Member	May 31, 2000	January 19, 2001
R. Glenn Hubbard	Chairman	May 11, 2001	February 28, 2003
Mark B. McClellan	Member	July 25, 2001	November 13, 2002
Randall S. Kroszner	Member	November 30, 2001	July 1, 2003
N. Gregory Mankiw	Chairman	May 29, 2003	February 18, 2005
Kristin J. Forbes	Member	November 21, 2003	June 3, 2005
Harvey S. Rosen	Member	November 21, 2003	
	Chairman	February 23, 2005	June 10, 2005
Ben S. Bernanke	Chairman	June 21, 2005	January 31, 2006
Katherine Baicker	Member	November 18, 2005	July 11, 2007
Matthew J. Slaughter	Member	November 18, 2005	March 1, 2007
Edward P. Lazear	Chairman	February 27, 2006	January 20, 2009
Donald B. Marron	Member	July 17, 2008	January 20, 2009
Christina D. Romer	Chair	January 29, 2009	September 3, 2010
Austan D. Goolsbee	Member	March 11, 2009	
	Chairman	September 10, 2010	August 5, 2011
Cecilia Elena Rouse	Member	March 11, 2009	February 28, 2011
Katharine G. Abraham	Member	April 19, 2011	April 19, 2013
Carl Shapiro	Member	April 19, 2011	May 4, 2012
Alan B. Krueger	Chairman	November 7, 2011	August 2, 2013
James H. Stock	Member	February 7, 2013	May 19, 2014
Jason Furman	Chairman	August 4, 2013	January 20, 2017
Betsey Stevenson	Member	August 6, 2013	August 7, 2015
Maurice Obstfeld	Member	July 21, 2014	August 28, 2015
Sandra E. Black	Member	August 10, 2015	January 20, 2017
Jay C. Shambaugh	Member	August 31, 2015	January 20, 2017
Kevin A. Hassett	Chairman	September 13, 2017	June 30, 2019
Richard V. Burkhauser	Member	September 28, 2017	May 18, 2019
Tomas J. Philipson	Member	August 31, 2017	
	Acting Chairman	July 1, 2019	
	Vice Chairman	July 24, 2019	June 22, 2020
Tyler B. Goodspeed	Member	May 22, 2019	
	Acting Chairman	June 23, 2020	
	Vice Chairman	June 23, 2020	

Report to the President on the Activities of the Council of Economic Advisers During 2020

The Employment Act of 1946 established the Council of Economic Advisers to provide the President with objective economic analysis on the development and implementation of policy for the full range of domestic and international economic issues that can affect the United States. Governed by a Chairman, who is appointed by the President and confirmed by the United States Senate, the Council has two additional Members who are also appointed by the President.

The Chairman and Members of the Council

On June 22, 2020, Tomas J. Philipson left the Council of Economic Advisers to return to the Harris School of Public Policy at the University of Chicago, where he is the Daniel Levin Professor of Public Policy Studies. In accordance with the Employment Act of 1946, on June 23, 2020, Tyler B. Goodspeed was designated Vice and Acting Chairman of the Council, having been appointed by the President as a Member of the Council on May 22, 2019.

Dr. Goodspeed previously served as Chief Economist for Macroeconomic Policy and Senior Economist for tax, public finance, and macroeconomics. Prior to joining the Council, he was on the Faculty of Economics at the University of Oxford and was a Lecturer in Economics at King's College London. He has published extensively on financial regulation, banking, and monetary economics, with particular attention to the role of access to credit in mitigating the effects of adverse aggregate shocks in historical contexts, especially exogenous environmental shocks. His research has appeared in three full-length monographs from academic presses, as well as numerous articles in peer-reviewed and edited journals. Dr. Goodspeed received his B.A., M.A., and Ph.D. from Harvard University, and M.Phil from the University of Cambridge, where he was a Gates Scholar. He is a current member of the American Economic Association, and was previously a member of the Royal Economic Society, Economic History Association, and Economic History Society, as well as an adjunct scholar at the Cato Institute.

Areas of Activity

Macroeconomic Policies

Throughout 2020, in fulfilling its mandate from the Employment Act of 1946, the Council continued "to gather timely and authoritative information concerning economic developments and economic trends, both current and prospective," and "to formulate and recommend national economic policy to promote employment, production, and purchasing power." The Council appraises the President and White House staff of new economic data and their significance on an ongoing basis, and advises on the policy options to promote the economic objectives specified in the 1946 Act. As core products of the Council, these regular appraisals include written memoranda, presentations, and studies. The Council also prepares in-depth briefings on certain topics as well as public reports that address macroeconomic issues.

In 2020, the Council worked closely with counterparts throughout the Federal government, particularly in the Department of the Treasury, National Economic Council, and Office of Management and Budget to design an effective policy response to the unprecedented macroeconomic developments in 2020, including but not limited to the Coronavirus Aid, Relief, and Economic Security Act and subsequent extensions, and to evaluate and report on the efficacy of those responses. One of the Council's public reports this year evaluated the economic effects of the Federal government's unprecedented response to the COVID-19 pandemic. According to the report, this historic policy response, coupled with a strong prepandemic economy, ameliorated a stark economic contraction while improving expectations for a recovery in 2021 and protecting the economic well-being of the Nation's most vulnerable households and industries. Following the legislated expiration of some of the provisions of the CARES Act, the Council worked with other components within the Executive Office of the President to advise on additional executive actions and follow-on legislation in response to the ongoing macroeconomic challenges of the COVID-19 pandemic.

The Council also published a report this year that assessed the impact of Opportunity Zones on poverty rates and job creation in underserved communities. The report finds that private sector investment grew in these areas as a result of tax incentives, leading to stark decreases in poverty in Opportunity Zones.

Working alongside the Department of the Treasury and the Office of Management and Budget, the Council participates in the "troika" process that generates the macroeconomic assumptions that underlie the Administration's budget proposals. The Council, under the leadership of the Acting Chairman, continued to initiate and lead this process of formulating policy-inclusive economic projections assuming full implementation of the Administration's economic policy agenda.

The Acting Chairman maintained the Council's tradition of meeting regularly with the Chairman and Members of the Board of Governors of the Federal Reserve System to exchange views and data insights on the economy.

Microeconomic Policies

The Council participated in discussions, internal to the Federal Government as well as external, on a range of issues in microeconomic policy. Topics included space policy, environmental reform, drug pricing reform, immigration reform, and a host of Federal aid policies in response to the ongoing pandemic. In particular, the Council worked closely with other components of the Executive Office of the President and agencies of the Federal Government to facilitate adequate aggregate supplies of personal protective equipment and ventilators.

Publication topics this year focused on the effects of school choice programs on the education system. The report shows that school choice expands educational opportunities particularly for low-income and minority students by allowing them to attend schools other than their local underperforming school districts and providing competition that spurs all schools to improve. One report published this year focused on the reversal of the Safer Affordable Fuel-Efficient (SAFE) Vehicle Rule. This is the single largest deregulatory effort by the Administration, hallmarking a pillar of the economic agenda, and providing thousands of dollars in savings for American citizens and auto manufacturers.

As part of an effort to disseminate information on the pandemic and the health of the economy, the Council created a data visualization dashboard in collaboration with the private sector and the Department of Health and Human Services. The dashboard displayed a host of variables on a state and national level ranging from small business openings to hospitalizations.

International Economics

The Council participated in the analysis of numerous issues in the area of international economics. The Council engages with a number of international organizations. The Council is a leading participant in the activities of the Organization for Economic Cooperation and Development (OECD), a forum for facilitating economic coordination and cooperation among the world's high-income countries. Council Members and Council staff have also engaged with the OECD working-party meetings on a range of issues and shaped the organization's agenda, with the Acting Chairman elected as Chair of the Economic Policy Committee, and a member of the Bureau of the Working Party 1.

In addition, the Council analyzed a number of proposals and scenarios in the area of international trade and investment. These included generating estimates of the benefits, as well as any trade-offs, of prospective trade agreements as well as revisions to existing agreements. The Council also worked with counterparts in the Department of the Treasury and United States Trade Representative on issues pertaining to international taxation in the digital economy.

In the fall of 2020, the United States brokered historic peace agreements between Israel and countries in the Arab League including Bahrain, the United Arab Emirates, Sudan, and Morocco. These pacts serve as a vital step toward ensuring economic growth and peace in the Middle East. Additionally, an agreement was brokered by the United States establishing economic normalization between Kosovo and Serbia following over 20 years of diplomatic discord.

With the onset of the pandemic, the Council also worked closely with members of the Coronavirus Task Force to analyze the potential economic costs and benefits of early nonpharmaceutical interventions, including the January 31, 2020, suspension of international travel from the People's Republic of China. The pandemic also generated profound focus on global supply chains. As such, the Council has participated in numerous interagency work streams on the security of these supply chains and potential reshoring of critical infrastructure and pharmaceutical capacity.

The Council continues to actively monitor the U.S. international trade and investment position and to engage with emerging issues in international economics, such as malicious cyber activity. The Council looks forward to continuing to analyze the United States' international economic position.

The Staff of the Council of Economic Advisers

Executive Office

Rachael S. Slobodien	Chief of Staff
Emily A. Tubb	Deputy Chief of Staff
Robert M. Fisher	General Counsel and Senior Economist
Cale A. Clingenpeel	Senior Adviser to the Chairman
N. Emma Ernst	Special Assistant for Strategy and Communications

Senior Research Staff

Kevin C. Corinth	Chief Economist
Joseph V. Balagtas	Senior Economist; Agriculture, International Trade, and Infrastructure
Andre J. Barbe	Senior Economist; International Trade
Aaron J. Cooke	Chief Economist for Macroeconomic Policy
Steven N. Braun	Director of Macroeconomic Forecasting
Aaron D. Hedlund	Chief Economist for Domestic Policy
LaVaughn M. Henry	Senior Economist; Banking and Finance
Ian A. Lange	Senior Economist; Energy
Aparna Mathur	Senior Economist; Labor and Tax
Deborah F. Minehart	Senior Economist; Industrial Organization
Stephen T. Parente	Chief Economist for Health Policy
Brandon J. Restrepo	Senior Economist; Agriculture, Domestic Policy, Health
Julia A. Tavlas	Strategic Adviser to the Council on National Security

Junior Research Staff

Remington A. Barrett	Research Economist; National Security and International Trade
Andrew M. Baxter	Economist; Deregulation and Macroeconomics
Adam D. Donoho	Staff Economist; Macroeconomics and International Trade
Alex J. Durante	Staff Economist; International Trade and Public Finance
Troy M. Durie	Staff Economist; International Trade, Macroeconomics

William O. Ensor .... Economist; International Trade, Macroeconomics

Luke D. Stuttgen .... Staff Economist; Health

Grayson R. Wiles .... Research Associate; Macroeconomics, Health, and Deregulation

Carson P. Wilson .... Economist; Labor

Statistical Office

Brian A. Amorosi .... Director of Statistical Office

Administrative Office

Megan M. Packer .... Director of Finance and Administration

Interns

Student interns provide invaluable help with research projects, day-to-day operations, and fact-checking. Interns during the year were: Akshay Aggarwal, Jenna Albezreh, Solveig Baylor, Reade Ben, Ann Bennett, Christian Brown, Sachin Das, Peter Deegan, Tivas Gupta, Adam Hoffman, Nicholas Kruppe, Hadley Kruse, Andrew Liang, Gregory Marchal, Kole Nichols, Annika Nordquist, Jacob Ouellet, Max Resnick, Peter Shane, Matthew Stenzel, Madeline VanHorn, Nikitha Vicas, Michael Wang, Robert Williams, Victor Xiao, Tiffany Yen, and Samuel Zwickel.

ERP Production

Alfred F. Imhoff .... Editor

Appendix B

Statistical Tables Relating to Income, Employment, and Production

Contents

Labor Market Indicators

Production and Business Activity

Prices

International Statistics

General Notes

Detail in these tables may not add to totals due to rounding.

Because of the formula used for calculating real gross domestic product (GDP), the chained (2012) dollar estimates for the detailed components do not add to the chained-dollar value of GDP or to any intermediate aggregate. The Department of Commerce (Bureau of Economic Analysis) no longer publishes chained-dollar estimates prior to 2002, except for selected series.

Because of the method used for seasonal adjustment, the sum or average of seasonally adjusted monthly values generally will not equal annual totals based on unadjusted values.

Unless otherwise noted, all dollar figures are in current dollars.

Symbols used:
p Preliminary.
... Not available (also, not applicable).
NSA Not seasonally adjusted.

Data in these tables reflect revisions made by source agencies through December 4, 2020.

Excel versions of these tables are available at www.gpo.gov/erp.

National Income or Expenditure

TABLE B–1. Percent changes in real gross domestic product, 1969–2020

[Percent change, fourth quarter over fourth quarter; quarterly changes at seasonally adjusted annual rates]

Year or quarter	Gross domestic product	Personal consumption expenditures			Gross private domestic investment							Change in private inventories
						Fixed investment						
							Nonresidential					
		Total	Goods	Services	Total	Total	Total	Structures	Equipment	Intellectual property products	Residential	
1969	2.0	3.1	2.0	4.2	2.2	2.5	5.5	6.4	5.2	4.5	-5.4	
1970	-.2	1.7	.0	3.4	-6.4	-.9	-4.4	-2.6	-5.8	-3.4	9.4	
1971	4.4	5.4	6.6	4.3	13.1	10.5	4.7	-1.1	8.5	4.8	25.2	
1972	6.9	7.3	8.5	6.2	15.0	12.0	11.5	5.1	17.0	6.2	12.9	
1973	4.0	1.8	.4	3.2	10.2	3.5	10.6	7.9	13.5	5.1	-10.5	
1974	-1.9	-1.6	-5.6	2.4	-10.4	-9.9	-3.9	-6.4	-3.7	1.6	-24.6	
1975	2.6	5.1	6.1	4.1	-9.8	-2.6	-5.9	-8.1	-6.7	2.8	7.8	
1976	4.3	5.4	6.4	4.5	15.2	12.1	7.8	3.8	9.0	11.8	23.8	
1977	5.0	4.2	4.9	3.7	14.9	12.1	11.9	5.7	17.2	4.8	12.6	
1978	6.7	4.0	3.5	4.4	14.3	13.1	16.0	21.7	14.5	10.3	6.8	
1979	1.3	1.7	.3	2.9	-3.4	1.1	5.5	8.8	2.7	9.4	-9.1	
1980	.0	.0	-2.5	2.2	-7.2	-4.8	-.9	2.7	-4.4	4.7	-15.3	
1981	1.3	.1	-.2	.3	6.7	1.5	9.0	14.1	4.6	12.1	-22.0	
1982	-1.4	3.5	3.6	3.4	-17.3	-8.0	-9.5	-13.5	-10.0	3.4	-1.7	
1983	7.9	6.6	8.3	5.3	31.3	18.3	10.4	-3.9	19.9	13.0	49.7	
1984	5.6	4.3	5.3	3.6	14.2	11.3	13.9	15.7	13.4	12.6	3.7	
1985	4.2	4.8	4.6	5.0	1.9	3.7	3.2	3.3	1.7	7.7	5.2	
1986	2.9	4.4	6.5	3.0	-4.1	.6	-3.2	-14.3	.8	5.4	11.8	
1987	4.5	2.8	.4	4.6	9.8	1.5	2.2	4.9	.1	4.2	-.5	
1988	3.8	4.6	4.5	4.7	-.5	3.7	5.1	-3.3	8.2	9.8	.1	
1989	2.7	2.4	1.8	2.7	.7	1.5	4.5	3.3	2.5	11.3	-6.5	
1990	.6	.8	-1.6	2.3	-6.5	-4.2	-.9	-3.2	-2.7	6.2	-13.6	
1991	1.2	.9	-.8	2.0	2.1	-1.9	-3.4	-12.8	-3.2	7.2	2.9	
1992	4.4	4.9	5.3	4.7	7.7	8.7	7.1	1.0	11.3	4.8	13.6	
1993	2.6	3.3	4.4	2.7	7.6	8.4	7.6	.2	13.1	2.9	10.6	
1994	4.1	3.8	5.5	2.8	11.5	6.6	8.5	1.6	12.5	5.8	1.6	
1995	2.2	2.8	2.3	3.0	.8	5.5	7.4	4.7	8.1	8.3	.1	
1996	4.4	3.4	4.8	2.7	11.2	9.9	11.3	10.9	11.1	12.1	5.6	
1997	4.5	4.5	5.3	4.0	11.4	8.3	9.7	4.4	10.7	12.4	4.0	
1998	4.9	5.6	8.1	4.3	9.7	11.5	11.6	4.3	14.8	11.5	11.3	
1999	4.8	5.1	6.6	4.3	8.5	7.2	8.4	-.1	9.5	13.3	3.5	
2000	3.0	4.4	4.0	4.7	4.3	5.9	8.5	10.8	8.5	6.6	-1.5	
2001	.2	2.5	4.9	1.2	-11.1	-4.7	-6.8	-10.6	-7.7	-2.1	2.0	
2002	2.1	2.1	1.7	2.4	4.4	-1.5	-5.1	-15.7	-3.7	.9	8.1	
2003	4.3	3.8	6.6	2.3	8.7	8.6	6.8	1.9	9.6	5.8	12.7	
2004	3.3	3.8	4.3	3.5	8.0	6.5	6.5	.3	9.8	5.7	6.6	
2005	3.1	3.0	3.0	3.0	6.1	5.8	6.1	1.5	8.7	5.1	5.2	
2006	2.6	3.2	4.6	2.5	-1.5	.0	8.1	9.0	7.1	9.3	-15.2	
2007	2.0	1.6	1.8	1.5	-1.8	-1.1	7.3	17.7	3.9	4.0	-21.2	
2008	-2.8	-1.8	-6.8	.9	-15.3	-11.1	-7.0	-.8	-15.9	.9	-24.7	
2009	.2	-.1	.6	-.4	-9.2	-10.5	-10.3	-27.1	-8.4	3.8	-11.5	
2010	2.6	2.7	4.3	1.9	12.1	6.1	8.9	-3.6	22.6	1.6	-5.7	
2011	1.6	1.2	.9	1.4	10.4	9.2	10.0	8.6	12.7	7.2	5.3	
2012	1.5	1.6	2.4	1.2	4.0	7.2	5.6	4.0	7.8	3.7	15.4	
2013	2.6	1.9	3.5	1.1	9.3	5.7	5.4	6.7	5.4	4.5	7.1	
2014	2.9	3.8	5.0	3.2	5.3	7.0	6.9	9.3	5.6	6.9	7.7	
2015	2.2	3.1	3.8	2.7	2.3	1.7	-.1	-7.3	1.5	3.3	9.2	
2016	2.1	2.7	3.6	2.3	1.2	2.4	1.8	3.5	-2.2	6.4	4.2	
2017	2.7	2.9	5.2	1.8	4.0	4.8	4.8	.0	7.5	4.9	4.7	
2018	2.5	2.4	2.9	2.1	5.9	4.0	6.5	1.2	7.0	9.4	-3.9	
2019	2.3	2.5	3.7	1.9	-1.0	1.5	1.4	1.9	-1.3	4.6	1.6	
2017: I	2.3	3.2	3.9	2.8	-1.2	7.1	5.9	7.9	4.7	5.9	11.7	
II	1.7	1.8	4.9	.4	3.7	1.6	2.4	-.7	5.1	1.1	-1.1	
III	2.9	2.3	4.1	1.5	7.6	1.2	2.1	-10.9	6.2	6.7	-1.7	
IV	3.9	4.2	7.7	2.6	6.3	9.5	9.2	4.7	14.1	6.0	10.5	
2018: I	3.8	2.0	2.1	2.0	11.0	8.5	12.2	21.6	10.1	8.8	-3.3	
II	2.7	3.2	4.2	2.7	-1.1	4.4	6.2	5.0	2.4	12.3	-1.7	
III	2.1	2.7	2.8	2.6	10.2	.8	2.6	-5.9	6.1	4.4	-5.4	
IV	1.3	1.6	2.6	1.1	3.9	2.6	5.0	-12.6	9.6	12.1	-5.2	
2019: I	2.9	1.8	2.5	1.5	3.9	2.9	4.2	8.2	2.0	4.5	-1.7	
II	1.5	3.7	7.7	1.9	-5.8	-.4	.0	1.6	-3.8	4.1	-2.1	
III	2.6	2.7	4.2	2.0	1.8	2.4	1.9	3.6	-1.7	5.3	4.6	
IV	2.4	1.6	.6	2.0	-3.7	1.0	-.3	-5.3	-1.7	4.6	5.8	
2020: I	-5.0	-6.9	.1	-9.8	-9.0	-1.4	-6.7	-3.7	-15.2	2.4	19.0	
II	-31.4	-33.2	-10.8	-41.8	-46.6	-29.2	-27.2	-33.6	-35.9	-11.4	-35.6	
III p	33.1	40.6	46.9	37.6	84.9	30.4	21.8	-15.8	66.6	6.0	62.3	

See next page for continuation of table.

TABLE B–1. Percent changes in real gross domestic product, 1969–2020—*Continued*

[Percent change, fourth quarter over fourth quarter; quarterly changes at seasonally adjusted annual rates]

Year or quarter	Net exports of goods and services			Government consumption expenditures and gross investment					Final sales of domestic product	Gross domestic purchases[1]	Final sales to private domestic purchasers[2]	Gross domestic income (GDI)[3]	Average of GDP and GDI
	Net exports	Exports	Imports	Total	Federal			State and local					
					Total	National defense	Non-defense						
1969		8.7	5.9	−1.2	−3.6	−4.6	−0.2	1.8	2.1	1.9	2.9	2.1	2.1
1970		5.9	3.0	−1.2	−5.8	−8.6	3.9	4.3	.7	−.3	1.1	−.8	−.5
1971		−4.5	1.3	−2.4	−7.3	−11.5	5.6	2.8	4.0	4.7	6.5	4.8	4.6
1972		19.5	17.9	−.1	−2.6	−5.8	6.1	2.3	6.4	6.8	8.3	7.1	7.0
1973		18.4	−.5	−.3	−3.6	−5.0	−.3	2.9	2.8	2.9	2.2	3.8	3.9
1974		3.1	−1.0	3.0	3.7	1.2	9.5	2.4	−1.7	−2.3	−3.5	−2.9	−2.4
1975		1.5	−5.6	3.0	.8	.5	1.4	4.9	3.9	2.0	3.4	2.7	2.6
1976		4.3	19.2	−1.3	−1.0	−2.1	1.3	−1.6	3.8	5.4	6.7	3.8	4.1
1977		−1.4	5.7	1.9	2.3	.1	6.8	1.7	4.5	5.6	5.9	6.0	5.5
1978		18.8	9.9	4.4	3.5	2.9	4.8	5.2	6.4	6.1	6.1	5.4	6.0
1979		10.5	.9	.9	1.2	2.4	−1.1	.7	2.2	.5	1.5	.8	1.0
1980		3.9	−9.3	.3	4.0	3.7	4.6	−2.9	.5	−1.4	−1.2	1.3	.6
1981		.7	6.2	2.5	6.0	7.9	2.0	−.7	.3	1.8	.4	1.2	1.2
1982		−12.2	−3.9	2.6	4.5	7.3	−1.6	.8	.4	−.7	.8	−1.3	−1.3
1983		5.5	24.6	1.9	2.7	6.5	−6.6	1.1	6.0	9.5	9.1	6.6	7.3
1984		9.1	18.9	6.3	7.1	5.6	11.5	5.4	5.0	6.5	5.9	6.7	6.1
1985		1.5	5.6	6.1	6.7	8.2	2.8	5.5	4.6	4.5	4.6	3.4	3.8
1986		10.6	7.9	4.7	5.3	4.7	6.8	4.1	3.9	2.9	3.5	2.7	2.8
1987		12.8	6.3	3.0	3.6	5.3	−1.0	2.4	3.0	4.1	2.5	5.5	5.0
1988		14.0	3.8	1.4	−1.4	−.8	−3.0	4.1	4.6	3.0	4.4	4.7	4.2
1989		10.2	2.6	2.5	.5	−1.3	5.8	4.3	2.9	2.1	2.2	1.0	1.9
1990		7.4	−.2	2.6	1.5	.0	5.4	3.6	1.0	−.1	−.3	1.0	.8
1991		9.2	5.7	.0	−2.3	−4.9	4.3	1.9	.5	.9	.3	.7	.9
1992		4.5	6.5	1.3	1.6	−.4	6.2	1.1	4.5	4.6	5.6	3.9	4.1
1993		4.4	9.9	−.7	−4.5	−5.4	−2.5	2.2	2.7	3.2	4.3	3.0	2.8
1994		10.8	12.2	.0	−4.2	−6.7	1.1	3.1	3.3	4.3	4.4	4.3	4.2
1995		9.4	4.8	−.6	−4.8	−5.0	−4.3	2.2	3.0	1.8	3.3	2.9	2.6
1996		10.1	11.1	2.6	1.1	.3	2.6	3.6	4.2	4.6	4.8	4.8	4.6
1997		8.3	14.2	1.7	.2	−.8	1.9	2.7	3.9	5.2	5.3	5.5	5.0
1998		2.6	11.0	2.8	−.3	−2.4	3.3	4.6	5.2	5.9	6.9	4.9	4.9
1999		6.3	12.0	3.9	3.5	3.9	3.9	4.1	4.5	5.5	5.6	4.5	4.7
2000		6.0	10.9	.4	−2.0	−3.3	.1	1.8	3.3	3.7	4.7	3.3	3.1
2001		−12.2	−7.8	4.9	5.5	4.7	6.7	4.6	1.4	.3	.9	.1	.1
2002		3.9	9.5	3.9	8.1	8.1	8.2	1.6	1.0	2.8	1.4	2.8	2.4
2003		7.2	5.7	1.9	6.5	8.9	2.5	−.7	4.3	4.3	4.8	2.8	3.6
2004		7.4	11.2	.8	2.6	2.8	2.4	−.2	3.0	4.0	4.3	3.8	3.6
2005		7.4	6.3	.9	1.8	1.8	1.9	.3	3.0	3.2	3.6	4.3	3.7
2006		10.3	4.3	1.9	2.4	3.1	1.3	1.6	2.9	2.1	2.5	2.7	2.6
2007		9.2	1.3	2.3	3.6	3.9	3.1	1.5	2.1	1.1	1.0	−.7	.7
2008		−2.4	−5.5	2.5	6.3	7.4	4.2	.3	−2.0	−3.3	−3.7	−2.7	−2.7
2009		1.2	−5.7	3.0	6.2	4.9	8.6	1.0	−.1	−.8	−2.1	.5	.3
2010		9.9	12.0	−1.3	1.9	1.3	3.0	−3.5	1.8	3.1	3.3	3.5	3.0
2011		4.6	3.8	−3.4	−3.5	−3.6	−3.2	−3.3	1.4	1.6	2.6	2.1	1.8
2012		2.1	.6	−2.1	−2.6	−4.7	1.2	−1.7	1.9	1.2	2.6	2.9	2.2
2013		6.0	3.0	−2.4	−6.1	−6.5	−5.5	.2	2.0	2.2	2.6	1.5	2.0
2014		2.9	6.5	.3	−1.1	−3.4	2.7	1.2	3.2	3.4	4.5	4.2	3.5
2015		−1.5	3.3	2.2	1.3	−.4	3.8	2.8	2.1	2.8	2.8	1.4	1.8
2016		1.5	2.8	1.5	.1	−.7	1.2	2.4	2.3	2.2	2.6	1.2	1.6
2017		5.8	5.6	1.1	1.2	2.2	−.1	1.1	2.8	2.8	3.2	2.9	2.8
2018		.5	3.0	1.5	3.0	4.2	1.1	.6	2.2	2.8	2.7	2.4	2.4
2019		.4	−1.9	3.0	4.8	5.6	3.7	1.9	2.8	1.9	2.3	1.9	2.1
2017: I		8.3	4.3	.0	−1.6	−1.8	−1.4	1.0	3.7	1.9	4.0	3.8	3.0
II		1.0	3.6	1.5	2.2	6.4	−3.7	1.2	1.4	2.1	1.8	3.3	2.5
III		2.6	1.7	.2	−.5	−1.5	1.0	.6	1.9	2.8	2.1	1.7	2.3
IV		11.5	13.1	2.8	5.0	6.0	3.6	1.6	4.4	4.3	5.2	2.8	3.4
2018: I		2.7	.3	1.5	1.9	−.5	5.5	1.2	3.4	3.4	3.3	3.6	3.7
II		1.9	−.1	2.9	3.5	5.7	.6	2.5	3.7	2.4	3.4	.8	1.7
III		−5.2	8.0	2.5	4.5	5.4	3.3	1.4	.5	3.9	2.3	4.6	3.3
IV		2.8	4.1	−.9	1.9	6.4	−4.4	−2.5	1.1	1.5	1.8	.6	1.0
2019: I		1.8	−2.1	2.5	1.3	5.6	−4.7	3.2	2.7	2.3	2.0	2.2	2.6
II		−4.5	1.7	5.0	9.2	4.4	16.9	2.6	2.5	2.2	2.8	1.2	1.3
III		.8	.5	2.1	4.8	5.6	3.5	.6	2.7	2.5	2.7	.8	1.7
IV		3.4	−7.5	2.4	4.0	6.6	.1	1.5	3.2	.8	1.5	3.3	2.8
2020: I		−9.5	−15.0	1.3	1.6	−.3	4.4	1.1	−3.6	−5.9	−5.8	−2.5	−3.7
II		−64.4	−54.1	2.5	16.4	3.8	37.6	−5.4	−28.1	−30.3	−32.4	−32.6	−32.0
III p		60.5	93.1	−4.9	−6.2	3.1	−18.1	−4.0	25.6	36.9	38.5	25.5	29.2

[1] Gross domestic product (GDP) less exports of goods and services plus imports of goods and services.
[2] Personal consumption expenditures plus gross private fixed investment.
[3] Gross domestic income is deflated by the implicit price deflator for GDP.

Note: Percent changes based on unrounded GDP quantity indexes.

Source: Department of Commerce (Bureau of Economic Analysis).

Table B–2. Contributions to percent change in real gross domestic product, 1969–2020

[Percentage points, except as noted; annual average to annual average, quarterly data at seasonally adjusted annual rates]

Year or quarter	Gross domestic product (percent change)	Personal consumption expenditures			Gross private domestic investment							
					Total	Fixed investment						Change in private inventories
						Total	Nonresidential				Residential	
		Total	Goods	Services			Total	Structures	Equipment	Intellectual property products		
1969	3.1	2.20	0.92	1.28	0.93	0.93	0.79	0.19	0.51	0.09	0.14	0.00
1970	.2	1.39	.23	1.16	−1.03	−.33	−.10	.01	−.11	.00	−.23	−.70
1971	3.3	2.29	1.23	1.06	1.63	1.08	−.01	−.06	.05	.01	1.08	.56
1972	5.3	3.66	1.90	1.76	1.90	1.85	.97	.12	.75	.11	.87	.06
1973	5.6	2.97	1.52	1.45	1.95	1.47	1.51	.30	1.12	.08	−.04	.48
1974	−.5	−.50	−1.08	.58	−1.24	−.98	.10	−.08	.14	.05	−1.08	−.26
1975	−.2	1.36	.20	1.16	−2.91	−1.68	−1.13	−.42	−.73	.01	−.54	−1.24
1976	5.4	3.41	2.03	1.38	2.91	1.54	.66	.09	.39	.18	.88	1.37
1977	4.6	2.59	1.26	1.33	2.47	2.23	1.26	.15	1.01	.11	.97	.24
1978	5.5	2.68	1.19	1.49	2.22	2.10	1.72	.52	1.08	.12	.38	.12
1979	3.2	1.44	.45	.99	.72	1.11	1.34	.51	.62	.20	−.22	−.40
1980	−.3	−.19	−.72	.53	−2.07	−1.18	.00	.26	−.35	.09	−1.19	−.89
1981	2.5	.85	.33	.52	1.64	.50	.87	.39	.28	.21	−.37	1.13
1982	−1.8	.88	.19	.69	−2.46	−1.16	−.43	−.09	−.47	.12	−.72	−1.31
1983	4.6	3.51	1.69	1.82	1.60	1.32	−.06	−.56	.32	.17	1.38	.28
1984	7.2	3.30	1.91	1.39	4.73	2.83	2.18	.58	1.29	.30	.65	1.90
1985	4.2	3.20	1.38	1.83	−.01	1.02	.91	.31	.39	.21	.11	−1.03
1986	3.5	2.58	1.45	1.13	.03	.34	−.24	−.49	.08	.17	.58	−.31
1987	3.5	2.15	.47	1.67	.53	.11	.01	−.11	.03	.10	.10	.41
1988	4.2	2.65	.96	1.69	.45	.59	.63	.02	.43	.18	−.05	−.13
1989	3.7	1.86	.64	1.21	.72	.55	.71	.07	.35	.29	−.16	.17
1990	1.9	1.28	.16	1.12	−.45	−.25	.14	.05	−.14	.22	−.38	−.21
1991	−.1	.12	−.49	.61	−1.09	−.84	−.48	−.38	−.28	.18	−.35	−.26
1992	3.5	2.36	.76	1.60	1.11	.83	.33	−.18	.34	.17	.49	.28
1993	2.8	2.24	.99	1.26	1.24	1.17	.84	−.01	.73	.12	.32	.07
1994	4.0	2.51	1.26	1.26	1.90	1.29	.91	.05	.75	.11	.38	.61
1995	2.7	1.91	.71	1.20	.55	.99	1.15	.16	.78	.20	−.15	−.44
1996	3.8	2.26	1.06	1.20	1.49	1.48	1.13	.15	.65	.33	.35	.02
1997	4.4	2.45	1.12	1.33	2.01	1.49	1.38	.21	.76	.41	.11	.52
1998	4.5	3.42	1.54	1.88	1.76	1.82	1.44	.16	.91	.37	.38	−.07
1999	4.8	3.42	1.83	1.59	1.62	1.65	1.36	.01	.89	.45	.29	−.03
2000	4.1	3.32	1.23	2.09	1.31	1.34	1.31	.24	.71	.36	.03	−.03
2001	1.0	1.66	.72	.94	−1.11	−.27	−.31	−.04	−.31	.04	.04	−.84
2002	1.7	1.71	.92	.80	−.16	−.64	−.94	−.56	−.35	−.03	.29	.48
2003	2.9	2.13	1.15	.98	.76	.77	.30	−.09	.26	.14	.47	−.02
2004	3.8	2.53	1.21	1.32	1.64	1.23	.67	.00	.49	.18	.57	.41
2005	3.5	2.39	.98	1.41	1.26	1.33	.92	.06	.60	.26	.41	−.07
2006	2.9	2.05	.87	1.19	.60	.50	1.00	.22	.57	.21	−.50	.10
2007	1.9	1.49	.65	.84	−.48	−.24	.89	.42	.25	.23	−1.13	−.25
2008	−.1	−.14	−.71	.56	−1.52	−1.05	.08	.23	−.29	.14	−1.14	−.46
2009	−2.5	−.85	−.70	−.15	−3.52	−2.70	−1.95	−.72	−1.22	−.02	−.74	−.83
2010	2.6	1.20	.62	.57	1.86	.44	.52	−.50	.92	.11	−.08	1.42
2011	1.6	1.29	.49	.80	.94	.99	1.00	.07	.69	.24	.00	−.05
2012	2.2	1.03	.48	.55	1.64	1.47	1.16	.34	.62	.20	.31	.17
2013	1.8	.99	.70	.29	1.11	.87	.54	.04	.28	.22	.34	.23
2014	2.5	1.99	.90	1.10	.95	1.07	.95	.33	.42	.20	.12	−.12
2015	3.1	2.55	1.03	1.53	.95	.65	.32	−.03	.19	.16	.33	.31
2016	1.7	1.87	.77	1.10	−.27	.30	.07	−.14	−.10	.32	.23	−.57
2017	2.3	1.79	.86	.93	.60	.64	.49	.12	.18	.18	.15	−.04
2018	3.0	1.85	.86	.98	1.08	.88	.91	.11	.45	.34	−.02	.20
2019	2.2	1.64	.78	.86	.30	.32	.39	−.02	.12	.29	−.07	−.02
2017: I	2.3	2.15	.83	1.32	−.23	1.17	.75	.24	.26	.25	.43	−1.41
II	1.7	1.23	1.04	.20	.61	.27	.31	−.02	.28	.05	−.04	.34
III	2.9	1.57	.86	.71	1.26	.21	.28	−.35	.35	.28	−.07	1.05
IV	3.9	2.82	1.61	1.20	1.07	1.57	1.18	.14	.78	.26	.39	−.50
2018: I	3.8	1.40	.45	.95	1.83	1.42	1.55	.60	.57	.38	−.13	.41
II	2.7	2.13	.88	1.25	−.19	.76	.82	.15	.15	.52	−.07	−.94
III	2.1	1.79	.60	1.19	1.72	.14	.36	−.19	.35	.19	−.22	1.58
IV	1.3	1.05	.53	.52	.69	.46	.66	−.40	.54	.52	−.21	.23
2019: I	2.9	1.25	.52	.73	.71	.50	.56	.24	.12	.20	−.06	.21
II	1.5	2.47	1.57	.90	−1.04	−.07	.01	.05	−.23	.19	−.08	−.97
III	2.6	1.83	.87	.96	.34	.42	.25	.11	−.10	.24	.17	−.09
IV	2.4	1.07	.12	.96	−.64	.17	−.04	−.16	−.10	.21	.22	−.82
2020: I	−5.0	−4.75	.03	−4.78	−1.56	−.23	−.91	−.11	−.91	.11	.68	−1.34
II	−31.4	−24.01	−2.06	−21.95	−8.77	−5.27	−3.67	−1.11	−2.03	−.53	−1.60	−3.50
III ᵖ	33.1	25.22	9.49	15.73	11.78	5.23	3.06	−.47	3.19	.34	2.17	6.55

See next page for continuation of table.

TABLE B–2. Contributions to percent change in real gross domestic product, 1969–2020—*Continued*

[Percentage points, except as noted; annual average to annual average, quarterly data at seasonally adjusted annual rates]

Year or quarter	Net exports of goods and services							Government consumption expenditures and gross investment					Final sales of domestic product
	Net exports	Exports			Imports			Total	Federal			State and local	
		Total	Goods	Services	Total	Goods	Services		Total	National defense	Non-defense		
1969	−0.03	0.25	0.20	0.05	−0.28	−0.20	−0.08	0.02	−0.34	−0.45	0.11	0.36	3.12
1970	.33	.54	.43	.11	−.21	−.14	−.07	−.50	−.80	−.83	.03	.30	.89
1971	−.18	.10	.00	.10	−.28	−.32	.04	−.45	−.80	−.97	.17	.35	2.74
1972	−.19	.42	.43	−.01	−.61	−.55	−.06	−.12	−.37	−.60	.22	.25	5.20
1973	.80	1.08	1.05	.02	−.28	−.33	.05	−.07	−.39	−.40	.01	.32	5.16
1974	.73	.56	.49	.08	.17	.17	.00	.47	.06	−.07	.14	.41	−.28
1975	.86	−.05	−.14	.09	.91	.85	.06	.49	.05	−.07	.13	.43	1.03
1976	−1.05	.36	.34	.02	−1.41	−1.31	−.10	.12	.01	−.04	.06	.10	4.01
1977	−.70	.19	.12	.07	−.89	−.82	−.07	.26	.21	.06	.15	.05	4.38
1978	.05	.80	.64	.17	−.76	−.66	−.10	.60	.23	.04	.19	.37	5.42
1979	.64	.80	.69	.11	−.16	−.13	−.02	.36	.20	.15	.05	.16	3.56
1980	1.64	.95	.88	.07	.69	.66	.03	.36	.38	.22	.16	−.02	.63
1981	−.15	.12	−.05	.17	−.26	−.18	−.09	.20	.43	.40	.03	−.23	1.41
1982	−.59	−.71	−.63	−.08	.12	.20	−.08	.37	.35	.47	−.11	.01	−.50
1983	−1.32	−.22	−.21	.00	−1.10	−.98	−.12	.79	.65	.51	.14	.14	4.31
1984	−1.54	.61	.41	.20	−2.16	−1.78	−.38	.74	.33	.38	−.04	.41	5.34
1985	−.39	.24	.20	.05	−.63	−.50	−.13	1.37	.78	.62	.16	.59	5.20
1986	−.29	.53	.27	.25	−.82	−.80	−.02	1.14	.61	.52	.09	.53	3.77
1987	.17	.77	.62	.15	−.60	−.39	−.21	.62	.38	.38	.01	.24	3.05
1988	.81	1.23	.99	.24	−.41	−.35	−.07	.26	−.15	−.04	−.12	.42	4.31
1989	.51	.97	.72	.26	−.46	−.37	−.09	.58	.15	−.02	.18	.43	3.51
1990	.40	.78	.56	.22	−.37	−.25	−.13	.65	.20	.02	.18	.45	2.09
1991	.62	.61	.45	.16	.01	−.04	.05	.25	.01	−.06	.07	.24	.15
1992	−.04	.66	.52	.14	−.70	−.76	.05	.10	−.15	−.31	.16	.25	3.24
1993	−.56	.31	.22	.09	−.87	−.82	−.05	−.17	−.32	−.32	.00	.15	2.68
1994	−.41	.84	.65	.19	−1.25	−1.15	−.10	.02	−.31	−.28	−.02	.32	3.41
1995	.12	1.02	.83	.19	−.90	−.84	−.06	.10	−.21	−.21	.00	.31	3.13
1996	−.15	.86	.68	.18	−1.01	−.91	−.10	.18	−.09	−.08	−.01	.27	3.76
1997	−.31	1.26	1.10	.16	−1.57	−1.40	−.17	.30	−.06	−.13	.07	.36	3.92
1998	−1.14	.26	.17	.08	−1.39	−1.18	−.21	.44	−.06	−.09	.03	.50	4.55
1999	−.87	.52	.31	.20	−1.39	−1.31	−.07	.58	.13	.06	.07	.46	4.78
2000	−.83	.86	.73	.13	−1.69	−1.44	−.25	.33	.02	−.04	.06	.31	4.16
2001	−.22	−.61	−.48	−.12	.39	.40	−.01	.67	.24	.13	.11	.43	1.84
2002	−.64	−.17	−.23	.06	−.47	−.40	−.07	.82	.47	.30	.18	.35	1.26
2003	−.45	.20	.19	.01	−.64	−.64	−.01	.41	.45	.35	.10	−.03	2.88
2004	−.67	.88	.57	.31	−1.55	−1.30	−.24	−.30	.31	.26	.05	−.01	3.39
2005	−.29	.69	.52	.17	−.97	−.88	−.09	.15	.15	.11	.04	.00	3.59
2006	−.10	.94	.70	.23	−1.04	−.82	−.21	.30	.17	.07	.10	.13	2.75
2007	.53	.93	.53	.40	−.41	−.28	−.12	.34	.14	.13	.01	.20	2.12
2008	1.04	.66	.48	.18	.38	.49	−.10	.48	.46	.33	.13	.02	.33
2009	1.13	−1.01	−1.00	−.01	2.14	2.08	.06	.70	.47	.29	.18	.23	−1.71
2010	−.49	1.35	1.12	.23	−1.84	−1.74	−.10	.00	.35	.16	.19	−.35	1.14
2011	−.01	.90	.61	.28	−.91	−.82	−.09	−.66	−.23	−.12	−.11	−.44	1.60
2012	.00	.46	.36	.10	−.46	−.38	−.09	−.42	−.16	−.18	.03	−.26	2.08
2013	.22	.48	.30	.18	−.26	−.25	−.01	−.47	−.44	−.34	−.10	−.03	1.61
2014	−.25	.57	.42	.14	−.81	−.75	−.06	−.17	−.19	−.19	.00	.02	2.65
2015	−.76	.06	−.03	.09	−.81	−.73	−.08	.33	.00	−.09	.09	.33	2.77
2016	−.21	.04	.04	−.01	−.25	−.17	−.08	.32	.04	−.02	.06	.28	2.28
2017	−.22	.47	.31	.15	−.68	−.56	−.12	.16	.02	.03	−.01	.14	2.37
2018	−.25	.36	.33	.03	−.62	−.60	−.01	.32	.18	.13	.06	.13	2.80
2019	−.18	−.01	−.01	−.01	−.16	−.06	−.10	.40	.26	.21	.05	.14	2.18
2017: I	.36	.98	.59	.39	−.62	−.46	−.16	.01	−.10	−.07	−.04	.11	3.69
II	−.39	.13	−.12	.25	−.52	−.32	−.20	.27	.14	.24	−.10	.13	1.38
III	.08	.33	.23	.10	−.25	−.14	−.11	.04	−.03	−.06	.03	.07	1.89
IV	−.49	1.36	1.24	.12	−1.85	−1.89	.04	.49	.32	.23	.09	.17	4.38
2018: I	.29	.34	.11	.23	−.05	−.19	.13	.26	.12	−.02	.14	.13	3.37
II	.25	.24	.67	−.43	.01	.01	.00	.50	.23	.21	.01	.27	3.64
III	−1.83	−.66	−.71	.05	−1.17	−1.08	−.09	.44	.29	.20	.08	.15	.54
IV	−.27	.34	.34	.00	−.61	−.39	−.23	−.16	.12	.24	−.12	−.28	1.09
2019: I	.55	.22	.31	−.08	.33	.34	−.01	.43	.09	.22	−.13	.34	2.73
II	−.79	−.54	−.74	.20	−.25	−.01	−.24	.86	.58	.17	.41	.28	2.46
III	.04	.10	.23	−.13	−.06	−.08	.02	.37	.31	.22	.09	.06	2.66
IV	1.52	.39	.19	.20	1.13	1.15	−.03	.42	.26	.26	.00	.16	3.18
2020: I	1.13	−1.12	−.20	−.92	2.25	1.36	.90	.22	.10	−.01	.11	.12	−3.62
II	.62	−9.51	−6.56	−2.95	10.13	7.32	2.80	.77	1.17	.18	.98	−.40	−27.88
III *p*	−3.18	4.95	4.88	.07	−8.12	−7.67	−.46	−.76	−.38	.17	−.55	−.38	26.51

Source: Department of Commerce (Bureau of Economic Analysis).

TABLE B–3. Gross domestic product, 2004–2020

[Quarterly data at seasonally adjusted annual rates]

Year or quarter	Gross domestic product	Personal consumption expenditures			Gross private domestic investment							
		Total	Goods	Services	Total	Fixed investment						Change in private inventories
						Total	Nonresidential				Residential	
							Total	Structures	Equipment	Intellectual property products		
Billions of dollars												
2004	12,213.7	8,212.7	2,902.0	5,310.6	2,281.3	2,217.2	1,467.4	307.7	721.9	437.8	749.8	64.1
2005	13,036.6	8,747.1	3,082.9	5,664.2	2,534.7	2,477.2	1,621.0	353.0	794.9	473.1	856.2	57.5
2006	13,814.6	9,260.3	3,239.7	6,020.7	2,701.0	2,632.0	1,793.8	425.2	862.3	506.3	838.2	69.0
2007	14,451.9	9,706.4	3,367.0	6,339.4	2,673.0	2,639.1	1,948.6	510.3	893.4	544.8	690.5	34.0
2008	14,712.8	9,976.3	3,363.2	6,613.1	2,477.6	2,506.9	1,990.9	571.1	845.4	574.4	516.0	−29.2
2009	14,448.9	9,842.2	3,180.0	6,662.2	1,929.7	2,080.4	1,690.4	455.8	670.3	564.4	390.0	−150.8
2010	14,992.1	10,185.8	3,317.8	6,868.0	2,165.5	2,111.6	1,735.0	379.8	777.0	578.2	376.6	53.9
2011	15,542.6	10,641.1	3,518.1	7,123.0	2,332.6	2,286.3	1,907.5	404.5	881.3	621.7	378.8	46.3
2012	16,197.0	11,006.8	3,637.7	7,369.1	2,621.8	2,550.5	2,118.5	479.4	983.4	655.7	432.0	71.2
2013	16,784.9	11,317.2	3,730.0	7,587.2	2,826.0	2,721.5	2,211.5	492.5	1,027.0	691.9	510.0	104.5
2014	17,527.3	11,822.8	3,863.0	7,959.8	3,044.2	2,960.2	2,400.1	577.6	1,091.9	730.5	560.2	84.0
2015	18,238.3	12,297.5	3,923.0	8,374.5	3,237.2	3,100.4	2,466.6	584.4	1,119.5	762.7	633.8	136.8
2016	18,745.1	12,770.0	3,998.4	8,771.6	3,188.3	3,160.0	2,460.5	560.3	1,088.6	811.7	699.5	28.4
2017	19,543.0	13,340.4	4,172.3	9,168.1	3,351.1	3,334.8	2,574.5	599.1	1,122.2	853.2	760.3	16.3
2018	20,611.9	13,993.3	4,371.9	9,621.4	3,632.9	3,575.1	2,776.7	631.4	1,213.4	931.8	798.5	57.7
2019	21,433.2	14,544.6	4,512.2	10,032.4	3,751.2	3,702.1	2,895.0	650.2	1,241.0	1,003.8	807.1	49.1
2017: I	19,237.4	13,153.2	4,108.1	9,045.1	3,266.2	3,278.5	2,532.5	600.1	1,094.3	838.0	746.0	−12.3
II	19,379.2	13,241.3	4,130.3	9,111.0	3,313.3	3,309.2	2,555.9	604.5	1,107.5	843.9	753.3	4.0
III	19,617.3	13,370.9	4,177.3	9,193.6	3,378.8	3,333.8	2,575.2	592.3	1,124.7	858.2	758.5	45.1
IV	19,938.0	13,596.0	4,273.4	9,322.7	3,446.3	3,417.8	2,634.2	599.3	1,162.4	872.5	783.6	28.5
2018: I	20,242.2	13,755.5	4,315.6	9,440.0	3,555.0	3,510.5	2,716.2	629.2	1,189.6	897.4	794.3	44.5
II	20,552.7	13,939.9	4,368.8	9,571.1	3,580.9	3,570.2	2,765.9	640.7	1,197.0	928.3	804.3	10.7
III	20,742.7	14,086.3	4,394.8	9,691.4	3,671.7	3,593.3	2,792.6	634.2	1,219.6	938.9	800.7	78.4
IV	20,909.9	14,191.4	4,408.3	9,783.1	3,723.9	3,626.5	2,831.9	621.5	1,247.6	962.8	794.7	97.3
2019: I	21,115.3	14,276.6	4,415.2	9,861.4	3,772.8	3,674.2	2,878.4	640.1	1,256.5	981.9	795.8	98.6
II	21,329.9	14,497.3	4,517.7	9,979.6	3,739.7	3,686.6	2,891.3	649.7	1,243.1	998.5	795.3	53.1
III	21,540.3	14,645.3	4,553.6	10,091.7	3,759.8	3,718.5	2,908.0	658.8	1,234.9	1,014.2	810.5	41.3
IV	21,747.4	14,759.2	4,562.4	10,196.8	3,732.6	3,729.2	2,902.3	652.3	1,229.3	1,020.7	827.0	3.4
2020: I	21,561.1	14,545.5	4,552.9	9,992.5	3,675.9	3,728.0	2,859.3	648.7	1,181.6	1,029.1	868.7	−52.1
II	19,520.1	13,097.3	4,361.5	8,735.8	3,128.6	3,427.0	2,646.8	584.0	1,057.2	1,005.6	780.2	−298.4
III p	21,157.1	14,394.2	4,866.1	9,528.1	3,680.3	3,682.3	2,781.7	560.3	1,199.1	1,022.3	900.6	−2.1
Billions of chained (2012) dollars												
2004	14,406.4	9,729.3	3,250.0	6,479.2	2,502.6	2,440.7	1,594.0	456.3	688.6	459.2	830.9	82.6
2005	14,912.5	10,075.9	3,384.7	6,689.5	2,670.6	2,618.7	1,716.4	466.1	760.0	493.1	885.4	63.7
2006	15,338.3	10,384.5	3,509.7	6,871.7	2,752.4	2,686.8	1,854.2	501.7	832.6	521.5	818.9	87.1
2007	15,626.0	10,615.3	3,607.6	7,003.6	2,684.1	2,653.5	1,982.1	568.6	865.8	554.3	665.8	40.6
2008	15,604.7	10,592.8	3,498.9	7,093.0	2,462.9	2,499.4	1,994.2	605.4	824.4	575.3	504.6	−32.7
2009	15,208.8	10,460.0	3,389.8	7,070.1	1,942.0	2,099.8	1,704.3	492.2	649.7	572.4	395.3	−177.3
2010	15,598.8	10,643.0	3,485.7	7,157.4	2,216.5	2,164.2	1,781.0	412.8	781.2	588.1	383.0	57.3
2011	15,840.7	10,843.8	3,561.8	7,282.1	2,362.1	2,317.8	1,935.4	424.1	886.2	624.8	382.5	46.7
2012	16,197.0	11,006.8	3,637.7	7,369.1	2,621.8	2,550.5	2,118.5	479.4	983.4	655.7	432.0	71.2
2013	16,495.4	11,166.9	3,752.2	7,415.5	2,801.5	2,692.1	2,206.0	485.5	1,029.2	691.4	485.5	108.7
2014	16,912.0	11,497.4	3,905.1	7,594.9	2,959.2	2,869.2	2,365.3	538.8	1,101.1	724.8	504.1	86.3
2015	17,432.2	11,934.3	4,090.9	7,849.0	3,121.8	2,979.0	2,420.3	534.1	1,134.6	752.4	555.4	137.6
2016	17,730.5	12,264.6	4,238.9	8,035.6	3,074.8	3,032.2	2,433.0	510.5	1,115.1	809.8	592.1	24.5
2017	18,144.1	12,587.2	4,410.6	8,195.5	3,183.4	3,147.4	2,524.2	531.7	1,150.3	844.2	615.7	15.8
2018	18,687.8	12,928.1	4,590.2	8,367.1	3,384.9	3,310.4	2,698.9	551.1	1,242.2	910.2	612.0	53.4
2019	19,091.7	13,240.2	4,760.5	8,520.5	3,442.6	3,371.7	2,776.8	547.7	1,267.7	968.2	601.5	48.5
2017: I	17,977.3	12,477.3	4,328.2	8,161.0	3,120.4	3,115.5	2,492.6	538.5	1,121.5	832.6	614.4	−18.9
II	18,054.1	12,533.1	4,380.8	8,169.3	3,149.1	3,127.7	2,507.3	537.6	1,135.5	834.8	612.7	.6
III	18,185.6	12,604.5	4,424.9	8,199.7	3,207.5	3,137.1	2,520.3	522.3	1,152.6	848.4	610.1	56.1
IV	18,359.4	12,733.7	4,508.3	8,251.9	3,256.7	3,209.2	2,576.4	528.4	1,191.4	860.9	625.5	25.3
2018: I	18,530.5	12,798.1	4,531.6	8,293.2	3,342.5	3,275.2	2,651.5	554.8	1,220.3	879.3	620.3	47.3
II	18,654.4	12,898.1	4,578.5	8,348.5	3,333.3	3,310.6	2,691.9	561.6	1,227.7	905.2	617.6	−4.9
III	18,752.4	12,983.0	4,610.7	8,401.7	3,415.4	3,317.0	2,709.5	553.2	1,245.9	914.9	609.1	79.1
IV	18,813.9	13,033.4	4,639.8	8,425.1	3,448.3	3,338.7	2,742.6	534.9	1,274.8	941.5	601.0	92.3
2019: I	18,950.3	13,093.2	4,668.6	8,457.5	3,481.3	3,362.3	2,770.8	545.5	1,281.1	951.9	598.4	101.7
II	19,020.6	13,212.8	4,756.3	8,498.3	3,429.9	3,358.6	2,771.0	547.8	1,268.6	961.5	595.2	49.4
III	19,141.7	13,301.3	4,805.2	8,541.5	3,445.7	3,378.9	2,783.9	552.6	1,263.3	974.0	601.9	44.0
IV	19,254.0	13,353.7	4,811.8	8,584.9	3,413.3	3,387.2	2,781.5	545.1	1,258.0	985.2	610.5	−1.1
2020: I	19,010.8	13,118.4	4,812.9	8,365.3	3,334.0	3,375.4	2,733.8	540.0	1,207.1	991.1	637.6	−80.9
II	17,302.5	11,860.3	4,677.4	7,306.9	2,849.8	3,096.3	2,525.5	487.5	1,080.1	961.5	571.3	−287.0
III p	18,583.5	12,915.9	5,149.7	7,913.5	3,323.1	3,308.6	2,653.4	467.0	1,227.1	975.7	644.8	−4.3

See next page for continuation of table.

| Year or quarter | Net exports of goods and services | | | Government consumption expenditures and gross investment | | | | | Final sales of domestic product | Gross domestic purchases [1] | Final sales to private domestic purchasers [2] | Gross domestic income (GDI) [3] | Average of GDP and GDI |
| | Net exports | Exports | Imports | Total | Federal | | | State and local | | | | | |
					Total	National defense	Non-defense						
	Billions of dollars												
2004	−619.1	1,177.6	1,796.7	2,338.9	891.7	569.9	321.9	1,447.1	12,149.7	12,832.8	10,429.8	12,236.1	12,224.9
2005	−721.2	1,305.2	2,026.4	2,476.0	947.5	609.4	338.0	1,528.5	12,979.1	13,757.8	11,224.3	13,089.3	13,063.0
2006	−770.9	1,472.6	2,243.5	2,624.2	1,000.7	640.8	359.9	1,623.5	13,745.6	14,585.5	11,892.3	14,021.8	13,918.2
2007	−718.4	1,660.9	2,379.3	2,790.8	1,050.5	679.3	371.2	1,740.3	14,417.9	15,170.3	12,345.5	14,434.5	14,443.2
2008	−723.1	1,837.1	2,560.1	2,982.0	1,150.6	750.3	400.2	1,831.4	14,742.1	15,435.9	12,483.2	14,530.3	14,621.6
2009	−396.5	1,582.0	1,978.4	3,073.5	1,218.2	787.6	430.6	1,855.3	14,599.7	14,845.4	11,922.6	14,259.0	14,354.0
2010	−513.9	1,846.3	2,360.2	3,154.6	1,297.9	828.0	469.9	1,856.7	14,938.1	15,506.0	12,297.4	14,932.1	14,962.1
2011	−579.5	2,103.0	2,682.5	3,148.4	1,298.9	834.0	465.0	1,849.4	15,496.3	16,122.0	12,927.4	15,599.4	15,571.0
2012	−568.6	2,191.3	2,759.9	3,137.0	1,286.5	814.2	472.4	1,850.5	16,125.8	16,765.6	13,557.4	16,436.8	16,316.9
2013	−490.8	2,273.4	2,764.2	3,132.4	1,226.6	764.2	462.4	1,905.8	16,680.3	17,275.6	14,038.7	16,941.8	16,863.3
2014	−507.7	2,371.7	2,879.4	3,168.0	1,215.0	743.4	471.6	1,953.0	17,443.3	18,034.9	14,783.0	17,813.9	17,670.6
2015	−526.6	2,265.9	2,792.4	3,230.2	1,220.8	729.7	491.0	2,009.4	18,101.5	18,764.9	15,397.9	18,475.6	18,357.0
2016	−512.5	2,227.2	2,739.7	3,299.3	1,234.7	728.7	506.0	2,064.6	18,716.7	19,257.6	15,930.0	18,837.3	18,791.2
2017	−555.5	2,374.6	2,930.1	3,407.0	1,263.9	747.2	516.6	2,143.2	19,526.7	20,098.5	16,675.2	19,674.4	19,608.7
2018	−609.5	2,528.7	3,138.2	3,595.2	1,339.4	794.3	545.1	2,255.7	20,554.1	21,221.3	17,568.4	20,669.9	20,640.9
2019	−610.5	2,514.8	3,125.2	3,747.9	1,419.2	852.4	566.7	2,328.7	21,384.1	22,043.7	18,246.7	21,420.4	21,426.8
2017: I	−543.6	2,326.4	2,869.9	3,361.6	1,246.5	733.2	513.3	2,115.1	19,249.7	19,781.0	16,431.6	19,352.2	19,294.8
II	−559.5	2,333.1	2,892.6	3,384.2	1,257.9	746.2	511.7	2,126.3	19,375.2	19,938.8	16,550.5	19,572.2	19,475.7
III	−543.6	2,370.1	2,913.7	3,411.1	1,262.7	746.4	516.4	2,148.4	19,572.2	20,160.9	16,704.7	19,750.4	19,683.9
IV	−575.5	2,468.7	3,044.1	3,471.1	1,288.3	763.0	525.3	2,182.9	19,909.5	20,513.4	17,013.8	20,022.8	19,980.4
2018: I	−589.8	2,507.2	3,097.0	3,521.5	1,308.1	770.2	537.9	2,213.4	20,197.7	20,832.0	17,266.0	20,319.8	20,281.0
II	−548.1	2,550.3	3,098.4	3,580.0	1,329.3	786.8	542.5	2,250.7	20,541.9	21,100.8	17,510.1	20,533.2	20,542.9
III	−646.4	2,523.9	3,170.3	3,631.2	1,352.0	802.0	550.1	2,279.1	20,664.4	21,389.2	17,679.6	20,847.3	20,795.0
IV	−653.4	2,533.4	3,186.9	3,648.0	1,368.4	818.4	550.0	2,279.6	20,812.5	21,563.3	17,818.0	20,979.1	20,944.5
2019: I	−615.5	2,523.5	3,139.0	3,681.5	1,388.8	833.0	555.8	2,292.7	21,016.7	21,730.9	17,950.8	21,147.8	21,131.6
II	−644.7	2,514.6	3,159.4	3,737.6	1,410.6	844.3	566.4	2,327.0	21,276.8	21,974.6	18,183.9	21,347.2	21,338.6
III	−631.8	2,505.2	3,137.1	3,767.1	1,429.3	857.7	571.6	2,337.8	21,499.0	22,172.2	18,363.8	21,465.3	21,502.8
IV	−549.8	2,515.7	3,065.4	3,805.3	1,447.9	874.7	573.3	2,357.4	21,744.0	22,297.2	18,488.4	21,721.2	21,734.3
2020: I	−494.3	2,438.7	2,933.0	3,834.1	1,452.6	873.8	578.8	2,381.6	21,613.3	22,055.4	18,273.4	21,671.3	21,616.2
II	−545.2	1,788.2	2,333.3	3,839.3	1,504.8	876.5	628.3	2,334.5	19,818.5	20,065.3	16,524.3	19,533.5	19,526.8
III *p*	−733.8	2,074.5	2,808.3	3,816.5	1,486.8	887.5	599.3	2,329.7	21,159.2	21,890.9	18,076.5	20,863.9	21,010.5
	Billions of chained (2012) dollars												
2004	−841.4	1,431.2	2,272.6	2,992.7	1,077.5	692.7	384.8	1,920.1	14,335.7	15,254.1	12,194.2	14,432.7	14,419.6
2005	−887.8	1,533.2	2,421.0	3,015.5	1,099.1	708.6	390.6	1,920.1	14,852.3	15,804.5	12,725.8	14,972.8	14,942.7
2006	−905.0	1,676.4	2,581.5	3,063.5	1,125.0	719.8	405.3	1,941.6	15,263.0	16,246.7	13,102.6	15,568.3	15,453.3
2007	−823.6	1,822.3	2,646.0	3,118.6	1,147.0	740.3	406.7	1,974.7	15,588.7	16,454.6	13,293.8	15,607.2	15,616.6
2008	−661.6	1,925.4	2,587.1	3,195.6	1,218.8	791.5	427.3	1,978.7	15,639.7	16,270.7	13,108.0	15,411.1	15,507.9
2009	−484.8	1,763.8	2,248.6	3,307.3	1,293.0	836.7	456.3	2,015.6	15,373.0	15,698.9	12,557.6	15,008.9	15,108.9
2010	−565.9	1,977.9	2,543.8	3,307.2	1,346.1	861.3	484.8	1,961.3	15,546.6	16,164.7	12,805.7	15,536.3	15,567.5
2011	−568.1	2,119.0	2,687.1	3,203.3	1,311.1	842.9	468.3	1,892.2	15,796.5	16,408.8	13,161.2	15,898.6	15,869.6
2012	−568.6	2,191.3	2,759.9	3,137.0	1,286.5	814.2	472.4	1,850.5	16,125.8	16,765.6	13,557.4	16,436.8	16,316.9
2013	−532.8	2,269.6	2,802.4	3,061.0	1,215.3	759.6	455.6	1,845.3	16,386.2	17,028.6	13,858.9	16,649.6	16,572.5
2014	−577.2	2,365.2	2,942.5	3,033.4	1,183.8	728.4	455.2	1,848.6	16,822.3	17,487.7	14,366.5	17,188.6	17,050.3
2015	−719.5	2,375.2	3,094.8	3,088.2	1,183.8	713.1	470.2	1,902.9	17,290.1	18,141.1	14,913.2	17,659.0	17,545.6
2016	−763.6	2,382.3	3,145.9	3,144.4	1,190.5	709.6	480.4	1,952.0	17,686.9	18,480.6	15,296.6	17,817.7	17,774.1
2017	−816.8	2,475.5	3,292.4	3,172.3	1,194.1	715.4	478.2	1,976.2	18,107.2	18,939.0	15,734.3	18,266.1	18,205.1
2018	−877.7	2,549.5	3,427.2	3,229.8	1,227.8	739.1	488.4	2,000.2	18,613.8	19,537.1	16,238.2	18,740.4	18,714.1
2019	−917.6	2,546.6	3,464.2	3,303.9	1,277.2	780.2	497.1	2,025.5	19,021.1	19,981.0	16,611.7	19,080.2	19,085.9
2017: I	−792.3	2,446.0	3,238.3	3,156.9	1,186.4	705.8	479.9	1,968.4	17,970.8	18,751.0	15,592.5	18,084.6	18,030.9
II	−815.0	2,451.9	3,266.9	3,169.0	1,192.7	716.9	475.4	1,974.2	18,031.4	18,847.6	15,660.6	18,233.8	18,143.9
III	−813.0	2,468.0	3,281.0	3,170.6	1,191.3	714.2	476.6	1,977.2	18,115.0	18,978.5	15,741.5	18,309.1	18,247.4
IV	−847.0	2,536.2	3,383.2	3,192.8	1,206.0	724.7	480.8	1,984.9	18,311.4	19,178.8	15,942.8	18,437.6	18,398.5
2018: I	−833.0	2,553.2	3,386.1	3,204.3	1,211.7	723.8	487.3	1,990.7	18,463.4	19,339.5	16,073.0	18,601.5	18,566.0
II	−820.2	2,565.2	3,385.4	3,227.3	1,222.3	733.9	488.0	2,003.0	18,630.7	19,453.6	16,208.3	18,636.7	18,645.6
III	−920.3	2,531.0	3,451.3	3,247.4	1,235.8	743.5	491.9	2,009.9	18,655.1	19,640.0	16,299.7	18,846.9	18,799.6
IV	−937.3	2,548.6	3,486.0	3,240.2	1,241.6	755.1	486.4	1,997.1	18,705.9	19,715.2	16,371.8	18,876.3	18,845.1
2019: I	−907.4	2,560.4	3,467.8	3,260.0	1,245.8	765.5	480.5	2,012.7	18,833.1	19,827.8	16,455.1	18,979.5	18,964.9
II	−951.4	2,531.4	3,482.9	3,300.3	1,273.6	773.7	499.7	2,025.5	18,949.6	19,937.4	16,571.1	19,036.1	19,028.3
III	−950.2	2,536.6	3,486.8	3,317.7	1,288.5	784.4	504.0	2,028.3	19,075.2	20,059.1	16,680.0	19,075.1	19,108.4
IV	−861.5	2,557.8	3,419.3	3,337.5	1,301.1	797.1	504.1	2,035.6	19,226.6	20,099.6	16,740.6	19,230.7	19,242.4
2020: I	−788.0	2,495.1	3,283.1	3,347.9	1,306.1	796.5	509.6	2,041.0	19,049.0	19,797.8	16,493.4	19,108.0	19,059.4
II	−775.1	1,927.4	2,702.5	3,368.7	1,356.8	804.0	551.9	2,013.1	17,540.5	18,087.5	14,956.2	17,314.4	17,308.5
III *p*	−1,016.4	2,169.5	3,185.9	3,327.0	1,335.3	810.3	524.9	1,992.7	18,567.4	19,564.5	16,224.0	18,326.0	18,454.7

[1] Gross domestic product (GDP) less exports of goods and services plus imports of goods and services.
[2] Personal consumption expenditures plus gross private fixed investment.
[3] For chained dollar measures, gross domestic income is deflated by the implicit price deflator for GDP.

Source: Department of Commerce (Bureau of Economic Analysis).

TABLE B–4. Percentage shares of gross domestic product, 1969–2020

[Percent of nominal GDP]

Year or quarter	Gross domestic product (percent)	Personal consumption expenditures			Gross private domestic investment								Change in private inventories
						Fixed investment							
							Nonresidential						
		Total	Goods	Services	Total	Total	Total	Structures	Equipment	Intellectual property products	Residential		
1969	100.0	59.3	29.9	29.4	17.1	16.2	11.8	3.7	6.4	1.7	4.4	0.9
1970	100.0	60.3	29.7	30.6	15.8	15.7	11.6	3.8	6.2	1.7	4.0	.2
1971	100.0	60.1	29.4	30.7	16.9	16.2	11.2	3.7	5.9	1.6	5.0	.7
1972	100.0	60.1	29.2	30.8	17.8	17.1	11.5	3.7	6.2	1.6	5.7	.7
1973	100.0	59.6	29.2	30.4	18.7	17.6	12.1	3.9	6.7	1.6	5.5	1.1
1974	100.0	60.2	29.2	31.0	17.8	16.9	12.4	4.0	6.8	1.7	4.5	.9
1975	100.0	61.2	29.2	32.0	15.3	15.6	11.7	3.6	6.4	1.7	4.0	-.4
1976	100.0	61.3	29.2	32.1	17.3	16.3	11.7	3.5	6.5	1.7	4.6	.9
1977	100.0	61.2	28.8	32.4	19.1	18.0	12.4	3.6	7.1	1.7	5.5	1.1
1978	100.0	60.5	28.2	32.3	20.3	19.2	13.4	4.0	7.7	1.7	5.9	1.1
1979	100.0	60.3	28.1	32.3	20.5	19.9	14.2	4.5	7.9	1.8	5.6	.7
1980	100.0	61.3	28.0	33.3	18.6	18.8	14.2	4.8	7.6	1.9	4.5	-.2
1981	100.0	60.3	27.1	33.2	19.7	18.8	14.7	5.2	7.5	2.0	4.0	.9
1982	100.0	61.9	26.9	35.0	17.4	17.8	14.5	5.3	7.0	2.2	3.3	-.4
1983	100.0	62.8	26.8	36.0	17.5	17.7	13.3	4.2	6.8	2.2	4.4	-.2
1984	100.0	61.7	26.3	35.4	20.3	18.7	14.0	4.4	7.2	2.4	4.7	1.6
1985	100.0	62.5	26.2	36.3	19.1	18.6	14.0	4.5	7.1	2.4	4.6	.5
1986	100.0	63.0	26.1	36.9	18.5	18.4	13.3	3.9	6.9	2.5	5.1	.1
1987	100.0	63.4	25.9	37.5	18.4	17.8	12.7	3.6	6.6	2.5	5.1	.6
1988	100.0	63.6	25.5	38.1	17.9	17.5	12.6	3.5	6.6	2.5	4.9	.4
1989	100.0	63.4	25.2	38.2	17.7	17.2	12.7	3.4	6.6	2.7	4.5	.5
1990	100.0	63.9	25.0	38.9	16.7	16.4	12.4	3.4	6.2	2.8	4.0	.2
1991	100.0	64.0	24.3	39.7	15.3	15.3	11.8	3.0	5.9	2.9	3.6	.0
1992	100.0	64.4	24.0	40.4	15.5	15.3	11.4	2.6	5.9	2.9	3.9	.3
1993	100.0	64.9	23.9	41.0	16.1	15.8	11.7	2.6	6.2	2.9	4.2	.3
1994	100.0	64.8	24.0	40.8	17.2	16.4	11.9	2.6	6.5	2.8	4.4	.9
1995	100.0	65.0	23.8	41.2	17.2	16.8	12.6	2.7	6.9	3.0	4.2	.4
1996	100.0	65.0	23.8	41.2	17.7	17.4	12.9	2.8	7.0	3.1	4.4	.4
1997	100.0	64.5	23.4	41.2	18.6	17.8	13.4	2.9	7.1	3.4	4.4	.8
1998	100.0	64.9	23.3	41.6	19.2	18.5	13.8	3.0	7.3	3.5	4.6	.7
1999	100.0	65.2	23.7	41.5	19.6	19.0	14.2	3.0	7.4	3.8	4.8	.6
2000	100.0	66.0	23.9	42.0	19.9	19.4	14.6	3.1	7.5	4.0	4.7	.5
2001	100.0	66.8	23.9	42.9	18.3	18.6	13.8	3.2	6.7	3.9	4.8	-.4
2002	100.0	67.1	23.8	43.4	17.7	17.5	12.4	2.6	6.0	3.7	5.1	.2
2003	100.0	67.4	23.8	43.6	17.7	17.6	12.0	2.5	5.9	3.7	5.6	.1
2004	100.0	67.2	23.8	43.5	18.7	18.2	12.0	2.5	5.9	3.6	6.1	.5
2005	100.0	67.1	23.6	43.4	19.4	19.0	12.4	2.7	6.1	3.6	6.6	.4
2006	100.0	67.0	23.5	43.6	19.6	19.1	13.0	3.1	6.2	3.7	6.1	.5
2007	100.0	67.2	23.3	43.9	18.5	18.3	13.5	3.5	6.2	• 3.8	4.8	.2
2008	100.0	67.8	22.9	44.9	16.8	17.0	13.5	3.9	5.7	3.9	3.5	-.2
2009	100.0	68.1	22.0	46.1	13.4	14.4	11.7	3.2	4.6	3.9	2.7	-1.0
2010	100.0	67.9	22.1	45.8	14.4	14.1	11.6	2.5	5.2	3.9	2.5	.4
2011	100.0	68.5	22.6	45.8	15.0	14.7	12.3	2.6	5.7	4.0	2.4	.3
2012	100.0	68.0	22.5	45.5	16.2	15.7	13.1	3.0	6.1	4.0	2.7	.4
2013	100.0	67.4	22.2	45.2	16.8	16.2	13.2	2.9	6.1	4.1	3.0	.6
2014	100.0	67.5	22.0	45.4	17.4	16.9	13.7	3.3	6.2	4.2	3.2	.5
2015	100.0	67.4	21.5	45.9	17.7	17.0	13.5	3.2	6.1	4.2	3.5	.7
2016	100.0	68.1	21.3	46.8	17.0	16.9	13.1	3.0	5.8	4.3	3.7	.2
2017	100.0	68.3	21.3	46.9	17.1	17.1	13.2	3.1	5.7	4.4	3.9	.1
2018	100.0	67.9	21.2	46.7	17.6	17.3	13.5	3.1	5.9	4.5	3.9	.3
2019	100.0	67.9	21.1	46.8	17.5	17.3	13.5	3.0	5.8	4.7	3.8	.2
2017: I	100.0	68.4	21.4	47.0	17.0	17.0	13.2	3.1	5.7	4.4	3.9	-.1
II	100.0	68.3	21.3	47.0	17.1	17.1	13.2	3.1	5.7	4.4	3.9	.0
III	100.0	68.2	21.3	46.9	17.2	17.0	13.1	3.0	5.7	4.4	3.9	.2
IV	100.0	68.2	21.4	46.8	17.3	17.1	13.2	3.0	5.8	4.4	3.9	.1
2018: I	100.0	68.0	21.3	46.6	17.6	17.3	13.4	3.1	5.9	4.4	3.9	.2
II	100.0	67.8	21.3	46.6	17.4	17.4	13.5	3.1	5.8	4.5	3.9	.1
III	100.0	67.9	21.2	46.7	17.7	17.3	13.5	3.1	5.9	4.5	3.9	.4
IV	100.0	67.9	21.1	46.8	17.8	17.3	13.5	3.0	6.0	4.6	3.8	.5
2019: I	100.0	67.6	20.9	46.7	17.9	17.4	13.6	3.0	6.0	4.7	3.8	.5
II	100.0	68.0	21.2	46.8	17.5	17.3	13.6	3.0	5.8	4.7	3.7	.2
III	100.0	68.0	21.1	46.9	17.5	17.3	13.5	3.1	5.7	4.7	3.8	.2
IV	100.0	67.9	21.0	46.9	17.2	17.1	13.3	3.0	5.7	4.7	3.8	.0
2020: I	100.0	67.5	21.1	46.3	17.0	17.3	13.3	3.0	5.5	4.8	4.0	-.2
II	100.0	67.1	22.3	44.8	16.0	17.6	13.6	3.0	5.4	5.2	4.0	-1.5
III p	100.0	68.0	23.0	45.0	17.4	17.4	13.1	2.6	5.7	4.8	4.3	.0

See next page for continuation of table.

[Percent of nominal GDP]

| Year or quarter | Net exports of goods and services | | | | | | | Government consumption expenditures and gross investment | | | | |
| | Net exports | Exports | | | Imports | | | Total | Federal | | | State and local |
		Total	Goods	Services	Total	Goods	Services		Total	National defense	Non-defense	
1969	0.1	5.1	3.8	1.3	5.0	3.6	1.3	23.5	12.9	10.0	2.9	10.6
1970	.4	5.6	4.2	1.4	5.2	3.8	1.4	23.5	12.4	9.4	3.0	11.2
1971	.1	5.4	4.0	1.4	5.4	4.0	1.4	23.0	11.5	8.4	3.1	11.4
1972	−.3	5.5	4.1	1.4	5.8	4.5	1.4	22.4	11.1	7.9	3.2	11.3
1973	.3	6.7	5.3	1.4	6.4	5.0	1.4	21.4	10.3	7.2	3.1	11.1
1974	−.1	8.2	6.7	1.5	8.2	6.8	1.5	22.1	10.3	7.1	3.2	11.8
1975	.9	8.2	6.7	1.6	7.3	5.9	1.4	22.6	10.3	7.0	3.3	12.3
1976	−.1	8.0	6.5	1.5	8.1	6.7	1.4	21.6	9.9	6.7	3.2	11.7
1977	−1.1	7.7	6.2	1.5	8.8	7.3	1.4	20.9	9.6	6.5	3.2	11.2
1978	−1.1	7.9	6.4	1.6	9.0	7.5	1.5	20.3	9.3	6.2	3.1	10.9
1979	−.9	8.8	7.1	1.6	9.6	8.1	1.5	20.0	9.2	6.1	3.0	10.8
1980	−.5	9.8	8.1	1.8	10.3	8.7	1.6	20.6	9.6	6.4	3.2	11.0
1981	−.4	9.5	7.6	1.9	9.9	8.4	1.6	20.4	9.8	6.7	3.1	10.6
1982	−.6	8.5	6.7	1.8	9.1	7.5	1.6	21.3	10.4	7.3	3.1	10.9
1983	−1.4	7.6	5.9	1.7	9.0	7.5	1.5	21.1	10.5	7.5	3.0	10.6
1984	−2.5	7.5	5.7	1.8	10.0	8.3	1.7	20.5	10.2	7.4	2.8	10.3
1985	−2.6	7.0	5.2	1.7	9.6	7.9	1.7	21.0	10.4	7.6	2.8	10.5
1986	−2.9	7.0	5.1	2.0	9.9	8.1	1.8	21.3	10.5	7.7	2.8	10.8
1987	−3.0	7.5	5.5	2.0	10.5	8.5	1.9	21.2	10.4	7.7	2.7	10.9
1988	−2.1	8.5	6.3	2.1	10.6	8.6	1.9	20.6	9.8	7.3	2.5	10.8
1989	−1.5	8.9	6.6	2.3	10.5	8.6	1.9	20.4	9.5	6.9	2.5	11.0
1990	−1.3	9.3	6.8	2.5	10.6	8.5	2.0	20.8	9.4	6.8	2.6	11.3
1991	−.5	9.7	7.0	2.7	10.1	8.1	2.0	21.1	9.5	6.7	2.7	11.6
1992	−.5	9.7	7.0	2.7	10.2	8.4	1.9	20.6	9.0	6.2	2.8	11.6
1993	−1.0	9.5	6.8	2.7	10.5	8.6	1.9	19.9	8.5	5.7	2.7	11.4
1994	−1.3	9.9	7.1	2.8	11.2	9.3	1.9	19.2	7.9	5.2	2.6	11.4
1995	−1.2	10.6	7.8	2.9	11.8	9.9	1.9	19.0	7.5	4.9	2.6	11.4
1996	−1.2	10.7	7.8	3.0	11.9	10.0	1.9	18.5	7.2	4.7	2.5	11.3
1997	−1.2	11.1	8.2	3.0	12.3	10.3	2.0	18.0	6.8	4.3	2.5	11.2
1998	−1.8	10.5	7.6	2.9	12.3	10.3	2.0	17.8	6.5	4.1	2.4	11.3
1999	−2.7	10.3	7.4	2.9	13.0	10.9	2.0	17.9	6.3	4.0	2.4	11.5
2000	−3.7	10.7	7.8	2.9	14.4	12.2	2.2	17.8	6.2	3.8	2.4	11.6
2001	−3.5	9.7	7.0	2.7	13.2	11.1	2.1	18.4	6.3	3.9	2.4	12.1
2002	−3.9	9.1	6.5	2.6	13.0	10.9	2.1	19.1	6.8	4.2	2.6	12.3
2003	−4.4	9.0	6.4	2.6	13.4	11.3	2.2	19.3	7.2	4.5	2.7	12.1
2004	−5.1	9.6	6.8	2.8	14.7	12.3	2.4	19.1	7.3	4.7	2.6	11.8
2005	−5.5	10.0	7.1	2.9	15.5	13.2	2.4	19.0	7.3	4.7	2.6	11.7
2006	−5.6	10.7	7.6	3.1	16.2	13.7	2.5	19.0	7.2	4.6	2.6	11.8
2007	−5.0	11.5	8.0	3.5	16.5	13.8	2.6	19.3	7.3	4.7	2.6	12.0
2008	−4.9	12.5	8.8	3.7	17.4	14.6	2.8	20.3	7.8	5.1	2.7	12.4
2009	−2.7	10.9	7.3	3.6	13.7	11.0	2.7	21.3	8.4	5.5	3.0	12.8
2010	−3.4	12.3	8.5	3.8	15.7	13.0	2.8	21.0	8.7	5.5	3.1	12.4
2011	−3.7	13.5	9.4	4.1	17.3	14.4	2.8	20.3	8.4	5.4	3.0	11.9
2012	−3.5	13.5	9.4	4.1	17.0	14.2	2.8	19.4	7.9	5.0	2.9	11.4
2013	−2.9	13.5	9.3	4.3	16.5	13.7	2.8	18.7	7.3	4.6	2.8	11.4
2014	−2.9	13.5	9.2	4.3	16.4	13.6	2.8	18.1	6.9	4.2	2.7	11.1
2015	−2.9	12.4	8.2	4.2	15.3	12.5	2.8	17.7	6.7	4.0	2.7	11.0
2016	−2.7	11.9	7.7	4.2	14.6	11.8	2.8	17.6	6.6	3.9	2.7	11.0
2017	−2.8	12.2	7.9	4.3	15.0	12.2	2.8	17.4	6.5	3.8	2.6	11.0
2018	−3.0	12.3	8.1	4.2	15.2	12.4	2.8	17.4	6.5	3.9	2.6	10.9
2019	−2.8	11.7	7.6	4.1	14.6	11.8	2.8	17.5	6.6	4.0	2.6	10.9
2017: I	−2.8	12.1	7.9	4.2	14.9	12.1	2.8	17.5	6.5	3.8	2.7	11.0
II	−2.9	12.0	7.8	4.3	14.9	12.1	2.8	17.5	6.5	3.9	2.6	11.0
III	−2.8	12.1	7.8	4.3	14.9	12.0	2.9	17.4	6.4	3.8	2.6	11.0
IV	−2.9	12.4	8.1	4.3	15.3	12.4	2.8	17.4	6.5	3.8	2.6	10.9
2018: I	−2.9	12.4	8.1	4.3	15.3	12.5	2.8	17.4	6.5	3.8	2.7	10.9
II	−2.7	12.4	8.2	4.2	15.1	12.3	2.8	17.4	6.5	3.8	2.6	11.0
III	−3.1	12.2	8.0	4.2	15.3	12.5	2.8	17.5	6.5	3.9	2.7	11.0
IV	−3.1	12.1	8.0	4.1	15.2	12.4	2.8	17.4	6.5	3.9	2.6	10.9
2019: I	−2.9	12.0	7.9	4.1	14.9	12.1	2.8	17.4	6.6	3.9	2.6	10.9
II	−3.0	11.8	7.6	4.1	14.8	12.0	2.8	17.5	6.6	4.0	2.7	10.9
III	−2.9	11.6	7.5	4.1	14.6	11.8	2.8	17.5	6.6	4.0	2.7	10.9
IV	−2.5	11.6	7.5	4.1	14.1	11.3	2.8	17.5	6.7	4.0	2.6	10.8
2020: I	−2.3	11.3	7.4	3.9	13.6	11.0	2.6	17.8	6.7	4.1	2.7	11.0
II	−2.8	9.2	5.8	3.3	12.0	9.9	2.1	19.7	7.7	4.5	3.2	12.0
III *p*	−3.5	9.8	6.7	3.2	13.3	11.2	2.0	18.0	7.0	4.2	2.8	11.0

Source: Department of Commerce (Bureau of Economic Analysis).

TABLE B–5. Chain-type price indexes for gross domestic product, 1969–2020

[Index numbers, 2012=100, except as noted; quarterly data seasonally adjusted]

Year or quarter	Gross domestic product	Personal consumption expenditures			Gross private domestic investment							
						Fixed investment						
							Nonresidential					
		Total	Goods	Services	Total	Total	Total	Structures	Equipment	Intellectual property products	Residential
1969	20.590	20.015	30.934	15.078	28.402	27.498	34.638	11.114	59.657	36.204	15.518
1970	21.676	20.951	32.114	15.913	29.624	28.699	36.295	11.845	61.891	37.929	16.016
1971	22.776	21.841	33.079	16.781	31.092	30.134	37.997	12.757	63.848	39.318	16.943
1972	23.760	22.586	33.926	17.491	32.388	31.420	39.297	13.674	64.686	40.490	17.975
1973	25.061	23.802	35.949	18.336	34.153	33.169	40.882	14.734	65.780	42.494	19.571
1974	27.309	26.280	40.436	19.890	37.559	36.449	44.857	16.770	70.713	46.461	21.593
1975	29.846	28.470	43.703	21.595	42.059	40.874	50.766	18.773	81.484	50.190	23.590
1976	31.490	30.032	45.413	23.093	44.384	43.232	53.562	19.692	86.486	52.408	25.117
1977	33.445	31.986	47.837	24.841	47.655	46.550	57.111	21.401	91.800	54.709	27.683
1978	35.798	34.211	50.773	26.750	51.517	50.444	60.930	23.468	96.900	57.557	31.082
1979	38.766	37.251	55.574	28.994	56.141	54.977	65.830	26.194	103.167	61.382	34.593
1980	42.278	41.262	61.797	32.009	61.395	60.105	71.641	28.629	112.249	66.123	38.325
1981	46.269	44.958	66.389	35.288	67.123	65.624	78.453	32.566	120.463	71.058	41.425
1982	49.130	47.456	68.198	38.058	70.679	69.311	82.911	35.136	125.415	75.093	43.646
1983	51.051	49.474	69.429	40.396	70.896	69.575	82.774	34.241	125.776	77.898	44.680
1984	52.894	51.343	70.742	42.498	71.661	70.253	83.036	34.540	124.748	80.081	46.003
1985	54.568	53.134	71.877	44.577	72.548	71.277	83.893	35.361	124.748	81.413	47.267
1986	55.673	54.290	71.541	46.408	74.178	73.021	85.365	36.039	127.254	82.047	49.351
1987	57.041	55.964	73.842	47.796	75.723	74.506	86.339	36.618	128.083	83.518	51.486
1988	59.055	58.151	75.788	50.082	77.627	76.586	88.514	38.171	129.854	86.129	53.278
1989	61.370	60.690	78.704	52.443	79.606	78.561	90.572	39.666	132.337	87.240	55.020
1990	63.676	63.355	81.927	54.846	81.270	80.278	92.516	40.948	135.042	88.147	56.288
1991	65.819	65.473	83.930	56.992	82.648	81.683	94.267	41.689	137.330	90.271	57.021
1992	67.321	67.218	84.943	59.018	82.647	81.728	93.960	41.699	137.121	89.373	57.723
1993	68.917	68.892	85.681	61.059	83.627	82.711	94.161	42.922	135.518	89.998	60.074
1994	70.386	70.330	86.552	62.719	84.875	83.983	94.904	44.437	135.277	90.468	62.247
1995	71.864	71.811	87.361	64.471	86.240	85.378	95.849	46.362	133.796	93.134	64.473
1996	73.178	73.346	88.321	66.240	86.191	85.450	95.267	47.540	130.762	93.544	65.856
1997	74.446	74.623	88.219	68.107	86.241	85.599	94.735	49.355	127.156	94.052	67.444
1998	75.267	75.216	86.893	69.549	85.608	85.133	93.248	51.612	121.451	93.595	69.223
1999	76.346	76.338	87.349	70.970	85.690	85.277	92.314	53.198	116.763	95.105	71.816
2000	78.069	78.235	89.082	72.938	86.815	86.486	92.718	55.283	114.224	97.814	75.004
2001	79.822	79.738	89.015	75.171	87.555	87.241	92.346	58.178	110.858	97.684	78.564
2002	81.039	80.789	88.166	77.123	87.841	87.500	91.863	60.603	108.531	96.376	80.510
2003	82.567	82.358	88.054	79.506	88.561	88.265	91.156	62.769	105.725	95.647	84.325
2004	84.778	84.411	89.292	81.965	91.148	90.843	92.055	67.416	104.841	95.335	90.243
2005	87.407	86.812	91.084	84.673	94.839	94.597	94.443	75.733	104.598	95.952	96.706
2006	90.074	89.174	92.306	87.616	98.176	97.958	96.745	84.749	103.560	97.088	102.355
2007	92.498	91.438	93.331	90.516	99.656	99.456	98.310	89.748	103.191	98.284	103.708
2008	94.264	94.180	96.122	93.235	100.474	100.296	99.832	94.335	102.542	99.834	102.249
2009	94.999	94.094	93.812	94.231	99.331	99.076	99.184	92.613	103.169	98.589	98.671
2010	96.109	95.705	95.183	95.957	97.687	97.568	97.416	92.006	99.417	98.306	98.317
2011	98.112	98.131	98.773	97.814	98.704	98.641	98.559	95.362	99.447	99.517	99.049
2012	100.000	100.000	100.000	100.000	100.000	100.000	100.000	100.000	100.000	100.000	100.000
2013	101.773	101.346	99.407	102.316	100.979	101.091	100.251	101.455	99.787	100.081	105.054
2014	103.647	102.830	98.920	104.804	102.922	103.172	101.469	107.198	99.169	100.791	111.118
2015	104.639	103.043	95.896	106.694	103.535	104.075	101.909	109.403	98.671	101.374	114.114
2016	105.736	104.121	94.325	109.160	103.520	104.214	101.131	109.763	97.621	100.232	118.134
2017	107.751	105.984	94.597	111.868	105.246	105.954	101.994	112.668	97.565	101.065	123.497
2018	110.322	108.239	95.244	114.991	107.217	107.998	102.882	114.563	97.685	102.372	130.470
2019	112.318	109.851	94.785	117.744	108.998	109.799	104.256	118.709	97.888	103.683	134.182
2017: I	107.031	105.421	94.913	110.837	104.517	105.234	101.600	111.439	97.577	100.649	121.429
II	107.368	105.654	94.283	111.530	105.093	105.807	101.942	112.438	97.538	101.089	122.950
III	107.968	106.084	94.403	112.125	105.608	106.272	102.184	113.392	97.574	101.167	124.339
IV	108.637	106.775	94.788	112.980	105.765	106.503	102.248	113.401	97.572	101.353	125.271
2018: I	109.292	107.485	95.232	113.832	106.395	107.188	102.442	113.387	97.487	102.057	128.032
II	110.165	108.081	95.419	114.650	107.097	107.847	102.754	114.053	97.500	102.552	130.203
III	110.671	108.501	95.317	115.356	107.553	108.333	103.073	114.628	97.885	102.617	131.433
IV	111.159	108.889	95.009	116.125	107.823	108.624	103.257	116.182	97.868	102.262	132.212
2019: I	111.497	109.042	94.571	116.605	108.501	109.279	103.885	117.323	98.081	103.149	132.981
II	112.181	109.726	94.985	117.436	108.971	109.767	104.341	118.610	97.992	103.848	133.615
III	112.602	110.108	94.766	118.154	109.232	110.049	104.457	119.236	97.758	104.129	134.663
IV	112.989	110.529	94.817	118.781	109.099	110.099	104.342	119.668	97.722	103.606	135.468
2020: I	113.380	110.882	94.599	119.456	109.764	110.446	104.589	120.124	97.888	103.838	136.256
II	112.860	110.435	93.248	119.560	109.739	110.678	104.800	119.803	97.879	104.585	136.583
III p	113.850	111.450	94.494	120.408	110.463	111.295	104.834	119.993	97.722	104.774	139.690

See next page for continuation of table.

[Index numbers, 2012=100, except as noted; quarterly data seasonally adjusted]

| Year or quarter | Exports and imports of goods and services | | | Government consumption expenditures and gross investment | | | | Final sales of domestic product | Personal consumption expenditures excluding food and energy | Gross domestic purchases[1] | Percent change[2] | | | |
| | | | | Federal | | | State and local | | | | Gross domestic product | Personal consumption expenditures | | Gross domestic purchases[1] |
	Exports	Imports	Total	Total	National defense	Non-defense						Total	Excluding food and energy	
1969	28.589	18.839	14.892	17.715	17.019	19.154	13.063	20.465	21.136	20.010	4.9	4.5	4.7	4.9
1970	29.711	19.954	16.078	19.109	18.294	20.906	14.117	21.547	22.126	21.087	5.3	4.7	4.7	5.4
1971	30.796	21.179	17.352	20.670	19.817	22.521	15.198	22.642	23.167	22.185	5.1	4.2	4.7	5.2
1972	32.145	22.662	18.662	22.485	21.883	23.579	16.163	23.624	23.912	23.175	4.3	3.4	3.2	4.5
1973	36.382	26.601	19.936	24.051	23.484	25.018	17.246	24.923	24.823	24.499	5.5	5.4	3.8	5.7
1974	44.807	38.058	21.852	25.971	25.404	26.904	19.157	27.154	26.788	26.986	9.0	10.4	7.9	10.2
1975	49.388	41.226	23.870	28.254	27.545	29.484	20.999	29.680	29.026	29.452	9.3	8.3	8.4	9.1
1976	51.009	42.467	25.181	30.012	29.345	31.124	22.024	31.326	30.791	31.071	5.5	5.5	6.1	5.5
1977	53.088	46.209	26.739	31.858	31.268	32.782	23.394	33.284	32.771	33.119	6.2	6.5	6.4	6.6
1978	56.317	49.466	28.507	34.008	33.561	34.612	24.914	35.637	34.943	35.474	7.0	7.0	6.6	7.1
1979	63.101	57.930	30.853	36.566	36.216	36.952	27.114	38.591	37.490	38.585	8.3	8.9	7.3	8.8
1980	69.503	72.166	34.045	40.099	39.919	40.106	30.081	42.084	40.936	42.602	9.1	10.8	9.2	10.4
1981	74.650	76.066	37.424	43.843	43.747	43.643	33.226	46.046	44.523	46.532	9.4	9.0	8.8	9.2
1982	75.006	73.506	39.969	46.943	47.039	46.289	35.401	48.921	47.417	49.214	6.2	5.6	6.5	5.8
1983	75.311	70.751	41.516	48.499	48.778	47.397	36.964	50.836	49.844	50.926	3.9	4.3	5.1	3.5
1984	76.016	70.139	43.317	50.637	51.013	49.279	38.544	52.671	51.911	52.649	3.6	3.8	4.1	3.4
1985	73.753	67.836	44.659	51.712	51.872	50.907	40.113	54.371	54.019	54.214	3.2	3.5	4.1	3.0
1986	72.523	67.834	45.409	51.957	51.894	51.748	41.269	55.492	55.883	55.345	2.0	2.2	3.5	2.1
1987	74.124	71.935	46.635	52.318	52.267	52.076	43.196	56.851	57.683	56.908	2.5	3.1	3.2	2.8
1988	77.920	75.377	48.177	54.025	53.904	53.974	44.640	58.890	60.134	58.921	3.5	3.9	4.2	3.5
1989	79.210	77.024	50.016	55.534	55.365	55.605	46.752	61.205	62.630	61.240	3.9	4.4	4.2	3.9
1990	79.657	79.233	52.113	57.250	57.162	57.093	49.153	63.519	65.168	63.663	3.8	4.4	4.1	4.0
1991	80.545	78.573	54.005	59.309	58.964	59.787	50.953	65.663	67.495	65.662	3.4	3.3	3.6	3.1
1992	80.153	78.636	55.642	60.824	60.678	60.825	52.690	67.169	69.547	67.190	2.3	2.7	3.0	2.3
1993	80.277	78.033	56.953	62.151	61.615	62.994	54.002	68.765	71.436	68.706	2.4	2.5	2.7	2.3
1994	81.210	78.766	58.463	63.861	63.229	64.898	55.394	70.239	73.034	70.147	2.1	2.1	2.2	2.1
1995	83.025	80.924	60.123	65.838	65.027	67.223	56.871	71.722	74.625	71.661	2.1	2.1	2.2	2.2
1996	81.923	79.514	61.355	66.937	66.114	68.344	58.177	73.055	76.040	72.908	1.8	2.1	1.9	1.7
1997	80.479	76.750	62.560	67.972	67.035	69.591	59.471	74.344	77.382	73.983	1.7	1.7	1.8	1.5
1998	78.574	72.618	63.624	68.841	67.871	70.518	60.630	75.200	78.366	74.476	1.1	.8	1.3	.7
1999	77.971	73.019	65.778	70.519	69.559	72.178	63.008	76.296	79.425	75.632	1.4	1.5	1.4	1.6
2000	79.467	76.221	68.601	72.886	71.908	74.578	66.032	78.037	80.804	77.575	2.3	2.5	1.7	2.6
2001	78.836	74.223	70.567	74.236	73.270	75.906	68.281	79.793	82.258	79.039	2.2	1.9	1.8	1.9
2002	78.201	73.242	72.393	76.631	75.714	78.222	69.815	81.004	83.639	80.125	1.5	1.3	1.7	1.4
2003	79.400	75.454	75.028	80.008	79.505	80.895	72.050	82.541	84.837	81.776	1.9	1.9	1.4	2.1
2004	82.284	79.060	78.153	82.760	82.263	83.637	75.369	84.751	86.515	84.126	2.7	2.5	2.0	2.9
2005	85.131	83.703	82.110	86.204	86.011	86.531	79.609	87.388	88.373	87.037	3.1	2.8	2.1	3.5
2006	87.842	86.909	85.661	88.949	89.022	88.799	83.617	90.058	90.392	89.783	3.1	2.7	2.3	3.2
2007	91.139	89.921	89.491	91.589	91.750	91.279	88.133	92.489	92.378	92.206	2.7	2.5	2.2	2.7
2008	95.410	98.960	93.308	94.381	94.801	93.597	92.558	94.259	94.225	94.849	1.9	3.0	2.0	2.9
2009	89.694	87.987	92.931	94.214	94.126	94.364	92.048	94.970	95.315	94.559	.8	−.1	1.2	−.3
2010	93.348	92.783	95.386	96.421	96.128	96.942	94.669	96.086	96.608	95.923	1.2	1.7	1.4	1.4
2011	99.242	99.826	98.285	99.070	98.946	99.289	97.739	98.100	98.139	98.246	2.1	2.5	1.6	2.4
2012	100.000	100.000	100.000	100.000	100.000	100.000	100.000	100.000	100.000	100.000	1.9	1.9	1.9	1.8
2013	100.168	98.636	102.332	100.931	100.609	101.478	103.279	101.795	101.526	101.468	1.8	1.3	1.5	1.5
2014	100.272	97.854	104.435	102.632	102.056	103.593	105.645	103.692	103.122	103.138	1.8	1.5	1.6	1.6
2015	95.395	90.001	104.598	103.128	102.334	104.428	105.598	104.737	104.404	103.411	1.0	.2	1.2	.3
2016	93.490	86.867	104.926	103.711	102.696	105.342	105.770	105.867	106.102	104.175	1.0	1.0	1.6	.7
2017	95.921	88.771	107.398	105.843	104.449	108.040	108.450	107.885	107.855	106.119	1.9	1.8	1.7	1.9
2018	99.183	91.334	111.312	109.089	107.477	111.619	112.775	110.470	110.005	108.602	2.4	2.1	2.0	2.3
2019	98.751	89.986	113.439	111.110	109.256	114.014	114.969	112.470	111.875	110.329	1.8	1.5	1.7	1.6
2017: I	95.121	88.409	106.487	105.072	103.888	106.955	107.454	107.166	107.251	105.470	2.0	2.2	1.8	2.2
II	95.169	88.330	106.794	105.466	104.097	107.625	107.708	107.502	107.619	105.773	1.3	.9	1.4	1.2
III	96.049	88.589	107.589	106.002	104.518	108.335	108.661	108.094	107.989	106.278	2.3	1.6	1.4	1.9
IV	97.346	89.756	108.721	106.831	105.294	109.244	109.978	108.777	108.561	106.953	2.5	2.6	2.1	2.0
2018: I	98.203	91.232	109.901	107.962	106.419	110.386	111.190	109.442	109.212	107.727	2.4	2.7	2.4	2.9
II	99.416	91.292	110.934	108.763	107.222	111.184	112.365	110.308	109.834	108.414	3.2	2.2	2.3	2.6
III	99.718	91.626	111.821	109.413	107.874	111.832	113.398	110.820	110.232	108.918	1.8	1.6	1.5	1.9
IV	99.394	91.186	112.592	110.218	108.394	113.073	114.148	111.312	110.743	109.348	1.8	1.4	1.9	1.6
2019: I	98.554	90.291	112.931	111.479	108.822	115.643	113.914	111.645	111.074	109.623	1.2	.6	1.2	1.0
II	99.335	90.485	113.256	110.761	109.118	113.332	114.890	112.333	111.666	110.211	2.5	2.5	2.1	2.2
III	98.763	89.745	113.547	110.921	109.345	113.390	115.262	112.758	112.192	110.557	1.5	1.4	1.9	1.3
IV	98.350	89.426	114.022	111.281	109.743	113.691	115.811	113.145	112.568	110.925	1.4	1.5	1.3	1.3
2020: I	97.739	89.113	114.527	111.205	109.701	113.561	116.688	113.514	113.027	111.324	1.4	1.3	1.6	1.4
II	92.774	86.125	113.972	110.901	109.014	113.834	115.969	113.039	112.809	110.930	−1.8	−1.6	−.8	−1.4
III p	95.620	87.928	114.715	111.340	109.533	114.153	116.915	114.011	113.790	111.846	3.6	3.7	3.5	3.3

[1] Gross domestic product (GDP) less exports of goods and services plus imports of goods and services.
[2] Quarterly percent changes are at annual rates.

Source: Department of Commerce (Bureau of Economic Analysis).

TABLE B–6. Gross value added by sector, 1969–2020

[Billions of dollars; quarterly data at seasonally adjusted annual rates]

Year or quarter	Gross domestic product	Business [1]			Households and institutions			General government [3]			Addendum: Gross housing value added
		Total	Nonfarm [1]	Farm	Total	Households	Nonprofit institutions serving households [2]	Total	Federal	State and local	
1969	1,017.6	782.7	759.9	22.8	87.0	57.1	30.0	147.9	76.9	70.9	73.0
1970	1,073.3	815.9	792.3	23.7	94.6	61.2	33.4	162.8	82.5	80.3	78.8
1971	1,164.9	882.5	857.2	25.4	104.5	67.2	37.4	177.8	87.5	90.3	86.4
1972	1,279.1	972.5	942.9	29.7	114.0	72.7	41.4	192.6	92.4	100.2	93.9
1973	1,425.4	1,094.0	1,047.2	46.8	124.6	78.5	46.1	206.8	96.4	110.4	101.4
1974	1,545.2	1,182.8	1,138.5	44.2	137.2	85.5	51.7	225.3	102.5	122.8	110.4
1975	1,684.9	1,284.8	1,239.2	45.6	151.6	93.7	58.0	248.4	110.5	138.0	121.3
1976	1,873.4	1,443.3	1,400.2	43.0	164.9	101.7	63.2	265.3	117.3	148.0	130.9
1977	2,081.8	1,616.2	1,572.7	43.5	179.9	110.7	69.2	285.7	125.2	160.6	144.2
1978	2,351.6	1,838.2	1,787.5	50.7	202.1	124.8	77.3	311.3	135.8	175.5	160.2
1979	2,627.3	2,062.8	2,002.7	60.1	226.3	139.5	86.9	338.2	145.4	192.8	177.7
1980	2,857.3	2,225.8	2,174.4	51.4	258.2	158.8	99.3	373.4	159.8	213.5	204.0
1981	3,207.0	2,502.0	2,437.0	65.0	291.6	179.2	112.4	413.5	178.3	235.2	231.6
1982	3,343.8	2,568.6	2,508.2	60.4	323.8	198.2	125.6	451.4	195.7	255.6	258.6
1983	3,634.0	2,801.9	2,757.0	44.9	352.5	213.6	138.9	479.7	207.1	272.6	280.6
1984	4,037.6	3,136.7	3,072.6	64.2	383.8	230.9	152.8	517.1	225.3	291.9	303.1
1985	4,339.0	3,369.6	3,305.9	63.7	411.8	248.2	163.6	557.5	240.0	317.6	333.8
1986	4,579.6	3,539.3	3,479.4	59.9	447.0	268.4	178.6	593.3	250.6	342.7	364.5
1987	4,855.2	3,735.2	3,673.2	62.0	489.5	289.8	199.7	630.4	261.0	369.4	392.1
1988	5,236.4	4,019.3	3,957.9	61.4	539.8	316.4	223.4	677.4	278.5	398.8	424.2
1989	5,641.6	4,326.7	4,252.8	73.9	586.0	341.4	244.6	728.8	292.8	436.1	452.7
1990	5,963.1	4,542.0	4,464.2	77.8	636.3	367.6	268.8	784.9	306.7	478.2	487.0
1991	6,158.1	4,645.0	4,574.7	70.4	677.3	386.6	290.7	835.8	323.5	512.2	515.3
1992	6,520.3	4,920.2	4,840.4	79.9	720.3	407.1	313.2	879.8	329.6	550.2	545.2
1993	6,858.6	5,177.4	5,106.2	71.3	772.8	437.6	335.1	908.3	331.5	576.9	578.4
1994	7,287.2	5,523.7	5,440.1	83.6	824.7	472.7	352.0	938.8	332.6	606.2	619.6
1995	7,639.7	5,795.1	5,726.7	68.4	877.8	506.9	370.9	966.9	333.0	633.9	662.6
1996	8,073.1	6,159.5	6,066.9	92.6	923.2	534.6	388.7	990.3	331.8	658.6	695.0
1997	8,577.6	6,578.8	6,490.6	88.1	975.9	565.7	410.2	1,022.9	333.5	689.3	731.9
1998	9,062.8	6,959.2	6,880.2	79.0	1,040.6	601.6	439.0	1,063.0	336.8	726.2	774.8
1999	9,630.7	7,400.1	7,329.2	70.9	1,112.4	645.2	467.3	1,118.1	345.0	773.1	826.2
2000	10,252.3	7,876.1	7,800.1	76.0	1,191.9	693.5	498.5	1,184.3	360.3	824.0	881.7
2001	10,581.8	8,062.0	7,983.9	78.1	1,267.2	744.7	522.6	1,252.6	370.3	882.3	943.5
2002	10,936.4	8,264.4	8,190.4	74.0	1,343.6	780.7	562.9	1,328.4	397.8	930.6	985.1
2003	11,458.2	8,642.4	8,551.3	91.1	1,411.0	816.6	594.4	1,404.8	434.7	970.1	1,016.4
2004	12,213.7	9,240.6	9,121.2	119.4	1,494.5	868.4	626.1	1,478.7	459.4	1,019.3	1,075.2
2005	13,036.6	9,898.0	9,793.5	104.5	1,583.3	933.4	649.8	1,555.4	488.4	1,067.0	1,151.9
2006	13,814.6	10,509.1	10,412.8	96.3	1,673.6	991.2	682.4	1,631.9	509.9	1,122.1	1,224.2
2007	14,451.9	10,994.6	10,878.9	115.7	1,730.3	1,016.9	713.4	1,726.9	535.7	1,191.2	1,273.4
2008	14,712.8	11,054.9	10,935.4	119.5	1,836.8	1,075.2	761.6	1,821.2	569.1	1,252.1	1,349.5
2009	14,448.9	10,669.9	10,566.8	103.1	1,895.5	1,097.0	798.5	1,883.5	603.0	1,280.5	1,393.8
2010	14,992.1	11,140.5	11,022.8	117.6	1,905.5	1,091.0	814.5	1,946.1	640.0	1,306.1	1,400.2
2011	15,542.6	11,612.9	11,460.7	152.2	1,956.8	1,108.0	848.8	1,972.9	659.8	1,313.1	1,445.7
2012	16,197.0	12,189.5	12,040.5	148.9	2,018.4	1,128.0	890.3	1,989.1	663.7	1,325.5	1,478.5
2013	16,784.9	12,670.5	12,485.9	184.6	2,075.0	1,157.0	918.0	2,039.3	658.4	1,380.9	1,511.2
2014	17,527.3	13,280.5	13,112.4	168.1	2,158.8	1,203.3	955.4	2,088.0	666.8	1,421.1	1,585.1
2015	18,238.3	13,841.5	13,694.1	147.4	2,255.9	1,252.3	1,003.6	2,141.0	673.7	1,467.3	1,690.4
2016	18,745.1	14,212.0	14,081.3	130.6	2,349.4	1,302.2	1,047.2	2,183.7	684.6	1,499.1	1,773.4
2017	19,543.0	14,854.4	14,714.3	140.1	2,447.3	1,362.4	1,084.9	2,241.3	700.3	1,541.0	1,854.6
2018	20,611.9	15,709.0	15,568.7	140.3	2,569.5	1,435.2	1,134.3	2,333.3	726.7	1,606.6	1,939.0
2019	21,433.2	16,329.8	16,193.8	136.1	2,686.3	1,501.0	1,185.3	2,417.1	751.2	1,665.9	2,031.7
2017: I	19,237.4	14,607.2	14,460.2	147.0	2,414.0	1,341.4	1,072.6	2,216.3	694.1	1,522.2	1,826.9
II	19,379.2	14,713.9	14,570.0	143.9	2,436.1	1,355.5	1,080.6	2,229.2	696.7	1,532.5	1,845.4
III	19,617.3	14,916.1	14,782.1	134.0	2,452.4	1,365.1	1,087.4	2,248.7	701.9	1,546.9	1,863.1
IV	19,938.0	15,180.3	15,045.0	135.4	2,486.6	1,387.5	1,099.2	2,271.0	708.4	1,562.5	1,883.2
2018: I	20,242.2	15,424.4	15,281.6	142.8	2,522.4	1,406.3	1,116.1	2,295.4	716.2	1,579.2	1,904.5
II	20,552.7	15,676.9	15,530.9	146.0	2,554.9	1,426.2	1,128.7	2,320.8	723.6	1,597.2	1,926.8
III	20,742.7	15,810.3	15,676.0	134.3	2,583.5	1,445.3	1,138.2	2,348.9	730.9	1,618.0	1,950.4
IV	20,909.9	15,924.3	15,786.4	137.9	2,617.2	1,463.1	1,154.1	2,368.3	736.3	1,632.0	1,974.3
2019: I	21,115.3	16,081.5	15,949.6	131.9	2,647.5	1,479.8	1,167.7	2,386.3	743.1	1,643.3	1,999.0
II	21,329.9	16,251.2	16,117.5	133.7	2,674.0	1,495.4	1,178.6	2,404.7	747.7	1,657.0	2,023.1
III	21,540.3	16,411.1	16,272.5	138.6	2,699.1	1,508.7	1,190.4	2,430.1	754.4	1,675.7	2,043.8
IV	21,747.4	16,575.6	16,435.5	140.1	2,724.7	1,520.1	1,204.6	2,447.1	759.5	1,687.7	2,061.1
2020: I	21,561.1	16,351.2	16,201.3	149.8	2,751.0	1,532.6	1,218.4	2,459.0	764.0	1,695.0	2,080.1
II	19,520.1	14,418.3	14,310.8	107.5	2,697.3	1,540.1	1,157.2	2,404.5	772.1	1,632.4	2,092.9
III [p]	21,157.1	15,966.6	15,831.4	135.2	2,754.5	1,549.8	1,204.7	2,436.1	782.9	1,653.2	2,106.7

[1] Gross domestic business value added equals gross domestic product excluding gross value added of households and institutions and of general government. Nonfarm value added equals gross domestic business value added excluding gross farm value added.

[2] Equals compensation of employees of nonprofit institutions, the rental value of nonresidential fixed assets owned and used by nonprofit institutions serving households, and rental income of persons for tenant-occupied housing owned by nonprofit institutions.

[3] Equals compensation of general government employees plus general government consumption of fixed capital.

Source: Department of Commerce (Bureau of Economic Analysis).

TABLE B-7. Real gross value added by sector, 1969–2020

[Billions of chained (2012) dollars; quarterly data at seasonally adjusted annual rates]

Year or quarter	Gross domestic product	Business [1]			Households and institutions			General government [3]			Addendum: Gross housing value added
		Total	Nonfarm [1]	Farm	Total	Households	Nonprofit institutions serving households [2]	Total	Federal	State and local	
1969	4,942.1	3,272.7	3,232.1	45.1	648.6	379.9	267.1	1,221.2	543.2	643.9	480.4
1970	4,951.3	3,271.3	3,227.9	46.4	660.5	388.7	269.5	1,226.5	525.5	672.7	496.4
1971	5,114.3	3,394.9	3,348.6	48.8	690.6	408.3	279.5	1,228.7	506.6	700.2	520.8
1972	5,383.3	3,616.6	3,574.1	48.8	717.9	425.2	289.6	1,232.9	487.2	724.6	545.5
1973	5,687.2	3,867.8	3,833.7	48.2	741.9	438.8	300.0	1,232.9	473.6	750.1	562.9
1974	5,656.5	3,808.8	3,776.2	47.2	772.2	458.4	310.3	1,257.1	473.8	777.4	590.5
1975	5,644.8	3,772.6	3,714.5	56.1	799.1	471.5	324.2	1,276.0	472.1	801.0	609.4
1976	5,949.0	4,027.5	3,980.8	53.4	809.4	477.7	328.4	1,286.8	473.3	811.7	615.4
1977	6,224.1	4,258.1	4,209.4	56.2	815.8	477.6	335.3	1,300.3	475.2	824.3	624.3
1978	6,568.6	4,529.7	4,490.5	54.1	846.3	500.5	342.1	1,325.1	481.5	843.7	646.7
1979	6,776.6	4,690.6	4,642.4	59.2	869.8	510.8	355.7	1,339.9	482.5	859.1	659.2
1980	6,759.2	4,648.3	4,602.9	57.6	896.0	525.3	367.4	1,359.9	490.3	871.1	682.5
1981	6,930.7	4,783.9	4,707.8	76.0	913.2	531.0	379.3	1,369.5	498.5	871.0	695.9
1982	6,805.8	4,646.5	4,563.8	79.7	940.9	538.3	401.1	1,385.7	507.7	876.9	712.1
1983	7,117.7	4,892.8	4,846.6	55.1	979.7	559.3	419.0	1,397.7	520.6	873.5	739.6
1984	7,632.8	5,326.8	5,256.6	73.5	1,002.2	569.8	431.3	1,418.3	534.1	879.0	753.8
1985	7,951.1	5,575.2	5,488.1	87.1	1,019.6	582.8	435.3	1,461.1	551.1	904.3	785.0
1986	8,226.4	5,777.7	5,695.5	83.3	1,051.5	594.4	456.5	1,500.5	564.4	930.7	806.3
1987	8,511.0	5,985.1	5,902.7	84.1	1,090.9	609.5	481.9	1,537.5	582.2	949.1	825.1
1988	8,866.5	6,241.4	6,171.6	74.8	1,146.9	634.8	513.6	1,580.7	593.4	981.6	852.3
1989	9,192.1	6,480.4	6,398.4	85.0	1,193.5	654.5	541.3	1,619.4	602.4	1,011.9	870.1
1990	9,365.5	6,584.1	6,494.1	91.7	1,231.8	667.2	568.3	1,659.8	612.9	1,042.2	887.5
1991	9,355.4	6,544.0	6,453.2	92.3	1,257.0	677.5	583.9	1,676.7	616.4	1,055.9	905.7
1992	9,684.9	6,821.1	6,715.4	106.6	1,288.8	692.8	600.7	1,683.9	606.3	1,073.9	927.7
1993	9,951.5	7,015.7	6,922.7	94.4	1,355.2	726.4	634.0	1,687.9	596.3	1,088.7	961.0
1994	10,352.4	7,354.0	7,241.3	114.3	1,400.9	763.3	641.4	1,689.5	579.7	1,107.7	1,002.0
1995	10,630.3	7,580.0	7,490.0	91.0	1,442.7	789.7	656.3	1,691.9	561.2	1,129.6	1,037.8
1996	11,031.4	7,931.9	7,827.1	105.3	1,471.4	805.9	669.0	1,695.2	547.8	1,147.1	1,055.7
1997	11,521.9	8,348.3	8,230.6	118.1	1,516.7	828.7	691.7	1,708.1	538.8	1,169.7	1,081.1
1998	12,038.3	8,781.0	8,666.5	114.0	1,567.5	850.2	722.2	1,726.8	533.1	1,194.6	1,106.4
1999	12,610.5	9,277.8	9,159.7	116.8	1,610.7	883.9	730.3	1,742.1	528.9	1,214.4	1,144.2
2000	13,131.0	9,728.6	9,593.7	138.2	1,640.6	923.9	717.8	1,770.3	531.7	1,240.0	1,184.9
2001	13,262.1	9,796.7	9,668.7	128.1	1,676.7	953.7	723.3	1,801.4	533.2	1,269.6	1,218.3
2002	13,493.1	9,968.0	9,835.5	133.5	1,702.5	960.1	743.4	1,835.6	542.6	1,294.4	1,221.4
2003	13,879.1	10,295.0	10,153.1	145.1	1,735.0	984.3	751.3	1,858.5	557.0	1,302.8	1,234.6
2004	14,406.4	10,736.4	10,581.6	159.8	1,803.1	1,024.9	778.7	1,871.5	565.1	1,307.5	1,278.2
2005	14,912.5	11,157.9	10,995.0	168.8	1,867.3	1,078.1	788.9	1,888.4	572.3	1,317.0	1,339.1
2006	15,338.3	11,533.3	11,370.8	165.5	1,898.7	1,107.0	790.9	1,903.9	576.7	1,328.3	1,376.2
2007	15,626.0	11,795.2	11,646.9	144.6	1,896.1	1,096.5	799.2	1,930.9	584.6	1,347.3	1,380.2
2008	15,604.7	11,679.1	11,527.0	148.5	1,953.1	1,131.2	821.4	1,970.9	606.3	1,365.3	1,424.7
2009	15,208.8	11,245.6	11,079.9	170.7	1,956.2	1,122.8	833.1	2,006.7	636.6	1,370.5	1,432.1
2010	15,598.8	11,607.3	11,443.9	165.1	1,975.0	1,126.3	848.6	2,016.3	658.0	1,358.5	1,449.0
2011	15,840.7	11,830.4	11,673.0	157.5	2,003.1	1,129.9	873.1	2,007.2	664.3	1,343.0	1,476.5
2012	16,197.0	12,189.5	12,040.5	148.9	2,018.4	1,128.0	890.3	1,989.1	663.7	1,325.5	1,478.5
2013	16,495.4	12,487.3	12,307.3	179.8	2,032.8	1,135.7	897.1	1,975.7	652.0	1,323.7	1,481.2
2014	16,912.0	12,877.1	12,695.0	181.6	2,064.8	1,158.6	906.3	1,971.9	646.9	1,324.7	1,520.0
2015	17,432.2	13,361.7	13,167.2	195.5	2,097.8	1,172.5	925.3	1,977.2	642.5	1,334.2	1,573.0
2016	17,730.5	13,609.4	13,405.9	207.3	2,131.0	1,189.2	941.7	1,995.6	645.2	1,349.7	1,604.6
2017	18,144.1	13,980.4	13,778.5	201.5	2,161.3	1,208.7	952.6	2,010.7	645.6	1,364.2	1,626.5
2018	18,687.8	14,469.2	14,258.5	211.5	2,202.9	1,238.3	964.6	2,028.2	648.5	1,378.7	1,650.1
2019	19,091.7	14,820.0	14,609.0	208.5	2,233.6	1,256.1	977.6	2,053.4	655.7	1,396.7	1,673.7
2017: I	17,977.3	13,828.7	13,621.7	210.6	2,150.1	1,202.0	948.1	2,005.5	645.7	1,359.0	1,619.5
II	18,054.1	13,895.0	13,691.5	204.7	2,158.2	1,207.9	950.3	2,008.2	644.8	1,362.6	1,625.6
III	18,185.6	14,019.5	13,821.2	195.6	2,162.4	1,208.4	953.9	2,012.6	645.6	1,366.1	1,629.4
IV	18,359.4	14,178.4	13,979.7	195.0	2,174.7	1,216.6	958.1	2,016.5	646.4	1,369.2	1,631.4
2018: I	18,530.5	14,334.8	14,127.3	207.4	2,188.2	1,226.7	961.5	2,019.2	646.4	1,371.8	1,639.7
II	18,654.4	14,442.3	14,230.6	213.2	2,198.6	1,235.0	963.7	2,026.0	648.7	1,376.3	1,646.3
III	18,752.4	14,523.7	14,312.6	211.4	2,208.2	1,242.5	965.8	2,033.4	650.6	1,381.8	1,653.4
IV	18,813.9	14,576.1	14,363.3	213.9	2,216.6	1,249.1	967.6	2,034.4	648.5	1,384.9	1,661.1
2019: I	18,950.3	14,705.9	14,498.7	203.1	2,225.8	1,255.0	970.9	2,033.5	642.3	1,390.4	1,669.5
II	19,020.6	14,753.3	14,542.6	208.7	2,231.1	1,256.3	974.9	2,050.7	656.3	1,393.4	1,673.1
III	19,141.7	14,858.9	14,646.3	210.9	2,236.6	1,256.9	979.7	2,061.8	661.0	1,399.9	1,675.6
IV	19,254.0	14,961.9	14,748.4	211.4	2,241.1	1,256.1	985.0	2,067.7	663.1	1,403.6	1,676.4
2020: I	19,010.8	14,730.3	14,507.8	229.2	2,238.7	1,251.4	987.3	2,054.8	666.6	1,387.7	1,673.3
II	17,302.5	13,133.0	12,933.6	206.4	2,164.4	1,250.4	914.7	1,990.7	672.9	1,319.2	1,673.2
III [p]	18,583.5	14,377.5	14,153.8	237.0	2,199.0	1,252.6	946.5	2,019.2	681.9	1,338.6	1,676.3

[1] Gross domestic business value added equals gross domestic product excluding gross value added of households and institutions and of general government. Nonfarm value added equals gross domestic business value added excluding gross farm value added.

[2] Equals compensation of employees of nonprofit institutions, the rental value of nonresidential fixed assets owned and used by nonprofit institutions serving households, and rental income of persons for tenant-occupied housing owned by nonprofit institutions.

[3] Equals compensation of general government employees plus general government consumption of fixed capital.

Source: Department of Commerce (Bureau of Economic Analysis).

Table B–8. Gross domestic product (GDP) by industry, value added, in current dollars and as a percentage of GDP, 1997–2019

[Billions of dollars; except as noted]

Year	Gross domestic product	Total private industries	Agriculture, forestry, fishing, and hunting	Mining	Construction	Total manufacturing	Durable goods	Nondurable goods	Utilities	Wholesale trade	Retail trade
						Value added					
1997	8,577.6	7,432.0	108.6	95.1	339.6	1,382.9	823.8	559.1	171.5	527.5	579.9
1998	9,062.8	7,871.5	99.8	81.7	379.8	1,430.6	850.7	579.9	163.7	563.7	626.9
1999	9,630.7	8,378.3	92.6	84.5	417.6	1,488.9	874.9	614.1	179.9	584.0	652.6
2000	10,252.3	8,929.3	98.3	110.6	461.3	1,550.2	924.8	625.4	180.1	622.6	685.5
2001	10,581.8	9,188.9	99.8	123.9	486.5	1,473.9	833.4	640.5	181.3	613.8	709.5
2002	10,936.4	9,462.0	95.6	112.4	493.6	1,468.5	832.8	635.7	177.6	613.1	732.6
2003	11,458.2	9,905.9	114.0	139.0	525.2	1,524.2	863.2	661.0	184.0	641.5	769.6
2004	12,213.7	10,582.5	142.9	166.5	584.6	1,608.1	905.1	703.0	199.2	697.1	795.6
2005	13,036.6	11,326.4	128.3	225.7	651.8	1,693.4	956.8	736.6	198.1	754.9	840.8
2006	13,814.6	12,022.6	125.1	273.3	697.1	1,793.8	1,004.4	789.4	226.8	811.5	869.9
2007	14,451.9	12,564.8	144.1	314.0	715.3	1,844.7	1,030.6	814.1	231.9	857.8	869.2
2008	14,712.8	12,731.2	147.2	392.2	648.9	1,800.8	999.7	801.1	241.7	884.3	848.7
2009	14,448.9	12,403.9	130.0	275.8	565.6	1,702.1	881.0	821.2	258.2	834.2	827.6
2010	14,992.1	12,884.1	146.3	305.8	525.1	1,797.0	964.3	832.7	278.8	888.9	851.5
2011	15,542.6	13,405.5	180.9	356.3	524.4	1,867.6	1,015.2	852.4	287.5	934.9	871.9
2012	16,197.0	14,037.5	179.6	358.8	553.4	1,927.1	1,061.7	865.3	279.7	997.4	908.4
2013	16,784.9	14,572.3	215.6	386.5	587.6	1,991.9	1,102.0	889.9	286.3	1,040.1	949.5
2014	17,527.3	15,255.9	201.0	416.4	636.9	2,050.2	1,134.1	916.1	298.1	1,088.2	974.5
2015	18,238.3	15,898.9	182.3	261.8	694.9	2,129.6	1,183.8	945.8	299.2	1,142.9	1,020.1
2016	18,745.1	16,360.2	166.6	218.0	746.9	2,099.7	1,186.4	913.4	301.7	1,133.6	1,052.8
2017	19,543.0	17,094.2	176.6	274.0	797.8	2,182.4	1,227.2	955.1	310.1	1,163.5	1,083.5
2018	20,611.9	18,062.2	178.6	330.8	848.2	2,314.4	1,287.6	1,026.8	321.8	1,210.9	1,115.8
2019	21,433.2	18,793.8	175.4	309.5	892.7	2,345.8	1,320.8	1,025.1	335.3	1,262.3	1,162.2
	Percent					*Industry value added as a percentage of GDP (percent)*					
1997	100.0	86.6	1.3	1.1	4.0	16.1	9.6	6.5	2.0	6.2	6.8
1998	100.0	86.9	1.1	.9	4.2	15.8	9.4	6.4	1.8	6.2	6.9
1999	100.0	87.0	1.0	.9	4.3	15.5	9.1	6.4	1.9	6.1	6.8
2000	100.0	87.1	1.0	1.1	4.5	15.1	9.0	6.1	1.8	6.1	6.7
2001	100.0	86.8	.9	1.2	4.6	13.9	7.9	6.1	1.7	5.8	6.7
2002	100.0	86.5	.9	1.0	4.5	13.4	7.6	5.8	1.6	5.6	6.7
2003	100.0	86.5	1.0	1.2	4.6	13.3	7.5	5.8	1.6	5.6	6.7
2004	100.0	86.6	1.2	1.4	4.8	13.2	7.4	5.8	1.6	5.7	6.5
2005	100.0	86.9	1.0	1.7	5.0	13.0	7.3	5.7	1.5	5.8	6.4
2006	100.0	87.0	.9	2.0	5.0	13.0	7.3	5.7	1.6	5.9	6.3
2007	100.0	86.9	1.0	2.2	4.9	12.8	7.1	5.6	1.6	5.9	6.0
2008	100.0	86.5	1.0	2.7	4.4	12.2	6.8	5.4	1.6	6.0	5.8
2009	100.0	85.8	.9	1.9	3.9	11.8	6.1	5.7	1.8	5.8	5.7
2010	100.0	85.9	1.0	2.0	3.5	12.0	6.4	5.6	1.9	5.9	5.7
2011	100.0	86.2	1.2	2.3	3.4	12.0	6.5	5.5	1.8	6.0	5.6
2012	100.0	86.7	1.1	2.2	3.4	11.9	6.6	5.3	1.7	6.2	5.6
2013	100.0	86.8	1.3	2.3	3.5	11.9	6.6	5.3	1.7	6.2	5.7
2014	100.0	87.0	1.1	2.4	3.6	11.7	6.5	5.2	1.7	6.2	5.6
2015	100.0	87.2	1.0	1.4	3.8	11.7	6.5	5.2	1.6	6.3	5.6
2016	100.0	87.3	.9	1.2	4.0	11.2	6.3	4.9	1.6	6.0	5.6
2017	100.0	87.5	.9	1.4	4.1	11.2	6.3	4.9	1.6	6.0	5.5
2018	100.0	87.6	.9	1.6	4.1	11.2	6.2	5.0	1.6	5.9	5.4
2019	100.0	87.7	.8	1.4	4.2	10.9	6.2	.4.8	1.6	5.9	5.4

[1] Consists of agriculture, forestry, fishing, and hunting; mining; construction; and manufacturing.

[2] Consists of utilities; wholesale trade; retail trade; transportation and warehousing; information; finance, insurance, real estate, rental, and leasing; professional and business services; educational services, health care, and social assistance; arts, entertainment, recreation, accommodation, and food services; and other services, except government.

Note: Data shown in Tables B–8 and B–9 are consistent with the 2020 annual revision of the industry accounts released in September 2020. For details see *Survey of Current Business*, October 2020.

See next page for continuation of table.

[Billions of dollars; except as noted]

Year	Private industries—Continued							Government	Private goods-producing industries[1]	Private services-producing industries[2]
	Transportation and warehousing	Information	Finance, insurance, real estate, rental, and leasing	Professional and business services	Educational services, health care, and social assistance	Arts, entertainment, recreation, accommodation, and food services	Other services, except government			
	Value added									
1997	257.3	394.1	1,612.4	840.6	590.6	301.8	230.3	1,145.6	1,926.1	5,505.9
1998	280.0	434.6	1,710.1	914.0	615.8	322.1	248.7	1,191.3	1,991.8	5,879.7
1999	290.0	485.0	1,837.1	997.2	653.9	354.1	260.8	1,252.3	2,083.7	6,294.6
2000	307.8	471.3	1,974.7	1,105.1	695.4	386.5	279.7	1,323.0	2,220.4	6,708.9
2001	308.1	502.4	2,128.1	1,155.5	749.9	390.7	265.6	1,392.9	2,184.1	7,004.8
2002	305.7	550.6	2,217.0	1,189.9	807.0	413.5	284.9	1,474.4	2,170.1	7,291.9
2003	321.4	564.9	2,295.9	1,247.4	862.8	432.1	283.8	1,552.3	2,302.4	7,603.5
2004	352.1	620.4	2,389.1	1,341.0	927.3	461.2	297.3	1,631.3	2,502.2	8,080.3
2005	375.8	642.3	2,606.2	1,446.4	970.5	481.2	310.7	1,710.3	2,699.3	8,627.1
2006	410.4	652.0	2,743.9	1,546.6	1,035.5	511.5	325.0	1,792.0	2,889.4	9,133.2
2007	413.9	706.9	2,848.3	1,666.7	1,087.9	533.5	330.5	1,887.1	3,018.1	9,546.7
2008	426.8	743.0	2,762.7	1,777.1	1,184.8	542.7	330.3	1,981.6	2,989.1	9,742.1
2009	404.6	721.9	2,867.7	1,688.7	1,267.5	533.3	326.5	2,045.1	2,673.6	9,730.3
2010	433.0	753.3	2,943.0	1,766.8	1,310.7	555.8	328.0	2,108.0	2,774.3	10,109.8
2011	451.4	759.8	3,045.3	1,856.7	1,354.7	580.9	333.1	2,137.1	2,929.3	10,476.3
2012	472.0	759.0	3,261.0	1,964.7	1,407.4	621.4	348.0	2,159.5	3,018.8	11,018.7
2013	491.1	828.9	3,322.8	2,017.3	1,447.2	651.3	356.3	2,212.5	3,181.6	11,390.8
2014	521.8	842.4	3,548.0	2,118.4	1,491.9	691.4	376.6	2,271.4	3,304.5	11,951.4
2015	565.8	906.9	3,749.0	2,236.9	1,571.0	746.8	391.6	2,339.4	3,268.6	12,630.3
2016	582.0	968.4	3,946.0	2,304.3	1,652.0	788.2	399.9	2,384.9	3,231.2	13,129.0
2017	607.0	1,005.4	4,116.8	2,431.0	1,707.2	824.5	414.3	2,448.7	3,430.9	13,663.4
2018	650.7	1,059.8	4,371.9	2,572.8	1,781.9	866.7	437.9	2,549.7	3,671.9	14,390.3
2019	696.7	1,127.5	4,541.8	2,710.7	1,865.4	907.2	461.3	2,639.5	3,723.4	15,070.4
	Industry value added as a percentage of GDP (percent)									
1997	3.0	4.6	18.8	9.8	6.9	3.5	2.7	13.4	22.5	64.2
1998	3.1	4.8	18.9	10.1	6.8	3.6	2.7	13.1	22.0	64.9
1999	3.0	5.0	19.1	10.4	6.8	3.7	2.7	13.0	21.6	65.4
2000	3.0	4.6	19.3	10.8	6.8	3.8	2.7	12.9	21.7	65.4
2001	2.9	4.7	20.1	10.9	7.1	3.7	2.5	13.2	20.6	66.2
2002	2.8	5.0	20.3	10.9	7.4	3.8	2.6	13.5	19.8	66.7
2003	2.8	4.9	20.0	10.9	7.5	3.8	2.5	13.5	20.1	66.4
2004	2.9	5.1	19.6	11.0	7.6	3.8	2.4	13.4	20.5	66.2
2005	2.9	4.9	20.0	11.1	7.4	3.7	2.4	13.1	20.7	66.2
2006	3.0	4.7	19.9	11.2	7.5	3.7	2.4	13.0	20.9	66.1
2007	2.9	4.9	19.7	11.5	7.5	3.7	2.3	13.1	20.9	66.1
2008	2.9	5.0	18.8	12.1	8.1	3.7	2.2	13.5	20.3	66.2
2009	2.8	5.0	19.8	11.7	8.8	3.7	2.3	14.2	18.5	67.3
2010	2.9	5.0	19.6	11.8	8.7	3.7	2.2	14.1	18.5	67.4
2011	2.9	4.9	19.6	11.9	8.7	3.7	2.1	13.7	18.8	67.4
2012	2.9	4.7	20.1	12.1	8.7	3.8	2.1	13.3	18.6	68.0
2013	2.9	4.9	19.8	12.0	8.6	3.9	2.1	13.2	19.0	67.9
2014	3.0	4.8	20.2	12.1	8.5	3.9	2.1	13.0	18.9	68.2
2015	3.1	5.0	20.6	12.3	8.6	4.1	2.1	12.8	17.9	69.3
2016	3.1	5.2	21.1	12.3	8.8	4.2	2.1	12.7	17.2	70.0
2017	3.1	5.1	21.1	12.4	8.7	4.2	2.1	12.5	17.6	69.9
2018	3.2	5.1	21.2	12.5	8.6	4.2	2.1	12.4	17.8	69.8
2019	3.3	5.3	21.2	12.6	8.7	4.2	2.2	12.3	17.4	70.3

Note (cont'd): Value added is the contribution of each private industry and of government to GDP. Value added is equal to an industry's gross output minus its intermediate inputs. Current-dollar value added is calculated as the sum of distributions by an industry to its labor and capital, which are derived from the components of gross domestic income.

Value added industry data shown in Tables B–8 and B–9 are based on the 2012 North American Industry Classification System (NAICS).

Source: Department of Commerce (Bureau of Economic Analysis).

TABLE B–9. Real gross domestic product by industry, value added, and percent changes, 1997–2019

Year	Gross domestic product	Private industries									
		Total private industries	Agriculture, forestry, fishing, and hunting	Mining	Construction	Manufacturing			Utilities	Wholesale trade	Retail trade
						Total manufacturing	Durable goods	Non-durable goods			

Year											
	Chain-type quantity indexes for value added (2012=100)										
1997	71.136	70.417	78.122	73.569	124.924	73.952	54.862	108.774	82.684	68.023	76.897
1998	74.324	73.791	76.225	76.540	130.646	76.995	59.373	106.919	78.993	74.707	84.286
1999	77.857	77.614	78.531	74.233	136.033	81.273	63.518	110.673	92.023	77.183	87.388
2000	81.070	81.097	90.102	65.831	141.541	87.116	70.928	111.745	93.244	81.126	90.310
2001	81.880	81.675	86.959	76.178	138.629	83.415	66.355	110.500	77.009	82.663	93.582
2002	83.306	83.128	90.001	78.193	134.131	84.146	67.757	109.712	79.706	83.546	97.689
2003	85.689	85.527	96.987	69.241	136.316	88.809	72.791	113.126	77.930	88.159	102.703
2004	88.945	89.042	104.744	69.643	141.182	95.078	78.019	120.927	82.678	91.924	104.467
2005	92.070	92.473	109.218	70.809	141.809	97.970	83.413	118.785	78.378	96.071	107.851
2006	94.698	95.475	111.013	81.679	138.846	103.527	89.812	122.532	83.261	98.749	108.686
2007	96.475	97.063	98.327	87.975	134.563	106.948	93.989	124.516	84.935	102.073	105.144
2008	96.343	96.460	100.402	85.158	121.446	104.777	94.526	118.051	89.475	101.967	101.290
2009	93.899	93.523	111.362	97.660	104.296	95.141	80.927	114.724	84.828	89.701	97.020
2010	96.306	95.938	107.954	86.193	98.928	100.289	91.144	112.361	95.043	95.040	99.094
2011	97.800	97.577	103.799	89.398	97.334	100.663	97.290	104.898	98.680	96.794	99.277
2012	100.000	100.000	100.000	100.000	100.000	100.000	100.000	100.000	100.000	100.000	100.000
2013	101.842	101.886	116.603	103.938	102.485	103.068	102.463	103.817	98.916	102.293	103.112
2014	104.415	104.833	117.923	115.332	104.396	104.832	103.973	105.900	95.102	106.201	105.005
2015	107.626	108.516	126.532	125.930	109.171	106.297	105.978	106.685	95.207	110.773	108.938
2016	109.468	110.497	133.001	119.044	113.337	105.467	105.792	105.033	99.972	109.412	112.981
2017	112.021	113.283	130.128	120.121	116.868	108.160	109.354	106.620	100.347	111.213	116.995
2018	115.378	116.940	135.540	126.039	120.122	112.745	114.590	110.399	100.876	111.878	120.068
2019	117.872	119.709	135.659	140.557	120.091	114.960	116.383	113.128	102.160	109.538	123.099
	Percent change from year earlier										
1997	4.4	5.5	8.9	4.9	0.9	7.3	9.8	3.8	–4.0	11.7	7.7
1998	4.5	4.8	–2.4	4.0	4.6	4.1	8.2	–1.7	–4.5	9.8	9.6
1999	4.8	5.2	3.0	–3.0	4.1	5.6	7.0	3.5	16.5	3.3	3.7
2000	4.1	4.5	14.7	–11.3	4.0	7.2	11.7	1.0	1.3	5.1	3.3
2001	1.0	.7	–3.5	15.7	–2.1	–4.2	–6.4	–1.1	–17.4	1.9	3.6
2002	1.7	1.8	3.5	2.6	–3.2	.9	2.1	–.7	3.5	1.1	4.4
2003	2.9	2.9	7.8	–11.4	1.6	5.5	7.4	3.1	–2.2	5.5	5.1
2004	3.8	4.1	8.0	.6	3.6	7.1	7.2	6.9	6.1	4.3	1.7
2005	3.5	3.9	4.3	1.7	.4	3.0	6.9	–1.8	–5.2	4.5	3.2
2006	2.9	3.2	1.6	15.4	–2.1	5.7	7.7	3.2	6.2	2.8	.8
2007	1.9	1.7	–11.4	7.7	–3.1	3.3	4.7	1.6	2.0	3.4	–3.3
2008	–.1	–.6	2.1	–3.2	–9.7	–2.0	.6	–5.2	5.3	–.1	–3.7
2009	–2.5	–3.0	10.9	14.7	–14.1	–9.2	–14.4	–2.8	–5.2	–12.0	–4.2
2010	2.6	2.6	–3.1	–11.7	–5.1	5.4	12.6	–2.1	12.0	6.0	2.1
2011	1.6	1.7	–3.8	3.7	–1.6	.4	6.7	–6.6	3.8	1.8	.2
2012	2.2	2.5	–3.7	11.9	2.7	–.7	2.8	–4.7	1.3	3.3	.7
2013	1.8	1.9	16.6	3.9	2.5	3.1	2.5	3.8	–1.1	2.3	3.1
2014	2.5	2.9	1.1	11.0	1.9	1.7	1.5	2.0	–3.9	3.8	1.8
2015	3.1	3.5	7.3	9.2	4.6	1.4	1.9	.7	.1	4.3	3.7
2016	1.7	1.8	5.1	–5.5	3.8	–.8	–.2	–1.5	5.0	–1.2	3.7
2017	2.3	2.5	–2.2	.9	3.1	2.6	3.4	1.5	.4	1.6	3.6
2018	3.0	3.2	4.2	4.9	2.8	4.2	4.8	3.5	.5	.6	2.6
2019	2.2	2.4	.1	11.5	.0	2.0	1.6	2.5	1.3	–2.1	2.5

[1] Consists of agriculture, forestry, fishing, and hunting; mining; construction; and manufacturing.
[2] Consists of utilities; wholesale trade; retail trade; transportation and warehousing; information; finance, insurance, real estate, rental, and leasing; professional and business services; educational services, health care, and social assistance; arts, entertainment, recreation, accommodation, and food services; and other services, except government.

See next page for continuation of table.

Year		Private industries—Continued						Government	Private goods-producing industries [1]	Private services-producing industries [2]
	Transportation and warehousing	Information	Finance, insurance, real estate, rental, and leasing	Professional and business services	Educational services, health care, and social assistance	Arts, entertainment, recreation, accommodation, and food services	Other services, except government			
					Chain-type quantity indexes for value added (2012=100)					
1997	85.155	45.779	64.494	63.672	65.203	78.811	115.601	87.669	81.548	67.403
1998	89.482	50.548	67.298	66.614	65.487	80.968	120.416	88.689	84.672	70.856
1999	90.225	56.651	71.498	69.758	67.685	85.402	121.187	89.756	88.733	74.618
2000	90.015	55.600	75.255	73.866	70.186	90.569	123.985	91.578	94.034	77.602
2001	83.969	58.897	79.439	75.941	71.869	87.406	111.728	92.511	91.428	79.044
2002	80.939	64.594	80.102	76.841	74.748	89.727	114.785	94.159	91.560	80.849
2003	83.784	66.612	81.058	79.221	77.673	92.055	111.552	95.294	94.958	82.982
2004	90.758	74.307	82.263	81.173	81.384	96.188	113.022	96.155	100.536	85.949
2005	95.120	79.284	87.902	84.782	82.907	96.474	113.811	97.036	102.929	89.658
2006	100.720	82.056	90.292	87.152	86.241	99.144	114.372	97.580	107.432	92.253
2007	99.935	90.123	91.815	90.025	86.891	98.599	111.727	98.528	108.998	93.847
2008	99.042	95.903	88.295	94.309	92.433	96.435	107.629	100.447	104.880	94.207
2009	93.111	93.560	92.578	88.315	95.708	90.853	101.336	100.560	97.869	92.358
2010	97.611	98.866	93.968	91.987	96.712	94.349	99.397	101.063	98.681	95.192
2011	99.380	100.275	95.903	95.662	98.366	97.660	98.508	100.747	98.817	97.237
2012	100.000	100.000	100.000	100.000	100.000	100.000	100.000	100.000	100.000	100.000
2013	101.455	109.095	99.099	101.293	101.289	102.128	99.257	99.297	103.878	101.342
2014	104.591	111.815	102.053	105.908	103.098	105.845	102.117	99.069	106.798	104.296
2015	107.458	123.540	104.722	109.519	106.991	109.145	102.740	99.194	110.207	108.048
2016	109.202	134.332	106.404	111.764	110.040	110.705	101.850	100.170	110.396	110.475
2017	113.438	142.999	107.752	116.740	111.644	113.123	102.665	101.231	112.949	113.318
2018	118.281	153.023	109.910	122.685	114.725	115.500	106.048	102.258	117.412	116.770
2019	122.016	163.905	111.467	128.212	117.930	117.225	107.483	103.244	119.991	119.585
					Percent change from year earlier					
1997	5.0	−0.7	5.0	7.6	1.9	6.0	4.9	1.3	6.2	5.2
1998	5.1	10.4	4.3	4.6	0.4	2.7	4.2	1.2	3.8	5.1
1999	.8	12.1	6.2	4.7	3.4	5.5	.6	1.2	4.8	5.3
2000	−.2	−1.9	5.3	5.9	3.7	6.1	2.3	2.0	6.0	4.0
2001	−6.7	5.9	5.6	2.8	2.4	−3.5	−9.9	1.0	−2.8	1.9
2002	−3.6	9.7	.8	1.2	4.0	2.7	2.7	1.8	.1	2.3
2003	3.5	3.1	1.2	3.1	3.9	2.6	−2.8	1.2	3.7	2.6
2004	8.3	11.6	1.5	2.5	4.8	4.5	1.3	.9	5.9	3.6
2005	4.8	6.7	6.9	4.4	1.9	.3	.7	.9	2.4	4.3
2006	5.9	3.5	2.7	2.8	4.0	2.8	.5	.6	4.4	2.9
2007	−.8	9.8	1.7	3.3	.8	−.5	−2.3	1.0	1.5	1.7
2008	−.9	6.4	−3.8	4.8	6.4	−2.2	−3.7	1.9	−3.8	.4
2009	−6.0	−2.4	4.9	−6.4	3.5	−5.8	−5.8	.1	−6.7	−2.0
2010	4.8	5.7	1.5	4.2	1.0	3.8	−1.9	.5	.8	3.1
2011	1.8	1.4	2.1	4.0	1.7	3.5	−.9	−.3	.1	2.1
2012	.6	−.3	4.3	4.5	1.7	2.4	1.5	−.7	1.2	2.8
2013	1.5	9.1	−.9	1.3	1.3	2.1	−.7	−.7	3.9	1.3
2014	3.1	2.5	3.0	4.6	1.8	3.6	2.9	−.2	2.8	2.9
2015	2.7	10.5	2.6	3.4	3.8	3.1	.6	.1	3.2	3.6
2016	1.6	8.7	1.6	2.0	2.8	1.4	−.9	1.0	.2	2.2
2017	3.9	6.5	1.3	4.5	1.5	2.2	.8	1.1	2.3	2.6
2018	4.3	7.0	2.0	5.1	2.8	2.1	3.3	1.0	4.0	3.0
2019	3.2	7.1	1.4	4.5	2.8	1.5	1.4	1.0	2.2	2.4

Note: Data are based on the 2012 North American Industry Classification System (NAICS).

See Note, Table B–8.

Source: Department of Commerce (Bureau of Economic Analysis).

TABLE B–10. Personal consumption expenditures, 1969–2020

[Billions of dollars; quarterly data at seasonally adjusted annual rates]

Year or quarter	Personal consumption expenditures	Goods Total	Durable Total[1]	Durable Motor vehicles and parts	Nondurable Total[1]	Nondurable Food and beverages purchased for off-premises consumption	Nondurable Gasoline and other energy goods	Services Total	Household consumption expenditures Total[1]	Household consumption expenditures Housing and utilities	Household consumption expenditures Health care	Household consumption expenditures Financial services and insurance	Addendum: Personal consumption expenditures excluding food and energy[2]
1969	603.6	304.7	90.5	37.4	214.2	95.4	25.0	299.0	289.5	101.0	42.1	27.7	469.3
1970	646.7	318.8	90.0	34.5	228.8	103.5	26.3	327.9	317.5	109.4	47.7	30.1	501.7
1971	699.9	342.1	102.4	43.2	239.7	107.1	27.6	357.8	346.1	120.0	53.7	33.1	548.5
1972	768.2	373.8	116.4	49.4	257.4	114.5	29.4	394.3	381.5	131.2	59.8	37.1	605.8
1973	849.6	416.6	130.5	54.4	286.1	126.7	34.3	432.9	419.2	143.5	67.2	39.9	668.5
1974	930.2	451.5	130.2	48.2	321.4	143.0	43.8	478.6	463.1	158.6	76.1	44.1	719.7
1975	1,030.5	491.3	142.2	52.6	349.2	156.6	48.0	539.2	522.2	176.5	89.0	51.8	797.3
1976	1,147.7	546.3	168.6	68.2	377.7	167.3	53.0	601.4	582.4	194.7	101.8	56.8	894.7
1977	1,274.0	600.4	192.0	79.8	408.4	179.8	57.8	673.6	653.0	217.8	115.7	65.1	998.6
1978	1,422.3	663.6	213.3	89.2	450.2	196.1	61.5	758.7	735.7	244.3	131.2	76.7	1,122.4
1979	1,585.4	737.9	226.3	90.2	511.6	218.4	80.4	847.5	821.4	273.4	148.8	83.6	1,239.7
1980	1,750.7	799.8	226.4	84.4	573.4	239.2	101.9	950.9	920.8	312.5	171.7	91.7	1,353.1
1981	1,934.0	869.4	243.9	93.0	625.4	255.3	113.4	1,064.6	1,030.4	352.1	201.9	98.5	1,501.5
1982	2,071.3	899.3	253.0	100.0	646.3	267.1	108.4	1,172.0	1,134.0	387.5	225.2	113.7	1,622.9
1983	2,281.6	973.8	295.0	122.9	678.8	277.0	106.5	1,307.8	1,267.1	421.2	253.1	141.0	1,817.2
1984	2,492.3	1,063.7	342.2	147.2	721.5	291.1	108.2	1,428.6	1,383.3	457.5	276.5	150.8	2,008.1
1985	2,712.8	1,137.6	380.4	170.1	757.2	303.0	110.5	1,575.2	1,527.3	500.6	302.2	178.2	2,210.3
1986	2,886.3	1,195.6	421.4	187.5	774.2	316.4	91.2	1,690.7	1,638.0	537.0	330.2	187.7	2,391.3
1987	3,076.3	1,256.3	442.0	188.2	814.3	324.3	96.4	1,820.0	1,764.3	571.6	366.0	189.5	2,566.6
1988	3,330.0	1,337.3	475.1	202.2	862.3	342.8	99.9	1,992.7	1,929.4	614.4	410.1	202.9	2,793.1
1989	3,576.8	1,423.8	494.3	207.8	929.5	365.4	110.4	2,153.0	2,084.9	655.2	451.2	222.3	3,002.1
1990	3,809.0	1,491.3	497.1	205.1	994.2	391.2	124.2	2,317.7	2,241.8	696.5	506.2	230.8	3,194.9
1991	3,943.4	1,497.4	477.2	185.7	1,020.3	403.0	121.1	2,446.0	2,365.9	735.2	555.8	250.1	3,314.4
1992	4,197.6	1,563.3	508.1	204.8	1,055.2	404.5	125.2	2,634.3	2,546.4	771.1	612.8	277.0	3,561.7
1993	4,452.0	1,642.3	551.5	224.7	1,090.8	413.5	126.9	2,809.6	2,719.6	814.9	648.8	314.0	3,796.6
1994	4,721.0	1,746.6	607.2	249.8	1,139.4	432.1	129.2	2,974.4	2,876.6	863.3	680.5	327.9	4,042.5
1995	4,962.6	1,815.5	635.7	255.7	1,179.8	443.7	133.4	3,147.1	3,044.7	913.7	719.9	347.0	4,267.2
1996	5,244.6	1,917.7	676.3	273.5	1,241.4	461.9	144.7	3,326.9	3,216.9	962.4	752.1	372.1	4,513.0
1997	5,536.8	2,006.5	715.5	293.1	1,291.0	474.8	147.7	3,530.3	3,424.7	1,009.8	790.9	408.9	4,787.8
1998	5,877.2	2,108.4	779.3	320.2	1,329.1	487.4	132.4	3,768.8	3,645.0	1,065.5	832.0	446.1	5,132.4
1999	6,279.1	2,287.1	855.6	350.7	1,431.5	515.5	146.5	3,992.0	3,853.8	1,123.1	863.6	486.4	5,491.2
2000	6,762.1	2,453.2	912.6	363.2	1,540.6	540.6	184.5	4,309.0	4,150.9	1,198.6	918.4	543.0	5,899.4
2001	7,065.6	2,525.6	941.5	383.3	1,584.1	564.0	178.0	4,540.0	4,361.0	1,287.5	996.6	525.7	6,174.0
2002	7,342.7	2,598.8	985.4	401.3	1,613.4	575.1	167.9	4,743.9	4,545.5	1,333.6	1,082.9	534.7	6,454.1
2003	7,723.1	2,722.6	1,017.8	401.5	1,704.8	599.6	196.4	5,000.5	4,795.0	1,394.1	1,154.0	560.3	6,766.8
2004	8,212.7	2,902.0	1,080.6	409.3	1,821.4	632.6	232.7	5,310.6	5,104.3	1,469.1	1,238.9	605.5	7,179.2
2005	8,747.1	3,082.9	1,128.6	410.0	1,954.3	668.2	283.8	5,664.2	5,453.9	1,583.6	1,320.5	659.0	7,605.3
2006	9,260.3	3,239.7	1,158.3	394.9	2,081.3	700.3	319.7	6,020.7	5,781.5	1,682.4	1,391.9	695.0	8,039.7
2007	9,706.4	3,367.0	1,188.0	400.6	2,179.0	737.3	345.5	6,339.4	6,090.6	1,758.2	1,478.2	737.2	8,413.4
2008	9,976.3	3,363.2	1,098.8	343.3	2,264.5	769.1	391.1	6,613.1	6,325.8	1,835.4	1,555.3	756.6	8,592.6
2009	9,842.2	3,180.0	1,012.1	318.6	2,167.9	772.9	287.0	6,662.2	6,373.0	1,877.7	1,632.7	711.3	8,567.0
2010	10,185.8	3,317.8	1,049.0	344.5	2,268.9	786.9	336.7	6,868.0	6,573.6	1,903.9	1,699.6	754.4	8,840.8
2011	10,641.1	3,518.1	1,093.5	365.2	2,424.6	819.5	413.8	7,123.0	6,811.1	1,955.9	1,757.1	797.9	9,188.9
2012	11,006.8	3,637.7	1,144.2	396.6	2,493.5	846.2	421.9	7,369.1	7,027.5	1,996.3	1,821.3	820.1	9,531.1
2013	11,317.2	3,730.0	1,189.4	417.5	2,540.6	864.0	418.2	7,587.2	7,234.6	2,055.3	1,858.2	858.4	9,815.1
2014	11,822.8	3,863.0	1,242.1	442.0	2,620.9	896.9	403.3	7,959.8	7,594.2	2,149.9	1,940.5	908.1	10,290.4
2015	12,297.5	3,923.0	1,307.6	475.3	2,615.4	921.0	309.4	8,374.5	8,002.9	2,257.9	2,057.3	957.3	10,841.4
2016	12,770.0	3,998.4	1,350.2	485.6	2,648.1	939.9	275.0	8,771.6	8,370.8	2,358.5	2,165.1	984.0	11,334.2
2017	13,340.4	4,172.3	1,410.7	503.6	2,761.6	970.2	309.0	9,168.1	8,751.4	2,459.5	2,248.3	1,052.4	11,835.3
2018	13,993.3	4,371.9	1,481.6	523.2	2,890.3	998.8	349.2	9,621.4	9,182.7	2,570.2	2,345.0	1,119.5	12,403.6
2019	14,544.6	4,512.2	1,534.4	521.8	2,977.9	1,025.7	335.4	10,032.4	9,593.2	2,681.2	2,450.8	1,176.1	12,940.9
2017: I	13,153.2	4,108.1	1,383.2	494.9	2,724.9	956.5	307.8	9,045.1	8,622.4	2,412.8	2,222.6	1,023.0	11,676.6
II	13,241.3	4,130.3	1,394.0	493.9	2,736.3	964.8	295.3	9,111.0	8,692.0	2,450.5	2,224.3	1,044.2	11,751.8
III	13,370.9	4,177.3	1,413.0	503.4	2,764.3	972.8	305.1	9,193.6	8,781.1	2,469.5	2,258.7	1,061.3	11,867.9
IV	13,596.0	4,273.4	1,452.6	522.4	2,820.8	986.4	327.8	9,322.7	8,910.1	2,505.2	2,287.6	1,081.1	12,044.7
2018: I	13,755.5	4,315.6	1,461.8	517.7	2,853.8	991.7	343.7	9,440.0	9,016.1	2,528.5	2,306.7	1,097.3	12,183.0
II	13,939.9	4,368.8	1,482.6	523.2	2,886.2	996.7	349.6	9,571.1	9,137.2	2,559.5	2,332.6	1,109.9	12,348.9
III	14,086.3	4,394.8	1,488.7	525.6	2,906.1	1,001.2	356.4	9,691.4	9,255.5	2,580.3	2,370.3	1,127.7	12,489.1
IV	14,191.4	4,408.3	1,493.2	526.4	2,915.1	1,005.6	347.3	9,783.1	9,321.9	2,612.5	2,370.5	1,143.3	12,593.3
2019: I	14,276.6	4,415.2	1,494.5	508.5	2,920.7	1,011.7	321.9	9,861.4	9,424.9	2,639.2	2,405.9	1,151.6	12,699.5
II	14,497.3	4,517.7	1,536.0	524.9	2,981.7	1,023.4	344.9	9,979.6	9,542.2	2,668.9	2,440.2	1,168.7	12,887.3
III	14,645.3	4,553.6	1,552.8	525.7	3,000.8	1,035.2	334.5	10,091.7	9,647.4	2,698.8	2,457.0	1,184.4	13,030.6
IV	14,759.2	4,562.4	1,554.1	528.2	3,008.2	1,032.4	340.4	10,196.8	9,758.5	2,717.8	2,500.3	1,199.5	13,146.2
2020: I	14,545.5	4,552.9	1,496.4	484.6	3,056.5	1,112.9	310.4	9,992.5	9,471.1	2,737.3	2,403.5	1,200.9	12,890.6
II	13,097.3	4,361.5	1,478.3	484.6	2,883.2	1,137.1	188.3	8,735.8	8,153.3	2,781.2	2,000.8	1,182.0	11,519.7
III ᵖ	14,394.2	4,866.1	1,753.7	585.4	3,112.4	1,145.8	247.9	9,528.1	9,053.0	2,800.4	2,386.1	1,213.2	12,749.1

[1] Includes other items not shown separately.
[2] Food consists of food and beverages purchased for off-premises consumption; food services, which include purchased meals and beverages, are not classified as food.

Source: Department of Commerce (Bureau of Economic Analysis).

TABLE B–11. Real personal consumption expenditures, 2002–2020

[Billions of chained (2012) dollars; quarterly data at seasonally adjusted annual rates]

| Year or quarter | Personal consumption expenditures | Goods | | | | | | Services | | | | | Addendum: Personal consumption expenditures excluding food and energy[2] |
| | | Total | Durable | | Nondurable | | | Total | Household consumption expenditures | | | | |
			Total[1]	Motor vehicles and parts	Total[1]	Food and beverages purchased for off-premises consumption	Gasoline and other energy goods		Total[1]	Housing and utilities	Health care	Financial services and insurance	
2002	9,088.7	2,947.6	820.2	416.9	2,157.5	744.5	455.2	6,151.1	5,966.4	1,707.6	1,440.7	700.3	7,716.7
2003	9,377.5	3,092.0	879.3	429.2	2,233.6	761.8	455.6	6,289.4	6,087.7	1,730.5	1,479.3	704.3	7,976.2
2004	9,729.3	3,250.0	952.1	441.1	2,306.5	779.5	459.4	6,479.2	6,275.1	1,773.8	1,531.2	728.5	8,298.2
2005	10,075.9	3,384.7	1,004.9	435.1	2,383.4	809.2	457.4	6,689.5	6,487.6	1,846.6	1,581.9	767.9	8,605.9
2006	10,384.5	3,509.7	1,049.3	419.0	2,461.6	834.0	456.3	6,871.7	6,640.7	1,882.5	1,618.2	785.8	8,894.3
2007	10,615.3	3,607.6	1,099.7	427.3	2,503.4	845.2	455.4	7,003.6	6,765.7	1,900.7	1,657.2	808.3	9,107.6
2008	10,592.8	3,498.9	1,036.4	373.1	2,463.9	831.0	437.5	7,093.0	6,815.4	1,921.2	1,697.9	825.0	9,119.2
2009	10,460.0	3,389.8	973.0	346.7	2,423.1	825.3	440.1	7,070.1	6,781.3	1,943.1	1,735.1	809.5	8,988.1
2010	10,643.0	3,485.7	1,027.3	360.0	2,461.3	837.7	437.9	7,157.4	6,859.0	1,966.8	1,761.7	810.5	9,151.3
2011	10,843.8	3,561.8	1,079.7	370.1	2,482.9	839.0	427.8	7,282.1	6,969.3	1,993.0	1,788.7	831.4	9,363.2
2012	11,006.8	3,637.7	1,144.2	396.6	2,493.5	846.2	421.9	7,369.1	7,027.5	1,996.3	1,821.3	820.1	9,531.1
2013	11,166.9	3,752.2	1,214.1	415.3	2,538.5	855.5	429.7	7,415.5	7,069.8	2,006.4	1,832.6	815.2	9,667.6
2014	11,497.4	3,905.1	1,301.6	439.4	2,605.3	871.4	430.0	7,594.9	7,249.6	2,039.9	1,892.8	817.9	9,978.8
2015	11,934.3	4,090.9	1,400.6	472.8	2,693.7	884.8	450.0	7,849.0	7,511.1	2,089.3	1,994.6	837.7	10,384.1
2016	12,264.6	4,238.9	1,481.9	488.7	2,762.0	912.4	452.1	8,035.6	7,682.2	2,121.4	2,074.9	820.9	10,682.3
2017	12,587.2	4,410.6	1,584.6	513.0	2,834.0	943.1	449.5	8,195.5	7,841.8	2,139.0	2,123.5	838.0	10,973.3
2018	12,928.1	4,590.2	1,692.7	535.1	2,910.3	965.9	447.0	8,367.1	8,002.5	2,167.3	2,174.1	840.3	11,275.5
2019	13,240.2	4,760.5	1,774.6	532.4	3,001.5	982.0	444.9	8,520.5	8,167.8	2,193.0	2,232.9	857.9	11,567.3
2017: I	12,477.3	4,328.2	1,536.8	500.3	2,797.7	933.2	445.2	8,161.0	7,798.6	2,123.5	2,111.4	834.1	10,887.5
II	12,533.1	4,380.8	1,561.3	502.3	2,826.3	937.6	453.3	8,169.3	7,813.7	2,139.9	2,105.1	836.0	10,920.1
III	12,604.5	4,424.9	1,594.7	515.4	2,838.7	944.3	450.9	8,199.7	7,850.9	2,139.2	2,131.4	841.1	10,990.2
IV	12,733.7	4,508.3	1,645.7	534.1	2,873.2	957.2	448.5	8,251.9	7,903.9	2,153.3	2,146.0	840.8	11,095.3
2018: I	12,798.1	4,531.6	1,661.9	531.0	2,881.2	961.6	447.6	8,293.2	7,938.2	2,156.1	2,154.1	838.6	11,155.8
II	12,898.1	4,578.5	1,690.6	536.4	2,900.9	964.3	448.3	8,348.5	7,986.4	2,166.4	2,165.1	837.4	11,243.7
III	12,983.0	4,610.7	1,703.9	535.7	2,920.1	967.1	445.1	8,401.7	8,039.5	2,168.7	2,193.3	840.7	11,330.3
IV	13,033.4	4,639.8	1,714.3	537.1	2,938.9	970.4	446.8	8,425.1	8,045.9	2,177.7	2,183.8	844.3	11,372.2
2019: I	13,093.2	4,668.6	1,718.3	520.6	2,962.9	969.6	446.6	8,457.5	8,100.1	2,183.0	2,208.0	853.8	11,433.9
II	13,212.8	4,756.3	1,770.5	534.6	3,001.0	979.9	446.7	8,498.3	8,145.6	2,190.4	2,229.4	853.7	11,541.4
III	13,301.3	4,805.2	1,797.8	535.1	3,023.9	991.6	444.8	8,541.5	8,188.4	2,199.5	2,234.0	858.2	11,615.1
IV	13,353.7	4,811.8	1,811.7	539.2	3,018.2	987.1	441.6	8,584.9	8,237.0	2,199.1	2,260.2	865.8	11,678.9
2020: I	13,118.4	4,812.9	1,752.0	495.9	3,070.6	1,055.9	421.3	8,365.3	7,949.2	2,197.4	2,161.7	861.4	11,405.3
II	11,860.3	4,677.4	1,744.6	497.3	2,947.9	1,040.9	342.0	7,306.9	6,832.2	2,220.6	1,782.7	859.0	10,212.1
III ᵖ	12,915.9	5,149.7	2,028.8	574.3	3,151.5	1,053.8	400.0	7,913.5	7,535.4	2,225.4	2,111.0	869.9	11,204.5

[1] Includes other items not shown separately.
[2] Food consists of food and beverages purchased for off-premises consumption; food services, which include purchased meals and beverages, are not classified as food.

Source: Department of Commerce (Bureau of Economic Analysis).

TABLE B–12. Private fixed investment by type, 1969–2020

[Billions of dollars; quarterly data at seasonally adjusted annual rates]

Year or quarter	Private fixed investment	Nonresidential											Residential		
		Total nonresidential	Structures	Equipment						Intellectual property products			Total residential¹	Structures	
				Total¹	Information processing equipment			Industrial equipment	Transportation equipment	Total¹	Software	Research and development²		Total¹	Single family
					Total	Computers and peripheral equipment	Other								
1969	164.4	120.0	37.7	65.2	12.8	2.4	10.4	19.1	18.9	17.2	1.8	11.0	44.4	43.4	19.7
1970	168.0	124.6	40.3	66.4	14.3	2.7	11.6	20.3	16.2	17.9	2.3	11.5	43.4	42.3	17.5
1971	188.6	130.4	42.7	69.1	14.9	2.8	12.2	19.5	18.4	18.7	2.4	11.9	58.2	56.9	25.8
1972	219.0	146.6	47.2	78.9	16.7	3.5	13.2	21.4	21.8	20.6	2.8	12.9	72.4	70.9	32.8
1973	251.0	172.7	55.0	95.1	19.9	3.5	16.3	26.0	26.6	22.7	3.2	14.6	78.3	76.6	35.2
1974	260.5	191.1	61.2	104.3	23.1	3.9	19.2	30.7	26.3	25.5	3.9	16.4	69.5	67.6	29.7
1975	263.5	196.8	61.4	107.6	23.8	3.6	20.2	31.3	25.2	27.8	4.8	17.5	66.7	64.8	29.6
1976	306.1	219.3	65.9	121.2	27.5	4.4	23.1	34.1	30.0	32.2	5.2	19.6	86.8	84.6	43.9
1977	374.3	259.1	74.6	148.7	33.7	5.7	28.0	39.4	39.3	35.8	5.5	21.8	115.2	112.8	62.2
1978	452.6	314.6	93.6	180.6	42.3	7.6	34.8	47.7	47.3	40.4	6.3	24.9	138.0	135.3	72.8
1979	521.7	373.8	117.7	208.1	50.3	10.2	40.2	56.2	53.6	48.1	8.1	29.1	147.8	144.7	72.3
1980	536.4	406.9	136.2	216.4	58.9	12.5	46.4	60.7	48.4	54.4	9.8	34.2	129.5	126.1	52.9
1981	601.4	472.9	167.3	240.9	69.6	17.1	52.5	65.5	50.6	64.8	11.8	39.7	128.5	124.9	52.0
1982	595.9	485.1	177.6	234.9	74.2	18.9	55.3	62.7	46.8	72.7	14.0	44.8	110.8	107.2	41.5
1983	643.3	482.2	154.3	246.5	83.7	23.9	59.8	58.9	53.5	81.3	16.4	49.6	161.1	156.9	72.5
1984	754.7	564.3	177.4	291.9	101.2	31.6	69.6	68.1	64.4	95.0	20.4	56.9	190.4	185.6	86.4
1985	807.8	607.8	194.5	307.9	106.6	33.7	72.9	72.5	69.0	105.3	23.8	63.0	200.1	195.0	87.4
1986	842.6	607.8	176.5	317.7	111.1	33.4	77.7	75.4	70.5	113.5	25.6	66.5	234.8	229.3	104.1
1987	865.0	615.2	174.2	320.9	112.2	35.8	76.4	76.7	68.1	120.1	29.0	69.2	249.8	244.0	117.2
1988	918.5	662.3	182.8	346.8	120.8	38.0	82.8	84.2	72.9	132.7	33.3	76.4	256.2	250.1	120.1
1989	972.0	716.0	193.7	372.2	130.7	43.1	87.6	93.3	67.9	150.1	40.6	84.1	256.0	249.9	120.9
1990	978.9	739.2	202.9	371.9	129.6	38.6	90.9	92.1	70.0	164.4	45.4	91.5	239.7	233.7	112.9
1991	944.7	723.6	183.6	360.8	129.2	37.7	91.5	89.3	71.5	179.1	48.7	101.0	221.2	215.4	99.4
1992	996.7	741.9	172.6	381.7	142.1	44.0	98.1	93.0	74.7	187.7	51.1	105.4	254.7	248.8	122.0
1993	1,086.0	799.2	177.2	425.1	153.3	47.9	105.4	102.2	89.4	196.9	57.2	106.3	286.8	280.7	140.1
1994	1,192.7	868.9	186.8	476.4	167.0	52.4	114.6	113.6	107.7	205.7	60.4	109.2	323.8	317.6	162.3
1995	1,286.3	962.2	207.3	528.1	188.4	66.1	122.3	129.0	116.1	226.8	65.5	121.2	324.1	317.7	153.5
1996	1,401.3	1,043.2	224.6	565.3	204.7	72.8	131.9	136.5	123.2	253.3	74.5	134.5	358.1	351.7	170.8
1997	1,524.7	1,149.1	250.3	610.9	222.8	81.4	141.4	140.4	135.5	288.0	93.8	148.1	375.6	369.3	175.2
1998	1,673.0	1,254.1	276.0	660.0	240.1	87.9	152.2	147.4	147.1	318.1	109.2	160.6	418.8	412.1	199.4
1999	1,826.2	1,364.5	285.7	713.6	259.8	97.2	162.5	149.1	174.4	365.1	136.6	177.5	461.8	454.5	223.8
2000	1,983.9	1,498.4	321.0	766.1	293.8	103.2	190.6	162.9	170.8	411.3	156.8	199.0	485.4	477.7	236.8
2001	1,973.1	1,460.1	333.5	711.5	265.9	87.6	178.4	151.9	154.2	415.0	157.7	202.7	513.1	505.2	249.1
2002	1,910.4	1,352.8	287.0	659.6	236.7	79.7	157.0	141.7	141.6	406.2	152.5	196.1	557.6	549.6	265.9
2003	2,013.0	1,375.9	286.6	670.6	242.7	79.9	162.8	143.4	134.1	418.7	155.0	201.0	637.1	628.8	310.6
2004	2,217.2	1,467.4	307.7	721.9	255.8	84.2	171.6	144.2	159.2	437.8	166.3	207.4	749.8	740.8	377.6
2005	2,477.2	1,621.0	353.0	794.9	267.0	84.2	182.8	162.4	179.6	473.1	178.6	224.7	856.2	846.6	433.5
2006	2,632.0	1,793.8	425.2	862.3	288.5	92.6	195.9	181.6	194.3	506.3	189.5	245.6	838.2	828.1	416.0
2007	2,639.1	1,948.6	510.3	893.4	310.9	95.4	215.5	194.1	188.8	544.8	206.4	268.0	690.5	680.6	305.2
2008	2,506.9	1,990.9	571.1	845.4	306.3	93.9	212.4	194.3	148.7	574.4	223.8	284.2	516.0	506.4	185.8
2009	2,080.4	1,690.4	455.8	670.3	275.6	88.9	186.7	153.7	74.9	564.4	226.0	274.6	390.0	381.2	105.3
2010	2,111.6	1,735.0	379.8	777.0	307.5	99.6	207.9	155.2	135.8	578.2	226.4	282.4	376.6	367.4	112.6
2011	2,286.3	1,907.5	404.5	881.3	313.3	95.6	217.7	191.5	177.8	621.7	249.8	303.4	378.8	369.1	108.2
2012	2,550.5	2,118.5	479.4	983.4	331.2	103.5	227.7	211.2	215.3	655.7	272.1	313.4	432.0	421.5	132.0
2013	2,721.5	2,211.5	492.5	1,027.0	341.7	102.1	239.6	209.3	242.5	691.9	283.7	337.9	510.0	499.0	170.8
2014	2,960.2	2,400.1	577.6	1,091.9	346.0	101.9	244.1	218.8	272.8	730.5	297.5	359.5	560.2	548.8	193.6
2015	3,100.4	2,466.6	584.4	1,119.5	352.8	101.3	251.5	218.2	306.3	762.7	307.1	378.3	633.8	622.1	221.1
2016	3,160.0	2,460.5	560.3	1,088.6	353.3	99.0	254.3	214.3	292.0	811.7	327.3	403.4	699.5	687.3	242.5
2017	3,334.8	2,574.5	599.1	1,122.2	371.3	106.1	265.2	227.9	292.0	853.2	349.2	420.0	760.3	747.9	270.2
2018	3,575.1	2,776.7	631.4	1,213.4	395.9	119.3	276.6	251.5	309.5	931.8	382.7	461.3	798.5	785.5	289.6
2019	3,702.1	2,895.0	650.2	1,241.0	397.2	121.6	275.7	260.9	310.3	1,003.8	411.2	501.9	807.1	793.9	280.0
2017: I	3,278.5	2,532.5	600.1	1,094.3	359.1	100.6	258.5	219.4	290.3	838.0	340.1	414.8	746.0	733.6	259.9
II	3,309.2	2,555.9	604.5	1,107.5	368.9	105.2	263.7	225.5	284.8	843.9	346.7	413.6	753.3	741.0	267.3
III	3,333.8	2,575.2	592.3	1,124.7	372.3	110.0	262.3	229.2	292.4	858.2	352.4	421.6	758.5	746.2	273.2
IV	3,417.8	2,634.2	599.3	1,162.4	384.9	108.6	276.3	237.7	300.4	872.5	357.5	430.0	783.6	770.8	280.2
2018: I	3,510.5	2,716.2	629.2	1,189.6	395.1	117.1	278.0	245.0	305.4	897.4	367.8	443.5	794.3	781.5	290.6
II	3,570.2	2,765.9	640.7	1,197.0	392.6	119.9	272.7	247.0	303.0	928.3	380.9	460.0	804.3	791.3	295.1
III	3,593.3	2,792.6	634.2	1,219.6	400.0	121.4	278.6	252.5	307.4	938.9	386.9	463.6	800.7	787.7	291.0
IV	3,626.5	2,831.9	621.5	1,247.6	396.0	118.8	277.2	261.3	322.2	962.8	395.3	478.2	794.7	781.7	281.6
2019: I	3,674.2	2,878.4	640.1	1,256.5	401.6	120.4	281.2	260.5	324.3	981.9	401.3	490.9	795.8	782.7	275.5
II	3,686.6	2,891.3	649.7	1,243.1	399.2	124.0	275.2	261.7	309.0	998.5	407.6	500.5	795.3	782.1	274.3
III	3,718.5	2,908.0	658.8	1,234.9	396.1	119.6	276.5	263.7	300.0	1,014.2	416.3	506.8	810.5	797.2	279.8
IV	3,729.2	2,902.3	652.3	1,229.3	392.1	122.3	269.7	257.8	307.8	1,020.7	419.6	509.4	827.0	813.6	290.3
2020: I	3,728.0	2,859.3	648.7	1,181.6	377.7	115.7	262.0	255.1	282.1	1,029.1	427.0	511.5	868.7	855.3	307.4
II	3,427.0	2,646.8	584.0	1,057.2	401.8	135.5	266.3	238.8	175.8	1,005.6	420.9	499.6	780.2	766.5	270.1
III ᵖ	3,682.3	2,781.7	560.3	1,199.1	443.0	147.7	295.3	249.4	236.3	1,022.3	427.6	513.4	900.6	885.1	287.2

¹ Includes other items not shown separately.
² Research and development investment includes expenditures for software.

Source: Department of Commerce (Bureau of Economic Analysis).

472 | Appendix B

TABLE B–13. Real private fixed investment by type, 2002–2020

[Billions of chained (2012) dollars; quarterly data at seasonally adjusted annual rates]

Year or quarter	Private fixed investment	Nonresidential Total nonresidential	Structures	Equipment Total[2]	Information processing equipment Total	Computers and peripheral equipment[1]	Other	Industrial equipment	Transportation equipment	Intellectual property products Total[2]	Software	Research and development[3]	Residential Total residential[2]	Structures Total[2]	Single family
2002	2,183.4	1,472.7	473.5	607.8	133.3	35.9	98.3	181.4	162.4	421.5	125.5	244.1	692.6	685.1	327.1
2003	2,280.6	1,509.4	456.6	634.3	150.4	40.2	111.1	182.2	150.3	437.7	133.5	246.1	755.5	747.7	362.0
2004	2,440.7	1,594.0	456.3	688.6	169.4	45.7	124.7	178.8	171.2	459.2	149.3	248.1	830.9	822.1	405.4
2005	2,618.7	1,716.4	466.1	760.0	187.6	51.8	136.5	194.2	192.1	493.1	163.4	261.6	885.4	876.3	432.8
2006	2,686.8	1,854.2	501.7	832.6	217.0	64.7	152.4	210.6	206.4	521.5	173.5	279.6	818.9	809.5	390.4
2007	2,653.5	1,982.1	568.6	865.8	247.2	73.9	173.3	217.3	197.7	554.3	191.1	296.1	665.8	656.6	283.5
2008	2,499.4	1,994.2	605.4	824.4	260.6	79.7	180.9	208.3	155.0	575.3	206.7	304.8	504.6	495.7	178.1
2009	2,099.8	1,704.3	492.2	649.7	247.5	81.1	166.5	162.7	72.5	572.4	212.9	297.4	395.3	386.9	105.3
2010	2,164.2	1,781.0	412.8	781.2	289.1	94.1	195.1	162.5	141.5	588.1	220.9	298.5	383.0	373.8	114.3
2011	2,317.8	1,935.4	424.1	886.2	303.2	93.9	209.3	194.9	181.8	624.8	245.2	311.0	382.5	372.4	109.1
2012	2,550.5	2,118.5	479.4	983.4	331.2	103.5	227.7	211.2	215.3	655.7	272.1	313.4	432.0	421.5	132.0
2013	2,692.1	2,206.0	485.5	1,029.2	351.8	103.0	248.8	208.4	238.5	691.4	287.2	333.8	485.5	474.1	161.8
2014	2,869.2	2,365.3	538.8	1,101.1	370.2	102.9	267.7	216.5	265.0	724.8	305.3	346.9	504.1	491.8	171.8
2015	2,979.0	2,420.3	534.1	1,134.6	393.3	103.4	291.0	216.7	292.8	752.4	320.2	357.1	555.4	542.0	191.5
2016	3,032.2	2,433.0	510.5	1,115.1	410.8	102.6	310.1	213.7	275.7	809.8	345.9	386.7	592.1	577.6	201.3
2017	3,147.4	2,524.2	531.7	1,150.3	441.2	110.5	332.7	225.4	271.4	844.2	374.6	392.3	615.7	600.3	214.8
2018	3,310.4	2,698.9	551.1	1,242.2	479.3	124.0	356.6	243.9	287.0	910.2	416.4	416.0	612.0	596.6	220.7
2019	3,371.7	2,776.8	547.7	1,267.7	493.9	130.7	363.8	249.1	285.7	968.2	449.3	440.5	601.5	586.0	206.8
2017: I	3,115.5	2,492.6	538.5	1,121.5	425.1	105.0	322.4	218.0	269.3	832.6	363.0	391.7	614.4	599.2	209.0
II	3,127.7	2,507.3	537.6	1,135.5	438.1	109.7	330.4	223.3	264.6	834.8	369.8	388.0	612.7	597.5	212.9
III	3,137.1	2,520.3	522.3	1,152.6	442.8	114.6	329.4	226.4	271.8	848.4	379.3	392.4	610.1	594.8	216.2
IV	3,209.2	2,576.4	528.4	1,191.4	458.9	112.6	348.8	233.9	279.8	860.9	385.5	397.1	625.5	609.7	221.1
2018: I	3,275.2	2,651.5	554.8	1,220.3	474.2	121.5	354.3	239.6	284.0	879.3	399.0	403.1	620.3	604.6	225.4
II	3,310.6	2,691.9	561.6	1,227.7	474.1	124.6	350.3	240.0	281.8	905.2	413.2	414.4	617.6	602.0	225.3
III	3,317.0	2,709.5	553.2	1,245.9	484.8	126.1	359.9	244.2	284.1	914.9	420.8	416.5	609.1	593.8	220.6
IV	3,338.7	2,742.6	534.9	1,274.8	483.9	123.8	361.8	251.7	298.0	941.5	432.6	430.0	601.0	585.9	211.6
2019: I	3,362.3	2,770.8	545.5	1,281.1	493.5	126.4	368.6	249.7	299.1	951.9	438.8	434.4	598.4	583.2	204.7
II	3,358.6	2,771.0	547.8	1,268.6	494.8	132.6	362.4	250.2	283.7	961.5	443.6	439.4	595.2	580.0	203.9
III	3,378.9	2,783.9	552.6	1,263.3	494.3	129.5	365.7	251.4	277.1	974.0	452.9	442.7	601.9	586.4	206.3
IV	3,387.2	2,781.5	545.1	1,258.0	492.9	134.4	358.3	245.3	283.0	985.2	461.8	445.3	610.5	594.6	212.3
2020: I	3,375.4	2,733.8	540.0	1,207.1	475.8	127.9	348.1	241.8	257.8	991.1	472.5	443.6	637.6	621.4	222.5
II	3,096.3	2,525.5	487.5	1,080.1	507.4	149.1	355.8	226.5	160.6	961.5	465.4	428.3	571.3	555.7	194.3
III p	3,308.6	2,653.4	467.0	1,227.1	559.1	162.5	394.3	236.0	218.3	975.7	474.5	436.3	644.8	627.8	202.3

[1] Because computers exhibit rapid changes in prices relative to other prices in the economy, the chained-dollar estimates should not be used to measure the component's relative importance or its contribution to the growth rate of more aggregate series. The quantity index for computers can be used to accurately measure the real growth rate of this series. For information on this component, see *Survey of Current Business* Table 5.3.1 (for growth rates), Table 5.3.2 (for contributions), and Table 5.3.3 (for quantity indexes).

[2] Includes other items not shown separately.

[3] Research and development investment includes expenditures for software.

Source: Department of Commerce (Bureau of Economic Analysis).

National Income or Expenditure | 473

TABLE B–14. Foreign transactions in the national income and product accounts, 1969–2020

[Billions of dollars; quarterly data at seasonally adjusted annual rates]

Year or quarter	Current receipts from rest of the world					Current payments to rest of the world									Balance on current account, NIPA[2]
	Total	Exports of goods and services			Income receipts	Total	Imports of goods and services			Income payments	Current taxes and transfer payments to rest of the world (net)				
		Total	Goods[1]	Services[1]			Total	Goods[1]	Services[1]		Total	From persons (net)	From government (net)	From business (net)	
1969	63.7	51.9	38.7	13.2	11.8	62.1	50.5	36.8	13.7	5.7	5.9	1.1	4.5	0.3	1.6
1970	72.5	59.7	45.0	14.7	12.8	68.8	55.8	40.9	14.9	6.4	6.6	1.3	4.9	.4	3.7
1971	77.0	63.0	46.2	16.8	14.0	76.7	62.3	46.6	15.8	6.4	7.9	1.4	6.1	.4	.3
1972	87.1	70.8	52.6	18.3	16.3	91.2	74.2	56.9	17.3	7.7	9.2	1.4	7.4	.5	–4.0
1973	118.8	95.3	75.8	19.5	23.5	109.9	91.2	71.8	19.3	10.9	7.9	1.6	5.6	.7	8.9
1974	156.5	126.7	103.5	23.2	29.8	150.5	127.5	104.5	22.9	14.3	8.7	1.4	6.4	1.0	6.0
1975	166.7	138.7	112.5	26.2	28.0	146.9	122.7	99.0	23.7	15.0	9.1	1.3	7.1	.7	19.8
1976	181.9	149.5	121.5	28.0	32.4	174.8	151.1	124.6	26.5	15.5	8.1	1.4	5.7	1.1	7.1
1977	196.5	159.3	128.4	30.9	37.2	207.5	182.4	152.6	29.8	16.9	8.1	1.4	5.3	1.4	–10.9
1978	233.1	186.9	149.9	37.0	46.3	245.8	212.3	177.4	34.8	24.7	8.8	1.6	5.9	1.4	–12.6
1979	298.5	230.1	187.3	42.9	68.3	299.6	252.7	212.8	39.9	36.4	10.6	1.7	6.8	2.0	–1.2
1980	359.9	280.8	230.4	50.3	79.1	351.4	293.8	248.6	45.3	44.9	12.6	2.0	8.3	2.4	8.5
1981	397.3	305.2	245.2	60.0	92.0	393.9	317.8	267.8	49.9	59.1	17.0	5.6	8.3	3.2	3.4
1982	384.2	283.2	222.6	60.7	101.0	387.5	303.2	250.5	52.6	64.5	19.8	6.7	9.7	3.4	–3.3
1983	378.9	277.0	214.0	62.9	101.9	413.9	328.6	272.7	56.0	64.8	20.5	7.0	10.1	3.4	–35.1
1984	424.2	302.4	231.3	71.1	121.9	514.3	405.1	336.3	68.8	85.6	23.6	7.9	12.2	3.5	–90.1
1985	415.9	303.2	227.5	75.7	112.7	530.2	417.2	343.3	73.9	87.3	25.7	8.3	14.4	2.9	–114.3
1986	432.3	321.0	231.4	89.6	111.3	575.0	452.9	370.0	82.9	94.4	27.8	9.1	15.4	3.2	–142.7
1987	487.2	363.9	265.6	98.4	123.3	641.3	508.7	414.8	93.9	105.8	26.8	10.0	13.4	3.4	–154.1
1988	596.7	444.6	332.1	112.5	152.1	712.4	554.0	452.1	101.9	129.5	29.0	10.8	13.7	4.5	–115.7
1989	682.0	504.3	374.8	129.5	177.7	774.3	591.0	484.8	106.2	152.9	30.4	11.6	14.2	4.6	–92.4
1990	740.7	551.9	403.3	148.6	188.8	815.6	629.7	508.1	121.7	154.2	31.7	12.2	14.7	4.8	–74.9
1991	763.3	594.9	430.1	164.8	168.4	755.4	623.5	500.7	122.8	136.8	–4.9	14.1	–24.0	5.0	7.9
1992	785.1	633.1	455.3	177.7	152.1	830.7	667.8	544.9	122.9	121.0	41.9	14.5	22.0	5.4	–45.6
1993	810.4	654.8	467.7	187.1	155.6	889.8	720.0	592.8	127.2	124.4	45.4	17.1	22.9	5.4	–79.4
1994	905.5	720.9	518.4	202.6	184.5	1,021.1	813.4	676.8	136.6	161.6	46.1	18.9	21.1	6.0	–115.6
1995	1,042.6	812.8	592.4	220.4	229.8	1,148.5	902.6	757.4	145.1	201.9	44.1	20.3	15.6	8.2	–105.9
1996	1,114.0	867.6	628.8	238.8	246.4	1,229.0	964.0	807.4	156.5	215.5	49.5	22.6	20.0	6.9	–115.0
1997	1,233.9	953.8	699.9	253.9	280.1	1,364.0	1,055.8	885.7	170.1	256.8	51.4	25.7	16.7	9.1	–130.1
1998	1,239.8	953.0	692.6	260.4	286.8	1,445.1	1,115.7	930.8	184.9	269.4	60.0	29.7	17.4	13.0	–205.3
1999	1,350.7	992.8	711.7	281.1	320.2	1,629.0	1,248.6	1,051.2	197.4	294.7	85.7	36.3	25.0	24.4	–278.3
2000	1,517.9	1,096.3	795.9	300.3	380.6	1,912.2	1,471.3	1,250.1	221.2	345.6	95.4	38.6	26.8	29.9	–394.3
2001	1,393.9	1,024.6	741.2	283.4	324.1	1,778.1	1,392.6	1,173.8	218.8	275.3	110.2	42.5	26.7	41.1	–384.2
2002	1,370.3	998.7	709.0	289.7	314.8	1,812.0	1,424.1	1,194.4	229.8	269.6	118.3	44.4	29.3	44.6	–441.6
2003	1,455.9	1,036.2	737.1	299.1	353.8	1,964.9	1,539.3	1,291.3	248.0	295.4	130.1	46.1	32.0	52.0	–508.9
2004	1,689.1	1,177.6	830.0	347.7	446.9	2,310.3	1,796.7	1,507.3	289.4	368.8	144.9	49.5	34.0	61.4	–621.2
2005	1,941.3	1,305.2	921.9	383.3	566.0	2,670.6	2,026.4	1,715.5	311.0	488.1	156.1	54.4	39.9	61.8	–729.3
2006	2,259.5	1,472.6	1,044.9	427.7	712.0	3,059.3	2,243.5	1,895.7	347.8	661.5	154.2	57.1	41.7	55.3	–799.8
2007	2,602.4	1,660.9	1,161.3	499.6	866.6	3,312.3	2,379.3	1,999.7	379.6	757.6	175.5	65.3	49.1	61.0	–710.0
2008	2,775.2	1,837.1	1,292.5	544.5	848.8	3,452.3	2,560.1	2,144.3	415.9	694.2	198.0	71.1	54.3	72.5	–677.1
2009	2,319.9	1,582.0	1,058.4	523.6	647.8	2,688.6	1,978.4	1,585.4	393.1	505.8	204.3	69.8	62.9	71.6	–368.7
2010	2,658.3	1,846.3	1,272.4	573.8	715.2	3,089.6	2,360.2	1,944.8	415.4	519.5	209.9	72.1	63.3	74.6	–431.3
2011	2,998.3	2,103.0	1,462.3	640.7	789.2	3,460.0	2,682.5	2,240.5	441.9	552.8	224.7	74.7	66.8	83.2	–461.7
2012	3,107.7	2,191.3	1,521.6	669.7	799.7	3,549.0	2,759.9	2,301.4	458.5	567.4	221.8	75.7	67.3	78.7	–441.3
2013	3,228.0	2,273.4	1,559.2	714.2	823.4	3,588.4	2,764.2	2,296.4	467.8	592.7	231.5	77.8	66.6	87.2	–360.5
2014	3,371.4	2,371.7	1,615.0	756.7	853.5	3,737.0	2,879.4	2,391.6	487.8	612.5	245.2	83.7	65.3	96.1	–365.6
2015	3,263.4	2,265.9	1,494.6	771.3	860.8	3,687.1	2,792.4	2,288.1	504.4	640.4	254.3	89.5	65.2	99.6	–423.7
2016	3,265.9	2,227.2	1,444.0	783.2	893.5	3,673.4	2,739.7	2,221.1	518.6	661.5	272.2	90.6	69.2	112.5	–407.4
2017	3,569.6	2,374.6	1,541.8	832.8	1,032.7	3,961.2	2,930.1	2,376.9	553.2	740.4	290.6	95.2	67.8	127.6	–391.5
2018	3,821.7	2,528.7	1,663.9	864.8	1,142.9	4,289.5	3,138.2	2,565.6	572.6	858.2	293.2	99.2	74.3	119.7	–467.8
2019	3,831.8	2,514.8	1,636.7	878.0	1,169.8	4,334.5	3,125.2	2,525.6	599.6	900.2	309.1	102.9	74.4	131.8	–502.8
2017: I	3,466.4	2,326.4	1,513.6	812.7	964.9	3,834.3	2,869.9	2,334.3	535.6	688.2	276.2	93.3	66.8	116.0	–367.9
II	3,469.5	2,333.1	1,504.9	828.2	987.7	3,902.5	2,892.6	2,342.1	550.5	720.1	289.8	94.1	63.3	132.4	–433.0
III	3,604.4	2,370.1	1,533.5	836.7	1,058.2	3,973.7	2,913.7	2,351.4	562.3	756.8	303.2	96.4	66.0	140.7	–369.3
IV	3,738.2	2,468.7	1,615.4	853.6	1,120.2	4,134.1	3,044.1	2,479.7	564.5	796.6	293.3	96.7	75.2	121.4	–395.9
2018: I	3,768.2	2,507.2	1,635.4	871.8	1,116.2	4,176.0	3,097.0	2,533.8	563.2	801.7	277.4	97.8	66.9	112.7	–407.8
II	3,854.3	2,550.3	1,693.5	856.8	1,153.4	4,250.7	3,098.4	2,531.8	566.6	861.9	290.4	98.8	76.5	115.0	–396.5
III	3,809.1	2,523.9	1,660.5	863.4	1,129.2	4,336.4	3,170.3	2,596.3	574.0	869.2	296.9	99.3	75.2	122.4	–527.3
IV	3,855.4	2,533.4	1,666.3	867.1	1,147.8	4,395.0	3,186.9	2,600.3	586.6	899.9	308.2	100.9	78.5	128.9	–539.6
2019: I	3,816.9	2,523.5	1,660.6	862.9	1,148.0	4,348.9	3,139.0	2,550.9	588.1	901.5	308.4	102.5	75.9	130.0	–532.0
II	3,844.1	2,514.6	1,631.1	883.5	1,184.3	4,379.9	3,159.4	2,556.4	603.0	913.2	307.3	103.3	70.1	133.9	–535.8
III	3,841.5	2,505.2	1,626.0	879.2	1,181.2	4,349.3	3,137.1	2,534.6	602.4	901.4	310.8	103.2	74.8	132.8	–507.8
IV	3,824.5	2,515.7	1,629.1	886.5	1,165.9	4,260.1	3,065.4	2,460.7	604.8	884.8	309.9	102.7	76.7	130.4	–435.6
2020: I	3,637.7	2,438.7	1,599.0	839.7	1,054.6	4,061.1	2,933.0	2,377.9	555.1	811.4	316.7	101.6	79.4	135.7	–423.4
II	2,793.4	1,788.2	1,135.1	653.1	866.0	3,359.6	2,333.3	1,927.8	405.5	714.2	312.1	100.9	81.8	129.4	–566.2
III p	3,181.1	2,074.5	1,407.8	666.7	961.6	3,892.4	2,808.3	2,374.9	433.4	773.6	310.6	98.9	82.2	129.5	–711.3

[1] Certain goods, primarily military equipment purchased and sold by the Federal Government, are included in services. Beginning with 1986, repairs and alterations of equipment were reclassified from goods to services.
[2] National income and product accounts (NIPA).

Source: Department of Commerce (Bureau of Economic Analysis).

TABLE B-15. Real exports and imports of goods and services, 2002–2020

[Billions of chained (2012) dollars; quarterly data at seasonally adjusted annual rates]

Year or quarter	Exports of goods and services						Imports of goods and services					
	Total	Goods[1]				Services[1]	Total	Goods[1]				Services[1]
		Total	Durable goods	Non-durable goods	Non-agricultural goods			Total	Durable goods	Non-durable goods	Non-petroleum goods	
2002	1,277.1	900.6	524.7	388.8	797.3	376.5	1,944.4	1,634.0	785.6	896.4	1,207.4	309.4
2003	1,305.0	927.1	542.4	396.4	821.8	377.8	2,040.1	1,729.0	831.2	948.7	1,276.4	310.5
2004	1,431.2	1,008.3	604.0	410.3	904.9	422.8	2,272.6	1,926.8	951.0	1,012.5	1,430.8	345.2
2005	1,533.2	1,085.4	663.4	423.3	975.8	447.6	2,421.0	2,062.3	1,036.9	1,053.0	1,543.4	358.6
2006	1,676.4	1,193.0	739.4	451.5	1,073.6	483.3	2,581.5	2,190.9	1,135.6	1,069.5	1,664.8	390.2
2007	1,822.3	1,276.1	796.6	475.7	1,148.3	546.0	2,646.0	2,236.0	1,168.3	1,078.9	1,714.6	409.2
2008	1,925.4	1,350.4	835.0	512.7	1,215.0	574.7	2,587.1	2,160.8	1,130.6	1,040.7	1,657.1	425.2
2009	1,763.8	1,190.3	694.5	499.9	1,060.0	572.9	2,248.6	1,830.1	902.3	948.3	1,375.9	415.9
2010	1,977.9	1,368.7	818.1	551.7	1,223.8	609.2	2,543.8	2,112.7	1,115.6	1,001.5	1,636.1	430.8
2011	2,119.0	1,465.3	893.7	571.6	1,321.6	653.8	2,687.1	2,242.5	1,227.0	1,016.2	1,769.8	444.6
2012	2,191.3	1,521.6	937.7	583.9	1,376.4	669.7	2,759.9	2,301.4	1,326.4	975.0	1,867.1	458.5
2013	2,269.6	1,570.0	960.1	609.9	1,422.9	699.5	2,802.4	2,341.9	1,385.9	956.1	1,932.5	460.6
2014	2,365.3	1,642.7	1,001.3	641.5	1,484.2	722.7	2,942.5	2,472.2	1,508.8	963.8	2,076.6	471.0
2015	2,375.2	1,636.9	979.1	659.7	1,475.5	737.3	3,094.8	2,612.0	1,607.5	1,004.2	2,205.9	485.0
2016	2,382.3	1,645.8	968.0	683.3	1,476.5	736.1	3,145.9	2,647.7	1,629.2	1,018.2	2,228.5	499.2
2017	2,475.5	1,712.5	998.3	722.0	1,540.3	762.9	3,292.4	2,772.1	1,745.8	1,019.3	2,343.7	521.5
2018	2,549.5	1,784.3	1,032.8	760.8	1,610.8	768.7	3,427.2	2,909.4	1,842.7	1,058.4	2,482.9	523.7
2019	2,446.6	1,782.5	1,005.2	790.6	1,610.2	767.6	3,464.2	2,923.4	1,848.3	1,067.0	2,512.0	543.1
2017: I	2,446.0	1,695.4	977.4	728.0	1,519.1	751.1	3,238.3	2,727.2	1,696.3	1,026.9	2,291.0	512.5
II	2,451.9	1,688.4	983.4	712.9	1,518.4	762.1	3,266.9	2,745.6	1,730.7	1,007.7	2,319.0	521.6
III	2,468.0	1,699.9	1,004.1	701.1	1,529.2	766.7	3,281.0	2,753.8	1,742.9	1,002.6	2,333.2	526.7
IV	2,536.2	1,766.4	1,028.5	746.2	1,594.6	771.9	3,383.2	2,862.0	1,813.4	1,039.8	2,431.8	525.1
2018: I	2,553.2	1,772.0	1,041.3	737.8	1,602.5	782.1	3,386.1	2,872.6	1,818.2	1,046.1	2,450.5	519.0
II	2,565.2	1,808.4	1,039.6	779.2	1,625.7	762.6	3,385.4	2,871.9	1,811.1	1,053.1	2,442.9	518.9
III	2,531.0	1,769.1	1,019.8	759.2	1,592.7	765.0	3,451.3	2,935.1	1,860.2	1,066.6	2,498.0	523.1
IV	2,548.8	1,787.9	1,030.7	767.1	1,622.4	765.2	3,486.0	2,957.9	1,881.3	1,068.0	2,540.1	533.8
2019: I	2,560.4	1,804.9	1,032.9	783.1	1,634.6	761.4	3,467.8	2,938.1	1,869.2	1,060.1	2,527.1	534.5
II	2,531.4	1,762.5	997.4	777.5	1,586.7	770.7	3,482.9	2,939.0	1,855.0	1,076.0	2,522.2	546.2
III	2,536.6	1,775.8	995.9	793.9	1,600.8	764.4	3,486.8	2,944.4	1,858.8	1,077.6	2,531.7	545.2
IV	2,557.8	1,786.8	994.5	807.8	1,618.8	774.0	3,419.3	2,872.2	1,810.3	1,054.2	2,467.0	546.5
2020: I	2,495.1	1,774.5	960.5	835.0	1,603.3	730.1	3,283.1	2,786.5	1,729.2	1,051.8	2,391.7	502.5
II	1,927.4	1,347.2	657.2	729.3	1,181.9	582.1	2,702.5	2,348.0	1,370.1	985.0	2,018.9	372.1
III[p]	2,169.5	1,611.2	857.8	774.2	1,428.0	583.3	3,185.9	2,826.6	1,775.3	1,038.8	2,445.0	394.1

[1] Certain goods, primarily military equipment purchased and sold by the Federal Government, are included in services. Repairs and alterations of equipment are also included in services.

Source: Department of Commerce (Bureau of Economic Analysis).

TABLE B–16. Sources of personal income, 1969–2020

[Billions of dollars; quarterly data at seasonally adjusted annual rates]

Year or quarter	Personal income	Compensation of employees							Proprietors' income with inventory valuation and capital consumption adjustments			Rental income of persons with capital consumption adjustment
		Total	Wages and salaries			Supplements to wages and salaries			Total	Farm	Nonfarm	
			Total	Private industries	Govern-ment	Total	Employer contributions for employee pension and insurance funds	Employer contributions for government social insurance				
1969	800.3	584.5	518.3	412.7	105.6	66.1	43.4	22.8	77.0	12.8	64.2	20.3
1970	865.0	623.3	551.6	434.3	117.2	71.8	47.9	23.8	77.8	12.9	64.9	20.7
1971	932.8	665.0	584.5	457.8	126.8	80.4	54.0	26.4	83.9	13.4	70.5	21.8
1972	1,024.5	731.3	638.8	500.9	137.9	92.5	61.4	31.2	95.1	17.0	78.1	22.7
1973	1,140.8	812.7	708.8	560.0	148.8	103.9	64.1	39.8	112.5	29.1	83.4	23.1
1974	1,251.8	887.7	772.3	611.8	160.5	115.4	70.7	44.7	112.2	23.5	88.7	23.2
1975	1,369.4	947.2	814.8	638.6	176.2	132.4	85.7	46.7	118.2	22.0	96.2	22.3
1976	1,502.6	1,048.3	899.7	710.8	188.9	148.6	94.2	54.4	131.0	17.2	113.8	20.3
1977	1,659.2	1,165.8	994.2	791.6	202.6	171.7	110.6	61.1	144.5	16.0	128.5	15.9
1978	1,863.7	1,316.8	1,120.6	900.6	220.0	196.2	124.7	71.5	166.0	19.9	146.1	16.5
1979	2,082.7	1,477.2	1,253.3	1,016.2	237.1	223.9	141.3	82.6	179.4	22.2	157.3	16.1
1980	2,323.6	1,622.2	1,373.4	1,112.0	261.5	248.8	159.9	88.9	171.6	11.7	159.9	19.0
1981	2,605.1	1,792.5	1,511.4	1,225.5	285.8	281.2	177.5	103.6	179.7	19.0	160.7	23.8
1982	2,791.6	1,893.0	1,587.5	1,280.0	307.5	305.5	195.7	109.8	171.2	13.3	157.9	23.8
1983	2,981.1	2,012.5	1,677.5	1,352.7	324.8	335.0	215.1	119.9	186.3	6.2	180.1	24.4
1984	3,292.7	2,215.9	1,844.9	1,496.8	348.1	371.0	231.9	139.0	228.2	20.9	207.3	24.7
1985	3,524.9	2,387.3	1,982.6	1,608.7	373.9	404.8	257.0	147.7	241.1	21.0	220.1	26.2
1986	3,733.1	2,542.1	2,102.3	1,705.1	397.2	439.7	281.9	157.9	256.5	22.8	233.7	18.3
1987	3,961.6	2,722.4	2,256.3	1,833.2	423.1	466.1	299.9	166.3	286.5	28.9	257.6	16.6
1988	4,283.4	2,948.0	2,439.8	1,987.7	452.0	508.2	323.6	184.6	325.5	26.8	298.7	22.5
1989	4,625.6	3,139.6	2,583.1	2,101.9	481.1	556.6	362.9	193.7	341.1	33.0	308.1	21.5
1990	4,913.8	3,340.4	2,741.2	2,222.2	519.0	599.2	392.7	206.5	353.2	32.2	321.0	28.2
1991	5,084.9	3,450.5	2,814.5	2,265.7	548.8	636.0	420.9	215.1	354.2	26.8	327.4	38.6
1992	5,420.9	3,668.2	2,965.5	2,393.5	572.0	702.7	474.3	228.4	400.2	34.8	365.4	60.6
1993	5,657.9	3,817.3	3,079.3	2,490.3	589.0	737.9	498.3	239.7	428.0	31.4	396.6	90.1
1994	5,947.1	4,006.2	3,236.6	2,627.1	609.5	769.6	515.5	254.1	456.6	34.7	422.0	113.7
1995	6,291.4	4,198.1	3,418.0	2,789.0	629.0	780.1	515.9	264.1	481.2	22.0	459.2	124.9
1996	6,678.5	4,416.9	3,616.5	2,968.4	648.1	800.5	525.7	274.8	543.8	37.3	506.4	142.5
1997	7,092.5	4,708.8	3,876.8	3,205.0	671.9	832.0	542.4	289.6	584.0	32.4	551.6	147.1
1998	7,606.7	5,071.1	4,181.6	3,480.3	701.3	889.5	582.3	307.2	640.2	28.5	611.7	165.2
1999	8,001.9	5,402.8	4,458.0	3,724.2	733.8	944.8	621.4	323.3	696.4	28.1	668.3	178.5
2000	8,652.6	5,848.1	4,825.9	4,046.1	779.8	1,022.2	677.0	345.2	753.9	31.5	722.4	183.5
2001	9,005.6	6,039.1	4,954.4	4,132.4	822.0	1,084.7	726.7	358.0	831.0	32.1	798.9	202.4
2002	9,159.0	6,135.6	4,996.3	4,123.4	872.9	1,139.3	773.2	366.0	869.8	19.9	849.8	211.1
2003	9,487.5	6,354.1	5,138.7	4,224.8	914.0	1,215.3	832.8	382.5	896.9	36.5	860.4	231.5
2004	10,035.1	6,720.1	5,421.6	4,469.2	952.3	1,298.5	889.7	408.8	962.0	51.5	910.5	248.9
2005	10,598.2	7,066.6	5,691.9	4,700.6	991.3	1,374.7	946.7	428.1	978.0	46.8	931.2	232.0
2006	11,381.7	7,479.9	6,057.0	5,022.4	1,034.5	1,422.9	975.6	447.3	1,049.6	33.1	1,016.6	202.3
2007	12,007.8	7,878.9	6,396.8	5,308.2	1,088.5	1,482.1	1,020.4	461.7	994.0	40.3	953.8	184.4
2008	12,442.2	8,057.0	6,534.2	5,390.4	1,143.9	1,522.7	1,051.3	471.4	960.9	40.2	920.7	256.7
2009	12,059.1	7,758.5	6,248.6	5,073.4	1,175.2	1,509.9	1,051.8	458.1	938.5	28.1	910.5	327.3
2010	12,551.6	7,924.9	6,372.1	5,180.9	1,191.2	1,552.9	1,083.9	469.0	1,108.7	39.0	1,069.7	394.2
2011	13,326.8	8,225.9	6,625.9	5,431.1	1,194.9	1,600.0	1,107.3	492.7	1,229.3	64.9	1,164.4	478.6
2012	14,010.1	8,566.7	6,927.5	5,729.2	1,198.3	1,639.2	1,125.9	513.3	1,347.3	60.9	1,286.4	518.0
2013	14,181.1	8,834.2	7,113.2	5,905.2	1,208.0	1,721.0	1,194.7	526.3	1,403.6	88.3	1,315.3	557.0
2014	14,991.7	9,249.1	7,475.2	6,238.3	1,236.9	1,773.9	1,227.5	546.4	1,447.7	69.8	1,377.9	604.6
2015	15,724.2	9,699.4	7,859.5	6,583.7	1,275.8	1,839.9	1,270.6	569.4	1,423.0	56.2	1,366.7	649.0
2016	16,160.7	9,963.9	8,089.1	6,780.9	1,308.2	1,874.7	1,293.5	581.2	1,424.8	36.0	1,388.7	682.7
2017	16,948.6	10,422.5	8,471.5	7,123.7	1,347.7	1,951.1	1,346.0	605.1	1,509.0	41.5	1,467.4	721.9
2018	17,851.8	10,950.1	8,894.2	7,491.7	1,402.5	2,055.9	1,430.7	625.2	1,585.9	43.0	1,542.9	759.3
2019	18,551.5	11,432.4	9,309.3	7,858.5	1,450.8	2,123.1	1,474.0	649.1	1,657.7	49.7	1,608.0	787.1
2017: I	16,633.7	10,223.1	8,308.8	6,977.3	1,331.5	1,914.2	1,319.2	595.1	1,493.4	47.3	1,446.1	709.0
II	16,828.4	10,335.3	8,399.9	7,059.8	1,340.1	1,935.4	1,334.6	600.8	1,502.7	44.7	1,457.9	713.2
III	17,036.6	10,476.9	8,515.3	7,162.7	1,352.7	1,961.6	1,353.7	607.9	1,507.8	37.1	1,470.7	725.9
IV	17,295.6	10,654.9	8,661.8	7,295.1	1,366.7	1,993.0	1,376.4	616.6	1,532.1	37.0	1,495.1	739.6
2018: I	17,548.6	10,776.1	8,756.4	7,376.1	1,380.3	2,019.7	1,402.3	617.4	1,557.7	40.8	1,516.9	745.3
II	17,750.3	10,882.3	8,836.3	7,442.4	1,393.9	2,046.0	1,424.4	621.6	1,570.7	42.3	1,528.4	752.4
III	17,976.5	11,034.1	8,963.2	7,550.7	1,412.5	2,070.9	1,441.7	629.2	1,588.4	34.0	1,554.4	768.2
IV	18,132.0	11,107.8	9,021.0	7,597.6	1,423.3	2,086.9	1,454.3	632.6	1,627.0	55.0	1,572.0	771.2
2019: I	18,366.7	11,335.3	9,228.7	7,796.4	1,432.3	2,106.6	1,462.5	644.1	1,627.5	44.2	1,583.4	776.6
II	18,480.9	11,391.7	9,274.9	7,832.5	1,442.3	2,116.8	1,469.8	646.9	1,628.5	36.9	1,591.6	786.7
III	18,597.6	11,438.0	9,311.3	7,852.3	1,459.0	2,126.6	1,477.6	649.0	1,677.0	58.9	1,618.1	789.7
IV	18,760.8	11,564.8	9,422.5	7,953.0	1,469.5	2,142.4	1,486.1	656.3	1,697.7	58.7	1,639.0	795.5
2020: I	18,951.0	11,674.4	9,526.1	8,044.5	1,481.6	2,148.3	1,482.3	666.0	1,706.0	56.4	1,649.6	802.3
II	20,457.3	10,949.5	8,908.8	7,487.2	1,421.6	2,040.7	1,400.1	640.5	1,511.9	38.9	1,473.0	796.1
III ᵖ	19,926.4	11,533.0	9,405.9	7,964.0	1,441.9	2,127.1	1,457.8	669.2	1,804.5	62.9	1,741.6	806.0

See next page for continuation of table.

[Billions of dollars; quarterly data at seasonally adjusted annual rates]

Year or quarter	Personal income receipts on assets			Personal current transfer receipts								Less: Contributions for government social insurance, domestic
					Government social benefits to persons						Other current transfer receipts, from business (net)	
	Total	Personal interest income	Personal dividend income	Total	Total [1]	Social security [2]	Medicare [3]	Medicaid	Unemployment insurance	Other		
1969	100.3	76.1	24.2	62.3	59.0	26.4	6.7	4.6	2.3	12.4	3.3	44.1
1970	114.9	90.6	24.3	74.7	71.7	31.4	7.3	5.5	4.2	16.0	2.9	46.4
1971	125.1	100.1	25.0	88.1	85.4	36.6	8.0	6.7	6.2	19.4	2.7	51.2
1972	136.6	109.8	26.8	97.9	94.8	40.9	8.8	8.2	6.0	21.4	3.1	59.2
1973	155.4	125.5	29.9	112.6	108.6	50.7	10.2	9.6	4.6	23.3	3.9	75.5
1974	180.6	147.4	33.2	133.3	128.6	57.6	12.7	11.2	7.0	28.4	4.7	85.2
1975	201.0	168.0	32.9	170.0	163.1	65.9	15.6	13.9	18.1	35.7	6.8	89.3
1976	220.0	181.0	39.0	184.3	177.6	74.5	18.8	15.5	16.4	38.7	6.7	101.3
1977	251.6	206.9	44.7	194.6	189.5	83.2	22.1	16.7	13.1	40.9	5.1	113.1
1978	285.8	235.1	50.7	209.9	203.4	91.4	25.5	18.6	9.4	44.9	6.5	131.3
1979	327.1	269.7	57.4	235.6	227.3	102.6	29.9	21.1	9.7	49.9	8.2	152.7
1980	396.9	332.9	64.0	280.1	271.5	118.6	36.2	23.9	16.1	62.1	8.6	166.2
1981	485.8	412.2	73.6	319.0	307.8	138.6	43.5	27.7	15.9	66.3	11.2	195.7
1982	557.0	479.5	77.6	355.5	343.1	153.7	50.9	30.2	25.2	66.8	12.4	208.9
1983	599.5	516.3	83.3	384.3	370.5	164.4	57.8	33.9	26.4	71.5	13.8	226.0
1984	680.8	590.1	90.6	400.6	380.9	173.0	64.7	36.6	16.0	74.3	19.7	257.5
1985	726.3	628.9	97.4	425.4	403.1	183.3	69.7	39.7	15.9	78.0	22.3	281.4
1986	768.2	662.1	106.0	451.6	428.6	193.6	75.3	43.6	16.5	83.0	22.9	303.4
1987	791.1	679.0	112.2	468.1	447.9	201.0	81.6	47.8	14.6	86.4	20.2	323.1
1988	851.4	721.7	129.7	497.5	476.9	213.9	86.3	53.0	13.3	93.6	20.6	361.5
1989	964.3	806.5	157.8	544.2	521.1	227.4	98.2	60.8	14.4	103.1	23.2	385.2
1990	1,005.3	836.5	168.8	596.9	574.7	244.1	107.6	73.1	18.2	113.9	22.2	410.1
1991	1,003.7	823.5	180.2	668.1	650.5	264.2	117.5	96.9	26.8	127.0	17.6	430.2
1992	998.8	809.8	189.1	748.0	731.8	281.8	132.6	116.2	39.6	142.9	16.3	455.0
1993	1,007.0	802.3	204.7	793.0	778.9	297.9	146.8	130.1	34.8	150.0	14.1	477.4
1994	1,049.8	814.6	235.2	829.0	815.7	312.2	164.4	139.4	23.9	156.1	13.3	508.2
1995	1,136.6	878.6	258.0	883.5	864.7	327.7	181.2	149.6	21.7	164.0	18.7	532.8
1996	1,201.2	899.0	302.2	929.2	906.3	342.0	194.9	158.2	22.3	167.6	22.9	555.1
1997	1,285.0	947.1	337.9	954.9	935.4	356.6	206.9	163.1	20.1	166.4	19.4	587.2
1998	1,370.9	1,015.5	355.4	983.9	957.9	369.2	205.6	170.2	19.7	170.0	26.0	624.7
1999	1,359.3	1,012.7	346.6	1,026.2	992.2	379.9	208.7	184.6	20.5	174.4	34.0	661.3
2000	1,485.7	1,102.2	383.5	1,087.3	1,044.9	401.4	219.1	199.5	20.7	179.1	42.4	705.8
2001	1,473.7	1,104.3	369.3	1,192.6	1,145.8	425.1	242.6	227.3	31.9	192.4	46.8	733.2
2002	1,408.9	1,010.1	398.8	1,285.2	1,251.0	446.9	259.7	250.0	53.5	211.3	34.2	751.5
2003	1,437.2	1,005.0	432.1	1,347.3	1,321.0	463.5	276.7	264.5	53.2	231.2	26.3	779.3
2004	1,512.1	950.4	561.7	1,421.2	1,404.5	485.5	304.4	289.8	36.4	254.3	16.8	829.2
2005	1,678.2	1,100.4	577.8	1,516.7	1,490.9	512.7	332.1	304.4	31.8	273.5	25.8	873.3
2006	1,958.6	1,235.8	722.8	1,613.8	1,593.0	544.1	399.1	299.1	30.4	281.5	20.8	922.5
2007	2,183.8	1,368.6	815.3	1,728.1	1,697.3	575.7	428.2	324.2	32.7	294.9	30.8	961.4
2008	2,200.9	1,396.3	804.6	1,955.1	1,919.3	605.5	461.6	338.3	51.1	417.7	35.8	988.4
2009	1,852.2	1,299.3	553.0	2,146.7	2,107.7	664.5	493.0	369.6	131.2	398.0	39.0	964.3
2010	1,782.3	1,238.5	543.9	2,325.2	2,281.4	690.2	513.4	396.9	138.9	484.2	43.7	983.7
2011	1,950.9	1,269.4	681.5	2,358.7	2,310.1	713.3	535.6	406.0	107.2	484.8	48.5	916.7
2012	2,165.6	1,330.5	835.1	2,363.0	2,322.6	762.1	554.7	417.5	83.6	434.4	40.4	950.5
2013	2,066.3	1,273.0	793.3	2,424.3	2,385.9	799.0	572.8	440.0	62.5	432.5	38.4	1,104.3
2014	2,302.2	1,349.0	953.2	2,541.5	2,498.6	834.6	600.0	490.9	35.5	453.5	42.9	1,153.6
2015	2,472.2	1,439.1	1,033.1	2,685.4	2,635.1	871.8	634.9	535.9	32.5	467.4	50.3	1,204.7
2016	2,551.7	1,474.3	1,077.4	2,776.8	2,717.1	895.5	662.1	562.7	32.3	466.8	59.7	1,239.1
2017	2,738.5	1,577.6	1,160.8	2,855.1	2,806.2	926.1	692.3	573.7	30.3	472.4	48.8	1,298.4
2018	2,946.7	1,641.6	1,305.1	2,970.3	2,922.9	972.4	734.2	589.8	27.9	478.9	47.4	1,360.4
2019	2,967.9	1,677.4	1,290.4	3,125.2	3,078.0	1,030.7	783.7	614.0	27.7	490.9	47.2	1,418.8
2017: I	2,653.3	1,551.7	1,101.6	2,831.7	2,778.8	916.5	679.5	572.4	30.9	473.7	52.9	1,276.8
II	2,728.0	1,572.8	1,155.2	2,838.5	2,789.3	922.0	687.5	567.9	30.2	471.0	49.2	1,289.3
III	2,761.3	1,585.4	1,175.9	2,869.2	2,822.2	929.0	696.3	578.8	30.3	473.9	47.0	1,304.5
IV	2,811.4	1,600.7	1,210.7	2,880.9	2,834.7	936.8	705.8	575.8	29.8	471.0	46.2	1,323.2
2018: I	2,874.8	1,619.2	1,255.6	2,937.8	2,890.9	960.7	716.1	581.8	29.2	485.0	46.9	1,343.1
II	2,934.4	1,634.5	1,299.9	2,963.3	2,916.0	968.3	727.5	592.6	27.9	481.1	47.3	1,352.8
III	2,971.8	1,650.1	1,321.8	2,983.0	2,935.4	976.5	739.9	595.1	27.4	476.6	47.6	1,369.1
IV	3,005.6	1,662.5	1,343.0	2,997.1	2,949.4	984.1	753.3	588.8	27.0	472.8	47.8	1,376.8
2019: I	2,950.7	1,652.0	1,298.7	3,085.2	3,037.5	1,018.9	767.4	599.4	28.0	496.5	47.7	1,408.7
II	2,970.2	1,682.6	1,287.6	3,118.6	3,071.0	1,026.7	779.7	615.0	27.5	492.4	47.5	1,414.7
III	2,970.1	1,681.7	1,288.3	3,141.9	3,094.8	1,034.3	789.9	622.3	27.6	488.9	47.1	1,419.0
IV	2,980.4	1,693.4	1,287.0	3,155.2	3,108.7	1,043.0	797.9	619.4	27.9	486.0	46.5	1,432.9
2020: I	2,984.3	1,679.7	1,304.6	3,235.5	3,189.6	1,068.5	804.7	624.1	43.4	510.4	45.9	1,451.5
II	2,910.2	1,637.0	1,273.2	5,678.4	5,627.4	1,075.4	824.1	668.8	1,084.6	1,832.5	50.6	1,388.4
III [p]	2,862.8	1,629.0	1,233.8	4,370.0	4,324.1	1,080.6	842.7	691.3	768.7	795.5	45.9	1,449.8

[1] Includes Veterans' benefits, not shown seperately.
[2] Includes old-age, survivors, and disability insurance benefits that are distributed from the federal old-age and survivors insurance trust fund and the disability insurance trust fund.
[3] Includes hospital and supplementary medical insurance benefits that are distributed from the federal hospital insurance trust fund and the supplementary medical insurance trust fund.

Source: Department of Commerce (Bureau of Economic Analysis).

Table B–17. Disposition of personal income, 1969–2020

[Billions of dollars, except as noted; quarterly data at seasonally adjusted annual rates]

Year or quarter	Personal income	Less: Personal current taxes	Equals: Disposable personal income	Less: Personal outlays				Equals: Personal saving	Percent of disposable personal income [2]		
				Total	Personal consumption expenditures	Personal interest payments [1]	Personal current transfer payments		Personal outlays		Personal saving
									Total	Personal consumption expenditures	
1969	800.3	104.5	695.8	619.8	603.6	13.9	2.2	76.1	89.1	86.7	10.9
1970	865.0	103.1	762.0	664.4	646.7	15.1	2.6	97.6	87.2	84.9	12.8
1971	932.8	101.7	831.1	719.2	699.9	16.4	2.8	111.9	86.5	84.2	13.5
1972	1,024.5	123.6	900.8	789.3	768.2	18.0	3.2	111.5	87.6	85.3	12.4
1973	1,140.8	132.4	1,008.4	872.6	849.6	19.6	3.4	135.8	86.5	84.3	13.5
1974	1,251.8	151.0	1,100.8	954.5	930.2	20.9	3.4	146.3	86.7	84.5	13.3
1975	1,369.4	147.6	1,221.8	1,057.8	1,030.5	23.4	3.8	164.0	86.6	84.3	13.4
1976	1,502.6	172.7	1,330.0	1,175.6	1,147.7	23.5	4.4	154.4	88.4	86.3	11.6
1977	1,659.2	197.9	1,461.4	1,305.4	1,274.0	26.6	4.8	155.9	89.3	87.2	10.7
1978	1,863.7	229.6	1,634.1	1,459.0	1,422.3	31.3	5.4	175.1	89.3	87.0	10.7
1979	2,082.7	268.9	1,813.8	1,627.0	1,585.4	35.5	6.0	186.8	89.7	87.4	10.3
1980	2,323.6	299.5	2,024.1	1,800.1	1,750.7	42.5	6.9	224.1	88.9	86.5	11.1
1981	2,605.1	345.8	2,259.3	1,993.9	1,934.0	48.4	11.5	265.5	88.3	85.6	11.8
1982	2,791.6	354.7	2,436.9	2,143.5	2,071.3	58.5	13.8	293.3	88.0	85.0	12.0
1983	2,981.1	352.9	2,628.2	2,364.2	2,281.6	67.4	15.1	264.0	90.0	86.8	10.0
1984	3,292.7	377.9	2,914.8	2,584.5	2,492.3	75.0	17.1	330.3	88.7	85.5	11.3
1985	3,524.9	417.8	3,107.1	2,822.1	2,712.8	90.6	18.8	284.9	90.8	87.3	9.2
1986	3,733.1	437.8	3,295.3	3,004.7	2,886.3	97.3	21.1	290.6	91.2	87.6	8.8
1987	3,961.6	489.6	3,472.0	3,196.6	3,076.3	97.1	23.2	275.4	92.1	88.6	7.9
1988	4,283.4	505.9	3,777.5	3,457.0	3,330.0	101.3	25.6	320.5	91.5	88.2	8.5
1989	4,625.6	567.7	4,057.8	3,717.9	3,576.8	113.1	28.0	340.0	91.6	88.1	8.4
1990	4,913.8	594.7	4,319.1	3,958.0	3,809.0	118.4	30.6	361.1	91.6	88.2	8.4
1991	5,084.9	588.9	4,496.0	4,100.0	3,943.4	119.9	36.7	396.0	91.2	87.7	8.8
1992	5,420.9	612.8	4,808.1	4,354.2	4,197.6	116.1	40.5	453.9	90.6	87.3	9.4
1993	5,657.9	648.8	5,009.2	4,611.5	4,452.0	113.9	45.6	397.7	92.1	88.9	7.9
1994	5,947.1	693.1	5,254.0	4,890.6	4,721.0	119.9	49.8	363.4	93.1	89.9	6.9
1995	6,291.4	748.4	5,543.0	5,155.9	4,962.6	140.4	52.9	387.1	93.0	89.5	7.0
1996	6,678.5	837.1	5,841.4	5,459.2	5,244.6	157.0	57.6	382.3	93.5	89.8	6.5
1997	7,092.5	931.8	6,160.7	5,770.4	5,536.8	169.7	63.9	390.3	93.7	89.9	6.3
1998	7,606.7	1,032.4	6,574.2	6,127.7	5,877.2	180.9	69.5	446.5	93.2	89.4	6.8
1999	8,001.9	1,111.9	6,890.0	6,542.9	6,279.1	187.5	76.3	347.1	95.0	91.1	5.0
2000	8,652.6	1,236.3	7,416.3	7,060.2	6,762.1	214.8	83.2	356.1	95.2	91.2	4.8
2001	9,005.6	1,239.0	7,766.5	7,377.2	7,065.6	220.0	91.5	389.4	95.0	91.0	5.0
2002	9,159.0	1,052.2	8,106.8	7,635.1	7,342.7	195.7	96.7	471.7	94.2	90.6	5.8
2003	9,487.5	1,003.5	8,484.0	8,015.1	7,723.1	190.9	101.1	468.9	94.5	91.0	5.5
2004	10,035.1	1,048.7	8,986.3	8,525.8	8,212.7	202.2	110.9	460.6	94.9	91.4	5.1
2005	10,598.2	1,212.5	9,385.8	9,095.7	8,747.1	230.5	118.1	290.1	96.9	93.2	3.1
2006	11,381.7	1,357.0	10,024.7	9,643.7	9,260.3	258.4	124.9	381.0	96.2	92.4	3.8
2007	12,007.8	1,492.5	10,515.3	10,129.4	9,706.4	284.6	138.4	385.9	96.3	92.3	3.7
2008	12,442.2	1,507.5	10,934.7	10,389.8	9,976.3	268.8	144.6	544.9	95.0	91.2	5.0
2009	12,059.1	1,152.4	10,906.7	10,240.5	9,842.2	254.0	144.3	666.2	93.9	90.2	6.1
2010	12,551.6	1,237.6	11,314.0	10,573.6	10,185.8	242.8	145.0	740.3	93.5	90.0	6.5
2011	13,326.8	1,453.7	11,873.1	11,024.0	10,641.1	232.1	150.8	849.1	92.8	89.6	7.2
2012	14,010.1	1,509.5	12,500.6	11,394.0	11,006.8	232.4	154.8	1,106.6	91.1	88.1	8.9
2013	14,181.1	1,676.4	12,504.7	11,705.0	11,317.2	229.5	158.3	799.7	93.6	90.5	6.4
2014	14,991.7	1,784.6	13,207.1	12,236.2	11,822.8	243.8	169.6	970.9	92.6	89.5	7.4
2015	15,724.2	1,939.9	13,784.3	12,745.6	12,297.5	264.7	183.5	1,038.7	92.5	89.2	7.5
2016	16,160.7	1,957.9	14,202.8	13,227.8	12,770.0	273.0	184.8	975.0	93.1	89.9	6.9
2017	16,948.6	2,046.7	14,901.9	13,830.9	13,340.4	297.3	193.3	1,071.0	92.8	89.5	7.2
2018	17,851.8	2,085.3	15,766.5	14,529.2	13,993.3	332.9	203.0	1,237.3	92.2	88.8	7.8
2019	18,551.5	2,202.9	16,348.6	15,117.4	14,544.6	362.3	210.5	1,231.2	92.5	89.0	7.5
2017: I	16,633.7	2,001.1	14,632.7	13,625.1	13,153.2	284.0	187.9	1,007.6	93.1	89.9	6.9
II	16,828.4	2,005.6	14,822.8	13,728.1	13,241.3	293.1	193.8	1,094.7	92.6	89.3	7.4
III	17,036.6	2,052.3	14,984.2	13,867.0	13,370.9	302.0	194.1	1,117.3	92.5	89.2	7.5
IV	17,295.6	2,127.9	15,167.8	14,103.4	13,596.0	310.1	197.3	1,064.3	93.0	89.6	7.0
2018: I	17,548.6	2,085.6	15,463.0	14,274.1	13,755.5	318.3	200.2	1,188.8	92.3	89.0	7.7
II	17,750.3	2,064.4	15,685.9	14,467.9	13,939.9	325.9	202.0	1,218.0	92.2	88.9	7.8
III	17,976.5	2,100.5	15,876.1	14,628.2	14,086.3	338.6	203.3	1,247.9	92.1	88.7	7.9
IV	18,132.0	2,090.7	16,041.3	14,746.8	14,191.4	348.9	206.5	1,294.5	91.9	88.5	8.1
2019: I	18,366.7	2,170.7	16,196.0	14,841.5	14,276.6	355.1	209.8	1,354.5	91.6	88.1	8.4
II	18,480.9	2,222.5	16,258.4	15,072.3	14,497.3	364.7	210.3	1,186.1	92.7	89.2	7.3
III	18,597.6	2,197.1	16,400.5	15,219.9	14,645.3	364.9	209.7	1,180.6	92.8	89.3	7.2
IV	18,760.8	2,221.2	16,539.6	15,335.8	14,759.2	364.6	212.0	1,203.8	92.7	89.2	7.3
2020: I	18,951.0	2,252.4	16,698.6	15,103.3	14,545.5	352.9	204.9	1,595.3	90.4	87.1	9.6
II	20,457.3	2,096.5	18,360.8	13,590.0	13,097.3	286.0	206.6	4,770.8	74.0	71.3	26.0
III ᵖ	19,926.4	2,186.6	17,739.8	14,880.5	14,394.2	287.6	198.7	2,859.3	83.9	81.1	16.1

[1] Consists of nonmortgage interest paid by households.
[2] Percents based on data in millions of dollars.

Source: Department of Commerce (Bureau of Economic Analysis).

TABLE B–18. Total and per capita disposable personal income and personal consumption expenditures, and per capita gross domestic product, in current and real dollars, 1969–2020

[Quarterly data at seasonally adjusted annual rates, except as noted]

Year or quarter	Disposable personal income: Total (billions of dollars) Current dollars	Chained (2012) dollars	Per capita (dollars) Current dollars	Chained (2012) dollars	Personal consumption expenditures: Total (billions of dollars) Current dollars	Chained (2012) dollars	Per capita (dollars) Current dollars	Chained (2012) dollars	Gross domestic product per capita (dollars) Current dollars	Chained (2012) dollars	Population (thousands)[1]
1969	695.8	3,476.5	3,432	17,148	603.6	3,015.9	2,977	14,876	5,019	24,377	202,736
1970	762.0	3,637.0	3,715	17,734	646.7	3,086.9	3,153	15,051	5,233	24,142	205,089
1971	831.1	3,805.2	4,002	18,321	699.9	3,204.8	3,370	15,430	5,609	24,625	207,692
1972	900.8	3,988.4	4,291	18,999	768.2	3,401.0	3,659	16,201	6,093	25,644	209,924
1973	1,008.4	4,236.5	4,758	19,989	849.6	3,569.4	4,009	16,841	6,725	26,834	211,939
1974	1,100.8	4,188.7	5,146	19,583	930.2	3,539.5	4,349	16,547	7,224	26,445	213,898
1975	1,221.8	4,291.4	5,657	19,869	1,030.5	3,619.7	4,771	16,759	7,801	26,136	215,981
1976	1,330.0	4,428.5	6,098	20,306	1,147.7	3,821.5	5,262	17,523	8,590	27,278	218,086
1977	1,461.4	4,568.8	6,634	20,740	1,274.0	3,983.0	5,783	18,081	9,450	28,254	220,289
1978	1,634.1	4,776.4	7,340	21,455	1,422.3	4,157.3	6,388	18,674	10,563	29,505	222,629
1979	1,813.8	4,869.1	8,057	21,630	1,585.4	4,256.1	7,043	18,907	11,672	30,104	225,106
1980	2,024.1	4,905.6	8,888	21,542	1,750.7	4,242.8	7,688	18,631	12,547	29,681	227,726
1981	2,259.3	5,025.4	9,823	21,849	1,934.0	4,301.6	8,408	18,702	13,943	30,132	230,008
1982	2,436.9	5,135.0	10,494	22,113	2,071.3	4,364.6	8,919	18,795	14,399	29,308	232,218
1983	2,628.2	5,312.2	11,216	22,669	2,281.6	4,611.7	9,737	19,680	15,508	30,374	234,333
1984	2,914.8	5,677.1	12,330	24,016	2,492.3	4,854.3	10,543	20,535	17,080	32,289	236,394
1985	3,107.1	5,847.6	13,027	24,518	2,712.8	5,105.6	11,374	21,407	18,192	33,337	238,506
1986	3,295.3	6,069.8	13,691	25,219	2,886.3	5,316.4	11,992	22,089	19,028	34,179	240,683
1987	3,472.0	6,204.1	14,297	25,548	3,076.3	5,496.9	12,668	22,636	19,993	35,047	242,843
1988	3,777.5	6,496.0	15,414	26,508	3,330.0	5,726.5	13,589	23,368	21,368	36,181	245,061
1989	4,057.8	6,686.2	16,403	27,027	3,576.8	5,893.5	14,458	23,823	22,805	37,157	247,387
1990	4,319.1	6,817.4	17,264	27,250	3,809.0	6,012.2	15,225	24,031	23,835	37,435	250,181
1991	4,496.0	6,867.0	17,734	27,086	3,943.4	6,023.0	15,554	23,757	24,290	36,900	253,530
1992	4,808.1	7,152.9	18,714	27,841	4,197.6	6,244.7	16,338	24,306	25,379	37,696	256,922
1993	5,009.2	7,271.1	19,245	27,935	4,452.0	6,462.2	17,104	24,828	26,350	38,234	260,282
1994	5,254.0	7,470.6	19,943	28,356	4,721.0	6,712.6	17,919	25,479	27,660	39,295	263,455
1995	5,543.0	7,718.9	20,792	28,954	4,962.6	6,910.7	18,615	25,923	28,658	39,875	266,588
1996	5,841.4	7,964.2	21,658	29,528	5,244.6	7,150.5	19,445	26,511	29,932	40,900	269,714
1997	6,160.7	8,255.8	22,570	30,246	5,536.8	7,419.7	20,284	27,183	31,424	42,211	272,958
1998	6,574.2	8,740.4	23,806	31,651	5,877.2	7,813.8	21,283	28,295	32,818	43,593	276,154
1999	6,890.0	9,025.6	24,666	32,312	6,279.1	8,225.4	22,479	29,447	34,478	45,146	279,328
2000	7,416.3	9,479.5	26,262	33,568	6,762.1	8,643.4	23,945	30,607	36,305	46,498	282,398
2001	7,766.5	9,740.1	27,230	34,149	7,065.6	8,861.1	24,772	31,067	37,100	46,497	285,225
2002	8,106.8	10,034.5	28,153	34,847	7,342.7	9,088.7	25,499	31,563	37,980	46,858	287,955
2003	8,484.0	10,301.4	29,192	35,446	7,723.1	9,377.5	26,574	32,267	39,426	47,756	290,626
2004	8,986.3	10,645.9	30,643	36,302	8,212.7	9,729.3	28,004	33,176	41,648	49,125	293,262
2005	9,385.8	10,811.6	31,710	36,526	8,747.1	10,075.9	29,552	34,041	44,044	50,381	295,993
2006	10,024.7	11,241.7	33,548	37,621	9,260.3	10,384.5	30,990	34,752	46,231	51,330	298,818
2007	10,515.3	11,499.9	34,854	38,118	9,706.4	10,615.3	32,173	35,186	47,902	51,794	301,696
2008	10,934.7	11,610.4	35,905	38,124	9,976.3	10,592.8	32,758	34,783	48,311	51,240	304,543
2009	10,906.7	11,591.3	35,499	37,727	9,842.2	10,460.0	32,034	34,045	47,028	49,501	307,240
2010	11,314.0	11,821.8	36,523	38,162	10,185.8	10,643.0	32,881	34,357	48,397	50,355	309,774
2011	11,873.1	12,099.3	38,054	38,778	10,641.1	10,843.8	34,105	34,755	49,814	50,770	312,010
2012	12,500.6	12,500.6	39,784	39,784	11,006.8	11,006.8	35,030	35,030	51,548	51,548	314,212
2013	12,504.7	12,338.6	39,527	39,002	11,317.2	11,166.9	35,774	35,298	53,057	52,142	316,357
2014	13,207.1	12,843.7	41,450	40,309	11,822.8	11,497.4	37,105	36,084	55,008	53,077	318,631
2015	13,784.3	13,377.2	42,953	41,684	12,297.5	11,934.3	38,320	37,188	56,832	54,320	320,918
2016	14,202.8	13,640.8	43,946	42,207	12,770.0	12,264.6	39,513	37,949	58,001	54,862	323,186
2017	14,901.9	14,060.5	45,821	43,234	13,340.4	12,587.2	41,019	38,703	60,091	55,790	325,220
2018	15,766.5	14,566.4	48,223	44,553	13,993.3	12,928.1	42,800	39,542	63,043	57,158	326,949
2019	16,348.6	14,882.5	49,763	45,301	14,544.6	13,240.2	44,272	40,302	65,240	58,113	328,527
2017: I	14,632.7	13,880.7	45,093	42,776	13,153.2	12,477.3	40,534	38,451	59,284	55,401	324,496
II	14,822.8	14,030.1	45,616	43,176	13,241.3	12,533.1	40,749	38,570	59,638	55,560	324,948
III	14,984.2	14,125.4	46,038	43,399	13,370.9	12,604.5	41,081	38,727	60,273	55,874	325,475
IV	15,167.8	14,205.8	46,532	43,581	13,596.0	12,733.7	41,710	39,065	61,166	56,324	325,963
2018: I	15,463.0	14,386.7	47,385	44,087	13,755.5	12,798.1	42,153	39,219	62,031	56,785	326,325
II	15,685.9	14,513.6	48,013	44,424	13,939.9	12,898.1	42,668	39,480	62,909	57,099	326,703
III	15,876.1	14,632.6	48,526	44,725	14,086.3	12,983.0	43,055	39,683	63,401	57,317	327,167
IV	16,041.3	14,732.3	48,966	44,970	14,191.4	13,033.4	43,319	39,784	63,827	57,429	327,602
2019: I	16,196.0	14,853.5	49,390	45,296	14,276.6	13,093.2	43,536	39,927	64,391	57,789	327,923
II	16,258.4	14,817.8	49,528	45,139	14,497.3	13,212.8	44,163	40,250	64,977	57,942	328,270
III	16,400.5	14,895.4	49,890	45,312	14,645.3	13,301.3	44,551	40,463	65,526	58,229	328,730
IV	16,539.6	14,964.5	50,244	45,459	14,759.2	13,353.7	44,835	40,566	66,064	58,490	329,186
2020: I	16,698.6	15,060.3	50,674	45,702	14,545.5	13,118.4	44,140	39,810	65,430	57,691	329,529
II	18,360.8	16,626.5	55,656	50,399	13,097.3	11,860.3	39,701	35,951	59,170	52,448	329,898
III[p]	17,739.8	15,917.9	53,697	48,182	14,394.2	12,915.9	43,570	39,095	64,041	56,251	330,368

[1] Population of the United States including Armed Forces overseas. Annual data are averages of quarterly data. Quarterly data are averages for the period.

Source: Department of Commerce (Bureau of Economic Analysis and Bureau of the Census).

Table B–19. Gross saving and investment, 1969–2020

[Billions of dollars, except as noted; quarterly data at seasonally adjusted annual rates]

Year or quarter	Total gross saving	Gross saving — Net saving — Total net saving	Net private saving — Total	Net private saving — Personal saving	Net private saving — Undistributed corporate profits [1]	Net government saving — Total	Net government saving — Federal	Net government saving — State and local	Consumption of fixed capital — Total	Consumption of fixed capital — Private	Consumption of fixed capital — Government
1969	233.1	108.2	110.3	76.1	34.2	−2.0	−5.1	3.1	124.9	89.4	35.5
1970	228.2	91.4	124.8	97.6	27.2	−33.4	−34.8	1.4	136.8	98.3	38.6
1971	246.1	97.2	149.4	111.9	37.5	−52.2	−50.9	−1.3	148.9	107.6	41.3
1972	277.6	116.6	159.6	111.5	48.0	−42.9	−49.0	6.1	161.0	117.5	43.5
1973	335.3	156.6	189.3	135.8	53.5	−32.7	−38.3	5.6	178.7	131.5	47.2
1974	349.2	142.3	186.0	146.3	39.7	−43.7	−41.3	−2.3	206.9	153.2	53.7
1975	348.1	109.6	218.3	164.0	54.3	−108.7	−97.9	−10.7	238.5	178.8	59.7
1976	399.3	139.1	224.4	154.4	70.0	−85.3	−80.9	−4.4	260.2	196.5	63.7
1977	459.4	169.6	242.5	155.9	86.6	−72.9	−73.4	.5	289.8	221.1	68.7
1978	548.0	220.8	278.0	175.1	102.9	−57.2	−62.0	4.9	327.2	252.1	75.1
1979	613.5	239.6	288.2	186.8	101.4	−48.6	−47.4	−1.2	373.9	290.7	83.1
1980	630.1	201.7	296.4	224.1	72.3	−94.7	−88.8	−5.9	428.4	335.0	93.5
1981	743.9	256.6	354.9	265.5	89.4	−98.2	−88.1	−10.2	487.2	381.9	105.3
1982	725.8	188.9	379.0	293.3	85.6	−190.1	−167.4	−22.8	537.0	420.4	116.6
1983	716.7	154.1	379.7	264.0	115.7	−225.6	−207.2	−18.4	562.6	438.8	123.8
1984	881.6	283.2	479.9	330.3	149.5	−196.7	−196.5	−.2	598.4	463.5	134.9
1985	881.0	240.8	442.5	284.9	157.5	−201.7	−199.2	−2.4	640.1	496.4	143.7
1986	864.5	179.2	399.1	290.6	108.5	−219.9	−215.9	−4.0	685.3	531.6	153.7
1987	948.9	218.5	398.6	275.4	123.2	−180.1	−165.7	−14.4	730.4	566.3	164.1
1988	1,076.6	292.1	463.4	320.5	142.9	−171.3	−160.0	−11.3	784.5	607.9	176.6
1989	1,109.8	271.5	450.2	340.0	110.3	−178.7	−159.4	−19.3	838.3	649.6	188.6
1990	1,113.4	224.8	464.4	361.1	103.2	−239.5	−203.3	−36.2	888.5	688.4	200.1
1991	1,153.4	221.0	529.5	396.0	133.5	−308.5	−248.4	−60.1	932.4	721.5	210.9
1992	1,147.6	187.4	592.8	453.9	139.0	−405.5	−334.5	−71.0	960.2	742.9	217.4
1993	1,163.4	159.9	545.9	397.7	148.2	−386.0	−313.5	−72.5	1,003.5	778.2	225.3
1994	1,295.1	239.5	559.0	363.4	195.7	−319.6	−255.6	−63.9	1,055.6	822.5	233.1
1995	1,426.3	303.9	616.5	387.1	229.4	−312.5	−242.1	−70.4	1,122.4	880.7	241.7
1996	1,578.9	403.6	636.8	382.3	254.5	−233.2	−179.4	−53.8	1,175.3	929.1	246.2
1997	1,780.5	541.2	675.1	390.3	284.9	−133.9	−92.0	−42.0	1,239.3	987.8	251.6
1998	1,930.6	620.8	649.5	446.5	203.0	−28.7	1.4	−30.1	1,309.7	1,052.2	257.6
1999	2,010.3	611.3	581.1	347.1	234.0	30.2	69.1	−38.9	1,398.9	1,132.2	266.7
2000	2,129.2	618.0	499.0	356.1	142.9	119.0	159.7	−40.6	1,511.2	1,231.5	279.7
2001	2,075.6	476.1	580.1	389.4	190.7	−104.0	15.0	−119.0	1,599.5	1,311.7	287.8
2002	2,005.2	347.2	797.9	471.7	326.2	−450.7	−267.8	−182.9	1,658.0	1,361.8	296.2
2003	1,995.8	276.7	855.4	468.9	386.5	−578.7	−397.4	−181.3	1,719.1	1,411.9	307.1
2004	2,168.6	346.7	889.2	460.6	428.6	−542.5	−393.5	−149.0	1,821.8	1,497.1	324.7
2005	2,371.4	400.4	796.9	290.1	506.9	−396.6	−293.8	−102.8	1,971.0	1,622.6	348.4
2006	2,659.3	535.1	842.1	381.0	461.1	−307.0	−221.9	−85.0	2,124.1	1,751.8	372.3
2007	2,537.6	284.8	673.8	385.9	287.9	−389.0	−259.7	−129.3	2,252.8	1,852.5	400.3
2008	2,247.6	−111.2	734.6	544.9	189.6	−845.8	−624.9	−220.9	2,358.8	1,931.8	427.0
2009	2,013.9	−357.5	1,227.0	666.2	560.8	−1,584.5	−1,243.2	−341.3	2,371.5	1,928.7	442.8
2010	2,318.7	−72.2	1,553.6	740.3	813.3	−1,625.8	−1,318.4	−307.5	2,390.9	1,933.8	457.2
2011	2,564.3	89.8	1,599.0	849.1	749.9	−1,509.2	−1,234.1	−275.1	2,474.5	1,997.3	477.2
2012	3,041.3	465.3	1,820.8	1,106.6	714.1	−1,355.5	−1,072.7	−282.8	2,576.0	2,082.4	493.6
2013	3,222.9	541.7	1,438.8	799.7	639.1	−897.1	−631.8	−265.3	2,681.2	2,176.6	504.6
2014	3,567.8	752.8	1,588.0	970.9	617.1	−835.3	−597.4	−237.9	2,815.0	2,298.5	516.6
2015	3,673.4	762.0	1,538.0	1,038.7	499.3	−776.0	−560.2	−215.8	2,911.4	2,388.5	522.9
2016	3,511.5	524.9	1,433.2	975.0	458.2	−908.3	−669.1	−239.2	2,986.6	2,458.3	528.3
2017	3,755.4	642.5	1,603.8	1,071.0	532.8	−961.3	−722.4	−238.8	3,112.9	2,569.7	543.2
2018	3,927.0	661.9	1,807.3	1,237.3	570.0	−1,145.4	−931.7	−213.7	3,265.0	2,699.0	566.1
2019	3,988.4	567.5	1,822.2	1,231.2	591.0	−1,254.7	−1,047.0	−207.7	3,420.9	2,832.7	588.3
2017: I	3,665.2	602.4	1,522.6	1,007.6	515.1	−920.2	−671.5	−248.7	3,062.8	2,526.0	536.8
II	3,735.0	637.8	1,609.6	1,094.7	514.9	−971.8	−698.1	−273.7	3,097.2	2,556.5	540.6
III	3,807.4	676.2	1,655.0	1,117.3	537.7	−978.7	−731.0	−247.8	3,131.2	2,585.7	545.5
IV	3,813.9	653.6	1,627.8	1,064.3	563.5	−974.3	−789.1	−185.1	3,160.3	2,610.4	549.9
2018: I	3,910.2	705.3	1,799.1	1,188.8	610.3	−1,093.8	−917.2	−176.5	3,204.8	2,648.6	556.2
II	3,868.6	620.1	1,788.9	1,218.0	570.9	−1,168.8	−942.3	−226.5	3,248.5	2,684.6	563.9
III	3,964.0	677.2	1,804.7	1,247.9	556.8	−1,127.5	−907.2	−220.3	3,286.8	2,717.4	569.4
IV	3,965.0	645.1	1,836.5	1,294.5	542.0	−1,191.4	−960.0	−231.4	3,319.9	2,745.2	574.7
2019: I	4,003.9	642.3	1,871.8	1,354.5	517.3	−1,229.5	−1,016.0	−213.5	3,361.6	2,781.3	580.3
II	3,971.2	566.8	1,775.0	1,186.1	588.9	−1,208.2	−1,033.0	−175.2	3,404.4	2,818.6	585.8
III	3,934.9	491.6	1,795.5	1,180.6	615.0	−1,303.9	−1,084.1	−219.8	3,443.3	2,851.9	591.4
IV	4,043.6	569.1	1,846.5	1,203.8	642.7	−1,277.3	−1,054.9	−222.4	3,474.4	2,878.9	595.6
2020: I	4,150.8	641.8	1,995.3	1,595.3	400.0	−1,353.5	−1,150.8	−202.7	3,509.0	2,908.7	600.3
II	3,362.1	−172.3	4,995.7	4,770.8	224.9	−5,168.0	−5,638.3	470.3	3,534.4	2,930.2	604.2
III p	3,465.9	−106.5	3,538.1	2,859.3	678.8	−3,644.5	−3,514.6	−129.9	3,572.3	2,961.6	610.7

[1] With inventory valuation and capital consumption adjustments.

See next page for continuation of table.

[Billions of dollars, except as noted; quarterly data at seasonally adjusted annual rates]

Year or quarter	Gross domestic investment, capital account transactions, and net lending, NIPA [2]						Statistical discrepancy	Addenda:						
	Gross domestic investment			Capital account transactions (net) [3]	Net lending or net borrowing (−), NIPA [2,4]			Gross private saving	Gross government saving			Net domestic investment	Gross saving as a percent of gross national income	Net saving as a percent of gross national income
	Total	Total	Gross private domestic investment	Gross government investment						Total	Federal	State and local			
1969	234.7	233.1	173.6	59.5	0.0	1.6	1.6	199.7	33.4	20.7	12.8	108.2	22.8	10.6
1970	233.6	229.8	170.0	59.8	.0	3.7	5.3	223.0	5.2	−7.2	12.4	93.0	21.2	8.5
1971	255.6	255.3	196.8	58.5	.0	.3	9.5	257.0	−10.9	−21.8	10.9	106.4	21.2	8.4
1972	284.8	288.8	228.1	60.7	.0	−4.1	7.2	277.1	.6	−18.8	19.4	127.8	21.7	9.1
1973	341.4	332.6	266.9	65.6	.0	8.8	6.1	320.8	14.5	−6.0	20.4	153.9	23.4	10.9
1974	356.6	350.7	274.5	76.2	.0	5.9	7.4	339.1	10.1	−6.0	16.0	143.8	22.5	9.2
1975	361.5	341.7	257.3	84.4	.1	19.8	13.3	397.1	−48.9	−59.2	10.3	103.1	20.7	6.5
1976	420.0	412.9	323.2	89.6	.1	7.0	20.7	420.9	−21.6	−39.2	17.6	152.6	21.4	7.4
1977	478.9	489.8	396.6	93.2	.1	−11.0	19.4	463.6	−4.2	−28.2	24.0	199.9	22.1	8.1
1978	571.3	583.9	478.4	105.6	.1	−12.7	23.3	530.1	17.9	−12.4	30.3	256.7	23.3	9.4
1979	658.6	659.8	539.7	120.1	.1	−1.3	45.1	579.0	34.6	7.2	27.3	285.9	23.5	9.2
1980	674.6	666.0	530.1	135.9	.1	8.4	44.4	631.4	−1.2	−28.4	27.1	237.6	22.1	7.1
1981	781.9	778.6	631.2	147.3	.1	3.3	38.1	736.8	7.1	−20.6	27.6	291.3	23.2	8.0
1982	734.7	738.0	581.0	156.9	.1	−3.4	8.8	739.5	−73.5	−92.0	18.4	201.0	21.5	5.6
1983	773.6	808.7	637.5	171.2	.1	−35.2	57.0	818.5	−101.8	−126.1	24.3	246.1	19.8	4.3
1984	923.2	1,013.3	820.1	193.2	.1	−90.2	41.6	943.4	−61.8	−105.9	44.1	414.9	21.9	7.0
1985	935.2	1,049.5	829.7	219.9	.1	−114.5	54.3	938.9	−57.9	−102.3	44.4	409.4	20.4	5.6
1986	944.6	1,087.2	849.1	238.1	.1	−142.8	80.1	930.7	−66.2	−112.4	46.2	401.9	19.1	4.0
1987	992.7	1,146.8	892.2	254.6	.1	−154.2	43.8	964.9	−16.0	−55.6	39.6	416.4	19.7	4.5
1988	1,079.6	1,195.4	937.0	258.4	.1	−115.9	3.0	1,071.3	5.3	−41.0	46.4	410.9	20.5	5.6
1989	1,177.8	1,270.1	999.7	270.4	.3	−92.7	68.0	1,099.9	9.9	−32.5	42.4	431.9	19.8	4.9
1990	1,208.9	1,283.8	993.4	290.4	7.4	−82.3	95.5	1,152.8	−39.4	−69.8	30.4	395.3	18.9	3.8
1991	1,246.3	1,238.4	944.3	294.1	5.3	2.6	93.0	1,250.9	−97.6	−108.3	10.8	306.0	18.9	3.6
1992	1,263.6	1,309.1	1,013.0	296.1	−1.3	−44.3	115.9	1,335.7	−188.1	−191.2	3.1	348.9	17.8	2.9
1993	1,319.3	1,398.7	1,106.8	291.9	.9	−80.2	156.0	1,324.1	−160.7	−166.5	5.8	395.2	17.3	2.4
1994	1,435.1	1,550.7	1,256.5	294.2	1.3	−116.9	140.0	1,381.6	−86.4	−105.3	18.8	495.0	18.1	3.3
1995	1,519.3	1,625.2	1,317.5	307.7	.4	−106.3	93.0	1,497.2	−70.9	−88.6	17.7	502.8	18.8	4.0
1996	1,637.0	1,752.0	1,432.1	320.0	.2	−115.2	58.1	1,565.9	13.0	−25.7	38.7	576.7	19.6	5.0
1997	1,792.1	1,922.2	1,595.6	326.6	.5	−130.6	11.6	1,662.9	117.6	62.3	55.3	682.9	20.7	6.3
1998	1,875.3	2,080.7	1,736.7	344.0	.2	−205.6	−55.2	1,701.7	228.9	156.8	72.1	770.9	21.1	6.8
1999	1,977.3	2,255.5	1,887.1	368.5	6.7	−285.0	−33.0	1,713.3	296.9	227.3	69.7	856.6	20.7	6.3
2000	2,033.0	2,427.3	2,038.4	388.9	4.6	−398.9	−96.3	1,730.5	398.8	322.8	76.0	916.0	20.5	6.0
2001	1,962.5	2,346.7	1,934.8	411.9	−11.9	−372.3	−113.1	1,891.8	183.8	179.5	4.4	747.2	19.3	4.4
2002	1,932.4	2,374.1	1,930.4	443.7	4.2	−445.8	−72.7	2,159.7	−154.5	−101.0	−53.5	716.1	18.1	3.1
2003	1,982.3	2,491.3	2,027.1	464.2	8.8	−517.7	−13.4	2,267.3	−271.6	−225.1	−46.4	772.2	17.3	2.4
2004	2,146.2	2,767.5	2,281.3	486.2	4.6	−625.8	−22.3	2,386.1	−217.8	−213.0	−4.8	945.6	17.6	2.8
2005	2,318.7	3,048.0	2,534.7	513.3	−.7	−728.6	−52.7	2,419.5	−48.1	−103.2	55.1	1,077.0	18.0	3.0
2006	2,452.1	3,251.8	2,701.0	550.9	7.7	−807.5	−207.2	2,593.9	65.4	−20.7	86.0	1,127.7	18.9	3.8
2007	2,555.0	3,265.0	2,673.0	592.0	6.4	−716.3	17.4	2,526.3	11.3	−46.9	58.2	1,012.2	17.4	2.0
2008	2,430.2	3,107.2	2,477.6	629.6	.8	−677.8	182.6	2,666.4	−418.8	−399.1	−19.7	748.4	15.3	−.8
2009	2,203.9	2,572.6	1,929.7	642.9	6.3	−375.0	189.9	3,155.7	−1,141.8	−1,009.5	−132.2	201.1	14.0	−2.5
2010	2,378.7	2,810.0	2,165.5	644.5	7.4	−438.7	60.0	3,487.4	−1,168.7	−1,074.6	−94.1	419.1	15.3	−.5
2011	2,507.4	2,969.2	2,332.6	636.6	9.5	−471.2	−56.8	3,596.3	−1,032.1	−979.2	−52.9	494.7	16.2	.6
2012	2,801.4	3,242.8	2,621.8	621.0	−.5	−440.8	−239.8	3,903.1	−861.9	−811.0	−50.8	666.8	18.2	2.8
2013	3,066.0	3,426.4	2,826.0	600.4	7.0	−367.4	−156.9	3,615.3	−392.4	−365.9	−26.5	745.2	18.8	3.2
2014	3,281.2	3,646.7	3,044.2	602.6	6.9	−372.5	−286.6	3,886.5	−318.7	−327.1	8.4	831.7	19.8	4.2
2015	3,436.1	3,859.8	3,237.2	622.6	8.3	−432.0	−237.3	3,926.5	−253.1	−288.7	35.6	948.4	19.6	4.1
2016	3,419.3	3,826.8	3,188.3	638.4	7.0	−414.5	−92.2	3,891.5	−380.0	−397.3	17.3	840.2	18.4	2.8
2017	3,623.9	4,015.5	3,351.1	664.3	16.0	−407.5	−131.4	4,173.4	−418.1	−445.4	27.3	902.6	18.8	3.2
2018	3,869.0	4,336.8	3,632.9	703.9	4.6	−472.4	−58.0	4,506.3	−579.3	−645.9	66.6	1,071.7	18.7	3.2
2019	4,001.2	4,504.0	3,751.2	752.8	6.7	−509.5	12.8	4,654.9	−666.5	−752.2	85.7	1,083.1	18.4	2.6
2017: I	3,550.5	3,918.4	3,266.2	652.2	8.9	−376.8	−114.8	4,048.7	−383.4	−396.7	13.3	855.5	18.7	3.1
II	3,542.0	3,975.0	3,313.3	661.7	8.4	−441.4	−193.0	4,166.1	−431.2	−422.0	−9.1	877.8	18.8	3.2
III	3,674.2	4,043.5	3,378.8	664.7	39.5	−408.8	−133.2	4,240.7	−433.3	−453.3	20.0	912.4	19.0	3.4
IV	3,729.0	4,124.9	3,446.3	678.7	7.2	−403.1	−84.8	4,238.2	−424.3	−509.5	85.2	964.6	18.7	3.2
2018: I	3,832.6	4,240.5	3,555.0	685.4	6.0	−413.9	−77.6	4,447.7	−537.5	−635.0	97.4	1,035.6	18.9	3.4
II	3,888.1	4,284.5	3,580.9	703.6	12.1	−408.5	19.5	4,473.5	−604.9	−657.4	52.5	1,036.0	18.6	3.0
III	3,859.4	4,386.7	3,671.7	715.0	2.2	−529.5	−104.6	4,522.1	−558.1	−620.1	62.0	1,099.9	18.8	3.2
IV	3,895.7	4,435.3	3,723.9	711.5	−1.9	−537.7	−69.3	4,581.7	−616.7	−671.3	54.5	1,115.4	18.7	3.0
2019: I	3,971.4	4,503.5	3,772.8	730.7	10.6	−542.7	−32.5	4,653.1	−649.2	−723.9	74.7	1,141.9	18.7	3.0
II	3,953.8	4,489.6	3,739.7	749.9	3.8	−539.6	−17.4	4,593.6	−622.4	−740.0	117.5	1,085.2	18.4	2.6
III	4,009.9	4,517.7	3,759.8	757.9	3.8	−511.5	75.0	4,647.4	−712.5	−788.3	75.8	1,074.4	18.1	2.3
IV	4,069.8	4,505.4	3,732.6	772.8	8.5	−444.2	26.2	4,725.3	−681.7	−756.6	74.8	1,031.0	18.4	2.6
2020: I	4,040.6	4,464.0	3,675.9	788.1	12.3	−435.7	−110.2	4,904.0	−753.2	−850.3	97.0	955.0	18.9	2.9
II	3,348.7	3,914.9	3,128.6	786.2	4.7	−570.9	−13.4	7,925.9	−4,563.8	−5,334.7	770.9	380.5	17.1	−.9
III p	3,759.1	4,470.5	3,680.3	790.2			293.2	6,499.7	−3,033.7	−3,208.8	175.1	898.2	16.5	−.5

[2] National income and product accounts (NIPA).
[3] Consists of capital transfers and the acquisition and disposal of nonproduced nonfinancial assets.
[4] Prior to 1982, equals the balance on current account, NIPA.

Source: Department of Commerce (Bureau of Economic Analysis).

TABLE B–20. Median money income (in 2019 dollars) and poverty status of families and people, by race, 2012-2019

Race, Hispanic origin, and year	Families[1]						People below poverty level[2]		Median money income (in 2019 dollars) of people 15 years old and over with income[3]			
			Below poverty level[2]						Males		Females	
	Number (millions)	Median money income (in 2019 dollars)[3]	Total		Female householder, no husband present		Number (millions)	Percent	All people	Year-round full-time workers	All people	Year-round full-time workers
			Number (millions)	Percent	Number (millions)	Percent						
TOTAL (all races)[4]												
2012	80.9	$69,433	9.5	11.8	4.8	30.9	46.5	15.0	$37,822	$56,540	$24,007	$44,643
2013[5]	81.2	70,150	9.1	11.2	4.6	30.6	45.3	14.5	38,725	56,000	24,253	44,627
2013[6]	82.3	71,970	9.6	11.7	5.2	32.2	46.3	14.8	39,167	56,522	24,322	44,739
2014	81.7	72,027	9.5	11.6	4.8	30.6	46.7	14.8	39,241	55,622	24,041	44,100
2015	82.2	76,290	8.6	10.4	4.4	28.2	43.1	13.5	40,076	56,380	25,649	45,057
2016	82.9	77,459	8.1	9.8	4.1	26.6	40.6	12.7	41,410	56,968	26,519	46,023
2017	83.1	79,198	7.8	9.3	4.0	25.7	39.7	12.3	42,130	58,231	26,580	46,284
2017[7]	83.5	79,404	7.8	9.3	4.0	26.2	39.6	12.3	42,129	57,885	27,009	47,799
2018	83.5	80,071	7.5	9.0	3.7	24.9	38.1	11.8	42,369	58,256	27,570	47,371
2019	83.7	86,011	6.6	7.8	3.3	22.2	34.0	10.5	44,310	60,876	29,407	50,129
WHITE, non-Hispanic[8]												
2012	54.0	79,738	3.8	7.1	1.7	23.4	18.9	9.7	43,229	62,747	25,548	47,044
2013[5]	53.8	79,833	3.7	6.9	1.6	22.6	18.8	9.6	44,105	62,060	26,141	47,031
2013[6]	54.7	82,041	4.0	7.3	1.9	25.8	19.6	10.0	44,912	64,720	26,089	47,353
2014	53.8	82,865	3.9	7.3	1.7	23.7	19.7	10.1	44,397	63,466	25,949	47,818
2015	53.8	86,897	3.5	6.4	1.6	21.7	17.8	9.1	45,546	65,556	27,656	49,309
2016	54.1	87,433	3.4	6.3	1.6	21.1	17.3	8.8	46,237	65,197	28,227	50,402
2017	53.9	89,538	3.2	6.0	1.4	19.8	17.0	8.7	47,804	65,102	28,280	51,061
2017[7]	54.2	90,699	3.2	5.9	1.4	20.2	16.6	8.5	48,175	64,996	29,005	52,729
2018	54.2	91,069	3.2	5.8	1.4	19.7	15.7	8.1	48,683	66,465	30,002	51,612
2019	54.3	97,101	2.7	5.0	1.1	17.1	14.2	7.3	50,565	70,297	31,338	53,733
BLACK[8]												
2012	9.8	45,199	2.3	23.7	1.6	37.8	10.9	27.2	27,803	44,594	22,335	39,162
2013[5]	9.9	45,716	2.3	22.8	1.6	38.5	11.0	27.2	27,322	45,680	22,034	38,980
2013[6]	9.9	46,048	2.2	22.4	1.7	36.7	10.2	25.2	27,614	44,408	23,159	37,840
2014	9.9	46,645	2.3	22.9	1.6	37.2	10.8	26.2	28,720	44,500	22,664	38,063
2015	9.8	49,403	2.1	21.1	1.5	33.9	10.0	24.1	29,572	44,974	23,323	40,032
2016	10.0	52,592	1.9	19.0	1.3	31.6	9.2	22.0	31,575	44,759	24,328	39,788
2017	10.0	52,769	1.8	18.2	1.3	30.8	9.0	21.2	31,405	45,553	24,654	39,088
2017[7]	10.0	52,824	1.9	18.9	1.4	31.9	9.2	21.7	30,637	44,431	24,954	39,968
2018	9.8	54,067	1.7	17.7	1.2	29.4	8.9	20.8	31,686	46,448	25,923	41,034
2019	10.0	58,518	1.6	16.3	1.1	27.3	8.1	18.8	31,261	46,811	27,020	42,098
ASIAN[8]												
2012	4.1	86,862	.4	9.4	.1	19.2	1.9	11.7	44,875	66,410	26,031	51,584
2013[5]	4.4	83,986	.4	8.7	.1	14.9	1.8	10.5	44,139	66,166	27,306	49,835
2013[6]	4.4	91,012	.4	10.2	.1	25.7	2.3	13.1	47,037	67,194	28,408	51,094
2014	4.5	89,430	.4	8.9	.1	18.9	2.1	12.0	44,213	64,605	27,447	52,264
2015	4.7	98,034	.4	8.0	.1	16.2	2.1	11.4	47,162	68,463	28,631	53,992
2016	4.7	99,609	.3	7.2	.1	19.4	1.9	10.1	49,635	71,351	28,521	54,376
2017	4.9	96,768	.4	7.8	.1	15.5	2.0	10.0	50,939	73,434	29,473	53,991
2017[7]	4.9	98,772	.4	7.4	.1	16.3	1.9	9.7	51,298	73,184	28,787	54,725
2018	5.1	103,078	.4	7.6	.1	19.6	2.0	10.1	52,726	72,530	31,752	58,194
2019	5.1	112,226	.3	5.7	.1	14.4	2.0	10.1	53,675	76,684	32,099	60,297
HISPANIC (any race)[8]												
2012	12.0	45,475	2.8	23.5	1.3	40.7	13.6	25.6	27,434	36,273	18,658	32,918
2013[5]	12.1	46,465	2.6	21.6	1.3	40.4	12.7	23.5	27,934	36,220	19,525	33,856
2013[6]	12.4	45,003	2.9	23.1	1.4	40.5	13.4	24.7	26,603	35,579	18,635	34,264
2014	12.5	48,767	2.7	21.5	1.3	37.9	13.1	23.6	28,835	37,957	19,009	33,325
2015	12.8	51,072	2.5	19.6	1.2	35.5	12.1	21.4	30,334	38,819	20,400	34,161
2016	13.0	54,445	2.3	17.3	1.1	32.7	11.1	19.4	32,506	40,679	21,207	34,131
2017	13.2	55,916	2.2	16.3	1.1	32.7	10.8	18.3	32,009	41,614	21,184	33,832
2017[7]	13.3	55,896	2.2	16.4	1.1	33.4	10.8	18.3	31,801	40,201	21,392	34,262
2018	13.3	56,091	2.1	15.5	1.0	30.8	10.5	17.6	31,986	41,091	22,080	35,806
2019	13.2	60,927	1.8	13.9	.9	26.8	9.5	15.7	32,285	41,992	23,420	36,905

[1] The term "family" refers to a group of two or more persons related by birth, marriage, or adoption and residing together. Every family must include a reference person.

[2] Poverty thresholds are updated each year to reflect changes in the consumer price index for all urban consumers (CPI-U).

[3] Adjusted by consumer price index research series (CPI-U-RS).

[4] Data for American Indians and Alaska natives, native Hawaiians and other Pacific Islanders, and those reporting two or more races are included in the total but not shown separately.

[5] The 2014 Current Population Survey (CPS) Annual Social and Economic Supplement (ASEC) included redesigned income questions, which were implemented to a subsample of the 98,000 addresses using a probability split panel design. These 2013 data are based on the 2014 ASEC sample of 68,000 addresses that received income questions similar to those used in the 2013 ASEC and are consistent with data in earlier years.

[6] These 2013 data are based on the 2014 ASEC sample of 30,000 addresses that received redesigned income questions and are consistent with data in later years.

[7] Reflects implementation of an updated processing system.

[8] The CPS allows respondents to choose more than one race. Data shown are for "white alone, non-Hispanic," "black alone," and "Asian alone" race categories. ("Black" is also "black or African American.") Family race and Hispanic origin are based on the reference person.

Note: For details see *Income and Poverty in the United States* in publication Series P–60 on the CPS ASEC.

Source: Department of Commerce (Bureau of the Census).

Table B–21. Real farm income, 1955–2020

[Billions of chained (2020) dollars]

Year	Income of farm operators from farming [1]							Net farm income
	Gross farm income						Production expenses	
	Total	Value of agricultural sector production				Direct Federal Government payments		
		Total	Crops [2,3]	Animals and animal products [3]	Farm-related income [4]			
1955	257.3	255.6	109.6	131.7	14.3	1.8	170.4	86.9
1956	252.4	248.3	107.3	127.1	13.9	4.1	168.8	83.7
1957	249.9	242.6	98.1	130.4	14.0	7.3	170.2	79.6
1958	273.4	265.8	105.3	145.8	14.6	7.6	181.0	92.4
1959	262.5	257.8	102.3	139.8	15.6	4.7	188.3	74.2
1960	263.7	258.9	107.1	135.8	16.0	4.8	187.1	76.6
1961	274.2	264.1	107.0	140.6	16.5	10.1	193.3	80.9
1962	282.9	271.2	111.3	143.1	16.8	11.7	202.3	80.6
1963	286.5	275.2	118.5	139.3	17.5	11.2	208.7	77.7
1964	275.2	261.0	109.8	133.2	18.1	14.2	207.0	68.3
1965	297.4	281.7	121.5	141.8	18.3	15.7	215.0	82.4
1966	313.7	293.3	113.8	160.7	18.7	20.4	226.9	86.8
1967	305.1	286.5	116.1	150.9	19.5	18.6	230.6	74.5
1968	300.4	280.3	109.6	151.2	19.5	20.1	229.0	71.4
1969	311.5	290.5	108.7	161.9	19.9	20.9	232.6	78.9
1970	308.5	289.0	107.7	161.4	20.0	19.5	233.2	75.4
1971	310.1	294.4	117.0	157.1	20.4	15.7	235.2	74.9
1972	340.4	321.5	124.2	176.6	20.7	19.0	247.3	93.1
1973	448.8	436.9	195.3	219.4	22.2	11.8	292.9	155.9
1974	409.1	406.8	204.6	178.3	23.9	2.2	295.5	113.5
1975	383.1	380.0	192.0	163.8	24.2	3.1	285.9	97.2
1976	371.6	369.0	174.6	168.4	26.0	2.6	298.8	72.8
1977	369.8	363.6	173.9	160.9	28.8	6.2	302.2	67.6
1978	408.0	398.4	179.8	186.9	31.6	9.6	327.9	80.0
1979	442.1	438.0	195.5	208.8	33.7	4.0	361.7	80.4
1980	401.5	398.0	173.1	189.1	35.8	3.5	358.1	43.4
1981	408.7	404.0	193.9	173.0	37.0	4.7	342.7	66.1
1982	379.9	371.8	166.2	163.2	42.5	8.1	324.7	55.2
1983	342.7	322.0	126.7	156.0	39.3	20.7	310.9	31.8
1984	361.1	343.0	167.1	154.8	21.0	18.1	305.3	55.8
1985	335.6	319.6	153.5	143.7	22.3	16.1	276.2	59.4
1986	318.9	294.7	129.3	144.5	20.9	24.1	255.3	63.6
1987	335.7	302.3	128.5	151.0	22.8	33.4	259.9	75.8
1988	342.5	314.7	133.4	151.4	29.9	27.9	266.2	76.3
1989	355.0	334.8	151.0	154.6	29.2	20.2	268.9	86.1
1990	353.2	336.6	148.6	160.8	27.2	16.6	270.6	82.6
1991	331.8	317.6	140.2	150.7	26.6	14.2	262.3	69.5
1992	338.7	323.2	150.4	147.2	25.6	15.5	254.0	84.7
1993	338.3	316.1	136.4	151.8	28.0	22.1	261.2	77.1
1994	349.1	336.4	162.3	145.0	29.1	12.7	264.2	84.9
1995	333.6	322.1	151.7	138.9	31.5	11.5	270.7	62.9
1996	366.4	355.0	179.7	143.0	32.2	11.4	274.8	91.6
1997	363.5	352.1	171.8	147.1	33.2	11.4	285.2	78.4
1998	351.4	332.7	154.3	142.3	36.2	18.7	280.2	71.2
1999	349.9	317.8	138.2	141.8	37.9	32.0	278.9	71.0
2000	352.0	318.1	138.3	144.3	35.6	33.8	278.1	73.8
2001	356.0	324.0	135.4	151.5	37.1	32.0	277.8	78.2
2002	323.5	306.1	137.4	131.1	37.6	17.4	268.6	54.9
2003	356.3	333.5	149.5	144.6	39.4	22.8	272.3	84.0
2004	395.5	378.1	167.8	166.7	43.6	17.4	278.2	117.2
2005	388.3	356.6	148.8	164.6	43.2	31.7	285.8	102.5
2006	366.3	346.4	149.8	150.6	45.9	19.9	293.8	72.5
2007	417.4	402.8	185.7	170.1	46.9	14.6	331.3	86.1
2008	439.6	424.9	209.6	168.1	47.2	14.8	345.6	94.1
2009	402.8	388.2	197.0	143.2	48.1	14.6	328.4	74.4
2010	421.8	407.1	198.8	165.9	42.3	14.7	330.5	91.2
2011	487.2	475.1	231.0	189.8	54.4	12.1	355.6	131.6
2012	511.4	499.3	242.0	192.3	65.0	12.1	401.8	109.6
2013	540.8	528.5	261.2	202.3	65.0	12.3	402.6	138.2
2014	530.2	519.5	226.3	235.1	58.0	10.7	429.0	101.2
2015	479.0	467.2	200.3	211.0	56.0	11.7	390.2	88.7
2016	443.3	429.3	203.6	177.9	47.9	14.0	376.3	67.0
2017	448.9	436.7	198.3	186.7	51.8	12.2	369.6	79.3
2018	438.1	424.1	191.9	182.8	49.3	14.1	354.3	83.8
2019	437.7	414.9	183.2	178.5	53.3	22.7	353.0	84.6
2020 [p]	463.2	416.7	196.6	167.0	53.1	46.5	343.6	119.6

[1] The GDP chain-type price index is used to convert the current-dollar statistics to 2020=100 equivalents.
[2] Crop receipts include proceeds received from commodities placed under Commodity Credit Corporation loans.
[3] The value of production equates to the sum of cash receipts, home consumption, and the value of the change in inventories.
[4] Includes income from forest products sold, the gross imputed rental value of farm dwellings, machine hire and custom work, and other sources of farm income such as commodity insurance indemnities.

Note: Data for 2020 are forecasts.

Source: Department of Agriculture (Economic Research Service).

Labor Market Indicators

Table B–22. Civilian labor force, 1929–2020

[Monthly data seasonally adjusted, except as noted]

Year or month	Civilian noninstitutional population [1]	Civilian labor force					Not in labor force	Civilian labor force participation rate [2]	Civilian employment/ population ratio [3]	Unemployment rate, civilian workers [4]
		Total	Employment			Unemployment				
			Total	Agricultural	Non-agricultural					
	Thousands of persons 14 years of age and over							Percent		
1929		49,180	47,630	10,450	37,180	1,550				3.2
1930		49,820	45,480	10,340	35,140	4,340				8.7
1931		50,420	42,400	10,290	32,110	8,020				15.9
1932		51,000	38,940	10,170	28,770	12,060				23.6
1933		51,590	38,760	10,090	28,670	12,830				24.9
1934		52,230	40,890	9,900	30,990	11,340				21.7
1935		52,870	42,260	10,110	32,150	10,610				20.1
1936		53,440	44,410	10,000	34,410	9,030				16.9
1937		54,000	46,300	9,820	36,480	7,700				14.3
1938		54,610	44,220	9,690	34,530	10,390				19.0
1939		55,230	45,750	9,610	36,140	9,480				17.2
1940	99,840	55,640	47,520	9,540	37,980	8,120	44,200	55.7	47.6	14.6
1941	99,900	55,910	50,350	9,100	41,250	5,560	43,990	56.0	50.4	9.9
1942	98,640	56,410	53,750	9,250	44,500	2,660	42,230	57.2	54.5	4.7
1943	94,640	55,540	54,470	9,080	45,390	1,070	39,100	58.7	57.6	1.9
1944	93,220	54,630	53,960	8,950	45,010	670	38,590	58.6	57.9	1.2
1945	94,090	53,860	52,820	8,580	44,240	1,040	40,230	57.2	56.1	1.9
1946	103,070	57,520	55,250	8,320	46,930	2,270	45,550	55.8	53.6	3.9
1947	106,018	60,168	57,812	8,256	49,557	2,356	45,850	56.8	54.5	3.9
	Thousands of persons 16 years of age and over									
1947	101,827	59,350	57,038	7,890	49,148	2,311	42,477	58.3	56.0	3.9
1948	103,068	60,621	58,343	7,629	50,714	2,276	42,447	58.8	56.6	3.8
1949	103,994	61,286	57,651	7,658	49,993	3,637	42,708	58.9	55.4	5.9
1950	104,995	62,208	58,918	7,160	51,758	3,288	42,787	59.2	56.1	5.3
1951	104,621	62,017	59,961	6,726	53,235	2,055	42,604	59.2	57.3	3.3
1952	105,231	62,138	60,250	6,500	53,749	1,883	43,093	59.0	57.3	3.0
1953	107,056	63,015	61,179	6,260	54,919	1,834	44,041	58.9	57.1	2.9
1954	108,321	63,643	60,109	6,205	53,904	3,532	44,678	58.8	55.5	5.5
1955	109,683	65,023	62,170	6,450	55,722	2,852	44,660	59.3	56.7	4.4
1956	110,954	66,552	63,799	6,283	57,514	2,750	44,402	60.0	57.5	4.1
1957	112,265	66,929	64,071	5,947	58,123	2,859	45,336	59.6	57.1	4.3
1958	113,727	67,639	63,036	5,586	57,450	4,602	46,088	59.5	55.4	6.8
1959	115,329	68,369	64,630	5,565	59,065	3,740	46,960	59.3	56.0	5.5
1960	117,245	69,628	65,778	5,458	60,318	3,852	47,617	59.4	56.1	5.5
1961	118,771	70,459	65,746	5,200	60,546	4,714	48,312	59.3	55.4	6.7
1962	120,153	70,614	66,702	4,944	61,759	3,911	49,539	58.8	55.5	5.5
1963	122,416	71,833	67,762	4,687	63,076	4,070	50,583	58.7	55.4	5.7
1964	124,485	73,091	69,305	4,523	64,782	3,786	51,394	58.7	55.7	5.2
1965	126,513	74,455	71,088	4,361	66,726	3,366	52,058	58.9	56.2	4.5
1966	128,058	75,770	72,895	3,979	68,915	2,875	52,288	59.2	56.9	3.8
1967	129,874	77,347	74,372	3,844	70,527	2,975	52,527	59.6	57.3	3.8
1968	132,028	78,737	75,920	3,817	72,103	2,817	53,291	59.6	57.5	3.6
1969	134,335	80,734	77,902	3,606	74,296	2,832	53,602	60.1	58.0	3.5
1970	137,085	82,771	78,678	3,463	75,215	4,093	54,315	60.4	57.4	4.9
1971	140,216	84,382	79,367	3,394	75,972	5,016	55,834	60.2	56.6	5.9
1972	144,126	87,034	82,153	3,484	78,669	4,882	57,091	60.4	57.0	5.6
1973	147,096	89,429	85,064	3,470	81,594	4,365	57,667	60.8	57.8	4.9
1974	150,120	91,949	86,794	3,515	83,279	5,156	58,171	61.3	57.8	5.6
1975	153,153	93,775	85,846	3,408	82,438	7,929	59,377	61.2	56.1	8.5
1976	156,150	96,158	88,752	3,331	85,421	7,406	59,991	61.6	56.8	7.7
1977	159,033	99,009	92,017	3,283	88,734	6,991	60,025	62.3	57.9	7.1
1978	161,910	102,251	96,048	3,387	92,661	6,202	59,659	63.2	59.3	6.1
1979	164,863	104,962	98,824	3,347	95,477	6,137	59,900	63.7	59.9	5.8
1980	167,745	106,940	99,303	3,364	95,938	7,637	60,806	63.8	59.2	7.1
1981	170,130	108,670	100,397	3,368	97,030	8,273	61,460	63.9	59.0	7.6
1982	172,271	110,204	99,526	3,401	96,125	10,678	62,067	64.0	57.8	9.7
1983	174,215	111,550	100,834	3,383	97,450	10,717	62,665	64.0	57.9	9.6
1984	176,383	113,544	105,005	3,321	101,685	8,539	62,839	64.4	59.5	7.5
1985	178,206	115,461	107,150	3,179	103,971	8,312	62,744	64.8	60.1	7.2
1986	180,587	117,834	109,597	3,163	106,434	8,237	62,752	65.3	60.7	7.0
1987	182,753	119,865	112,440	3,208	109,232	7,425	62,888	65.6	61.5	6.2
1988	184,613	121,669	114,968	3,169	111,800	6,701	62,944	65.9	62.3	5.5
1989	186,393	123,869	117,342	3,199	114,142	6,528	62,523	66.5	63.0	5.3

[1] Not seasonally adjusted.
[2] Civilian labor force as percent of civilian noninstitutional population.
[3] Civilian employment as percent of civilian noninstitutional population.
[4] Unemployed as percent of civilian labor force.

See next page for continuation of table.

TABLE B–22. Civilian labor force, 1929–2020—*Continued*

[Monthly data seasonally adjusted, except as noted]

Year or month	Civilian noninstitutional population [1]	Civilian labor force Total	Employment Total	Employment Agricultural	Employment Non-agricultural	Unemployment	Not in labor force	Civilian labor force participation rate [2]	Civilian employment/ population ratio [3]	Unemployment rate, civilian workers [4]
	Thousands of persons 16 years of age and over							Percent		
1990	189,164	125,840	118,793	3,223	115,570	7,047	63,324	66.5	62.8	5.6
1991	190,925	126,346	117,718	3,269	114,449	8,628	64,578	66.2	61.7	6.8
1992	192,805	128,105	118,492	3,247	115,245	9,613	64,700	66.4	61.5	7.5
1993	194,838	129,200	120,259	3,115	117,144	8,940	65,638	66.3	61.7	6.9
1994	196,814	131,056	123,060	3,409	119,651	7,996	65,758	66.6	62.5	6.1
1995	198,584	132,304	124,900	3,440	121,460	7,404	66,280	66.6	62.9	5.6
1996	200,591	133,943	126,708	3,443	123,264	7,236	66,647	66.8	63.2	5.4
1997	203,133	136,297	129,558	3,399	126,159	6,739	66,837	67.1	63.8	4.9
1998	205,220	137,673	131,463	3,378	128,085	6,210	67,547	67.1	64.1	4.5
1999	207,753	139,368	133,488	3,281	130,207	5,880	68,385	67.1	64.3	4.2
2000 [5]	212,577	142,583	136,891	2,464	134,427	5,692	69,994	67.1	64.4	4.0
2001	215,092	143,734	136,933	2,299	134,635	6,801	71,359	66.8	63.7	4.7
2002	217,570	144,863	136,485	2,311	134,174	8,378	72,707	66.6	62.7	5.8
2003	221,168	146,510	137,736	2,275	135,461	8,774	74,658	66.2	62.3	6.0
2004	223,357	147,401	139,252	2,232	137,020	8,149	75,956	66.0	62.3	5.5
2005	226,082	149,320	141,730	2,197	139,532	7,591	76,762	66.0	62.7	5.1
2006	228,815	151,428	144,427	2,206	142,221	7,001	77,387	66.2	63.1	4.6
2007	231,867	153,124	146,047	2,095	143,952	7,078	78,743	66.0	63.0	4.6
2008	233,788	154,287	145,362	2,168	143,194	8,924	79,501	66.0	62.2	5.8
2009	235,801	154,142	139,877	2,103	137,775	14,265	81,659	65.4	59.3	9.3
2010	237,830	153,889	139,064	2,206	136,858	14,825	83,941	64.7	58.5	9.6
2011	239,618	153,617	139,869	2,254	137,615	13,747	86,001	64.1	58.4	8.9
2012	243,284	154,975	142,469	2,186	140,283	12,506	88,310	63.7	58.6	8.1
2013	245,679	155,389	143,929	2,130	141,799	11,460	90,290	63.2	58.6	7.4
2014	247,947	155,922	146,305	2,237	144,068	9,617	92,025	62.9	59.0	6.2
2015	250,801	157,130	148,834	2,422	146,411	8,296	93,671	62.7	59.3	5.3
2016	253,538	159,187	151,436	2,460	148,976	7,751	94,351	62.8	59.7	4.9
2017	255,079	160,320	153,337	2,454	150,883	6,982	94,759	62.9	60.1	4.4
2018	257,791	162,075	155,761	2,425	153,336	6,314	95,716	62.9	60.4	3.9
2019	259,175	163,539	157,538	2,425	155,113	6,001	95,636	63.1	60.8	3.7
2018: Jan	256,780	161,068	154,486	2,443	152,053	6,582	95,712	62.7	60.2	4.1
Feb	256,934	161,783	155,142	2,430	152,659	6,641	95,151	63.0	60.4	4.1
Mar	257,097	161,684	155,191	2,340	152,714	6,493	95,414	62.9	60.4	4.0
Apr	257,272	161,742	155,324	2,330	153,007	6,418	95,529	62.9	60.4	4.0
May	257,454	161,874	155,665	2,353	153,353	6,209	95,579	62.9	60.5	3.8
June	257,642	162,269	155,750	2,398	153,383	6,519	95,373	63.0	60.5	4.0
July	257,843	162,173	155,993	2,483	153,519	6,180	95,670	62.9	60.5	3.8
Aug	258,066	161,768	155,601	2,377	153,329	6,167	96,297	62.7	60.3	3.8
Sept	258,290	162,078	156,032	2,487	153,528	6,045	96,212	62.8	60.4	3.7
Oct	258,514	162,605	156,482	2,407	153,989	6,123	95,909	62.9	60.5	3.8
Nov	258,708	162,662	156,628	2,549	154,102	6,034	96,045	62.9	60.5	3.7
Dec	258,888	163,111	156,825	2,491	154,266	6,286	95,777	63.0	60.6	3.9
2019: Jan	258,239	163,142	156,627	2,546	154,112	6,516	95,097	63.2	60.7	4.0
Feb	258,392	163,047	156,866	2,488	154,354	6,181	95,345	63.1	60.7	3.8
Mar	258,537	162,935	156,741	2,336	154,346	6,194	95,602	63.0	60.6	3.8
Apr	258,693	162,546	156,696	2,389	154,369	5,850	96,147	62.8	60.6	3.6
May	258,861	162,782	156,844	2,423	154,486	5,938	96,079	62.9	60.6	3.6
June	259,037	163,133	157,148	2,330	154,835	5,985	95,905	63.0	60.7	3.7
July	259,225	163,373	157,346	2,400	155,035	6,027	95,852	63.0	60.7	3.7
Aug	259,432	163,894	157,895	2,414	155,546	5,999	95,538	63.2	60.9	3.7
Sept	259,638	164,051	158,298	2,416	155,816	5,753	95,587	63.2	61.0	3.5
Oct	259,845	164,401	158,544	2,473	155,970	5,857	95,444	63.3	61.0	3.6
Nov	260,020	164,347	158,536	2,356	156,167	5,811	95,673	63.2	61.0	3.5
Dec	260,181	164,556	158,803	2,533	156,241	5,753	95,625	63.2	61.0	3.5
2020: Jan	259,502	164,606	158,714	2,404	156,345	5,892	94,896	63.4	61.2	3.6
Feb	259,628	164,546	158,759	2,467	156,281	5,787	95,082	63.4	61.1	3.5
Mar	259,758	162,913	155,772	2,399	153,358	7,140	96,845	62.7	60.0	4.4
Apr	259,896	156,481	133,403	2,424	131,053	23,078	103,415	60.2	51.3	14.7
May	260,047	158,227	137,242	2,341	134,966	20,985	101,820	60.8	52.8	13.3
June	260,204	159,932	142,182	2,297	139,944	17,750	100,273	61.5	54.6	11.1
July	260,373	159,870	143,532	2,128	141,487	16,338	100,503	61.4	55.1	10.2
Aug	260,558	160,838	147,288	2,159	145,156	13,550	99,720	61.7	56.5	8.4
Sept	260,742	160,143	147,563	2,257	145,235	12,580	100,599	61.4	56.6	7.9
Oct	260,925	160,867	149,806	2,529	147,222	11,061	100,058	61.7	57.4	6.9
Nov	261,085	160,467	149,732	2,399	147,277	10,735	100,618	61.5	57.3	6.7

[5] Beginning in 2000, data for agricultural employment are for agricultural and related industries; data for this series and for nonagricultural employment are not strictly comparable with data for earlier years. Because of independent seasonal adjustment for these two series, monthly data will not add to total civilian employment.

Note: Labor force data in Tables B–22 through B–28 are based on household interviews and usually relate to the calendar week that includes the 12th of the month. Historical comparability is affected by revisions to population controls, changes in occupational and industry classification, and other changes to the survey. In recent years, updated population controls have been introduced annually with the release of January data, so data are not strictly comparable with earlier periods. Particularly notable changes were introduced for data in the years 1953, 1960, 1962, 1972, 1973, 1978, 1980, 1990, 1994, 1997, 1998, 2000, 2003, 2008 and 2012. For definitions of terms, area samples used, historical comparability of the data, comparability with other series, etc., see *Employment and Earnings* or concepts and methodology of the CPS at http://www.bls.gov/cps/documentation.htm#concepts.

Source: Department of Labor (Bureau of Labor Statistics).

[Thousands of persons 16 years of age and over, except as noted; monthly data seasonally adjusted]

Year or month	All civilian workers	By sex and age			By race or ethnicity [1]									
		Men 20 years and over	Women 20 years and over	Both sexes 16–19	White			Black or African American			Asian	Hispanic or Latino ethnicity		
					Total	Men 20 years and over	Women 20 years and over	Total	Men 20 years and over	Women 20 years and over	Total	Total	Men 20 years and over	Women 20 years and over
1975	85,846	48,018	30,726	7,104	76,411	43,192	26,731	7,894	3,998	3,388	....	3,663	2,117	1,224
1976	88,752	49,190	32,226	7,336	78,853	44,171	27,958	8,227	4,120	3,599	....	3,720	2,109	1,288
1977	92,017	50,555	33,775	7,688	81,700	45,326	29,306	8,540	4,273	3,758	....	4,079	2,335	1,370
1978	96,048	52,143	35,836	8,070	84,936	46,594	30,975	9,102	4,483	4,047	....	4,527	2,568	1,537
1979	98,824	53,308	37,434	8,083	87,259	47,546	32,357	9,359	4,606	4,174	....	4,785	2,701	1,638
1980	99,303	53,101	38,492	7,710	87,715	47,419	33,275	9,313	4,498	4,267	....	5,527	3,142	1,886
1981	100,397	53,582	39,590	7,225	88,709	47,846	34,275	9,355	4,520	4,329	....	5,813	3,325	2,029
1982	99,526	52,891	40,086	6,549	87,903	47,209	34,710	9,189	4,414	4,347	....	5,805	3,354	2,040
1983	100,834	53,487	41,004	6,342	88,893	47,618	35,476	9,375	4,531	4,428	....	6,072	3,523	2,127
1984	105,005	55,769	42,793	6,444	92,120	49,461	36,823	10,119	4,871	4,773	....	6,651	3,825	2,357
1985	107,150	56,562	44,154	6,434	93,736	50,061	37,907	10,501	4,992	4,977	....	6,888	3,994	2,456
1986	109,597	57,569	45,556	6,472	95,660	50,818	39,050	10,814	5,150	5,128	....	7,219	4,174	2,615
1987	112,440	58,726	47,074	6,640	97,789	51,649	40,242	11,309	5,357	5,365	....	7,790	4,444	2,872
1988	114,968	59,781	48,383	6,805	99,812	52,466	41,316	11,658	5,509	5,548	....	8,250	4,680	3,047
1989	117,342	60,837	49,745	6,759	101,584	53,292	42,346	11,953	5,602	5,727	....	8,573	4,853	3,172
1990	118,793	61,678	50,535	6,581	102,261	53,685	42,796	12,175	5,692	5,884	....	9,845	5,609	3,567
1991	117,718	61,178	50,634	5,906	101,182	53,103	42,862	12,074	5,706	5,874	....	9,828	5,623	3,603
1992	118,492	61,496	51,328	5,669	101,669	53,357	43,327	12,151	5,681	5,978	....	10,027	5,757	3,693
1993	120,259	62,355	52,099	5,805	103,045	54,021	43,910	12,382	5,793	6,095	....	10,361	5,992	3,800
1994	123,060	63,294	53,606	6,161	105,190	54,676	45,116	12,835	5,964	6,320	....	10,788	6,189	3,989
1995	124,900	64,085	54,396	6,419	106,490	55,254	45,643	13,279	6,137	6,556	....	11,127	6,367	4,116
1996	126,708	64,897	55,311	6,500	107,808	55,977	46,164	13,542	6,167	6,762	....	11,642	6,655	4,341
1997	129,558	66,284	56,613	6,661	109,856	56,986	47,063	13,969	6,325	7,013	....	12,726	7,307	4,705
1998	131,463	67,135	57,278	7,051	110,931	57,500	47,342	14,556	6,530	7,290	....	13,291	7,570	4,928
1999	133,488	67,761	58,555	7,172	112,235	57,934	48,098	15,056	6,702	7,663	....	13,720	7,576	5,290
2000	136,891	69,634	60,067	7,189	114,424	59,119	49,145	15,156	6,741	7,703	6,043	15,735	8,859	5,903
2001	136,933	69,776	60,417	6,740	114,430	59,245	49,369	15,006	6,627	7,741	6,180	16,190	9,100	6,121
2002	136,485	69,734	60,420	6,332	114,013	59,124	49,448	14,872	6,652	7,610	6,215	16,590	9,341	6,367
2003	137,736	70,415	61,402	5,919	114,235	59,348	49,823	14,739	6,586	7,636	5,756	17,372	10,063	6,541
2004	139,252	71,572	61,773	5,907	115,239	60,159	50,040	14,909	6,681	7,707	5,994	17,930	10,385	6,752
2005	141,730	73,050	62,702	5,978	116,949	61,255	50,589	15,313	6,901	7,876	6,244	18,632	10,872	6,913
2006	144,427	74,431	63,834	6,162	118,833	62,259	51,359	15,765	7,079	8,068	6,522	19,613	11,391	7,321
2007	146,047	75,337	64,799	5,911	119,792	62,806	51,996	16,051	7,245	8,240	6,839	20,382	11,827	7,662
2008	145,362	74,750	65,039	5,573	119,126	62,304	52,124	15,953	7,151	8,260	6,917	20,346	11,769	7,707
2009	139,877	71,341	63,699	4,837	114,996	59,626	51,231	15,025	6,628	7,956	6,635	19,647	11,256	7,649
2010	139,064	71,230	63,456	4,378	114,168	59,438	50,997	15,010	6,680	7,944	6,705	19,906	11,438	7,788
2011	139,869	72,182	63,360	4,327	114,469	60,118	50,881	15,051	6,765	7,906	6,867	20,269	11,685	7,918
2012	142,469	73,403	64,640	4,426	114,769	60,193	50,911	15,856	7,104	8,313	7,705	21,878	12,212	8,858
2013	143,929	74,176	65,295	4,458	115,379	60,511	51,198	16,151	7,304	8,408	8,136	22,514	12,638	9,056
2014	146,305	75,471	66,287	4,548	116,788	61,289	51,798	16,362	7,613	8,663	8,325	23,492	13,202	9,431
2015	148,834	76,776	67,323	4,734	117,944	61,959	52,161	17,472	7,938	9,032	8,706	24,400	13,624	9,853
2016	151,436	78,084	68,387	4,965	119,313	62,575	52,771	17,982	8,228	9,219	9,213	25,249	14,055	10,217
2017	153,337	78,919	69,344	5,074	120,176	63,009	53,179	18,587	8,500	9,514	9,448	25,938	14,355	10,543
2018	155,761	80,211	70,424	5,126	121,461	63,719	53,682	19,091	8,745	9,751	9,832	27,012	14,873	11,045
2019	157,538	80,917	71,470	5,150	122,441	64,070	54,304	19,381	8,883	9,910	10,179	27,805	15,204	11,516
2019: Jan	156,627	80,474	71,004	5,149	121,812	63,869	53,895	19,211	8,714	9,833	9,991	27,558	15,068	11,386
Feb	156,866	80,677	71,169	5,019	122,119	64,067	54,143	19,140	8,744	9,819	10,046	27,499	15,127	11,328
Mar	156,741	80,570	71,056	5,115	122,111	63,937	54,102	19,093	8,765	9,776	10,082	27,562	15,192	11,324
Apr	156,696	80,609	71,136	4,951	121,964	63,915	54,120	19,235	8,823	9,860	9,969	27,364	15,034	11,337
May	156,844	80,761	71,038	5,044	121,970	64,041	54,003	19,302	8,840	9,947	10,057	27,507	15,185	11,341
June	157,148	80,780	71,209	5,159	122,199	64,015	54,054	19,216	8,773	9,858	10,302	27,621	15,099	11,396
July	157,346	80,975	71,120	5,250	122,213	64,007	54,060	19,502	8,956	9,893	10,163	27,610	15,028	11,493
Aug	157,895	81,046	71,665	5,184	122,566	64,099	54,379	19,485	8,937	9,944	10,227	27,876	15,191	11,609
Sept	158,298	81,146	71,990	5,162	122,955	64,224	54,709	19,550	8,976	9,987	10,262	28,156	15,320	11,723
Oct	158,544	81,196	72,130	5,218	123,028	64,173	54,755	19,571	9,003	9,984	10,409	28,279	15,310	11,834
Nov	158,536	81,377	71,881	5,278	123,077	64,247	54,666	19,527	9,019	9,929	10,429	28,339	15,498	11,675
Dec	158,803	81,390	72,200	5,213	123,175	64,238	54,834	19,712	9,034	9,906	10,214	28,286	15,393	11,736
2020: Jan	158,714	81,345	72,097	5,273	123,332	64,341	54,807	19,549	8,918	10,067	10,017	28,397	15,571	11,701
Feb	158,759	81,202	72,179	5,378	123,189	64,204	54,692	19,730	8,945	10,207	10,312	28,531	15,519	11,834
Mar	155,772	79,832	70,886	5,054	121,042	63,120	53,878	19,208	8,812	9,830	10,037	27,672	15,037	11,507
Apr	133,403	69,977	59,947	3,479	104,065	55,776	45,563	16,240	7,448	8,351	8,499	22,579	12,776	9,060
May	137,242	71,672	61,638	3,932	107,499	57,263	47,195	16,523	7,583	8,426	8,475	23,241	13,154	9,326
June	142,182	73,641	64,426	4,114	111,538	58,898	49,440	16,927	7,670	8,693	8,717	24,711	13,590	10,158
July	143,532	74,184	65,113	4,235	112,226	59,054	49,822	17,161	7,827	8,785	9,163	24,885	13,728	10,217
Aug	147,288	75,945	66,637	4,706	115,354	60,425	51,124	17,528	8,051	8,949	9,462	25,886	14,213	10,649
Sept	147,563	76,231	66,289	5,043	115,496	60,738	50,794	17,537	7,967	8,997	9,568	25,834	14,463	10,307
Oct	149,806	77,049	67,615	5,142	117,181	61,335	51,742	17,970	8,169	9,244	9,611	26,619	14,785	10,711
Nov	149,732	76,747	67,881	5,104	116,673	60,843	51,756	18,106	8,184	9,345	9,701	26,702	14,705	10,861

[1] Beginning in 2003, persons who selected this race group only. Persons whose ethnicity is identified as Hispanic or Latino may be of any race. Prior to 2003, persons who selected more than one race were included in the group they identified as the main race. Data for "black or African American" were for "black" prior to 2003. See Employment and Earnings or concepts and methodology of the Current Population Survey (CPS) at http://www.bls.gov/cps/documentation.htm#concepts for details.

Note: Detail will not sum to total because data for all race groups are not shown here.

See footnote 5 and Note, Table B–22.

Source: Department of Labor (Bureau of Labor Statistics).

[Thousands of persons 16 years of age and over, except as noted; monthly data seasonally adjusted]

Year or month	All civilian workers	By sex and age			By race or ethnicity [1]									
		Men 20 years and over	Women 20 years and over	Both sexes 16–19	White			Black or African American			Asian	Hispanic or Latino ethnicity		
					Total	Men 20 years and over	Women 20 years and over	Total	Men 20 years and over	Women 20 years and over	Total	Total	Men 20 years and over	Women 20 years and over
1975	7,929	3,476	2,684	1,767	6,421	2,841	2,166	1,369	571	469	....	508	225	160
1976	7,406	3,098	2,588	1,719	5,914	2,504	2,045	1,334	528	477	....	485	217	166
1977	6,991	2,794	2,535	1,663	5,441	2,211	1,946	1,393	512	528	....	456	195	153
1978	6,202	2,328	2,292	1,583	4,698	1,797	1,713	1,330	462	510	....	452	175	168
1979	6,137	2,308	2,276	1,555	4,664	1,773	1,699	1,319	473	513	....	434	168	160
1980	7,637	3,353	2,615	1,669	5,884	2,629	1,964	1,553	636	574	....	620	284	190
1981	8,273	3,615	2,895	1,763	6,343	2,825	2,143	1,731	703	671	....	678	321	212
1982	10,678	5,089	3,613	1,977	8,241	3,991	2,715	2,142	954	793	....	929	461	293
1983	10,717	5,257	3,632	1,829	8,128	4,098	2,643	2,272	1,002	878	....	961	491	302
1984	8,539	3,932	3,107	1,499	6,372	2,992	2,264	1,914	815	747	....	800	393	258
1985	8,312	3,715	3,129	1,468	6,191	2,834	2,283	1,864	757	750	....	811	401	269
1986	8,237	3,751	3,032	1,454	6,140	2,857	2,213	1,840	765	728	....	857	438	278
1987	7,425	3,369	2,709	1,347	5,501	2,584	1,922	1,684	666	706	....	751	374	241
1988	6,701	2,987	2,487	1,226	4,944	2,268	1,766	1,547	617	642	....	732	351	234
1989	6,528	2,867	2,467	1,194	4,770	2,149	1,758	1,544	619	625	....	750	342	276
1990	7,047	3,239	2,596	1,212	5,186	2,431	1,852	1,565	664	633	....	876	425	289
1991	8,628	4,195	3,074	1,359	6,560	3,284	2,248	1,723	745	698	....	1,092	575	339
1992	9,613	4,717	3,469	1,427	7,169	3,620	2,512	2,011	886	800	....	1,311	675	418
1993	8,940	4,287	3,288	1,365	6,655	3,263	2,400	1,844	801	729	....	1,248	629	418
1994	7,996	3,627	3,049	1,320	5,892	2,735	2,197	1,666	682	685	....	1,187	558	431
1995	7,404	3,239	2,819	1,346	5,459	2,465	2,042	1,538	593	620	....	1,140	530	404
1996	7,236	3,146	2,783	1,306	5,300	2,363	1,998	1,592	639	643	....	1,132	495	438
1997	6,739	2,882	2,585	1,271	4,836	2,140	1,784	1,560	585	673	....	1,069	471	401
1998	6,210	2,580	2,424	1,205	4,484	1,920	1,688	1,426	524	622	....	1,026	436	376
1999	5,880	2,433	2,285	1,162	4,273	1,813	1,616	1,309	480	561	....	945	374	376
2000	5,692	2,376	2,235	1,081	4,121	1,731	1,595	1,241	499	512	227	954	388	371
2001	6,801	3,040	2,599	1,162	4,969	2,275	1,849	1,416	573	582	288	1,138	495	436
2002	8,378	3,896	3,228	1,253	6,137	2,943	2,269	1,693	695	738	389	1,353	636	496
2003	8,774	4,209	3,314	1,251	6,311	3,125	2,276	1,787	760	772	366	1,441	693	555
2004	8,149	3,791	3,150	1,208	5,847	2,785	2,172	1,729	733	755	277	1,342	635	504
2005	7,591	3,392	3,013	1,186	5,350	2,450	2,054	1,700	699	734	259	1,191	536	464
2006	7,001	3,131	2,751	1,119	5,002	2,281	1,927	1,549	640	656	205	1,081	497	414
2007	7,078	3,259	2,718	1,101	5,143	2,408	1,930	1,445	622	588	229	1,220	576	446
2008	8,924	4,297	3,342	1,285	6,509	3,179	2,384	1,788	811	732	285	1,678	860	567
2009	14,265	7,555	5,157	1,552	10,648	5,746	3,745	2,606	1,286	1,032	522	2,706	1,474	911
2010	14,825	7,763	5,534	1,528	10,916	5,828	3,960	2,852	1,396	1,165	543	2,843	1,519	1,001
2011	13,747	6,898	5,450	1,400	9,889	5,046	3,818	2,831	1,360	1,204	518	2,629	1,345	984
2012	12,506	5,984	5,125	1,397	8,915	4,347	3,564	2,544	1,152	1,119	483	2,514	1,195	995
2013	11,460	5,568	4,565	1,327	8,033	3,994	3,102	2,429	1,082	1,069	448	2,257	1,090	855
2014	9,617	4,585	3,926	1,106	6,540	3,141	2,623	2,141	973	943	436	1,878	864	764
2015	8,296	3,959	3,371	966	5,662	2,751	2,249	1,846	835	811	347	1,726	820	686
2016	7,751	3,675	3,151	925	5,345	2,594	2,100	1,655	737	724	349	1,548	720	627
2017	6,982	3,287	2,868	827	4,765	2,288	1,923	1,501	663	657	333	1,401	632	585
2018	6,314	2,976	2,578	759	4,354	2,094	1,743	1,322	582	573	304	1,323	591	547
2019	6,001	2,819	2,435	746	4,159	1,967	1,664	1,251	571	527	280	1,248	553	497
2019: Jan	6,516	3,112	2,639	765	4,448	2,165	1,755	1,404	660	570	318	1,400	628	569
Feb	6,181	2,911	2,497	773	4,157	1,970	1,668	1,417	667	544	320	1,248	561	465
Mar	6,194	2,995	2,451	747	4,286	2,083	1,676	1,344	630	542	318	1,357	641	517
Apr	5,850	2,812	2,304	734	3,947	1,900	1,538	1,352	628	556	225	1,198	581	433
May	5,938	2,808	2,401	730	4,121	1,938	1,670	1,265	579	533	260	1,197	543	480
June	5,985	2,788	2,447	751	4,120	1,928	1,704	1,223	528	546	225	1,252	564	503
July	6,027	2,796	2,465	767	4,185	1,980	1,666	1,220	543	537	290	1,305	625	450
Aug	5,999	2,806	2,451	742	4,286	1,965	1,773	1,119	550	456	299	1,213	528	510
Sept	5,753	2,695	2,323	735	4,063	1,886	1,639	1,135	512	491	259	1,137	473	468
Oct	5,857	2,715	2,411	730	4,094	1,941	1,644	1,133	482	511	305	1,203	531	485
Nov	5,811	2,679	2,411	721	4,115	1,957	1,633	1,148	485	516	276	1,236	485	521
Dec	5,753	2,618	2,383	752	4,022	1,839	1,602	1,238	557	530	264	1,231	483	558
2020: Jan	5,892	2,743	2,415	734	3,957	1,938	1,517	1,241	526	550	315	1,275	543	541
Feb	5,787	2,799	2,323	665	3,957	1,950	1,555	1,216	554	514	262	1,322	516	607
Mar	7,140	3,344	2,954	843	4,979	2,402	2,000	1,387	665	543	433	1,771	807	738
Apr	23,078	10,483	10,966	1,628	17,176	7,869	8,071	3,247	1,432	1,644	1,438	5,263	2,561	2,288
May	20,985	9,385	9,920	1,681	15,162	6,862	7,099	3,334	1,388	1,671	1,493	4,977	2,338	2,184
June	17,750	8,354	8,154	1,242	12,470	5,790	5,707	3,083	1,492	1,420	1,392	4,195	1,999	1,841
July	16,338	7,720	7,607	1,011	11,392	5,367	5,302	2,933	1,402	1,371	1,245	3,675	1,761	1,664
Aug	13,550	6,567	6,078	905	9,118	4,485	4,000	2,621	1,225	1,224	1,133	3,040	1,549	1,255
Sept	12,580	6,065	5,561	954	8,717	4,238	3,774	2,420	1,150	1,120	933	2,964	1,386	1,272
Oct	11,061	5,513	4,715	832	7,513	3,810	3,094	2,166	1,057	936	787	2,567	1,310	1,054
Nov	10,735	5,468	4,438	829	7,359	3,797	2,941	2,078	1,028	929	695	2,451	1,243	964

[1] See footnote 1 and Note, Table B–23.

Note: See footnote 5 and Note, Table B–22.

Source: Department of Labor (Bureau of Labor Statistics).

[Percent [1]; monthly data seasonally adjusted]

Year or month	All civilian workers	Men				Women				Both sexes 16–19 years	By race or ethnicity [2]			
		20 years and over	20–24 years	25–54 years	55 years and over	20 years and over	20–24 years	25–54 years	55 years and over		White	Black or African American	Asian	Hispanic or Latino ethnicity
1975	61.2	80.3	84.5	94.4	49.4	46.0	64.1	55.1	23.1	54.0	61.5	58.8	....	60.8
1976	61.6	79.8	85.2	94.2	47.8	47.0	65.0	56.8	23.0	54.5	61.8	59.0	....	60.8
1977	62.3	79.7	85.6	94.2	47.4	48.1	66.5	58.5	22.9	56.0	62.5	59.8	....	61.6
1978	63.2	79.8	85.9	94.3	47.2	49.6	68.3	60.6	23.1	57.8	63.3	61.5	....	62.9
1979	63.7	79.8	86.4	94.4	46.6	50.6	69.0	62.3	23.2	57.9	63.9	61.4	....	63.6
1980	63.8	79.4	85.9	94.2	45.6	51.3	68.9	64.0	22.8	56.7	64.1	61.0	....	64.0
1981	63.9	79.0	85.5	94.1	44.5	52.1	69.6	65.3	22.7	55.4	64.3	60.8	....	64.1
1982	64.0	78.7	84.9	94.0	43.8	52.7	69.8	66.3	22.7	54.1	64.3	61.0	....	63.6
1983	64.0	78.5	84.8	93.8	43.0	53.1	69.9	67.1	22.4	53.5	64.3	61.5	....	63.8
1984	64.4	78.3	85.0	93.9	41.8	53.7	70.4	68.2	22.2	53.9	64.6	62.2	....	64.9
1985	64.8	78.1	85.0	93.9	41.0	54.7	71.8	69.6	22.0	54.5	65.0	62.9	....	64.6
1986	65.3	78.1	85.8	93.8	40.4	55.5	72.4	70.8	22.1	54.7	65.5	63.3	....	65.4
1987	65.6	78.0	85.2	93.7	40.4	56.2	73.0	71.9	22.0	54.7	65.8	63.8	....	66.4
1988	65.9	77.9	85.0	93.6	39.9	56.8	72.7	72.7	22.3	55.3	66.2	63.8	....	67.4
1989	66.5	78.1	85.3	93.7	39.6	57.7	72.4	73.6	23.0	55.9	66.7	64.2	....	67.6
1990	66.5	78.2	84.4	93.4	39.4	58.0	71.3	74.0	22.9	53.7	66.9	64.0	....	67.4
1991	66.2	77.7	83.5	93.1	38.5	57.9	70.1	74.1	22.6	51.6	66.6	63.3	....	66.5
1992	66.4	77.7	83.3	93.0	38.4	58.5	70.9	74.6	22.8	51.3	66.8	63.9	....	66.8
1993	66.3	77.3	83.2	92.6	37.7	58.5	70.9	74.6	22.8	51.5	66.8	63.2	....	66.2
1994	66.6	76.8	83.1	91.7	37.8	59.3	71.0	75.3	24.0	52.7	67.1	63.4	....	66.1
1995	66.6	76.7	83.1	91.6	37.9	59.4	70.3	75.6	23.9	53.5	67.1	63.7	....	65.8
1996	66.8	76.8	82.5	91.8	38.3	59.9	71.3	76.1	23.9	52.3	67.2	64.1	....	66.5
1997	67.1	77.0	82.5	91.8	38.9	60.5	72.7	76.7	24.6	51.6	67.5	64.7	....	67.9
1998	67.1	76.8	82.0	91.8	39.1	60.4	73.0	76.5	25.0	52.8	67.3	65.6	....	67.9
1999	67.1	76.7	81.9	91.7	39.6	60.7	73.2	76.8	25.6	52.0	67.3	65.8	....	67.7
2000	67.1	76.7	82.6	91.6	40.1	60.6	73.1	76.7	26.1	52.0	67.3	65.8	67.2	69.7
2001	66.8	76.5	81.6	91.3	40.9	60.6	72.7	76.4	27.0	49.6	67.0	65.3	67.2	69.5
2002	66.6	76.3	80.7	91.0	42.0	60.5	72.1	75.9	28.5	47.4	66.8	64.8	67.2	69.1
2003	66.2	75.9	80.0	90.6	42.6	60.6	70.8	75.6	30.0	44.5	66.5	64.3	66.4	68.3
2004	66.0	75.8	79.6	90.5	43.2	60.3	70.5	75.3	30.5	43.9	66.3	63.8	65.9	68.6
2005	66.0	75.8	79.1	90.5	44.2	60.4	70.1	75.3	31.4	43.7	66.3	64.2	66.1	68.0
2006	66.2	75.9	79.6	90.6	44.9	60.5	69.5	75.5	32.3	43.7	66.5	64.1	66.2	68.7
2007	66.0	75.9	78.7	90.9	45.2	60.6	70.1	75.4	33.2	41.3	66.4	63.7	66.5	68.8
2008	66.0	75.7	78.7	90.5	46.0	60.9	70.0	75.8	33.9	40.2	66.3	63.7	67.0	68.5
2009	65.4	74.8	76.2	89.7	46.3	60.8	69.6	75.6	34.7	37.5	65.8	62.4	66.0	68.0
2010	64.7	74.1	74.5	89.3	46.4	60.3	68.3	75.2	35.1	34.9	65.1	62.2	64.7	67.5
2011	64.1	73.4	74.7	88.7	46.3	59.8	67.8	74.7	35.1	34.1	64.5	61.4	64.6	66.5
2012	63.7	73.0	74.5	88.7	46.8	59.3	67.4	74.5	35.1	34.3	64.0	61.5	63.9	66.4
2013	63.2	72.5	73.9	88.4	46.5	58.8	67.5	73.9	35.1	34.5	63.5	61.2	64.6	66.0
2014	62.9	71.9	73.9	88.2	45.9	58.5	67.7	73.9	34.9	34.0	63.1	61.2	63.6	66.1
2015	62.7	71.7	73.0	88.3	45.9	58.2	68.3	73.7	34.7	34.3	62.8	61.5	62.8	65.9
2016	62.8	71.7	73.0	88.5	46.2	58.3	68.0	74.3	34.7	35.2	62.9	61.6	63.2	65.8
2017	62.9	71.6	74.1	88.6	46.1	58.5	68.5	75.0	34.7	35.2	62.8	62.3	63.6	66.1
2018	62.9	71.6	73.2	89.0	46.2	58.5	69.0	75.3	34.7	35.1	62.8	62.3	63.5	66.3
2019	63.1	71.6	74.0	89.1	46.3	58.9	70.4	76.0	35.0	35.3	63.0	62.5	64.0	66.8
2019: Jan	63.2	71.8	73.6	89.4	46.4	58.9	69.3	75.9	35.0	35.4	63.0	62.7	64.3	67.3
Feb	63.1	71.7	73.4	89.4	46.4	58.8	70.1	75.8	35.2	34.7	63.0	62.5	64.6	66.7
Mar	63.0	71.7	74.2	89.5	46.0	58.7	69.9	75.7	35.0	35.1	63.0	62.1	64.0	66.9
Apr	62.8	71.5	74.1	89.1	45.9	58.6	70.2	75.5	34.9	34.1	62.8	62.5	62.6	66.0
May	62.9	71.6	75.5	88.8	46.2	58.6	70.7	75.6	34.5	34.6	62.8	62.4	63.1	66.2
June	63.0	71.5	74.5	88.7	46.3	58.7	70.2	75.9	34.7	35.4	62.9	61.9	63.6	66.4
July	63.0	71.6	74.2	88.9	46.7	58.6	70.7	75.4	35.1	36.1	62.9	62.7	63.7	66.4
Aug	63.2	71.6	73.2	89.0	46.5	59.0	70.5	76.3	35.0	35.5	63.1	62.3	64.1	66.7
Sept	63.2	71.6	73.9	89.1	46.3	59.1	71.0	76.3	35.1	35.3	63.2	62.5	64.2	67.0
Oct	63.3	71.6	74.1	89.1	46.3	59.2	71.4	76.5	35.1	35.6	63.2	65.3	67.3
Nov	63.2	71.6	73.4	89.3	46.5	59.0	70.0	76.5	35.0	35.9	63.2	62.3	64.7	67.4
Dec	63.2	71.5	73.3	89.2	46.4	59.2	70.3	76.8	35.0	35.7	63.2	63.1	63.6	67.1
2020: Jan	63.4	71.8	75.1	89.3	46.6	59.2	70.6	77.0	34.8	36.1	63.4	62.6	63.9	67.8
Feb	63.4	71.7	74.6	89.3	46.6	59.2	71.3	77.0	34.9	36.4	63.3	63.1	64.4	68.1
Mar	62.7	70.9	74.8	89.3	45.9	58.6	68.9	76.4	34.6	35.5	62.7	62.0	63.8	67.1
Apr	60.2	68.6	65.3	86.4	44.6	56.3	63.7	73.6	33.4	30.8	60.3	58.6	60.7	63.3
May	60.8	69.0	67.2	87.2	44.3	56.8	64.9	74.3	33.4	33.9	61.0	59.6	60.8	64.1
June	61.5	69.8	67.6	87.9	45.0	57.5	66.4	75.4	33.8	32.3	61.6	60.0	61.4	65.5
July	61.4	69.7	69.2	87.6	44.9	57.6	66.4	75.1	34.3	31.7	61.4	60.2	63.4	64.6
Aug	61.7	70.1	70.8	88.1	44.9	57.6	65.6	74.9	34.6	33.9	61.8	60.4	63.8	65.3
Sept	61.4	69.9	71.6	87.7	44.9	56.8	66.5	74.2	33.7	36.2	61.6	59.7	63.0	64.9
Oct	61.7	70.1	73.3	87.9	44.7	57.2	68.6	74.6	33.6	36.1	61.8	60.2	62.9	65.6
Nov	61.5	69.7	73.2	87.4	44.6	57.1	68.5	74.5	33.6	35.9	61.5	60.3	62.8	65.4

[1] Civilian labor force as percent of civilian noninstitutional population in group specified.
[2] See footnote 1, Table B–23.

Note: Data relate to persons 16 years of age and over, except as noted.

See footnote 5 and Note, Table B–22.

Source: Department of Labor (Bureau of Labor Statistics).

[Percent [1]; monthly data seasonally adjusted]

Year or month	All civilian workers	Men 20 years and over	Men 20–24 years	Men 25–54 years	Men 55 years and over	Women 20 years and over	Women 20–24 years	Women 25–54 years	Women 55 years and over	Both sexes 16–19 years	White	Black or African American	Asian	Hispanic or Latino ethnicity
1975	56.1	74.8	72.4	89.0	47.0	42.3	56.0	51.0	21.9	43.3	56.7	50.1	....	53.4
1976	56.8	75.1	74.9	89.5	45.7	43.5	57.3	52.9	21.9	44.2	57.5	50.8	....	53.8
1977	57.9	75.6	76.3	90.1	45.5	44.8	59.0	54.8	21.9	46.1	58.6	51.4	....	55.4
1978	59.3	76.4	78.0	91.0	45.7	46.6	61.4	57.3	22.3	48.3	60.0	53.6	....	57.2
1979	59.9	76.5	78.9	91.1	45.2	47.7	62.4	59.0	22.5	48.5	60.6	53.8	....	58.3
1980	59.2	74.6	75.1	89.4	44.1	48.1	61.8	60.1	22.1	46.6	60.0	52.3	....	57.6
1981	59.0	74.0	74.2	89.0	42.9	48.6	61.8	61.2	21.9	44.6	60.0	51.3	....	57.4
1982	57.8	71.8	71.0	86.5	41.6	48.4	60.6	61.2	21.6	41.5	58.9	49.4	....	54.9
1983	57.9	71.4	71.3	86.1	40.6	48.8	60.9	62.0	21.4	41.5	58.9	49.5	....	55.1
1984	59.5	73.2	74.9	88.4	39.8	50.1	62.7	63.9	21.3	43.7	60.5	52.3	....	57.9
1985	60.1	73.3	75.3	88.7	39.3	51.0	64.1	65.3	21.1	44.4	61.0	53.4	....	57.8
1986	60.7	73.3	76.3	88.5	38.8	52.0	64.9	66.6	21.3	44.6	61.5	54.1	....	58.5
1987	61.5	73.8	76.8	89.0	39.0	53.1	66.1	68.2	21.3	45.5	62.3	55.6	....	60.5
1988	62.3	74.2	77.5	89.5	38.6	54.0	66.6	69.3	21.7	46.8	63.1	56.3	....	61.9
1989	63.0	74.5	77.8	89.9	38.3	54.9	66.4	70.4	22.4	47.5	63.8	56.9	....	62.2
1990	62.8	74.3	76.7	89.1	38.0	55.2	65.2	70.6	22.2	45.3	63.7	56.7	....	61.9
1991	61.7	72.7	73.8	87.5	36.8	54.6	63.2	70.1	21.9	42.0	62.6	55.4	....	59.8
1992	61.5	72.1	73.1	86.8	36.4	54.8	63.6	70.1	21.8	41.0	62.4	54.9	....	59.1
1993	61.7	72.3	73.8	87.0	35.9	55.0	64.0	70.4	22.0	41.7	62.7	55.0	....	59.1
1994	62.5	72.6	74.6	87.2	36.2	56.2	64.5	71.5	23.1	43.4	63.5	56.1	....	59.5
1995	62.9	73.0	75.4	87.6	36.5	56.5	64.0	72.2	23.0	44.2	63.8	57.1	....	59.7
1996	63.2	73.2	74.7	87.9	37.0	57.0	64.9	72.8	23.1	43.5	64.1	57.4	....	60.6
1997	63.8	73.7	75.2	88.4	37.7	57.8	66.8	73.5	23.8	43.4	64.6	58.2	....	62.6
1998	64.1	73.9	75.4	88.8	38.0	58.0	67.3	73.6	24.4	45.1	64.7	59.7	....	63.1
1999	64.3	74.0	75.6	89.0	38.5	58.5	68.0	74.1	24.9	44.7	64.8	60.6	....	63.4
2000	64.4	74.2	76.6	89.0	39.1	58.4	67.9	74.2	25.5	45.2	64.9	60.9	64.8	65.7
2001	63.7	73.3	74.2	87.9	39.6	58.1	67.3	73.4	26.3	42.3	64.2	59.7	64.2	64.9
2002	62.7	72.3	72.5	86.6	40.3	57.5	65.6	72.3	27.5	39.6	63.4	58.1	63.2	63.9
2003	62.3	71.7	71.5	85.9	40.7	57.5	64.2	72.0	28.9	36.8	63.0	57.4	62.4	63.1
2004	62.3	71.9	71.6	86.3	41.5	57.4	64.3	71.8	29.4	36.4	63.1	57.2	63.0	63.8
2005	62.7	72.4	71.5	86.9	42.7	57.6	64.5	72.0	30.4	36.5	63.4	57.7	63.4	64.0
2006	63.1	72.9	72.7	87.3	43.5	58.0	64.2	72.5	31.4	36.9	63.8	58.4	64.2	65.2
2007	63.0	72.8	71.7	87.5	43.7	58.2	65.0	72.5	32.2	34.8	63.6	58.4	64.3	64.9
2008	62.2	71.6	69.7	86.0	44.2	57.9	63.8	72.3	32.7	32.6	62.8	57.3	64.3	63.3
2009	59.3	67.6	63.3	81.5	43.0	56.2	61.1	70.2	32.6	28.4	60.2	53.2	61.2	59.7
2010	58.5	66.8	61.3	81.0	42.8	55.5	59.4	69.3	32.9	25.9	59.4	52.3	59.9	59.0
2011	58.4	67.0	63.0	81.4	43.1	55.0	58.7	69.0	32.9	25.8	59.4	51.7	60.0	58.9
2012	58.6	67.5	63.8	82.5	43.8	55.0	59.2	69.2	33.1	26.1	59.4	53.0	60.1	59.5
2013	58.6	67.4	63.5	82.8	43.8	54.9	59.8	69.3	33.3	26.6	59.4	53.2	61.2	60.0
2014	59.0	67.8	64.9	83.6	43.9	55.2	60.9	70.0	33.4	27.3	59.7	54.3	60.4	61.2
2015	59.3	68.1	65.1	84.4	44.1	55.4	62.5	70.3	33.5	28.5	59.9	55.7	60.4	61.6
2016	59.7	68.5	66.2	85.0	44.4	55.7	63.0	71.1	33.5	29.7	60.2	56.4	60.9	62.0
2017	60.1	68.8	67.9	85.4	44.6	56.1	64.2	72.1	33.6	30.3	60.4	57.6	61.5	62.7
2018	60.4	69.0	67.6	86.2	44.7	56.4	64.7	72.8	33.7	30.6	60.7	58.3	61.6	63.2
2019	60.8	69.2	68.3	86.4	45.1	56.9	66.4	73.7	34.0	30.9	61.0	58.7	62.3	63.9
2019: Jan	60.7	69.1	67.5	86.4	44.9	56.8	64.8	73.4	34.0	30.8	60.8	58.4	62.3	64.0
Feb	60.7	69.2	67.9	86.5	45.1	56.9	65.3	73.4	34.3	30.1	60.9	58.2	62.6	63.8
Mar	60.6	69.1	67.7	86.7	44.7	56.7	66.0	73.2	34.1	30.6	60.9	58.0	62.1	63.8
Apr	60.6	69.1	68.4	86.4	44.7	56.8	66.4	73.3	33.9	29.7	60.8	58.4	61.2	63.2
May	60.6	69.2	69.2	86.2	45.0	56.6	66.7	73.3	33.4	30.2	60.8	58.5	61.5	63.4
June	60.7	69.1	69.0	86.1	45.1	56.7	66.6	73.6	33.6	30.9	60.9	58.2	62.2	63.6
July	60.7	69.2	68.6	86.2	45.5	56.6	66.6	73.0	34.1	31.5	60.8	59.0	62.0	63.4
Aug	60.9	69.2	67.4	86.3	45.4	57.0	66.1	74.0	34.0	31.1	61.0	58.9	62.2	63.9
Sept	61.0	69.3	68.5	86.4	45.2	57.2	67.2	74.0	34.2	30.9	61.2	59.0	62.6	64.4
Oct	61.0	69.3	68.5	86.5	45.2	57.3	68.0	74.2	34.1	31.3	61.2	59.0	63.5	64.5
Nov	61.0	69.4	68.1	86.7	45.3	57.0	66.1	74.1	34.1	31.6	61.2	58.8	63.0	64.6
Dec	61.0	69.3	68.0	86.6	45.4	57.3	66.5	74.4	34.1	31.2	61.2	59.3	62.0	64.3
2020: Jan	61.2	69.5	70.0	86.6	45.4	57.3	66.1	74.7	34.0	31.7	61.4	58.9	61.9	64.9
Feb	61.1	69.3	69.6	86.5	45.3	57.4	67.0	74.7	34.0	32.4	61.3	59.4	62.8	65.1
Mar	60.0	68.1	65.2	85.9	44.3	56.3	63.2	73.6	33.5	30.5	60.2	57.8	61.1	63.0
Apr	51.3	59.6	50.0	76.0	39.2	47.6	45.9	63.5	28.3	21.0	51.8	48.8	51.9	51.3
May	52.8	61.0	52.1	77.9	39.8	48.9	49.3	65.0	28.9	23.7	53.4	49.6	51.7	52.8
June	54.6	62.7	54.8	79.5	41.0	51.1	52.7	67.7	30.2	24.8	55.4	50.8	52.9	56.0
July	55.1	63.1	56.9	79.8	41.3	51.6	53.9	67.9	31.0	25.6	55.7	51.5	55.8	56.3
Aug	56.5	64.5	60.7	81.6	41.6	52.7	56.4	69.2	31.9	28.4	57.3	52.5	57.0	58.4
Sept	56.6	64.7	62.4	81.5	42.1	52.4	58.4	68.7	31.2	30.5	57.3	52.5	57.4	58.2
Oct	57.4	65.4	64.8	82.2	42.4	53.4	61.8	70.0	31.7	31.1	58.1	53.7	58.1	59.9
Nov	57.3	65.1	64.6	81.9	42.0	53.6	62.1	70.2	31.7	30.9	57.8	54.1	58.6	59.9

[1] Civilian employment as percent of civilian noninstitutional population in group specified.

[2] See footnote 1, Table B–23.

Note: Data relate to persons 16 years of age and over, except as noted.

See footnote 5 and Note, Table B–22.

Source: Department of Labor (Bureau of Labor Statistics).

TABLE B–27. Civilian unemployment rate, 1975–2020

[Percent [1]; monthly data seasonally adjusted]

Year or month	All civilian workers	By sex and age			By race or ethnicity [2]				U-6 measure of labor underutilization [3]	By educational attainment (25 years & over)			
		Men 20 years and over	Women 20 years and over	Both sexes 16–19	White	Black or African American	Asian	Hispanic or Latino ethnicity		Less than a high school diploma	High school graduates, no college	Some college or associate degree	Bachelor's degree and higher [4]
1975	8.5	6.8	8.0	19.9	7.8	14.8	....	12.2	....	....	....	....	....
1976	7.7	5.9	7.4	19.0	7.0	14.0	....	11.5	....	....	....	....	....
1977	7.1	5.2	7.0	17.8	6.2	14.0	....	10.1	....	....	....	....	....
1978	6.1	4.3	6.0	16.4	5.2	12.8	....	9.1	....	....	....	....	....
1979	5.8	4.2	5.7	16.1	5.1	12.3	....	8.3	....	....	....	....	....
1980	7.1	5.9	6.4	17.8	6.3	14.3	....	10.1	....	....	....	....	....
1981	7.6	6.3	6.8	19.6	6.7	15.6	....	10.4	....	....	....	....	....
1982	9.7	8.8	8.3	23.2	8.6	18.9	....	13.8	....	....	....	....	....
1983	9.6	8.9	8.1	22.4	8.4	19.5	....	13.7	....	....	....	....	....
1984	7.5	6.6	6.8	18.9	6.5	15.9	....	10.7	....	....	....	....	....
1985	7.2	6.2	6.6	18.6	6.2	15.1	....	10.5	....	....	....	....	....
1986	7.0	6.1	6.2	18.3	6.0	14.5	....	10.6	....	....	....	....	....
1987	6.2	5.4	5.4	16.9	5.3	13.0	....	8.8	....	....	....	....	....
1988	5.5	4.8	4.9	15.3	4.7	11.7	....	8.2	....	....	....	....	....
1989	5.3	4.5	4.7	15.0	4.5	11.4	....	8.0	....	....	....	....	....
1990	5.6	5.0	4.9	15.5	4.8	11.4	....	8.2	....	....	....	....	....
1991	6.8	6.4	5.7	18.7	6.1	12.5	....	10.0	....	....	....	....	....
1992	7.5	7.1	6.3	20.1	6.6	14.2	....	11.6	....	11.5	6.8	5.6	3.2
1993	6.9	6.4	5.9	19.0	6.1	13.0	....	10.8	....	10.8	6.3	5.2	2.9
1994	6.1	5.4	5.4	17.6	5.3	11.5	....	9.9	10.9	9.8	5.4	4.5	2.6
1995	5.6	4.8	4.9	17.3	4.9	10.4	....	9.3	10.1	9.0	4.8	4.0	2.4
1996	5.4	4.6	4.8	16.7	4.7	10.5	....	8.9	9.7	8.7	4.7	3.7	2.2
1997	4.9	4.2	4.4	16.0	4.2	10.0	....	7.7	8.9	8.1	4.3	3.3	2.0
1998	4.5	3.7	4.1	14.6	3.9	8.9	....	7.2	8.0	7.1	4.0	3.0	1.8
1999	4.2	3.5	3.8	13.9	3.7	8.0	....	6.4	7.4	6.7	3.5	2.8	1.8
2000	4.0	3.3	3.6	13.1	3.5	7.6	3.6	5.7	7.0	6.3	3.4	2.7	1.7
2001	4.7	4.2	4.1	14.7	4.2	8.6	4.5	6.6	8.1	7.2	4.2	3.3	2.3
2002	5.8	5.3	5.1	16.5	5.1	10.2	5.9	7.5	9.6	8.4	5.3	4.5	2.9
2003	6.0	5.6	5.1	17.5	5.2	10.8	6.0	7.7	10.1	8.8	5.5	4.8	3.1
2004	5.5	5.0	4.9	17.0	4.8	10.4	4.4	7.0	9.6	8.5	5.0	4.2	2.7
2005	5.1	4.4	4.6	16.6	4.4	10.0	4.0	6.0	8.9	7.6	4.7	3.9	2.3
2006	4.6	4.0	4.1	15.4	4.0	8.9	3.0	5.2	8.2	6.8	4.3	3.6	2.0
2007	4.6	4.1	4.0	15.7	4.1	8.3	3.2	5.6	8.3	7.1	4.4	3.6	2.0
2008	5.8	5.4	4.9	18.7	5.2	10.1	4.0	7.6	10.5	9.0	5.7	4.6	2.6
2009	9.3	9.6	7.5	24.3	8.5	14.8	7.3	12.1	16.2	14.6	9.7	8.0	4.6
2010	9.6	9.8	8.0	25.9	8.7	16.0	7.5	12.5	16.7	14.9	10.3	8.4	4.7
2011	8.9	8.7	7.9	24.4	7.9	15.8	7.0	11.5	15.9	14.1	9.4	8.0	4.3
2012	8.1	7.5	7.3	24.0	7.2	13.8	5.9	10.3	14.7	12.4	8.3	7.1	4.0
2013	7.4	7.0	6.5	22.9	6.5	13.1	5.2	9.1	13.8	11.0	7.5	6.4	3.7
2014	6.2	5.7	5.6	19.6	5.3	11.3	5.0	7.4	12.0	9.0	6.0	5.4	3.2
2015	5.3	4.9	4.8	16.9	4.6	9.6	3.8	6.6	10.4	8.0	5.4	4.5	2.6
2016	4.9	4.5	4.4	15.7	4.3	8.4	3.6	5.8	9.6	7.4	5.2	4.1	2.5
2017	4.4	4.0	4.0	14.0	3.8	7.5	3.4	5.1	8.5	6.5	4.6	3.8	2.3
2018	3.9	3.6	3.5	12.9	3.5	6.5	3.0	4.7	7.7	5.6	4.1	3.3	2.1
2019	3.7	3.4	3.3	12.7	3.3	6.1	2.7	4.3	7.2	5.4	3.7	3.0	2.1
2019: Jan	4.0	3.7	3.6	12.9	3.5	6.8	3.1	4.8	8.0	5.7	3.7	3.4	2.4
Feb	3.8	3.5	3.4	13.3	3.3	6.9	3.1	4.3	7.2	5.3	3.7	3.1	2.2
Mar	3.8	3.6	3.3	12.7	3.4	6.6	3.1	4.7	7.4	5.8	3.7	3.4	2.0
Apr	3.6	3.4	3.1	12.9	3.1	6.6	2.2	4.2	7.3	5.3	3.4	3.1	2.1
May	3.6	3.4	3.3	12.6	3.3	6.2	2.5	4.2	7.2	5.4	3.6	2.8	2.1
June	3.7	3.3	3.3	12.7	3.3	6.0	2.1	4.3	7.2	5.3	3.9	3.0	2.1
July	3.7	3.3	3.3	12.7	3.3	5.9	2.8	4.5	6.9	5.2	3.6	3.2	2.1
Aug	3.7	3.3	3.3	12.5	3.4	5.4	2.8	4.2	7.2	5.4	3.6	3.0	2.1
Sept	3.5	3.2	3.1	12.5	3.2	5.5	2.5	3.9	6.9	4.8	3.6	2.9	2.0
Oct	3.6	3.2	3.2	12.3	3.2	5.5	2.8	4.1	6.9	5.5	3.7	2.8	2.1
Nov	3.5	3.2	3.2	12.0	3.2	5.6	2.6	4.2	6.8	5.3	3.7	2.9	2.0
Dec	3.5	3.1	3.2	12.6	3.2	5.9	2.5	4.2	6.7	5.2	3.7	2.7	1.9
2020: Jan	3.6	3.3	3.2	12.2	3.1	6.0	3.0	4.3	6.9	5.5	3.8	2.8	2.0
Feb	3.5	3.3	3.1	11.0	3.1	5.8	2.5	4.4	7.0	5.7	3.6	3.0	1.9
Mar	4.4	4.0	4.0	14.3	4.0	6.7	4.1	6.0	8.7	6.8	4.4	3.7	2.5
Apr	14.7	13.0	15.5	31.9	14.2	16.7	14.5	18.9	22.8	21.2	17.3	15.0	8.4
May	13.3	11.6	13.9	29.9	12.4	16.8	15.0	17.6	21.2	19.9	15.3	13.3	7.4
June	11.1	10.2	11.2	23.2	10.1	15.4	13.8	14.5	18.0	16.6	12.1	10.9	6.9
July	10.2	9.4	10.5	19.3	9.2	14.6	12.0	12.9	16.5	15.4	10.8	10.0	6.7
Aug	8.4	8.0	8.4	16.1	7.3	13.0	10.7	10.5	14.2	12.6	9.8	8.0	5.3
Sept	7.9	7.4	7.7	15.9	7.0	12.1	8.9	10.3	12.8	10.6	9.0	8.1	4.8
Oct	6.9	6.7	6.5	13.9	6.0	10.8	7.6	8.8	12.1	9.8	8.1	6.5	4.2
Nov	6.7	6.7	6.1	14.0	5.9	10.3	6.7	8.4	12.0	9.0	7.7	6.3	4.2

[1] Unemployed as percent of civilian labor force in group specified.
[2] See footnote 1, Table B–23.
[3] Total unemployed, plus all persons marginally attached to the labor force, plus total employed part time for economic reasons, as a percent of the civilian labor force plus all persons marginally attached to the labor force.
[4] Includes persons with bachelor's, master's, professional, and doctoral degrees.

Note: Data relate to persons 16 years of age and over, except as noted.

See Note, Table B–22.

Source: Department of Labor (Bureau of Labor Statistics).

TABLE B–28. Unemployment by duration and reason, 1975–2020

[Thousands of persons, except as noted; monthly data seasonally adjusted [1]]

Year or month	Un-employ-ment	Duration of unemployment						Reason for unemployment					
		Less than 5 weeks	5–14 weeks	15–26 weeks	27 weeks and over	Average (mean) duration (weeks)[2]	Median duration (weeks)	Job losers[3]			Job leavers	Re-entrants	New entrants
								Total	On layoff	Other			
1975	7,929	2,940	2,484	1,303	1,203	14.2	8.4	4,386	1,671	2,714	827	1,892	823
1976	7,406	2,844	2,196	1,018	1,348	15.8	8.2	3,679	1,050	2,628	903	1,928	895
1977	6,991	2,919	2,132	913	1,028	14.3	7.0	3,166	865	2,300	909	1,963	953
1978	6,202	2,865	1,923	766	648	11.9	5.9	2,585	712	1,873	874	1,857	885
1979	6,137	2,950	1,946	706	535	10.8	5.4	2,635	851	1,784	880	1,806	817
1980	7,637	3,295	2,470	1,052	820	11.9	6.5	3,947	1,488	2,459	891	1,927	872
1981	8,273	3,449	2,539	1,122	1,162	13.7	6.9	4,267	1,430	2,837	923	2,102	981
1982	10,678	3,883	3,311	1,708	1,776	15.6	8.7	6,268	2,127	4,141	840	2,384	1,185
1983	10,717	3,570	2,937	1,652	2,559	20.0	10.1	6,258	1,780	4,478	830	2,412	1,216
1984	8,539	3,350	2,451	1,104	1,634	18.2	7.9	4,421	1,171	3,250	823	2,184	1,110
1985	8,312	3,498	2,509	1,025	1,280	15.6	6.8	4,139	1,157	2,982	877	2,256	1,039
1986	8,237	3,448	2,557	1,045	1,187	15.0	6.9	4,033	1,090	2,943	1,015	2,160	1,029
1987	7,425	3,246	2,196	943	1,040	14.5	6.5	3,566	943	2,623	965	1,974	920
1988	6,701	3,084	2,007	801	809	13.5	5.9	3,092	851	2,241	983	1,809	816
1989	6,528	3,174	1,978	730	646	11.9	4.8	2,983	850	2,133	1,024	1,843	677
1990	7,047	3,265	2,257	822	703	12.0	5.3	3,387	1,028	2,359	1,041	1,930	688
1991	8,628	3,480	2,791	1,246	1,111	13.7	6.8	4,694	1,292	3,402	1,004	2,139	792
1992	9,613	3,376	2,830	1,453	1,954	17.7	8.7	5,389	1,260	4,129	1,002	2,285	937
1993	8,940	3,262	2,584	1,297	1,798	18.0	8.3	4,848	1,115	3,733	976	2,198	919
1994	7,996	2,728	2,408	1,237	1,623	18.8	9.2	3,815	977	2,838	791	2,786	604
1995	7,404	2,700	2,342	1,085	1,278	16.6	8.3	3,476	1,030	2,446	824	2,525	579
1996	7,236	2,633	2,287	1,053	1,262	16.7	8.3	3,370	1,021	2,349	774	2,512	580
1997	6,739	2,538	2,138	995	1,067	15.8	8.0	3,037	931	2,106	795	2,338	569
1998	6,210	2,622	1,950	763	875	14.5	6.7	2,822	866	1,957	734	2,132	520
1999	5,880	2,568	1,832	755	725	13.4	6.4	2,622	848	1,774	783	2,005	469
2000	5,692	2,558	1,815	669	649	12.6	5.9	2,517	852	1,664	780	1,961	434
2001	6,801	2,853	2,196	951	801	13.1	6.8	3,476	1,067	2,409	835	2,031	459
2002	8,378	2,893	2,580	1,369	1,535	16.6	9.1	4,607	1,124	3,483	866	2,368	536
2003	8,774	2,785	2,612	1,442	1,936	19.2	10.1	4,838	1,121	3,717	818	2,477	641
2004	8,149	2,696	2,382	1,293	1,779	19.6	9.8	4,197	998	3,199	858	2,408	686
2005	7,591	2,667	2,304	1,130	1,490	18.4	8.9	3,667	933	2,734	872	2,386	666
2006	7,001	2,614	2,121	1,031	1,235	16.8	8.3	3,321	921	2,400	827	2,237	616
2007	7,078	2,542	2,232	1,061	1,243	16.8	8.5	3,515	976	2,539	793	2,142	627
2008	8,924	2,932	2,804	1,427	1,761	17.9	9.4	4,789	1,176	3,614	896	2,472	766
2009	14,265	3,165	3,828	2,775	4,496	24.4	15.1	9,160	1,630	7,530	882	3,187	1,035
2010	14,825	2,771	3,267	2,371	6,415	33.0	21.4	9,250	1,431	7,819	889	3,466	1,220
2011	13,747	2,677	2,993	2,061	6,016	39.3	21.4	8,106	1,230	6,876	956	3,401	1,284
2012	12,506	2,644	2,866	1,859	5,136	39.4	19.3	6,877	1,183	5,694	967	3,345	1,316
2013	11,460	2,584	2,759	1,807	4,310	36.5	17.0	6,073	1,136	4,937	932	3,207	1,247
2014	9,617	2,471	2,432	1,497	3,218	33.7	14.0	4,878	1,007	3,871	824	2,829	1,086
2015	8,296	2,399	2,302	1,267	2,328	29.2	11.6	4,063	974	3,089	819	2,535	879
2016	7,751	2,362	2,226	1,158	2,005	27.5	10.6	3,740	966	2,774	858	2,330	823
2017	6,982	2,270	2,008	1,017	1,687	25.0	10.0	3,434	956	2,479	778	2,079	690
2018	6,314	2,170	1,876	917	1,350	22.7	9.3	2,990	852	2,138	794	1,928	602
2019	6,001	2,086	1,789	860	1,266	21.6	9.1	2,786	823	1,963	814	1,810	591
2019: Jan	6,516	2,319	1,999	898	1,259	20.6	9.0	3,060	940	2,120	816	1,944	607
Feb	6,181	2,169	1,809	928	1,279	22.0	9.4	2,863	828	2,036	841	1,902	619
Mar	6,194	2,116	1,812	936	1,305	22.2	9.5	2,826	866	1,959	780	2,002	605
Apr	5,850	1,906	1,835	860	1,227	22.8	9.3	2,660	722	1,938	728	1,899	535
May	5,938	2,158	1,572	822	1,298	24.1	9.1	2,674	865	1,810	809	1,850	602
June	5,985	1,949	1,832	776	1,413	22.1	9.4	2,744	805	1,939	889	1,850	537
July	6,027	2,222	1,795	909	1,170	19.7	9.0	2,796	828	1,968	832	1,794	597
Aug	5,999	2,218	1,746	831	1,251	22.1	9.0	2,864	812	2,052	784	1,785	577
Sept	5,753	1,869	1,778	806	1,318	21.7	9.4	2,575	729	1,846	840	1,669	673
Oct	5,857	1,978	1,747	884	1,259	21.6	9.2	2,691	772	1,919	846	1,698	622
Nov	5,811	2,026	1,753	865	1,219	20.2	9.2	2,804	768	2,036	776	1,663	581
Dec	5,753	2,065	1,730	812	1,186	20.8	9.0	2,686	807	1,880	829	1,655	551
2020: Jan	5,892	2,059	1,755	887	1,166	21.9	9.3	2,665	742	1,923	836	1,838	557
Feb	5,787	2,013	1,803	825	1,102	20.9	9.1	2,723	801	1,922	777	1,803	505
Mar	7,140	3,542	1,794	808	1,164	17.1	7.0	3,946	1,848	2,099	727	1,778	509
Apr	23,078	14,283	7,004	833	939	6.1	2.0	20,626	18,063	2,563	570	1,477	389
May	20,985	3,875	14,814	1,078	1,164	9.9	7.7	18,291	15,343	2,948	554	1,645	536
June	17,750	2,838	11,496	1,903	1,391	15.7	13.6	14,272	10,565	3,707	565	2,356	563
July	16,338	3,202	5,169	6,484	1,501	17.9	15.0	12,924	9,225	3,699	571	2,358	513
Aug	13,550	2,281	3,134	6,517	1,624	20.2	16.7	10,307	6,160	4,147	589	2,095	554
Sept	12,580	2,552	2,732	4,918	2,405	20.7	17.8	9,135	4,637	4,498	801	2,146	537
Oct	11,061	2,500	2,275	2,617	3,556	21.2	19.3	7,712	3,205	4,507	769	2,009	528
Nov	10,735	2,467	2,413	1,857	3,941	23.2	18.8	7,485	2,764	4,721	721	1,924	560

[1] Because of independent seasonal adjustment of the various series, detail will not sum to totals.
[2] Beginning with 2011, includes unemployment durations of up to 5 years; prior data are for up to 2 years.
[3] Beginning with 1994, job losers and persons who completed temporary jobs.

Note: Data relate to persons 16 years of age and over.

See Note, Table B–22.

Source: Department of Labor (Bureau of Labor Statistics).

[Thousands of jobs; monthly data seasonally adjusted]

Year or month	Total non-agricultural employment	Private industries										
		Total private	Goods-producing industries						Private service-providing industries		
			Total	Mining and logging	Construction	Manufacturing			Total	Trade, transportation, and utilities [1]	
						Total	Durable goods	Non-durable goods		Total	Retail trade
1975	77,069	62,250	21,318	802	3,608	16,909	10,266	6,643	40,932	15,583	8,604
1976	79,502	64,501	22,025	832	3,662	17,531	10,640	6,891	42,476	16,105	8,970
1977	82,593	67,334	22,972	865	3,940	18,167	11,132	7,035	44,362	16,741	9,363
1978	86,826	71,014	24,156	902	4,322	18,932	11,770	7,162	46,858	17,633	9,882
1979	89,933	73,865	24,997	1,008	4,562	19,426	12,220	7,206	48,869	18,276	10,185
1980	90,533	74,158	24,263	1,077	4,454	18,733	11,679	7,054	49,895	18,387	10,249
1981	91,297	75,117	24,118	1,180	4,304	18,634	11,611	7,023	50,999	18,577	10,369
1982	89,689	73,706	22,550	1,163	4,024	17,363	10,610	6,753	51,156	18,430	10,377
1983	90,295	74,284	22,110	997	4,065	17,048	10,326	6,722	52,174	18,642	10,640
1984	94,548	78,389	23,435	1,014	4,501	17,920	11,050	6,870	54,954	19,624	11,227
1985	97,532	81,000	23,585	974	4,793	17,819	11,034	6,784	57,415	20,350	11,738
1986	99,500	82,661	23,318	829	4,937	17,552	10,795	6,757	59,343	20,765	12,082
1987	102,116	84,960	23,470	771	5,090	17,609	10,767	6,842	61,490	21,271	12,422
1988	105,378	87,838	23,909	770	5,233	17,906	10,969	6,938	63,929	21,942	12,812
1989	108,051	90,124	24,045	750	5,309	17,985	11,004	6,981	66,079	22,477	13,112
1990	109,526	91,112	23,723	765	5,263	17,695	10,737	6,958	67,389	22,633	13,186
1991	108,425	89,879	22,588	739	4,780	17,068	10,220	6,848	67,291	22,247	12,900
1992	108,799	90,012	22,095	689	4,608	16,799	9,946	6,853	67,918	22,091	12,831
1993	110,931	91,942	22,219	666	4,779	16,774	9,901	6,872	69,723	22,343	13,024
1994	114,393	95,118	22,774	659	5,095	17,020	10,132	6,889	72,344	23,090	13,494
1995	117,400	97,968	23,156	641	5,274	17,241	10,373	6,868	74,812	23,793	13,900
1996	119,828	100,289	23,409	637	5,536	17,237	10,486	6,751	76,880	24,197	14,146
1997	122,941	103,278	23,886	654	5,813	17,419	10,705	6,714	79,392	24,656	14,393
1998	126,146	106,237	24,354	645	6,149	17,560	10,911	6,649	81,883	25,139	14,613
1999	129,228	108,921	24,465	598	6,545	17,322	10,831	6,491	84,456	25,722	14,974
2000	132,011	111,221	24,649	599	6,787	17,263	10,877	6,386	86,572	26,174	15,284
2001	132,073	110,955	23,873	606	6,826	16,441	10,336	6,105	87,082	25,931	15,242
2002	130,634	109,121	22,557	583	6,716	15,259	9,485	5,774	86,564	25,442	15,029
2003	130,331	108,748	21,816	572	6,735	14,509	8,964	5,546	86,931	25,228	14,922
2004	131,769	110,148	21,882	591	6,976	14,315	8,925	5,390	88,266	25,470	15,063
2005	134,034	112,230	22,190	628	7,336	14,227	8,956	5,271	90,039	25,892	15,285
2006	136,435	114,462	22,530	684	7,691	14,155	8,981	5,174	91,931	26,206	15,359
2007	137,981	115,763	22,233	724	7,630	13,879	8,808	5,071	93,530	26,556	15,526
2008	137,224	114,714	21,335	767	7,162	13,406	8,463	4,943	93,380	26,219	15,289
2009	131,296	108,741	18,558	694	6,016	11,847	7,284	4,564	90,184	24,834	14,528
2010	130,345	107,855	17,751	705	5,518	11,528	7,064	4,464	90,104	24,565	14,446
2011	131,914	109,828	18,047	788	5,533	11,726	7,273	4,453	91,781	24,990	14,674
2012	134,157	112,237	18,420	848	5,646	11,927	7,470	4,457	93,817	25,399	14,847
2013	136,364	114,511	18,738	863	5,856	12,020	7,548	4,472	95,773	25,783	15,085
2014	138,940	117,058	19,226	891	6,151	12,185	7,674	4,512	97,832	26,303	15,363
2015	141,825	119,796	19,610	813	6,461	12,336	7,765	4,571	100,186	26,606	15,611
2016	144,336	122,112	19,750	668	6,728	12,354	7,714	4,640	102,362	27,179	15,832
2017	146,608	124,258	20,084	676	6,969	12,439	7,741	4,699	104,174	27,393	15,846
2018	148,908	126,454	20,704	727	7,288	12,688	7,946	4,742	105,750	27,607	15,786
2019	150,939	128,346	21,067	735	7,492	12,840	8,059	4,781	107,279	27,715	15,644
2019: Jan	150,134	127,628	21,023	746	7,452	12,825	8,059	4,766	106,605	27,711	15,697
Feb	150,135	127,622	20,994	741	7,423	12,830	8,062	4,768	106,628	27,688	15,667
Mar	150,282	127,754	21,011	741	7,443	12,827	8,056	4,771	106,743	27,665	15,643
Apr	150,492	127,939	21,039	741	7,469	12,829	8,056	4,773	106,900	27,671	15,631
May	150,577	128,026	21,050	743	7,478	12,829	8,056	4,773	106,976	27,667	15,619
June	150,759	128,206	21,076	741	7,497	12,838	8,064	4,774	107,130	27,686	15,613
July	150,953	128,366	21,085	736	7,504	12,845	8,067	4,778	107,281	27,692	15,614
Aug	151,160	128,523	21,087	731	7,508	12,848	8,066	4,782	107,436	27,688	15,614
Sept	151,368	128,718	21,106	731	7,524	12,851	8,066	4,785	107,612	27,712	15,623
Oct	151,553	128,908	21,086	735	7,541	12,810	8,019	4,791	107,822	27,750	15,645
Nov	151,814	129,155	21,131	724	7,539	12,868	8,064	4,804	108,024	27,762	15,631
Dec	151,998	129,319	21,136	715	7,555	12,866	8,064	4,802	108,183	27,809	15,672
2020: Jan	152,212	129,498	21,149	712	7,593	12,844	8,052	4,792	108,349	27,832	15,669
Feb	152,463	129,718	21,205	714	7,639	12,852	8,058	4,794	108,513	27,830	15,672
Mar	151,090	128,362	21,086	706	7,574	12,806	8,031	4,775	107,276	27,723	15,587
Apr	130,303	108,527	18,698	653	6,556	11,489	7,126	4,363	89,829	24,475	13,288
May	133,028	111,763	19,374	633	7,012	11,729	7,269	4,460	92,389	24,858	13,674
June	137,809	116,492	19,859	626	7,171	12,062	7,534	4,528	96,633	25,852	14,532
July	139,570	118,018	19,925	620	7,202	12,103	7,561	4,542	98,093	26,136	14,785
Aug	141,063	119,046	19,978	619	7,226	12,133	7,559	4,574	99,068	26,494	15,046
Sept	141,774	119,976	20,075	621	7,261	12,193	7,604	4,589	99,901	26,588	15,062
Oct [p]	142,384	120,853	20,182	623	7,333	12,226	7,620	4,606	100,671	26,749	15,157
Nov [p]	142,629	121,197	20,237	624	7,360	12,253	7,642	4,611	100,960	26,870	15,122

[1] Includes wholesale trade, transportation and warehousing, and utilities, not shown separately.

Note: Data in Tables B–29 and B–30 are based on reports from employing establishments and relate to full- and part-time wage and salary workers in nonagricultural establishments who received pay for any part of the pay period that includes the 12th of the month. Not comparable with labor force data (Tables B–22 through B–28), which include proprietors, self-employed persons, unpaid family workers, and private household workers; which count persons as

See next page for continuation of table.

Table B–29. Employees on nonagricultural payrolls, by major industry, 1975–2020—*Continued*

[Thousands of jobs; monthly data seasonally adjusted]

| Year or month | Private industries—Continued | | | | | | Government | | | |
| | Private service-providing industries—Continued | | | | | | | | | |
	Information	Financial activities	Professional and business services	Education and health services	Leisure and hospitality	Other services	Total	Federal	State	Local
1975	2,061	4,047	6,056	5,497	5,544	2,144	14,820	2,882	3,179	8,758
1976	2,111	4,155	6,310	5,756	5,794	2,244	15,001	2,863	3,273	8,865
1977	2,185	4,348	6,611	6,052	6,065	2,359	15,258	2,859	3,377	9,023
1978	2,287	4,599	6,997	6,427	6,411	2,505	15,812	2,893	3,474	9,446
1979	2,375	4,843	7,339	6,768	6,631	2,637	16,068	2,894	3,541	9,633
1980	2,361	5,025	7,571	7,077	6,721	2,755	16,375	3,000	3,610	9,765
1981	2,382	5,163	7,809	7,364	6,840	2,865	16,180	2,922	3,640	9,619
1982	2,317	5,209	7,875	7,526	6,874	2,924	15,982	2,884	3,640	9,458
1983	2,253	5,334	8,065	7,781	7,078	3,021	16,011	2,915	3,662	9,434
1984	2,398	5,553	8,493	8,211	7,489	3,186	16,159	2,943	3,734	9,482
1985	2,437	5,815	8,900	8,679	7,869	3,366	16,533	3,014	3,832	9,687
1986	2,445	6,128	9,241	9,086	8,156	3,523	16,838	3,044	3,893	9,901
1987	2,507	6,385	9,639	9,543	8,446	3,699	17,156	3,089	3,967	10,100
1988	2,585	6,500	10,121	10,096	8,778	3,907	17,540	3,124	4,076	10,339
1989	2,622	6,562	10,588	10,652	9,062	4,116	17,927	3,136	4,182	10,609
1990	2,688	6,614	10,881	11,024	9,288	4,261	18,415	3,196	4,305	10,914
1991	2,677	6,561	10,746	11,556	9,256	4,249	18,545	3,110	4,355	11,081
1992	2,641	6,559	11,001	11,948	9,437	4,240	18,787	3,111	4,408	11,267
1993	2,668	6,742	11,527	12,362	9,732	4,350	18,989	3,063	4,488	11,438
1994	2,738	6,910	12,207	12,872	10,100	4,428	19,275	3,018	4,576	11,682
1995	2,843	6,866	12,878	13,360	10,501	4,572	19,432	2,949	4,635	11,849
1996	2,940	7,018	13,497	13,761	10,777	4,690	19,539	2,877	4,606	12,056
1997	3,084	7,255	14,371	14,185	11,018	4,825	19,664	2,806	4,582	12,276
1998	3,218	7,565	15,183	14,570	11,232	4,976	19,909	2,772	4,612	12,525
1999	3,419	7,753	15,994	14,939	11,543	5,087	20,307	2,769	4,709	12,829
2000	3,630	7,783	16,704	15,252	11,862	5,168	20,790	2,865	4,786	13,139
2001	3,629	7,900	16,514	15,814	12,036	5,258	21,118	2,764	4,905	13,449
2002	3,395	7,956	16,016	16,398	11,986	5,372	21,513	2,766	5,029	13,718
2003	3,188	8,078	16,029	16,835	12,173	5,401	21,583	2,761	5,002	13,820
2004	3,118	8,105	16,440	17,230	12,493	5,409	21,621	2,730	4,982	13,909
2005	3,061	8,197	17,003	17,676	12,816	5,395	21,804	2,732	5,032	14,041
2006	3,038	8,367	17,619	18,154	13,110	5,438	21,974	2,732	5,075	14,167
2007	3,032	8,348	17,998	18,676	13,427	5,494	22,218	2,734	5,122	14,362
2008	2,984	8,206	17,792	19,228	13,436	5,515	22,509	2,762	5,177	14,571
2009	2,804	7,838	16,634	19,630	13,077	5,367	22,555	2,832	5,169	14,554
2010	2,707	7,695	16,783	19,975	13,049	5,331	22,490	2,977	5,137	14,376
2011	2,674	7,697	17,389	20,318	13,353	5,360	22,086	2,859	5,078	14,150
2012	2,676	7,784	17,992	20,769	13,768	5,430	21,920	2,820	5,055	14,045
2013	2,706	7,886	18,575	21,086	14,254	5,483	21,853	2,769	5,046	14,037
2014	2,726	7,977	19,124	21,439	14,696	5,567	21,882	2,733	5,050	14,098
2015	2,750	8,123	19,695	22,029	15,160	5,622	22,029	2,757	5,077	14,195
2016	2,794	8,287	20,114	22,639	15,660	5,691	22,224	2,795	5,110	14,319
2017	2,814	8,451	20,508	23,188	16,051	5,770	22,350	2,805	5,165	14,379
2018	2,839	8,590	20,950	23,638	16,295	5,831	22,455	2,800	5,173	14,481
2019	2,860	8,746	21,313	24,177	16,576	5,893	22,594	2,834	5,177	14,583
2019: Jan	2,843	8,676	21,126	23,900	16,496	5,853	22,506	2,811	5,170	14,525
Feb	2,841	8,690	21,164	23,918	16,473	5,854	22,513	2,814	5,175	14,524
Mar	2,851	8,707	21,176	23,981	16,494	5,869	22,528	2,815	5,175	14,538
Apr	2,845	8,721	21,226	24,046	16,507	5,884	22,553	2,823	5,169	14,561
May	2,853	8,727	21,253	24,076	16,519	5,881	22,551	2,826	5,158	14,567
June	2,865	8,732	21,294	24,131	16,526	5,896	22,553	2,829	5,157	14,567
July	2,862	8,753	21,337	24,204	16,528	5,905	22,587	2,831	5,168	14,588
Aug	2,861	8,768	21,377	24,262	16,570	5,910	22,637	2,857	5,184	14,596
Sept	2,866	8,771	21,402	24,323	16,631	5,907	22,650	2,857	5,181	14,612
Oct	2,865	8,792	21,444	24,363	16,701	5,907	22,645	2,844	5,184	14,617
Nov	2,874	8,804	21,481	24,436	16,744	5,923	22,659	2,850	5,181	14,628
Dec	2,883	8,814	21,503	24,465	16,784	5,925	22,679	2,847	5,184	14,648
2020: Jan	2,894	8,823	21,523	24,534	16,808	5,935	22,714	2,855	5,190	14,669
Feb	2,894	8,845	21,550	24,586	16,867	5,941	22,745	2,867	5,199	14,679
Mar	2,888	8,827	21,456	24,408	16,124	5,850	22,728	2,886	5,162	14,680
Apr	2,609	8,566	19,254	21,805	8,549	4,571	21,776	2,893	4,993	13,890
May	2,569	8,585	19,414	22,193	9,954	4,816	21,265	2,885	4,956	13,424
June	2,576	8,605	19,725	22,760	11,933	5,182	21,317	2,883	4,973	13,461
July	2,565	8,620	19,887	22,979	12,566	5,340	21,552	2,912	4,964	13,676
Aug	2,588	8,648	20,071	23,154	12,704	5,409	22,017	3,164	4,988	13,865
Sept	2,641	8,685	20,198	23,214	13,117	5,458	21,798	3,128	4,921	13,749
Oct *p*	2,613	8,715	20,429	23,276	13,387	5,502	21,531	2,986	4,854	13,691
Nov *p*	2,614	8,730	20,489	23,330	13,418	5,509	21,432	2,900	4,854	13,678

Note (cont'd): employed when they are not at work because of industrial disputes, bad weather, etc., even if they are not paid for the time off; which are based on a sample of the working-age population; and which count persons only once—as employed, unemployed, or not in the labor force. In the data shown here, persons who work at more than one job are counted each time they appear on a payroll.

Establishment data for employment, hours, and earnings are classified based on the 2017 North American Industry Classification System (NAICS). For further description and details see *Employment and Earnings*.

Source: Department of Labor (Bureau of Labor Statistics).

TABLE B–30. Hours and earnings in private nonagricultural industries, 1975–2020

[Monthly data seasonally adjusted]

	All employees							Production and nonsupervisory employees [1]						
	Average weekly hours	Average hourly earnings		Average weekly earnings				Average weekly hours	Average hourly earnings		Average weekly earnings			
Year or month				Level		Percent change from year earlier					Level		Percent change from year earlier	
		Current dollars	1982–84 dollars [2]	Current dollars	1982–84 dollars [2]	Current dollars	1982–84 dollars [2]	Current dollars	Current dollars	1982–84 dollars [3]	Current dollars	1982–84 dollars [3]	Current dollars	1982–84 dollars [3]
1975	....	....	....	....	....	....	....	36.0	$4.74	$8.76	$170.45	$315.06	5.4	–3.4
1976	....	....	....	....	....	....	....	36.0	5.06	8.85	182.36	318.81	7.0	1.2
1977	....	....	....	....	....	....	....	35.9	5.44	8.93	195.34	320.76	7.1	.6
1978	....	....	....	....	....	....	....	35.8	5.88	8.96	210.17	320.38	7.6	–.1
1979	....	....	....	....	....	....	....	35.6	6.34	8.67	225.46	308.43	7.3	–3.7
1980	....	....	....	....	....	....	....	35.2	6.84	8.25	240.83	290.51	6.8	–5.8
1981	....	....	....	....	....	....	....	35.2	7.43	8.13	261.29	285.88	8.5	–1.6
1982	....	....	....	....	....	....	....	34.7	7.86	8.11	272.98	281.71	4.5	–1.5
1983	....	....	....	....	....	....	....	34.9	8.20	8.22	286.34	286.91	4.9	1.8
1984	....	....	....	....	....	....	....	35.1	8.49	8.22	298.08	288.56	4.1	.6
1985	....	....	....	....	....	....	....	34.9	8.73	8.17	304.37	284.72	2.1	–1.3
1986	....	....	....	....	....	....	....	34.7	8.92	8.21	309.69	285.17	1.7	.2
1987	....	....	....	....	....	....	....	34.7	9.14	8.12	317.33	282.07	2.5	–1.1
1988	....	....	....	....	....	....	....	34.6	9.44	8.07	326.50	279.06	2.9	–1.1
1989	....	....	....	....	....	....	....	34.5	9.81	8.00	338.42	276.04	3.7	–1.1
1990	....	....	....	....	....	....	....	34.3	10.20	7.91	349.63	271.03	3.3	–1.8
1991	....	....	....	....	....	....	....	34.1	10.51	7.83	358.46	266.91	2.5	–1.5
1992	....	....	....	....	....	....	....	34.2	10.77	7.79	368.17	266.40	2.7	–.2
1993	....	....	....	....	....	....	....	34.3	11.05	7.78	378.74	266.53	2.9	.0
1994	....	....	....	....	....	....	....	34.5	11.34	7.79	391.17	268.66	3.3	.8
1995	....	....	....	....	....	....	....	34.3	11.65	7.78	399.93	266.98	2.2	–.6
1996	....	....	....	....	....	....	....	34.3	12.04	7.81	413.17	268.12	3.3	.4
1997	....	....	....	....	....	....	....	34.5	12.51	7.94	431.75	273.95	4.5	2.2
1998	....	....	....	....	....	....	....	34.5	13.01	8.15	448.36	280.75	3.8	2.5
1999	....	....	....	....	....	....	....	34.3	13.48	8.26	463.09	283.76	3.3	1.1
2000	....	....	....	....	....	....	....	34.3	14.01	8.29	480.90	284.72	3.8	.3
2001	....	....	....	....	....	....	....	33.9	14.54	8.38	493.53	284.46	2.6	–.1
2002	....	....	....	....	....	....	....	33.9	14.96	8.50	506.48	287.94	2.6	1.2
2003	....	....	....	....	....	....	....	33.7	15.36	8.54	517.68	287.92	2.2	.0
2004	....	....	....	....	....	....	....	33.7	15.68	8.50	528.65	286.53	2.1	–.5
2005	....	....	....	....	....	....	....	33.8	16.12	8.44	543.94	284.79	2.9	–.6
2006	....	....	....	....	....	....	....	33.9	16.74	8.49	566.94	287.64	4.2	1.0
2007	34.4	$20.92	$10.09	$719.74	$347.13			33.8	17.41	8.59	589.09	290.53	3.9	1.0
2008	34.3	21.56	10.01	738.96	343.22	2.7	–1.1	33.6	18.06	8.56	607.10	287.65	3.1	–1.0
2009	33.8	22.17	10.33	749.74	349.47	1.5	1.8	33.1	18.60	8.87	615.82	293.77	1.4	2.1
2010	34.1	22.56	10.35	769.57	352.92	2.6	1.0	33.4	19.04	8.90	636.02	297.25	3.3	1.2
2011	34.3	23.03	10.24	790.74	351.54	2.8	–.4	33.6	19.43	8.77	652.72	294.58	2.6	–.9
2012	34.5	23.49	10.23	809.46	352.56	2.4	.3	33.7	19.73	8.72	665.54	294.19	2.0	–.1
2013	34.4	23.95	10.28	824.91	354.10	1.9	.4	33.7	20.13	8.78	677.62	295.49	1.8	.4
2014	34.5	24.46	10.33	844.80	356.85	2.4	.8	33.7	20.60	8.85	694.74	298.47	2.5	1.0
2015	34.5	25.01	10.55	864.07	364.56	2.3	2.2	33.7	21.03	9.07	708.70	305.72	2.0	2.4
2016	34.4	25.64	10.68	881.09	367.11	2.0	.7	33.6	21.53	9.20	723.20	308.96	2.0	1.1
2017	34.4	26.32	10.74	906.19	369.69	2.8	.7	33.7	22.05	9.22	742.48	310.59	2.7	.5
2018	34.5	27.11	10.80	936.37	372.90	3.3	.9	33.8	22.71	9.26	766.99	312.87	3.3	.7
2019	34.4	28.00	10.95	963.09	376.71	2.9	1.0	33.6	23.51	9.43	790.67	317.26	3.1	1.4
2019: Jan	34.5	27.58	10.92	951.51	376.76	3.6	2.0	33.8	23.11	9.39	781.12	317.48	4.0	2.7
Feb	34.4	27.69	10.94	952.54	376.23	3.2	1.7	33.6	23.19	9.40	779.18	315.77	2.9	1.6
Mar	34.5	27.76	10.93	957.72	376.91	3.4	1.5	33.7	23.28	9.40	784.54	316.70	3.5	1.7
Apr	34.4	27.81	10.91	956.66	375.24	3.0	1.0	33.7	23.33	9.38	786.22	316.14	3.2	1.2
May	34.4	27.87	10.92	958.73	375.73	3.0	1.2	33.6	23.42	9.41	786.91	316.23	3.0	1.3
June	34.4	27.96	10.95	961.82	376.59	2.8	1.1	33.6	23.47	9.43	788.59	316.78	2.9	1.4
July	34.3	28.05	10.95	962.12	375.70	2.9	1.0	33.5	23.54	9.43	788.59	315.88	2.7	1.0
Aug	34.4	28.16	10.99	968.70	377.96	3.2	1.4	33.6	23.64	9.46	794.30	317.98	3.1	1.6
Sept	34.4	28.16	10.97	968.70	377.52	2.8	1.1	33.6	23.70	9.48	796.32	318.47	3.4	1.8
Oct	34.4	28.24	10.98	971.46	377.66	2.9	1.1	33.6	23.76	9.47	798.34	318.35	3.4	1.9
Nov	34.3	28.34	10.99	972.06	377.02	3.0	.9	33.5	23.81	9.47	797.64	317.41	2.9	1.0
Dec	34.3	28.37	10.98	973.09	376.52	2.4	.1	33.6	23.84	9.46	801.02	317.83	2.9	.6
2020: Jan	34.3	28.43	10.98	975.15	376.77	2.5	.0	33.6	23.88	9.47	802.37	318.08	2.7	.2
Feb	34.4	28.52	11.01	981.09	378.73	3.0	.7	33.7	23.96	9.49	807.45	319.90	3.6	1.3
Mar	34.1	28.69	11.12	978.33	379.27	2.2	.6	33.4	24.10	9.59	804.94	320.38	2.6	1.2
Apr	34.2	30.03	11.73	1,027.03	401.34	7.4	7.0	33.5	25.12	10.09	841.52	337.96	7.0	6.9
May	34.7	29.70	11.61	1,030.59	402.94	7.5	7.2	34.1	24.97	10.03	851.48	342.12	8.2	8.2
June	34.6	29.32	11.40	1,014.47	394.41	5.5	4.7	34.0	24.73	9.87	840.82	335.73	6.6	6.0
July	34.6	29.35	11.34	1,015.51	392.51	5.5	4.5	34.0	24.64	9.77	837.76	332.20	6.2	5.2
Aug	34.7	29.45	11.34	1,021.92	393.53	5.5	4.1	34.1	24.78	9.78	845.00	333.59	6.4	4.9
Sept	34.8	29.47	11.33	1,025.56	394.13	5.9	4.4	34.1	24.76	9.75	844.32	332.49	6.0	4.4
Oct [p]	34.8	29.49	11.33	1,026.25	394.22	5.6	4.4	34.2	24.80	9.76	848.16	333.91	6.2	4.9
Nov [p]	34.8	29.58	....	1,029.38	....	5.9	....	34.2	24.87	....	850.55	....	6.6	....

[1] Production employees in goods-producing industries and nonsupervisory employees in service-providing industries. These groups account for four-fifths of the total employment on private nonfarm payrolls.

[2] Current dollars divided by the consumer price index for all urban consumers (CPI-U) on a 1982–84=100 base.

[3] Current dollars divided by the consumer price index for urban wage earners and clerical workers (CPI-W) on a 1982–84=100 base.

Note: See Note, Table B–29.

Source: Department of Labor (Bureau of Labor Statistics).

TABLE B–31. Employment cost index, private industry, 2002–2020

Year and month	Total private			Goods-producing			Service-providing[1]			Manufacturing		
	Total compensation	Wages and salaries	Benefits[2]	Total compensation	Wages and salaries	Benefits[2]	Total compensation	Wages and salaries	Benefits[2]	Total compensation	Wages and salaries	Benefits[2]
Indexes on NAICS basis, December 2005=100; not seasonally adjusted												
December:												
2002	90.0	92.2	84.7	89.0	92.6	82.3	90.4	92.1	85.8	88.7	92.8	81.3
2003	93.6	95.1	90.2	92.6	94.9	88.2	94.0	95.2	91.0	92.4	95.1	87.3
2004	97.2	97.6	96.2	96.9	97.2	96.3	97.3	97.7	96.1	96.9	97.4	96.0
2005	100.0	100.0	100.0	100.0	100.0	100.0	100.0	100.0	100.0	100.0	100.0	100.0
2006	103.2	103.2	103.1	102.5	102.9	101.7	103.4	103.3	103.7	101.8	102.3	100.8
2007	106.3	106.6	105.6	105.0	106.0	103.2	106.7	106.8	106.6	103.8	104.9	101.7
2008	108.9	109.4	107.7	107.5	109.0	104.7	109.4	109.6	108.9	105.9	107.7	102.5
2009	110.2	110.8	108.7	108.6	110.0	105.8	110.8	111.1	109.9	107.0	108.9	103.6
2010	112.5	112.8	111.9	111.1	111.6	110.1	113.0	113.1	112.6	110.0	110.7	108.8
2011	115.0	114.6	115.9	113.8	113.5	114.4	115.3	114.9	116.4	113.1	112.7	113.9
2012	117.1	116.6	118.2	115.6	115.4	116.0	117.6	117.0	119.1	114.9	114.8	115.0
2013	119.4	119.0	120.5	117.7	117.6	118.0	120.0	119.4	121.5	117.0	117.2	116.6
2014	122.2	121.6	123.5	120.3	120.1	120.7	122.8	122.1	124.6	119.8	119.8	119.8
2015	124.5	124.2	125.1	123.2	123.2	123.1	124.9	124.5	125.9	122.8	123.0	122.5
2016	127.2	127.1	127.3	125.8	126.2	124.9	127.7	127.4	128.3	125.5	126.2	124.3
2017	130.5	130.6	130.2	128.9	129.3	128.0	131.0	131.0	131.2	128.9	129.3	128.0
2018	134.4	134.7	133.6	131.9	133.0	129.6	135.2	135.2	135.1	131.6	132.9	129.1
2019	138.0	138.7	136.2	135.8	137.5	132.5	138.7	139.1	137.6	135.3	137.1	131.9
2020: Mar	139.4	140.4	136.9	136.7	138.5	133.0	140.2	140.9	138.4	136.2	138.4	132.2
June	140.1	140.9	138.0	137.7	139.6	133.9	140.8	141.3	139.5	137.2	139.3	133.4
Sept	140.7	141.7	138.5	138.2	140.2	134.2	141.5	142.1	140.1	137.6	139.8	133.5
Indexes on NAICS basis, December 2005=100; seasonally adjusted												
2019: Mar	135.5	135.9	134.6	133.0	134.1	130.8	136.2	136.4	136.0	132.8	134.1	130.4
June	136.3	136.8	135.1	134.0	135.2	131.5	137.0	137.2	136.5	133.7	135.1	131.1
Sept	137.3	137.9	135.8	135.1	136.5	132.2	138.0	138.3	137.2	134.6	136.2	131.6
Dec	138.2	138.9	136.5	135.9	137.6	132.6	138.9	139.3	137.9	135.5	137.3	132.0
2020: Mar	139.3	140.3	136.8	136.6	138.4	133.0	140.1	140.9	138.3	136.2	138.3	132.2
June	139.9	140.8	137.8	137.6	139.5	133.8	140.6	141.2	139.2	137.1	139.1	133.3
Sept	140.6	141.5	138.5	138.1	140.1	134.1	141.4	142.0	140.1	137.7	139.9	133.5
Percent change from 12 months earlier, not seasonally adjusted												
December:												
2002	3.1	2.6	4.2	3.5	2.9	4.8	3.0	2.6	4.1	3.7	2.9	5.3
2003	4.0	3.1	6.5	4.0	2.5	7.2	4.0	3.4	6.1	4.2	2.5	7.4
2004	3.8	2.6	6.7	4.6	2.4	9.2	3.5	2.6	5.6	4.9	2.4	10.0
2005	2.9	2.5	4.0	3.2	2.9	3.8	2.8	2.4	4.1	3.2	2.7	4.2
2006	3.2	3.2	3.1	2.5	2.9	1.7	3.4	3.3	3.7	1.8	2.3	.8
2007	3.0	3.3	2.4	2.4	3.0	1.5	3.2	3.4	2.8	2.0	2.5	.9
2008	2.4	2.6	2.0	2.4	2.8	1.5	2.5	2.6	2.2	2.0	2.7	.8
2009	1.2	1.3	.9	1.0	.9	1.1	1.3	1.4	.9	1.0	1.1	1.1
2010	2.1	1.8	2.9	2.3	1.5	4.1	2.0	1.8	2.5	2.8	1.7	5.0
2011	2.2	1.6	3.6	2.4	1.7	3.9	2.0	1.6	3.4	2.8	1.8	4.7
2012	1.8	1.7	2.0	1.6	1.7	1.4	2.0	1.8	2.3	1.6	1.9	1.0
2013	2.0	2.1	1.9	1.8	1.9	1.7	2.0	2.1	2.0	1.8	2.1	1.4
2014	2.3	2.2	2.5	2.2	2.1	2.3	2.3	2.3	2.6	2.4	2.2	2.7
2015	1.9	2.1	1.3	2.4	2.6	2.0	1.7	2.0	1.0	2.5	2.7	2.3
2016	2.2	2.3	1.8	2.1	2.4	1.5	2.2	2.3	1.9	2.2	2.6	1.5
2017	2.6	2.8	2.3	2.5	2.5	2.5	2.6	2.8	2.3	2.7	2.5	3.0
2018	3.0	3.1	2.6	2.3	2.9	1.3	3.2	3.2	3.0	2.1	2.8	.9
2019	2.7	3.0	1.9	3.0	3.4	2.2	2.6	2.9	1.9	2.8	3.2	2.2
2020: Mar	2.8	3.3	1.6	2.7	3.2	1.7	2.9	3.3	1.7	2.5	3.1	1.3
June	2.7	2.9	2.0	2.7	3.2	1.7	2.7	2.9	2.0	2.5	3.0	1.8
Sept	2.4	2.7	2.0	2.3	2.7	1.4	2.5	2.7	2.1	2.3	2.7	1.4
Percent change from 3 months earlier, seasonally adjusted												
2019: Mar	0.7	0.7	0.5	0.8	0.8	0.9	0.6	0.7	0.4	0.8	0.8	0.9
June	.6	.7	.4	.8	.8	.5	.6	.6	.4	.7	.7	.5
Sept	.7	.8	.5	.8	1.0	.5	.7	.8	.5	.7	.8	.4
Dec	.7	.7	.5	.6	.8	.3	.7	.7	.5	.7	.8	.3
2020: Mar	.8	1.0	.2	.5	.6	.3	.9	1.1	.3	.5	.7	.2
June	.4	.4	.7	.7	.8	.6	.4	.2	.7	.7	.6	.8
Sept	.5	.5	.5	.4	.4	.2	.6	.6	.6	.4	.6	.2

[1] On Standard Industrial Classification (SIC) basis, data are for service-producing industries.
[2] Employer costs for employee benefits.

Note: Changes effective with the release of March 2006 data (in April 2006) include changing industry classification to NAICS from SIC and rebasing data to December 2005=100. Historical SIC data are available through December 2005.

Data exclude farm and household workers.

Source: Department of Labor (Bureau of Labor Statistics).

[Index numbers, 2012=100; quarterly data seasonally adjusted]

Year or quarter	Labor productivity (output per hour)		Output [1]		Hours of all persons [2]		Compensation per hour [3]		Real compensation per hour [4]		Unit labor costs		Implicit price deflator [5]	
	Business sector	Nonfarm business sector	Business sector	Nonfarm business sector	Business sector	Nonfarm business sector	Business sector	Nonfarm business sector	Business sector	Nonfarm business sector	Business sector	Nonfarm business sector	Business sector	Nonfarm business sector
1970	42.2	43.5	26.8	26.8	63.6	61.7	12.1	12.2	65.2	65.9	28.6	28.0	24.9	24.5
1971	43.9	45.2	27.9	27.8	63.4	61.5	12.8	12.9	66.2	67.0	29.1	28.6	26.0	25.6
1972	45.4	46.8	29.7	29.7	65.4	63.5	13.6	13.8	68.2	69.1	30.0	29.5	26.9	26.4
1973	46.8	48.2	31.7	31.8	67.9	66.1	14.7	14.8	69.3	70.0	31.4	30.8	28.3	27.3
1974	46.0	47.4	31.2	31.4	68.0	66.2	16.0	16.2	68.2	69.0	34.9	34.2	31.1	30.2
1975	47.6	48.7	31.0	30.9	65.0	63.3	17.8	17.9	69.2	69.9	37.3	36.8	34.1	33.4
1976	49.2	50.4	33.0	33.1	67.2	65.6	19.2	19.3	70.7	71.2	39.0	38.4	35.8	35.2
1977	50.1	51.3	34.9	35.0	69.8	68.2	20.7	20.9	71.7	72.4	41.4	40.8	38.0	37.4
1978	50.7	52.0	37.2	37.3	73.3	71.7	22.5	22.7	72.6	73.4	44.3	43.7	40.6	39.8
1979	50.7	51.9	38.5	38.6	75.9	74.3	24.6	24.9	72.7	73.4	48.6	47.9	44.0	43.1
1980	50.7	51.9	38.1	38.2	75.2	73.7	27.3	27.6	72.4	73.2	53.8	53.1	47.9	47.2
1981	51.8	52.6	39.2	39.1	75.7	74.3	29.8	30.2	72.4	73.3	57.6	57.4	52.3	51.8
1982	51.5	52.2	38.1	37.9	73.9	72.6	32.1	32.4	73.4	74.2	62.2	62.1	55.3	55.0
1983	53.3	54.4	40.1	40.3	75.3	74.0	33.5	33.9	73.5	74.3	62.8	62.3	57.3	56.9
1984	54.8	55.6	43.7	43.7	79.7	78.6	35.0	35.3	73.7	74.4	63.8	63.6	58.9	58.5
1985	56.1	56.6	45.7	45.6	81.5	80.6	36.8	37.1	74.9	75.5	65.5	65.5	60.4	60.2
1986	57.7	58.2	47.4	47.3	82.2	81.2	38.8	39.2	77.8	78.4	67.3	67.3	61.3	61.1
1987	58.0	58.6	49.1	49.0	84.7	83.7	40.3	40.7	78.0	78.7	69.5	69.4	62.4	62.2
1988	58.9	59.5	51.2	51.3	87.0	86.1	42.4	42.8	79.3	79.9	72.1	71.8	64.4	64.1
1989	59.6	60.1	53.2	53.1	89.3	88.4	43.7	44.0	78.2	78.7	73.4	73.2	66.8	66.5
1990	60.7	61.1	54.0	53.9	88.9	88.3	46.5	46.7	79.2	79.6	76.5	76.3	69.0	68.7
1991	61.7	62.1	53.7	53.6	87.0	86.3	48.6	48.9	80.0	80.4	78.8	78.7	71.0	70.9
1992	64.6	64.9	56.0	55.8	86.6	85.9	51.6	51.9	82.9	83.4	79.9	80.0	72.1	72.1
1993	64.7	65.0	57.6	57.5	89.0	88.5	52.4	52.6	82.0	82.3	81.0	80.9	73.8	73.8
1994	65.0	65.4	60.3	60.1	92.8	91.9	52.8	53.1	80.9	81.4	81.1	81.1	75.1	75.1
1995	65.5	66.1	62.2	62.2	94.9	94.1	54.0	54.4	80.9	81.5	82.5	82.2	76.5	76.5
1996	67.1	67.5	65.1	65.0	97.0	96.3	56.0	56.3	81.7	82.1	83.4	83.3	77.7	77.5
1997	68.6	68.8	68.5	68.4	99.9	99.3	58.2	58.5	83.2	83.5	84.9	84.9	78.8	78.9
1998	70.7	71.0	72.0	72.0	101.9	101.4	61.7	61.9	86.9	87.2	87.2	87.2	79.3	79.4
1999	73.5	73.7	76.1	76.1	103.5	103.3	64.7	64.7	89.2	89.3	87.9	87.9	79.8	80.0
2000	76.1	76.1	79.8	79.7	104.9	104.7	69.1	69.3	92.3	92.4	90.9	91.0	81.0	81.3
2001	78.2	78.2	80.4	80.3	102.8	102.7	72.3	72.3	93.8	93.8	92.5	92.4	82.3	82.6
2002	81.5	81.6	81.8	81.7	100.3	100.1	73.9	74.0	94.4	94.5	90.7	90.7	82.9	83.3
2003	84.7	84.7	84.5	84.3	99.7	99.6	76.7	76.7	95.8	95.8	90.5	90.6	83.9	84.2
2004	87.3	87.1	88.1	87.9	100.9	100.9	80.3	80.2	97.7	97.6	92.0	92.1	86.1	86.2
2005	89.2	89.0	91.5	91.3	102.6	102.6	83.2	83.2	97.9	97.8	93.2	93.4	88.7	89.1
2006	90.3	90.0	94.6	94.4	104.8	104.9	86.4	86.3	98.4	98.4	95.7	95.9	91.1	91.6
2007	91.7	91.6	96.8	96.7	105.5	105.6	90.3	90.1	100.0	99.8	98.4	98.4	93.2	93.4
2008	92.7	92.6	95.8	95.7	103.3	103.4	92.8	92.7	99.0	98.9	100.0	100.1	94.7	94.9
2009	96.1	95.9	92.3	92.0	96.0	96.0	93.6	93.5	100.2	100.2	97.4	97.5	94.9	95.4
2010	99.3	99.2	95.2	95.0	95.9	95.9	95.3	95.3	100.4	100.4	95.9	96.1	96.0	96.3
2011	99.2	99.2	97.1	96.9	97.8	97.8	97.3	97.4	99.4	99.5	98.1	98.2	98.2	98.2
2012	100.0	100.0	100.0	100.0	100.0	100.0	100.0	100.0	100.0	100.0	100.0	100.0	100.0	100.0
2013	100.9	100.5	102.4	102.2	101.5	101.7	101.5	101.3	100.0	99.8	100.6	100.8	101.5	101.5
2014	101.6	101.4	105.6	105.4	103.9	104.0	104.1	104.1	100.9	100.9	102.5	102.7	103.1	103.3
2015	103.1	103.0	109.6	109.4	106.3	106.2	107.2	107.4	103.7	103.9	104.0	104.3	103.6	104.0
2016	103.5	103.3	111.6	111.3	107.9	107.8	108.3	108.6	103.5	103.7	104.7	105.1	104.4	105.0
2017	104.8	104.6	114.7	114.4	109.4	109.4	112.2	112.4	104.9	105.1	107.1	107.5	106.3	106.8
2018	106.4	106.1	118.7	118.4	111.5	111.6	116.0	116.2	105.9	106.0	109.0	109.5	108.6	109.2
2019	108.2	107.9	121.6	121.3	112.3	112.4	120.2	120.4	107.8	107.9	111.1	111.5	110.2	110.8
2017: I	104.4	104.2	113.4	113.1	108.7	108.6	110.6	110.8	104.0	104.1	105.9	106.3	105.6	106.2
II	104.4	104.2	114.0	113.7	109.2	109.2	111.3	111.4	104.5	104.7	106.6	107.0	105.9	106.4
III	105.1	104.8	115.0	114.8	109.4	109.5	112.8	112.9	105.4	105.4	107.3	107.7	106.4	107.0
IV	105.3	105.2	116.3	116.1	110.5	110.4	114.1	114.4	105.8	106.0	108.4	108.8	107.1	107.6
2018: I	106.0	105.8	117.6	117.3	110.9	110.9	114.9	115.0	105.6	105.8	108.3	108.8	107.6	108.2
II	106.5	106.1	118.5	118.2	111.3	111.4	115.4	115.4	105.5	105.5	108.3	108.8	108.5	109.1
III	106.5	106.2	119.1	118.9	111.8	111.9	116.7	116.8	106.2	106.3	109.5	110.0	108.9	109.5
IV	106.7	106.4	119.6	119.3	112.1	112.1	117.1	117.3	106.2	106.4	109.8	110.3	109.3	109.9
2019: I	107.7	107.4	120.6	120.4	112.1	112.1	119.6	119.8	108.3	108.4	111.1	111.6	109.4	110.0
II	108.3	107.9	121.0	120.8	111.8	111.9	120.1	120.2	107.9	108.0	111.0	111.4	110.2	110.8
III	108.3	108.0	121.9	121.6	112.6	112.7	120.1	120.2	107.4	107.5	110.9	111.3	110.4	111.1
IV	108.7	108.4	122.7	122.5	113.0	113.0	121.0	121.2	107.6	107.7	111.4	111.8	110.8	111.4
2020: I	108.7	108.3	120.8	120.5	111.2	111.2	123.6	123.9	109.6	109.8	113.8	114.4	111.0	111.7
II	111.2	111.1	107.7	107.4	96.9	96.7	129.2	129.7	115.6	115.9	116.2	116.7	109.8	110.6
III [p]	112.9	112.4	118.0	117.6	104.5	104.6	128.1	128.2	113.1	113.2	113.5	114.0	111.1	111.9

[1] Output refers to real gross domestic product in the sector.
[2] Hours at work of all persons engaged in sector, including hours of employees, proprietors, and unpaid family workers. Estimates based primarily on establishment data.
[3] Wages and salaries of employees plus employers' contributions for social insurance and private benefit plans. Also includes an estimate of wages, salaries, and supplemental payments for the self-employed.
[4] Hourly compensation divided by consumer price index. The trend for 1978-2019 is based on the consumer price index research series (CPI-U-RS). The change for prior years and recent quarters is based on the consumer price index for all urban consumers (CPI-U).
[5] Current dollar output divided by the output index.

Source: Department of Labor (Bureau of Labor Statistics).

TABLE B–33. Changes in productivity and related data, business and nonfarm business sectors, 1970–2020

[Percent change from preceding period; quarterly data at seasonally adjusted annual rates]

Year or quarter	Output per hour of all persons		Output [1]		Hours of all persons [2]		Compensation per hour [3]		Real compensation per hour [4]		Unit labor costs		Implicit price deflator [5]	
	Business sector	Nonfarm business sector	Business sector	Nonfarm business sector	Business sector	Nonfarm business sector	Business sector	Nonfarm business sector	Business sector	Nonfarm business sector	Business sector	Nonfarm business sector	Business sector	Nonfarm business sector
1970	2.0	1.5	0.0	-0.1	-2.0	-1.6	7.5	7.0	1.7	1.2	5.4	5.4	4.3	4.4
1971	4.1	3.9	3.8	3.7	-.3	-.2	6.0	6.1	1.6	1.7	1.9	2.1	4.2	4.3
1972	3.4	3.5	6.5	6.7	3.0	3.1	6.3	6.5	3.0	3.2	2.9	2.9	3.4	3.1
1973	3.0	3.1	6.9	7.3	3.8	4.1	7.9	7.6	1.6	1.3	4.8	4.4	5.2	3.5
1974	-1.7	-1.6	-1.5	-1.5	.2	.1	9.3	9.5	-1.5	-1.4	11.2	11.3	9.8	10.4
1975	3.5	2.8	-1.0	-1.6	-4.3	-4.3	10.7	10.5	1.4	1.3	6.9	7.6	9.7	10.7
1976	3.3	3.5	6.8	7.2	3.3	3.6	8.0	7.8	2.1	1.9	4.5	4.1	5.2	5.4
1977	1.8	1.7	5.7	5.7	3.8	3.9	8.0	8.2	1.4	1.6	6.1	6.4	5.9	6.2
1978	1.2	1.4	6.4	6.7	5.1	5.2	8.4	8.6	1.3	1.5	7.1	7.1	6.9	6.5
1979	.1	-.2	3.6	3.4	3.4	3.6	9.7	9.5	.2	.0	9.5	9.8	8.4	8.4
1980	.0	.0	-.9	-.9	-.9	-.8	10.7	10.8	-.4	-.4	10.7	10.8	8.9	9.5
1981	2.2	1.5	2.9	2.3	.8	.8	9.4	9.6	.0	.2	7.1	8.0	9.2	9.6
1982	-.5	-.8	-2.9	-3.1	-2.4	-2.3	7.5	7.4	1.4	1.2	8.0	8.2	5.7	6.2
1983	3.4	4.1	5.3	6.2	1.8	2.0	4.4	4.5	.1	.2	1.0	.4	3.6	3.5
1984	2.9	2.2	8.9	8.5	5.9	6.1	4.4	4.3	.2	.1	1.5	2.0	2.8	2.8
1985	2.3	1.8	4.7	4.4	2.3	2.6	5.1	4.9	1.6	1.4	2.7	3.1	2.6	3.1
1986	2.8	3.0	3.6	3.8	.8	.8	5.7	5.8	3.8	4.0	2.8	2.7	1.4	1.4
1987	.6	.6	3.6	3.6	3.0	3.0	3.8	3.8	.3	.3	3.2	3.2	1.9	1.9
1988	1.5	1.6	4.3	4.6	2.7	2.9	5.3	5.1	1.6	1.5	3.7	3.4	3.2	3.1
1989	1.2	.9	3.8	3.7	2.6	2.7	3.0	2.9	-1.3	-1.4	1.8	2.0	3.7	3.6
1990	2.0	1.7	1.6	1.5	-.4	-.2	6.3	6.0	1.3	1.0	4.2	4.2	3.3	3.4
1991	1.6	1.6	-.6	-.6	-2.2	-2.2	4.6	4.8	1.0	1.1	3.0	3.1	2.9	3.1
1992	4.7	4.5	4.2	4.1	-.4	-.4	6.1	6.2	3.6	3.6	1.4	1.7	1.6	1.7
1993	.1	.1	2.9	3.1	2.8	3.0	1.5	1.2	-1.0	-1.3	1.4	1.1	2.3	2.3
1994	.6	.7	4.8	4.6	4.2	3.9	.7	1.0	-1.3	-1.1	.1	.3	1.8	1.9
1995	.7	1.1	3.1	3.4	2.3	2.3	2.4	2.5	.0	.1	1.7	1.4	1.8	1.8
1996	2.5	2.1	4.6	4.5	2.1	2.3	3.6	3.5	.9	.8	1.1	1.3	1.6	1.4
1997	2.2	1.9	5.2	5.2	3.0	3.2	4.0	3.9	1.8	1.7	1.8	1.9	1.5	1.7
1998	3.1	3.1	5.2	5.3	2.0	2.2	5.9	5.8	4.5	4.4	2.7	2.6	.6	.7
1999	4.0	3.8	5.7	5.7	1.6	1.8	4.8	4.7	2.7	2.5	.8	.8	.6	.8
2000	3.4	3.3	4.9	4.7	1.4	1.4	6.9	7.0	3.4	3.5	3.4	3.6	1.5	1.6
2001	2.8	2.7	.7	.8	-2.0	-1.9	4.6	4.4	1.7	1.5	1.7	1.6	1.6	1.6
2002	4.3	4.3	1.7	1.7	-2.4	-2.5	2.2	2.3	.6	.7	-1.9	-1.9	.7	.8
2003	4.0	3.8	3.3	3.2	-.6	-.6	3.8	3.7	1.5	1.4	-.2	-.1	1.3	1.1
2004	3.0	2.9	4.3	4.2	1.2	1.3	4.7	4.6	1.9	1.8	1.6	1.6	2.5	2.3
2005	2.2	2.2	3.9	3.9	1.7	1.7	3.6	3.7	.2	.3	1.4	1.4	3.1	3.3
2006	1.1	1.1	3.4	3.4	2.2	2.3	3.9	3.8	.6	.6	2.7	2.7	2.7	2.8
2007	1.6	1.7	2.3	2.4	.6	.7	4.5	4.3	1.6	1.5	2.8	2.6	2.3	2.0
2008	1.1	1.1	-1.0	-1.0	-2.1	-2.1	2.8	2.9	-1.0	-.9	1.6	1.7	1.5	1.6
2009	3.6	3.6	-3.7	-3.9	-7.1	-7.2	.9	.9	1.2	1.3	-2.7	-2.5	.2	.5
2010	3.3	3.4	3.2	3.3	-.1	-.1	1.8	1.9	.1	.2	-1.5	-1.5	1.2	1.0
2011	-.1	.0	1.9	2.0	2.0	2.0	2.1	2.2	-1.0	-.9	2.2	2.2	2.3	1.9
2012	.8	.9	3.0	3.1	2.3	2.3	2.8	2.7	.6	.5	2.0	1.8	1.9	1.9
2013	.9	.5	2.4	2.2	1.5	1.7	1.5	1.3	.0	-.2	.6	.8	1.5	1.5
2014	.7	.9	3.1	3.2	2.4	2.3	2.6	2.8	.9	1.1	1.9	1.9	1.6	1.8
2015	1.5	1.6	3.8	3.7	2.3	2.1	2.9	3.1	2.8	3.0	1.4	1.6	.4	.7
2016	.4	.3	1.9	1.8	1.5	1.5	1.1	1.1	-.2	-.2	.7	.7	.8	1.0
2017	1.3	1.2	2.7	2.8	1.4	1.5	3.6	3.5	1.4	1.3	2.3	2.2	1.7	1.7
2018	1.6	1.4	3.5	3.5	1.9	2.0	3.4	3.4	.9	.9	1.8	1.9	2.2	2.2
2019	1.7	1.7	2.4	2.5	.7	.7	3.6	3.6	1.8	1.8	1.9	1.9	1.5	1.5
2017: I	.6	1.0	2.5	2.4	1.9	1.3	3.3	3.9	.4	1.0	2.7	2.9	2.0	1.5
II	-.2	-.1	1.9	2.1	2.1	2.2	2.4	2.4	2.0	2.0	2.6	2.5	1.0	1.0
III	3.0	2.5	3.6	3.8	.6	1.3	5.7	5.2	3.5	3.0	2.7	2.7	1.9	2.0
IV	.6	1.3	4.6	4.7	4.0	3.3	4.6	5.5	1.5	2.3	4.1	4.1	2.5	2.5
2018: I	2.9	2.3	4.5	4.3	1.6	2.0	2.7	2.2	-.6	-1.0	-.2	.0	2.0	2.1
II	1.7	1.1	3.0	3.0	1.3	1.8	1.7	1.3	-.5	-.9	-.1	.2	3.6	3.6
III	.1	.5	2.3	2.3	2.1	1.8	4.7	5.1	2.5	2.9	4.5	4.5	1.1	1.4
IV	.7	.8	1.5	1.4	.8	.7	1.5	1.8	.3	.5	.9	1.0	1.4	1.4
2019: I	3.6	3.7	3.6	3.8	.0	.1	8.8	8.7	7.9	7.7	5.0	4.8	.4	.4
II	2.2	2.0	1.3	1.2	-.9	-.7	1.7	1.4	-1.3	-1.6	-.5	-.6	3.0	3.0
III	.2	.3	2.9	2.9	2.7	2.6	-.1	-.2	-1.9	-2.0	-.3	-.4	1.1	1.0
IV	1.4	1.6	2.8	2.8	1.4	1.2	3.1	3.3	.7	.9	1.7	1.7	1.2	1.2
2020: I	.0	-.3	-6.0	-6.4	-6.0	-6.1	9.0	9.2	7.7	7.9	9.0	9.6	.8	.8
II	9.6	10.6	-36.8	-36.8	-42.4	-42.9	19.4	20.0	23.7	24.4	8.9	8.5	-4.3	-3.6
III [p]	6.4	4.9	43.7	43.5	35.1	36.8	-3.3	-4.4	-8.1	-9.1	-9.1	-8.9	4.7	4.4

[1] Output refers to real gross domestic product in the sector.
[2] Hours at work of all persons engaged in the sector. See footnote 2, Table B–32.
[3] Wages and salaries of employees plus employers' contributions for social insurance and private benefit plans. Also includes an estimate of wages, salaries, and supplemental payments for the self-employed.
[4] Hourly compensation divided by a consumer price index. See footnote 4, Table B–32.
[5] Current dollar output divided by the output index.

Note: Percent changes are calculated using index numbers to three decimal places and may differ slightly from percent changes based on indexes in Table B–32, which are rounded to one decimal place.

Source: Department of Labor (Bureau of Labor Statistics).

Production and Business Activity

TABLE B–34. Industrial production indexes, major industry divisions, 1975–2020

[2012=100, except as noted; monthly data seasonally adjusted]

Year or month	Total industrial production [1]		Manufacturing					Mining	Utilities
	Index, 2012=100	Percent change from year earlier [2]	Total [1]	Percent change from year earlier [2]	Durable	Nondurable	Other (non-NAICS) [1]		
1975	42.2	−8.9	39.2	−10.6	24.8	62.6	117.4	89.1	50.5
1976	45.5	7.9	42.7	9.0	27.1	68.3	121.1	89.7	52.9
1977	48.9	7.6	46.4	8.6	29.8	73.0	132.7	91.8	55.1
1978	51.6	5.5	49.2	6.1	32.1	75.6	137.3	94.6	56.5
1979	53.2	3.0	50.7	3.1	33.7	76.1	140.2	97.5	57.7
1980	51.8	−2.6	48.9	−3.6	32.2	73.7	145.0	99.3	58.1
1981	52.5	1.3	49.4	1.0	32.5	74.4	148.4	101.8	58.9
1982	49.8	−5.2	46.7	−5.5	29.7	73.3	150.2	96.8	57.0
1983	51.1	2.7	49.0	4.8	31.2	76.7	154.5	91.7	57.4
1984	55.7	8.9	53.7	9.8	35.6	80.2	161.6	97.6	60.8
1985	56.4	1.2	54.6	1.6	36.4	80.7	168.0	95.7	62.3
1986	56.9	1.0	55.8	2.2	37.0	83.0	171.4	88.8	62.9
1987	59.9	5.2	59.0	5.7	39.2	87.4	181.2	89.6	65.9
1988	63.0	5.2	62.1	5.3	42.1	90.4	180.4	91.9	69.9
1989	63.6	.9	62.6	.8	42.6	90.9	177.9	91.0	72.1
1990	64.2	1.0	63.1	.8	42.7	92.4	175.8	92.2	73.5
1991	63.2	−1.5	61.9	−1.9	41.4	92.1	168.6	90.3	75.3
1992	65.1	2.9	64.2	3.7	43.6	94.5	165.1	88.6	75.3
1993	67.2	3.3	66.5	3.6	46.1	95.9	166.3	88.4	77.9
1994	70.8	5.3	70.4	5.9	50.0	99.2	164.9	90.0	79.5
1995	74.0	4.6	74.0	5.1	54.1	100.9	164.8	89.9	82.3
1996	77.4	4.5	77.6	4.9	59.1	101.2	163.3	91.5	84.6
1997	83.0	7.2	84.2	8.4	66.1	105.0	177.1	93.2	84.5
1998	87.8	5.8	89.8	6.7	73.0	106.7	187.6	91.5	86.8
1999	91.7	4.4	94.3	5.1	79.3	107.3	193.0	86.9	89.5
2000	95.2	3.9	98.2	4.1	85.0	107.8	192.5	88.8	92.0
2001	92.3	−3.1	94.6	−3.7	81.6	104.7	180.0	89.0	91.7
2002	92.6	.4	95.1	.5	82.0	106.0	173.9	84.9	94.4
2003	93.8	1.3	96.4	1.3	84.2	106.2	169.0	85.1	96.0
2004	96.4	2.7	99.4	3.1	88.2	107.8	169.7	85.0	97.4
2005	99.6	3.3	103.4	4.1	93.4	110.5	169.2	84.0	99.5
2006	101.8	2.3	106.1	2.6	97.8	111.2	167.2	86.1	99.2
2007	104.4	2.5	109.0	2.8	102.7	112.5	157.7	86.8	102.3
2008	100.8	−3.5	103.8	−4.8	99.2	105.8	143.9	88.0	101.9
2009	89.2	−11.5	89.5	−13.8	80.6	97.7	120.4	83.1	99.0
2010	94.1	5.5	94.7	5.8	89.2	99.8	111.3	87.2	102.8
2011	97.1	3.1	97.5	2.9	94.7	99.9	106.1	92.6	102.4
2012	100.0	3.0	100.0	2.6	100.0	100.0	100.0	100.0	100.0
2013	102.0	2.0	100.9	.9	102.1	100.0	95.0	106.3	102.2
2014	105.2	3.1	102.0	1.1	105.1	99.3	93.8	117.8	103.5
2015	104.1	−1.0	101.5	−.5	103.9	99.6	90.4	113.9	102.7
2016	102.1	−2.0	100.7	−.8	101.7	100.4	88.0	102.6	102.3
2017	104.4	2.3	102.7	2.0	104.0	102.3	87.5	110.1	101.5
2018	108.6	3.9	105.0	2.3	107.5	104.3	78.9	123.8	105.9
2019	109.4	.8	104.8	−.2	108.2	103.5	73.2	132.7	104.8
2019: Jan	110.1	3.6	105.8	2.4	108.9	104.7	75.7	132.1	104.4
Feb	109.6	2.7	105.3	.8	108.5	104.0	76.3	130.3	105.0
Mar	109.7	2.3	105.2	.7	108.5	103.9	75.2	130.1	106.8
Apr	109.0	.7	104.3	−.6	107.6	103.0	74.7	133.4	103.3
May	109.2	1.7	104.4	.3	108.0	102.9	73.5	133.1	105.2
June	109.3	1.0	105.0	.2	108.4	103.6	73.8	133.6	100.9
July	109.1	.4	104.6	−.6	108.4	102.8	73.0	130.7	105.3
Aug	109.9	.3	105.2	−.5	108.9	103.6	72.6	133.7	104.6
Sept	109.5	−.2	104.5	−1.1	107.8	103.3	72.4	133.6	106.1
Oct	109.0	−.8	103.9	−1.6	106.6	103.4	72.2	133.4	106.5
Nov	110.0	−.4	104.9	−.9	108.8	103.2	70.3	132.6	109.7
Dec	109.7	−.8	105.1	−1.2	108.5	104.0	69.1	133.8	103.4
2020: Jan	109.2	−.8	105.0	−.8	107.9	104.3	70.5	135.2	98.6
Feb	109.3	−.2	104.9	−.3	108.1	104.0	71.8	133.0	102.2
Mar	104.5	−4.7	99.6	−5.3	99.7	101.8	66.8	130.7	99.1
Apr	91.3	−16.3	83.9	−19.6	77.8	92.0	56.3	121.8	100.9
May	92.1	−15.7	87.0	−16.6	83.1	93.1	57.2	108.0	100.2
June [p]	97.6	−10.7	93.5	−10.9	93.5	96.0	58.1	110.6	101.5
July [p]	101.7	−6.7	97.4	−6.8	100.1	97.5	57.4	114.9	106.7
Aug [p]	102.5	−6.7	98.8	−6.0	101.1	99.2	59.6	113.5	104.9
Sept [p]	102.1	−6.7	98.9	−5.4	101.2	99.1	61.3	114.9	99.4
Oct [p]	103.2	−5.3	99.9	−3.9	102.1	100.3	60.4	114.2	103.3

[1] Total industry and total manufacturing series include manufacturing as defined in the North American Industry Classification System (NAICS) plus those industries—logging and newspaper, periodical, book, and directory publishing—that have traditionally been considered to be manufacturing and included in the industrial sector.

[2] Percent changes based on unrounded indexes.

Note: Data based on NAICS; see footnote 1.

Source: Board of Governors of the Federal Reserve System.

Table B–35. Capacity utilization rates, 1975–2020

[Percent [1]; monthly data seasonally adjusted]

Year or month	Total industry [2]	Manufacturing				Mining	Utilities	Stage-of-process		
		Total [2]	Durable goods	Nondurable goods	Other (non-NAICS) [2]			Crude	Primary and semi-finished	Finished
1975	75.8	73.7	71.8	76.1	77.3	89.5	85.2	84.0	75.2	73.7
1976	79.8	78.4	76.5	81.2	77.6	89.6	85.7	87.0	80.2	76.9
1977	83.4	82.5	81.1	84.4	83.2	89.5	86.9	89.1	84.6	79.9
1978	85.1	84.4	83.8	85.3	85.1	89.7	87.2	88.7	86.3	82.3
1979	85.0	84.0	84.0	83.9	85.6	91.2	87.2	90.0	85.9	81.7
1980	80.8	78.7	77.5	79.7	86.8	91.3	85.5	89.4	78.8	79.4
1981	79.5	76.9	75.1	78.8	87.5	90.9	84.4	89.3	77.1	77.5
1982	73.6	70.9	66.4	76.4	87.4	84.1	80.0	82.3	70.4	73.1
1983	74.9	73.5	68.8	79.4	88.0	79.8	79.3	79.9	74.5	73.0
1984	80.4	79.4	76.9	82.1	89.5	85.8	81.9	85.8	81.2	77.2
1985	79.2	78.1	75.8	80.5	90.4	84.4	81.7	83.8	79.8	76.6
1986	78.6	78.4	75.4	81.8	88.8	77.6	80.9	79.2	79.7	77.1
1987	81.1	80.9	77.6	84.7	90.5	80.3	83.5	82.8	82.8	78.7
1988	84.2	83.9	81.9	86.2	88.6	84.1	86.8	86.3	85.8	81.6
1989	83.7	83.2	81.7	84.9	85.4	85.1	86.8	86.8	84.6	81.6
1990	82.4	81.5	79.3	84.2	83.7	86.9	86.6	87.9	82.6	80.5
1991	79.9	78.6	75.4	82.3	80.8	85.4	87.8	85.5	80.0	78.2
1992	80.6	79.6	77.1	82.7	80.1	85.2	86.4	85.9	81.5	78.2
1993	81.5	80.5	78.6	82.7	81.4	85.8	88.2	85.8	83.3	78.4
1994	83.5	82.8	81.5	84.6	81.5	86.8	88.3	87.8	86.3	79.2
1995	83.9	83.1	82.1	84.5	82.2	87.6	89.3	89.0	86.4	79.7
1996	83.4	82.1	81.6	83.1	80.6	90.5	90.7	89.1	85.6	79.3
1997	84.1	83.0	82.3	83.8	85.6	91.8	90.1	90.4	86.0	80.3
1998	82.8	81.6	80.7	82.2	86.8	89.3	92.6	87.1	84.2	80.3
1999	81.8	80.5	80.2	80.1	87.2	86.2	94.2	86.1	84.3	78.0
2000	81.5	79.7	79.7	78.9	87.5	90.5	94.3	88.5	84.0	76.9
2001	76.2	73.8	71.6	75.7	82.9	89.8	90.1	85.5	77.4	72.6
2002	74.9	73.0	70.1	75.9	81.6	86.0	87.6	83.2	77.4	70.5
2003	76.0	74.0	71.1	76.8	81.5	87.8	85.7	85.0	78.2	71.3
2004	78.2	76.5	74.2	78.7	82.4	88.2	84.5	86.5	80.2	73.4
2005	80.1	78.5	76.7	80.3	81.9	88.5	85.1	86.7	81.9	75.7
2006	80.6	78.8	77.9	79.8	79.8	90.1	83.7	88.1	81.5	76.4
2007	80.8	78.9	78.8	79.3	76.3	89.4	85.9	88.7	81.2	77.1
2008	77.8	74.7	74.9	74.1	77.3	90.0	84.2	87.5	77.0	73.9
2009	68.5	65.5	61.4	69.8	69.6	80.3	80.6	77.9	65.8	68.1
2010	73.5	70.7	68.8	73.3	66.2	83.9	83.0	83.2	71.8	71.2
2011	76.1	73.5	72.6	75.2	65.4	85.9	81.5	84.5	74.4	73.7
2012	76.9	74.5	75.1	75.0	63.1	87.3	78.4	85.5	74.7	74.8
2013	77.2	74.4	74.9	74.9	62.2	87.2	79.9	86.0	75.5	73.8
2014	78.6	75.2	76.2	75.1	63.7	90.5	80.8	88.4	76.7	74.6
2015	76.9	75.3	75.3	76.3	63.8	84.2	79.9	82.7	76.3	75.1
2016	75.0	74.2	73.1	76.2	64.2	77.6	78.8	78.4	75.2	73.6
2017	76.5	75.1	74.2	76.8	66.3	84.3	77.0	83.7	75.7	74.2
2018	78.7	76.6	76.1	78.0	62.3	90.2	79.3	88.8	77.5	75.4
2019	77.8	75.6	75.6	76.6	59.1	90.4	76.9	88.6	75.9	74.7
2019: Jan	79.0	76.7	76.6	77.9	60.8	92.4	77.3	90.6	77.2	75.4
Feb	78.5	76.3	76.2	77.4	61.4	90.7	77.6	89.1	76.7	75.3
Mar	78.4	76.2	76.1	77.2	60.5	90.1	78.7	88.2	76.7	75.5
Apr	77.8	75.4	75.4	76.4	60.2	91.9	75.9	89.6	75.7	74.5
May	77.8	75.4	75.5	76.2	59.3	91.3	77.2	89.1	76.0	74.4
June	77.7	75.7	75.7	76.7	59.6	91.3	73.9	88.7	75.2	75.2
July	77.4	75.3	75.6	76.0	59.0	88.9	76.9	86.8	75.6	74.8
Aug	77.8	75.7	75.9	76.5	58.7	90.6	76.3	88.6	75.8	74.9
Sept	77.4	75.1	75.0	76.2	58.5	90.2	77.2	88.4	75.7	74.1
Oct	77.0	74.6	74.1	76.1	58.4	89.7	77.3	88.3	75.1	73.6
Nov	77.6	75.2	75.5	75.9	56.9	88.8	79.5	87.7	75.8	74.7
Dec	77.2	75.3	75.2	76.4	56.0	89.2	74.8	87.9	74.9	74.6
2020: Jan	76.9	75.2	74.7	76.7	57.4	90.5	71.1	88.7	74.6	73.8
Feb	76.9	75.2	74.9	76.4	58.5	89.1	73.5	87.6	75.0	74.0
Mar	73.6	71.4	69.1	74.8	54.6	87.7	71.1	86.3	71.3	70.1
Apr	64.2	60.1	53.9	67.6	46.2	81.9	72.2	80.4	62.4	58.8
May	64.8	62.4	57.6	68.5	47.1	72.8	71.5	73.8	63.7	61.7
June [p]	68.7	67.0	64.7	70.6	48.0	74.7	72.3	75.5	67.0	67.3
July [p]	71.7	69.9	69.4	71.7	47.6	77.8	75.8	77.8	69.7	70.8
Aug [p]	72.2	70.9	70.1	73.0	49.6	77.1	74.3	77.9	70.1	71.7
Sept [p]	72.0	71.0	70.1	73.0	51.3	78.2	70.2	78.5	69.7	71.3
Oct [p]	72.8	71.7	70.8	73.9	50.7	77.9	72.7	78.7	71.0	71.7

[1] Output as percent of capacity.
[2] See footnote 1 and Note, Table B–34.

Source: Board of Governors of the Federal Reserve System.

TABLE B–36. New private housing units started, authorized, and completed and houses sold, 1975–2020

[Thousands; monthly data at seasonally adjusted annual rates]

Year or month	New housing units started Total	Type of structure 1 unit	Type of structure 2 to 4 units[2]	Type of structure 5 units or more	New housing units authorized[1] Total	Type of structure 1 unit	Type of structure 2 to 4 units	Type of structure 5 units or more	New housing units completed	New houses sold
1975	1,160.4	892.2	64.0	204.3	939.2	675.5	63.8	199.8	1,317.2	549
1976	1,537.5	1,162.4	85.8	289.2	1,296.2	893.6	93.1	309.5	1,377.2	646
1977	1,987.1	1,450.9	121.7	414.4	1,690.0	1,126.1	121.3	442.7	1,657.1	819
1978	2,020.3	1,433.3	125.1	462.0	1,800.5	1,182.6	130.6	487.3	1,867.5	817
1979	1,745.1	1,194.1	122.0	429.0	1,551.8	981.5	125.4	444.8	1,870.8	709
1980	1,292.2	852.2	109.5	330.5	1,190.6	710.4	114.5	365.7	1,501.6	545
1981	1,084.2	705.4	91.2	287.7	985.5	564.3	101.8	319.4	1,265.7	436
1982	1,062.2	662.6	80.1	319.6	1,000.5	546.4	88.3	365.8	1,005.5	412
1983	1,703.0	1,067.6	113.5	522.0	1,605.2	901.5	133.7	570.1	1,390.3	623
1984	1,749.5	1,084.2	121.4	543.9	1,681.8	922.4	142.6	616.8	1,652.2	639
1985	1,741.8	1,072.4	93.5	576.0	1,733.3	956.6	120.1	656.6	1,703.3	688
1986	1,805.4	1,179.4	84.0	542.0	1,769.4	1,077.6	108.4	583.5	1,756.4	750
1987	1,620.5	1,146.4	65.1	408.7	1,534.8	1,024.4	89.3	421.1	1,668.8	671
1988	1,488.1	1,081.3	58.7	348.0	1,455.6	993.8	75.7	386.1	1,529.8	676
1989	1,376.1	1,003.3	55.3	317.6	1,338.4	931.7	66.9	339.8	1,422.8	650
1990	1,192.7	894.8	37.6	260.4	1,110.8	793.9	54.3	262.6	1,308.0	534
1991	1,013.9	840.4	35.6	137.9	948.8	753.5	43.1	152.1	1,090.8	509
1992	1,199.7	1,029.9	30.9	139.0	1,094.9	910.7	45.8	138.4	1,157.5	610
1993	1,287.6	1,125.7	29.4	132.6	1,199.1	986.5	52.4	160.2	1,192.7	666
1994	1,457.0	1,198.4	35.2	223.5	1,371.6	1,068.5	62.2	241.0	1,346.9	670
1995	1,354.1	1,076.2	33.8	244.1	1,332.5	997.3	63.8	271.5	1,312.6	667
1996	1,476.8	1,160.9	45.3	270.8	1,425.6	1,069.5	65.8	290.3	1,412.9	757
1997	1,474.0	1,133.7	44.5	295.8	1,441.1	1,062.4	68.4	310.3	1,400.5	804
1998	1,616.9	1,271.4	42.6	302.9	1,612.3	1,187.6	69.2	355.5	1,474.2	886
1999	1,640.9	1,302.4	31.9	306.6	1,663.5	1,246.7	65.8	351.1	1,604.9	880
2000	1,568.7	1,230.9	38.7	299.1	1,592.3	1,198.1	64.9	329.3	1,573.7	877
2001	1,602.7	1,273.3	36.6	292.8	1,636.7	1,235.6	66.0	335.2	1,570.8	908
2002	1,704.9	1,358.6	38.5	307.9	1,747.7	1,332.6	73.7	341.4	1,648.4	973
2003	1,847.7	1,499.0	33.5	315.2	1,889.2	1,460.9	82.5	345.8	1,678.7	1,086
2004	1,955.8	1,610.5	42.3	303.0	2,070.1	1,613.4	90.4	366.2	1,841.9	1,203
2005	2,068.3	1,715.8	41.1	311.4	2,155.3	1,682.0	84.0	389.3	1,931.4	1,283
2006	1,800.9	1,465.4	42.7	292.8	1,838.9	1,378.2	76.6	384.1	1,979.4	1,051
2007	1,355.0	1,046.0	31.7	277.3	1,398.4	979.9	59.6	359.0	1,502.8	776
2008	905.5	622.0	17.5	266.0	905.4	575.6	34.4	295.4	1,119.7	485
2009	554.0	445.1	11.6	97.3	583.0	441.1	20.7	121.1	794.4	375
2010	586.9	471.2	11.4	104.3	604.6	447.3	22.0	135.3	651.7	323
2011	608.8	430.6	10.9	167.3	624.1	418.5	21.6	184.0	584.9	306
2012	780.6	535.3	11.4	233.9	829.7	518.7	25.9	285.1	649.2	368
2013	924.9	617.6	13.6	293.7	990.8	620.8	29.0	341.1	764.4	429
2014	1,003.3	647.9	13.7	341.7	1,052.1	640.3	29.9	382.0	883.8	437
2015	1,111.8	714.5	11.5	385.8	1,182.6	696.0	32.1	454.5	968.2	501
2016	1,173.8	781.5	11.5	380.8	1,206.6	750.8	34.8	421.1	1,059.7	561
2017	1,203.0	848.9	11.4	342.7	1,282.0	820.0	37.2	424.8	1,152.9	613
2018	1,249.9	875.8	13.9	360.3	1,328.8	855.3	39.7	433.8	1,184.9	617
2019	1,290.0	887.7	13.4	388.9	1,386.0	862.1	42.6	481.4	1,255.1	683
2019: Jan	1,272	953	....	302	1,316	812	47	457	1,256	637
Feb	1,137	785	....	347	1,305	811	37	457	1,328	665
Mar	1,203	840	....	358	1,327	824	38	465	1,332	700
Apr	1,267	864	....	381	1,330	800	48	482	1,334	664
May	1,268	821	....	435	1,338	827	37	474	1,230	600
June	1,235	865	....	359	1,273	843	46	384	1,166	726
July	1,212	875	....	326	1,366	851	46	469	1,258	661
Aug	1,377	911	....	451	1,471	896	42	533	1,263	706
Sept	1,274	906	....	357	1,437	900	36	501	1,123	726
Oct	1,340	911	....	417	1,503	929	48	526	1,274	706
Nov	1,371	933	....	419	1,510	935	41	534	1,222	696
Dec	1,587	1,047	....	520	1,457	940	43	474	1,312	731
2020: Jan	1,617	989	....	619	1,536	977	43	516	1,305	774
Feb	1,567	1,034	....	514	1,438	994	45	399	1,297	716
Mar	1,269	880	....	376	1,356	884	46	426	1,280	612
Apr	934	679	....	240	1,066	666	33	367	1,212	570
May	1,038	728	....	302	1,216	746	42	428	1,180	698
June	1,265	891	....	367	1,258	840	40	378	1,245	840
July	1,487	992	....	485	1,483	977	45	461	1,338	979
Aug[p]	1,373	1,022	....	330	1,476	1,038	52	386	1,216	1,001
Sept[p]	1,459	1,108	....	345	1,545	1,113	44	388	1,406	1,002
Oct[p]	1,530	1,179	....	334	1,544	1,128	57	359	1,343	999

[1] Authorized by issuance of local building permits in permit-issuing places: 20,100 places beginning with 2014; 19,300 for 2004–2013; 19,000 for 1994–2003; 17,000 for 1984–93; 16,000 for 1978–83; and 14,000 for 1975–77.
[2] Monthly data do not meet publication standards because tests for identifiable and stable seasonality do not meet reliability standards.

Note: One-unit estimates prior to 1999, for new housing units started and completed and for new houses sold, include an upward adjustment of 3.3 percent to account for structures in permit-issuing areas that did not have permit authorization.

Source: Department of Commerce (Bureau of the Census).

TABLE B–37. Manufacturing and trade sales and inventories, 1979–2020

[Amounts in millions of dollars; monthly data seasonally adjusted]

Year or month	Total manufacturing and trade			Manufacturing			Merchant wholesalers [1]			Retail trade			Retail and food services sales
	Sales [2]	Inven- tories [3]	Ratio [4]	Sales [2]	Inven- tories [3]	Ratio [4]	Sales [2]	Inven- tories [3]	Ratio [4]	Sales [2, 5]	Inven- tories [3]	Ratio [4]	
SIC: [6]													
1979	297,701	452,640	1.52	143,936	242,157	1.68	79,051	99,679	1.26	74,713	110,804	1.48	
1980	327,233	508,924	1.56	154,391	265,215	1.72	93,099	122,631	1.32	79,743	121,078	1.52	
1981	355,822	545,786	1.53	168,129	283,413	1.69	101,180	129,654	1.28	86,514	132,719	1.53	
1982	347,625	573,908	1.67	163,351	311,852	1.95	95,211	127,428	1.36	89,062	134,628	1.49	
1983	369,286	590,287	1.56	172,547	312,379	1.78	99,225	130,075	1.28	97,514	147,833	1.44	
1984	410,124	649,780	1.53	190,682	339,516	1.73	112,199	142,452	1.23	107,243	167,812	1.49	
1985	422,583	664,039	1.56	194,538	334,749	1.73	113,459	147,409	1.28	114,586	181,881	1.52	
1986	430,419	662,738	1.55	194,657	322,654	1.68	114,960	153,574	1.32	120,803	186,510	1.56	
1987	457,735	709,848	1.50	206,326	338,109	1.59	122,968	163,903	1.29	128,442	207,836	1.55	
1988	497,157	767,222	1.49	224,619	369,374	1.57	134,521	178,801	1.30	138,017	219,047	1.54	
1989	527,039	815,455	1.52	236,698	391,212	1.63	143,760	187,009	1.28	146,581	237,234	1.58	
1990	545,909	840,594	1.52	242,686	405,073	1.65	149,506	195,833	1.29	153,718	239,688	1.56	
1991	542,815	834,609	1.53	239,847	390,950	1.65	148,306	200,448	1.33	154,661	243,211	1.54	
1992	567,176	842,809	1.48	250,394	382,510	1.54	154,150	208,302	1.32	162,632	251,997	1.52	
NAICS: [6]													
1992	540,199	835,800	1.53	242,002	378,609	1.57	147,261	196,914	1.31	150,936	260,277	1.67	167,842
1993	567,195	863,125	1.50	251,708	379,806	1.50	154,018	204,842	1.30	161,469	278,477	1.68	179,425
1994	609,854	926,395	1.46	269,843	399,934	1.44	164,575	221,978	1.29	175,436	304,483	1.66	194,186
1995	654,689	985,385	1.48	289,973	424,802	1.44	179,915	238,392	1.29	184,801	322,191	1.72	204,219
1996	686,923	1,004,646	1.45	299,766	430,366	1.44	190,362	241,058	1.27	196,796	333,222	1.67	216,983
1997	723,443	1,045,495	1.42	319,558	443,227	1.37	198,154	258,454	1.26	205,731	343,814	1.64	227,178
1998	742,391	1,077,183	1.44	324,984	448,373	1.39	202,260	272,297	1.32	215,147	356,513	1.62	237,746
1999	786,178	1,137,260	1.40	335,991	463,004	1.35	216,597	290,182	1.30	233,591	384,074	1.59	257,249
2000	833,868	1,195,894	1.41	350,715	480,748	1.35	234,546	309,191	1.29	248,606	405,955	1.59	273,961
2001	818,160	1,118,552	1.42	330,875	427,353	1.38	232,096	297,536	1.32	255,189	393,663	1.58	281,576
2002	823,234	1,139,523	1.36	326,227	423,028	1.29	236,294	301,310	1.26	260,713	415,185	1.55	288,256
2003	854,700	1,147,795	1.34	334,616	408,302	1.25	248,190	308,274	1.22	271,894	431,219	1.56	301,038
2004	926,002	1,241,744	1.30	359,081	441,222	1.19	277,501	340,128	1.17	289,421	460,394	1.56	320,550
2005	1,005,821	1,314,317	1.27	395,173	474,639	1.17	303,208	367,978	1.17	307,440	471,700	1.51	340,479
2006	1,069,032	1,408,790	1.28	417,963	523,476	1.20	328,438	398,902	1.17	322,631	486,412	1.49	357,863
2007	1,128,176	1,487,939	1.28	443,288	563,065	1.22	351,956	424,296	1.17	332,932	500,578	1.49	369,978
2008	1,160,722	1,466,005	1.31	455,750	543,514	1.26	377,030	445,343	1.20	327,943	477,148	1.52	365,965
2009	988,802	1,331,784	1.38	368,648	505,294	1.39	319,115	397,325	1.29	301,039	429,165	1.47	338,706
2010	1,088,890	1,449,943	1.27	409,273	553,772	1.28	361,447	441,609	1.15	318,171	454,562	1.39	357,081
2011	1,206,660	1,565,507	1.26	457,658	606,940	1.29	407,090	487,381	1.15	341,913	471,186	1.35	383,192
2012	1,267,248	1,654,631	1.28	474,727	625,266	1.30	434,002	523,147	1.17	358,519	506,218	1.38	402,199
2013	1,303,229	1,718,588	1.29	484,145	629,795	1.29	447,546	544,044	1.19	371,538	544,749	1.41	416,814
2014	1,340,932	1,779,034	1.31	490,630	640,456	1.31	463,682	576,183	1.22	386,620	562,395	1.44	434,638
2015	1,294,787	1,809,516	1.39	459,918	635,557	1.39	441,036	583,909	1.33	393,833	590,050	1.46	445,791
2016	1,285,806	1,838,756	1.42	446,225	630,332	1.41	435,168	595,265	1.35	404,413	613,159	1.50	459,182
2017	1,349,179	1,897,688	1.38	465,664	656,797	1.38	462,419	613,124	1.30	421,096	627,767	1.48	478,734
2018	1,431,072	1,990,841	1.36	496,996	680,658	1.35	494,954	653,268	1.28	439,122	656,915	1.46	500,135
2019	1,453,310	2,028,040	1.39	501,430	700,021	1.38	497,530	664,316	1.34	454,351	663,703	1.46	518,167
2019: Jan	1,436,780	2,007,300	1.40	501,894	684,722	1.36	491,466	660,917	1.34	443,420	661,661	1.49	505,036
Feb	1,442,334	2,017,149	1.40	504,836	687,324	1.36	495,031	664,232	1.34	442,467	665,593	1.50	504,686
Mar	1,456,358	2,016,658	1.38	505,483	689,832	1.36	500,950	663,989	1.33	449,925	662,837	1.47	512,602
Apr	1,452,320	2,025,356	1.39	501,769	690,915	1.38	498,539	669,063	1.34	452,012	665,378	1.47	515,088
May	1,455,735	2,030,786	1.40	502,328	692,041	1.38	500,208	670,708	1.34	453,199	668,037	1.47	516,913
June	1,456,955	2,028,955	1.39	503,236	693,423	1.38	499,680	670,767	1.34	454,039	664,765	1.46	518,397
July	1,458,222	2,033,707	1.39	501,784	694,316	1.38	499,320	669,812	1.34	457,118	669,579	1.46	521,831
Aug	1,458,482	2,030,685	1.39	500,722	693,512	1.39	497,892	670,065	1.35	459,868	667,108	1.45	524,477
Sept	1,452,800	2,027,087	1.40	499,133	695,292	1.39	497,621	664,199	1.33	456,046	667,596	1.46	521,030
Oct	1,452,303	2,029,254	1.40	499,112	696,003	1.39	494,479	664,015	1.34	458,712	669,236	1.46	523,587
Nov	1,460,383	2,026,330	1.39	499,407	697,814	1.40	500,216	664,584	1.33	460,760	663,932	1.44	525,014
Dec	1,460,174	2,028,040	1.39	501,346	700,021	1.40	498,316	664,316	1.33	460,512	663,703	1.44	525,467
2020: Jan	1,468,389	2,022,853	1.38	499,594	698,880	1.40	504,733	660,230	1.31	464,062	663,743	1.43	529,616
Feb	1,460,413	2,013,829	1.38	497,544	696,428	1.40	500,955	655,712	1.31	461,914	661,689	1.43	527,273
Mar	1,384,176	2,007,046	1.45	470,383	689,026	1.46	475,572	648,727	1.36	438,221	669,293	1.53	483,949
Apr	1,184,954	1,979,748	1.67	404,544	685,869	1.70	397,676	650,023	1.63	382,734	643,856	1.68	412,766
May	1,285,801	1,933,282	1.50	416,573	686,935	1.65	420,440	642,489	1.53	448,788	603,858	1.35	488,218
June	1,396,172	1,912,335	1.37	458,275	690,353	1.51	458,074	634,233	1.38	479,823	587,749	1.22	529,962
July	1,443,470	1,914,153	1.33	479,889	686,399	1.43	479,882	633,155	1.32	483,699	594,599	1.23	535,923
Aug	1,455,958	1,919,935	1.32	481,216	686,479	1.43	485,744	636,155	1.31	488,998	597,301	1.22	543,404
Sept [p]	1,466,012	1,933,753	1.32	483,743	686,099	1.42	486,039	640,405	1.32	496,230	607,249	1.22	551,934
Oct [p]		1,945,722		488,600	687,258	1.41		646,229		497,695	612,235	1.23	553,329

[1] Excludes manufacturers' sales branches and offices.
[2] Annual data are averages of monthly not seasonally adjusted figures.
[3] Seasonally adjusted, end of period. Inventories beginning with January 1982 for manufacturing and December 1980 for wholesale and retail trade are not comparable with earlier periods.
[4] Inventory/sales ratio. Monthly inventories are inventories at the end of the month to sales for the month. Annual data beginning with 1982 are the average of monthly ratios for the year. Annual data for 1979–81 are the ratio of December inventories to monthly average sales for the year.
[5] Food services included on Standard Industrial Classification (SIC) basis and excluded on North American Industry Classification System (NAICS) basis. See last column for retail and food services sales.
[6] Effective in 2001, data classified based on NAICS. Data on NAICS basis available beginning with 1992. Earlier data based on SIC. Data on both NAICS and SIC basis include semiconductors.

Source: Department of Commerce (Bureau of the Census).

Prices

Table B-38. Changes in consumer price indexes, 1977–2020

[For all urban consumers; percent change]

Year or month	All items	All items less food and energy					Food			Energy[4]		C-CPI-U[5]
		Total[1]	Shelter[2]	Medical care[3]	Apparel	New vehicles	Total[1]	At home	Away from home	Total[1,3]	Gasoline	
						December to December, NSA						
1977	6.7	6.5	8.8	8.9	4.3	7.2	8.1	7.9	7.9	7.2	4.8	
1978	9.0	8.5	11.4	8.8	3.1	6.2	11.8	12.5	10.4	7.9	8.6	
1979	13.3	11.3	17.5	10.1	5.5	7.4	10.2	9.7	11.4	37.5	52.1	
1980	12.5	12.2	15.0	9.9	6.8	7.4	10.2	10.5	9.6	18.0	18.9	
1981	8.9	9.5	9.9	12.5	3.5	6.8	4.3	2.9	7.1	11.9	9.4	
1982	3.8	4.5	2.4	11.0	1.6	1.4	3.1	2.3	5.1	1.3	-6.7	
1983	3.8	4.8	4.7	6.4	2.9	3.3	2.7	1.8	4.1	-.5	-1.6	
1984	3.9	4.7	5.2	6.1	2.0	2.5	3.8	3.6	4.2	.2	-2.5	
1985	3.8	4.3	6.0	6.8	2.8	3.6	2.6	2.0	3.8	1.8	3.0	
1986	1.1	3.8	4.6	7.7	.9	5.6	3.8	3.7	4.3	-19.7	-30.7	
1987	4.4	4.2	4.8	5.8	4.8	1.8	3.5	3.5	3.7	8.2	18.6	
1988	4.4	4.7	4.5	6.9	4.7	2.2	5.2	5.6	4.4	.5	-1.8	
1989	4.6	4.4	4.9	8.5	1.0	2.4	5.6	6.2	4.6	5.1	6.5	
1990	6.1	5.2	5.2	9.6	5.1	2.0	5.3	5.8	4.5	18.1	36.8	
1991	3.1	4.4	3.9	7.9	3.4	3.2	1.9	1.3	2.9	-7.4	-16.2	
1992	2.9	3.3	2.9	6.6	1.4	2.3	1.5	1.5	1.4	2.0	2.0	
1993	2.7	3.2	3.0	5.4	.9	3.3	2.9	3.5	1.9	-1.4	-5.9	
1994	2.7	2.6	3.0	4.9	-1.6	3.3	2.9	3.5	1.9	2.2	6.4	
1995	2.5	3.0	3.5	3.9	.1	1.9	2.1	2.0	2.2	-1.3	-4.2	
1996	3.3	2.6	2.9	3.0	-.2	1.8	4.3	4.9	3.1	8.6	12.4	
1997	1.7	2.2	3.4	2.8	1.0	-.9	1.5	1.0	2.6	-3.4	-6.1	
1998	1.6	2.4	3.3	3.4	-.7	.0	2.3	2.1	2.5	-8.8	-15.4	
1999	2.7	1.9	2.5	3.7	-.5	-.3	1.9	1.7	2.3	13.4	30.1	
2000	3.4	2.6	3.4	4.2	-1.8	.0	2.8	2.9	2.4	14.2	13.9	2.6
2001	1.6	2.7	4.2	4.7	-3.2	-.1	2.8	2.6	3.0	-13.0	-24.9	1.3
2002	2.4	1.9	3.1	5.0	-1.8	-2.0	1.5	.8	2.3	10.7	24.8	2.0
2003	1.9	1.1	2.2	3.7	-2.1	-1.8	3.6	4.5	2.3	6.9	6.8	1.7
2004	3.3	2.2	2.7	4.2	-.2	.6	2.7	2.4	3.0	16.6	26.1	3.2
2005	3.4	2.2	2.6	4.3	-1.1	-.4	2.3	1.7	3.2	17.1	16.1	2.9
2006	2.5	2.6	4.2	3.6	.9	-.9	2.1	1.4	3.2	2.9	6.4	2.3
2007	4.1	2.4	3.1	5.2	-.3	-.3	4.9	5.6	4.0	17.4	29.6	3.7
2008	.1	1.8	1.9	2.6	-1.0	-3.2	5.9	6.6	5.0	-21.3	-43.1	.2
2009	2.7	1.8	.3	3.4	1.9	4.9	-.5	-2.4	1.9	18.2	53.5	2.5
2010	1.5	.8	.4	3.3	-1.1	-.2	1.5	1.7	1.3	7.7	13.8	1.3
2011	3.0	2.2	1.9	3.5	4.6	3.2	4.7	6.0	2.9	6.6	9.9	2.9
2012	1.7	1.9	2.2	3.2	1.8	1.6	1.8	1.3	2.5	.5	1.7	1.5
2013	1.5	1.7	2.5	2.0	.6	.4	1.1	.4	2.1	.5	-1.0	1.3
2014	.8	1.6	2.9	3.0	-2.0	.5	3.4	3.7	3.0	-10.6	-21.0	.5
2015	.7	2.1	3.2	2.6	-.9	.2	.8	-.4	2.6	-12.6	-19.7	.4
2016	2.1	2.2	3.6	4.1	-.1	.3	-.2	-2.0	2.3	5.4	9.1	1.8
2017	2.1	1.8	3.2	1.8	-1.6	-.5	1.6	.9	2.5	6.9	10.7	1.7
2018	1.9	2.2	3.2	2.0	-.1	-.3	1.6	.6	2.8	-.3	-2.1	1.5
2019	2.3	2.3	3.2	4.6	-1.2	.1	1.8	.7	3.1	3.4	7.9	1.8
						Change from year earlier, NSA						
2019: Jan	1.6	2.2	3.2	1.9	0.1	0.0	1.6	0.6	2.8	-4.8	-10.1	1.3
Feb	1.5	2.1	3.4	1.7	-.8	.3	2.0	1.2	2.9	-5.0	-9.1	1.3
Mar	1.9	2.0	3.4	1.7	-2.2	.7	2.1	1.4	3.0	-.4	-.7	1.5
Apr	2.0	2.1	3.4	1.9	-3.0	1.2	1.8	.7	3.1	1.7	3.1	1.6
May	1.8	2.0	3.3	2.1	-3.1	.9	2.0	1.2	2.9	-.5	-.2	1.4
June	1.6	2.1	3.5	2.0	-1.3	.6	1.9	.9	3.1	-3.4	-5.4	1.3
July	1.8	2.2	3.5	2.6	-.5	.3	1.8	.6	3.2	-2.0	-3.3	1.5
Aug	1.7	2.4	3.4	3.5	1.0	.2	1.7	.5	3.2	-4.4	-7.1	1.5
Sept	1.7	2.4	3.5	3.5	-.3	.1	1.8	.6	3.2	-4.8	-8.2	1.4
Oct	1.8	2.3	3.3	4.3	-2.3	.1	2.1	1.0	3.3	-4.2	-7.3	1.4
Nov	2.1	2.3	3.3	4.2	-1.6	-.1	2.0	1.0	3.2	-.6	-1.2	1.6
Dec	2.3	2.3	3.2	4.6	-1.2	.1	1.8	.7	3.1	• 3.4	7.9	1.8
2020: Jan	2.5	2.3	3.3	4.5	-1.3	.1	1.8	.7	3.1	6.2	12.8	2.0
Feb	2.3	2.4	3.3	4.6	-.9	.4	1.8	.8	3.0	2.8	5.6	1.8
Mar	1.5	2.1	3.0	4.7	-1.6	-.4	1.9	1.1	3.0	-5.7	-10.2	1.1
Apr	.3	1.4	2.6	4.8	-5.7	-.6	3.5	4.1	2.8	-17.7	-32.0	-.2
May	.1	1.2	2.5	4.9	-7.9	-.3	4.0	4.8	2.9	-18.9	-33.8	-.4
June	.6	1.2	2.4	5.1	-7.3	-.2	4.5	5.6	3.1	-12.6	-23.4	.2
July	1.0	1.6	2.3	5.0	-6.5	.5	4.1	4.6	3.4	-11.2	-20.3	.6
Aug	1.3	1.7	2.3	4.5	-5.9	.7	4.1	4.6	3.5	-9.0	-16.8	.9
Sept	1.4	1.7	2.0	4.2	-6.0	1.0	3.9	4.1	3.8	-7.7	-15.4	1.0
Oct	1.2	1.6	2.0	2.9	-5.5	1.5	3.9	4.0	3.9	-9.2	-18.0	.9

[1] Includes other items not shown separately.
[2] Data beginning with 1983 incorporate a rental equivalence measure for homeowners' costs.
[3] Commodities and services.
[4] Household energy--electricity, utility (piped) gas service, fuel oil, etc.--and motor fuel.
[5] Chained consumer price index (C-CPI-U) introduced in 2002. Reflects the effect of substitution that consumers make across item categories in response to changes in relative prices. Data for 2020 are subject to revision.

Source: Department of Labor (Bureau of Labor Statistics).

TABLE B-39. Price indexes for personal consumption expenditures, and percent changes, 1972-2020

[Chain-type price index numbers, 2012=100; monthly data seasonally adjusted]

Year or month	Personal consumption expenditures (PCE)						Percent change from year earlier					
	Total	Goods	Services	Food[1]	Energy goods and services[2]	PCE less food and energy	Total	Goods	Services	Food[1]	Energy goods and services[2]	PCE less food and energy
1972	22.586	33.926	17.491	22.371	10.716	23.912	3.4	2.6	4.2	4.8	2.6	3.2
1973	23.802	35.949	18.336	25.202	11.640	24.823	5.4	6.0	4.8	12.7	8.6	3.8
1974	26.280	40.436	19.890	29.034	15.176	26.788	10.4	12.5	8.5	15.2	30.4	7.9
1975	28.470	43.703	21.595	31.217	16.672	29.026	8.3	8.1	8.6	7.5	9.9	8.4
1976	30.032	45.413	23.093	31.798	17.791	30.791	5.5	3.9	6.9	1.9	6.7	6.1
1977	31.986	47.837	24.841	33.671	19.294	32.771	6.5	5.3	7.6	5.9	8.4	6.4
1978	34.211	50.773	26.750	36.892	20.380	34.943	7.0	6.1	7.7	9.6	5.6	6.6
1979	37.251	55.574	28.994	40.516	25.414	37.490	8.9	9.5	8.4	9.8	24.7	7.3
1980	41.262	61.797	32.009	43.922	33.203	40.936	10.8	11.2	10.4	8.4	30.6	9.2
1981	44.958	66.389	35.288	47.051	37.668	44.523	9.0	7.4	10.2	7.1	13.4	8.8
1982	47.456	68.198	38.058	48.289	38.326	47.417	5.6	2.7	7.8	2.6	1.7	6.5
1983	49.474	69.429	40.396	48.844	38.684	49.844	4.3	1.8	6.1	1.1	.9	5.1
1984	51.343	70.742	42.498	50.312	39.172	51.911	3.8	1.9	5.2	3.0	1.3	4.1
1985	53.134	71.877	44.577	50.859	39.585	54.019	3.5	1.6	4.9	1.1	1.1	4.1
1986	54.290	71.541	46.408	52.056	34.685	55.883	2.2	-.5	4.1	2.4	-12.4	3.5
1987	55.964	73.842	47.796	53.699	35.069	57.683	3.1	3.2	3.0	3.2	1.1	3.2
1988	58.151	75.788	50.082	55.300	35.337	60.134	3.9	2.6	4.8	3.0	.8	4.2
1989	60.690	78.704	52.443	58.216	37.425	62.630	4.4	3.8	4.7	5.3	5.9	4.2
1990	63.355	81.927	54.846	61.060	40.589	65.168	4.4	4.1	4.6	4.9	8.5	4.1
1991	65.473	83.930	56.992	62.977	40.769	67.495	3.3	2.4	3.9	3.1	.4	3.6
1992	67.218	84.943	59.018	63.461	40.959	69.547	2.7	1.2	3.6	.8	.5	3.0
1993	68.892	85.681	61.059	64.348	41.331	71.436	2.5	.9	3.5	1.4	.9	2.7
1994	70.330	86.552	62.719	65.426	41.493	73.034	2.1	1.0	2.7	1.7	.4	2.2
1995	71.811	87.361	64.471	66.844	41.819	74.625	2.1	.9	2.8	2.2	.8	2.2
1996	73.346	88.321	66.240	68.883	43.777	76.040	2.1	1.1	2.7	3.1	4.7	1.9
1997	74.623	88.219	68.107	70.195	44.236	77.382	1.7	-.1	2.8	1.9	1.0	1.8
1998	75.216	86.893	69.549	71.077	40.502	78.366	.8	-1.5	2.1	1.3	-8.4	1.3
1999	76.338	87.349	70.970	72.241	42.143	79.425	1.5	.5	2.0	1.6	4.1	1.4
2000	78.235	89.082	72.938	73.933	49.843	80.804	2.5	2.0	2.8	2.3	18.3	1.7
2001	79.738	89.015	75.171	76.089	51.088	82.258	1.9	-.1	3.1	2.9	2.5	1.8
2002	80.789	88.166	77.123	77.239	48.110	83.639	1.3	-1.0	2.6	1.5	-5.8	1.7
2003	82.358	88.054	79.506	78.701	54.190	84.837	1.9	-.1	3.1	1.9	12.6	1.4
2004	84.411	89.292	81.965	81.157	60.339	86.515	2.5	1.4	3.1	3.1	11.3	2.0
2005	86.812	91.084	84.673	82.575	70.752	88.373	2.8	2.0	3.3	1.7	17.3	2.1
2006	89.174	92.306	87.616	83.963	78.812	90.392	2.7	1.3	3.5	1.7	11.4	2.3
2007	91.438	93.331	90.516	87.239	83.557	92.378	2.5	1.1	3.3	3.9	6.0	2.2
2008	94.180	96.122	93.235	92.552	95.464	94.225	3.0	3.0	3.0	6.1	14.3	2.0
2009	94.094	93.812	94.231	93.651	77.393	95.315	-.1	-2.4	1.1	1.2	-18.9	1.2
2010	95.705	95.183	95.957	93.931	85.120	96.608	1.7	1.5	1.8	.3	10.0	1.4
2011	98.131	98.773	97.814	97.682	98.601	98.139	2.5	3.8	1.9	4.0	15.8	1.6
2012	100.000	100.000	100.000	100.000	100.000	100.000	1.9	1.2	2.2	2.4	1.4	1.9
2013	101.346	99.407	102.316	100.989	99.109	101.526	1.3	-.6	2.3	1.0	-.9	1.5
2014	102.830	98.920	104.804	102.925	98.279	103.122	1.5	-.5	2.4	1.9	-.8	1.6
2015	103.043	95.896	106.694	104.086	80.641	104.404	.2	-3.1	1.8	1.1	-17.9	1.2
2016	104.121	94.325	109.160	103.007	74.781	106.102	1.0	-1.6	2.3	-1.0	-7.3	1.6
2017	105.984	94.597	111.868	102.870	81.286	107.855	1.8	.3	2.5	-.1	8.7	1.7
2018	108.239	95.244	114.991	103.410	87.805	110.005	2.1	.7	2.8	.5	8.0	2.0
2019	109.851	94.785	117.744	104.442	85.928	111.875	1.5	-.5	2.4	1.0	-2.1	1.7
2019: Jan	108.872	94.443	116.412	103.974	82.391	111.002	1.5	-.9	2.6	.8	-5.2	1.8
Feb	109.003	94.502	116.581	104.425	83.531	111.045	1.4	-.9	2.4	1.3	-5.2	1.7
Mar	109.252	94.769	116.821	104.623	85.916	111.174	1.5	-.3	2.3	1.4	-.1	1.6
Apr	109.609	95.000	117.245	104.270	87.955	111.493	1.6	-.4	2.5	.8	1.5	1.7
May	109.720	95.015	117.410	104.538	87.373	111.632	1.5	-.4	2.4	1.3	-.4	1.6
June	109.849	94.940	117.653	104.505	85.789	111.874	1.5	-.6	2.4	1.1	-3.3	1.7
July	110.042	94.921	117.964	104.403	86.605	112.057	1.5	-.5	2.5	.9	-1.8	1.7
Aug	110.115	94.751	118.174	104.329	85.413	112.216	1.5	-.5	2.5	.8	-4.5	1.9
Sept	110.167	94.626	118.324	104.450	84.764	112.302	1.4	-.7	2.4	.8	-4.8	1.7
Oct	110.377	94.784	118.563	104.584	86.194	112.448	1.4	-.6	2.4	1.1	-4.3	1.7
Nov	110.461	94.760	118.707	104.628	86.865	112.501	1.4	-.3	2.2	.9	-.8	1.6
Dec	110.750	94.908	119.073	104.571	88.334	112.753	1.6	.4	2.2	.8	3.7	1.6
2020: Jan	110.917	94.946	119.312	104.875	87.832	112.949	1.9	.5	2.5	.9	6.6	1.8
Feb	111.014	94.836	119.524	105.359	86.028	113.121	1.8	.4	2.5	.9	3.0	1.9
Mar	110.717	94.017	119.533	105.958	80.854	113.013	1.3	-.8	2.3	1.3	-5.9	1.7
Apr	110.131	92.939	119.265	108.471	73.041	112.526	.5	-2.2	1.7	4.0	-17.0	.9
May	110.314	92.920	119.577	109.335	71.529	112.755	.5	-2.2	1.8	4.6	-18.1	1.0
June	110.859	93.885	119.838	109.901	74.846	113.145	.9	-1.1	1.9	5.2	-12.8	1.1
July	111.160	94.284	120.070	108.908	76.701	113.476	1.0	-.7	1.8	4.3	-11.4	1.3
Aug	111.506	94.684	120.376	108.795	77.347	113.846	1.3	-.1	1.9	4.3	-9.4	1.5
Sept[p]	111.684	94.512	120.778	108.478	77.882	114.049	1.4	-.1	2.1	3.9	-8.1	1.6
Oct[p]	111.684	94.319	120.905	108.606	77.954	114.033	1.2	-.5	2.0	3.8	-9.6	1.4

[1] Food consists of food and beverages purchased for off-premises consumption; food services, which include purchased meals and beverages, are not classified as food.
[2] Consists of gasoline and other energy goods and of electricity and gas services.

Source: Department of Commerce (Bureau of Economic Analysis).

Money Stock, Credit, and Finance

TABLE B–40. Money stock and debt measures, 1980–2020

[Averages of daily figures, except debt end-of-period basis; billions of dollars, seasonally adjusted]

Year and month	M1 Sum of currency, demand deposits, travelers checks, and other checkable deposits	M2 M1 plus savings deposits, retail MMMF balances, and small time deposits [1]	Debt Debt of domestic nonfinancial sectors [2]	Percent change		
				From year or 6 months earlier [3]		From previous period [4]
				M1	M2	Debt
December:						
1980	408.5	1,599.8	4,051.5	7.0	8.6	9.6
1981	436.7	1,755.5	4,464.7	6.9	9.7	10.2
1982	474.8	1,905.9	4,900.3	8.7	8.6	10.2
1983	521.4	2,123.5	5,497.7	9.8	11.4	12.1
1984	551.6	2,306.4	6,308.4	5.8	8.6	14.8
1985	619.8	2,492.1	7,341.7	12.4	8.1	16.1
1986	724.7	2,728.0	8,216.7	16.9	9.5	12.0
1987	750.2	2,826.4	8,936.1	3.5	3.6	9.0
1988	786.7	2,988.2	9,753.9	4.9	5.7	9.2
1989	792.9	3,152.5	10,501.9	.8	5.5	7.5
1990	824.7	3,271.8	11,218.1	4.0	3.8	6.6
1991	897.0	3,372.2	11,746.7	8.8	3.1	4.7
1992	1,024.9	3,424.7	12,298.0	14.3	1.6	4.7
1993	1,129.6	3,474.5	13,021.3	10.2	1.5	5.8
1994	1,150.7	3,486.4	13,701.7	1.9	.3	5.2
1995	1,127.5	3,629.5	14,386.1	-2.0	4.1	4.9
1996	1,081.3	3,810.4	15,135.9	-4.1	5.0	5.2
1997	1,072.3	4,022.8	15,974.2	-.8	5.6	5.6
1998	1,095.0	4,365.0	17,053.6	2.1	8.5	6.8
1999	1,122.2	4,627.4	18,222.3	2.5	6.0	6.7
2000	1,088.6	4,913.7	19,095.4	-3.0	6.2	4.7
2001	1,183.2	5,421.6	20,165.0	8.7	10.3	5.7
2002	1,220.2	5,759.7	21,513.5	3.1	6.2	6.7
2003	1,306.2	6,054.2	23,214.5	7.0	5.1	7.8
2004	1,376.0	6,405.0	26,126.6	5.3	5.8	9.2
2005	1,374.3	6,668.0	28,411.2	-.1	4.1	8.8
2006	1,366.6	7,057.5	30,854.9	-.6	5.8	8.5
2007	1,373.4	7,458.0	33,352.6	.5	5.7	8.2
2008	1,601.7	8,181.0	35,132.5	16.6	9.7	5.8
2009	1,692.8	8,483.4	36,108.3	5.7	3.7	3.7
2010	1,836.7	8,789.3	37,524.1	8.5	3.6	4.5
2011	2,164.2	9,651.1	38,749.3	17.8	9.8	3.7
2012	2,461.2	10,445.7	40,395.8	13.7	8.2	4.6
2013	2,664.5	11,015.0	41,954.9	8.3	5.5	4.1
2014	2,940.3	11,668.0	43,488.7	10.4	5.9	3.8
2015	3,093.8	12,330.1	45,204.6	5.2	5.7	4.4
2016	3,339.8	13,198.9	47,172.4	8.0	7.0	4.4
2017	3,607.3	13,835.7	49,277.9	8.0	4.8	4.2
2018	3,746.4	14,351.7	51,894.0	3.9	3.7	4.7
2019	3,976.9	15,307.1	54,333.1	6.2	6.7	4.7
2019: Jan	3,740.4	14,434.6		3.4	4.0	
Feb	3,759.6	14,464.3		4.0	3.8	
Mar	3,729.8	14,511.8	52,659.3	1.4	4.0	5.9
Apr	3,780.9	14,558.7		3.3	4.5	
May	3,792.4	14,654.3		5.1	5.7	
June	3,832.8	14,782.6	53,110.1	4.6	6.0	3.5
July	3,858.1	14,862.1		6.3	5.9	
Aug	3,853.2	14,933.3		5.0	6.5	
Sept	3,903.0	15,022.9	53,888.3	9.3	7.0	5.9
Oct	3,922.8	15,149.9		7.5	8.1	
Nov	3,947.4	15,251.2		8.2	8.1	
Dec	3,976.9	15,307.1	54,333.1	7.5	7.1	3.3
2020: Jan	3,975.1	15,402.1		6.1	7.3	
Feb	4,003.1	15,446.9		7.8	6.9	
Mar	4,256.7	15,989.9	55,781.6	18.1	12.9	10.7
Apr	4,799.0	17,020.1		44.7	24.7	
May	5,035.3	17,868.6		55.1	34.3	
June	5,215.0	18,164.0	59,303.6	62.3	37.3	25.3
July	5,331.8	18,322.2		68.3	37.9	
Aug	5,391.2	18,404.0		69.4	38.3	
Sept	5,502.6	18,648.3		58.5	33.3	
Oct ᵖ	5,580.5	18,812.1		32.6	21.1	

[1] Money market mutual fund (MMMF). Savings deposits include money market deposit accounts.
[2] Consists of outstanding debt securities and loans of the U.S. Government, State and local governments, and private nonfinancial sectors. Quarterly data shown in last month of quarter. End-of-year data are for fourth quarter.
[3] Annual changes are from December to December; monthly changes are from six months earlier at an annual rate.
[4] Debt growth of domestic nonfinancial sectors is the seasonally adjusted borrowing flow divided by the seasonally adjusted level of debt outstanding in the previous period. Annual changes are from fourth quarter to fourth quarter; quarterly changes are from previous quarter at an annual rate.

Note: For further information on the composition of M1 and M2, see the H.6 release.
For further information on the debt of domestic nonfinancial sectors and the derivation of debt growth, see the Z.1 release.

Source: Board of Governors of the Federal Reserve System.

TABLE B–41. Consumer credit outstanding, 1970–2020

[Amount outstanding (end of month); millions of dollars, seasonally adjusted]

Year and month	Total consumer credit [1]	Revolving	Nonrevolving [2]
December:			
1970	131,551.6	4,961.5	126,590.1
1971	146,930.2	8,245.3	138,684.8
1972	166,189.1	9,379.2	156,809.9
1973	190,086.3	11,342.2	178,744.1
1974	198,917.8	13,241.3	185,676.6
1975	204,002.0	14,495.3	189,506.7
1976	225,721.6	16,489.1	209,232.5
1977	260,562.7	37,414.8	223,147.9
1978	306,100.4	45,691.0	260,409.4
1979	348,589.1	53,596.4	294,992.7
1980	351,920.1	54,970.1	296,950.0
1981	371,301.4	60,928.0	310,373.4
1982	389,848.7	66,348.3	323,500.4
1983	437,068.9	79,027.3	358,041.6
1984	517,279.0	100,385.6	416,893.4
1985	599,711.2	124,465.8	475,245.4
1986	654,750.2	141,068.2	513,682.1
1987	686,318.8	160,853.9	525,464.9
1988 [3]	731,917.8	184,593.1	547,324.6
1989	794,612.2	211,229.8	583,382.3
1990	808,230.6	238,642.6	569,588.0
1991	798,029.0	263,768.6	534,260.4
1992	806,118.7	278,449.7	527,669.0
1993	865,650.6	309,908.0	555,742.6
1994	997,301.7	365,569.6	631,732.2
1995	1,140,744.4	443,920.1	696,824.3
1996	1,253,437.1	507,516.6	745,920.5
1997	1,324,757.3	540,005.6	784,751.8
1998	1,420,996.4	581,414.8	839,581.7
1999	1,531,106.0	610,696.5	920,409.5
2000	1,716,969.7	682,646.4	1,034,323.4
2001	1,867,852.9	714,840.7	1,153,012.1
2002	1,972,112.2	750,947.5	1,221,164.8
2003	2,077,360.7	768,258.3	1,309,102.4
2004	2,192,246.2	799,552.2	1,392,694.0
2005	2,290,928.1	829,518.4	1,461,409.8
2006	2,456,715.7	923,876.8	1,532,838.9
2007	2,609,476.5	1,001,625.3	1,607,851.2
2008	2,643,789.0	1,003,997.0	1,639,791.9
2009	2,555,016.6	916,076.6	1,638,940.0
2010	2,646,811.3	839,102.7	1,807,708.6
2011	2,756,392.9	840,259.2	1,916,133.6
2012	2,913,229.0	840,170.8	2,073,058.2
2013	3,090,924.8	854,400.8	2,236,524.0
2014	3,311,893.1	887,701.6	2,424,191.4
2015	3,390,629.3	898,650.7	2,491,978.6
2016	3,620,760.2	960,339.1	2,660,421.1
2017	3,813,046.3	1,018,081.3	2,794,965.0
2018	3,998,146.8	1,054,588.3	2,943,558.4
2019	4,180,684.8	1,094,209.4	3,086,475.4
2019: Jan	4,015,597.7	1,058,442.9	2,957,154.8
Feb	4,031,900.6	1,062,189.9	2,969,710.7
Mar	4,044,181.2	1,061,107.0	2,983,074.1
Apr	4,061,756.0	1,067,840.6	2,993,915.4
May	4,076,543.8	1,072,247.3	3,004,296.5
June	4,088,481.2	1,073,352.8	3,015,128.4
July	4,110,781.5	1,084,681.1	3,026,100.4
Aug	4,125,415.2	1,084,665.8	3,040,749.4
Sept	4,138,204.5	1,084,925.6	3,053,278.9
Oct	4,151,113.2	1,087,983.8	3,063,129.4
Nov	4,157,840.2	1,082,728.9	3,075,111.3
Dec	4,180,684.8	1,094,209.4	3,086,475.4
2020: Jan	4,190,270.2	1,092,712.8	3,097,557.4
Feb	4,209,622.6	1,098,736.5	3,110,886.1
Mar	4,195,694.8	1,078,068.7	3,117,626.1
Apr	4,131,087.5	1,020,395.2	3,110,692.3
May	4,117,682.8	996,669.0	3,121,013.8
June	4,137,343.6	994,974.4	3,142,369.2
July	4,152,000.1	994,304.9	3,157,695.2
Aug	4,145,071.4	984,593.5	3,160,478.0
Sept [p]	4,161,285.1	988,569.0	3,172,716.0

[1] Covers most short- and intermediate-term credit extended to individuals. Credit secured by real estate is excluded.
[2] Includes automobile loans and all other loans not included in revolving credit, such as loans for mobile homes, education, boats, trailers, or vacations. These loans may be secured or unsecured. Beginning with 1977, includes student loans extended by the Federal Government and by SLM Holding Corporation.
[3] Data newly available in January 1989 result in breaks in these series between December 1988 and subsequent months.

Source: Board of Governors of the Federal Reserve System.

Table B–42. Bond yields and interest rates, 1949–2020

[Percent per annum]

Year	U.S. Treasury securities Bills (at auction) [1] 3-month	6-month	Constant maturities [2] 3-year	10-year	30-year	Corporate bonds (Moody's) Aaa [3]	Baa	High-grade municipal bonds (Standard & Poor's)	Home mortgage yields [4]	Prime rate charged by banks [5]	Discount window (Federal Reserve Bank of New York) [5,6] Primary credit	Adjustment credit	Federal funds rate [7]
1949	1.102	....	....	....	....	2.66	3.42	2.21	....	2.00	....	1.50	....
1950	1.218	....	....	....	....	2.62	3.24	1.98	....	2.07	....	1.59	....
1951	1.552	....	....	....	....	2.86	3.41	2.00	....	2.56	....	1.75	....
1952	1.766	....	....	....	....	2.96	3.52	2.19	....	3.00	....	1.75	....
1953	1.931	....	2.47	2.85	....	3.20	3.74	2.72	....	3.17	....	1.99	....
1954	.953	....	1.63	2.40	....	2.90	3.51	2.37	....	3.05	....	1.60	....
1955	1.753	....	2.47	2.82	....	3.06	3.53	2.53	....	3.16	....	1.89	1.79
1956	2.658	....	3.19	3.18	....	3.36	3.88	2.93	....	3.77	....	2.77	2.73
1957	3.267	....	3.98	3.65	....	3.89	4.71	3.60	....	4.20	....	3.12	3.11
1958	1.839	....	2.84	3.32	....	3.79	4.73	3.56	....	3.83	....	2.15	1.57
1959	3.405	3.832	4.46	4.33	....	4.38	5.05	3.95	....	4.48	....	3.36	3.31
1960	2.93	3.25	3.98	4.12	....	4.41	5.19	3.73	....	4.82	....	3.53	3.21
1961	2.38	2.61	3.54	3.88	....	4.35	5.08	3.46	....	4.50	....	3.00	1.95
1962	2.78	2.91	3.47	3.95	....	4.33	5.02	3.18	....	4.50	....	3.00	2.71
1963	3.16	3.25	3.67	4.00	....	4.26	4.86	3.23	....	4.50	....	3.23	3.18
1964	3.56	3.69	4.03	4.19	....	4.40	4.83	3.22	....	4.50	....	3.55	3.50
1965	3.95	4.05	4.22	4.28	....	4.49	4.87	3.27	....	4.54	....	4.04	4.07
1966	4.88	5.08	5.23	4.93	....	5.13	5.67	3.82	....	5.63	....	4.50	5.11
1967	4.32	4.63	5.03	5.07	....	5.51	6.23	3.98	....	5.63	....	4.19	4.22
1968	5.34	5.47	5.68	5.64	....	6.18	6.94	4.51	....	6.31	....	5.17	5.66
1969	6.68	6.85	7.02	6.67	....	7.03	7.81	5.81	....	7.96	....	5.87	8.21
1970	6.43	6.53	7.29	7.35	....	8.04	9.11	6.51	....	7.91	....	5.95	7.17
1971	4.35	4.51	5.66	6.16	....	7.39	8.56	5.70	7.54	5.73	....	4.88	4.67
1972	4.07	4.47	5.72	6.21	....	7.21	8.16	5.27	7.38	5.25	....	4.50	4.44
1973	7.04	7.18	6.96	6.85	....	7.44	8.24	5.18	8.04	8.03	....	6.45	8.74
1974	7.89	7.93	7.84	7.56	....	8.57	9.50	6.09	9.19	10.81	....	7.83	10.51
1975	5.84	6.12	7.50	7.99	....	8.83	10.61	6.89	9.05	7.86	....	6.25	5.82
1976	4.99	5.27	6.77	7.61	....	8.43	9.75	6.49	8.87	6.84	....	5.50	5.05
1977	5.27	5.52	6.68	7.42	7.75	8.02	8.97	5.56	8.85	6.83	....	5.46	5.54
1978	7.22	7.58	8.29	8.41	8.49	8.73	9.49	5.90	9.64	9.06	....	7.46	7.94
1979	10.05	10.02	9.70	9.43	9.28	9.63	10.69	6.39	11.20	12.67	....	10.29	11.20
1980	11.51	11.37	11.51	11.43	11.27	11.94	13.67	8.51	13.74	15.26	....	11.77	13.35
1981	14.03	13.78	14.46	13.92	13.45	14.17	16.04	11.23	16.63	18.87	....	13.42	16.39
1982	10.69	11.08	12.93	13.01	12.76	13.79	16.11	11.57	16.04	14.85	....	11.01	12.24
1983	8.63	8.75	10.45	11.10	11.18	12.04	13.55	9.47	13.24	10.79	....	8.50	9.09
1984	9.53	9.77	11.92	12.46	12.41	12.71	14.19	10.15	13.88	12.04	....	8.80	10.23
1985	7.47	7.64	9.64	10.62	10.79	11.37	12.72	9.18	12.43	9.93	....	7.69	8.10
1986	5.98	6.03	7.06	7.67	7.78	9.02	10.39	7.38	10.19	8.33	....	6.32	6.80
1987	5.82	6.05	7.68	8.39	8.59	9.38	10.58	7.73	10.21	8.21	....	5.66	6.66
1988	6.69	6.92	8.26	8.85	8.96	9.71	10.83	7.76	10.34	9.32	....	6.20	7.57
1989	8.12	8.04	8.55	8.49	8.45	9.26	10.18	7.24	10.32	10.87	....	6.93	9.21
1990	7.51	7.47	8.26	8.55	8.61	9.32	10.36	7.25	10.13	10.01	....	6.98	8.10
1991	5.42	5.49	6.82	7.86	8.14	8.77	9.80	6.89	9.25	8.46	....	5.45	5.69
1992	3.45	3.57	5.30	7.01	7.67	8.14	8.98	6.41	8.39	6.25	....	3.25	3.52
1993	3.02	3.14	4.44	5.87	6.59	7.22	7.93	5.63	7.31	6.00	....	3.00	3.02
1994	4.29	4.66	6.27	7.09	7.37	7.96	8.62	6.19	8.38	7.15	....	3.60	4.21
1995	5.51	5.59	6.25	6.57	6.88	7.59	8.20	5.95	7.93	8.83	....	5.21	5.83
1996	5.02	5.09	5.99	6.44	6.71	7.37	8.05	5.75	7.81	8.27	....	5.02	5.30
1997	5.07	5.18	6.10	6.35	6.61	7.26	7.86	5.55	7.60	8.44	....	5.00	5.46
1998	4.81	4.85	5.14	5.26	5.58	6.53	7.22	5.12	6.94	8.35	....	4.92	5.35
1999	4.66	4.76	5.49	5.65	5.87	7.04	7.87	5.43	7.44	8.00	....	4.62	4.97
2000	5.85	5.92	6.22	6.03	5.94	7.62	8.36	5.77	8.05	9.23	....	5.73	6.24
2001	3.44	3.39	4.09	5.02	5.49	7.08	7.95	5.19	6.97	6.91	....	3.40	3.88
2002	1.62	1.69	3.10	4.61	5.43	6.49	7.80	5.05	6.54	4.67	....	1.17	1.67
2003	1.01	1.06	2.10	4.01	....	5.67	6.77	4.73	5.83	4.12	2.12	....	1.13
2004	1.38	1.57	2.78	4.27	....	5.63	6.39	4.63	5.84	4.34	2.34	....	1.35
2005	3.16	3.40	3.93	4.29	....	5.24	6.06	4.29	5.87	6.19	4.19	....	3.22
2006	4.73	4.80	4.77	4.80	4.91	5.59	6.48	4.42	6.41	7.96	5.96	....	4.97
2007	4.41	4.48	4.35	4.63	4.84	5.56	6.48	4.42	6.34	8.05	5.86	....	5.02
2008	1.48	1.71	2.24	3.66	4.28	5.63	7.45	4.80	6.03	5.09	2.39	....	1.92
2009	.16	.29	1.43	3.26	4.08	5.31	7.30	4.64	5.04	3.25	.50	....	.16
2010	.14	.20	1.11	3.22	4.25	4.94	6.04	4.16	4.69	3.25	.72	....	.18
2011	.06	.10	.75	2.78	3.91	4.64	5.66	4.29	4.45	3.25	.75	....	.10
2012	.09	.13	.38	1.80	2.92	3.67	4.94	3.14	3.66	3.25	.75	....	.14
2013	.06	.09	.54	2.35	3.45	4.24	5.10	3.96	3.98	3.25	.75	....	.11
2014	.03	.06	.90	2.54	3.34	4.16	4.85	3.78	4.17	3.25	.75	....	.09
2015	.06	.17	1.02	2.14	2.84	3.89	5.00	3.48	3.85	3.26	.76	....	.13
2016	.33	.46	1.00	1.84	2.59	3.67	4.72	3.07	3.65	3.51	1.01	....	.39
2017	.94	1.05	1.58	2.33	2.89	3.74	4.44	3.36	3.99	4.10	1.60	....	1.00
2018	1.94	2.10	2.63	2.91	3.11	3.93	4.80	3.53	4.54	4.91	2.41	....	1.83
2019	2.08	2.07	1.94	2.14	2.58	3.39	4.38	3.38	3.94	5.28	2.78	....	2.16

[1] High bill rate at auction, issue date within period, bank-discount basis. On or after October 28, 1998, data are stop yields from uniform-price auctions. Before that date, they are weighted average yields from multiple-price auctions.

See next page for continuation of table.

TABLE B–42. Bond yields and interest rates, 1949–2020—*Continued*

[Percent per annum]

Year and month	U.S. Treasury securities Bills (at auction)[1] 3-month	6-month	Constant maturities[2] 3-year	10-year	30-year	Corporate bonds (Moody's) Aaa[3]	Baa	High-grade municipal bonds (Standard & Poor's)	Home mortgage yields[4]	Prime rate charged by banks[5] High-low	Discount window (Federal Reserve Bank of New York)[5,6] Primary credit High-low	Adjustment credit High-low	Federal funds rate[7]
2016: Jan	0.25	0.44	1.14	2.09	2.86	4.00	5.45	3.01	3.87	3.50–3.50	1.00–1.00	....	0.34
Feb	.32	.44	.90	1.78	2.62	3.96	5.34	3.21	3.66	3.50–3.50	1.00–1.00		.38
Mar	.32	.48	1.04	1.89	2.68	3.82	5.13	3.28	3.69	3.50–3.50	1.00–1.00		.36
Apr	.23	.37	.92	1.81	2.62	3.62	4.79	3.04	3.61	3.50–3.50	1.00–1.00		.37
May	.27	.41	.97	1.81	2.63	3.65	4.68	2.95	3.60	3.50–3.50	1.00–1.00		.37
June	.29	.41	.86	1.64	2.45	3.50	4.53	2.84	3.57	3.50–3.50	1.00–1.00		.38
July	.31	.40	.79	1.50	2.23	3.28	4.22	2.57	3.44	3.50–3.50	1.00–1.00		.39
Aug	.30	.43	.85	1.56	2.26	3.32	4.24	2.77	3.44	3.50–3.50	1.00–1.00		.40
Sept	.32	.48	.90	1.63	2.35	3.41	4.31	2.86	3.46	3.50–3.50	1.00–1.00		.40
Oct	.34	.48	.99	1.76	2.50	3.51	4.38	3.13	3.47	3.50–3.50	1.00–1.00		.40
Nov	.44	.57	1.22	2.14	2.86	3.86	4.71	3.36	3.77	3.50–3.50	1.00–1.00		.41
Dec	.52	.64	1.49	2.49	3.11	4.06	4.83	3.81	4.20	3.75–3.50	1.25–1.00		.54
2017: Jan	.52	.61	1.48	2.43	3.02	3.92	4.66	3.68	4.15	3.75–3.75	1.25–1.25		.65
Feb	.53	.64	1.47	2.42	3.03	3.95	4.64	3.74	4.17	3.75–3.75	1.25–1.25		.66
Mar	.72	.84	1.59	2.48	3.08	4.01	4.68	3.78	4.20	4.00–3.75	1.50–1.25		.79
Apr	.81	.94	1.44	2.30	2.94	3.87	4.57	3.54	4.05	4.00–4.00	1.50–1.50		.90
May	.89	1.02	1.48	2.30	2.96	3.85	4.55	3.47	4.01	4.00–4.00	1.50–1.50		.91
June	.99	1.09	1.49	2.19	2.80	3.68	4.37	3.06	3.90	4.25–4.00	1.75–1.50		1.04
July	1.08	1.12	1.54	2.32	2.88	3.70	4.39	3.03	3.97	4.25–4.25	1.75–1.75		1.15
Aug	1.03	1.12	1.48	2.21	2.80	3.63	4.31	3.23	3.88	4.25–4.25	1.75–1.75		1.16
Sept	1.04	1.15	1.51	2.20	2.78	3.63	4.30	3.27	3.81	4.25–4.25	1.75–1.75		1.15
Oct	1.08	1.22	1.68	2.36	2.88	3.60	4.32	3.31	3.90	4.25–4.25	1.75–1.75		1.15
Nov	1.23	1.35	1.81	2.35	2.80	3.57	4.27	3.03	3.92	4.25–4.25	1.75–1.75		1.16
Dec	1.35	1.48	1.96	2.40	2.77	3.51	4.22	3.21	3.95	4.50–4.25	2.00–1.75		1.30
2018: Jan	1.43	1.59	2.15	2.58	2.88	3.55	4.26	3.29	4.03	4.50–4.50	2.00–2.00		1.41
Feb	1.53	1.72	2.36	2.86	3.13	3.82	4.51	3.54	4.33	4.50–4.50	2.00–2.00		1.42
Mar	1.70	1.87	2.42	2.84	3.09	3.87	4.64	3.58	4.44	4.75–4.50	2.25–2.00		1.51
Apr	1.76	1.93	2.52	2.87	3.07	3.85	4.67	3.55	4.47	4.75–4.75	2.25–2.25		1.69
May	1.87	2.03	2.66	2.98	3.13	4.00	4.83	3.38	4.59	4.75–4.75	2.25–2.25		1.70
June	1.91	2.08	2.65	2.91	3.05	3.96	4.83	3.15	4.57	5.00–4.75	2.50–2.25		1.82
July	1.96	2.12	2.70	2.89	3.01	3.87	4.79	3.45	4.53	5.00–5.00	2.50–2.50		1.91
Aug	2.03	2.18	2.71	2.89	3.04	3.88	4.77	3.58	4.55	5.00–5.00	2.50–2.50		1.91
Sept	2.13	2.28	2.84	3.00	3.15	3.98	4.88	3.63	4.63	5.25–5.00	2.75–2.50		1.95
Oct	2.24	2.39	2.94	3.15	3.34	4.14	5.07	3.88	4.83	5.25–5.25	2.75–2.75		2.19
Nov	2.34	2.46	2.91	3.12	3.36	4.22	5.22	3.64	4.87	5.25–5.25	2.75–2.75		2.20
Dec	2.38	2.49	2.67	2.83	3.10	4.02	5.13	3.69	4.64	5.50–5.25	3.00–2.75		2.27
2019: Jan	2.41	2.47	2.52	2.71	3.04	3.93	5.12	3.61	4.46	5.50–5.50	3.00–3.00		2.40
Feb	2.40	2.45	2.48	2.68	3.02	3.79	4.95	3.57	4.37	5.50–5.50	3.00–3.00		2.40
Mar	2.41	2.45	2.37	2.57	2.98	3.77	4.84	3.43	4.27	5.50–5.50	3.00–3.00		2.41
Apr	2.38	2.39	2.31	2.53	2.94	3.69	4.70	3.27	4.14	5.50–5.50	3.00–3.00		2.42
May	2.35	2.36	2.16	2.40	2.82	3.67	4.63	3.11	4.07	5.50–5.50	3.00–3.00		2.39
June	2.20	2.14	1.78	2.07	2.57	3.42	4.46	2.87	3.80	5.50–5.50	3.00–3.00		2.38
July	2.13	2.03	1.80	2.06	2.57	3.29	4.28	3.32	3.77	5.50–5.50	3.00–3.00		2.40
Aug	1.97	1.91	1.51	1.63	2.12	2.98	3.87	3.61	3.62	5.25–5.00	2.75–2.50		2.13
Sept	1.93	1.85	1.59	1.70	2.16	3.03	3.91	3.57	3.61	5.00–4.75	2.50–2.25		2.04
Oct	1.68	1.66	1.53	1.71	2.19	3.01	3.93	3.67	3.69	4.75–4.75	2.25–2.25		1.83
Nov	1.55	1.55	1.61	1.81	2.28	3.06	3.94	3.26	3.70	4.75–4.75	2.25–2.25		1.55
Dec	1.54	1.55	1.63	1.86	2.30	3.01	3.88	3.26	3.72	4.75–4.75	2.25–2.25		1.55
2020: Jan	1.53	1.53	1.52	1.76	2.22	2.94	3.77	3.00	3.62	4.75–4.75	2.25–2.25		1.55
Feb	1.54	1.50	1.31	1.50	1.97	2.78	3.61	2.66	3.47	4.75–4.75	2.25–2.25		1.58
Mar	.46	.45	.50	.87	1.46	3.02	4.29	3.07	3.45	4.75–3.25	2.25–0.25		.65
Apr	.15	.17	.28	.66	1.27	2.43	4.13	2.86	3.31	3.25–3.25	0.25–0.25		.05
May	.12	.15	.22	.67	1.38	2.49	3.95	2.69	3.23	3.25–3.25	0.25–0.25		.05
June	.16	.18	.22	.73	1.49	2.41	3.65	2.69	3.16	3.25–3.25	0.25–0.25		.08
July	.13	.15	.17	.62	1.31	2.14	3.31	1.75	3.02	3.25–3.25	0.25–0.25		.09
Aug	.10	.12	.16	.65	1.36	2.25	3.27	1.88	2.94	3.25–3.25	0.25–0.25		.10
Sept	.11	.12	.16	.68	1.42	2.31	3.36	2.10	2.89	3.25–3.25	0.25–0.25		.09
Oct	.10	.11	.19	.79	1.57	2.35	3.44	2.15	2.83	3.25–3.25	0.25–0.25		.09
Nov	.09	.10	.22	.87	1.62	2.30	3.30	2.10	2.77	3.25–3.25	0.25–0.25		.09

[2] Yields on the more actively traded issues adjusted to constant maturities by the Department of the Treasury. The 30-year Treasury constant maturity series was discontinued on February 18, 2002, and reintroduced on February 9, 2006.
[3] Beginning with December 7, 2001, data for corporate Aaa series are industrial bonds only.
[4] Contract interest rate on commitments for 30-year first-lien prime conventional conforming home purchase mortgage with a loan-to-value of 80 percent.
[5] For monthly data, high and low for the period.
[6] Primary credit replaced adjustment credit as the Federal Reserve's principal discount window lending program effective January 9, 2003.
[7] Beginning March 1, 2016, the daily effective federal funds rate is a volume-weighted median of transaction-level data collected from depository institutions in the Report of Selected Money Market Rates (FR 2420). Between July 21, 1975 and February 29, 2016, the daily effective rate was a volume-weighted mean of rates on brokered trades. Prior to that, the daily effective rate was the rate considered most representative of the day's transactions, usually the one at which most transactions occurred.

Sources: Department of the Treasury, Board of Governors of the Federal Reserve System, Federal Home Loan Mortgage Corporation, Moody's Investors Service, Bloomberg, and Standard & Poor's.

TABLE B–43. Mortgage debt outstanding by type of property and of financing, 1960–2019

[Billions of dollars]

End of year or quarter	All proper-ties	Farm proper-ties	Nonfarm properties				Nonfarm properties by type of mortgage					
							Government underwritten				Conventional [2]	
			Total	1- to 4-family houses	Multi-family proper-ties	Com-mercial proper-ties	Total [1]	1- to 4-family houses			Total	1- to 4-family houses
								Total	FHA-insured	VA-guaran-teed		
1960	208.4	12.8	195.6	141.4	20.8	33.4	62.3	56.4	26.7	29.7	133.2	84.9
1961	229.0	13.9	215.1	154.0	23.6	37.4	65.6	59.1	29.5	29.6	149.5	94.9
1962	252.4	15.2	237.2	168.3	26.7	42.2	69.4	62.2	32.3	29.9	167.9	106.1
1963	279.3	16.8	262.4	185.1	30.0	47.3	73.4	65.9	35.0	30.9	189.0	119.2
1964	307.0	18.9	288.1	203.2	34.6	51.2	77.2	69.2	38.3	30.9	210.9	133.1
1965	334.5	21.2	313.3	219.4	38.2	55.7	81.2	73.1	42.0	31.1	232.2	146.3
1966	358.5	23.1	335.5	232.7	41.3	61.5	84.1	76.1	44.8	31.3	251.4	156.7
1967	382.1	25.0	357.0	246.0	44.8	66.2	88.2	79.9	47.4	32.5	268.9	166.0
1968	411.4	27.2	384.2	262.9	48.3	73.0	93.4	84.4	50.6	33.8	290.8	178.5
1969	439.9	29.0	410.9	278.7	53.2	79.1	100.2	90.2	54.5	35.7	310.7	188.5
1970	469.4	30.5	438.9	292.2	60.1	86.5	109.2	97.3	59.9	37.3	329.6	195.0
1971	517.9	32.4	485.5	318.4	70.1	97.0	120.7	105.2	65.7	39.5	364.8	213.2
1972	589.8	35.4	554.4	357.4	82.9	114.2	131.1	113.0	68.2	44.7	423.3	244.4
1973	666.5	39.8	626.7	399.8	93.2	133.7	135.0	116.2	66.2	50.0	491.7	283.6
1974	728.4	44.9	683.5	435.2	100.0	148.3	140.2	121.3	65.1	56.2	543.3	313.9
1975	785.6	49.9	735.7	474.0	100.7	161.0	147.0	127.7	66.1	61.6	588.7	346.3
1976	870.5	55.4	815.1	535.0	105.9	174.2	154.0	133.5	66.5	67.0	661.1	401.5
1977	999.2	63.9	935.3	627.7	114.3	193.3	161.7	141.6	68.0	73.6	773.5	486.1
1978	1,150.7	72.8	1,077.9	738.3	125.2	214.5	176.4	153.4	71.4	82.0	901.5	584.9
1979	1,317.0	86.8	1,230.3	855.8	135.0	239.4	199.0	172.9	81.0	92.0	1,031.3	682.8
1980	1,457.8	97.5	1,360.3	957.9	142.5	259.9	225.1	195.2	93.6	101.6	1,135.3	762.7
1981	1,579.5	107.2	1,472.3	1,030.2	142.4	299.7	238.9	207.6	101.3	106.2	1,233.4	822.6
1982	1,661.3	111.3	1,550.0	1,070.2	146.1	333.7	248.9	217.9	108.0	109.9	1,301.1	852.3
1983	1,850.6	113.7	1,736.9	1,186.3	161.2	389.4	279.8	248.8	127.4	121.4	1,457.1	937.4
1984	2,092.0	112.4	1,979.6	1,321.5	186.1	471.9	294.8	265.9	136.7	129.1	1,684.7	1,055.7
1985	2,368.5	94.1	2,274.5	1,526.9	205.9	541.7	328.3	288.8	153.0	135.8	1,946.1	1,238.1
1986	2,655.6	84.1	2,571.5	1,730.1	239.4	602.0	370.5	328.6	185.5	143.1	2,201.0	1,401.5
1987	2,954.3	75.8	2,878.5	1,928.5	258.4	691.6	431.4	387.9	235.5	152.4	2,447.0	1,540.6
1988	3,271.9	70.8	3,201.1	2,162.8	274.5	763.7	459.7	414.2	258.8	155.4	2,741.4	1,748.6
1989	3,523.6	68.8	3,454.8	2,369.6	287.0	798.2	486.8	440.1	282.8	157.3	2,967.9	1,929.5
1990	3,779.5	67.6	3,711.8	2,606.8	287.4	817.6	517.9	470.9	310.9	160.0	3,193.9	2,135.9
1991	3,930.7	67.5	3,863.2	2,774.7	284.1	804.4	537.2	493.3	330.6	162.7	3,326.0	2,281.4
1992	4,040.8	67.9	3,972.9	2,942.1	270.9	759.9	533.3	489.8	326.0	163.8	3,439.6	2,452.3
1993	4,171.5	68.4	4,103.1	3,101.1	267.8	734.2	513.4	469.5	303.2	166.2	3,589.7	2,631.7
1994	4,336.3	69.9	4,266.3	3,278.6	268.5	719.2	559.3	514.2	336.8	177.3	3,707.0	2,764.4
1995	4,522.1	71.7	4,450.3	3,446.4	274.4	729.5	584.3	537.1	352.3	184.7	3,866.1	2,909.4
1996	4,802.8	74.4	4,728.4	3,682.8	286.7	758.9	620.3	571.2	379.2	192.0	4,108.1	3,111.6
1997	5,115.9	78.5	5,037.4	3,917.6	298.8	821.1	656.7	605.7	405.7	200.0	4,380.8	3,311.8
1998	5,603.2	83.1	5,520.1	4,275.8	334.5	909.8	674.0	623.8	417.9	205.9	4,846.1	3,652.0
1999	6,209.6	87.2	6,122.4	4,701.2	375.2	1,046.0	731.5	678.8	462.3	216.5	5,390.9	4,022.4
2000	6,766.6	84.7	6,681.9	5,125.0	404.5	1,152.5	773.1	719.9	499.9	220.1	5,908.8	4,405.0
2001	7,450.1	88.5	7,361.6	5,678.0	446.1	1,237.4	727.7	718.5	497.4	221.2	6,588.9	4,959.5
2002	8,358.7	95.4	8,263.3	6,434.4	486.3	1,342.6	759.3	704.0	486.2	217.7	7,504.0	5,730.4
2003	9,364.8	83.2	9,281.6	7,260.3	559.7	1,461.6	709.2	653.3	438.7	214.6	8,572.5	6,607.1
2004	10,646.7	95.7	10,551.0	8,292.1	609.3	1,649.6	660.2	604.1	398.1	206.0	9,890.8	7,688.0
2005	12,112.9	104.8	12,008.1	9,448.5	674.3	1,885.3	606.6	550.4	348.4	202.0	11,401.5	8,898.1
2006	13,525.6	108.0	13,417.5	10,530.8	717.5	2,169.2	600.2	543.5	336.9	206.6	12,817.4	9,987.3
2007	14,609.7	112.7	14,497.0	11,252.3	810.6	2,434.1	609.2	552.6	342.6	210.0	13,887.8	10,699.7
2008	14,690.0	134.7	14,555.3	11,150.9	852.9	2,551.5	807.2	750.7	534.0	216.7	13,748.1	10,400.2
2009	14,445.1	146.0	14,299.1	10,960.9	862.7	2,475.5	1,005.0	944.3	752.6	191.7	13,294.1	10,016.6
2010	13,892.8	154.1	13,738.7	10,523.4	862.9	2,352.4	1,227.6	1,156.1	934.4	221.7	12,511.1	9,367.3
2011	13,567.8	167.2	13,400.6	10,281.3	863.3	2,255.9	1,368.6	1,291.3	1,036.0	255.3	12,032.0	8,990.1
2012	13,331.3	173.4	13,157.9	10,047.7	891.2	2,219.0	1,544.8	1,459.7	1,165.4	294.2	11,613.0	8,588.0
2013	13,344.5	185.2	13,159.3	9,959.6	940.9	2,258.8	3,927.2	3,832.6	3,480.8	351.8	9,232.1	6,127.1
2014	13,486.8	196.8	13,290.0	9,936.6	1,009.1	2,344.3	4,130.9	4,028.1	3,615.3	412.8	9,159.1	5,908.5
2015	13,883.3	208.8	13,674.5	10,076.4	1,118.8	2,479.3	4,432.7	4,326.7	3,851.3	475.4	9,241.8	5,749.7
2016	14,331.9	226.0	14,105.9	10,277.1	1,236.3	2,592.5	4,764.8	4,654.9	4,106.9	548.1	9,341.0	5,622.2
2017	14,892.0	236.2	14,655.8	10,581.5	1,358.6	2,715.7	5,079.1	4,958.2	4,344.3	613.9	9,576.8	5,623.4
2018	15,429.1	245.7	15,183.4	10,871.8	1,480.6	2,831.0	5,380.0	5,246.5	4,562.3	684.2	9,803.4	5,625.3
2019	15,519.8	250.9	15,268.9	10,901.4	1,505.5	2,862.0	5,416.7	5,281.4	4,588.7	692.7	9,852.2	5,620.0
2019: I	15,519.8	250.9	15,268.9	10,901.4	1,505.5	2,862.0	5,416.7	5,281.4	4,588.7	692.7	9,852.2	5,620.0
II	15,654.4	256.2	15,398.2	10,984.1	1,529.8	2,884.4	5,479.8	5,343.7	4,643.4	700.3	9,918.4	5,640.4
III	15,856.1	261.5	15,594.6	11,085.5	1,577.6	2,931.5	5,563.7	5,425.5	4,713.2	712.3	10,030.9	5,660.0
IV	16,008.4	266.8	15,741.6	11,157.6	1,617.7	2,966.4	5,664.1	5,522.9	4,788.6	734.3	10,077.5	5,634.6
2020: I	16,139.0	270.5	15,868.5	11,219.4	1,637.4	3,011.7	5,758.4	5,616.5	4,866.4	750.1	10,110.2	5,602.9
II [p]	16,284.1	274.2	16,010.0	11,303.8	1,671.8	3,034.3	5,852.3	5,709.4	4,939.6	769.8	10,157.7	5,594.5

[1] Includes Federal Housing Administration (FHA)–insured multi-family properties, not shown separately.
[2] Derived figures. Total includes multi-family and commercial properties with conventional mortgages, not shown separately.

Source: Board of Governors of the Federal Reserve System, based on data from various Government and private organizations.

[Billions of dollars]

End of year or quarter	Total	Major financial institutions			Other holders		
		Total	Depository Institutions[1,2]	Life insurance companies	Federal and related agencies[3]	Mortgage pools or trusts[4]	Individuals and others
1960	208.4	156.4	114.6	41.8	11.3	0.2	40.5
1961	229.0	171.1	126.9	44.2	11.9	.3	45.7
1962	252.4	190.5	143.6	46.9	12.2	.4	49.3
1963	279.3	214.6	164.1	50.5	11.3	.5	52.9
1964	307.0	238.8	183.6	55.2	11.6	.6	56.0
1965	334.5	262.4	202.4	60.0	12.7	.9	58.6
1966	358.5	279.5	214.8	64.6	16.2	1.3	61.5
1967	382.1	296.4	228.9	67.5	18.9	2.0	64.7
1968	411.4	317.3	247.3	70.0	22.6	2.5	69.0
1969	439.9	336.6	264.6	72.0	27.9	3.2	72.2
1970	469.4	352.9	278.5	74.4	33.6	4.8	78.2
1971	517.9	389.2	313.7	75.5	36.8	9.5	82.3
1972	589.8	443.8	366.8	76.9	40.1	14.4	91.5
1973	666.5	500.7	419.4	81.4	46.6	18.0	101.1
1974	728.4	539.3	453.1	86.2	60.7	21.5	106.9
1975	785.6	576.1	486.9	89.2	72.6	28.5	108.4
1976	870.5	640.7	549.1	91.6	76.0	40.7	113.2
1977	999.2	735.3	638.4	96.8	83.7	56.8	123.4
1978	1,150.7	837.5	731.3	106.2	100.2	70.4	142.7
1979	1,317.0	928.6	810.2	118.4	121.2	94.8	172.4
1980	1,457.8	988.0	857.0	131.1	142.9	114.0	213.0
1981	1,579.5	1,034.1	896.4	137.7	160.4	129.0	256.0
1982	1,661.3	1,019.6	877.6	142.0	176.9	178.5	286.3
1983	1,850.6	1,108.4	957.4	151.0	188.5	244.8	309.0
1984	2,092.0	1,248.2	1,091.5	156.7	201.6	300.0	342.2
1985	2,368.5	1,368.7	1,196.9	171.8	213.0	392.4	394.4
1986	2,655.6	1,483.3	1,289.5	193.8	202.1	549.5	420.6
1987	2,954.3	1,631.5	1,419.1	212.4	188.5	700.8	433.4
1988	3,271.9	1,797.8	1,564.9	232.9	192.5	785.7	495.9
1989	3,523.6	1,897.4	1,643.2	254.2	197.8	922.2	506.1
1990	3,779.5	1,918.8	1,651.0	267.9	239.0	1,085.9	535.7
1991	3,930.7	1,846.2	1,586.7	259.5	266.0	1,269.6	549.0
1992	4,040.8	1,770.5	1,528.5	242.0	286.1	1,440.0	544.3
1993	4,171.5	1,770.1	1,546.3	223.9	326.1	1,561.1	514.2
1994	4,336.3	1,824.7	1,608.9	215.8	315.6	1,696.9	499.1
1995	4,522.1	1,900.1	1,687.0	213.1	307.9	1,812.0	502.0
1996	4,802.8	1,982.2	1,773.7	208.5	294.4	1,989.1	537.1
1997	5,115.9	2,084.2	1,877.1	207.0	285.2	2,166.5	580.1
1998	5,603.2	2,194.7	1,981.0	213.8	291.9	2,487.1	629.5
1999	6,209.6	2,394.5	2,163.5	231.0	319.8	2,832.3	663.1
2000	6,766.6	2,619.2	2,383.0	236.2	339.9	3,097.5	710.1
2001	7,450.1	2,791.0	2,547.9	243.1	372.0	3,532.4	754.7
2002	8,358.7	3,089.4	2,839.3	250.1	432.3	3,978.4	858.6
2003	9,364.8	3,387.5	3,126.4	261.2	694.1	4,330.3	952.9
2004	10,646.7	3,926.5	3,653.0	273.5	703.2	4,834.5	1,182.5
2005	12,112.9	4,396.5	4,110.8	285.7	665.4	5,710.0	1,341.1
2006	13,525.6	4,784.0	4,479.8	304.1	687.5	6,629.5	1,424.7
2007	14,609.7	5,065.5	4,738.4	327.1	725.5	7,434.4	1,384.3
2008	14,690.0	5,045.8	4,702.0	343.8	801.1	7,592.7	1,250.4
2009	14,445.1	4,779.4	4,452.0	327.4	816.1	7,649.8	1,199.8
2010	13,892.8	4,585.2	4,266.1	319.2	5,127.5	3,108.4	1,071.7
2011	13,567.8	4,450.3	4,115.7	334.6	5,033.9	3,034.3	1,049.2
2012	13,331.3	4,438.2	4,091.3	346.9	4,935.0	2,947.6	1,010.5
2013	13,344.5	4,412.3	4,046.1	366.3	4,993.2	2,773.5	1,165.5
2014	13,486.8	4,546.7	4,158.5	388.2	4,987.7	2,742.7	1,209.8
2015	13,883.3	4,804.2	4,373.6	430.7	5,036.6	2,793.6	1,248.9
2016	14,331.9	5,096.7	4,631.2	465.5	5,146.9	2,826.6	1,261.7
2017	14,892.0	5,308.0	4,801.3	506.7	5,313.6	2,971.9	1,298.6
2018	15,429.1	5,487.5	4,919.4	568.1	5,457.0	3,143.9	1,340.7
2019	16,008.4	5,710.4	5,091.2	619.2	5,634.5	3,262.6	1,401.0
2019: I	15,519.8	5,518.4	4,936.9	581.6	5,480.6	3,162.9	1,357.8
II	15,654.4	5,592.2	5,001.7	590.4	5,510.1	3,184.2	1,367.9
III	15,856.1	5,648.9	5,043.5	605.4	5,583.9	3,231.2	1,392.1
IV	16,008.4	5,710.4	5,091.2	619.2	5,634.5	3,262.6	1,401.0
2020: I	16,139.0	5,754.3	5,125.6	628.7	5,692.4	3,307.9	1,384.3
II [p]	16,284.1	5,775.7	5,144.5	631.2	5,832.5	3,278.9	1,397.0

[1] Includes savings banks and savings and loan associations. Data reported by Federal Savings and Loan Insurance Corporation–insured institutions include loans in process for 1987 and exclude loans in process beginning with 1988.

[2] Includes loans held by nondeposit trust companies but not loans held by bank trust departments.

[3] Includes Government National Mortgage Association (GNMA or Ginnie Mae), Federal Housing Administration, Veterans Administration, Farmers Home Administration (FmHA), Federal Deposit Insurance Corporation, Resolution Trust Corporation (through 1995), and in earlier years Reconstruction Finance Corporation, Homeowners Loan Corporation, Federal Farm Mortgage Corporation, and Public Housing Administration. Also includes U.S.-sponsored agencies such as Federal National Mortgage Association (FNMA or Fannie Mae), Federal Land Banks, Federal Home Loan Mortgage Corporation (FHLMC or Freddie Mac), Federal Agricultural Mortgage Corporation (Farmer Mac, beginning 1994), Federal Home Loan Banks (beginning 1997), and mortgage pass-through securities issued or guaranteed by GNMA, FHLMC, FNMA, FmHA, or Farmer Mac. Other U.S. agencies (amounts small or current separate data not readily available) included with "individuals and others."

[4] Includes private mortgage pools.

Source: Board of Governors of the Federal Reserve System, based on data from various Government and private organizations.

Money Stock, Credit, and Finance | 509

Government Finance

Table B-45. Federal receipts, outlays, surplus or deficit, and debt, fiscal years 1955–2020
[Billions of dollars; fiscal years]

Fiscal year or period	Total			On-budget			Off-budget			Federal debt (end of period)		Addendum: Gross domestic product
	Receipts	Outlays	Surplus or deficit (–)	Receipts	Outlays	Surplus or deficit (–)	Receipts	Outlays	Surplus or deficit (–)	Gross Federal	Held by the public	
1955	65.5	68.4	–3.0	60.4	64.5	–4.1	5.1	4.0	1.1	274.4	226.6	406.3
1956	74.6	70.6	3.9	68.2	65.7	2.5	6.4	5.0	1.5	272.7	222.2	438.2
1957	80.0	76.6	3.4	73.2	70.6	2.6	6.8	6.0	.8	272.3	219.3	463.4
1958	79.6	82.4	–2.8	71.6	74.9	–3.3	8.0	7.5	.5	279.7	226.3	473.5
1959	79.2	92.1	–12.8	71.0	83.1	–12.1	8.3	9.0	–.7	287.5	234.7	504.6
1960	92.5	92.2	.3	81.9	81.3	.5	10.6	10.9	–.2	290.5	236.8	534.3
1961	94.4	97.7	–3.3	82.3	86.0	–3.8	12.1	11.7	.4	292.6	238.4	546.6
1962	99.7	106.8	–7.1	87.4	93.3	–5.9	12.3	13.5	–1.3	302.9	248.0	585.7
1963	106.6	111.3	–4.8	92.4	96.4	–4.0	14.2	15.0	–.8	310.3	254.0	618.2
1964	112.6	118.5	–5.9	96.2	102.8	–6.5	16.4	15.7	.6	316.1	256.8	661.7
1965	116.8	118.2	–1.4	100.1	101.7	–1.6	16.7	16.5	.2	322.3	260.8	709.3
1966	130.8	134.5	–3.7	111.7	114.8	–3.1	19.1	19.7	–.6	328.5	263.7	780.5
1967	148.8	157.5	–8.6	124.4	137.0	–12.6	24.4	20.4	4.0	340.4	266.6	836.5
1968	153.0	178.1	–25.2	128.1	155.8	–27.7	24.9	22.3	2.6	368.7	289.5	897.6
1969	186.9	183.6	3.2	157.9	158.4	–.5	29.0	25.2	3.7	365.8	278.1	980.3
1970	192.8	195.6	–2.8	159.3	168.0	–8.7	33.5	27.6	5.9	380.9	283.2	1,046.7
1971	187.1	210.2	–23.0	151.3	177.3	–26.1	35.8	32.8	3.0	408.2	303.0	1,116.6
1972	207.3	230.7	–23.4	167.4	193.5	–26.1	39.9	37.2	2.7	435.9	322.4	1,216.2
1973	230.8	245.7	–14.9	184.7	200.0	–15.2	46.1	45.7	.3	466.3	340.9	1,352.7
1974	263.2	269.4	–6.1	209.3	216.5	–7.2	53.9	52.9	1.1	483.9	343.7	1,482.8
1975	279.1	332.3	–53.2	216.6	270.8	–54.1	62.5	61.6	.9	541.9	394.7	1,606.9
1976	298.1	371.8	–73.7	231.7	301.1	–69.4	66.4	70.7	–4.3	629.0	477.4	1,786.1
Transition quarter	81.2	96.0	–14.7	63.2	77.3	–14.1	18.0	18.7	–.7	643.6	495.5	471.6
1977	355.6	409.2	–53.7	278.7	328.7	–49.9	76.8	80.5	–3.7	706.4	549.1	2,024.3
1978	399.6	458.7	–59.2	314.2	369.6	–55.4	85.4	89.2	–3.8	776.6	607.1	2,273.4
1979	463.3	504.0	–40.7	365.3	404.9	–39.6	98.0	99.1	–1.1	829.5	640.3	2,565.6
1980	517.1	590.9	–73.8	403.9	477.0	–73.1	113.2	113.9	–.7	909.0	711.9	2,791.9
1981	599.3	678.2	–79.0	469.1	543.0	–73.9	130.2	135.3	–5.1	994.8	789.4	3,133.2
1982	617.8	745.7	–128.0	474.3	594.9	–120.6	143.5	150.9	–7.4	1,137.3	924.6	3,313.4
1983	600.6	808.4	–207.8	453.2	660.9	–207.7	147.3	147.4	–.1	1,371.7	1,137.3	3,536.0
1984	666.4	851.8	–185.4	500.4	685.6	–185.3	166.1	166.2	–.1	1,564.6	1,307.0	3,949.2
1985	734.0	946.3	–212.3	547.9	769.4	–221.5	186.2	176.9	9.2	1,817.4	1,507.3	4,265.1
1986	769.2	990.4	–221.2	568.9	806.8	–237.9	200.2	183.5	16.7	2,120.5	1,740.6	4,526.2
1987	854.3	1,004.0	–149.7	640.9	809.2	–168.4	213.4	194.8	18.6	2,346.0	1,889.8	4,767.6
1988	909.2	1,064.4	–155.2	667.7	860.0	–192.3	241.5	204.4	37.1	2,601.1	2,051.6	5,138.6
1989	991.1	1,143.7	–152.6	727.4	932.8	–205.4	263.7	210.9	52.8	2,867.8	2,190.7	5,554.7
1990	1,032.0	1,253.0	–221.0	750.3	1,027.9	–277.6	281.7	225.1	56.6	3,206.3	2,411.6	5,898.8
1991	1,055.0	1,324.2	–269.2	761.1	1,082.5	–321.4	293.9	241.7	52.2	3,598.2	2,689.0	6,093.2
1992	1,091.2	1,381.5	–290.3	788.8	1,129.2	–340.4	302.4	252.3	50.1	4,001.8	2,999.7	6,416.2
1993	1,154.3	1,409.4	–255.1	842.4	1,142.8	–300.4	311.9	266.6	45.3	4,351.0	3,248.4	6,775.3
1994	1,258.6	1,461.8	–203.2	923.5	1,182.4	–258.8	335.0	279.4	55.7	4,643.3	3,433.1	7,176.8
1995	1,351.8	1,515.7	–164.0	1,000.7	1,227.1	–226.4	351.1	288.7	62.4	4,920.6	3,604.4	7,560.4
1996	1,453.1	1,560.5	–107.4	1,085.6	1,259.6	–174.0	367.5	300.9	66.6	5,181.5	3,734.1	7,951.3
1997	1,579.2	1,601.1	–21.9	1,187.2	1,290.5	–103.2	392.0	310.6	81.4	5,369.2	3,772.3	8,451.0
1998	1,721.7	1,652.5	69.3	1,305.9	1,335.9	–29.9	415.8	316.6	99.2	5,478.2	3,721.1	8,930.8
1999	1,827.5	1,701.8	125.6	1,383.0	1,381.1	1.9	444.5	320.8	123.7	5,605.5	3,632.4	9,479.4
2000	2,025.2	1,789.0	236.2	1,544.6	1,458.2	86.4	480.6	330.8	149.8	5,628.7	3,409.8	10,117.4
2001	1,991.1	1,862.8	128.2	1,483.6	1,516.0	–32.4	507.5	346.8	160.7	5,769.9	3,319.6	10,526.5
2002	1,853.1	2,010.9	–157.8	1,337.8	1,655.2	–317.4	515.3	355.7	159.7	6,198.4	3,540.4	10,833.6
2003	1,782.3	2,159.9	–377.6	1,258.5	1,796.9	–538.4	523.8	363.0	160.8	6,760.0	3,913.4	11,283.8
2004	1,880.1	2,292.8	–412.7	1,345.4	1,913.3	–568.0	534.7	379.5	155.2	7,354.7	4,295.5	12,025.4
2005	2,153.6	2,472.0	–318.3	1,576.1	2,069.7	–493.6	577.5	402.2	175.3	7,905.3	4,592.2	12,834.2
2006	2,406.9	2,655.1	–248.2	1,798.5	2,233.0	–434.5	608.4	422.1	186.3	8,451.4	4,829.0	13,638.4
2007	2,568.0	2,728.7	–160.7	1,932.9	2,275.0	–342.2	635.1	453.6	181.5	8,950.7	5,035.1	14,290.8
2008	2,524.0	2,982.5	–458.6	1,865.9	2,507.8	–641.8	658.0	474.8	183.3	9,986.1	5,803.1	14,743.3
2009	2,105.0	3,517.7	–1,412.7	1,451.0	3,000.7	–1,549.7	654.0	517.0	137.0	11,875.9	7,544.7	14,431.8
2010	2,162.7	3,457.1	–1,294.4	1,531.0	2,902.4	–1,371.4	631.7	554.7	77.0	13,528.8	9,018.9	14,838.8
2011	2,303.5	3,603.1	–1,299.6	1,737.7	3,104.5	–1,366.8	565.8	498.6	67.2	14,764.2	10,128.2	15,403.7
2012	2,450.0	3,526.6	–1,076.6	1,880.5	3,019.0	–1,138.5	569.5	507.6	61.9	16,050.9	11,281.1	16,056.4
2013	2,775.1	3,454.9	–679.8	2,101.8	2,821.1	–719.2	673.3	633.8	39.5	16,719.4	11,982.7	16,603.8
2014	3,021.5	3,506.3	–484.8	2,285.9	2,800.2	–514.3	735.6	706.1	29.5	17,794.5	12,779.9	17,335.6
2015	3,249.9	3,691.9	–442.0	2,479.5	2,948.8	–469.3	770.4	743.1	27.3	18,120.1	13,116.7	18,106.1
2016	3,268.0	3,852.6	–584.7	2,457.8	3,077.9	–620.2	810.2	774.7	35.5	19,539.5	14,167.6	18,581.6
2017	3,316.2	3,981.6	–665.4	2,465.6	3,180.4	–714.9	850.6	801.2	49.4	20,205.7	14,665.4	19,316.6
2018	3,329.9	4,109.0	–779.1	2,475.2	3,260.5	–785.3	854.7	848.6	6.2	21,462.3	15,749.6	20,368.9
2019	3,464.2	4,448.3	–984.2	2,549.9	3,541.7	–991.8	914.3	906.6	7.7	22,669.5	16,800.7	21,223.8
2020 (estimates) [1]	3,420.0	6,551.9	–3,131.9	2,454.5	5,596.3	–3,141.8	965.4	955.6	9.8	26,901.1	21,019.1	20,996.4

[1] Estimates from *Final Monthly Treasury Statement*, issued October 2020.

Note: Fiscal years through 1976 were on a July 1–June 30 basis; beginning with October 1976 (fiscal year 1977), the fiscal year is on an October 1–September 30 basis. The transition quarter is the three-month period from July 1, 1976 through September 30, 1976.

See *Budget of the United States Government, Fiscal Year 2021*, for additional information.

Sources: Department of Commerce (Bureau of Economic Analysis), Department of the Treasury, and Office of Management and Budget.

TABLE B–46. Federal receipts, outlays, surplus or deficit, and debt, as percent of gross domestic product, fiscal years 1949–2020

[Percent; fiscal years]

Fiscal year or period	Receipts	Outlays		Surplus or deficit (−)	Federal debt (end of period)	
		Total	National defense		Gross Federal	Held by public
1949	14.3	14.0	4.8	0.2	91.4	77.5
1950	14.2	15.3	4.9	−1.1	92.2	78.6
1951	15.8	13.9	7.2	1.9	78.1	65.5
1952	18.5	19.0	12.9	−.4	72.6	60.1
1953	18.2	19.9	13.8	−1.7	69.6	57.2
1954	18.0	18.3	12.7	−.3	70.0	58.0
1955	16.1	16.8	10.5	−.7	67.5	55.8
1956	17.0	16.1	9.7	.9	62.2	50.7
1957	17.3	16.5	9.8	.7	58.8	47.3
1958	16.8	17.4	9.9	−.6	59.1	47.8
1959	15.7	18.3	9.7	−2.5	57.0	46.5
1960	17.3	17.3	9.0	.1	54.4	44.3
1961	17.3	17.9	9.1	−.6	53.5	43.6
1962	17.0	18.2	8.9	−1.2	51.7	42.3
1963	17.2	18.0	8.6	−.8	50.2	41.1
1964	17.0	17.9	8.3	−.9	47.8	38.8
1965	16.5	16.7	7.1	−.2	45.4	36.8
1966	16.8	17.2	7.4	−.5	42.1	33.8
1967	17.8	18.8	8.5	−1.0	40.7	31.9
1968	17.0	19.8	9.1	−2.8	41.1	32.3
1969	19.1	18.7	8.4	.3	37.3	28.4
1970	18.4	18.7	7.8	−.3	36.4	27.1
1971	16.8	18.8	7.1	−2.1	36.6	27.1
1972	17.0	19.0	6.5	−1.9	35.8	26.5
1973	17.1	18.2	5.7	−1.1	34.5	25.2
1974	17.8	18.2	5.4	−.4	32.6	23.2
1975	17.4	20.7	5.4	−3.3	33.7	24.6
1976	16.7	20.8	5.0	−4.1	35.2	26.7
Transition quarter	17.2	20.3	4.7	−3.1	34.1	26.3
1977	17.6	20.2	4.8	−2.7	34.9	27.1
1978	17.6	20.2	4.6	−2.6	34.2	26.7
1979	18.1	19.6	4.5	−1.6	32.3	25.0
1980	18.5	21.2	4.8	−2.6	32.6	25.5
1981	19.1	21.6	5.0	−2.5	31.8	25.2
1982	18.6	22.5	5.6	−3.9	34.3	27.9
1983	17.0	22.9	5.9	−5.9	38.8	32.2
1984	16.9	21.6	5.8	−4.7	39.6	33.1
1985	17.2	22.2	5.9	−5.0	42.6	35.3
1986	17.0	21.9	6.0	−4.9	46.8	38.5
1987	17.9	21.1	5.9	−3.1	49.2	39.6
1988	17.7	20.7	5.7	−3.0	50.6	39.9
1989	17.8	20.6	5.5	−2.7	51.6	39.4
1990	17.5	21.2	5.1	−3.7	54.4	40.9
1991	17.3	21.7	4.5	−4.4	59.1	44.1
1992	17.0	21.5	4.6	−4.5	62.4	46.8
1993	17.0	20.8	4.3	−3.8	64.2	47.9
1994	17.5	20.4	3.9	−2.8	64.7	47.8
1995	17.9	20.0	3.6	−2.2	65.1	47.7
1996	18.3	19.6	3.3	−1.4	65.2	47.0
1997	18.7	18.9	3.2	−.3	63.5	44.6
1998	19.3	18.5	3.0	.8	61.3	41.7
1999	19.3	18.0	2.9	1.3	59.1	38.3
2000	20.0	17.7	2.9	2.3	55.6	33.7
2001	18.9	17.7	2.9	1.2	54.8	31.5
2002	17.1	18.6	3.2	−1.5	57.2	32.7
2003	15.8	19.1	3.6	−3.3	59.9	34.7
2004	15.6	19.1	3.8	−3.4	61.2	35.7
2005	16.8	19.3	3.9	−2.5	61.6	35.8
2006	17.6	19.5	3.8	−1.8	62.0	35.4
2007	18.0	19.1	3.9	−1.1	62.6	35.2
2008	17.1	20.2	4.2	−3.1	67.7	39.4
2009	14.6	24.4	4.6	−9.8	82.3	52.3
2010	14.6	23.3	4.7	−8.7	91.2	60.8
2011	15.0	23.4	4.6	−8.4	95.8	65.8
2012	15.3	22.0	4.2	−6.7	100.0	70.3
2013	16.7	20.8	3.8	−4.1	100.7	72.2
2014	17.4	20.2	3.5	−2.8	102.6	73.7
2015	17.9	20.4	3.3	−2.4	100.1	72.4
2016	17.6	20.7	3.2	−3.1	105.2	76.2
2017	17.2	20.6	3.1	−3.4	104.6	75.9
2018	16.3	20.2	3.1	−3.8	105.4	77.3
2019	16.3	21.0	3.2	−4.6	106.8	79.2
2020 (estimates)[1]	16.3	31.2	3.5	−14.9	128.1	100.1

[1] Estimates from *Final Monthly Treasury Statement*, issued October 2020.

Note: See Note, Table B–45.

Sources: Department of the Treasury and Office of Management and Budget.

TABLE B–47. Federal receipts and outlays, by major category, and surplus or deficit, fiscal years 1955–2020

[Billions of dollars; fiscal years]

Fiscal year or period	Receipts (on-budget and off-budget)					Outlays (on-budget and off-budget)										Surplus or deficit (−) (on-budget and off-budget)
	Total	Individual income taxes	Corporation income taxes	Social insurance and retirement receipts	Other	Total	National defense		International affairs	Health	Medicare	Income security	Social security	Net interest	Other	
							Total	Department of Defense, military								
1955	65.5	28.7	17.9	7.9	11.0	68.4	42.7		2.2	0.3		5.1	4.4	4.9	8.9	−3.0
1956	74.6	32.2	20.9	9.3	12.2	70.6	42.5		2.4	.4		4.7	5.5	5.1	10.1	3.9
1957	80.0	35.6	21.2	10.0	13.2	76.6	45.4		3.1	.5		5.4	6.7	5.4	10.1	3.4
1958	79.6	34.7	20.1	11.2	13.6	82.4	46.8		3.4	.5		7.5	8.2	5.6	10.3	−2.8
1959	79.2	36.7	17.3	11.7	13.5	92.1	49.0		3.1	.7		8.2	9.7	5.8	15.5	−12.8
1960	92.5	40.7	21.5	14.7	15.6	92.2	48.1		3.0	.8		7.4	11.6	6.9	14.4	.3
1961	94.4	41.3	21.0	16.4	15.7	97.7	49.6		3.2	.9		9.7	12.5	6.7	15.2	−3.3
1962	99.7	45.6	20.5	17.0	16.5	106.8	52.3	50.1	5.6	1.2		9.2	14.4	6.9	17.2	−7.1
1963	106.6	47.6	21.6	19.8	17.6	111.3	53.4	51.1	5.3	1.5		9.3	15.8	7.7	18.3	−4.8
1964	112.6	48.7	23.5	22.0	18.5	118.5	54.8	52.6	4.9	1.8		9.7	16.6	8.2	22.6	−5.9
1965	116.8	48.8	25.5	22.2	20.3	118.2	50.6	48.8	5.3	1.8		9.5	17.5	8.6	25.0	−1.4
1966	130.8	55.4	30.1	25.5	19.8	134.5	58.1	56.6	5.6	2.5	0.1	9.7	20.7	9.4	28.5	−3.7
1967	148.8	61.5	34.0	32.6	20.7	157.5	71.4	70.1	5.6	3.4	2.7	10.3	21.7	10.3	32.1	−8.6
1968	153.0	68.7	28.7	33.9	21.7	178.1	81.9	80.4	5.3	4.4	4.6	11.8	23.9	11.1	35.1	−25.2
1969	186.9	87.2	36.7	39.0	23.9	183.6	82.5	80.8	4.6	5.2	5.7	13.1	27.3	12.7	32.6	3.2
1970	192.8	90.4	32.8	44.4	25.2	195.6	81.7	80.1	4.3	5.9	6.2	15.6	30.3	14.4	37.2	−2.8
1971	187.1	86.2	26.8	47.3	26.8	210.2	78.9	77.5	4.2	6.8	6.6	22.9	35.9	14.8	40.0	−23.0
1972	207.3	94.7	32.2	52.6	27.8	230.7	79.2	77.6	4.8	8.7	7.5	27.6	40.2	15.5	47.3	−23.4
1973	230.8	103.2	36.2	63.1	28.3	245.7	76.7	75.0	4.1	9.4	8.1	28.3	49.1	17.3	52.8	−14.9
1974	263.2	119.0	38.6	75.1	30.6	269.4	79.3	77.9	5.7	10.7	9.6	33.7	55.9	21.4	52.9	−6.1
1975	279.1	122.4	40.6	84.5	31.5	332.3	86.5	84.9	7.1	12.9	12.9	50.2	64.7	23.2	74.9	−53.2
1976	298.1	131.6	41.4	90.8	34.3	371.8	89.6	87.9	6.4	15.7	15.8	60.8	73.9	26.7	82.8	−73.7
Transition quarter	81.2	38.8	8.5	25.2	8.6	96.0	22.3	21.8	2.5	3.9	4.3	15.0	19.8	6.9	21.4	−14.7
1977	355.6	157.6	54.9	106.5	36.6	409.2	97.2	95.1	6.4	17.3	19.3	61.0	85.1	29.9	93.0	−53.7
1978	399.6	181.0	60.0	121.0	37.7	458.7	104.5	102.3	7.5	18.5	22.8	61.5	93.9	35.5	114.7	−59.2
1979	463.3	217.8	65.7	138.9	40.8	504.0	116.3	113.6	7.5	20.5	26.5	66.4	104.1	42.6	120.2	−40.7
1980	517.1	244.1	64.6	157.8	50.6	590.9	134.0	130.9	12.7	23.2	32.1	86.5	118.5	52.5	131.3	−73.8
1981	599.3	285.9	61.1	182.7	69.5	678.2	157.5	153.9	13.1	26.9	39.1	100.3	139.6	68.8	133.0	−79.0
1982	617.8	297.7	49.2	201.5	69.3	745.7	185.3	180.7	12.3	27.4	46.6	108.1	156.0	85.0	125.0	−128.0
1983	600.6	288.9	37.0	209.0	65.6	808.4	209.9	204.4	11.8	28.6	52.6	123.0	170.7	89.8	121.8	−207.8
1984	666.4	298.4	56.9	239.4	71.8	851.8	227.4	220.9	−15.9	30.4	57.5	113.4	178.2	111.1	117.9	−185.4
1985	734.0	334.5	61.3	265.2	73.0	946.3	252.7	245.1	16.2	33.5	65.8	129.0	188.6	129.5	131.0	−212.3
1986	769.2	349.0	63.1	283.9	73.2	990.4	273.4	265.4	14.1	35.9	70.2	120.7	198.8	136.0	141.3	−221.2
1987	854.3	392.6	83.9	303.3	74.5	1,004.0	282.0	273.9	11.6	40.0	75.1	124.1	207.4	138.6	125.2	−149.7
1988	909.2	401.2	94.5	334.3	79.2	1,064.4	290.4	281.9	10.5	44.5	78.9	130.4	219.3	151.8	138.7	−155.2
1989	991.1	445.7	103.3	359.4	82.7	1,143.7	303.6	294.8	9.6	48.4	85.0	137.6	232.5	169.0	158.2	−152.6
1990	1,032.0	466.9	93.5	380.0	91.5	1,253.0	299.3	289.7	13.8	57.7	98.1	148.8	248.6	184.3	202.4	−221.0
1991	1,055.0	467.8	98.1	396.0	93.1	1,324.2	273.3	262.3	15.8	71.1	104.5	172.6	269.0	194.4	223.4	−269.2
1992	1,091.2	476.0	100.3	413.7	101.3	1,381.5	298.3	286.8	16.1	89.4	119.0	199.7	287.6	199.3	172.1	−290.3
1993	1,154.3	509.7	117.5	428.3	98.8	1,409.4	291.1	278.5	17.2	99.3	130.6	210.1	304.6	198.7	157.8	−255.1
1994	1,258.6	543.1	140.4	461.5	113.7	1,461.8	281.6	268.6	17.1	107.1	144.7	217.2	319.6	202.9	171.5	−203.2
1995	1,351.8	590.2	157.0	484.5	120.1	1,515.7	272.1	259.4	16.4	115.4	159.9	223.8	335.8	232.1	160.3	−164.0
1996	1,453.1	656.4	171.8	509.4	115.4	1,560.5	265.7	253.1	13.5	119.3	174.2	229.7	349.7	241.1	167.3	−107.4
1997	1,579.2	737.5	182.3	539.4	120.1	1,601.1	270.5	258.3	15.2	123.8	190.0	235.0	365.3	244.0	157.4	−21.9
1998	1,721.7	828.6	188.7	571.8	132.6	1,652.5	268.2	255.8	13.1	131.4	192.8	237.7	379.2	241.1	189.0	69.3
1999	1,827.5	879.5	184.7	611.8	151.5	1,701.8	274.8	261.2	15.2	141.0	190.4	242.4	390.0	229.8	218.1	125.6
2000	2,025.2	1,004.5	207.3	652.9	160.6	1,789.0	294.4	281.0	17.2	154.5	197.1	253.7	409.4	222.9	239.7	236.2
2001	1,991.1	994.3	151.1	694.0	151.7	1,862.8	304.7	290.2	16.5	172.2	217.4	269.7	433.0	206.2	243.2	128.2
2002	1,853.1	858.3	148.0	700.8	146.0	2,010.9	348.5	331.8	22.3	196.5	230.9	312.7	456.0	170.9	273.2	−157.8
2003	1,782.3	793.7	131.8	713.0	143.9	2,159.9	404.7	387.1	21.2	219.6	249.4	334.6	474.7	153.1	302.6	−377.6
2004	1,880.1	809.0	189.4	733.4	148.4	2,292.8	455.8	436.4	26.9	240.1	269.4	333.0	495.5	160.2	311.8	−412.7
2005	2,153.6	927.2	278.3	794.1	154.0	2,472.0	495.3	474.1	34.6	250.6	298.6	345.8	523.3	184.0	339.8	−318.3
2006	2,406.9	1,043.9	353.9	837.8	171.2	2,655.1	521.8	499.3	29.5	252.8	329.9	352.4	548.5	226.6	393.5	−248.2
2007	2,568.0	1,163.5	370.2	869.6	164.7	2,728.7	551.3	528.5	28.5	266.4	375.4	365.9	586.2	237.1	317.9	−160.7
2008	2,524.0	1,145.7	304.3	900.2	173.7	2,982.5	616.1	594.6	28.9	280.6	390.8	431.2	617.0	252.8	365.2	−458.6
2009	2,105.0	915.3	138.2	890.9	160.5	3,517.7	661.0	636.7	37.5	334.4	430.1	533.1	683.0	186.9	651.7	−1,412.7
2010	2,162.7	898.5	191.4	864.8	207.9	3,457.1	693.5	666.7	45.2	369.1	451.6	622.1	706.7	196.2	372.6	−1,294.4
2011	2,303.5	1,091.5	181.1	818.8	212.1	3,603.1	705.6	678.1	45.7	372.5	485.7	597.3	730.8	230.0	435.7	−1,299.6
2012	2,450.0	1,132.2	242.3	845.3	230.2	3,526.6	677.9	650.9	36.8	346.8	471.8	541.2	773.3	220.4	458.4	−1,076.6
2013	2,775.1	1,316.4	273.5	947.8	237.4	3,454.9	633.4	607.8	46.5	358.3	497.8	536.4	813.6	220.9	348.0	−679.8
2014	3,021.5	1,394.6	320.7	1,023.5	282.7	3,506.3	603.5	577.9	46.9	409.5	511.7	513.6	850.5	229.0	341.7	−484.8
2015	3,249.9	1,540.8	343.8	1,065.3	300.0	3,691.9	589.7	562.5	52.0	482.3	546.2	508.8	887.8	223.2	402.0	−442.0
2016	3,268.0	1,546.1	299.6	1,115.1	307.3	3,852.6	593.4	565.4	45.3	511.3	594.5	514.1	916.1	240.0	437.9	−584.7
2017	3,316.2	1,587.1	297.0	1,161.9	270.1	3,981.6	598.7	568.9	46.3	533.2	597.3	503.4	944.9	262.6	495.3	−665.4
2018	3,329.9	1,683.5	204.7	1,170.7	270.9	4,109.0	631.1	600.7	49.0	551.2	588.7	495.3	987.8	325.0	480.9	−779.1
2019	3,464.2	1,717.9	230.2	1,243.4	272.7	4,448.3	686.0	654.0	52.7	584.8	651.0	514.8	1,044.4	375.2	539.4	−984.2
2020 (estimates) [1]	3,420.0	1,608.7	211.8	1,310.0	289.5	6,551.9	726.2	690.4	67.7	748.3	776.2	1,262.6	1,095.8	344.7	1,530.5	−3,131.9

[1] Estimates from *Final Monthly Treasury Statement*, issued October 2020.

Note: See Note, Table B–45.

Sources: Department of the Treasury and Office of Management and Budget.

TABLE B–48. Federal receipts, outlays, surplus or deficit, and debt, fiscal years 2015–2020

[Millions of dollars; fiscal years]

Description	Actual					Estimates [1]
	2015	2016	2017	2018	2019	2020
RECEIPTS, OUTLAYS, AND SURPLUS OR DEFICIT						
Total:						
Receipts	3,249,890	3,267,965	3,316,184	3,329,907	3,464,161	3,419,955
Outlays	3,691,850	3,852,616	3,981,630	4,109,044	4,448,316	6,551,872
Surplus or deficit (–)	–441,960	–584,651	–665,446	–779,137	–984,155	–3,131,917
On-budget:						
Receipts	2,479,518	2,457,785	2,465,566	2,475,160	2,549,858	2,454,527
Outlays	2,948,773	3,077,943	3,180,429	3,260,472	3,541,699	5,596,291
Surplus or deficit (–)	–469,255	–620,158	–714,863	–785,312	–991,841	–3,141,764
Off-budget:						
Receipts	770,372	810,180	850,618	854,747	914,303	965,428
Outlays	743,077	774,673	801,201	848,572	906,617	955,581
Surplus or deficit (–)	27,295	35,507	49,417	6,175	7,686	9,846
OUTSTANDING DEBT, END OF PERIOD						
Gross Federal debt	18,120,106	19,539,450	20,205,704	21,462,277	22,669,466	26,901,109
Held by Federal Government accounts	5,003,414	5,371,826	5,540,265	5,712,710	5,868,720	5,882,037
Held by the public	13,116,692	14,167,624	14,665,439	15,749,567	16,800,746	21,019,071
Federal Reserve System	2,461,947	2,463,456	2,465,418	2,313,209	2,113,329	....
Other	10,654,745	11,704,168	12,200,021	13,436,358	14,687,417	....
RECEIPTS BY SOURCE						
Total: On-budget and off-budget	3,249,890	3,267,965	3,316,184	3,329,907	3,464,161	3,419,955
Individual income taxes	1,540,802	1,546,075	1,587,120	1,683,538	1,717,857	1,608,662
Corporation income taxes	343,797	299,571	297,048	204,733	230,245	211,845
Social insurance and retirement receipts	1,065,257	1,115,065	1,161,897	1,170,701	1,243,372	1,309,955
On-budget	294,885	304,885	311,279	315,954	329,069	....
Off-budget	770,372	810,180	850,618	854,747	914,303	....
Excise taxes	98,279	95,026	83,823	94,986	99,452	86,782
Estate and gift taxes	19,232	21,354	22,768	22,983	16,672	17,624
Customs duties and fees	35,041	34,838	34,574	41,299	70,784	68,550
Miscellaneous receipts	147,482	156,036	128,954	111,667	85,779	116,538
Deposits of earnings by Federal Reserve System	96,468	115,672	81,287	70,750	52,793	....
All other	51,014	40,364	47,667	40,917	32,986	....
OUTLAYS BY FUNCTION						
Total: On-budget and off-budget	3,691,850	3,852,616	3,981,630	4,109,044	4,448,316	6,551,872
National defense	589,659	593,372	598,722	631,130	686,003	726,151
International affairs	52,040	45,306	46,309	48,996	52,739	67,660
General science, space, and technology	29,412	30,174	30,394	31,534	32,410	34,059
Energy	6,841	3,721	3,856	2,169	5,041	7,168
Natural resources and environment	36,033	39,082	37,896	39,140	37,844	40,691
Agriculture	18,500	18,344	18,872	21,789	38,257	49,153
Commerce and housing credit	–37,905	–34,077	–26,685	–9,470	–25,715	571,657
On-budget	–36,195	–32,716	–24,412	–8,005	–24,612	....
Off-budget	–1,710	–1,361	–2,273	–1,465	–1,103	....
Transportation	89,533	92,566	93,552	92,785	97,116	146,156
Community and regional development	20,669	20,140	24,907	42,159	26,876	83,619
Education, training, employment, and social services	122,035	109,709	143,953	95,503	136,752	236,723
Health	482,257	511,325	533,152	551,219	584,816	748,293
Medicare	546,202	594,536	597,307	588,706	650,996	776,224
Income security	508,800	514,098	503,443	495,289	514,787	1,262,558
Social security	887,753	916,067	944,878	987,791	1,044,409	1,095,817
On-budget	30,990	32,522	37,393	35,752	36,130	....
Off-budget	856,763	883,545	907,485	952,039	1,008,279	....
Veterans benefits and services	159,781	174,557	176,584	178,895	199,843	218,674
Administration of justice	51,906	55,768	57,944	60,418	65,740	72,102
General government	20,956	23,146	23,821	23,885	23,436	176,825
Net interest	223,181	240,033	262,551	324,975	375,158	344,705
On-budget	319,149	330,608	349,063	408,784	457,662	....
Off-budget	–95,968	–90,575	–86,512	–83,809	–82,504	....
Allowances						
Undistributed offsetting receipts	–115,803	–95,251	–89,826	–97,869	–98,192	–106,362
On-budget	–99,795	–78,315	–72,327	–79,676	–80,137	....
Off-budget	–16,008	–16,936	–17,499	–18,193	–18,055	....

[1] Estimates from *Final Monthly Treasury Statement*, issued October 2020.

Note: See Note, Table B–45.

Sources: Department of the Treasury and Office of Management and Budget.

Federal and State and local government current receipts and expenditures, national income and product accounts (NIPA) basis, 1969–2020

[Billions of dollars; quarterly data at seasonally adjusted annual rates]

Year or quarter	Total government			Federal Government			State and local government			Addendum: Grants-in-aid to State and local governments
	Current receipts	Current expenditures	Net government saving (NIPA)	Current receipts	Current expenditures	Net Federal Government saving (NIPA)	Current receipts	Current expenditures	Net State and local government saving (NIPA)	
1969	282.7	284.7	−2.0	191.8	197.0	−5.1	104.5	101.4	3.1	13.7
1970	285.8	319.2	−33.4	185.1	219.9	−34.8	119.1	117.6	1.4	18.3
1971	302.3	354.5	−52.2	190.7	241.6	−50.9	133.7	135.0	−1.3	22.1
1972	345.6	388.5	−42.9	219.0	268.0	−49.0	157.1	151.0	6.1	30.5
1973	388.8	421.5	−32.7	249.2	287.6	−38.3	173.0	167.4	5.6	33.5
1974	430.2	473.9	−43.7	278.5	319.8	−41.3	186.6	189.0	−2.3	34.9
1975	441.2	549.9	−108.7	276.8	374.8	−97.9	208.0	218.7	−10.7	43.6
1976	505.7	591.0	−85.3	322.6	403.5	−80.9	232.2	236.6	−4.4	49.1
1977	567.4	640.3	−72.9	363.9	437.3	−73.4	258.3	257.8	.5	54.8
1978	646.1	703.3	−57.2	423.8	485.9	−62.0	285.8	280.9	4.9	63.5
1979	729.3	777.9	−48.6	487.0	534.4	−47.4	306.3	307.5	−1.2	64.0
1980	799.9	894.6	−94.7	533.7	622.5	−88.8	335.9	341.8	−5.9	69.7
1981	919.1	1,017.4	−98.2	621.1	709.1	−88.1	367.5	377.6	−10.2	69.4
1982	940.9	1,131.0	−190.1	618.7	786.0	−167.4	388.5	411.3	−22.8	66.3
1983	1,002.1	1,227.7	−225.6	644.8	851.9	−207.2	425.3	443.7	−18.4	67.9
1984	1,115.0	1,311.7	−196.7	711.2	907.7	−196.5	476.1	476.3	−.2	72.3
1985	1,217.0	1,418.7	−201.7	775.7	975.0	−199.2	517.5	519.9	−2.4	76.2
1986	1,292.9	1,512.8	−219.9	817.9	1,033.8	−215.9	557.4	561.3	−4.0	82.4
1987	1,406.6	1,586.7	−180.1	899.5	1,065.2	−165.7	585.5	599.9	−14.4	78.4
1988	1,507.1	1,678.3	−171.3	962.4	1,122.4	−160.0	630.4	641.7	−11.3	85.7
1989	1,632.0	1,810.7	−178.7	1,042.5	1,201.8	−159.4	681.4	700.7	−19.3	91.8
1990	1,713.3	1,952.9	−239.5	1,087.6	1,290.9	−203.3	730.1	766.3	−36.2	104.4
1991	1,763.7	2,072.2	−308.5	1,107.8	1,356.2	−248.4	779.9	840.0	−60.1	124.0
1992	1,848.7	2,254.2	−405.5	1,154.4	1,488.9	−334.5	836.1	907.0	−71.0	141.7
1993	1,953.3	2,339.3	−386.0	1,231.0	1,544.6	−313.5	878.0	950.4	−72.5	155.7
1994	2,097.6	2,417.2	−319.6	1,329.3	1,585.0	−255.6	935.1	999.1	−63.9	166.8
1995	2,223.9	2,536.5	−312.5	1,417.4	1,659.5	−242.1	981.0	1,051.4	−70.4	174.5
1996	2,388.6	2,621.8	−233.2	1,536.3	1,715.7	−179.4	1,033.7	1,087.5	−53.8	181.5
1997	2,565.9	2,699.9	−133.9	1,667.4	1,759.4	−92.0	1,086.7	1,128.7	−42.0	188.1
1998	2,738.6	2,767.4	−28.7	1,789.8	1,788.4	1.4	1,149.6	1,179.7	−30.1	200.8
1999	2,910.1	2,879.9	30.2	1,906.6	1,837.5	69.1	1,222.7	1,261.6	−38.9	219.2
2000	3,139.4	3,020.4	119.0	2,068.4	1,908.7	159.7	1,304.1	1,344.8	−40.6	233.1
2001	3,124.4	3,228.3	−104.0	2,032.2	2,017.2	15.0	1,353.4	1,472.4	−119.0	261.3
2002	2,968.3	3,418.9	−450.7	1,870.8	2,138.6	−267.8	1,386.2	1,569.1	−182.9	288.7
2003	3,045.9	3,624.6	−578.7	1,895.6	2,293.0	−397.4	1,472.0	1,653.3	−181.3	321.7
2004	3,275.7	3,818.2	−542.5	2,027.7	2,421.2	−393.5	1,580.3	1,729.3	−149.0	332.3
2005	3,679.3	4,075.9	−396.6	2,304.4	2,598.1	−293.8	1,718.5	1,821.3	−102.8	343.5
2006	4,013.4	4,320.4	−307.0	2,538.3	2,760.2	−221.9	1,816.2	1,901.2	−85.0	341.0
2007	4,210.8	4,599.8	−389.0	2,667.8	2,927.5	−259.7	1,902.1	2,031.4	−129.3	359.1
2008	4,125.0	4,970.8	−845.8	2,580.7	3,205.6	−624.9	1,915.5	2,136.4	−220.9	371.2
2009	3,696.6	5,281.1	−1,584.5	2,239.5	3,482.6	−1,243.2	1,915.2	2,256.6	−341.3	458.1
2010	3,933.2	5,559.0	−1,625.8	2,444.0	3,762.4	−1,318.4	1,994.4	2,301.8	−307.5	505.2
2011	4,130.6	5,639.9	−1,509.2	2,572.8	3,806.9	−1,234.1	2,030.4	2,305.4	−275.1	472.5
2012	4,312.2	5,667.6	−1,355.5	2,700.3	3,773.0	−1,072.7	2,056.3	2,339.1	−282.8	444.4
2013	4,834.6	5,731.7	−897.1	3,139.0	3,770.8	−631.8	2,145.7	2,411.0	−265.3	450.1
2014	5,054.5	5,889.8	−835.3	3,292.0	3,889.4	−597.4	2,257.5	2,495.4	−237.9	495.0
2015	5,288.1	6,064.1	−776.0	3,448.0	4,008.3	−560.2	2,373.2	2,588.9	−215.8	533.1
2016	5,338.0	6,246.3	−908.3	3,463.3	4,132.5	−669.1	2,431.5	2,670.7	−239.2	556.8
2017	5,479.8	6,441.0	−961.3	3,524.3	4,246.8	−722.4	2,515.2	2,754.0	−238.8	559.8
2018	5,628.2	6,773.6	−1,145.4	3,567.6	4,499.3	−931.7	2,643.2	2,856.8	−213.7	582.6
2019	5,846.0	7,100.7	−1,254.7	3,711.2	4,758.1	−1,047.0	2,742.9	2,950.7	−207.7	608.1
2017: I	5,443.7	6,363.9	−920.2	3,523.7	4,195.3	−671.5	2,481.0	2,729.6	−248.7	561.0
II	5,421.5	6,393.3	−971.8	3,504.1	4,202.2	−698.1	2,459.7	2,733.4	−273.7	542.3
III	5,487.0	6,465.7	−978.7	3,531.0	4,261.9	−731.0	2,518.9	2,766.7	−247.8	562.9
IV	5,567.0	6,541.2	−974.3	3,538.5	4,327.7	−789.1	2,601.3	2,786.4	−185.1	572.9
2018: I	5,547.4	6,641.2	−1,093.8	3,492.4	4,409.6	−917.2	2,636.5	2,813.0	−176.5	581.5
II	5,569.6	6,738.3	−1,168.8	3,527.5	4,469.8	−942.3	2,620.1	2,846.6	−226.5	578.0
III	5,689.4	6,816.9	−1,127.5	3,617.6	4,524.8	−907.2	2,656.0	2,876.4	−220.3	584.3
IV	5,706.6	6,898.0	−1,191.4	3,633.0	4,593.0	−960.0	2,660.0	2,891.4	−231.4	586.5
2019: I	5,774.5	7,004.0	−1,229.5	3,674.1	4,690.1	−1,016.0	2,694.6	2,908.1	−213.5	594.2
II	5,864.3	7,072.5	−1,208.2	3,704.5	4,737.5	−1,033.0	2,772.3	2,947.5	−175.2	612.5
III	5,841.0	7,144.9	−1,303.9	3,702.4	4,786.4	−1,084.1	2,748.9	2,968.8	−219.8	610.3
IV	5,904.2	7,181.5	−1,277.3	3,763.7	4,818.6	−1,054.9	2,755.9	2,978.3	−222.4	615.4
2020: I	5,910.2	7,263.7	−1,353.5	3,753.1	4,903.9	−1,150.8	2,785.0	2,987.7	−202.7	627.8
II	5,526.6	10,694.6	−5,168.0	3,468.8	9,107.1	−5,638.3	3,454.7	2,984.4	470.3	1,396.9
III p	5,829.9	9,474.3	−3,644.5	3,687.7	7,202.3	−3,514.6	2,870.4	3,000.2	−129.9	728.2

Note: Federal grants-in-aid to State and local governments are reflected in Federal current expenditures and State and local current receipts. Total government current receipts and expenditures have been adjusted to eliminate this duplication.

Source: Department of Commerce (Bureau of Economic Analysis).

TABLE B–50. State and local government revenues and expenditures, fiscal years 1956–2018

[Millions of dollars]

Fiscal year [1]	General revenues by source [2]							General expenditures by function [2]				
	Total	Property taxes	Sales and gross receipts taxes	Individual income taxes	Corporation net income taxes	Revenue from Federal Government	All other [3]	Total [4]	Education	Highways	Public welfare [4]	All other [4,5]
1956	34,670	11,749	8,691	1,538	890	3,335	8,467	36,715	13,224	6,953	3,139	13,399
1957	38,164	12,864	9,467	1,754	984	3,843	9,252	40,375	14,134	7,816	3,485	14,940
1958	41,219	14,047	9,829	1,759	1,018	4,865	9,701	44,851	15,919	8,567	3,818	16,547
1959	45,306	14,983	10,437	1,994	1,001	6,377	10,514	48,887	17,283	9,592	4,136	17,876
1960	50,505	16,405	11,849	2,463	1,180	6,974	11,634	51,876	18,719	9,428	4,404	19,325
1961	54,037	18,002	12,463	2,613	1,266	7,131	12,562	56,201	20,574	9,844	4,720	21,063
1962	58,252	19,054	13,494	3,037	1,308	7,871	13,488	60,206	22,216	10,357	5,084	22,549
1963	62,891	20,089	14,456	3,269	1,505	8,722	14,850	64,815	23,776	11,135	5,481	24,423
1963–64	68,443	21,241	15,762	3,791	1,695	10,002	15,952	69,302	26,286	11,664	5,766	25,586
1964–65	74,000	22,583	17,118	4,090	1,929	11,029	17,251	74,678	28,563	12,221	6,315	27,579
1965–66	83,036	24,670	19,085	4,760	2,038	13,214	19,269	82,843	33,287	12,770	6,757	30,029
1966–67	91,197	26,047	20,530	5,825	2,227	15,370	21,198	93,350	37,919	13,932	8,218	33,281
1967–68	101,264	27,747	22,911	7,308	2,518	17,181	23,599	102,411	41,158	14,481	9,857	36,915
1968–69	114,550	30,673	26,519	8,908	3,180	19,153	26,117	116,728	47,238	15,417	12,110	41,963
1969–70	130,756	34,054	30,322	10,812	3,738	21,857	29,973	131,332	52,718	16,427	14,679	47,508
1970–71	144,927	37,852	33,233	11,900	3,424	26,146	32,372	150,674	59,413	18,095	18,226	54,940
1971–72	167,535	42,877	37,518	15,227	4,416	31,342	36,156	168,549	65,813	19,021	21,117	62,598
1972–73	190,222	45,283	42,047	17,994	5,425	39,264	40,210	181,357	69,713	18,615	23,582	69,447
1973–74	207,670	47,705	46,098	19,491	6,015	41,820	46,542	199,222	75,833	19,946	25,085	78,358
1974–75	228,171	51,491	49,815	21,454	6,642	47,034	51,735	230,722	87,858	22,528	28,156	92,180
1975–76	256,176	57,001	54,547	24,575	7,273	55,589	57,191	256,731	97,216	23,907	32,604	103,004
1976–77	285,157	62,527	60,641	29,246	9,174	62,444	61,125	274,215	102,780	23,058	35,906	112,472
1977–78	315,960	66,422	67,596	33,176	10,738	69,592	68,435	296,984	110,758	24,609	39,140	122,478
1978–79	343,236	64,944	74,247	36,932	12,128	75,164	79,822	327,517	119,448	28,440	41,898	137,731
1979–80	382,322	68,499	79,927	42,080	13,321	83,029	95,467	369,086	133,211	33,311	47,288	155,276
1980–81	423,404	74,969	85,971	46,426	14,143	90,294	111,599	407,449	145,784	34,603	54,105	172,957
1981–82	457,654	82,067	93,613	50,738	15,028	87,282	128,925	436,733	154,282	34,520	57,996	189,935
1982–83	486,753	89,105	100,247	55,129	14,258	90,007	138,008	466,516	163,876	36,655	60,906	205,080
1983–84	542,730	96,457	114,097	64,871	16,798	96,935	153,571	505,008	176,108	39,419	66,414	223,068
1984–85	598,121	103,757	126,376	70,361	19,152	106,158	172,317	553,899	192,686	44,989	71,479	244,745
1985–86	641,486	111,709	135,005	74,365	19,994	113,099	187,314	605,623	210,819	49,368	75,868	269,568
1986–87	686,860	121,203	144,091	83,935	22,425	114,857	200,350	657,134	226,619	52,355	82,650	295,510
1987–88	726,762	132,212	156,452	88,350	23,663	117,602	208,482	704,921	242,683	55,621	89,090	317,527
1988–89	786,129	142,400	166,336	97,806	25,926	125,824	227,838	762,360	263,898	58,105	97,879	342,479
1989–90	849,502	155,613	177,885	105,640	23,566	136,802	249,996	834,818	288,148	61,057	110,518	375,094
1990–91	902,207	167,999	185,570	109,341	22,242	154,099	262,955	908,108	309,302	64,937	130,402	403,467
1991–92	979,137	180,337	197,731	115,638	23,880	179,174	282,376	981,253	324,652	67,351	158,723	430,526
1992–93	1,041,643	189,744	209,649	123,235	26,417	198,663	293,935	1,030,434	342,287	68,370	170,705	449,072
1993–94	1,100,490	197,141	223,628	128,810	28,320	215,492	307,099	1,077,665	353,287	72,067	183,394	468,916
1994–95	1,169,505	203,451	237,268	137,931	31,406	228,771	330,677	1,149,863	378,273	77,109	196,703	497,779
1995–96	1,222,821	209,440	248,993	146,844	32,009	234,891	350,645	1,193,276	398,859	79,092	197,354	517,971
1996–97	1,289,237	218,877	261,418	159,042	33,820	244,847	371,233	1,249,984	418,416	82,062	203,779	545,727
1997–98	1,365,762	230,150	274,883	175,630	34,412	255,048	395,639	1,318,042	450,365	87,214	208,120	572,343
1998–99	1,434,029	239,672	290,993	189,309	33,922	270,628	409,505	1,402,369	483,259	93,018	218,957	607,134
1999–2000	1,541,322	249,178	309,290	211,661	36,059	291,950	443,186	1,506,797	521,612	101,336	237,336	646,512
2000–01	1,647,161	263,689	320,217	226,334	35,296	324,033	477,592	1,626,063	563,572	107,235	261,622	693,634
2001–02	1,684,879	279,191	324,123	202,832	28,152	360,546	490,035	1,736,866	594,694	115,295	285,464	741,413
2002–03	1,763,212	296,683	337,787	199,407	31,369	389,264	508,702	1,821,917	621,335	117,696	310,783	772,102
2003–04	1,887,397	317,941	361,027	215,215	33,716	423,112	536,386	1,908,543	655,182	117,215	340,523	795,622
2004–05	2,026,034	335,779	384,266	242,273	43,256	438,558	581,902	2,012,110	688,314	126,350	365,295	832,151
2005–06	2,197,475	364,559	417,735	268,667	53,081	452,975	640,458	2,123,663	728,917	136,502	373,846	884,398
2006–07	2,330,611	388,905	440,470	290,278	60,955	464,914	685,089	2,264,035	774,170	145,011	389,259	955,595
2007–08	2,421,977	409,540	449,945	304,902	57,231	477,441	722,919	2,406,183	826,061	153,831	408,920	1,017,372
2008–09	2,429,672	434,818	434,128	270,942	46,280	537,949	705,555	2,500,796	851,689	154,338	437,184	1,057,586
2009–10	2,510,846	443,947	435,571	261,510	44,108	623,801	701,909	2,542,231	860,118	155,912	460,230	1,065,971
2010–11	2,618,037	445,771	463,979	285,293	48,422	726,966	647,606	2,583,805	862,271	153,895	494,682	1,072,957
2011–12	2,598,745	445,854	482,172	307,897	48,877	580,604	733,341	2,595,947	870,321	159,498	491,158	1,074,971
2012–13	2,687,495	453,458	503,553	339,666	52,853	583,294	754,672	2,631,945	878,957	160,260	518,035	1,074,693
2013–14	2,768,260	465,100	522,014	343,001	54,558	602,175	781,412	2,723,022	906,016	165,051	547,889	1,104,066
2014–15	2,920,320	484,251	544,359	368,862	57,130	658,012	807,707	2,844,289	934,353	171,084	616,515	1,122,338
2015–16	3,018,372	504,593	559,625	375,310	53,581	693,989	831,274	2,964,238	973,025	177,982	655,532	1,157,699
2016–17	3,121,060	525,513	580,661	384,717	52,836	710,096	867,238	3,076,039	1,012,871	181,705	681,388	1,200,075
2017–18	3,289,962	547,039	611,372	425,716	56,059	739,662	910,115	3,205,237	1,046,262	186,752	721,277	1,250,946

[1] Fiscal years not the same for all governments. See Note.
[2] Excludes revenues or expenditures of publicly owned utilities and liquor stores and of insurance-trust activities. Intergovernmental receipts and payments between State and local governments are also excluded.
[3] Includes motor vehicle license taxes, other taxes, and charges and miscellaneous revenues.
[4] Includes intergovernmental payments to the Federal Government.
[5] Includes expenditures for libraries, hospitals, health, employment security administration, veterans' services, air transportation, sea and inland port facilities, parking facilities, police protection, fire protection, correction, protective inspection and regulation, sewerage, natural resources, parks and recreation, housing and community development, solid waste management, financial administration, judicial and legal, general public buildings, other government administration, interest on general debt, and other general expenditures, not elsewhere classified.

Note: Except for States listed, data for fiscal years listed from 1963–64 to 2017–18 are the aggregation of data for government fiscal years that ended in the 12-month period from July 1 to June 30 of those years; Texas used August and Alabama and Michigan used September as end dates. Data for 1963 and earlier years include data for government fiscal years ending during that particular calendar year.

Source: Department of Commerce (Bureau of the Census).

TABLE B–51. U.S. Treasury securities outstanding by kind of obligation, 1980–2020

[Billions of dollars]

End of fiscal year or month	Total Treasury securities outstanding [1]	Marketable							Nonmarketable				
		Total [2]	Treasury bills	Treasury notes	Treasury bonds	Treasury inflation-protected securities			Total	U.S. savings securities [3]	Foreign series [4]	Government account series	Other [5]
						Total	Notes	Bonds					
1980	906.8	594.5	199.8	310.9	83.8				312.3	73.0	25.2	189.8	24.2
1981	996.8	683.2	223.4	363.6	96.2				313.6	68.3	20.5	201.1	23.7
1982	1,141.2	824.4	277.9	442.9	103.6				316.8	67.6	14.6	210.5	24.1
1983	1,376.3	1,024.0	340.7	557.5	125.7				352.3	70.6	11.5	234.7	35.6
1984	1,560.4	1,176.6	356.8	661.7	158.1				383.8	73.7	8.8	259.5	41.8
1985	1,822.3	1,360.2	384.2	776.4	199.5				462.1	78.2	6.6	313.9	63.3
1986	2,124.9	1,564.3	410.7	896.9	241.7				560.5	87.8	4.1	365.9	102.8
1987	2,349.4	1,676.0	378.3	1,005.1	277.6				673.4	98.5	4.4	440.7	129.8
1988	2,601.4	1,802.9	398.5	1,089.6	299.9				798.5	107.8	6.3	536.5	148.0
1989	2,837.9	1,892.8	406.6	1,133.2	338.0				945.2	115.7	6.8	663.7	159.0
1990	3,212.7	2,092.8	482.5	1,218.1	377.2				1,119.9	123.9	36.0	779.4	180.6
1991	3,664.5	2,390.7	564.6	1,387.4	423.4				1,273.9	135.4	41.6	908.4	188.5
1992	4,063.8	2,677.5	634.3	1,566.3	461.8				1,386.3	150.3	37.0	1,011.0	188.0
1993	4,410.7	2,904.9	658.4	1,734.2	497.4				1,505.8	169.1	42.5	1,114.3	179.9
1994	4,691.7	3,091.6	697.3	1,867.5	511.8				1,600.1	178.6	42.0	1,211.7	167.8
1995	4,953.0	3,260.4	742.5	1,980.3	522.6				1,692.6	183.5	41.0	1,324.3	143.8
1996	5,220.8	3,418.4	761.2	2,098.7	543.5				1,802.4	184.1	37.5	1,454.7	126.1
1997	5,407.6	3,439.6	701.9	2,122.2	576.2	24.4	24.4		1,968.0	182.7	34.9	1,608.5	141.9
1998	5,518.7	3,331.0	637.6	2,009.1	610.4	58.8	41.9	17.0	2,187.6	180.8	35.1	1,777.3	194.4
1999	5,647.3	3,233.0	653.2	1,828.8	643.7	92.4	67.6	24.8	2,414.3	180.0	31.0	2,005.2	198.1
2000	5,622.1	2,992.8	616.2	1,611.3	635.3	115.0	81.6	33.4	2,629.4	177.7	25.4	2,242.9	183.3
2001	5,807.5	2,930.7	734.9	1,433.0	613.0	134.9	95.1	39.7	2,876.7	186.5	18.3	2,492.1	179.9
2002	6,228.2	3,136.7	868.3	1,521.6	593.0	138.9	93.7	45.1	3,091.5	193.3	12.5	2,707.3	178.4
2003	6,783.2	3,460.7	918.2	1,799.5	576.9	166.1	120.0	46.1	3,322.5	201.6	11.0	2,912.2	197.7
2004	7,379.1	3,846.1	961.5	2,109.6	552.0	223.0	164.5	58.5	3,533.0	204.2	5.9	3,130.0	192.9
2005	7,932.7	4,084.9	914.3	2,328.8	520.7	307.1	229.1	78.0	3,847.8	203.6	3.1	3,380.6	260.5
2006	8,507.0	4,303.0	911.5	2,447.2	534.7	395.6	293.9	101.7	4,203.9	203.7	3.0	3,722.7	274.5
2007	9,007.7	4,448.1	958.1	2,458.0	561.1	456.9	335.7	121.2	4,559.5	197.1	3.0	4,026.8	332.6
2008	10,024.7	5,236.0	1,489.8	2,624.8	582.9	524.5	380.2	144.3	4,788.7	194.3	3.0	4,297.7	293.8
2009	11,909.8	7,009.7	1,992.5	3,773.8	679.8	551.7	396.2	155.5	4,900.1	192.5	4.9	4,454.3	248.4
2010	13,561.6	8,498.3	1,788.5	5,255.9	849.9	593.8	421.1	172.7	5,063.3	188.7	4.2	4,645.3	225.1
2011	14,790.3	9,624.5	1,477.5	6,412.5	1,020.4	705.7	509.4	196.3	5,165.8	185.1	3.0	4,793.9	183.8
2012	16,066.2	10,749.7	1,616.0	7,120.7	1,198.2	807.7	584.7	223.0	5,316.5	183.8	3.0	4,939.3	190.4
2013	16,738.2	11,596.2	1,530.0	7,758.0	1,366.2	936.4	685.5	250.8	5,142.0	180.0	3.0	4,803.1	156.0
2014	17,824.1	12,294.2	1,411.0	8,167.8	1,534.1	1,044.7	765.2	279.5	5,529.9	176.7	3.0	5,212.5	137.7
2015	18,150.6	12,853.8	1,358.0	8,372.7	1,688.3	1,135.4	832.1	303.3	5,296.9	172.8	.3	5,013.5	110.3
2016	19,573.4	13,660.6	1,647.0	8,631.0	1,825.5	1,210.0	881.6	328.3	5,912.8	167.5	.3	5,604.1	141.0
2017	20,244.9	14,199.8	1,801.9	8,805.5	1,951.7	1,286.5	933.3	353.2	6,045.1	161.7	.3	5,771.1	112.0
2018	21,516.1	15,278.0	2,239.9	9,154.4	2,127.8	1,376.4	993.4	383.0	6,238.0	156.8	.3	5,977.6	103.4
2019	22,719.4	16,347.3	2,377.0	9,762.8	2,319.1	1,455.7	1,044.9	410.8	6,372.1	152.3	.3	6,133.7	85.8
2020	26,945.4	20,374.9	5,028.9	10,663.8	2,673.5	1,523.2	1,092.7	430.5	6,570.5	148.6	.3	6,196.3	225.3
2019: Jan	21,982.4	15,619.8	2,299.1	9,355.8	2,190.5	1,403.8	1,015.6	388.2	6,362.6	155.2	.3	6,114.0	93.1
Feb	22,115.5	15,769.7	2,396.0	9,376.3	2,201.0	1,407.7	1,012.4	395.3	6,345.8	154.9	.3	6,097.9	92.8
Mar	22,028.0	15,939.0	2,480.0	9,414.3	2,217.0	1,421.1	1,025.1	396.0	6,089.0	154.5	.3	5,840.6	93.7
Apr	22,027.7	15,880.9	2,384.0	9,491.4	2,233.0	1,390.3	992.6	397.7	6,146.8	154.1	.3	5,902.6	89.8
May	22,026.4	15,941.3	2,353.9	9,516.4	2,258.5	1,410.3	1,010.4	399.9	6,085.2	153.7	.3	5,846.6	84.6
June	22,023.5	15,931.2	2,250.9	9,554.4	2,274.5	1,432.7	1,030.8	401.9	6,092.4	153.4	.3	5,859.0	79.7
July	22,022.4	15,968.1	2,205.9	9,642.2	2,290.6	1,432.5	1,029.6	402.9	6,054.2	153.0	.3	5,825.5	75.5
Aug	22,460.5	16,146.3	2,331.9	9,656.4	2,303.1	1,440.0	1,029.9	410.1	6,314.2	152.6	.3	6,084.6	76.7
Sept	22,719.4	16,347.3	2,377.0	9,762.8	2,319.1	1,455.7	1,044.9	410.8	6,372.1	152.3	.3	6,133.7	85.8
Oct	23,008.4	16,514.1	2,456.1	9,834.9	2,335.1	1,474.4	1,063.6	410.8	6,494.3	152.0	.3	6,251.8	90.1
Nov	23,076.2	16,627.8	2,515.1	9,830.4	2,363.1	1,487.6	1,076.5	411.1	6,448.5	151.8	.3	6,200.0	96.4
Dec	23,201.4	16,682.1	2,416.9	9,929.2	2,379.1	1,507.4	1,095.3	412.0	6,519.2	151.3	.3	6,262.4	105.3
2020: Jan	23,223.8	16,720.0	2,404.3	9,998.7	2,395.6	1,499.6	1,087.7	411.9	6,503.8	150.7	.3	6,251.6	101.3
Feb	23,410.0	16,918.5	2,564.6	9,994.3	2,413.5	1,506.3	1,086.8	419.5	6,491.4	150.3	.3	6,236.6	104.3
Mar	23,686.9	17,162.8	2,657.4	10,092.5	2,429.6	1,525.5	1,104.4	421.0	6,524.1	150.0	.3	6,261.8	112.0
Apr	24,974.2	18,535.6	4,001.8	10,163.7	2,446.6	1,492.9	1,070.7	422.2	6,438.6	150.1	.3	6,173.0	115.2
May	25,746.3	19,232.0	4,629.9	10,176.7	2,472.7	1,502.2	1,080.8	421.4	6,514.2	150.0	.3	6,192.1	171.8
June	26,477.4	19,906.0	5,079.6	10,314.5	2,533.4	1,509.5	1,090.9	418.6	6,571.4	149.8	.3	6,208.6	212.8
July	26,525.0	20,007.9	5,078.9	10,427.6	2,573.0	1,486.7	1,068.2	418.5	6,517.1	149.4	.3	6,157.0	210.4
Aug	26,728.8	20,190.7	5,076.7	10,524.0	2,624.5	1,501.9	1,073.5	428.4	6,538.1	149.0	.3	6,174.3	214.5
Sept	26,945.4	20,374.9	5,028.9	10,663.8	2,673.5	1,523.2	1,092.7	430.5	6,570.5	148.6	.3	6,196.3	225.3
Oct	27,135.6	20,442.4	4,985.3	10,729.2	2,697.1	1,545.1	1,113.2	431.9	6,693.2	148.2	.3	6,314.1	230.7
Nov	27,446.3	20,692.4	4,943.7	10,919.1	2,786.6	1,561.2	1,128.7	432.5	6,753.9	147.8	.3	6,375.7	230.1

[1] Data beginning with January 2001 are interest-bearing and non-interest-bearing securities; prior data are interest-bearing securities only.

[2] Data from 1986 to 2002 and 2005 forward include Federal Financing Bank securities, not shown separately. Beginning with data for January 2014, includes Floating Rate Notes, not shown separately.

[3] Through 1996, series is U.S. savings bonds. Beginning 1997, includes U.S. retirement plan bonds, U.S. individual retirement bonds, and U.S. savings notes previously included in "other" nonmarketable securities.

[4] Nonmarketable certificates of indebtedness, notes, bonds, and bills in the Treasury foreign series of dollar-denominated and foreign-currency-denominated issues.

[5] Includes depository bonds; retirement plan bonds through 1996; Rural Electrification Administration bonds; State and local bonds; special issues held only by U.S. Government agencies and trust funds and the Federal home loan banks; for the period July 2003 through February 2004, depositary compensation securities; and for the period August 2008 through April 2016, Hope bonds for the HOPE For Homeowners Program.

Note: The fiscal year is on an October 1–September 30 basis.

Source: Department of the Treasury.

TABLE B–52. Estimated ownership of U.S. Treasury securities, 2006–2020

[Billions of dollars]

End of month	Total public debt [1]	Federal Reserve and Intragovernmental holdings [2]	Held by private investors									
			Total privately held	Depository institutions [3]	U.S. savings bonds [4]	Pension funds		Insurance companies	Mutual funds [6]	State and local governments	Foreign and international [7]	Other investors [8]
						Private [5]	State and local governments					
2006: Mar	8,371.2	4,257.2	4,114.0	113.0	206.0	116.8	152.9	200.3	254.2	515.7	2,082.1	473.0
June	8,420.0	4,389.2	4,030.8	119.5	205.2	117.7	149.6	196.1	243.4	531.6	1,977.8	490.1
Sept	8,507.0	4,432.8	4,074.2	113.6	203.7	125.8	149.3	196.8	234.2	542.3	2,025.3	483.2
Dec	8,680.2	4,558.1	4,122.1	114.8	202.4	139.8	153.4	197.9	248.2	570.5	2,103.1	392.0
2007: Mar	8,849.7	4,576.6	4,273.1	119.8	200.3	139.7	156.3	185.4	263.2	608.3	2,194.8	405.2
June	8,867.7	4,715.1	4,152.6	110.4	198.6	139.9	162.3	168.9	257.6	637.8	2,192.0	285.1
Sept	9,007.7	4,738.0	4,269.7	119.7	197.1	140.5	153.2	155.1	292.7	643.1	2,235.3	332.9
Dec	9,229.2	4,833.5	4,395.7	129.8	196.5	141.0	144.2	141.9	343.5	647.8	2,353.2	297.8
2008: Mar	9,437.6	4,694.7	4,742.9	125.0	195.4	143.7	135.4	152.1	466.7	646.4	2,506.3	371.9
June	9,492.0	4,685.8	4,806.2	112.7	195.0	145.0	135.5	159.4	440.3	635.1	2,587.4	395.9
Sept	10,024.7	4,692.7	5,332.0	130.0	194.3	147.0	136.7	163.4	631.4	614.0	2,802.4	512.9
Dec	10,699.8	4,806.4	5,893.4	105.0	194.1	147.4	129.9	171.4	758.2	601.4	3,077.2	708.9
2009: Mar	11,126.9	4,785.2	6,341.7	125.7	194.0	155.4	137.0	191.0	721.1	588.2	3,265.7	963.7
June	11,545.3	5,026.8	6,518.5	140.8	193.6	164.1	144.6	200.0	711.8	588.5	3,460.8	914.2
Sept	11,909.8	5,127.1	6,782.7	198.2	192.5	167.2	145.6	210.2	668.5	583.6	3,570.6	1,046.3
Dec	12,311.3	5,276.9	7,034.4	202.5	191.3	175.6	151.4	222.0	668.8	585.6	3,685.1	1,152.1
2010: Mar	12,773.1	5,259.8	7,513.3	269.3	190.2	183.0	153.6	225.7	678.5	585.0	3,877.9	1,350.1
June	13,201.8	5,345.1	7,856.7	266.1	189.6	190.8	150.1	231.8	676.8	584.4	4,070.0	1,497.1
Sept	13,561.6	5,350.5	8,211.1	322.8	188.7	198.2	145.2	240.6	671.0	586.0	4,324.2	1,534.4
Dec	14,025.2	5,656.2	8,368.9	319.3	187.9	206.8	153.7	248.4	721.7	595.7	4,435.6	1,499.9
2011: Mar	14,270.0	5,958.9	8,311.1	321.0	186.7	215.8	157.9	253.5	749.4	585.3	4,481.4	1,360.1
June	14,343.1	6,220.4	8,122.7	279.4	186.0	251.8	158.0	254.8	753.7	572.2	4,690.6	976.1
Sept	14,790.3	6,328.0	8,462.4	293.8	185.1	373.6	155.7	259.6	788.7	557.9	4,912.1	935.8
Dec	15,222.8	6,439.6	8,783.3	279.7	185.2	391.9	160.7	297.3	927.9	562.2	5,006.9	971.4
2012: Mar	15,582.3	6,397.2	9,185.1	317.0	184.8	406.6	169.4	298.1	1,015.4	567.4	5,145.1	1,081.2
June	15,855.5	6,475.8	9,379.7	303.2	184.7	427.4	171.2	293.6	997.8	585.4	5,310.9	1,105.4
Sept	16,066.2	6,446.8	9,619.4	338.2	183.8	453.9	181.7	292.6	1,080.7	596.9	5,476.1	1,015.4
Dec	16,432.7	6,523.7	9,909.1	347.7	182.5	468.0	183.6	292.7	1,031.8	599.6	5,573.8	1,229.4
2013: Mar	16,771.6	6,656.8	10,114.8	338.9	181.7	463.4	193.4	284.3	1,066.7	615.6	5,725.0	1,245.7
June	16,738.2	6,773.3	9,964.9	300.2	180.9	444.5	187.7	276.2	1,000.1	612.6	5,595.0	1,367.8
Sept	16,738.2	6,834.2	9,904.0	293.2	180.0	347.8	187.5	273.2	986.1	624.3	5,652.8	1,359.1
Dec	17,352.0	7,205.3	10,146.6	321.1	179.2	464.9	181.3	271.2	983.3	633.6	5,792.6	1,319.5
2014: Mar	17,601.2	7,301.5	10,299.7	368.4	178.3	474.3	184.3	276.8	1,060.4	632.0	5,948.3	1,177.0
June	17,632.6	7,461.0	10,171.6	409.5	177.6	482.6	198.3	287.7	986.2	638.8	6,018.7	972.1
Sept	17,824.1	7,490.8	10,333.2	471.1	176.7	490.7	198.7	298.1	1,075.8	628.7	6,069.2	924.1
Dec	18,141.4	7,578.9	10,562.6	516.8	175.9	507.1	199.2	307.0	1,121.8	654.5	6,157.7	922.4
2015: Mar	18,152.1	7,521.3	10,630.8	518.1	174.9	447.8	176.7	305.1	1,170.4	663.3	6,172.6	1,001.8
June	18,152.0	7,536.5	10,615.5	518.5	173.9	373.8	185.7	304.3	1,139.8	652.8	6,163.1	1,103.5
Sept	18,150.6	7,488.7	10,661.9	519.1	172.8	305.3	171.0	306.6	1,195.1	646.0	6,105.9	1,240.2
Dec	18,922.2	7,711.2	11,211.0	547.4	171.6	504.7	174.5	306.7	1,318.3	680.9	6,146.2	1,360.6
2016: Mar	19,264.9	7,801.4	11,463.6	562.9	170.3	524.4	170.4	315.5	1,404.1	695.0	6,284.4	1,336.6
June	19,381.6	7,911.2	11,470.4	580.6	169.0	537.9	185.0	329.8	1,434.2	712.6	6,279.1	1,242.2
Sept	19,573.4	7,863.5	11,709.9	627.6	167.5	545.6	203.8	341.2	1,600.4	735.8	6,155.9	1,332.1
Dec	19,976.9	8,005.6	11,971.3	663.9	165.8	538.0	218.8	330.2	1,705.4	742.5	6,006.3	1,600.5
2017: Mar	19,846.4	7,941.1	11,905.3	658.6	164.2	444.2	239.5	338.2	1,669.1	749.7	6,075.3	1,566.4
June	19,844.6	7,943.4	11,901.1	621.9	162.8	425.9	262.8	348.2	1,608.5	735.1	6,151.9	1,584.0
Sept	20,244.9	8,036.9	12,208.0	611.8	161.7	570.8	266.5	359.4	1,697.8	714.8	6,301.9	1,523.3
Dec	20,492.7	8,132.1	12,360.6	638.3	160.4	432.0	289.4	372.6	1,797.5	731.6	6,211.3	1,727.6
2018: Mar	21,089.9	8,086.6	13,003.3	639.7	159.0	589.5	300.1	361.6	1,977.1	714.0	6,223.4	2,038.9
June	21,195.3	8,106.9	13,088.5	665.3	157.8	604.8	307.3	225.6	1,843.4	728.7	6,225.0	2,330.5
Sept	21,516.1	8,068.1	13,447.9	683.9	156.8	615.2	301.7	225.9	1,898.2	733.5	6,225.9	2,606.9
Dec	21,974.1	8,095.0	13,879.1	771.5	155.7	636.9	367.9	203.7	2,023.3	716.0	6,270.1	2,734.0
2019: Mar	22,028.0	7,999.1	14,028.9	771.3	154.5	440.6	358.9	203.6	2,058.3	714.5	6,474.0	2,853.1
June	22,023.5	7,945.2	14,078.4	810.0	153.4	447.7	388.8	206.4	1,951.2	676.7	6,625.9	2,818.3
Sept	22,719.4	8,023.6	14,695.8	911.7	152.3	670.6	349.0	214.3	2,217.3	696.1	6,923.5	2,561.0
Dec	23,201.4	8,359.9	14,841.5	937.5	151.3	684.8	353.0	215.3	2,350.6	740.3	6,844.2	2,564.6
2020: Mar	23,686.9	9,279.7	14,407.2	948.5	150.0	733.4	352.1	243.9	2,384.6	740.1	6,949.5	1,905.1
June	26,477.4	10,157.7	16,319.6	1,157.0	149.8	740.7	337.6	242.0	3,568.2	834.7	7,046.6	2,243.0
Sept	26,945.4	10,371.9	16,573.5	....	148.6	....	....	....	....	....	7,071.0	....

[1] Face value.
[2] Federal Reserve holdings exclude Treasury securities held under repurchase agreements.
[3] Includes U.S. chartered depository institutions, foreign banking offices in U.S., banks in U.S. affiliated areas, credit unions, and bank holding companies.
[4] Current accrual value includes myRA.
[5] Includes Treasury securities held by the Federal Employees Retirement System Thrift Savings Plan "G Fund."
[6] Includes money market mutual funds, mutual funds, and closed-end investment companies.
[7] Includes nonmarketable foreign series, Treasury securities, and Treasury deposit funds. Excludes Treasury securities held under repurchase agreements in custody accounts at the Federal Reserve Bank of New York. Estimates reflect benchmarks to this series at differing intervals; for further detail, see Treasury Bulletin and http://www.treasury.gov/resource-center/data-chart-center/tic/pages/index.aspx.
[8] Includes individuals, Government-sponsored enterprises, brokers and dealers, bank personal trusts and estates, corporate and noncorporate businesses, and other investors.

Source: Department of the Treasury.

Corporate Profits and Finance

TABLE B–53. Corporate profits with inventory valuation and capital consumption adjustments, 1969–2020

[Billions of dollars; quarterly data at seasonally adjusted annual rates]

Year or quarter	Corporate profits with inventory valuation and capital consumption adjustments	Taxes on corporate income	Corporate profits after tax with inventory valuation and capital consumption adjustments		
			Total	Net dividends	Undistributed profits with inventory valuation and capital consumption adjustments
1969	98.4	37.0	61.5	27.3	34.2
1970	86.2	31.3	55.0	27.8	27.2
1971	100.6	34.8	65.8	28.4	37.5
1972	117.2	39.1	78.1	30.1	48.0
1973	133.4	45.6	87.8	34.2	53.5
1974	125.7	47.2	78.5	38.8	39.7
1975	138.9	46.3	92.6	38.3	54.3
1976	174.3	59.4	114.9	44.9	70.0
1977	205.8	68.5	137.3	50.7	86.6
1978	238.6	77.9	160.7	57.8	102.9
1979	249.0	80.7	168.2	66.8	101.4
1980	223.6	75.5	148.1	75.8	72.3
1981	247.5	70.3	177.2	87.8	89.4
1982	229.9	51.3	178.6	92.9	85.6
1983	279.8	66.4	213.3	97.7	115.7
1984	337.9	81.5	256.4	106.9	149.5
1985	354.5	81.6	272.9	115.3	157.5
1986	324.4	91.9	232.5	124.0	108.5
1987	366.0	112.7	253.3	130.1	123.2
1988	414.5	124.3	290.2	147.3	142.9
1989	414.3	124.4	289.9	179.6	110.3
1990	417.7	121.8	295.9	192.7	103.2
1991	452.6	117.8	334.8	201.3	133.5
1992	477.2	131.9	345.3	206.3	139.0
1993	524.6	155.0	369.5	221.3	148.2
1994	624.8	172.7	452.1	256.4	195.7
1995	706.2	194.4	511.8	282.3	229.4
1996	789.5	211.4	578.1	323.6	254.5
1997	869.7	224.8	645.0	360.1	284.9
1998	808.5	221.8	586.6	383.6	203.0
1999	834.9	227.4	607.5	373.5	234.0
2000	786.6	233.4	553.1	410.2	142.9
2001	758.7	170.1	588.6	397.9	190.7
2002	911.7	160.7	751.0	424.9	326.2
2003	1,056.3	213.8	842.5	456.0	386.5
2004	1,289.3	278.5	1,010.8	582.2	428.6
2005	1,488.6	379.7	1,108.9	602.0	506.9
2006	1,646.3	430.1	1,216.1	755.1	461.1
2007	1,533.2	391.8	1,141.4	853.5	287.9
2008	1,285.8	255.9	1,029.9	840.3	189.6
2009	1,386.8	203.9	1,182.9	622.1	560.8
2010	1,728.7	272.3	1,456.5	643.2	813.3
2011	1,809.8	280.8	1,529.0	779.1	749.9
2012	1,997.4	334.6	1,662.8	948.7	714.1
2013	2,010.7	362.6	1,648.1	1,009.0	639.1
2014	2,120.2	407.1	1,713.1	1,096.1	617.1
2015	2,060.5	396.3	1,664.2	1,164.9	499.3
2016	2,023.7	376.2	1,647.6	1,189.4	458.2
2017	2,114.5	311.3	1,803.2	1,270.4	532.8
2018	2,243.0	282.9	1,960.1	1,390.1	570.0
2019	2,250.5	298.7	1,951.8	1,360.8	591.0
2017: I	2,064.1	313.3	1,750.8	1,235.7	515.1
II	2,103.0	319.6	1,783.3	1,268.4	514.9
III	2,136.0	322.1	1,813.9	1,276.2	537.7
IV	2,155.0	290.2	1,864.7	1,301.2	563.5
2018: I	2,206.0	255.8	1,950.2	1,339.9	610.3
II	2,225.3	277.4	1,947.9	1,377.0	570.9
III	2,258.1	288.2	1,969.8	1,413.0	556.8
IV	2,282.5	310.1	1,972.4	1,430.4	542.0
2019: I	2,181.2	294.6	1,886.6	1,369.3	517.3
II	2,263.2	304.9	1,958.2	1,369.3	588.9
III	2,246.5	283.0	1,963.4	1,348.5	615.0
IV	2,311.3	312.3	1,998.9	1,356.3	642.7
2020: I	2,035.0	255.6	1,779.5	1,379.5	400.0
II	1,826.1	236.8	1,589.4	1,364.5	224.9
III ᴾ	2,321.4	294.3	2,027.1	1,348.3	678.8

Source: Department of Commerce (Bureau of Economic Analysis).

TABLE B–54. Corporate profits by industry, 1969–2020

[Billions of dollars; quarterly data at seasonally adjusted annual rates]

Year or quarter	Total	Corporate profits with inventory valuation adjustment and without capital consumption adjustment												Rest of the world
		Domestic industries												
		Total	Financial			Nonfinancial								
			Total	Federal Reserve banks	Other	Total	Manu-factur-ing	Trans-porta-tion [1]	Utilities	Whole-sale trade	Retail trade	Infor-mation	Other	
SIC: [2]														
1969	90.8	84.2	13.6	3.1	10.6	70.6	41.6	11.1		4.9	6.4		6.5	6.6
1970	79.7	72.6	15.5	3.5	12.0	57.1	32.0	8.8		4.6	6.1		5.8	7.1
1971	94.7	86.8	17.9	3.3	14.6	68.9	40.0	9.6		5.4	7.3		6.7	7.9
1972	109.3	99.7	19.5	3.3	16.1	80.3	47.6	10.4		7.2	7.5		7.6	9.5
1973	126.6	111.7	21.1	4.5	16.6	90.6	55.0	10.2		8.8	7.0		10.0	14.9
1974	123.3	105.8	20.8	5.7	15.1	85.1	51.0	9.1		12.2	2.8		10.0	17.5
1975	144.2	129.6	20.4	5.6	14.8	109.2	63.0	11.7		14.3	8.4		11.8	14.6
1976	182.1	165.6	25.6	5.9	19.7	140.0	82.5	17.5		13.7	10.9		15.3	16.5
1977	212.8	193.7	32.6	6.1	26.5	161.1	91.5	21.2		16.4	12.8		19.2	19.1
1978	246.7	223.8	40.8	7.6	33.1	183.1	105.8	25.5		16.7	13.1		22.0	22.9
1979	261.0	226.4	41.8	9.4	32.3	184.6	107.1	21.6		20.0	10.7		25.2	34.6
1980	240.6	205.2	35.2	11.8	23.5	169.9	97.6	22.2		18.5	7.0		24.6	35.5
1981	252.0	222.3	30.3	14.4	15.9	192.0	112.5	25.1		23.7	10.7		20.1	29.7
1982	224.8	192.2	27.2	15.2	12.0	165.0	89.6	28.1		20.7	14.3		12.3	32.6
1983	256.4	221.4	36.2	14.6	21.6	185.2	97.3	34.3		21.9	19.3		12.3	35.1
1984	294.3	257.7	34.7	16.4	18.3	223.0	114.2	44.7		30.4	21.5		12.1	36.6
1985	289.7	251.6	46.5	16.3	30.2	205.1	107.1	39.1		24.6	22.8		11.4	38.1
1986	273.3	233.8	56.4	15.5	40.8	177.4	75.6	39.3		24.4	23.4		14.7	39.5
1987	314.6	266.5	60.3	16.2	44.1	206.2	101.8	42.0		18.9	23.3		20.3	48.0
1988	366.2	309.2	66.9	18.1	48.8	242.3	132.8	46.8		20.4	19.8		22.5	57.0
1989	373.1	305.9	78.3	20.6	57.6	227.6	122.3	41.9		22.0	20.9		20.5	67.1
1990	391.2	315.1	89.6	21.8	67.8	225.5	120.9	43.5		19.4	20.3		21.3	76.1
1991	434.2	357.8	120.4	20.7	99.7	237.3	109.3	54.5		22.3	26.9		24.3	76.5
1992	459.7	386.6	132.4	18.3	114.1	254.2	108.9	57.7		25.3	28.1		33.4	73.1
1993	501.9	425.0	119.9	16.7	103.2	305.1	122.9	70.1		26.5	39.7		45.8	76.9
1994	589.3	511.3	125.9	18.5	107.4	385.4	162.6	83.9		31.4	46.3		61.2	78.0
1995	667.0	574.0	140.3	22.9	117.3	433.7	199.8	89.0		28.0	43.9		73.1	92.9
1996	741.8	639.8	147.9	22.5	125.3	492.0	220.4	91.2		39.9	52.0		88.5	102.0
1997	811.0	703.4	162.2	24.3	137.9	541.2	248.5	81.0		48.1	63.4		100.3	107.6
1998	743.8	641.1	138.9	25.6	113.3	502.1	220.4	72.6		50.6	72.3		86.3	102.8
1999	761.9	640.2	154.6	26.7	127.9	485.6	219.4	49.3		46.8	72.5		97.6	121.7
2000	729.8	584.1	149.7	31.2	118.5	434.4	205.9	33.8		50.4	68.9		75.4	145.7
NAICS: [2]														
1998	743.8	641.1	138.9	25.6	113.3	502.1	193.5	12.8	33.3	57.3	62.5	33.1	109.7	102.8
1999	761.9	640.2	154.6	26.7	127.9	485.6	184.5	7.2	34.4	55.6	59.5	20.8	123.5	121.7
2000	729.8	584.1	149.7	31.2	118.5	434.4	175.6	9.5	24.3	59.5	51.3	−11.9	126.1	145.7
2001	697.1	528.3	195.0	28.9	166.1	333.3	75.1	−.7	22.5	51.1	71.3	−26.4	140.2	168.8
2002	797.4	640.6	265.3	23.5	241.9	375.3	78.3	−6.5	10.5	53.5	83.3	5.0	151.2	156.8
2003	955.7	796.7	302.8	20.0	282.7	494.0	123.9	4.4	13.2	56.6	87.9	28.1	179.9	158.9
2004	1,217.5	1,022.4	346.0	20.0	326.0	676.3	186.2	12.0	21.1	72.7	94.0	61.6	228.8	195.1
2005	1,629.2	1,403.4	409.5	26.5	383.0	993.9	279.7	28.4	32.4	96.0	133.2	100.7	333.5	225.7
2006	1,812.2	1,572.5	413.1	33.8	379.3	1,159.4	352.9	40.8	55.2	105.0	133.6	115.2	356.8	239.7
2007	1,708.3	1,370.5	300.2	36.0	264.2	1,070.3	321.1	23.3	49.6	102.8	119.4	120.5	333.6	337.8
2008	1,344.5	954.2	94.6	35.1	59.5	859.7	240.0	29.3	30.4	92.7	82.2	98.8	286.3	390.2
2009	1,470.1	1,121.3	362.7	47.3	315.3	758.7	164.7	21.7	23.4	88.9	107.9	87.0	265.1	348.8
2010	1,786.4	1,400.6	405.8	71.6	334.3	994.8	281.8	44.6	30.6	99.3	115.9	102.3	320.4	385.8
2011	1,750.2	1,337.7	378.4	76.0	302.4	959.3	296.0	30.6	10.2	97.2	115.1	95.7	314.5	412.6
2012	2,144.7	1,739.3	482.4	71.7	410.6	1,256.9	403.0	54.4	13.8	137.9	155.7	112.0	380.1	405.4
2013	2,165.9	1,767.1	430.7	79.7	351.1	1,336.3	446.9	45.2	28.3	146.4	153.3	137.6	378.6	398.8
2014	2,266.6	1,861.7	483.1	103.5	379.6	1,378.6	458.7	55.7	32.8	150.6	157.3	126.6	397.0	404.9
2015	2,184.6	1,789.4	447.2	100.7	346.5	1,342.1	427.2	61.0	20.2	152.4	169.3	135.5	376.4	395.2
2016	2,124.3	1,704.4	455.8	92.0	363.8	1,248.6	332.7	63.9	9.4	126.6	170.5	157.4	388.1	420.0
2017	2,130.5	1,633.3	435.6	78.2	357.3	1,197.7	304.7	58.7	14.0	122.0	149.1	138.0	411.1	497.2
2018	2,132.0	1,619.5	418.2	68.0	350.2	1,201.3	337.6	52.8	21.7	105.7	146.5	139.2	397.7	512.5
2019	2,232.0	1,726.5	470.5	52.4	418.1	1,256.0	336.5	56.4	27.2	111.3	168.0	130.8	425.8	505.4
2018: I	2,088.9	1,552.9	423.2	73.7	349.5	1,129.7	276.2	48.5	22.7	111.3	149.5	134.9	386.7	536.0
II	2,112.5	1,599.8	419.6	70.5	349.1	1,180.2	348.1	46.6	23.3	94.9	137.7	143.4	386.2	512.7
III	2,149.9	1,657.4	414.6	66.9	347.6	1,242.8	365.3	52.0	22.3	103.9	157.5	144.0	397.8	492.5
IV	2,176.8	1,667.8	415.3	61.0	354.3	1,252.5	360.9	64.2	18.6	112.9	141.2	134.6	420.1	509.0
2019: I	2,154.9	1,670.5	460.1	53.0	407.1	1,210.4	324.5	54.7	26.2	103.9	155.5	136.2	409.4	484.4
II	2,246.4	1,740.2	472.3	56.6	415.8	1,267.8	344.9	54.4	28.2	110.5	165.6	140.0	424.3	506.2
III	2,231.7	1,717.2	466.7	50.7	416.0	1,250.5	341.0	59.5	27.1	113.4	166.8	108.4	434.3	514.5
IV	2,294.9	1,778.3	482.9	49.4	433.5	1,295.4	335.7	57.0	27.3	117.4	184.2	138.7	435.1	516.6
2020: I	2,053.5	1,580.4	444.7	68.5	376.2	1,135.7	302.2	37.8	22.5	108.3	167.1	126.7	371.0	473.1
II	1,844.3	1,460.7	471.1	77.3	393.8	989.6	197.6	19.2	29.0	101.4	205.1	109.5	327.8	383.6
III [p]	2,337.9	1,914.8	495.8	94.0	401.7	1,419.0								423.2

[1] Data on Standard Industrial Classification (SIC) basis include transportation and public utilities. Those on North American Industry Classification System (NAICS) basis include transporation and warehousing. Utilities classified separately in NAICS (as shown beginning 1998).

[2] SIC-based industry data use the 1987 SIC for data beginning in 1987 and the 1972 SIC for prior data. NAICS-based data use 2002 NAICS.

Note: Industry data on SIC basis and NAICS basis are not necessarily the same and are not strictly comparable.

Source: Department of Commerce (Bureau of Economic Analysis).

End of year	Common stock prices (end of period) [1]									Common stock yields (Standard & Poor's) (percent) [5]	
	New York Stock Exchange (NYSE) indexes [2]						Dow Jones industrial average [2]	Standard & Poor's composite index (1941–43=10) [2]	Nasdaq composite index (Feb. 5, 1971=100) [2]	Dividend-price ratio [6]	Earnings-price ratio [7]
	Composite (Dec. 31, 2002= 5,000) [3]	December 31, 1965=50									
		Composite	Industrial	Transportation	Utility [4]	Finance					
1949							200.52	16.76		6.59	15.48
1950							235.42	20.41		6.57	13.99
1951							269.23	23.77		6.13	11.82
1952							291.90	26.57		5.80	9.47
1953		13.60					280.90	24.81		5.80	10.26
1954		19.40					404.39	35.98		4.95	8.57
1955		23.71					488.40	45.48		4.08	7.95
1956		24.35					499.47	46.67		4.09	7.55
1957		21.11					435.69	39.99		4.35	7.89
1958		28.85					583.65	55.21		3.97	6.23
1959		32.15					679.36	59.89		3.23	5.78
1960		30.94					615.89	58.11		3.47	5.90
1961		38.93					731.14	71.55		2.98	4.62
1962		33.81					652.10	63.10		3.37	5.82
1963		39.92					762.95	75.02		3.17	5.50
1964		45.65					874.13	84.75		3.01	5.32
1965	528.69	50.00	50.00	50.00	50.00	50.00	969.26	92.43		3.00	5.59
1966	462.28	43.72	43.13	47.56	90.38	44.91	785.69	80.33		3.40	6.63
1967	569.18	53.83	56.59	49.66	86.76	53.80	905.11	96.47		3.20	5.73
1968	622.79	58.90	61.69	56.27	91.64	76.48	943.75	103.86		3.07	5.67
1969	544.86	51.53	54.74	37.85	77.54	67.87	800.36	92.06		3.24	6.08
1970	531.12	50.23	52.91	35.70	81.64	64.34	838.92	92.15		3.83	6.45
1971	596.68	56.43	60.53	49.56	78.78	73.83	890.20	102.09	114.12	3.14	5.41
1972	681.79	64.48	70.33	47.69	84.34	83.34	1,020.02	118.05	133.73	2.84	5.50
1973	547.93	51.82	56.60	37.53	68.66	64.51	850.86	97.55	92.19	3.06	7.12
1974	382.03	36.13	39.15	26.36	53.30	39.84	616.24	68.56	59.82	4.47	11.59
1975	503.73	47.64	52.73	32.98	66.94	45.20	852.41	90.19	77.62	4.31	9.15
1976	612.01	57.88	63.36	42.57	82.54	59.23	1,004.65	107.46	97.88	3.77	8.90
1977	555.12	52.50	56.43	40.50	81.08	53.85	831.17	95.10	105.05	4.62	10.79
1978	566.96	53.62	58.87	41.58	75.38	55.01	805.01	96.11	117.98	5.28	12.03
1979	655.04	61.95	70.24	50.64	73.80	63.45	838.74	107.94	151.14	5.47	13.46
1980	823.27	77.86	91.52	76.19	76.90	70.83	963.99	135.76	202.34	5.26	12.66
1981	751.90	71.11	80.89	66.85	80.10	73.68	875.00	122.55	195.84	5.20	11.96
1982	856.79	81.03	93.02	73.63	86.94	85.00	1,046.54	140.64	232.41	5.81	11.60
1983	1,006.41	95.18	111.35	98.09	92.48	94.32	1,258.64	164.93	278.60	4.40	8.03
1984	1,013.91	96.38	110.58	90.61	103.14	97.63	1,211.57	167.24	247.35	4.64	10.02
1985	1,285.66	121.59	139.27	113.97	126.38	131.29	1,546.67	211.28	324.93	4.25	8.12
1986	1,465.31	138.59	160.11	117.65	147.54	140.05	1,895.95	242.17	348.83	3.49	6.09
1987	1,461.61	138.23	167.04	118.57	134.62	114.57	1,938.83	247.08	330.47	3.08	5.48
1988	1,652.25	156.26	189.42	146.60	149.38	128.19	2,168.57	277.72	381.38	3.64	8.01
1989	2,062.30	195.04	232.76	178.33	204.00	156.15	2,753.20	353.40	454.82	3.45	7.42
1990	1,908.45	180.49	223.60	141.49	182.60	122.06	2,633.66	330.22	373.84	3.61	6.47
1991	2,426.04	229.44	285.82	201.87	204.26	172.68	3,168.83	417.09	586.34	3.24	4.79
1992	2,539.92	240.21	294.39	214.72	209.66	200.83	3,301.11	435.71	676.95	2.99	4.22
1993	2,739.44	259.08	315.26	270.48	229.92	216.82	3,754.09	466.45	776.80	2.78	4.46
1994	2,653.37	250.94	318.10	222.46	198.41	195.80	3,834.44	459.27	751.96	2.82	5.83
1995	3,484.15	329.51	413.29	301.96	252.90	274.25	5,117.12	615.93	1,052.13	2.56	6.09
1996	4,148.07	392.30	494.38	352.30	259.91	351.17	6,448.27	740.74	1,291.03	2.19	5.24
1997	5,405.19	511.19	630.38	466.25	335.19	495.96	7,908.25	970.43	1,570.35	1.77	4.57
1998	6,299.94	595.81	743.65	482.38	445.94	521.42	9,181.43	1,229.23	2,192.69	1.49	3.46
1999	6,876.10	650.30	828.21	466.70	511.15	516.61	11,497.12	1,469.25	4,069.31	1.25	3.17
2000	6,945.57	656.87	803.29	462.76	440.54	646.95	10,786.85	1,320.28	2,470.52	1.15	3.63
2001	6,236.39	589.80	735.71	438.81	329.84	593.69	10,021.50	1,148.08	1,950.40	1.32	2.95
2002	5,000.00	472.87	583.95	395.81	233.08	510.46	8,341.63	879.82	1,335.51	1.61	2.92
2003 [3]	6,440.30	572.56	735.50	519.58	265.58	655.12	10,453.92	1,111.92	2,003.37	1.77	3.84

[1] End of period.

[2] Includes stocks as follows: for NYSE, all stocks listed; for Dow Jones industrial average, 30 stocks; for Standard & Poor's (S&P) composite index, 500 stocks; and for Nasdaq composite index, over 5,000.

[3] The NYSE relaunched the composite index on January 9, 2003, incorporating new definitions, methodology, and base value. (The composite index based on December 31, 1965=50 was discontinued.) Subset indexes on financial, energy, and health care were released by the NYSE on January 8, 2004 (see Table B–56). NYSE indexes shown in this table for industrials, utilities, transportation, and finance were discontinued.

[4] Effective April 1993, the NYSE doubled the value of the utility index to facilitate trading of options and futures on the index. Indexes prior to 1993 reflect the doubling.

[5] Based on 500 stocks in the S&P composite index.

[6] Aggregate cash dividends (based on latest known annual rate) divided by aggregate market value based on Wednesday closing prices. Monthly data are averages of weekly figures; annual data are averages of monthly figures.

[7] Quarterly data are ratio of earnings (after taxes) for four quarters ending with particular quarter-to-price index for last day of that quarter. Annual data are averages of quarterly ratios.

Sources: New York Stock Exchange, Dow Jones & Co., Inc., Standard & Poor's, and Nasdaq Stock Market.

| End of year or month | Common stock prices (end of period) [1] | | | | | | | Common stock yields (Standard & Poor's) (percent) [4] | |
| | New York Stock Exchange (NYSE) indexes (December 31, 2002=5,000) [2, 3] | | | | Dow Jones industrial average [2] | Standard & Poor's composite index (1941–43=10) [2] | Nasdaq composite index (Feb. 5, 1971=100) [2] | Dividend-price ratio [5] | Earnings-price ratio [6] |
	Composite	Financial	Energy	Health care					
2000	6,945.57				10,786.85	1,320.28	2,470.52	1.15	3.63
2001	6,236.39				10,021.50	1,148.08	1,950.40	1.32	2.95
2002	5,000.00	5,000.00	5,000.00	5,000.00	8,341.63	879.82	1,335.51	1.61	2.92
2003	6,440.30	6,676.42	6,321.05	5,925.97	10,453.92	1,111.92	2,003.37	1.77	3.84
2004	7,250.06	7,493.92	7,934.49	6,119.07	10,783.01	1,211.92	2,175.44	1.72	4.89
2005	7,753.95	7,996.94	10,109.61	6,458.20	10,717.50	1,248.29	2,205.32	1.83	5.36
2006	9,139.02	9,552.22	11,967.88	6,958.64	12,463.15	1,418.30	2,415.29	1.87	5.78
2007	9,740.32	8,300.68	15,283.81	7,170.42	13,264.82	1,468.36	2,652.28	1.86	5.29
2008	5,757.05	3,848.42	9,434.01	5,340.73	8,776.39	903.25	1,577.03	2.37	3.54
2009	7,184.96	4,721.02	11,415.03	6,427.27	10,428.05	1,115.10	2,269.15	2.40	1.86
2010	7,964.02	4,958.62	12,520.29	6,501.53	11,577.51	1,257.64	2,652.87	1.98	6.04
2011	7,477.03	4,062.88	12,409.61	7,045.61	12,217.56	1,257.60	2,605.15	2.05	6.77
2012	8,443.51	5,114.54	12,606.06	7,904.06	13,104.14	1,426.19	3,019.51	2.24	6.20
2013	10,400.33	6,353.68	14,557.54	10,245.31	16,576.66	1,848.36	4,176.59	2.14	5.57
2014	10,839.24	6,707.16	12,533.54	11,967.04	17,823.07	2,058.90	4,736.05	2.04	5.25
2015	10,143.42	6,305.68	9,343.81	12,385.19	17,425.03	2,043.94	5,007.41	2.10	4.59
2016	11,056.89	6,961.56	11,503.76	11,907.20	19,762.60	2,238.83	5,383.12	2.19	4.17
2017	12,808.84	8,235.89	11,470.58	14,220.58	24,719.22	2,673.61	6,903.39	1.97	4.22
2018	11,374.39	6,969.48	9,341.44	15,158.38	23,327.46	2,506.85	6,635.28	1.90	4.66
2019	13,913.03	8,700.11	10,037.30	18,070.10	28,538.44	3,230.78	8,972.60	1.93	4.53
2018: Jan	13,367.96	8,637.58	11,843.94	15,051.71	26,149.39	2,823.81	7,411.48	1.82	
Feb	12,652.55	8,246.24	10,625.83	14,357.41	25,029.20	2,713.83	7,273.01	1.89	
Mar	12,452.06	8,029.25	10,863.28	14,040.86	24,103.11	2,640.87	7,063.45	1.90	4.37
Apr	12,515.36	7,995.25	11,878.26	14,198.80	24,163.15	2,648.05	7,066.27	1.95	
May	12,527.14	7,877.77	12,056.61	14,292.95	24,415.84	2,705.27	7,442.12	1.92	
June	12,504.25	7,781.67	12,131.49	14,464.62	24,271.41	2,718.37	7,510.30	1.90	4.51
July	12,963.28	8,097.12	12,282.46	15,409.93	25,415.19	2,816.29	7,671.79	1.85	
Aug	13,016.89	8,109.69	11,837.21	15,887.99	25,964.82	2,901.52	8,109.54	1.82	
Sept	13,082.52	7,979.54	12,169.73	16,299.34	26,458.31	2,913.98	8,046.35	1.81	4.47
Oct	12,208.06	7,543.04	10,915.63	15,506.53	25,115.76	2,711.74	7,305.90	1.89	
Nov	12,457.55	7,713.77	10,478.32	16,505.42	25,538.46	2,760.17	7,330.54	1.95	
Dec	11,374.39	6,969.48	9,341.44	15,158.38	23,327.46	2,506.85	6,635.28	2.10	5.28
2019: Jan	12,299.03	7,613.43	10,351.36	15,655.94	24,999.67	2,704.10	7,281.74	2.07	
Feb	12,644.81	7,770.10	10,560.79	15,932.89	25,916.00	2,784.49	7,532.53	1.98	
Mar	12,696.88	7,685.02	10,679.94	16,182.85	25,928.68	2,834.40	7,729.32	1.96	4.74
Apr	13,060.65	8,138.15	10,699.48	15,706.22	26,592.91	2,945.83	8,095.39	1.90	
May	12,264.49	7,663.98	9,679.30	15,380.82	24,815.04	2,752.06	7,453.15	1.95	
June	13,049.71	8,064.09	10,334.74	16,347.65	26,599.96	2,941.76	8,006.24	1.94	4.60
July	13,066.60	8,130.16	9,973.03	16,209.28	26,864.27	2,980.38	8,175.42	1.88	
Aug	12,736.88	7,824.31	9,138.41	16,119.87	26,403.28	2,926.46	7,962.88	1.96	
Sept	13,004.74	8,115.96	9,564.95	15,990.79	26,916.83	2,976.74	7,999.34	1.92	4.46
Oct	13,171.81	8,293.63	9,423.40	16,716.08	27,046.23	3,037.56	8,292.36	1.93	
Nov	13,545.21	8,516.89	9,445.81	17,407.66	28,051.41	3,140.98	8,665.47	1.87	
Dec	13,913.03	8,700.11	10,037.30	18,070.10	28,538.44	3,230.78	8,972.60	1.84	4.32
2020: Jan	13,614.10	8,535.85	9,007.57	17,753.73	28,256.03	3,225.52	9,150.94	1.80	
Feb	12,380.97	7,701.35	7,770.44	16,364.87	25,409.36	2,954.22	8,567.37	1.84	
Mar	10,301.87	5,972.42	5,319.36	15,554.24	21,917.16	2,584.59	7,700.10	2.30	4.50
Apr	11,372.34	6,467.31	6,190.56	17,500.36	24,345.72	2,912.43	8,889.55	2.20	
May	11,802.95	6,612.69	6,262.28	18,041.17	25,383.11	3,044.31	9,489.87	2.08	
June	11,893.78	6,709.21	6,242.11	17,505.30	25,812.88	3,100.29	10,058.77	1.95	3.20
July	12,465.05	6,849.26	6,024.80	18,380.12	26,428.32	3,271.12	10,745.27	1.89	
Aug	13,045.60	7,181.16	6,014.26	18,853.66	28,430.05	3,500.31	11,775.46	1.78	
Sept	12,701.88	6,860.62	5,161.75	18,559.43	27,781.70	3,363.00	11,167.51	1.79	2.92
Oct	12,429.28	6,761.94	4,912.48	17,847.94	26,501.60	3,269.96	10,911.59	1.76	
Nov	14,006.46	7,887.93	6,232.84	19,390.40	29,638.64	3,621.63	12,198.74	1.69	

[1] End of year or month.
[2] Includes stocks as follows: for NYSE, all stocks listed (in 2020, over 2,800); for Dow Jones industrial average, 30 stocks; for Standard & Poor's (S&P) composite index, 500 stocks; and for Nasdaq composite index, in 2020, over 2,900.
[3] The NYSE relaunched the composite index on January 9, 2003, incorporating new definitions, methodology, and base value. Subset indexes on financial, energy, and health care were released by the NYSE on January 8, 2004.
[4] Based on 500 stocks in the S&P composite index.
[5] Aggregate cash dividends (based on latest known annual rate) divided by aggregate market value based on Wednesday closing prices. Monthly data are averages of weekly figures, annual data are averages of monthly figures.
[6] Quarterly data are ratio of earnings (after taxes) for four quarters ending with particular quarter-to-price index for last day of that quarter. Annual data are averages of quarterly ratios.

Sources: New York Stock Exchange, Dow Jones & Co., Inc., Standard & Poor's, and Nasdaq Stock Market.

International Statistics

TABLE B–57. U.S. international transactions, 1969–2020

[Millions of dollars; quarterly data seasonally adjusted]

Year or quarter	Goods[2] Exports	Goods Imports	Goods Balance on goods	Services Exports	Services Imports	Services Balance on services	Balance on goods and services	Primary income receipts and payments Receipts	Payments	Balance on primary income	Balance on secondary Income[3]	Balance on current account	Current account balance as a percentage of GDP
1969	36,414	35,807	607	12,806	13,323	–517	90	10,913	4,869	6,044	–5,735	399	0.0
1970	42,469	39,866	2,603	14,171	14,519	–348	2,255	11,748	5,514	6,234	–6,156	2,331	.2
1971	43,319	45,579	–2,260	16,358	15,401	959	–1,301	12,706	5,436	7,270	–7,402	–1,433	–.1
1972	49,381	55,797	–6,416	17,842	16,867	973	–5,443	14,764	6,572	8,192	–8,544	–5,796	–.5
1973	71,410	70,499	911	19,832	18,843	989	1,900	21,809	9,656	12,153	–6,914	7,140	.5
1974	98,306	103,811	–5,505	22,591	21,378	1,212	–4,293	27,587	12,084	15,503	–9,248	1,961	.1
1975	107,088	98,185	8,903	25,497	21,996	3,500	12,403	25,351	12,565	12,786	–7,076	18,117	1.1
1976	114,745	124,228	–9,483	27,971	24,570	3,402	–6,082	29,374	13,312	16,062	–5,686	4,296	.2
1977	120,816	151,907	–31,091	31,486	27,640	3,845	–27,247	32,355	14,218	18,137	–5,227	–14,336	–.7
1978	142,075	176,002	–33,927	36,353	32,189	4,164	–29,763	42,087	21,680	20,407	–5,788	–15,143	–.6
1979	184,439	212,007	–27,568	39,693	36,689	3,003	–24,566	63,835	32,961	30,874	–6,593	–285	.0
1980	224,250	249,750	–25,500	47,585	41,492	6,093	–19,407	72,605	42,533	30,072	–8,349	2,318	.1
1981	237,044	265,067	–28,023	57,355	45,503	11,851	–16,172	86,529	53,626	32,903	–11,702	5,029	.2
1982	211,157	247,642	–36,485	64,078	51,750	12,330	–24,156	96,522	61,359	35,163	–16,545	–5,537	–.2
1983	201,799	268,901	–67,102	64,307	54,973	9,335	–57,767	96,031	59,643	36,388	–17,311	–38,691	–1.1
1984	219,926	332,418	–112,492	71,168	67,748	3,418	–109,074	115,639	80,574	35,065	–20,334	–94,344	–2.3
1985	215,915	338,088	–122,173	73,156	72,863	294	–121,879	105,046	79,324	25,722	–21,999	–118,155	–2.7
1986	223,344	368,425	–145,081	86,690	80,147	6,543	–138,539	102,798	87,304	15,494	–24,131	–147,176	–3.2
1987	250,208	409,765	–159,557	98,661	90,788	7,874	–151,683	113,603	99,309	14,294	–23,265	–160,655	–3.3
1988	320,230	447,189	–126,959	110,920	98,525	12,394	–114,566	141,666	122,981	18,685	–25,274	–121,153	–2.3
1989	359,916	477,665	–117,749	127,087	102,480	24,607	–93,142	166,384	146,560	19,824	–26,169	–99,487	–1.8
1990	387,401	498,438	–111,037	147,833	117,660	30,173	–80,865	176,894	148,345	28,549	–26,654	–78,969	–1.3
1991	414,083	491,020	–76,937	164,260	118,459	45,802	–31,136	155,327	131,198	24,129	9,904	2,897	.0
1992	439,631	536,528	–96,897	177,251	119,566	57,685	–39,212	139,082	114,845	24,237	–36,635	–51,613	–.8
1993	456,943	589,394	–132,451	185,920	123,780	62,141	–70,311	141,606	116,287	25,319	–39,811	–84,805	–1.2
1994	502,859	668,690	–165,831	200,395	133,057	67,338	–98,493	169,447	152,302	17,145	–40,265	–121,612	–1.7
1995	575,204	749,374	–174,170	219,183	141,397	77,786	–96,384	213,661	192,771	20,890	–38,074	–113,567	–1.5
1996	612,113	803,113	–191,000	239,489	152,554	86,935	–104,065	229,530	207,212	22,318	–43,017	–124,764	–1.5
1997	678,366	876,794	–198,428	256,087	165,932	90,155	–108,273	261,357	248,752	12,607	–45,062	–140,726	–1.6
1998	670,416	918,637	–248,221	262,758	180,677	82,081	–166,140	266,244	261,978	4,266	–53,187	–215,062	–2.4
1999	698,524	1,035,592	–337,068	278,001	196,742	81,258	–255,809	302,540	292,566	9,974	–40,777	–286,612	–3.0
2000	784,940	1,231,722	–446,782	298,023	220,927	77,096	–369,686	365,612	350,980	14,632	–46,863	–401,918	–3.9
2001	731,331	1,153,701	–422,370	284,035	222,039	61,997	–360,373	311,364	288,120	23,244	–56,953	–394,082	–3.7
2002	698,036	1,173,281	–475,245	288,059	233,480	54,579	–420,666	306,391	288,886	17,506	–52,949	–456,110	–4.2
2003	730,446	1,272,089	–541,643	297,740	252,340	45,401	–496,243	346,931	317,677	29,254	–55,300	–522,289	–4.6
2004	823,584	1,488,349	–664,766	344,536	290,609	53,927	–610,838	432,839	386,256	46,583	–71,634	–635,890	–5.2
2005	913,016	1,695,820	–782,804	378,487	312,225	66,262	–716,542	536,294	492,108	44,186	–76,876	–749,232	–5.7
2006	1,040,905	1,878,194	–837,289	423,086	349,329	73,756	–763,533	669,919	653,945	15,974	–69,088	–816,646	–5.9
2007	1,165,151	1,986,347	–821,196	495,664	385,464	110,199	–710,997	816,938	752,582	64,356	–89,910	–736,550	–5.1
2008	1,308,795	2,141,287	–832,492	540,791	420,650	120,142	–712,350	820,244	708,225	112,019	–96,192	–696,523	–4.7
2009	1,070,331	1,580,025	–509,694	522,461	407,538	114,923	–394,771	653,222	537,684	115,539	–100,496	–379,729	–2.6
2010	1,290,279	1,938,950	–648,671	582,041	436,456	145,584	–503,087	723,223	553,311	169,911	–98,834	–432,009	–2.9
2011	1,498,887	2,239,886	–740,999	644,665	458,188	186,477	–554,522	791,469	589,038	202,431	–103,211	–455,302	–2.9
2012	1,562,630	2,303,749	–741,119	684,823	469,610	215,213	–525,906	791,679	593,754	197,925	–90,134	–418,115	–2.6
2013	1,593,708	2,294,247	–700,539	719,529	465,819	253,710	–446,829	811,561	616,041	195,520	–85,545	–336,854	–2.0
2014	1,635,563	2,385,480	–749,917	756,705	490,932	265,773	–484,144	845,926	645,623	200,303	–83,978	–367,819	–2.1
2015	1,511,381	2,273,249	–761,868	768,362	497,755	270,607	–491,261	825,100	639,724	185,376	–101,470	–407,355	–2.2
2016	1,457,393	2,207,195	–749,801	780,530	511,898	268,632	–481,169	857,819	660,798	197,021	–110,716	–394,865	–2.1
2017	1,557,003	2,356,345	–799,343	830,388	544,836	285,552	–513,791	997,524	739,731	257,793	–109,272	–365,269	–1.9
2018	1,676,950	2,557,251	–880,301	862,433	562,069	300,364	–579,937	1,108,472	857,298	251,174	–120,931	–449,693	–2.2
2019	1,652,437	2,516,767	–864,331	875,825	588,359	287,466	–576,865	1,135,691	899,347	236,344	–139,705	–480,226	–2.2
2017: I	384,339	578,214	–193,876	202,555	132,006	70,549	–123,326	232,348	171,880	60,469	–21,036	–83,894	–1.7
II	380,739	581,175	–200,436	206,436	135,618	70,818	–129,618	238,095	179,854	58,241	–30,983	–102,359	–2.1
III	386,644	582,360	–195,716	208,590	138,409	70,181	–125,535	255,766	189,031	66,734	–27,433	–86,234	–1.8
IV	405,282	614,597	–209,315	212,808	138,804	74,004	–135,311	271,315	198,966	72,349	–29,820	–92,782	–1.9
2018: I	412,989	630,894	–217,905	217,360	138,310	79,050	–138,855	270,402	200,215	70,187	–27,918	–96,587	–1.9
II	426,060	630,865	–204,805	213,617	139,042	74,575	–130,230	279,752	215,258	64,494	–29,678	–95,414	–1.9
III	419,341	646,224	–226,883	215,287	140,810	74,477	–152,406	273,725	217,087	56,638	–29,473	–125,241	–2.4
IV	418,561	649,269	–230,708	216,170	143,907	72,263	–158,445	284,593	224,738	59,855	–33,861	–132,452	–2.5
2019: I	419,048	635,180	–216,133	215,162	144,267	70,895	–145,237	278,452	225,153	53,298	–34,677	–126,616	–2.4
II	411,069	635,641	–224,572	220,326	147,964	72,362	–152,210	287,535	228,069	59,467	–34,948	–127,691	–2.4
III	410,930	632,059	–221,129	219,259	147,788	71,471	–149,658	286,761	225,140	61,621	–33,556	–121,594	–2.3
IV	411,390	613,887	–202,497	221,079	148,341	72,738	–129,759	282,943	220,985	61,958	–36,524	–104,324	–1.9
2020: I	403,533	595,281	–191,748	202,019	136,747	65,272	–126,476	256,527	204,491	52,036	–37,075	–111,516	–2.1
II [p]	288,885	508,223	–219,338	155,768	101,328	54,440	–164,898	209,389	180,176	29,213	–34,856	–170,541	–3.5

[1] Current and capital account statistics in the international transactions accounts differ slightly from statistics in the National Income and Product Accounts (NIPAs) because of adjustments made to convert the international statistics to national accounting concepts. A reconciliation can be found in NIPA table 4.3B.
[2] Adjusted from Census data to align with concepts and definitions used to prepare the international and national economic accounts. The adjustments are necessary to supplement coverage of Census data, to eliminate duplication of transactions recorded elsewhere in the international accounts, to value transactions according to a standard definition, and for earlier years, to record transactions in the appropriate period.

See next page for continuation of table.

Table B–57. U.S. international transactions, 1969–2020—*Continued*

[Millions of dollars; quarterly data seasonally adjusted]

Year or quarter	Balance on capital account [1]	Financial account											Statistical discrepancy
		Net U.S. acquisition of financial assets excluding financial derivatives [net increase in assets / financial outflow (+)]					Net U.S. incurrence of liabilities excluding financial derivatives [net increase in liabilities / financial inflow (+)]				Financial derivatives other than reserves, net transactions	Net lending (+) or net borrowing (–) from financial account transactions [5]	
		Total	Direct investment assets	Portfolio investment assets	Other investment assets	Reserve assets [4]	Total	Direct investment liabilities	Portfolio investment liabilities	Other investment liabilities			
1969	....	11,584	5,960	1,549	2,896	1,179	12,702	1,263	719	10,720	....	–1,118	–1,517
1970	....	9,336	7,590	1,076	3,151	–2,481	7,226	1,464	11,710	–5,948	....	2,110	–219
1971	....	12,474	7,618	1,113	6,092	–2,349	23,687	368	28,835	–5,516	....	–11,213	–9,779
1972	....	14,497	7,747	619	6,127	4	22,171	948	13,123	8,100	....	–7,674	–1,879
1973	....	22,874	11,353	672	11,007	–158	18,388	2,800	4,790	10,798	....	4,486	–2,654
1974	....	34,745	9,052	1,853	22,373	1,467	35,228	4,761	5,500	24,967	....	–483	–2,444
1975	....	39,703	14,244	6,247	18,363	849	16,870	2,603	12,761	1,506	....	22,833	4,717
1976	....	51,269	11,949	8,885	27,877	2,558	37,840	4,347	16,165	17,328	....	13,429	9,134
1977	....	34,785	11,891	5,459	17,060	375	52,770	3,728	37,615	11,427	....	–17,985	–3,651
1978	....	61,130	16,057	3,626	42,179	–732	66,275	7,896	30,083	28,296	....	–5,145	9,997
1979	....	66,053	25,223	12,430	27,267	1,133	40,693	11,876	–13,502	42,319	....	25,360	25,647
1980	....	86,968	19,222	6,042	53,550	8,154	62,036	16,918	23,825	21,293	....	24,932	22,614
1981	....	114,147	9,624	15,650	83,697	5,176	85,684	25,196	17,509	42,979	....	28,463	23,433
1982	....	142,722	19,397	12,395	105,965	4,965	109,897	27,475	19,695	62,727	....	32,825	38,362
1983	....	74,690	20,844	2,063	50,588	1,195	95,715	18,688	18,382	58,645	....	–21,025	17,666
1984	....	50,740	26,770	3,498	17,340	3,132	126,413	34,832	38,695	52,886	....	–75,673	18,673
1985	....	47,064	21,241	3,008	18,957	3,858	146,544	22,057	68,004	56,483	....	–99,480	18,677
1986	....	107,252	19,524	8,984	79,057	–313	223,854	30,946	104,497	88,411	....	–116,602	30,570
1987	....	84,058	39,795	7,903	45,508	–9,148	251,863	63,232	79,631	109,000	....	–167,805	–7,149
1988	....	105,747	21,701	4,589	75,544	3,913	244,008	56,910	86,786	100,312	....	–138,261	–17,108
1989	–207	182,908	50,973	31,166	75,476	25,293	230,302	75,801	74,852	79,649	....	–47,394	52,299
1990	–7,221	103,985	59,934	30,557	11,336	2,158	162,109	71,247	25,767	65,095	....	–58,124	28,066
1991	–5,129	75,753	49,253	32,053	210	–5,763	119,586	34,535	72,562	12,489	....	–43,833	–41,601
1992	1,449	84,899	58,755	50,684	–20,639	–3,901	178,842	30,315	92,199	56,328	....	–93,943	–43,776
1993	–714	199,399	82,799	137,917	–22,696	1,379	278,607	50,211	174,387	54,009	....	–79,208	6,313
1994	–1,112	188,758	89,988	54,088	50,028	–5,346	312,995	55,942	131,849	125,204	....	–124,237	–1,514
1995	–221	363,555	110,041	143,506	100,266	9,742	446,393	69,067	254,431	122,895	....	–82,838	30,951
1996	–8	424,548	103,024	160,179	168,013	–6,668	559,027	97,644	392,107	69,276	....	–134,479	–9,706
1997	–256	502,024	121,352	121,036	258,626	1,010	720,999	122,150	311,105	287,744	....	–218,975	–77,995
1998	–7	385,936	174,751	132,186	72,216	6,783	452,901	211,152	225,878	15,871	....	–66,965	148,106
1999	–6,428	526,612	247,484	141,007	146,868	–8,747	765,215	312,449	278,697	174,069	....	–238,603	54,437
2000	–4,217	587,682	186,371	159,713	241,308	290	1,066,074	349,124	441,966	274,984	....	–478,392	–72,257
2001	12,170	386,313	146,041	106,919	128,442	4,911	788,345	172,946	431,492	184,357	....	–402,032	–20,120
2002	–3,825	319,175	178,984	79,532	56,978	3,681	821,844	111,056	504,155	206,634	....	–502,668	–42,734
2003	–8,499	371,104	195,218	133,059	44,351	–1,524	911,660	117,107	550,163	244,390	....	–540,556	–9,768
2004	–4,344	1,058,661	374,006	191,956	495,505	–2,806	1,600,881	213,642	867,340	519,899	....	–542,220	98,014
2005	950	562,996	52,591	267,290	257,210	–14,094	1,277,056	142,345	832,037	302,673	....	–714,059	34,223
2006	–7,439	1,324,623	283,800	493,366	549,830	–2,373	2,120,480	298,464	1,126,735	695,280	–29,710	–825,567	–1,482
2007	–6,057	1,563,467	523,889	380,807	658,649	122	2,190,087	346,615	1,156,612	686,860	–6,222	–632,841	109,765
2008	–172	–317,592	343,584	–284,269	–381,754	4,848	462,408	341,091	523,683	–402,367	32,947	–747,053	–50,358
2009	–5,877	131,082	312,597	375,883	–609,654	52,256	325,644	161,082	357,352	–192,789	–44,816	–239,379	146,227
2010	–6,891	958,737	349,829	199,620	407,454	1,835	1,391,042	264,039	820,434	306,569	–14,076	–446,381	–7,481
2011	–9,020	492,556	436,615	85,365	–45,301	15,877	983,522	263,499	311,626	408,397	–35,006	–525,972	–61,650
2012	931	176,937	377,239	248,760	–453,522	4,460	632,034	250,343	747,017	–365,327	7,064	–448,032	–30,849
2013	–6,559	649,753	392,796	481,298	–221,242	–3,099	1,052,068	288,131	511,987	251,949	2,222	–400,093	–56,681
2014	–6,535	866,702	387,528	582,676	–99,920	–3,583	1,109,443	251,857	697,607	159,979	–54,335	–297,076	77,278
2015	–7,940	197,359	302,072	160,410	–258,831	–6,292	503,468	511,434	213,910	–221,876	–27,035	–333,144	82,151
2016	–6,606	335,233	299,814	36,283	–2,955	2,090	706,693	474,388	231,265	1,040	7,827	–363,633	37,838
2017	12,394	1,188,188	405,375	569,375	215,127	–1,690	1,546,281	366,966	790,796	388,489	23,998	–334,095	18,779
2018	–4,196	358,971	–151,298	335,263	170,017	4,989	758,291	261,480	303,073	193,736	–20,404	–419,724	34,165
2019	–6,244	440,751	188,469	46,570	201,053	4,659	797,960	351,629	179,980	266,350	–38,340	–395,549	90,921
2017: I	–2,116	347,090	115,669	141,588	90,074	–241	412,154	99,067	160,102	152,986	–5,609	–70,674	15,336
II	–1,999	321,857	83,096	154,279	84,331	150	446,786	91,677	259,549	95,560	9,306	–115,623	–11,264
III	18,213	395,144	126,052	175,975	93,177	–61	504,352	103,950	294,391	106,011	18,600	–90,608	–22,587
IV	–1,703	124,097	80,558	97,533	–52,455	–1,539	182,989	72,302	76,754	33,933	1,701	–57,190	37,295
2018: I	–1,406	320,758	–58,184	289,989	88,959	–7	446,162	65,445	301,122	79,595	29,139	–96,265	1,727
II	–2,912	–223,399	–105,044	–17,704	–103,719	3,068	–135,152	9,475	–18,368	–126,259	–15,723	–103,970	–5,644
III	–455	109,691	74,289	83,451	–47,872	–177	114,982	137,899	12,157	–35,075	–11,505	–16,796	108,900
IV	576	151,921	–62,359	–20,473	232,649	2,105	332,299	48,662	8,164	275,474	–22,315	–202,693	–70,817
2019: I	–2,542	84,497	–11,846	–40,720	136,855	208	158,290	117,543	–18,569	59,315	–21,383	–95,175	33,983
II	–848	158,966	115,561	45,025	–3,980	2,359	317,227	99,461	146,049	71,717	–9,642	–167,903	–39,364
III	–835	142,221	25,574	20,460	94,305	1,882	238,964	78,119	105,660	55,185	–6,382	–103,125	19,303
IV	–2,019	55,067	59,180	21,806	–26,128	210	83,479	56,506	–53,160	80,133	–933	–29,345	76,998
2020: I	–2,971	830,858	–9,065	115,814	724,354	–245	952,306	52,201	–20,547	920,653	–21,611	–143,059	–28,572
II p	–1,052	–147,602	35,861	–29,818	–158,606	4,960	–4,777	–8,510	338,957	–335,225	60,256	–82,569	89,025

[3] Includes U.S. government and private transfers, such as U.S. government grants and pensions, fines and penalties, withholding taxes, personal transfers, insurance-related transfers, and other current transfers.

[4] Consists of monetary gold, special drawing rights (SDRs), the U.S. reserve position in the International Monetary Fund (IMF), and other reserve assets, including foreign currencies.

[5] Net lending means that U.S. residents are net suppliers of funds to foreign residents, and net borrowing means the opposite.

Source: Department of Commerce (Bureau of Economic Analysis).

TABLE B–58. U.S. international trade in goods on balance of payments (BOP) and Census basis, and trade in services on BOP basis, 1991–2020

[Billions of dollars; monthly data seasonally adjusted]

Year or month	Goods: Exports (f.a.s. value)[1,2]							Goods: Imports (customs value)[6]							Services (BOP basis)	
	Total, BOP basis[3,4]	Census basis (by end-use category)						Total, BOP basis[4]	Census basis (by end-use category)						Exports[4]	Imports[4]
		Total, Census basis[3,5]	Foods, feeds, and beverages	Industrial supplies and materials	Capital goods except automotive	Automotive vehicles, parts, and engines	Consumer goods (nonfood) except automotive		Total, Census basis[5]	Foods, feeds, and beverages	Industrial supplies and materials	Capital goods except automotive	Automotive vehicles, parts, and engines	Consumer goods (nonfood) except automotive		
1991	414.1	421.7	35.7	109.7	166.7	40.0	45.9	491.0	488.5	26.5	131.6	120.7	85.7	108.0	164.3	118.5
1992	439.6	448.2	40.3	109.1	175.9	47.0	51.4	536.5	532.7	27.6	138.6	134.3	91.8	122.7	177.3	119.6
1993	456.9	465.1	40.6	111.8	181.7	52.4	54.7	589.4	580.7	27.9	145.6	152.4	102.4	134.0	185.9	123.8
1994	502.9	512.6	42.0	121.4	205.0	57.8	60.0	668.7	663.3	31.0	162.1	184.4	118.3	146.3	200.4	133.1
1995	575.2	584.7	50.5	146.2	233.0	61.8	64.4	749.4	743.5	33.2	181.8	221.4	123.8	159.9	219.2	141.4
1996	612.1	625.1	55.5	147.7	253.0	65.0	70.1	803.1	795.3	35.7	204.5	228.1	128.9	172.0	239.5	152.6
1997	678.4	689.2	51.5	158.2	294.5	74.0	77.4	876.8	869.7	39.7	213.8	253.3	139.8	193.8	256.1	165.9
1998	670.4	682.1	46.4	148.3	299.4	72.4	80.3	918.6	911.9	41.2	200.1	269.5	148.7	217.0	262.8	180.7
1999	698.5	695.8	46.0	147.5	310.8	75.3	80.9	1,035.6	1,024.6	43.6	221.4	295.7	179.0	241.9	278.0	196.7
2000	784.9	781.9	47.9	172.6	356.9	80.4	89.4	1,231.7	1,218.0	46.0	299.0	347.0	195.9	281.8	298.0	220.9
2001	731.3	729.1	49.4	160.1	321.7	75.4	88.3	1,153.7	1,141.0	46.6	273.9	298.0	189.8	284.3	284.0	222.0
2002	698.0	693.1	49.6	156.8	290.4	78.9	84.4	1,173.3	1,161.4	49.7	267.7	283.3	203.7	307.8	288.1	233.5
2003	730.4	724.8	55.0	173.0	293.7	80.6	89.9	1,272.1	1,257.1	55.8	313.8	295.9	210.1	333.9	297.7	252.3
2004	823.6	814.9	56.6	203.9	327.5	89.2	103.2	1,488.3	1,469.7	62.1	412.8	343.6	228.2	372.9	344.5	290.6
2005	913.0	901.1	59.0	233.0	358.4	98.4	115.3	1,695.8	1,673.5	68.1	523.8	379.3	239.4	407.2	378.5	312.2
2006	1,040.9	1,026.0	66.0	276.0	404.0	107.3	129.1	1,878.2	1,853.9	74.9	602.0	418.3	256.6	442.6	423.1	349.3
2007	1,165.2	1,148.2	84.3	316.4	433.0	121.3	146.0	1,986.3	1,957.0	81.7	634.7	444.5	256.7	474.6	495.7	385.5
2008	1,308.8	1,287.4	108.3	388.0	457.7	121.5	161.3	2,141.3	2,103.6	89.0	779.5	453.7	231.2	481.6	540.8	420.7
2009	1,070.3	1,056.0	93.9	296.5	391.2	81.7	149.5	1,580.0	1,559.6	81.6	462.4	370.5	157.7	427.3	522.5	407.5
2010	1,290.3	1,278.5	107.7	391.7	447.5	112.0	165.2	1,939.0	1,913.9	91.7	603.1	449.4	225.1	483.2	582.0	436.5
2011	1,498.9	1,482.5	126.2	501.1	494.0	133.0	175.3	2,239.9	2,208.0	107.5	755.8	510.8	254.6	514.1	644.7	458.2
2012	1,562.6	1,545.8	133.0	501.2	527.2	146.2	181.7	2,303.7	2,276.3	110.3	730.6	548.7	297.8	516.9	684.8	469.6
2013	1,593.7	1,578.5	136.2	508.2	534.4	152.7	188.8	2,294.2	2,268.0	115.1	681.5	555.7	308.8	531.7	719.5	465.8
2014	1,635.6	1,621.9	143.7	505.8	551.5	159.8	199.0	2,385.5	2,356.4	125.9	667.0	594.1	328.6	551.7	756.7	490.9
2015	1,511.4	1,503.3	127.7	427.0	539.5	151.9	197.7	2,273.2	2,248.8	127.8	486.0	602.5	349.2	594.2	768.4	497.8
2016	1,457.4	1,451.5	130.5	397.3	519.7	150.4	193.7	2,207.2	2,186.8	130.0	443.3	589.7	349.9	583.1	780.5	511.9
2017	1,557.0	1,547.2	132.8	465.2	533.4	157.9	197.7	2,356.3	2,339.6	137.8	507.0	639.8	358.2	601.4	830.4	544.8
2018	1,677.0	1,665.7	133.1	541.2	563.1	158.8	206.0	2,557.3	2,537.7	147.3	575.1	691.3	371.5	646.1	862.4	562.1
2019	1,652.4	1,643.2	131.1	529.8	547.9	162.5	205.7	2,516.8	2,497.5	150.5	521.5	677.8	375.9	653.6	875.8	588.4
2019: Jan	138.9	138.2	10.9	44.3	46.6	13.5	17.5	211.2	209.6	12.4	43.9	57.0	31.8	55.7	71.4	48.0
Feb	139.2	138.3	10.6	43.5	47.8	13.7	17.6	210.2	208.5	12.0	42.8	57.3	31.7	55.4	71.6	47.9
Mar	141.0	140.1	10.9	44.7	47.6	13.8	17.7	213.7	212.1	12.9	45.2	57.9	31.8	54.8	72.2	48.4
Apr	136.4	135.5	11.2	44.3	44.7	13.2	17.2	209.7	208.1	12.8	44.5	55.8	31.0	54.9	72.9	48.7
May	139.1	138.3	11.2	44.2	45.9	13.7	17.9	215.1	213.3	12.7	46.0	56.9	32.7	55.3	73.8	49.1
June	135.5	134.8	11.1	43.8	44.8	13.5	16.2	210.8	209.3	12.6	42.7	56.9	32.3	54.3	73.7	50.2
July	137.5	136.7	11.1	43.0	45.6	13.9	17.6	212.1	210.3	12.7	44.1	55.7	32.4	55.5	73.0	49.4
Aug	137.4	136.6	11.6	43.9	44.3	14.1	17.0	212.0	210.2	12.6	42.8	57.0	31.8	56.4	73.2	49.3
Sept	136.1	135.4	10.6	43.8	45.0	13.4	17.0	208.0	206.5	12.7	42.1	56.0	31.0	54.5	73.1	49.0
Oct	136.9	136.1	10.5	44.8	44.9	13.3	16.8	204.0	202.5	12.5	41.9	56.1	29.2	52.3	73.6	49.4
Nov	136.9	136.2	10.8	44.2	45.4	13.5	16.8	202.3	200.9	12.3	41.2	55.4	30.2	51.9	73.7	49.3
Dec	137.7	136.9	10.9	45.3	45.1	13.0	16.5	207.6	206.2	12.3	44.4	55.9	30.1	52.7	73.8	49.5
2020: Jan	137.2	136.4	10.9	45.7	44.6	13.2	16.5	203.4	201.9	13.0	42.3	55.2	29.2	52.6	72.0	49.3
Feb	138.5	137.7	11.1	46.6	44.7	13.5	15.9	198.2	196.6	12.5	40.9	52.0	30.6	50.7	71.2	48.4
Mar	127.8	127.6	10.8	43.0	42.5	11.2	14.8	193.7	192.5	12.8	41.1	53.9	27.9	46.9	58.8	39.0
Apr	95.7	95.7	10.8	33.9	32.3	3.8	10.4	167.4	166.4	12.1	41.4	48.2	13.4	43.8	53.4	33.6
May	90.0	89.9	10.4	30.0	31.5	3.4	10.9	166.1	165.3	12.1	43.7	47.5	9.0	45.7	54.0	33.5
June	103.1	102.9	10.0	32.8	35.2	8.3	12.3	174.8	173.8	12.4	35.4	49.8	18.6	50.5	54.6	34.0
July	115.5	115.3	10.2	35.3	37.7	12.2	14.9	196.4	195.3	12.8	39.8	53.9	26.4	54.0	54.5	35.1
Aug	119.0	118.7	11.3	39.2	36.3	12.2	15.1	202.9	201.8	13.5	38.2	54.7	28.0	57.8	54.9	35.9
Sept	122.7	122.5	12.9	39.3	37.7	12.5	15.3	203.4	201.9	13.5	36.9	55.5	31.2	55.8	55.4	36.7
Oct[p]	126.3	126.2	12.4	41.0	39.1	12.7	16.2	207.8	206.6	13.3	38.2	56.9	32.2	57.2	55.7	37.4

[1] Department of Defense shipments of grant-aid military supplies and equipment under the Military Assistance Program are excluded from total exports through 1985 and included beginning 1986.
[2] F.a.s. (free alongside ship) value basis at U.S. port of exportation for exports.
[3] Beginning with data for 1989, exports have been adjusted for undocumented exports to Canada and are included in the appropriate end-use categories. For prior years, only total exports include this adjustment.
[4] Beginning with data for 1999, exports of goods under the U.S. Foreign Military Sales program and fuel purchases by foreign air and ocean carriers in U.S. ports are included in goods exports (BOP basis) and excluded from services exports. Beginning with data for 1999, imports of petroleum abroad by U.S. military agencies and fuel purchases by U.S. air and ocean carriers in foreign ports are included in goods imports (BOP basis) and excluded from services imports.
[5] Total includes "other" exports or imports, not shown separately.
[6] Total arrivals of imported goods other than in-transit shipments.
[7] Total includes revisions not reflected in detail.
[8] Total exports are on a revised statistical month basis; end-use categories are on a statistical month basis.
Note: Goods on a Census basis are adjusted to a BOP basis by the Bureau of Economic Analysis, in line with concepts and definitions used to prepare international and national accounts. The adjustments are necessary to supplement coverage of Census data, to eliminate duplication of transactions recorded elsewhere in international accounts, to value transactions according to a standard definition, and for earlier years, to record transactions in the appropriate period.
Data include international trade of the U.S. Virgin Islands, Puerto Rico, and U.S. Foreign Trade Zones.
Source: Department of Commerce (Bureau of the Census and Bureau of Economic Analysis).

[Millions of dollars]

Item	2000	2005	2010	2014	2015	2016	2017	2018	2019
EXPORTS									
Total, all countries................................	1,082,963	1,291,503	1,872,320	2,392,268	2,279,743	2,237,923	2,387,391	2,539,383	2,528,262
Europe	298,654	366,823	510,935	615,176	607,894	615,047	654,053	707,327	729,607
Euro area [1]	174,591	214,207	292,815	351,688	350,099	356,767	377,059	404,262	426,565
France	30,821	35,241	45,279	51,305	50,064	51,397	53,848	58,685	60,289
Germany	45,379	55,246	75,023	78,948	81,185	82,737	88,542	93,732	96,701
Italy	16,666	18,557	22,787	25,532	24,622	25,049	27,235	32,576	33,500
United Kingdom	73,995	83,456	104,891	120,981	126,707	125,224	131,145	147,212	147,801
Canada	204,237	246,292	307,571	379,809	341,326	327,982	348,765	369,598	361,226
Latin America and Other Western Hemisphere ..	228,633	259,832	416,623	588,680	550,636	516,623	553,504	590,942	576,822
Brazil	22,112	21,574	53,766	71,353	58,672	52,497	63,811	66,263	67,278
Mexico	127,581	141,856	187,487	270,941	267,798	261,524	275,601	299,355	289,798
Venezuela	9,476	9,396	15,918	17,935	14,211	9,976	7,455	9,140	3,624
Asia and Pacific	301,451	342,228	523,350	651,454	633,794	641,003	695,065	729,294	715,837
China	21,862	50,685	113,577	166,367	163,323	169,351	186,727	179,196	164,479
India	6,730	13,294	29,243	36,013	38,833	41,202	47,683	56,477	58,690
Japan	101,554	93,383	104,991	114,169	106,578	107,772	114,135	122,511	125,021
Korea, Republic of	35,106	37,866	56,700	67,835	66,239	65,369	73,447	80,566	81,442
Singapore	24,557	26,657	39,743	42,060	43,033	45,204	50,491	55,263	54,614
Taiwan	30,604	29,103	36,896	40,304	39,013	38,931	37,166	41,909	42,873
Middle East................	28,616	48,702	70,477	102,145	102,150	98,902	97,015	98,141	100,262
Africa	17,203	22,890	40,278	51,999	41,215	35,659	36,341	41,299	41,541
IMPORTS									
Total, all countries	1,452,649	2,008,045	2,375,406	2,876,412	2,771,004	2,719,093	2,901,181	3,119,320	3,105,126
Europe	359,220	493,562	566,372	704,997	704,906	698,834	742,279	807,435	852,446
Euro area [1]	216,802	304,574	341,235	438,742	444,221	440,207	464,665	505,195	538,486
France	41,344	47,725	56,563	66,101	66,240	64,578	68,611	72,331	78,343
Germany	75,709	110,076	114,861	159,108	158,862	149,258	153,602	159,340	162,903
Italy	31,593	39,768	37,779	52,124	53,787	55,174	60,542	66,204	69,612
United Kingdom	70,963	84,200	96,034	112,020	115,039	108,704	113,542	123,546	126,163
Canada	253,313	319,543	310,340	387,994	334,254	317,096	341,337	362,587	363,893
Latin America and Other Western Hemisphere ..	255,760	362,652	468,191	559,536	527,898	515,871	543,652	587,433	597,258
Brazil	15,340	26,401	30,095	38,938	36,153	32,717	35,729	36,881	37,601
Mexico	148,493	188,384	248,695	324,751	327,767	325,707	346,048	378,572	393,950
Venezuela	19,192	34,662	33,394	30,805	16,217	11,451	12,688	13,460	2,113
Asia and Pacific	507,527	682,521	841,359	1,060,863	1,060,061	1,078,868	1,152,093	1,226,299	1,181,797
China	103,340	251,791	377,619	484,565	499,676	479,708	524,006	559,235	472,322
India	12,480	23,426	44,940	68,100	69,768	72,564	76,875	83,176	87,439
Japan	164,972	162,613	147,993	170,186	164,764	167,233	172,519	178,725	180,529
Korea, Republic of	45,726	51,175	59,292	80,515	82,525	79,644	80,165	85,106	88,853
Singapore	21,837	19,242	23,668	23,007	25,192	25,061	27,648	36,080	36,224
Taiwan	44,272	40,690	41,740	47,145	47,635	46,066	49,641	53,244	61,657
Middle East................	44,500	81,361	95,039	119,806	79,369	72,940	79,631	88,394	69,763
Africa	31,075	69,516	93,001	42,125	32,708	34,214	42,102	45,638	39,890
BALANCE (excess of exports +)									
Total, all countries	−369,687	−716,542	−503,087	−484,144	−491,261	−481,169	−513,791	−579,937	−576,865
Europe	−60,566	−126,739	−55,436	−89,822	−97,012	−83,786	−88,225	−100,108	−122,839
Euro area [1]	−42,211	−90,367	−48,420	−87,053	−94,122	−83,440	−87,607	−100,933	−111,921
France	−10,523	−12,484	−11,284	−14,796	−16,176	−13,181	−14,763	−13,647	−18,054
Germany	−30,331	−54,830	−39,838	−80,161	−77,678	−66,520	−65,060	−65,607	−66,202
Italy	−14,928	−21,211	−14,991	−26,593	−29,165	−30,125	−33,307	−33,628	−36,112
United Kingdom	3,033	−744	8,856	8,962	11,667	16,520	17,603	23,665	21,637
Canada	−49,076	−73,252	−2,770	−8,185	7,072	10,885	7,428	7,011	−2,667
Latin America and Other Western Hemisphere ..	−27,127	−102,820	−51,567	29,144	22,739	752	9,852	3,509	−20,435
Brazil	6,772	−4,826	23,672	32,415	22,519	19,778	28,084	29,384	29,678
Mexico	−20,912	−46,528	−61,208	−53,812	−59,969	−64,183	−70,447	−79,217	−104,152
Venezuela	−9,716	−25,266	−17,476	−12,870	−2,006	−1,475	−5,233	−4,319	1,511
Asia and Pacific	−206,077	−340,293	−318,009	−409,408	−458,003	−437,865	−457,029	−497,005	−465,960
China	−81,478	−201,106	−264,042	−318,198	−336,353	−310,357	−337,279	−380,040	−307,841
India	−5,749	−10,132	−15,698	−32,088	−30,936	−31,362	−29,193	−26,699	−28,749
Japan	−63,419	−69,230	−43,002	−56,017	−58,186	−59,461	−58,384	−56,213	−55,508
Korea, Republic of	−10,620	−13,308	−2,593	−12,681	−16,286	−14,274	−6,718	−4,540	−7,411
Singapore	2,719	7,415	16,076	19,052	17,841	20,143	22,842	19,184	18,391
Taiwan	−13,668	−11,587	−4,843	−6,842	−8,621	−7,135	−12,475	−11,336	−18,785
Middle East................	−15,883	−32,659	−24,561	−17,661	22,781	25,962	17,384	9,747	30,499
Africa	−13,872	−46,625	−52,723	9,874	8,507	1,445	−5,762	−4,339	1,651

[1] Euro area consists of Austria, Belgium, Finland, France, Germany, Ireland, Italy, Luxembourg, Netherlands, Portugal, Spain and Greece (beginning in 2001), Slovenia (2007), Cyprus and Malta (2008), Slovakia (2009), Estonia (2011), Latvia (2014), and Lithuania (2015).

Note: Data are on a balance of payments basis. For further details, and additional data by country, see *Survey of Current Business*, October 2020.

Source: Department of Commerce (Bureau of Economic Analysis).

Table B–60. Foreign exchange rates, 2000–2020

[Foreign currency units per U.S. dollar, except as noted; certified noon buying rates in New York]

Period	Australia (dollar)[1]	Brazil (real)	Canada (dollar)	China, P.R. (yuan)	EMU Members (euro)[1,2]	India (rupee)	Japan (yen)	Mexico (peso)	South Korea (won)	Sweden (krona)	Switzerland (franc)	United Kingdom (pound)[1]
March 1973	1.4129	......	0.9967	2.2401	......	7.55	261.90	0.013	398.85	4.4294	3.2171	2.4724
2000	.5815	1.8301	1.4855	8.2784	0.9232	45.00	107.80	9.459	1,130.90	9.1735	1.6904	1.5156
2001	.5169	2.3527	1.5487	8.2770	.8952	47.22	121.57	9.337	1,292.01	10.3425	1.6891	1.4396
2002	.5437	2.9213	1.5704	8.2771	.9454	48.63	125.22	9.663	1,250.31	9.7233	1.5567	1.5025
2003	.6524	3.0750	1.4008	8.2772	1.1321	46.59	115.94	10.793	1,192.08	8.0787	1.3450	1.6347
2004	.7365	2.9262	1.3017	8.2768	1.2438	45.26	108.15	11.290	1,145.24	7.3480	1.2428	1.8330
2005	.7627	2.4352	1.2115	8.1936	1.2449	44.00	110.11	10.894	1,023.75	7.4710	1.2459	1.8204
2006	.7535	2.1738	1.1340	7.9723	1.2563	45.19	116.31	10.906	954.32	7.3718	1.2532	1.8434
2007	.8391	1.9461	1.0734	7.6058	1.3711	41.18	117.76	10.928	928.97	6.7550	1.1999	2.0020
2008	.8537	1.8326	1.0660	6.9477	1.4726	43.39	103.39	11.143	1,098.71	6.5846	1.0816	1.8545
2009	.7927	1.9976	1.1412	6.8307	1.3935	48.33	93.68	13.498	1,274.63	7.6539	1.0860	1.5661
2010	.9200	1.7600	1.0298	6.7696	1.3261	45.65	87.78	12.624	1,155.74	7.2053	1.0432	1.5452
2011	1.0332	1.6723	.9887	6.4630	1.3931	46.58	79.70	12.427	1,106.94	6.4878	.8862	1.6043
2012	1.0359	1.9535	.9995	6.3093	1.2859	53.37	79.82	13.154	1,126.16	6.7721	.9377	1.5853
2013	.9683	2.1570	1.0300	6.1478	1.3281	58.51	97.60	12.758	1,094.67	6.5124	.9269	1.5642
2014	.9034	2.3512	1.1043	6.1620	1.3297	61.00	105.74	13.302	1,052.29	6.8576	.9147	1.6484
2015	.7522	3.3360	1.2791	6.2827	1.1096	64.11	121.05	15.874	1,130.96	8.4350	.9628	1.5284
2016	.7445	3.4839	1.3243	6.6400	1.1072	67.16	108.66	18.667	1,159.34	8.5541	.9848	1.3555
2017	.7671	3.1910	1.2984	6.7569	1.1301	65.07	112.10	18.884	1,129.04	8.5430	.9842	1.2890
2018	.7481	3.6513	1.2957	6.6090	1.1817	68.37	110.40	19.218	1,099.29	8.6945	.9784	1.3363
2019	.6952	3.9440	1.3269	6.9081	1.1194	70.38	109.02	19.247	1,165.80	9.4604	.9937	1.2768
2019: I	.7122	3.7696	1.3297	6.7447	1.1354	70.42	110.19	19.204	1,124.80	9.1783	.9971	1.3031
II	.7003	3.9167	1.3378	6.8195	1.1237	69.53	109.95	19.111	1,166.07	9.4439	1.0028	1.2859
III	.6857	3.9688	1.3205	7.0150	1.1120	70.39	107.33	19.421	1,193.90	9.5878	.9856	1.2329
IV	.6837	4.1124	1.3197	7.0448	1.1075	71.21	108.68	19.248	1,175.54	9.6143	.9894	1.2880
2020: I	.6569	4.4720	1.3459	6.9786	1.1022	72.52	108.93	20.085	1,194.01	9.6829	.9680	1.2788
II	.6578	5.3736	1.3854	7.0841	1.1016	75.85	107.52	23.331	1,219.13	9.6838	.9634	1.2418
III	.7154	5.3790	1.3321	6.9153	1.1698	74.35	106.10	22.091	1,187.62	8.8608	.9194	1.2927

Trade-weighted value of the U.S. dollar

Period	Nominal			Real[6]		
	Broad index (January 2006=100)[3]	Advanced foreign economies index (January 2006=100)[4]	Emerging market economies index (January 2006=100)[5]	Broad index (January 2006=100)[3]	Advanced foreign economies index (January 2006=100)[4]	Emerging market economies index (January 2006=100)[5]
2000	....	....	....	....	....	....
2001	....	....	....	....	....	....
2002	....	....	....	....	....	....
2003	....	....	....	....	....	....
2004	....	....	....	....	....	....
2005	....	....	....	....	....	....
2006	98.6064	97.6875	99.8131	98.9391	98.3178	99.7537
2007	93.8253	92.0825	96.1230	94.2810	93.6310	95.1295
2008	90.8968	88.4455	94.1511	90.9956	90.8429	91.2339
2009	96.7688	92.8046	102.0228	95.3507	94.7051	96.1509
2010	93.0664	90.1032	97.1794	90.8021	92.0125	89.6511
2011	88.7923	84.8159	94.0346	86.3062	87.3150	85.3374
2012	91.6492	87.9861	96.5675	88.5092	90.8406	86.2309
2013	92.7655	90.6103	96.0743	88.8030	93.8332	84.0355
2014	95.5919	93.3976	98.9816	90.8264	97.0040	85.0587
2015	108.1589	108.1256	109.5474	101.2856	111.8249	91.8621
2016	113.0548	109.3062	118.1998	105.4934	113.9736	97.6718
2017	112.7924	108.8922	118.0915	104.9396	114.1265	96.5580
2018	112.0078	106.4267	119.0263	104.0831	112.1945	96.5658
2019	115.7182	110.1298	122.7845	107.0934	116.6247	98.4125
2019: I	114.4908	109.3956	121.0275	106.0727	115.4700	97.5080
II	115.3739	110.2733	121.9276	106.8373	116.6030	97.9743
III	116.4899	110.4769	124.0091	107.8440	117.1091	99.3667
IV	116.4571	110.3251	124.0981	107.6194	117.3167	98.8000
2020: I	117.8812	111.2690	126.0629	108.6315	118.4348	99.7293
II	122.1671	112.3253	133.8825	112.1821	119.1939	105.4947
III	117.7298	107.2406	130.1547	108.7043	114.8500	102.7665

[1] U.S. dollars per foreign currency unit.
[2] European Economic and Monetary Union (EMU) members consists of Austria, Belgium, Finland, France, Germany, Ireland, Italy, Luxembourg, Netherlands, Portugal, Spain and Greece (beginning in 2001), Slovenia (2007), Cyprus and Malta (2008), Slovakia (2009), Estonia (2011), Latvia (2014), and Lithuania (2015).
[3] Weighted average of the foreign exchange value of the U.S. dollar against the currencies of a broad group of major U.S. trading partners.
[4] Subset of the broad index. Consists of currencies of the Euro area, Australia, Canada, Japan, Sweden, Switzerland, and the United Kingdom.
[5] Subset of the broad index currencies that are emerging market economies. For details, see *Revisions to the Federal Reserve Dollar Indexes*, January 2019.
[6] Adjusted for changes in consumer price indexes for the United States and other countries.

Source: Board of Governors of the Federal Reserve System.

TABLE B-61. Growth rates in real gross domestic product by area and country, 2002-2021

[Percent change]

Area and country	2002-2011 annual average	2012	2013	2014	2015	2016	2017	2018	2019	2020[1]	2021[1]
World	4.1	3.5	3.5	3.5	3.4	3.3	3.8	3.5	2.8	−4.4	5.2
Advanced economies	1.7	1.2	1.4	2.1	2.4	1.8	2.5	2.2	1.7	−5.8	3.9
Of which:											
United States	1.8	2.2	1.8	2.5	3.1	1.7	2.3	3.0	2.2	−4.3	3.1
Euro area[2]	1.1	−.9	−.2	1.4	2.0	1.9	2.6	1.8	1.3	−8.3	5.2
Germany	1.1	.4	.4	2.2	1.5	2.2	2.6	1.3	.6	−6.0	4.2
France	1.3	.3	.6	1.0	1.1	1.1	2.3	1.8	1.5	−9.8	6.0
Italy	0.2	−3.0	−1.8	.0	.8	1.3	1.7	.8	.3	−10.6	5.2
Spain	1.6	−3.0	−1.4	1.4	3.8	3.0	2.9	2.4	2.0	−12.8	7.2
Japan	0.6	1.5	2.0	.4	1.2	.5	2.2	.3	.7	−5.3	2.3
United Kingdom	1.5	1.5	2.1	2.6	2.4	1.9	1.9	1.3	1.5	−9.8	5.9
Canada	2.0	1.8	2.3	2.9	.7	1.0	3.2	2.0	1.7	−7.1	5.2
Other advanced economies	3.7	2.2	2.5	3.0	2.3	2.5	3.1	2.7	1.7	−3.8	3.6
Emerging market and developing economies	6.5	5.4	5.1	4.7	4.3	4.5	4.8	4.5	3.7	−3.3	6.0
Regional groups:											
Emerging and Developing Asia	8.6	7.0	6.9	6.8	6.8	6.8	6.7	6.3	5.5	−1.7	8.0
China	10.7	7.9	7.8	7.3	6.9	6.8	6.9	6.7	6.1	1.9	8.2
India[3]	7.7	5.5	6.4	7.4	8.0	8.3	7.0	6.1	4.2	−10.3	8.8
ASEAN-5[4]	5.4	6.2	5.0	4.7	5.0	5.1	5.5	5.3	4.9	−3.4	6.2
Emerging and Developing Europe	4.8	3.1	3.1	1.8	1.0	1.9	4.1	3.3	2.1	−4.6	3.9
Russia	4.8	4.0	1.8	.7	−2.0	.2	1.8	2.5	1.3	−4.1	2.8
Latin America and the Caribbean	3.6	2.9	2.9	1.3	.4	−.6	1.4	1.1	.0	−8.1	3.6
Brazil	3.9	1.9	3.0	.5	−3.5	−3.3	1.3	1.3	1.1	−5.8	2.8
Mexico	1.9	3.6	1.4	2.8	3.3	2.6	2.1	2.2	−.3	−9.0	3.5
Middle East and Central Asia	5.6	5.1	3.1	3.1	2.7	4.5	2.6	2.1	1.4	−4.1	3.0
Saudi Arabia	4.5	5.4	2.7	3.7	4.1	1.7	−.7	2.4	.3	−5.4	3.1
Sub-Saharan Africa	5.9	4.8	5.1	5.2	3.2	1.5	3.1	3.3	3.2	−3.0	3.1
Nigeria	8.7	4.3	5.4	6.3	2.7	−1.6	.8	1.9	2.2	−4.3	1.7
South Africa	3.5	2.2	2.5	1.8	1.2	.4	1.4	.8	.2	−8.0	3.0

[1] All figures are forecasts as published by the International Monetary Fund.

[2] Euro area consists of Austria, Belgium, Finland, France, Germany, Ireland, Italy, Luxembourg, Netherlands, Portugal, Spain and Greece (beginning in 2001), Slovenia (2007), Cyprus and Malta (2008), Slovakia (2009), Estonia (2011), Latvia (2014), and Lithuania (2015).

[3] Data and forecasts are presented on a fiscal year basis and output growth is based on GDP at market prices.

[4] Consists of Indonesia, Malaysia, Philippines, Thailand, and Vietnam.

Note: For details on data shown in this table, see *World Economic Outlook*, October 2020, published by the International Monetary Fund.

Source: International Monetary Fund.